S0-CWX-257

DOMESTIC RELATIONS:

Law and Skills

By

WILLIAM P. STATSKY
Professor of Law
Antioch School of Law

Foreword by
Professor Sanford J. Fox

PARALEGAL SERIES

ST. PAUL, MINN.
WEST PUBLISHING CO.
1978

Printed in the United States of America

Library of Congress Cataloging in Publication Data

Statsky, William P
Domestic relations.

(Paralegal series)
Includes index.
1. Domestic relations—United States. I. Title.
KF505.S8 346'.73'015 78–7303

ISBN 0-8299-2007-2

Statsky Dom.Relations
1st Reprint—1980

To my own domestic relations—
Pat, Jessica, Gabriel,
Lena, Joe, Brenda, Deacon,
Bob, Commie, Mike D. and (Jessica
says it is OK to add:) myself

*

FOREWORD

The emergence of paralegal services in recent years has posed several challenges to the legal profession. Since law practice requires a range of skills, from the most mundane to the most sophisticated, there inevitably arises some apprehension that professional work, and its remuneration, at the former end of the spectrum will be lost to the newly arriving paraprofessionals. A sufficiently strident and organized protest against this loss of gainful employment could put the practicing bar in a position to handicap, if not to block outright, the future development of legal paraprofessionals. In some ways, the issues are not dissimilar from those emanating from the tax practice of accountants or the probate work of fiduciary institutions, although unlike such clashes the bar has had with those whom it has charged with the unauthorized practice of law, paraprofessionalism seeks to become part of a natural, evolutionary development of the practice of law itself.

The goal of paraprofessionalism is to aid, not to displace; its method is to facilitate, not to replicate. A lawyer with paraprofessional resources should be a more thorough and competent lawyer. The pressures to short-cut legal research felt by all save the largest firms—and even there from time to time—should diminish significantly as paraprofessional services become increasingly available. And it is, of course, not only the client who benefits from growth of the informational base on which advise is based. The litigation process, trial as well as appellate, stands to gain substantially in terms of efficiency and accuracy as the scope of preparation reflects paraprofessional activity.

All of these salutory effects depend on the assumption that the practicing bar is willing and able to follow an evolutionary path toward a greater commitment to the more intellectually rigorous and creative aspects of practice, although it would not be inconsistent with other developments in western culture if paraprofessionalism rather led to expanded professional leisure. But if we anticipate a persisting work ethic, there arises the question of how well founded is this "willing and able" assumption. To what extent is the bar prepared to assume responsibilities on a new plane of professionalism laid open by the entry of paraprofessionals?

The relevance of this question is striking in light of Professor Statsky's new book. He has prepared no mere manual of office procedures designed to facilitate learning how the litigation department relates to the probate department, or a handbook to prevent getting lost in a law library. This volume presents instead a methodology for gaining a thorough grounding in the fields of domestic relations law. It is a superb teaching tool. The paraprofessional who masters the skills required of him in a training program utilizing this book makes the central challenge to the bar in the nature of: "Do something I can't." Ultimately, the challenge is to those of us on the academic side of the law, for without some real confidence that professional legal education prepares students for intellectual rigor at a high level and for creative thought, the line between Professor Statsky's paraprofessionals and law school graduates may become all too blurred.

SANFORD J. FOX
Professor of Law,
Boston College Law School

OTHER SKILLS TEXTS BY THE SAME AUTHOR

Introduction to Paralegalism: Perspectives, Problems and Skills (West Publishing Co., 1974)

1977 Supplement to *Introduction to Paralegalism*

Legislative Analysis: How to Use Statutes and Regulations (West Publishing Co., 1975)

Case Analysis and Fundamentals of Legal Writing (West Publishing Co., 1977) (with J. Wernet)

Teaching Advocacy: Learner-Focused Training for Paralegals (National Paralegal Institute, 1974)

*

THE MEANING OF "YOUR STATE"

Throughout the skills assignments of this book, you will see reference to the phrase, "your state," e. g., the state code of your state. The objective of the assignments is to assist the student to relate the law outlined in the chapters of this book to the specific law of a particular state: "your state." The phrase, "your state" can have several meanings:

—the state where you intend to use your paralegal * skills—where you hope to be employed

—the state where you are studying to become a paralegal (which may be different from the state where you will be employed)

—the state where you are now working (which may be different from the state where you hope to be employed)

If you know for sure in what state you will be employed as a paralegal, it is highly recommended that you select this state as the focus of the assignments in this book.

Your selection of a state may depend in part on the availability of certain law books. In Chapter Two, *infra* pp. 37–38, the library law books dealing with Family Law to which you should have access are listed.

---

* A paralegal is a person with legal skills who works under the supervision of a lawyer or who is otherwise authorized by law to use those legal skills.

*

SUMMARY OF CONTENTS

SUMMARY OF CONTENTS

SUMMARY OF CONTENTS

*

TABLE OF CONTENTS

TABLE OF CONTENTS

CHAPTER THREE: THE DYNAMICS OF WORKING IN A FAMILY LAW OFFICE—Cont'd

TABLE OF CONTENTS

TABLE OF CONTENTS

TABLE OF CONTENTS

CHAPTER FIFTEEN: SEPARATION AGREEMENTS: LEGAL ISSUES AND DRAFTING OPTIONS—Continued

CHAPTER SIXTEEN: GROUNDS FOR DIVORCE—Cont'd

CHAPTER SEVENTEEN: DIVORCE PROCEDURE, ALIMONY, PROPERTY DIVISION, CHILD SUPPORT AND CUSTODY—Continued

TABLE OF CONTENTS

TABLE OF CONTENTS

APPENDICES

†

Superior Court of the District of Columbia
Photo by Pat Farrell

DOMESTIC RELATIONS: LAW AND SKILLS

Chapter One

THE SKILLS OF A FAMILY LAW PRACTICE

SECTION A. INTRODUCTION: THE SCOPE OF FAMILY LAW

What is the law of domestic relations? What kinds of problems are covered in this area of the law? Suppose that you are a paralegal working for Karen Smith, an attorney in your state. One of the clients of the office is Susan Miller who lives out of state. The attorney receives the following telegram from Ms. Miller:

2/7/79

Karen Smith:

I am leaving town in a week to come to live with my mother. She will help me move everything so that I can take up residence in your state. I must see you as soon as I arrive. My husband has threatened me and the children. I will bring the twins with me. I don't know where my oldest boy is. He is probably with his father getting into more trouble.

Susan Miller

Karen Smith asks you to prepare a list of potential problems that could be involved in the Miller case. The list can be used as a checklist of topics that will have to be covered during the interview [1] with Ms. Miller next week. By examining the list, you will obtain some idea of the scope of law that is part of a Family Law practice.

1. For more on client interviewing, see infra pp. 79–107. See also, Statsky, W., "Legal Interviewing" in *Introduction to Paralegalism: Perspectives, Problems and Skills* pp. 265–95 (1974), and p. 64 of the 1977 Supplement to the *Introduction* book.

2/10/79

Memo to: Karen Smith, Esq.
From: Your Name, Paralegal

Re: Susan Miller case
Our File Number: 79–235

You have asked me to prepare a list of potential problems that could be involved in the Miller case. The only facts we know thus far are those contained in her 2/7/79 telegram to you. She and two of her three children will be coming to live with her mother in this state. She says that her husband has threatened her and the children. She thinks her oldest son is with his father and that he will probably be getting into trouble. Here is a preliminary overview of problems that we need to look out for:

A. CRIMINAL LAW [2]

1. Has Mr. Miller committed a crime? What kind of threats did he make? Did he assault his wife and children?
2. Has he failed to support his family? If so, is the non-support serious enough to warrant criminal action against him?
3. Even if he has committed a crime, would it be wise for Ms. Miller to ask the district attorney to prosecute?
4. Is there any danger of further criminal acts by her husband? If so, what can be done, if anything, to prevent them?

B. DIVORCE/SEPARATION/ANNULMENT LAW [3]

5. What does Ms. Miller want?
6. Does she know what her husband wants to do?
7. Does she have grounds for a divorce?
8. Does she have grounds for an annulment? (Were the Millers validly married?)
9. Does she have grounds for a judicial separation?
10. Does Mr. Miller have grounds for a divorce, annulment or separation against his wife?

C. LAW OF CUSTODY [4]

11. Does Ms. Miller want permanent custody of all three children? (Is she the natural mother of all

2. Infra p. 434ff.

3. Infra p. 223ff.

4. Infra p. 376ff.

three? Is he their natural father? Any paternity problems?)

12. If she does not want a divorce or separation, how can she obtain custody of the children?

13. Does she want anyone else (e. g., her mother or other relative) to be given temporary or permanent custody of any of the children?

D. SUPPORT LAW [5]

14. Is Mr. Miller adequately supporting his wife?

15. Is he adequately supporting the three children?

16. Can she obtain a court order forcing him to support them while she is deciding whether or not she wants to terminate the marital relationship?

17. If she files for divorce, annulment or judicial separation, can she obtain a temporary support order while the case is in progress?

18. If she files for divorce, annulment or judicial separation, and loses, can she still obtain a support order against him?

19. Would a support order do any good? Does Mr. Miller have assets (personal property or real property) against which a support order can be enforced?

20. If he cannot be relied upon for support and she cannot work, does she qualify for public assistance?

E. CONTRACT/AGENCY LAW [6]

21. While she is living apart from her husband, can she enter into contracts with merchants for the purchase of food, clothing, furniture, transportation, etc. and make *him* pay for them?

22. Has she already entered into such contracts?

23. Has she ever worked for him or otherwise acted as his agent?

24. Has he ever worked for her or otherwise acted as her agent?

25. Have any of the children (particularly the older child) entered into any contracts under their own names? If so, who is liable for such contracts? Can they be cancelled or disaffirmed?

F. REAL AND PERSONAL PROPERTY LAW [7]

26. Do either or both of them own any real property, e. g., land? If so, how is the real property owned?

5. Infra p. 369ff.

6. Infra pp. 435–36.

7. Infra p. 371ff.

Individually? As tenants by the entirety? Who provided the consideration for the purchase?

27 What rights does she have in his property?

28. What rights does he have in her property?

29. What is his income? Can his wages be garnished?

30. What other personal property exists? Cars? Bank accounts? Stocks? Bonds? Furniture? Etc. Who owns the property?

G. TORT LAW [8]

31. Has he committed any torts against her? (E. g., assault, conversion)

32. Can one spouse sue another in tort?

H. CIVIL PROCEDURE/CONFLICT OF LAW [9]

33. If a court action is brought (e. g., divorce, custody, separate maintenance), what court would have jurisdiction? A court in this state? A court in the state where he resides? A federal court?

34. How can service of process be made?

35. If she sues and obtains a judgment in this state, can it be enforced in another state?

I. EVIDENCE [10]

36. What factual claims will Ms. Miller be making, e. g., that when her husband made a particular agreement with her, he never intended to carry it out; that he has assets which could be used to support his family which he is not using, etc.?

37. What testimonial evidence (oral statements of witnesses) exists to support her claims?

38. How much of this evidence is admissible in court?

39. How much of the admissible evidence is likely to be believed by a judge or jury?

40. What other relevant evidence should be pursued, e. g., documentary evidence such as marriage and birth certificates, records of purchases, etc.?

41. Whose depositions need to be taken, if any?

J. JUVENILE LAW [11]

42. Can a neglect petition be brought against Mr. Miller? Against Ms. Miller?

8. Infra pp. 477–482.

9. Infra p. 343ff.

10. Infra p. 367.

11. Infra p. 459ff.

43. Why is she upset about her eldest son? Has he committed any "acts of delinquency?" How old is he?

44. Is he a Person in Need of Supervision?

K. TAX LAW [12]

45. Have Mr. Miller and his wife filed joint tax returns in the past?

46. Are there any refunds due (or money owed) on past returns?

47. In a property settlement following a divorce or separation, what would be the most advantageous settlement for Ms. Miller for tax purposes?

48. What arrangement might Mr. Miller seek in order to seek the best tax posture? What is negotiable? What will he be willing to give up in order to obtain his tax objectives?

L. PROFESSIONAL RESPONSIBILITIES/ETHICS [13]

49. Is Mr. Miller represented by counsel? If so, can we contact Mr. Miller directly, or must all communications to him be made through his attorney. If he is not yet represented, are there limitations on what we can and cannot say to him?

50. If Ms. Miller can find her eldest son, can she simply take him away from her husband when the latter is not around? Would this be illegal? What advice would we have to give in this situation?

The purpose of this book is to examine many of the above questions that could arise in a case such as Miller v. Miller. More specifically, the purpose is to equip you with the *skills* needed to be able to raise and to answer such questions that could arise *in your state.*

SECTION B. THE SKILLS ASSIGNMENTS: GENERAL INSTRUCTIONS

The study of law should always have two components:

(1) *knowledge* of what the law is, and,

(2) *skills* to use that knowledge in the delivery of legal services to clients.

Knowledge without skills is as useless (and as potentially dangerous) as skills without knowledge.

12. Infra p. 411ff.

13. Infra p. 59ff.

(1) Knowledge

This book contains a great deal of information and knowledge about Family Law. Even if this book were devoted to the law of one state, however, it could not possibly contain all of the Family Law of that state. This is so not only because the law is constantly changing, but more importantly because of the nature of law itself. A fundamental principle of our legal system is that as the facts in a problem change, so the law itself governing those facts may change.[14] You will get a better sense of what this means later when you begin some of the legal analysis assignments.[15] The point is: since there are an infinite variety of facts possible, no one could have a complete knowledge of the law that governs all of the facts that could exist.

(2) Skills

First and foremost, this book is about the following skills as they are used in the delivery of legal services to clients with Family Law problems:

(a) legal analysis;

(b) drafting (e. g., complaints);

(c) interviewing;

(d) investigation;

(e) legal research (into the Family Law of your state);

(f) supervising and "being supervised";

(g) law office management.

Not all of these skills will be given equal emphasis in this book. Paralegals working in Family Law practices do not all perform the same tasks. The above skills, however, will equip the paralegal to handle most situations that can arise in the Family Law practice where s/he works. Without these skills, it must be frankly admitted, you will be lost. This will be so no matter how much *knowledge* of law you can memorize. Instructions given to you by your supervisors will tend to fall on deaf ears if you do not have at least a preliminary grasp of these skills. It is not uncommon for a supervisor to give instructions to a paralegal on an assignment and assume that the paralegal knows as much about the area of the law as the supervisor. What to do in such a situation? A major recourse of the paralegal is to use the basic skills referred to above. In short, the skills will enable you to stand on your own two feet in a busy law office under the supervision of attorneys and senior paralegals; they will enable you to make a maximum contribution to the office.

14. For more on the importance of facts in our legal system, see Chapter 10, "The Role of Facts in Our Legal System," in Statsky, W., & Wernet, J., *Case Analysis and Fundamentals of Legal Writing*, 153ff (1977).

15. Infra p. 16.

THE SKILLS ASSIGNMENTS IN THIS BOOK

Throughout the chapters of this book, you will find nine major kinds of skills assignments:

1. The State Code Assignment.
2. The Legal Analysis Assignment.
3. The Complaint Drafting Assignment.
4. The Agreement Drafting Assignment.
5. The Court Opinion Assignment.
6. The Checklist Formulation Assignment.
7. The Interrogatory Assignment.
8. The Flow Chart Assignment.
9. The Law Office Management Assignment.

On the pages where these assignments are found, you will be given *specific instructions.* In addition, a set of *general instructions* will be available for each of the nine categories of assignments. These general instructions will be found on the following pages of this chapter. Hence, throughout the remaining chapters of this book, you will be referred back to this chapter for *General Instructions* on the assignments so that these instructions will not have to be repeated constantly.

Before proceeding to the General Instructions, it is necessary that you learn:

How to Ride the Cartwheel

Many of the assignments will ask you to go examine some of the law books containing Family Law material. These law books will be mentioned in greater detail in Chapter Two.[16] One of our major objectives is to increase your ability to use books such as:

manuals	formbooks
codes	digests
encyclopedias	legal newspapers

In the practice of Family Law, the lawyer and the paralegal go to these materials *regularly* for reasons such as:

—finding a standard form in a practice book which will have to be adapted to the needs of a current client;

—checking the court rules to determine how many days a client has to file a court document;

16. Supra p. 37ff.

—checking the state statutory code to find out for the first time (or to refresh one's memory) what the law is on a particular problem, e. g., what the grounds for an annulment are;

—finding case law, e. g., to determine whether your state courts have ever rendered a decision on a set of facts similar to the facts of a current client;

—etc.

The skills of being able to handle the above tasks should be learned *while* you are studying Family Law. You should not have to wait until you have completed a legal research course and you do not have to do so. The assignments in this book are designed to train you in these skills while you are studying the basic principles of Family Law. Furthermore, in order to do the assignments, you do not have to have access to a large law library.[17]

What is needed in order to be able to use a law book—any law book? [18] Each law book (or set of law books) has its own peculiar features and structure. In all honesty, it must be admitted that many of these books are difficult to use because they are poorly organized. *If, however, you are able to use the index and the table of contents of these books,*[19] *seventy percent of the battle has been won.* Using the index and the table of contents is a skill in itself. The CARTWHEEL is a technique designed to assist you in acquiring this skill.

The objective of the CARTWHEEL can be simply stated: to get you into the habit of trying to phrase every word involved in the client's problem *fifteen to twenty different ways!* When you go to the index or table of contents of a law book, you naturally begin looking up the words and phrases which you think should lead you to the relevant material in the book. If you do not find anything on point, two conclusions are possible:

1. There is nothing on point in the law book.
2. You looked up the wrong words in the index and table of contents.

Most people make the mistake of thinking that the first conclusion is accurate. Nine times out of ten, the second conclusion is the reason why the student fails to find material in the law book that was relevant to the Family Law problem of the client. The solution is to be able to phrase a word in as many different ways and in as many different contexts as possible. Hence, the CARTWHEEL.

17. For a list of the law books to which you should have access, see pp. 37–38.

18. See generally, Statsky, W., "Legal Research and Analysis" in *Introduction to Paralegalism: Perspectives, Problems and Skills*, pp. 360–512 (1974).

19. Id. at p. 424ff.

Suppose that the problem of the client involved, among other things, a wedding. The structure of the CARTWHEEL would be as follows:

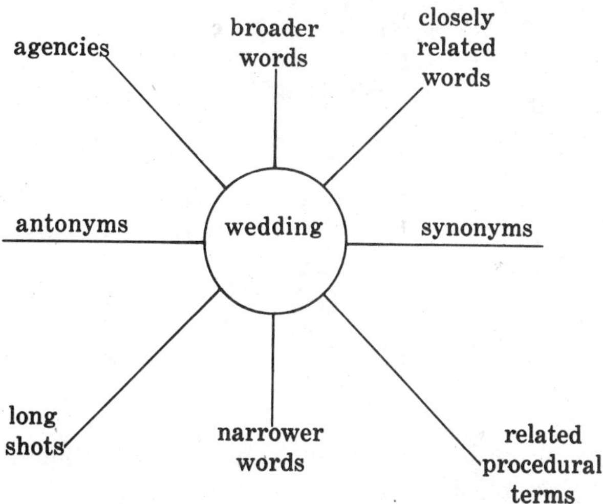

[B7882]

The first step in using the index and table of contents in any law book is to look up the word "wedding" in that index and table.. Assuming that you are not successful with this word (either because the word is not in the index and table, or because the page or section references after the word in the index and table do not lead you to relevant material in the body of the book), the next step is to think of as many different phrasings and contexts of the word "wedding" as possible. Here is where the steps of the CARTWHEEL can be useful:

THE CARTWHEEL: USING THE INDEX AND TABLE OF CONTENTS OF LAW BOOKS

1. Identify all the *major words* from the facts of the client's problem (most of these facts can be obtained from the intake memorandum written following the initial interview with the client.) Place each word or small set of words in the center of the CARTWHEEL.
2. In the index and table of contents, look up all of these words.
3. Identify the *broader* categories of these major words.
4. In the index and table of contents, look up all of these broader categories.
5. Identify the *narrower* categories of these words.
6. In the index and table of contents, look up all of these narrower categories.
7. Identify all of the *synonyms* of these words.
8. In the index and table of contents, look up all of these synonyms.
9. Identify all of the *antonyms* of these words.
10. In the index and table of contents, look up all of these antonyms.
11. Identify all *closely related* words.
12. In the index and table of contents, look up all of these closely related words.
13. Identify all *procedural* terms related to these words.
14. In the index and table of contents, look up all of these procedural terms.
15. Identify all *agencies*, if any, which might have some connection to these words.
16. In the index and table of contents, look up all of these agencies.
17. Identify all *long shots*.
18. In the index and table of contents, look up all of these long shots.

NOTE: The above categories are not mutually exclusive.

[B7861]

If we were to apply these 18 steps of the CARTWHEEL to the word "wedding," here are some of the words and phrases that would be checked in the index and table of contents of every law book that deals with Family Law:

BROADER WORDS: celebration, ceremony, rite, ritual, formality, festivity, etc.

NARROWER WORDS: civil wedding, church wedding, golden wedding, proxy wedding, sham wedding, shot-gun marriage, etc.

SYNONYMS: marriage, nuptial, etc.

ANTONYMS: alienation, annulment, divorce, separation, etc.

CLOSELY RELATED WORDS: matrimony, marital, domestic, husband, wife, bride, anniversary, custom, children, blood test, pre-marital, spouse, relationship, family, home, consummation, cohabitation, sexual relations, betrothal, minister, wedlock, oath, contract, name change, domicile, residence, etc.

PROCEDURAL TERMS: action, suit, statute of limitations, complaint, discovery, defense, petition, jurisdiction, etc.

AGENCIES: Bureau of Vital Statistics, County Clerk, License Bureau, Secretary of State, Justice of the Peace, etc.

LONG SHOTS: dowry, common law, single, blood relationship, fraud, religion, license, illegitimate, remarriage, antenuptial, alimony, bigamy, pregnancy, gifts, chastity, community property, impotence, incest, virginity, support, custody, consent, paternity, etc.

As indicated in the chart, there may be some overlapping of the categories; they are not mutually exclusive. Also, it is *not* significant whether you place a word in one category or another so long as the word comes to your mind as you comb through the index and table of contents. The CARTWHEEL is, in effect, a *word association game* which should become second nature to you with practice. Perhaps you might think that some of the word selections in the above categories are a bit farfetched. The problem, however, is that you simply will not know for sure whether a word will be fruitful until you try it. To be imaginative, one must be prepared to take some risks.

Paralegal in the law library
Photo by Michael Diamond

Assignment # 1

(a) Make a list of words that come to your mind under all the categories of the CARTWHEEL when your starting point is the word "cruelty."

(b) Make a list of words that come to your mind under all the categories of the CARTWHEEL when your starting point is the word "support."

Assignment # 2

(a) The statutory code [20] of your state probably has a number of different statutes that deal with the rights and obligations of children. Go to the indexes and tables of contents of your state statutory code and use them to help you find as many such statutes as you can. Use the CARTWHEEL to help your mind think of many different phrasings and contexts for the word "children." For each statute that you find, give its citation [21] and a brief summary of what it says about children.

20. See supra p. 13ff.

21. A citation to a statute will contain the name of the statutory code, the title and/or section number being referred to, and the date of the statutory code being used, e. g., Mass.Ann. Laws, Ch. 12, § 54 (1966). The mark § means section. The citation in the example means section 54 in chapter 12 of the Massachusetts Annotated Laws. See also infra p. 15.

(b) Repeat the above assignment for the word "woman." Find as many statutes in your statutory code as you can (using the CARTWHEEL as an aid) that treat the rights and obligations of a woman. For each statute, provide a citation and a brief summary.

We now turn to the GENERAL INSTRUCTIONS for the nine skills assignments of this book:

1. STATE CODE ASSIGNMENT

A great deal of Family Law grows out of the statutory law of your state. This law, of course, will be found within the state statutory code written by your state legislature. Here are some examples of what statutory codes look like:

It is extremely important that you become acquainted with the Family Law sections of your statutory code as soon as possible. Many of the assignments in the chapters of this book ask you to examine your statutory code on a particular Family Law topic. If you do not have access to the statutory code of your state, you will obviously not be able to do these assignments. Be sure to check all the leads to law libraries in your area mentioned in Chapter Two [22] before you conclude that no statutory code exists for you to use.

The General Instructions to use for all statutory code assignments are as follows:

GENERAL INSTRUCTIONS FOR THE STATUTORY CODE ASSIGNMENTS

1. Be sure that you are using the latest edition of your statutory code.
2. Statutes can be changed or repealed, and new statutes can be added. To find out about such changes, repeals and additions:
   - (a) check the pocket part [23] of every volume;
   - (b) look for Replacement Volumes; [24]
   - (c) look for Supplement Volumes; [25]
   - (d) shepardize the statute; [26]
3. Find as many indexes and tables of contents [27] within the code as you can. There will often be a General Index at the end of the entire set of the volumes. In addition, there will usually be smaller indexes after each volume or series of volumes that cover the same topic area.
4. Carefully employ the CARTWHEEL technique (supra pp. 7-11) to assist you in using the indexes and tables of contents within the code skillfully.
5. If there are Notes of Decisions [28] following the statute, these notes may be of assistance to you in understanding the statutes. The Notes are small paragraph summaries of court opinions that have interpreted the statute. (Caution: statutes are sometimes changed after opinions interpreting them are written.[29])

22. Infra p. 37.

23. See *Introduction*, supra note 1 at p. 380.

24. Id. at 381.

25. Id. at 383.

26. Id. at 505ff. To shepardize a statute means to find out what has happened to the statute since it was enacted. This is done by using a set of volumes called Shepard's Citations. You go to the Shepard volumes that cover the statutes of your state. At the beginning of many of these volumes there will be explanatory material telling you how to use the volumes, i. e., how to shepardize the statute.

27. See *Introduction*, supra note 1 at p. 424ff.

28. Id. at 401.

29. See *Case Analysis*, supra note 14 at p. 354.

6. Give a complete citation[30] to every statute you mention. The citation must include:
   (a) the title or chapter number of the statute;
   (b) the abbreviated name of the code;
   (c) the number of the section within the statute to which you are referring;
   (d) the subsection number, if any;
   (e) the date of the code you are using.
7. When you quote from a statute, always put quotation marks around the language you are quoting.
8. If you are asked to interpret or apply any statutory language to the facts of a hypothetical problem,[31] consult the General Instructions for the Legal Analysis Assignments (infra pp. 16–19).
9. If you cannot find what you are looking for in the statutory code, proceed as follows:
   (a) Repeat step 4 above. Frequently, the problem is the failure to use the indexes and tables of contents creatively. Do the CARTWHEEL exercise again to try to come up with more words and phrases to be checked in the indexes and tables of contents of the statutory code.
   (b) Check the court rules of your state courts[32] to determine whether they treat the topic you are pursuing.
   (c) Check the constitution of your state[33] to determine whether it treats the topic you are pursuing.
   (d) Find out if any court opinions have been written by your state courts on the topic you are pursuing. For the techniques of finding court opinions, see infra p. 27.

[B7862]

Assignment # 3

At the beginning of this book on pp. XI–XIII there is a SUMMARY OF CONTENTS of the entire book. You will note that there are blank spaces on the right hand side of the page which are to be filled in by you after you check the statutory code of your state. For each topic treated in this book, you should try to locate the section numbers of statutes that cover the same topic. Chapter Sixteen, for example, treats the topic of the grounds for divorce. Go to your statutory code. Use the index and table of contents within the code to locate statutes that cover this same topic of divorce grounds. If there is only one statutory section in your code that covers this topic, write that sec-

30. Id. at 550–551.

31. See generally, Statsky, W., *Legislative Analysis: How to Use Statutes and Regulations* (1975).

32. See *Introduction*, supra note 1 at p. 382.

33. Id. at p. 452.

tion number in the blank space corresponding to Chapter Sixteen in the SUMMARY OF CONTENTS. If there is more than one statutory section that cover this topic, write the first section number in that blank space. When you complete this assignment, you will have, at a glance, page references in this book and statutory references on the same topics. If you cannot find any statutes on any of the topics listed in the SUMMARY OF CONTENTS, leave the spaces next to those topics blank.

2. LEGAL ANALYSIS ASSIGNMENT

What is legal reasoning or legal analysis? [34] The process can be diagrammed as follows:

FACTS + RULE = APPLICATION OF RULE TO FACTS

[B7863]

For example:

FACTS: George and Helen are married. One day after a big argument, George walks out of the house and says, "Good by. Find someone else to take care of you." When he walked out the door, he had resolved to stay away forever. One day later, after George calmed down, he changed his mind and decided to return to Helen.

RULE: One spouse *abandons* another by leaving without any intention of returning.

APPLICATION OF RULE TO FACTS: When George walked out of the house resolving to stay away forever, he "left without any intention of returning." This is abandonment. The fact that he later changed his mind is not significant to a determination of whether abandonment existed. The critical question is the state of mind of the spouse at the time the spouse left.

The application of the rule to the facts is often the most difficult part of legal analysis. This is usually due to one of two reasons:

(a) a word or phrase in the rule is ambiguous, or

(b) you feel that you need more facts than you are given.

34. On legal analysis, see generally, Statsky, W., *Legislative Analysis: How to Use Statutes and Regulations* (1975) and Statsky, W. & Wernet, J., *Case Analysis and Fundamentals of Legal Writing* (1977).

(A) Ambiguity in the Rule

In our example involving George and Helen, suppose that the facts were as follows:

FACTS: George and Helen are married. One day after a big argument, George walks out of the apartment and says, "Good by. Find someone else to take care of you." He moves upstairs to another apartment in the same building which is vacant and which he and his wife jointly own. When he walked out the door of the apartment, he had resolved to stay away forever. One day later, after he calmed down, he changed his mind and decided to return to Helen.

RULE: One spouse *abandons* another by leaving without any intention of returning.

There is an ambiguity in the rule. What does "leaving" mean? At least two interpretations are possible:

—"leaving" means moving out of the entire building;

—"leaving" means moving out of whatever part of the building in which both spouses normally live.

Which is the correct definition of "leaving"? The difference in the definitions is critical. Depending on which definition is adopted, a different result is reached:

—according to the first definition, George would not have abandoned Helen because he did not move out of the entire building;

—according to the second definition, George did abandon Helen since he moved out of the apartment where they both normally lived; under this definition, he can commit abandonment without moving out of the entire building.

Your task in legal analysis is to be sensitive to such ambiguity in rules that you are trying to apply to facts. Unfortunately, most students are not. They do not like to search for ambiguity; they accept language at face value. You are urged to look at every word in the rule that you are applying and ask yourself:

What is the definition of this word? Is more than one definition possible? If your answer is no, think harder! Are you sure that both sides of the controversy would agree on the definition of the word you are examining?

The biggest mistake made in legal analysis is hitting the reader over the head with one conclusion. Don't try to impress the readers of your analysis with the certitude and inevitability of the analysis. Where ambiguity exists, find it and write about it. The sign of good legal analysis is a perceptive eye which articulates both sides of the controversy. Just because you personally believe that one side is more correct than the other, it does not mean that you can ignore the position that you think is wrong. State *all* sides. If you want to give your own personal opinion as to which side would win, you may do so, but only after you have put yourself in the shoes of both sides and have articulated what each side would argue. Students will often say, "I can't think of what the other side would argue." What these students must do is to re-think their analysis. Go through each word/phrase in the rule being applied and determine whether more than one interpretation or definition is possible.

Once you have identified ambiguity in the rule being applied, and once you have carefully spelled out how each side to the controversy would handle the ambiguity, what do you do next? How can you resolve the ambiguity? You would have to do legal research, e. g., to find out whether any courts have interpreted the words/phrases that are ambiguous. For purposes of the legal analysis assignments in this book, however, you should not do any legal research unless the instructions in the assignment tell you to do so.

(B) The Need for More Facts

In the process of trying to connect rules to facts, you may sometimes feel that you need more facts than those given in the assignment. You want the additional facts because you think they would be needed in order to be more sure of the arguments on the applicability of the rule. When you find yourself in such a situation, state what additional facts you would like to have and *state why they would be helpful to your analysis.*

In the example involving George and Helen above, suppose the facts provided that George told Helen, "Good by. Find someone else to take care of you", but you are not told whether he walked out. In your analysis, you would have to point out that the facts do not state what George did after he made this statement to Helen. You need additional facts. You need to know whether he left the building or any part of the building after he made the statement. The rule refers to "leaving" and you don't know whether he left. All you can do in the analysis is to say that "*if* George left after the statement, then . . . ."

Suppose also that you did not know whether George left with the intent of never returning. Clearly you would need additional facts to help resolve the intent issue. For example:

—Did he take his clothes with him?

—Did he speak to anyone else after he left about what he was doing?

—How far away did he go when he left?

—Did he change his address officially, e. g., at the post office?

—Did he call Helen or otherwise contact her after he left? If so, how long after he left, how often and about what?

—etc.

State why you need the additional facts. For example, if George took his clothes with him when he left, it would be some indication that his departure was permanent, i. e., that he had no intention of returning when he left. This should be stated as such in your legal analysis.

GENERAL INSTRUCTIONS FOR THE LEGAL ANALYSIS ASSIGNMENTS

1. The starting point in the legal analysis exercise is the set of facts provided in the assignment. It is to this set of facts that you must apply the rule or rules.
2. Where do you find the rule or rules to apply to the facts?
   (a) By examining the text of the chapter immediately preceding the assignment,
   (b) By going to the state code of your state—if you are told to do so in the assignment.
   (c) By stating what you think the rule should be (use this third approach only as a last resort).
3. Carefully examine each word/phrase in the rule being applied.
4. Define each important word/phrase in the rule.
5. Determine whether more than one definition exists for each such important word/phrase.
6. If more than one definition is possible, state each definition and show what effect the different definitions would have on the results of the analysis. How would each side use the definition most favorable to itself?
7. Carefully examine each of the facts given to you in the assignment.
8. Note any differences in the fact situation given in the assignment with comparable fact situations discussed in the text of the chapter immediately preceding the assignment. You will have to assess for yourself whether such fact differences are significant.
9. If you determine that you need more facts to provide the analysis, state what facts you need and why you would like to have the additional facts. Specifically, how will the additional facts assist in completing the analysis?
10. Analyze the facts from the perspective of both sides. Do not be dogmatic in your analysis. Whenever possible, show how the facts might be interpreted differently by both sides.
11. Do not do any legal research on the assignment unless you are specifically instructed to do so, e. g., see instruction 2(b) above.

[B7864]

3. COMPLAINT DRAFTING ASSIGNMENT

A complaint is a court document filed by a party suing another party which begins the litigation. The complaint states a grievance—called a cause of action—against the other party. A cause of action is simply a legally acceptable reason for suing.[35] In many of the assignments of this book, you will be asked to draft a complaint. The basic structure of a complaint can be seen in the following example:

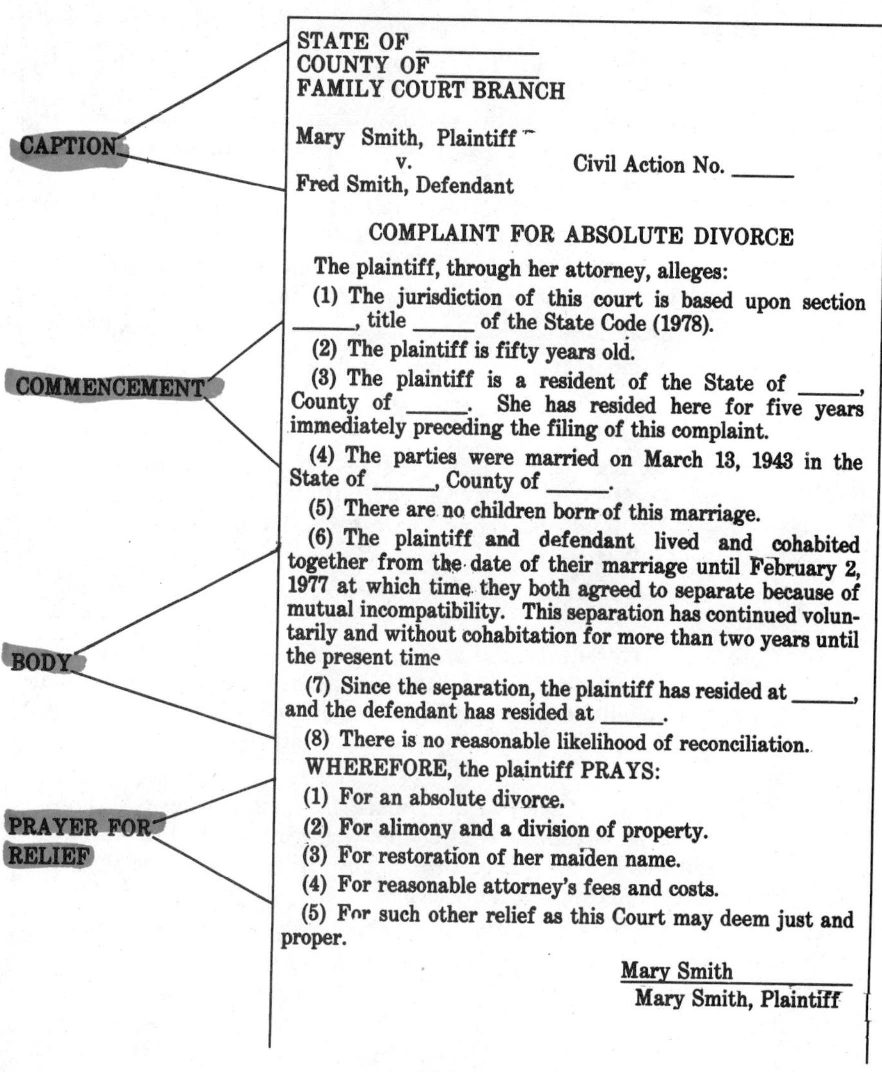

STATE OF ________
COUNTY OF ________
FAMILY COURT BRANCH

Mary Smith, Plaintiff
v. Civil Action No. _____
Fred Smith, Defendant

COMPLAINT FOR ABSOLUTE DIVORCE

The plaintiff, through her attorney, alleges:

(1) The jurisdiction of this court is based upon section _____, title _____ of the State Code (1978).

(2) The plaintiff is fifty years old.

(3) The plaintiff is a resident of the State of _____, County of _____. She has resided here for five years immediately preceding the filing of this complaint.

(4) The parties were married on March 13, 1943 in the State of _____, County of _____.

(5) There are no children born of this marriage.

(6) The plaintiff and defendant lived and cohabited together from the date of their marriage until February 2, 1977 at which time they both agreed to separate because of mutual incompatibility. This separation has continued voluntarily and without cohabitation for more than two years until the present time

(7) Since the separation, the plaintiff has resided at _____, and the defendant has resided at _____.

(8) There is no reasonable likelihood of reconciliation.

WHEREFORE, the plaintiff PRAYS:

(1) For an absolute divorce.

(2) For alimony and a division of property.

(3) For restoration of her maiden name.

(4) For reasonable attorney's fees and costs.

(5) For such other relief as this Court may deem just and proper.

Mary Smith
Mary Smith, Plaintiff

---

35. See *Case Analysis*, supra note 34 at pp. 47, 54, 56, 66, 80, 125ff, 178.

Linda Stout
Linda Stout
Attorney for Plaintiff
234 Main St.
_____, _____07237
966–8631

STATE of __________ } ss
COUNTY of __________ }

VERIFICATION

Mary Smith, being first duly sworn on oath according to law, deposes and says that she has read the foregoing complant by her subscribed and that the matters stated therein are true to the best of her knowledge, information and belief.

Mary Smith
Mary Smith

Subscribed and sworn to before me on this _____ day of _____, 19__.

____
Notary Public

My commission expires _____

IM–442

GENERAL INSTRUCTIONS FOR THE COMPLAINT DRAFTING ASSIGNMENT

1. Your objective is to draft a complaint that would be acceptable to a trial court in your state.
2. Go to your state statutory code and read everything you can about complaints in general and about complaints involving divorce and other domestic relations matters in particular. To help you use the statutory code, use the CARTWHEEL techniques, supra p. 7. For more on using the codes, see supra p. 14.
3. Go to the court rules of the courts of your state and read everything you can about complaints in general and about complaints involving divorce and other domestic relations matters in particular. To help you use the court rules, use the CARTWHEEL techniques, supra p. 7.
4. Some state codes and court rules have standard form complaints which may be helpful. Caution, however, must be exercised in using standard forms. See How to Avoid Abusing a Standard Form, infra p. 23.
5. Many states have practice manuals, formbooks or other practice materials written by attorneys. On identifying such texts for your state, see infra p. 42. These materials often contain standard form complaints which may be helpful. See How to Avoid Abusing a Standard Form, infra p. 23.
6. In the complaint drafting assignments of this book, you will often need additional facts in order to do the complaint, e. g., the names of the parties, their addresses, some of the basic facts that prompted the plaintiff to file the complaint, etc. What-

ever facts are missing should be made up by you so long as your facts are consistent with the limited facts that are provided in the assignment.

7. The caption of the complaint should conform to local practice. Normally, it contains:
   (a) the name of the court;
   (b) the parties' names and litigation capacity (plaintiff, defendant, etc.);
   (c) the docket number assigned by the court;
   (d) the title of the pleading (complaint for . . .).
8. Each paragraph is usually numbered separately. The content of each paragraph should be limited to a single allegation or to a small number of allegations that are closely related.
9. The commencement or beginning of the complaint should conform to local practice. Often it consists of a statement of the court's subject-matter jurisdiction (its power to hear this kind of case—see infra p. 352) and the basic facts that cover the residency of the plaintiff and the existence of a marriage.
10. The body of the complaint contains the statement of the plaintiff's cause of action. In a divorce action, for example, this would consist the grounds for the divorce.
11. The cause of action should be stated briefly and concisely. Avoid long recitations of the facts.
12. You cannot draft a complaint unless you know every component or element of the cause of action. For a divorce on the ground of separation, for example, there must be a voluntary living apart for a designated period of time and the time apart must be consecutive. There must be allegations of fact in the complaint that cover each of these elements of the ground.
13. Where will you find out what the elements of the cause of action are? By examining the law of your state.
14. With the exception of the citation to the statute on subject-matter jurisdiction referred to above in instruction, you do not give citations to statutes, court rules or opinions in the complaint. Limit yourself to the statement of facts—the essential facts.
15. If you are not sure of a fact, you can state it "on information and belief."
16. If the plaintiff has more than one cause of action or theory of recovery, s/he should state all of them. Each should be separately stated and numbered, I, II, III, etc. Each separate theory or cause of action is called a COUNT.
17. The prayer for relief should conform to local practice. It should contain everything the plaintiff is seeking in separately numbered paragraphs.
18. The signatures and verification should conform to local practice. The verification is a sworn statement that the contents of the pleading are true.

You will often have the need to check a standard form before you begin your own drafting. This can be useful so long as you know how to avoid abusing the form. The guidelines listed in the following chart should be kept in mind.

HOW TO AVOID ABUSING A STANDARD FORM

1. A standard form is an example of the document or instrument that is being drafted, e. g., pleading, contract or other agreement.
2. Standard forms are found in a number of places, e. g., form books, manuals, practice texts, in some statutory codes, in some court rules.
3. Most standard forms are written by private attorneys. Occasionally, however, a standard form will be written by the legislature or by the court as the suggested or required format to be used.
4. Considerable care must be exercised in the use of a standard form. Such forms can be very deceptive in that they appear to require little more than a filling in of the blanks. The intelligent use of the forms usually requires much more.
5. The cardinal rule is: adapt the form to the particulars of the client's case on which you are working.
6. Do not be afraid of changing the printed language of the form if you have a good reason for doing so. Whenever you make such a change, bring it to the attention of your supervisor for approval.
7. Forms often have boilerplate language, e. g., "wherefore," "hereinafter," "party of the first part." You should know the difference between essential language and boilerplate language in the form.
8. You should never use a standard form unless and until you have satisfied yourself that you know the meaning of *every* word and phrase on the form whether it is boilerplate or essential. The great temptation of most form users is to ignore what they don't understand because the form has been used so often in the past without any apparent difficulty. Don't give in to this temptation. Find out what everything means by:
   (a) using a legal dictionary;
   (b) asking your supervisor;
   (c) asking other knowledgeable people;
   (d) doing other legal research.
9. You need to know whether the entire form or any part of it has ever been litigated in court. You would have to do legal research in the area of the law relevant to the form in order to find this out.
10. Once you have found a form that appears useful, look around for another form that covers the same topic. Analyze the different forms available. Which one is preferable? Why? The

important point is: keep questioning the validity of the form. Be very skeptical about the utilization of any form.

11. Don't leave any blank spaces on the form.
12. If the form was written for another state, be sure that the form is adapted to the law of your state.
13. Occasionally you may go to an old case file to find a document in that file that might be used as a model for the similar document that you need to draft on a current case. All of the above cautions apply equally to the adaptation of documents from closed case files.

[B7866]

Looking for "model" documents in the closed case files
Photo by Michael Diamond

4. AGREEMENT DRAFTING ASSIGNMENT

Several times in this book, you will be asked to draft an agreement, e. g., a separation agreement. The general instructions on this assignment follow:

GENERAL INSTRUCTIONS FOR THE AGREEMENT DRAFTING ASSIGNMENT

1. Unless otherwise indicated most of the facts that you will need to draft the agreement will have to be created by you—make them up. For example, you can make up the names of the parties to the agreement, their addresses, number of children, economic circumstances or whatever you need to write the agreement. The only standard you need to apply in creating facts is reasonableness. Limit yourself to facts that you think would be normal or reasonable under the circumstances.
2. If you were not making up the facts, you would obviously have to obtain them from the client. This is done through extensive interviewing in order to obtain all the information needed.
3. It is always useful to obtain copies of similar agreements that were written in the past for other clients and/or to obtain copies of model agreements commonly found in form books, manuals, practice books, etc. Such material may provide effective starting points for your own drafting. Caution, however, must be exercised in using such material. See How to Avoid Abusing a Standard Form, supra p. 23.
4. It is critical that you know the law of the area covered by the agreement. What can and cannot be accomplished by the agreement? What legal pitfalls must be avoided? Research in the area of the law, therefore, is an essential precondition of drafting.
5. For purposes of the agreement drafting assignments in this book, however, you do not have to do any legal research unless your instructor tells you to do so. You should find all the law that you need by reading the chapter text immediately preceding the drafting assignment you are doing.
6. Tax considerations are often very important. You should know the tax consequences of every clause in the agreement.
7. Know what the client wants to accomplish by the agreement. Know the specific client objectives. It is too general, for example, to say that the client wants to divide the property of the spouses in an equitable manner. A more specific objective would be to have the other spouse use the vacation home for ten years or until s/he remarries, whichever occurs earlier. Have all the specific objectives in mind when you draft. Each clause in the agreement should relate to one or more of the objectives. Your drafting guide is your statement of objectives.

8. At the beginning of the agreement, label the kind of agreement that it is, e. g., SEPARATION AGREEMENT. Also at the beginning, state the names and addresses of the parties entering the agreement.

9. Number each paragraph consecutively (1, 2, 3, etc.). Limit the subject-matter of each paragraph to a single topic, or to closely related topics. Be as narrow as possible in selecting the topic of a paragraph. For example, in a separation agreement dealing with the disposition of the property that the spouses accumulated during the marriage, each paragraph should cover a separate category of property. Similarly, there should be separately numbered paragraphs covering custody of the children, visitation rights, alimony, etc.

10. A major mistake made by drafters is to assume that everyone will have the same definition of words. Key words should always be defined. What is a key word? Any word that is important and that could have more than one meaning. The word "property," for example, has several meanings, e. g., real property, personal property, property in one's possession now, property to be received in the future, etc. What meaning did the parties intend for the word, "property?" Such words should be carefully defined in the agreement.

11. One sign of an effective agreement is a fair one. It does not make much sense to try to take unfair advantage of the other side in the drafting of the agreement since the result may be an unworkable agreement leading to considerable delay, animosity and litigation expense. The cooperation of both sides is necessary to make the agreement work. An important incentive to such cooperation is a feeling by both parties that the agreement is fair.

[B7867]

5. COURT OPINION ASSIGNMENT

There are two reasons why you need to know how to locate court opinions on Family Law topics:

(a) To find the *common law.* The common law is judge-made law created in the absence of controlling statutory law.[36] There is a considerable amount of Family Law that is part of the common law.

(b) To find court opinions that have interpreted statutes on Family Law.

Equity.

36. See *Case Analysis*, supra note 34 at pp. 8, 93, 129, 221, 254, 353, 390.

GENERAL INSTRUCTIONS FOR THE COURT OPINION ASSIGNMENT

1. The objective of the assignment is to find opinions on the Family Law issue being studied. In the law library there are a number of books which can provide you with leads to such opinions. The major leads (which will be explained in greater detail below) are:
   - (a) Notes of Decisions [37] found within most statutory codes that are annotated.[38]
   - (b) The state digest [39] or the regional digest covering opinions of your state or the American Digest System.
   - (c) American Law Reports.[40]
   - (d) Footnote references in handbooks, hornbooks,[41] manuals, legal encyclopedias,[42] etc.
   - (e) Words and Phrases.
   - (f) Attorneys and paralegals experienced in Family Law.
2. It may be that you are not familiar with all the law books mentioned above. Do *not* wait for a course in legal research to begin learning how to use these books. Start *now* by asking questions about the books. Ask librarians, fellow students, teachers, practicing attorneys and paralegals, etc. Above all, go "browse" through these books as often as you can. Read the Preface or other introductory material in the books to get an idea of how to use them. It is going to be difficult [43] and time consuming, so begin now.
3. NOTES OF DECISIONS: to know how to use these Notes, you must first know how to use a statutory code. (Review the General Instructions for the Statutory Code Assignments, supra p. 14) The Notes contain summaries of opinions that have interpreted statutes. Hence in order to find these Notes you must first find a statute that covers the topic under examination. If opinions exist interpreting this statute, they will be summarized in the Notes following the statute. Be sure to check for more recent Notes in the pocket parts [44] of the code. If a lot of Notes exist after a particular statute, there will often be an index to the Notes before the Notes begin.
4. DIGESTS: digests are volumes of small paragraph summaries of court opinions. A digest is, in effect, a massive index to court opinions, and hence are often called "case finders." There

37. See also *Introduction*, supra note 1 at 401, 441, 467, 475, 493, 495, 499.

38. Id. at 370, 398, 430.

39. Id. at 375, 400, 410, 438ff., 445, 456, 493.

40. Id. at 366, 373, 458.

41. Id. at 378, 384.

42. Id. at 377.

43. See Id. at 440ff. on "How to Start Legal Research."

44. Id. at pp. 380, 387, 391, 401, 411, 433, 453.

are three kinds of digests—all of which contain the same basic material and format:

(a) State Digest. Many states have their own digest, i. e., small paragraph summaries of all the opinions written by the courts in a particular state.

(b) Regional Digest. There are a number of regional digests each one of which covers the opinions written by the state courts of several neighboring states. If you have access to such digests, find the one that covers the opinions of your state courts.

(c) American Digest System. This is the most comprehensive digest of all, covering the opinions of every court in the country. Under a digest topic and number you will find opinion summaries organized alphabetically by state. Hence under any such topic and number, look for the abbreviation of your state.

Whatever digest you use, your starting point should be the indexes and the tables of contents within the digest. To use these indexes effectively, apply the CARTWHEEL techniques (supra p. 7).

5. AMERICAN LAW REPORTS: these volumes contain the full text of selected court opinions plus extensive research material following the opinions. This material is called an annotation. Often within these annotations, there is a state-by-state breakdown (organized alphabetically by state) of the legal issues treated in the opinion. Hence, when you find an annotation on a Family Law topic, you will have references to court opinions in each state on that topic. There are several units of the American Law Reports volumes: ALR, ALR2d, ALR3d and ALR Fed. Each unit has its own index features. In addition, there are several Quick Index volumes. For all these indexes, use the CARTWHEEL techniques to gain access to the volumes (supra p. 7).

6. FOOTNOTE REFERENCES IN OTHER BOOKS: often the most valuable parts of handbooks, hornbooks, manuals and legal encyclopedias are the footnotes in these books. The footnotes usually give citations to court opinions on the topics being discussed in the body of the text. Hence, use the CARTWHEEL techniques (supra p. 7) to gain access to these books and find discussions on the Family Law topic you are examining. Once you find such discussions, see if there are any footnotes provided, and if so, see if there are any references (citations) to court opinions of your state. If you are in a set of books that has extensive footnotes, such as either of the major legal encyclopedias (Corpus Juris Secundum and American Jurisprudence 2nd), the court opinion references in the footnotes may be organized alphabetically by state which will make it easier for you to determine if opinions of your state are provided.

7. WORDS AND PHRASES: this is a multi-volume set of books containing thousands of definitions of legal terms. The definitions are quotations from court opinions. Use the CARTWHEEL techniques (supra pp. 7–11) to try to find court opinions of your state on the Family Law topic under examination.
8. EXPERIENCED ATTORNEYS AND PARALEGALS: never be reluctant to go to attorneys or paralegals in the field of Family Law to ask them for a lead to a court opinion of your state on a particular topic, or to ask them for suggestions on how you might go about finding such an opinion. It is suggested, however, that for your own education you *first* try locating the opinions *on your own* through the Notes of Decisions, digests, annotations of ALR, footnote references in handbooks, hornbooks, manuals and legal encyclopedias, and finally, through the Words and Phrases volumes.[45]

[B7869]

6. CHECKLIST FORMULATION ASSIGNMENT

It is important that you learn how to write checklists that could be part of a manual. Every rule that you are told about or that you read about can be "translated" into a checklist. Such checklist formulation should eventually become second nature to you. The sooner you start thinking in terms of do's, don't's, models, etc., the better.

Suppose that you have before you the following statute of your state:

> § 1742. No marriage shall be solemnized without a license issued by the county clerk of any county of this state not more than thirty days prior to the date of the solemnization of the marriage.

One way to handle this statute is to create a checklist of questions that you would ask a client in order to determine whether the statute applies. Some of the questions would be:

1. Did you have a marriage license?
2. Where did you get the license? Did you obtain it from a county clerk in this state?
3. On what date did you obtain the license?
4. On what date did you go through the marriage ceremony (solemnization)? Were there thirty days between the date you got the license and the date of the ceremony?

These are the questions that must be asked as part of a large number of questions concerning the validity of a particular marriage. If you were creating a manual, the above four questions in your checklist

45. See id. at p. 361.

for section 1742 could go under the manual topic of "Marriage Formation" or "Marriage License." Whenever you have a class on this topic or whenever you analyze any law on this topic (e. g., section 1742), you translate the lecture into checklists such as the brief one presented above.

To be sure, there are checklists written by others already in existence. They are found, for example, in manuals and practice books.[46] Why create your own? First of all, your checklists are *not* intended as a substitute for those in manuals or practice books. You will undoubtedly make extensive use of the latter. You are encouraged to do so. Your checklists will supplement the others. More significantly, two of the best ways for you to learn how to use manuals are (a) to write checklists of your own and (b) to see the connection between the law, (e. g., a statute) and the guidelines and techniques within a checklist. Your understanding of the checklists will be increased if you begin to see how they relate to the law itself. Hence, the emphasis placed on checklists (particularly within the assignments of this book) are intended in large measure to increase the effectiveness of your use of manuals and practice books in the area of domestic relations law.

GENERAL INSTRUCTIONS FOR THE CHECKLIST FORMULATION ASSIGNMENT

1. The starting point in all the checklist formulation assignments will be a rule. The rule will be found within a statute or a court opinion to which you will be referred.
2. Your objective is to make a list of questions that you would ask yourself and/or a client and/or a witness for the purpose of determining whether the rule might apply.
3. Study the rule carefully.
4. Make sure that you understand the rule.[47] Closely analyze it. Make inquiries on what you do not understand in the rule. Consult a legal dictionary. Read closely related rules in order to see the rule you are examining in context. Read the rule again.
5. Break the rule down into small units. Approach the rule piecemeal.
6. For each segment of the rule, design a question or a series of questions.
7. Every time the rule says that something must be done, create a question or a series of questions designed to determine whether it was done.
8. Every time the rule says that something must not be done, create a question or a series of questions designed to determine whether it was not done.

46. Supra p. 7 and infra p. 37.

47. See generally, *Legislative Analysis* supra note 34.

9. Every time the rule imposes a precondition (i. e., *if* such and such occurs, *then* . . . .), create a question or a series of questions designed to determine whether the precondition occurred.
10. Be alert to the word "and" in the rule. It usually refers to additional requirements. Create questions designed to determine whether all the additional requirements were met.
11. Be alert to the word "or" in the rule. It usually refers to alternative requirements. Create questions designed to determine which, if any, of the alternatives were met.
12. If you have been diligent in creating checklists, you will be taking major steps toward the creation of your own manual. The checklists could become part of your Family Law manual. (For other components of such a manual, see the General Instructions for the Law Office Management Assignment, infra p. 35)

[B7919]

7. INTERROGATORY ASSIGNMENT

Interrogatories are a written set of questions addressed by one party in litigation to another before trial.[48] The purpose of the interrogatories is to obtain factual information about the other party's case in order to prepare for trial. The instructions for the interrogatory assignment are as follows:

GENERAL INSTRUCTIONS FOR THE INTERROGATORIES ASSIGNMENT

1. Your objective in writing the questions, i. e., the interrogatories, is to obtain as much information as possible from the other side in order to assist you in preparing your own case.
2. You must limit yourself to questions that are relevant to the litigation. The definition of "relevant", however, is very broad so that you usually have a fair amount of leeway in asking questions. So long as the questions are not unduly detailed and unduly burdensome and expensive for the other side to answer, the questions will usually be allowed. The party to whom you are addressing the interrogatories has the right to object to any of your questions on the ground that they are harassing.
3. It can be useful to try to find sample interrogatories in manuals, form books and other practice materials. Such interrogatories, of course, would have to be adapted to the particular needs of the client's case on which you are currently working. On the dangers of using such forms, see How to Avoid Abusing a Standard Form, supra p. 23.

48. See *Introduction*, supra note 1 at pp. 49, 303, 312, 331, 352, 353ff.

4. It can also be useful to go to the closed case file of another case that contains interrogatories in order to try to adapt them. Again, the use of such materials is but a point of departure. Great care must be used in determining what, if anything, can be borrowed from other interrogatories.

5. Before you draft your interrogatories, you should know the case (on which you are working) inside and out. You should have read all pleadings filed to date, e. g., complaint, answer, all the correspondence in the file, the intake memorandum, etc. Many ideas for questions will come from this knowledge. Of course, for purposes of most of the assignments in this book, you will not have access to such data since the assignments will be based on hypothetical cases. In such situations, use your imagination.

6. In the Checklist Formulation instructions, you saw how you can devise a set of questions based upon a particular rule in order to determine whether that rule applied. See supra p. 29. The same principle of question formulation applies here. Interrogatories are used in litigation. The essence of litigation involves alleged violation of rights and obligations. Rights and obligations are based upon rules. The rules are being interpreted and applied through the litigation. The questions asked should relate to these rules, i. e., to a determination of whether the facts support the application of the rule.

7. The goal of the questions is to elicit facts. Your major concern is always, "what are the facts?"

8. Structure your fact questions around the basic Who, What, Where, When, Why inquiries.

9. It is sometimes useful to ask your questions in such a way that the "story" of the facts comes out chronologically.

10. Be constantly concerned about dates, full names, addresses, exact amounts, etc.

11. Always ask what witnesses the other side intends to rely on to support its version of the facts.

12. Always ask what documentation the other side has relied upon to support its version of the facts.

13. Phrase the questions so that the person answering will have to indicate whether s/he is talking from first hand knowledge, second hand knowledge (hearsay), etc.

14. As to each fact, ask questions calculated to elicit the respondent's ability to comment on the fact, e. g., how far away was s/he, does s/he wear glasses, etc.

15. Avoid complicated and difficult-to-read questions. Be direct and concise.

8. FLOW CHART ASSIGNMENT

A Flow Chart is a step by step account of litigation or of any process. A number of assignments in this book ask you to prepare a flow chart on a particular legal process under discussion. The instructions for this assignment are as follows:

GENERAL INSTRUCTIONS FOR THE FLOW CHART ASSIGNMENT

1. Design the flow chart based upon the law of your state.
2. The two primary sources of information for the flow chart are your state code and the court rules for the courts in your state. See General Instructions for the State Code Assignment, supra p. 14. See also the CARTWHEEL techniques for using codes and court rules, supra p. 7.
3. It is also possible for you to obtain information for the flow chart from manuals, form books and other practice material. It is recommended, however, that you try to obtain the information directly from the code and the court rules. This is so for two reasons. The practice materials may be out of date. Furthermore, the intelligent use of practice materials requires that the student know how to check the accuracy and timeliness of such materials by going to the primary sources—the code and the court rules (and occasionally, the state constitution).
4. The flow chart must be chronological, moving from the first step of the process to the last step.
5. The structure and graphics of the flow chart can be varied:
   (a) it may be presented as a series of boxes (one step per box) with all the boxes connected by arrows to show the progression of the process,
   (b) it may be presented in the form of a list of brief paragraphs with each numbered paragraph stating one step,
   (c) it may be presented in the form of an outline with the major headings being the key phases of the process, e. g., agency contact, pre-trial, etc. (See Appendix A, infra p. 483.)

   You will note that two of the flow chart assignments in this book are structured as numbered boxes arranged vertically (infra p. 241 and p. 398). It is not necessary that this structure be used for all the flow chart assignments. See also Appendix A, infra p. 483 for another kind of flow chart.
6. The information in the flow chart must be procedural. The concern is to obtain all the mechanics of the process. The flow chart should not contain information on substantive liability matters, e. g., on the definition of cruelty as a ground for divorce.
7. For each item of information in the flow chart, state the source of your information, i. e., give the citation to the statute or court rule that provided you with the procedural information you used in the flow chart.

[B7883]

8. Statutory codes and court rules often have sections that deal with all (or a large number of) cases. Such sections are often listed in the index and tables of contents of the codes and court rules under "Civil Procedure," "Actions," "Court Procedure," "Courts," etc. You should check these sections to see what, if anything, they say about the topic of your flow chart.

9. In addition, there may be special sections of your statutory code and court rules that cover the procedural steps that are peculiar to the topic of your flow chart.

10. The major phases of litigation are as follows: pre-trial; trial; appeal; and enforcement. Within these phases, the number of specific steps can be numerous. Some of the steps that you may have to cover are as follows:

—what agency, if any, has jurisdiction over the case;
—what is the application process at the agency;
—what court(s) have jurisdiction;
—how is service of process made;
—how is venue determined;
—what format must be used for the complaint;
—how is the complaint served and filed;
—what format must be used for the answer;
—how is the answer served and filed;
—any special rules for counterclaims;
—any special motions that can be made, e. g., motion to dismiss;
—what rules govern pre-trial discovery:
  deposition;
  interrogatories;
  requests for admissions;
  court ordered examinations (physical & mental);
—sanctions that can be imposed for violation of the discovery rules;
—what preliminary orders can be requested and how must the request be made;
—when and how can a jury request be made;
—what rules govern the issuing of the final judgment;
—how many days does a party have to appeal;
—what court has jurisdiction to hear the appeal;
—how can a judgment be enforced;
—etc.

Again, the above list is not exhaustive. If there are other steps or more detailed steps that apply to the process you are flow charting for your state, you should accurately list those steps that apply for your state.

[B7884]

9. LAW OFFICE MANAGEMENT ASSIGNMENT

The law office management assignment under discussion here does not involve a study of every detail of the administration of a law office from a business perspective. Rather, the assignments will focus on certain aspects of a Family Law practice. You will be asked to interview lawyers, paralegals and secretaries who are working in the field of domestic relations law in order to obtain the perspective of the practitioners on the topic under discussion.

GENERAL INSTRUCTIONS FOR THE LAW OFFICE MANAGEMENT ASSIGNMENT

1. Most of the assignments can be completed through interviews with lawyers, paralegals and secretaries working in the field of domestic relations law.
2. The interviews can be in person or on the phone. It is recommended that you do not use the mails except to ask brief questions.
3. How do you locate practicing lawyers, paralegals and secretaries in the field of domestic relations law? The following are some suggestions:

   —check a directory of lawyers, e. g., Martindale and Hubbell;
   —check with your local bar association;
   —ask your teacher for leads;
   —check with the nearest paralegal association;
   —check with the nearest association of legal secretaries;
   —check with the placement office of your school;
   —etc.
4. Everybody is busy, particularly those working in a law office. You must not give the impression that you are going to take up a lot of time.
5. Have a checklist of questions ready. Come prepared. Do not give the impression that you are not sure what you want.
6. If the person you are interviewing says, "How long will this take?" simply say that it will not take long. Find out if the person will let you begin asking a few questions now. Then say: "You can stop me as soon as you think I'm taking up too much of your time." Get the person to start talking about the topic of your interview as soon as possible. The more the two of you are talking about how long the interview will take, the less likely will the interview ever begin.

6\. Begin with very specific questions, e. g., approximately how many divorce cases did you work on last year? Then move to the broader questions, e. g., do you think that your office will be making greater use of paralegals on a particular kind of case?

7\. Review the instructions for the Flow Chart assignment, supra p. 33. Your interviews for the Law Office Management assignments will be facilitated if you have at least a general idea of what a flow chart is and how one is constructed. This does not mean that you cannot do the Law Office Management assignments until you have done the Flow Chart assignments.

[B7871]

Chapter Two

LAW BOOKS AND LEGAL INSTITUTIONS: A GUIDE TO FAMILY LAW IN YOUR STATE

SECTION A. INTRODUCTION

As soon as possible, it will be essential for you to become familiar with the law books that contain material on the Family Law of your state. Your study of Family Law may begin now, but it will by no means end with your completion of this course. Law books are critical tools of the lawyer's trade; the same is true of the paralegal. No course can cover all of Family Law. Hence, *one of the main objectives of a course in Family Law is to teach you how to keep on learning Family Law after the course is over.* This is done, in large measure, by assisting you to use the law books that contain material on Family Law in your state. Before discussing these law books, a word should be said about where they can be located. Finding a law library and obtaining permission to use it are not always easy undertakings.

SECTION B. FINDING A LAW LIBRARY

What is a law library? One image that may come to your mind is a huge building with thousands of thick, expensive law books. On the other hand, there are law libraries that contain five to ten books within someone's office. Of course, the definition of a great law library is one (big or small) that contains the book you happen to need at a particular time.

LOCATING A LAW LIBRARY

With a little ingenuity, you should be able to gain access to several law libraries in your area of the state. Thirteen different locations are possible:

1. THE LAW LIBRARY IN A PARALEGAL SCHOOL

Not all paralegal schools have large law libraries. For the Family Law practitioner, the essentials consist of a relatively small number of books:

—a state practice manual [1] (if any exist);

1. For more on practice manuals, see Statsky, W., *Introduction to Paralegalism: Perspectives, Problems and Skills*, pp. 378, 380 (1974).

—the court rules of the courts with jurisdiction[2] over Family Law problems in your state;

—those volumes of your state statutory code[3] which contain statutes on Family Law matters (perhaps three or four volumes);

—those volumes of the state digest (if one exists) which contain small paragraph summaries of court opinions on several major Family Law topics (perhaps three or four volumes).

2. THE LAW LIBRARY OF A NEARBY LAW SCHOOL

There are approximately 250 law schools in the United States. Almost all of them have comprehensive law libraries. The biggest difficulty with respect to using these libraries is obtaining permission. A number of approaches are possible:

—wait until someone tells you that you *can't* use it; walk around as if you belong there until someone tells you otherwise;

—ask the librarian of the law school for permission;

—ask the dean of the law school for permission;

—have one of your teachers or the director of your program contact the librarian or dean for permission.

3. THE LAW LIBRARY OF A BAR ASSOCIATION

In your area there may be several bar associations: state, county, city. Normally, the bar association will contain a law library. Permission could be sought from a number of people: any member of the association, the librarian, the president, the executive director or other officer of the association, the chairperson of the paralegal or legal assistant committee of the bar (if one exists), etc.

4. YOUR PUBLIC LIBRARY

Public libraries, particularly the larger ones, often have a section containing law books. The chances are that the collection will be small and out of date, but it is worth exploring.

5. THE LAW LIBRARY OF A COURT

Courts usually have comprehensive law libraries, especially appeals courts. Unfortunately, the judges may be unwilling to share these facilities with students. No harm in asking, however.

In the following locations, the problem, again, will be permission. As indicated above, some ingenuity and a contact are often needed.

6. THE LAW LIBRARY OF LARGE AND MEDIUM SIZE LAW FIRMS

2. For more on jurisdiction, see infra p. 350ff.

3. Supra p. 14.

7. THE LAW LIBRARY OF INDIVIDUAL PRIVATE ATTORNEYS

8. THE LAW LIBRARY OF THE LEGISLATURE

If you live near a state legislature, a city council, a county board of executives, etc.

9. THE LAW LIBRARY OF THE DISTRICT ATTORNEY, PROSECUTOR OR ATTORNEY GENERAL

10. THE LAW LIBRARY OF THE CITY SOLICITOR OR CORPORATION COUNSEL

11. THE LAW LIBRARY OF THE PUBLIC DEFENDER

12. THE LAW LIBRARY WITHIN A FEDERAL, STATE OR LOCAL ADMINISTRATIVE AGENCY

Especially within the general counsel's office of the agency or in the office of any attorney within the agency.

13. A UNIVERSITY/COLLEGE LIBRARY

Even if the university or college does not have a law school or a paralegal school, it might have some law books.

There is one other law library that you need to consider: your own. It is not too soon for you to start collecting your own law books beginning with your course books on law. If the books you purchase are used to further your career, they may be tax deductible. To be sure, you will not be able to afford to buy many books early in your career.

Never buy any law book without checking with at least two lawyers or paralegals on the *practical* value of the book. Ask them how often *they* consult the book on an average day. Do not let your eyes deceive you; it is not necessarily wise to purchase a book simply because it treats an area of the law you need to know something about.

SECTION C. THE LAW BOOKS ON FAMILY LAW: COMPILING YOUR OWN BIBLIOGRAPHY

There are two kinds of law books that are relevant to a Family Law practice: books containing primary authority and those containing secondary authority.

1. PRIMARY AUTHORITY

Primary authority is the law itself: *statutes* written by legislatures, *constitutions* written by the founders of the nation or state, *opinions* written by the courts, and *regulations* written by administrative agencies. What law books contain primary authority?

Statutes: Statutory Codes, Session Laws, Statutes at Large, etc.[4]

Constitutions: At the beginning of Statutory Codes.

Opinions: Reporters.[5]

Regulations: Code of Regulations, loose-leaf services.[6]

Court Rules: In a volume called Court Rules and/or within the Statutory Code.

2. SECONDARY AUTHORITY

Secondary authority contains leads to and information about primary authority. For example:

Digests: [7] small paragraph summaries of court opinions.

Manuals, Form Books, Practice Books: [8] summaries of the law with an emphasis on "how-to-do-it".

Legal Encyclopedias, Hornbooks, Treatises, Law Reviews: more scholarly summaries and commentary on the law.[9]

Legal Newspapers: current events in the local courts and other legal matters.

Shepards: [10] a system of informing you about the subsequent history of court opinions (e. g., since the opinion was written, has it been overruled, has it been cited by other opinions).

The next Assignment (# 4) is designed to begin your acquaintance with law books that have something to do with Family Law in your state. You will be asked to identify a number of different law books. How will you find out whether the law books exist in your state, and if so, where they can be located?

—check the card catalogs of law libraries;

—solicit leads from law librarians, law book salespersons, teachers, practicing attorneys, practicing paralegals, your fellow students, anyone else who has some familiarity with Family Law in your state.

4. See *Introduction*, supra note 1 at pp. 363, 366, 383, 392, 398, 401, 417, 454, 467, 482.

5. Id. at pp. 370ff., 381, 390, 458ff.

6. Id. at p. 367.

7. See supra p. 27.

8. Supra p. 23.

9. See generally, *Introduction* supra note 1 at pp. 360–512.

10. Id. at pp. 373, 389, 409, 433ff., 459, 505ff., 559.

Assignment # 4 will not make you an expert in the use of the law books mentioned. It will simply get you started.

For every law book that you come across, remember the following points:

ESSENTIAL QUESTIONS TO ASK YOURSELF ABOUT EVERY LAW BOOK

1. What kind or kinds of primary authority does the book contain?
2. If the book contains secondary authority, who is the author and/or editor?
3. Who published the book?
4. Has there been more than one edition of the book? If so, what edition are you examining?
5. What is the latest date on the copyright page?
6. How is the book brought up to date? Pocket Parts? Supplemental volumes?
7. If the book is part of a set, how many volumes are there in the set?
8. Is there a general index? If so, where it is located? Are there other, more narrow, indexes in the book or books? If so, where are they located?
9. Same questions as in no. 8 with reference to tables of contents.
10. Are there any other tables in the book or books, e. g., abbreviation tables? If so, locate and describe the purpose of each.
11. Does the book or books contain a Preface or other Introductory/Explanatory features? If so, where are they located and how useful are they?

[B7872]

If you are able to answer the above eleven questions about a law book, you have begun to master its structure, to "psyche it out," to make it part of your inventory of resources.

One final point before you begin Assignment # 4. Among the most important features of any law book are its index and table of contents. (As indicated, you must be alert to the fact that many books have more than one index and table of contents.) In the first chapter of this book, we discussed the techniques of using these features via the CARTWHEEL.[11] You should briefly review these techniques now before you do the following assignment.

11. Supra p. 7.

Assignment # 4

Compile a bibliography of Family Law in your state. Specifically, use the law libraries available to you and answer these questions:

(a) Name all Manuals, Practice Books and Form Books that (in whole or in part) cover any Family Law topics in your state. For an overview of such topics see the table of contents listings in this book, supra pp. XIV–XXIV.

(b) Go to your statutory code. Find and cite [12] any one statute on each of the following topics: marriage, annulment, illegitimacy, divorce, alimony, custody, adoption. Briefly state what each statute is about.

(c) For every court in your state that can handle Family Law cases,[13] determine where the court rules of that court are located. In how many different law books can they be found? (You may want to call the clerk of that court for help on this question.)

(d) For every administrative agency of the government that has anything to do with Family Law problems,[14] determine where the regulations (if any) of that agency are printed. (If necessary, call the agency and ask where its regulations are printed.)

(e) Go to a digest containing small paragraph summaries of court opinions in your state.[15] If it is a digest published by West (as most are), pick any five digest topics and key numbers [16] for each of the following areas of law: marriage, annulment, illegitimacy, divorce, alimony, custody and adoption. Simply state the digest topics and key numbers you have selected (five—picked at random—for each of these areas of the law).

(f) Is there a legal newspaper in your state? If so, what is it called? Locate current and/or back issues and identify any two items in the newspaper that have something to do with Family Law matters in your state, e. g., an article on a new divorce law, a report of a recent court opinion in the area.

(g) What is the *Family Law Reporter*? How would it be helpful in finding out about the Family Law of your state?

12. For the definition of a cite (or a citation) see supra p. 15.

13. See infra p. 43.

14. See infra p. 44 for a sample list of such agencies. Also examine Assignment # 6, infra p. 44.

15. Supra p. 27.

16. For example, Divorce, Remarriage 🔑386(4).

SECTION D. LEGAL INSTITUTIONS: COURTS AND AGENCIES

1. COURTS

Here our concern is as follows: what courts in your state have trial court jurisdiction (sometimes called original jurisdiction [17]) over Family Law problems? These courts may have different names in different states, e. g., Family Court, Domestic Relations Court, Juvenile Court, Superior Court, District Court, Circuit Court, etc. The word jurisdiction here refers simply to the *power* of the court to handle certain kinds of cases. If a court has concurrent jurisdiction over a matter, it means that more than one court in the state can hear the case. Exclusive jurisdiction, on the other hand, means that only one court can hear that particular kind of case.

How can you determine which courts in your state have jurisdiction over Family Law problems and what the limitations are, if any, on that jurisdiction? Several ways exist:

(1) examine all state statutes in the statutory code on the judicial system of your state;

(2) examine all constitutional provisions in the state constitution on the judicial system of your state;

(3) examine the court rules of each court in your state;

(4) ask court clerks, experienced lawyers and experienced paralegals;

(5) examine Manuals, Practice Books and Form Books.

While the latter two sources of information (4 and 5) can be quite reliable, it is highly recommended early in your career that you learn to consult the primary sources of information: statutes, constitutions and court rules (1, 2 and 3 above).

Assignment # 5

(a) What courts in your state have trial court jurisdiction over Family Law problems? For each court, make a list of each kind of Family Law problem it can hear. (See also General Instructions for the State Code Assignment, supra p. 14.)

(b) The above assignment led you to certain jurisdiction rules. Prepare checklists that can be used to determine whether these rules apply. (See also General Instructions for the Checklist Formulation Assignment, supra p. 29.)

17. For more on jurisdiction, see Statsky, W. and Wernet, J., *Case Analysis and Fundamentals of Legal Writing*, pp. 12–13 (1977).

2. ADMINISTRATIVE AGENCIES

Unlike other areas of the law, there is *not* a great deal of involvement of administrative agencies of the government in Family Law. (The main exception concerns children where a number of agencies are often involved.) The following are typical, although the names of the agencies may differ from state to state: Bureau of Vital Statistics, Adoption Department, Child Welfare Agency, Marriage Conciliation Bureau, etc.

Assignment # 6

Make a list of every agency in your state that handles children in trouble, husband-wife difficulties or any other Family Law problem. Some agencies may have only a partial involvement with problems of the family, e. g., a welfare department or a social security office. Include these agencies in your list. Select any two of these agencies. Write, call or visit these two agencies and ask for copies of the following:

—program literature describing the services of the agency;

—sample application forms that the public uses to obtain the benefits and services of the agency;

—an annual report on the activity of the agency;

—samples of the agency's regulations.

As you collect this data, exchange it among your classmates for agencies that you have not checked yourself. Be prepared to give a class presentation on the workings of a particular agency and its relationship to the topics you will be studying in this course.

Chapter Three

THE DYNAMICS OF WORKING IN A FAMILY LAW OFFICE

SECTION A. HOW TO BE SUPERVISED

The central question of this chapter is: how to survive in a busy law office handling a substantial number of Family Law cases? The first survival technique is to have a realistic understanding of what you could find during your first month on the job. The following list is an outline of some of the circumstances you might confront as a new employee. To be sure, not everyone will face all of the difficulties mentioned below. In fact, you may be lucky enough to avoid all of them. For the sake of caution, however, you should be aware of some of the more troublesome problems that could exist:

—the Family Law you learned in school was not enough to enable you to handle every assignment you are given on the job;

—your supervisors give you a lot of instructions and in the process assume that you know a lot more than you do;

—when you receive your first few assignments, you panic momentarily with the strange feeling that you don't remember anything you learned;

—your supervisor tells you to forget everything you learned because "we do things differently here";

—some of the attorneys are suspicious of paralegals—they are not quite sure what you are trained to do—you've got to prove yourself;

—one or more of the secretaries who have been at the firm some time are suspicious and perhaps resentful of your presence—they think that they should have been upgraded into the job you were given;

—the office moves at a frantic pace with seemingly no time to think;

—etc.

What to do when confronted with such situations? One way out is to learn *how to be supervised.*

Many paralegals are supervisors themselves. They could be supervising secretaries, clerks, investigators or other paralegals. One of the best ways to learn how to supervise someone else[1] is to learn how to be supervised. It does *not* come naturally. Unfortunately, very few people know how to supervise effectively. Even fewer know how to be supervised effectively.

Being supervised effectively means two interrelated things:

(1) to carry out an assigned responsibility according to the instructions of the supervisor,

(2) to take maximum advantage of each assignment to develop your knowledge and skills.

Both of these objectives may sound relatively easy. You may feel that you are already an expert at carrying out assigned tasks and at learning while doing. Are you?

If you asked a supervisor to assess the quality of the people s/he has supervised, you might be told that one in twenty is a "good worker." Can you say that you are the one in twenty? Most people get 15–20 minutes of productive work time out of each work hour. How much productive time do you think that you are able to get? It is not an understatement to say that 99 out of 100 of us *do not know what our supervisors really think of us.*

Assignment # 7

Think of the last five people who have supervised you in an employment setting. (If you have not yet worked enough to have had five work supervisors, select other settings in which others had to supervise you, e. g., school/church projects, other volunteer activity.) For each supervisor, answer the following questions:

(a) What would their general impression be of you as a worker?

(b) What negative comments would they make about you as a worker?

(c) If any of the supervisors could have replaced you, would s/he have done so? Why or why not?

Most of us would have a great deal of difficulty answering the questions in Assignment # 7 above with honesty and objectivity. When we think about our prior work settings that have been less than fully satisfactory, our inclination is to blame someone else for what went wrong. While it may be true that others deserve some blame, we need to look at our own participation, our own shortcomings, our own responsibility for what happened.

Step one, therefore in the process of learning how to be supervised is to try to answer the questions, "who am I as a worker?" "What

1. See Statsky, W., "Techniques for Supervising Paralegals," 22 *The Practical Lawyer* 81 (no. 4) (June 1, 1976).

are my strengths and weaknesses?" "Would I hire myself?" "Where do I need improvement?" "Does my ego interfere with my performance?" "Am I afraid to say, 'I don't understand'?" "Do I know how to ask for help?"

We now turn to a number of concrete suggestions to maintain a healthy supervisor-supervisee relationship:

1. DON'T PLAY KING'S CLOTHES WITH THE INSTRUCTIONS THAT YOU RECEIVE

Recall the story of the king's clothes. The king was naked, but everybody kept saying what a beautiful wardrobe he had on. As new people arrived, they saw that he had no clothes, but they heard everyone talking as if he was fully dressed. The new people did not want to appear stupid, so they too began admiring the king's wardrobe. When paralegals are receiving instructions on an assignment, they play king's clothes when they pretend that they understand all the instructions when in fact they do not. They do not want to appear to be uninformed or unintelligent. They do not want to give the impression that they are not sure of themselves. For obvious reasons, this is a serious mistake.

Whenever you are given an assignment in a new area, i. e., an assignment on something that you have not done before, there should be a great deal that you don't understand. This is particularly true during your first few months on the job when everything is new! Don't pretend to be something that you are not. Don't pretend that you have knowledge and skills that you don't have yet. Constantly ask questions about new things. Don't be reluctant to ask for explanations. Learn how to ask for help. *It will not be a sign of weakness.* Quite the contrary. People who want to make sure that they fully understand all their instructions soon gain a reputation for responsibility and conscientiousness.

2. REPEAT THE INSTRUCTIONS TO YOUR SUPERVISOR BEFORE YOU LEAVE THE ROOM

Once your supervisor has told you what s/he wants you to do, do not leave the room in silence or with the general observation, "I'll get on that right away." Repeat the instructions back to the supervisor *as you understand them.* Make sure that you and your supervisor are on the same waive length by explaining back what you think you were told to do. This will be an excellent opportunity for the supervisor to determine what you did or did not understand, and to provide you with clarifications where needed.

Your supervisor will not always be sure of what s/he wants you to do. By trying to obtain clarity on the instructions, you are providing the supervisor with the opportunity to think through what s/he wants done. In the middle of the session with you, the supervisor may change his/her mind on what is to be done.

3. WRITE YOUR INSTRUCTIONS DOWN

Never go to your supervisor without pen and paper. Preferably, keep an Instructions Notebook in which you record the following information:

—notes on what you are supposed to do;

—the date you are given the assignment;

—the date the supervisor expects you to complete all or part of the assignment.

The notes will serve as your memory bank. Whenever any questions arise about what you were supposed to do, you have something concrete to which to refer.

4. IF THE INSTRUCTIONS APPEAR TO BE COMPLICATED, ASK YOUR SUPERVISOR TO SEGMENT THE INSTRUCTIONS INTO SEPARATE TASKS AND TO PLACE A PRIORITY ON THE PERFORMANCE OF THE TASKS

As you receive instructions, you may sometimes feel overwhelmed by all that is being asked of you. Many supervisors do not give instructions in clear logical patterns. They may talk in a rambling, stream-of-consciousness fashion. When confronted with this situation, simply say:

> "OK, but can you break that down for me a little more in terms of what you want me to do first? I think I will be able to do the entire assignment, but it would help if I approach it one step at a time. Where do you want me to start?"

5. AS OFTEN AS POSSIBLE, WRITE YOUR INSTRUCTIONS AND WHAT YOU DO IN THE FORM OF CHECKLISTS

A methodical mind is one that views a project in "do-able" steps and that tackles one step at a time. You need to have a methodical mind in order to function in a busy law office. One of the best ways to develop such a mind is to think in terms of checklists. A checklist is simply a chronological sequencing of tasks that must be done in order to complete a project. We have already seen how to translate a rule into a checklist.[2] The same process can be used to convert the instructions from your supervisor into checklists of how to do a particular job. In the process of actually carrying out the instructions, you go through many steps—all of which you could put into a detailed checklist. The steps you went through to complete the task become a checklist of things to do in order to complete such a task. To be

2. See General Instructions for the Checklist Drafting Assignment, supra p. 29.

sure, it can be time consuming to draft checklists. Keep in mind, however, that:

—the checklists can be invaluable for other employees who are given similar assignments in the future;

—the checklists will be a benefit to you in organizing your own time and in assuring completeness.

You will not be able to draft checklists for everything that you do. Perhaps you will not be able to write more than one checklist a week. Perhaps you will have to use some of your own time to write the checklists. Whatever time you can devote to checklist writing will be profitably spent so long as you are serious about getting them written and in using them. They may have to be re-written or modified later. This should not deter you from the task of writing the checklists since most things that are worth doing require testing and reassessment.

Once you have a number of checklists, you have the makings of a how-to-do-it manual that you have written yourself.

6. FIND OUT WHAT MANUALS AND CHECKLISTS ALREADY EXIST IN YOUR OFFICE

It does not make sense to reinvent the wheel. If manuals and checklists already exist in your office on the topic of your assignments, you should find and use them. The problem is that the how-to-do-it information is usually buried in the heads of the attorneys, paralegals and secretaries of the office. No one has taken the time to write it all down. If this is not the case, you should find out where it is written down and try to adapt what you find to the particular assignment on which you are working.

7. ASK FOR A MODEL

One of the best ways of making sure that you know what the supervisor wants is by asking whether s/he knows of any models that you could use as a guide for what you are being asked to do. Such models may be found in closed case files, manuals, form books, practice texts, etc.[3] As pointed out in chapter one, however, great care must be used in using such material.[4] Every new legal problem is potentially unique. What will work in one case may not work in another. A model is a guide, a starting point and nothing more.

8. DO SOME INDEPENDENT LEGAL RESEARCH ON YOUR OWN ON THE INSTRUCTIONS YOU ARE GIVEN

Often you will be told what to do without being given more than a cursory explanation of why it needs to be done that way. All of the instructions you are given have some basis in the law. A com-

3. See supra p. 7.

4. See How to Avoid Abusing A Standard Form, supra p. 23.

plaint, for example, is served on an opposing party in a designated way because the law has imposed rules on how such service is to be made. You may be asked to serve a complaint in a certain way without being told what section of the state code (or of your court rules) *requires* it to be served in that way. It would be highly impractical for you to be able to read all the law that is the foundation for the instructions you are given. It is not necessary to do so and you would not have time to do so.

What you can do, however, is to select certain instructions on certain assignments and do some background legal research [5] in order to gain a greater appreciation for why the instructions were necessary to accomplish the task. You will probably have to do such legal research on your own time unless the assignment you are given includes some legal research. The research can be time consuming, but you will find it to be enormously educational. It can place a totally new perspective on the assignment, and indeed, on your entire job.

9. ASK SECRETARIES AND OTHER PARALEGALS FOR HELP

Secretaries and other paralegals that have worked in the office for a long period of time can be very helpful to you if you approach them properly.[6] Everybody wants to feel important. Everybody wants to be respected. When someone asks for something in such a way as to give the impression that s/he is entitled to what is being sought, difficulties usually result. Think of how you would like to be approached if you were in the position of the secretary or other paralegal. What would turn you off? What would make you want to go out of your way to cooperate with and assist a new paralegal employee who needs your help? Your answers (and sensitivity) to questions such as these will go a long way toward enabling you to draw on the experience of others in the office.

10. OBTAIN FEEDBACK ON AN ASSIGNMENT BEFORE THE DATE IT IS DUE

Unless the assignment you are given is a very simple one, do not wait until the date that it is due to communicate with your supervisor. Of course, if you are having trouble with the assignment, you will want to check with your supervisor as soon as possible and as often as necessary. It would be a mistake, however, to contact the supervisor only when trouble arises. To be sure, you should limit your contacts with any busy supervisor to essential contacts. You could take the following approach to your supervisor:

"Everything seems to be going fine on the project you gave me. I expect to have it in to you on time. I'm wondering, however, if

5. On finding law in state codes and in court opinions, see supra pp. 13–15 and 26–29.

6. For more on the interrelationship of secretaries and paralegals in a law office, see Statsky, W., *Introduction to Paralegalism: Perspectives, Problems and Skills*, pp. 8ff. (1974).

> you could give me a few moments of your time so that I can bring you up to date on where I am so that you can let me know if I am on the right track?"

Perhaps this contact could take place on the phone or during a brief office visit. Suppose that you have gone astray on the assignment without knowing it? It is obviously better to discover this before the assignment is turned in than on the date it is due. The more communication you have with your supervisor, the more likely it is that you will catch such errors before a great deal of time is wasted.

11. ASK TO PARTICIPATE IN OFFICE TRAINING PROGRAMS, CONTINUING LEGAL EDUCATION SEMINARS OF THE LOCAL BAR ASSOCIATION AND OF THE LOCAL PARALEGAL ASSOCIATIONS

Sometimes there are training sessions for new attorneys conducted in the law firm. You should ask that you be included in some or all of such sessions. Bar associations and paralegal associations often conduct all day seminars on legal topics relevant to your work. Seek permission to attend them if they are held during work hours.

12. ASK TO BE EVALUATED REGULARLY

For a number of reasons, evaluations are not given or are unhelpful when they are given:

—evaluations can be time consuming;

—evaluators are reluctant to say anything negative, especially in writing;

—most people don't like to be evaluated: it's too threatening to our ego.

The major antidote is to let your supervisor know that you want to be evaluated and that you can handle criticism. If you are defensive when you are criticized, you will find that the evaluations of your performance will go on behind your back. Such a work environment is obviously very unhealthy. Consider this approach that a paralegal might take to his/her supervisor:

> "I want to know what you think of my work. I want to know where you think I need improvement. That's the only way I'm going to learn. I also want to know when I'm doing things correctly, but I'm mainly interested in your suggestions on what I can do to increase my skills."

If you take this approach *and mean it,* the chances are good that you will receive some very constructive criticism.

In addition to the occasional oral evaluations that you might ask for, you may want to use an evaluation form which could be filled out in a short period of time by each of your supervisors. A sample of such a form follows. You will note that the form is centered around basic legal skills.[7] It is a sign of your own responsibility and maturity that you take the initiative in obtaining evaluations of your performance.

PERFORMANCE EVALUATION			
NAME OF PARALEGAL:			
NAME OF SUPERVISOR COMPLETING THIS EVALUATION:			
DATE THIS EVALUATION WAS COMPLETED:			
PERIOD COVERED BY THIS EVALUATION:			
(Instructions for filling out this form: for each of the following eight skill areas, circle the appropriate word in each of the three corresponding columns)			
SKILL AREAS BEING EVALUATED	EXPOSURE OF PARALEGAL TO THIS SKILL AREA	COMPLEXITY OF PARALEGAL'S TASKS IN THIS SKILL AREA	PERFORMANCE OF PARALEGAL IN THIS SKILL AREA
1. Interviewing	Extensive Minimal None	Very Complex Average Complexity Simple	Excellent Good Fair Poor
2. Investigation	Extensive Minimal None	Very Complex Average Complexity Simple	Excellent Good Fair Poor
3. Legal Writing e.g., preliminary drafts of complaint, interrogatories	Extensive Minimal None	Very Complex Average Complexity Simple	Excellent Good Fair Poor
4. Digesting, e.g., depositions	Extensive Minimal None	Very Complex Average Complexity Simple	Excellent Good Fair Poor
5. File Maintenance	Extensive Minimal None	Very Complex Average Complexity Simple	Excellent Good Fair Poor
6. Office Administration, generally, e.g., scheduling	Extensive Minimal None	Very Complex Average Complexity Simple	Excellent Good Fair Poor
7. Legal Research	Extensive Minimal None	Very Complex Average Complexity Simple	Excellent Good Fair Poor
8. Initiative/ Motivation			Excellent Good Fair Poor

IM-443

7. The form has been adapted from similar forms developed by the Urban Law Institute of Antioch School of Law.

The advantage of the above form is that it should take only moments for each supervisor to use. All that is needed is the circling of a small number of words. The disadvantage is that there is not a great detail provided by the evaluation. The reality, however, is that supervisors are not going to have the time to provide you with lengthy, narrative evaluations. The above evaluation form simply provides an outline of what has been happening and how the supervisor feels about it all. During oral conversations with the supervisor, you should be able to receive more comprehensive assessments of strengths and weaknesses. Hopefully, the form will be a catalyst for such conversations.

The form lists eight "skill areas being evaluated." Other areas could be added. Some of the areas listed can be broken down into narrower areas. You can adapt the form to the particular needs of the law office setting in which you find yourself. The objective is an evaluation instrument that is not burdensome to the supervisor, that helps the supervisor organize his/her thoughts about what you have been doing and that provides you with some useful information about your current standing.

SECTION B. ASSESSING YOUR OWN BIASES

Your involvement in a domestic relations case may come at a number of stages:

(a) you might do the comprehensive client interview after the attorney has decided to take the case and has established the attorney-client relationship through a contract called the retainer (involving the fee, the scope of the representation etc.);

(b) you may undertake field investigation in order to uncover and verify facts relevant to the case;

(c) you may handle intermediate client contact in order to obtain and exchange needed information;

(d) you may be asked to undertake legal research on the case and prepare drafts of certain documents, e. g., the divorce complaint;

(e) you may be scheduling client appointments, witness interviews and making a variety of arrangements centered around certain court dates.

No matter what stage of a case you are working on, you need to be aware of how your personal feelings about the case might effect your work on the case. How would you answer the following question:

> Are you the type of person who is objective enough that you can assist a person even though you have a personal distaste for what that person wants to do or what that person has done? yes.

In all likelihood, you would quickly answer "yes" to this question. We all like to feel that we are level headed and not susceptible to letting our own prejudices interfere with the job we have to accomplish. Some individuals do in fact possess this characteristic of objectivity. Most of us, however, are not as adept in hiding our humanness, our personal likes and dislikes, our value judgments.

Assignment # 8

The following fact situations involve aspects of domestic relations cases. Identify the potential difficulties that an individual working in the law office would have in each situation. Focus on the extent to which such an individual might be hampered in delivering legal services because of the personal reactions and feelings that the individual might have toward the client.

A.

Mr. Smith, the client, is being sued by his estranged wife for custody of their two small children. Mr. and Mrs. Smith live separately, but Mr. Smith has had custody of the children during most of their lives while Mrs. Smith has been in the hospital. Mrs. Smith has charged that Mr. Smith beats the children, leaves them with neighbors and day care centers for most of the day and is an alcoholic. Your investigation reveals that Mrs. Smith will probably be able to prove all these allegations in court.

B.

Mrs. Jones is being sued by Mr. Jones for divorce on the ground of adultery. Mrs. Jones is the client of your office. Thus far your investigation has revealed that there is considerable doubt over whether Mrs. Jones did in fact commit the act of adultery. During the course of your conversation with Mrs. Jones, she tells you that she is a prostitute.

C.

Jane Anderson is seeking an abortion. She is not married. The father of the child wants to prevent her from having the abortion. Jane comes to your office for legal help. She wants to know what her rights are. You are a devout Catholic assigned to work on the case.

D.

Tom Donaldson is a client of your office. You have been asked to work on the case which involves a charge by his former wife that he has failed to pay her the court ordered alimony payments and that those payments should be increased substantially because of her needs and his recently improved financial status. Your job is to help Tom collect a large volume of records concerning his past alimony payments and his present financial worth. There is no one else in the office who is available to do this record gathering but you. It is clear, however, that Tom does not like you. On a number of occasions, he has indirectly questioned your ability.

Having analyzed the fact situations involved in the above assignment, do you still feel the same about your assessment of your own objectivity? Clearly, we cannot wish our personal feelings away nor pretend that they do not exist. Nor are there any absolute rules or techniques that apply to every situation that you will be asked to handle. Nor are the following admonitions very helpful: "be objective," "be dispassionate," "don't get personally involved," "control your feelings." They are not very helpful as guidelines because they are too general and more significantly because, when viewed in the abstract, most of us will conclude that the admonitions are not needed since we want to believe that we are always objective, dispassionate, detached and in control.

Perhaps the best that we can do is to recognize that there are facts and circumstances that arouse our feelings and that tempt us to impose our own value judgments. Perhaps if we know where we are vulnerable, we will be in a better position to prevent our reactions from interfering with our work. It is not desirable for you to be totally dispassionate and removed. A paralegal who is cold, unfeeling and incapable of empathy is as bad as one who scolds a client for doing what is improper. It is clearly not improper for a paralegal to express sympathy, surprise and perhaps even shock at what unfolds from the client's life story. If these feelings are genuine, and if they would be normal reactions to the situation at a given moment, then they should be expressed.[8] Again, however, the problem is *how to draw the line between the expression* of these feelings, on the one hand, and the expression of feelings in such a way that you will interfere with your ability to communicate with the client now and in the future. As you gain experience in the art of dealing with people, you will hopefully develop styles and techniques that will enable you to avoid going over that line too often. The starting point in this development is the recognition that it is *not* difficult to find yourself going over the line, that you will often *not* be aware that you have been close to, or over, the line and that the main antidote available to you is your own willingness and ability to assess when you are in the danger zone.

8. See Statsky, W., "Legal Interviewing," in *Introduction to Paralegalism: Perspectives, Problems and Skills*, pp. 265ff. (1974).

Assignment # 9

(a) Think about your past and present contacts with people who have irritated you the most. Make a specific list of what bothered you about these people. Suppose that you are working in a law office where a client did one of the things on your list. What would you do?

(b) In the relationship between husband and wife, child and parent, there are undoubtedly many things which a husband, wife or child could do which would be wrong (i. e., illegal, immoral, improper) according to your personal system of values. Make a list of the ten things that could be done by husband, wife or child to each other (e. g., husband to wife, child to parent, etc.) which would be most offensive to your sense of values. Assume that a client in the office where you work (a stranger to you) has done one of these ten things and is being challenged in court by someone because of it. Your office is defending the client against this challenge. What difficulties do you see for yourself in being able to assist this client? Answer this question for ten different clients who did one of the ten things on your "Ten-most-Improper-Behavior" list.

SECTION C. WHAT DOES THE CLIENT WANT?

There are a number of assumptions that can be made about many clients with domestic relations problems:

1. The client is not sure what s/he wants in spite of what the client says s/he wants.
2. The client is not aware of what legal and non-legal options are available to help solve whatever problems exist.
3. The domestic relations problem probably involves other legal problems about which the client is unaware and about which even you may be unaware at the outset.

Suppose that a client walks into the office and says "I want to get a divorce." The following observations *might* be possible about this client:

(a) The client has an incorrect understanding of what a divorce is.

(b) The client says she wants a divorce because she thinks that this is the only legal remedy available to solve her problem.

(c) If the client knew that other remedies existed (e. g., annulment, separation) she would consider these options.

(d) What the client is really troubled about is the fact that her husband beats the kids and a divorce is the only way which she thinks can put a stop to it.

(e) The client consciously or unconsciously wants and needs an opportunity to tell someone how bad the world is treating her, and if given this opportunity, she may not want to terminate her marriage.

(f) If the client knew that marriage counseling was available in the community, she would consider using it before taking the dramatic step of going to a law office for a divorce.

If any or all of these observations are correct, think of how damaging it would be for someone in the law office to take out the standard divorce forms and quickly fill them out immediately after the client says, "I want a divorce." This response would not be appropriate because there was no probing beneath the statement to determine what in fact was on the client's mind. It may be, after all factors are examined, that the client *does* want a divorce. The danger, however, is that the client wants something else, but is steered in the direction of a divorce because no other options are presented to her, because no one takes the time to listen to her and to help her express ideas, intentions and desires that are lurking beneath the otherwise clear statement, "I want a divorce." While it is true that many clients walk into law offices and speak only of divorces and separation agreements, they frequently would be receptive to and even anxious for reconciliation.[9]

This is not to say that you must be prepared to psychoanalyze every client, nor that you must always distrust what the client tells you. It is rather a recognition of the fact that *most people are confused about the law and make requests based upon misinformation as to what courses of action are available to solve problems.* Common sense tells us to avoid taking all statements at face value. People under emotional distress, particularly in situations of family conflict, need to be treated with sensitivity. We should not expect them to be able to express their intentions with clarity all the time because of the emotions involved and because of the sometimes complicated nature of the law.

Assignment # 10

A client walks into the office where you work and makes the statements below. What areas do you think it would be reasonable to probe in order to determine if the statement is an accurate reflection of what the client wants? What misunderstandings do you think the client might have? What further questions would you want to ask in order to be sure that you have identified what the client wants?

9. Sachs, S. and Goldman, H., "The Crucial First Interview in a Divorce Case," 1 *Family Law Reporter* 4013, 4014 (Jan. 7, 1975).

A.

"I want to commit my husband to a mental institution."

B.

"I can't control my teenage son anymore. I want him placed in a juvenile home."

C.

"I want to put my baby daughter up for adoption."

Chapter Four

ETHICS AND THE FAMILY LAW PRACTICE

Every lawyer is subject to the Canons of Ethics (sometimes called the Code of Professional Responsibility) of his/her state. The violation of these ethical rules could result in disbarment. The ethical rules do not directly apply to paralegals working for lawyers. A paralegal cannot be disbarred or otherwise disciplined for violation of the Canons. A lawyer, however, is responsible for the conduct of the paralegal working for him/her. Hence, impropriety on the part of the paralegal could lead to the disciplining *of the employing lawyer* by the bar association and the court in the state that regulates the conduct of lawyers and the practice of law.[1]

Assignment # 11

(1) Give the full citation to the ethical rules that govern the conduct of lawyers in your state.

(2) What is the name of the bar association committee in your state that has jurisdiction over the ethical standards of lawyers? What discipline powers does this committee have over lawyers?

(3) If a lawyer is dissatisfied with the ruling of the above committee concerning his/her ethical conduct, to what court can the lawyer appeal?

(To find answers to the above questions, check your state statutory code and your state constitution. See General Instructions for the State Code Assignment, supra p. 14. In addition, you may want to contact your state bar association.)

(4) Draft a flow chart of all the procedural steps that must be taken for the disciplining of a lawyer for unethical conduct. (See also General Instructions for the Flow Chart Assignment, supra p. 33.)

Many states have adopted the ethical rules of the American Bar Association, the *Code of Professional Responsibility*. This *Code* consists of Disciplinary Rules (abbreviated DR) which state the requirements of professional behavior, and of Ethical Considerations (abbreviated EC) which elaborate upon the Disciplinary Rules. In the following chart, there is an outline of some of the ethical rules of the

1. See generally, "Ethics, the Authorized and the Unauthorized Practice of Law," in Statsky, W., *Introduction to Paralegalism: Perspectives, Problems and Skills*, pp. 96ff (1974). In the 1977 *Supplement*, see pp. 52ff. See also Drinker, H., "Problems of Professional Ethics in Matrimonial Litigation," 66 *Harvard Law Review* 443 (1953).

Code of Professional Responsibility with examples of how the rules might be *violated* in a Family Law practice.

ETHICS CHART		
THE ETHICAL RULE	CODE OF PROFESSIONAL RESPONSIBILITY REFERENCE	EXAMPLE OF HOW THIS RULE MIGHT BE VIOLATED IN A FAMILY LAW PRACTICE
1. A lawyer shall not engage in conduct involving dishonesty, fraud, deceit, or misrepresentation.	DR 1–102(A)(4) EC 1–5	A lawyer representing the husband tells the lawyer representing the wife that the husband does not own any land. The lawyer making this statement knows that it is not true.
2. A lawyer who knows that another lawyer is dishonest must report that lawyer.	DR 1–103(A) EC 1–4	Lawyer "X" knows that lawyer "Y" is misappropriating money from the latter's clients. Lawyer "X" fails to report Lawyer "Y" to the bar association.
3. A lawyer shall not publicize him or herself. It is permissible, however, to advertise the price of certain legal services.	DR 2–101(B) EC 2–9	A lawyer cannot buy advertising space claiming to be the "Best Divorce Lawyer in Town."
4. The letterhead of a lawyer must be dignified and not misleading. A paralegal's name cannot be printed on the lawyer's letterhead.	DR 2–102(A)(4) EC 2–10	
5. A lawyer cannot recommend that s/he be hired by a non-lawyer when the latter has not sought his/her advice about hiring a lawyer.	DR 2–103(A)	A lawyer is talking with a stranger at a social gathering. The stranger tells the lawyer that he had not lived with his wife for five years. The lawyer says, "Well, if you ever want a divorce lawyer, give me a call."
6. A lawyer shall not charge a clearly excessive fee. (A contingent fee is one which is paid based upon whether or not the client wins in court, i.e., the fee is contingent on the outcome. Contingent fee arrangements are rarely justified in Family Law cases.)	DR 2–106(A) EC 2–17	A lawyer represents a woman on a simple, uncontested divorce case. The lawyer spends a total of six hours on the case. The lawyer sends the woman a bill for $4,000.
7. A lawyer shall not divide a fee with another lawyer (who is not a partner in the same firm) unless the client consents.	DR 2–107	A client hires a lawyer. The lawyer is not familiar with the law of the case and makes an arrangement with a more experienced lawyer to help on the case. This other lawyer will receive one half of the fee. The client is unaware of this arrangement.

8. Generally, once a lawyer has been retained by a client and has filed a notice of appearance with the court, the lawyer cannot quit without court permission.	DR 2–2–110 EC 2–32	A client has an argument with his lawyer. The lawyer has already commenced a court action on behalf of the client. The argument is so serious that he will not pay the lawyer's fee. The lawyer tells the client to "get yourself another lawyer." The lawyer does not tell the court that he has quit.
9. A lawyer cannot aid a non-lawyer in the unauthorized practice of law. A lawyer employing a paralegal must see to it that the paralegal does not improperly engage in the practice of law. The public must not be misled into thinking the paralegal is a lawyer. (a) In most states, a paralegal can sign correspondence on firm stationary so long as the title used by the paralegal would not mislead the public. (b) In most states, a paralegal can have his/her own business card on which the name of the law firm is printed. (c) In communications with the public, the paralegal should make clear that s/he is not a lawyer. (d) A paralegal cannot be paid on a fixed fee or sliding scale basis directly related to the amount recovered.	DR 3–101(A) EC 3–6	
10. Generally, a lawyer cannot reveal the confidences or secrets of a client without the client's permission. The lawyer must see to it that his/her paralegal employees also preserve the confidences and secrets of clients.	DR 4–101(B)(1) DR 4–101(D) EC 4–1 EC 4–2	A lawyer represents a woman in a divorce proceeding. During a consultation, she tells the lawyer that her business partner does not know about the divorce. By coincidence, the lawyer also represents the business partner on another matter. In casual conversation with the latter, the lawyer mentions the fact that he is handling the divorce of the partner. The above lawyer has a paralegal working on the divorce case doing legal research. When the paralegal goes home after work, he tells his wife all about the interesting divorce case on which he is working. Both the lawyer and the paralegal have improperly revealed confidences of the client.

11. A lawyer shall not acquire a proprietary interest in the subject of the litigation s/he is handling.	DR 5–103(A)	A lawyer is representing a wife in a divorce action. One of the disputed issues is how to divide a business as part of the property settlement. Before the case has been resolved, the lawyer purchases a substantial share of the business.
12. A lawyer shall not accept multiple employment if the exercise of his/her independent professional judgment on behalf of a client will be or is likely to be adversely affected by his/her representation of another client.	DR 5–105(A) DR 5–105(B) EC 5–14 EC 5–15 EC 5–16	A husband and wife are thinking about a divorce. They have two young children and substantial property that would have to be divided. During their married life, they have always used a particular lawyer whom they both trust. They ask this lawyer to represent them both in the divorce. The lawyer agrees.
13. A lawyer shall not handle a legal matter without preparation adequate in the circumstances.	DR 6–101(A)(3) EC 6–4	A lawyer has a case load of 500 divorce cases. His/her office is a constant shambles. Appointments are often missed due to his/her poorly organized schedule.
14. A lawyer shall not: (a) Represent someone in a case which is brought merely to harass or to injure someone. (b) Knowingly advance a claim or defense that is unwarranted under existing law. (c) Knowingly use perjured testimony or false evidence. (d) Knowingly make a false statement of law or fact. (e) Participate in the creation or preservation of evidence which is obviously false. (f) Counsel or assist his/her client in conduct that the lawyer knows to be illegal or fraudulent. If the lawyer learns that the client has perpetrated a fraud on a person or on a tribunal, the lawyer shall ask the client to rectify the situation. If the client refuses, the lawyer must bring the fraud to the attention of the person or tribunal involved.	DR 7–102(A)(1) DR 7–102(A)(2) DR 7–102(A)(3) DR 7–102(A)(4) DR 7–102(A)(5) DR 7–102(A)(6) DR 7–102(A)(7) EC 7–4 EC 7–5 EC 7–6 EC 7–10 DR 2–109(A)(1) DR 2–109(A)(2)	A lawyer represents a husband who wants to sue his wife for a divorce on the grounds of adultery. The husband has told the lawyer that he does not care whether or not he gets the divorce. He is so angry at his wife that he only wants to humiliate her in public. A lawyer advises a wife to obtain a Mexican divorce through the mail even though the lawyer knows that such "mail-order" divorces are illegal. During a deposition, a husband states that his net worth is $45,000. The husband's lawyer knows that this figure is grossly low, but says nothing to anyone at any time. A husband and wife agree to obtain a divorce. The wife will claim the husband deserted her. The husband will not dispute this claim even though both he and his wife know that no desertion ever took place. The lawyers for both spouses suspect what is going on but ignore it.

15. A lawyer shall not communicate with a party s/he knows is represented by a lawyer without obtaining the permission of that lawyer. If the person is not represented, the lawyer should not communicate with that person except to suggest that a lawyer be hired. (The latter restriction applies only when the unrepresented person has an interest that is adverse to the interest of the lawyer's client.)	DR 7–104(A)(1) DR 7–104(A)(2) EC 7–18	A lawyer represents a wife who is thinking about divorcing her husband. Without checking to determine whether the husband is represented, the lawyer calls the husband to inform him of the impending divorce and to ask him questions about his financial situation.
16. A lawyer shall not threaten to bring criminal charges solely to obtain an advantage in a civil matter.	DR 7–105(A) EC 7–21	A husband and wife are having a dispute over who should be awarded custody of their child. The wife's attorney tells the husband's attorney that the wife is contemplating criminal prosecution for nonsupport in view of the husband's position on the custody question.
17. In presenting a matter to a tribunal, a lawyer shall disclose legal authority in the controlling jurisdiction known to him/her to be directly adverse to the position of his/her client and which is not disclosed by the opposing lawyer.	DR 7–106(B)(1) EC 7–23	A lawyer representing a wife asks the court for a special order. There is a very old opinion in the state which says that the order is inappropriate in this kind of case. Neither the court nor the lawyer for the husband know about this old case. The wife's lawyer does know about it but never mentions this case in the petition for the special order.
18. A lawyer shall not advise or cause a person to secret him or herself or to leave the jurisdiction of a tribunal for the purpose of making him/her unavailable as a witness.	DR 7–109(B)	A wife has filed a divorce action against her husband on the ground of adultery. The lawyer for the husband contacts the person with whom the husband has had the alleged adulterous relationship and tells her that she does not have to testify if she does not want to. "If you are called to appear, simply ignore it."
19. A lawyer shall not pay a witness a contingent witness fee.	DR 7–109(C)	In a custody dispute, the lawyer for the wife hires a child psychologist who will testify for the wife. The psychologist will be paid $200 if the wife loses the custody battle and $500 if she wins.
20. Generally, a lawyer should not communicate with a judge or other official before whom a case is pending without letting the other side know about the communication.	DR 7–110(B)	A lawyer representing a mother in an adoption proceeding meets the judge hearing the case. The meeting is at a social gathering. The lawyer discusses the case unknown to the lawyer for the father in this adoption dispute.

21. A lawyer should avoid even the appearance of impropriety.	DR 9–101 EC 9–2	A lawyer representing a wife in a divorce proceeding receives funds from the husband which are part of the property settlement. The wife asks the lawyer to hold the funds for her. The lawyer has only one bank account into which he deposits the wife's funds. It is a checking account. The lawyer has commingled a client's funds with the general operating funds of the firm. The lawyer has no intention of improperly using the client's funds and in fact does not do so.

IM–452

Assignment # 12

A lawyer represents an unmarried pregnant mother. He pays the hospital expenses for the delivery of the baby. He also arranges for the adoption of the baby. The adoptive parents pay him a fee for his services on the adoption. Included in the agreed-upon fee will be the reimbursement of the money the lawyer paid to the hospital for the delivery of the baby. Any ethical problems? (See also General Instructions for the Legal Analysis Assignment, supra p. 16.)

Assignment # 13

Has the state bar association or any local bar association in your state issued any ethical opinions that involve paralegals? If so, what do the opinions say? (For the complete text of many ethical opinions and bar association reports dealing with paralegals, see the 1977 Supplement to *Introduction to Paralegalism: Perspectives, Problems and Skills* (1974)).

Assignment # 14

Find an opinion from a court in your state in which a lawyer was disciplined for unethical conduct. Why was the lawyer disciplined? If possible, try to find a case in which the lawyer's unethical conduct occurred during his/her representation of a client on a Family Law case. (See also General Instructions for the Court Opinion Assignment, supra p. 26.)

OPINION OF THE ARIZONA BAR COMMITTEE ON RULES OF PROFESSIONAL CONDUCT[2]

OPINION NO. 76–25, November 19, 1976.
Released April 15, 1977.

QUESTION:

The Family Law Committee of the State Bar of Arizona has requested a determination of whether one attorney may represent

2. 3 *Family Law Reporter* 3097 (5/3/77).

both parties to a dissolution of marriage proceeding by filing a joint petition for dissolution of marriage.

CODE PROVISIONS INVOLVED:

Canon 4. A lawyer should preserve the confidences and secrets of a client.

Canon 5. A lawyer should exercise independent professional judgment on behalf of a client.

EC 5–14. Maintaining the independence of professional judgment required of a lawyer precludes his acceptance or continuation of employment that will adversely affect his judgment on behalf of or dilute his loyalty to a client. This problem arises whenever a lawyer is asked to represent two or more clients who may have differing interests, whether such interests be conflicting, inconsistent, diverse, or otherwise discordant.

EC 5–15. If a lawyer is requested to undertake or to continue representation of multiple clients having potentially differing interests, he must weigh carefully the possibility that his judgment may be impaired or his loyalty divided if he accepts or continues the employment. He should resolve all doubts against the propriety of the representation. A lawyer should never represent in litigation multiple clients with differing interests; and there are few situations in which he would be justified in representing in litigation multiple clients with potentially differing interests. If a lawyer accepted such employment and the interests did become actually differing, he would have to withdraw from employment with likelihood of resulting hardship on the clients; and for this reason it is preferable that he refuse the employment initially. On the other hand, there are many instances in which a lawyer may properly serve multiple clients with potentially differing interests in matters not involving litigation. If the interests vary only slightly, it is generally likely that the lawyer will not be subjected to an adverse influence and that he can retain his independent judgment on behalf of each client; and if the interests become differing, withdrawal is less likely to have a disruptive effect upon the causes of his clients.

EC 5–16. In those instances in which a lawyer is justified in representing two or more clients having differing interests, it is nevertheless essential that each client be given the opportunity to evaluate his need for representation free of any potential conflict and to obtain other counsel if he so desires. Thus before a lawyer may represent multiple clients, he should explain fully to each client the implications of the common representation and should accept or continue employment only if the clients consent. If there are present other circumstances that might cause any of the multiple clients to question the undivided loyalty of the lawyer, he should also advise all of the clients of those circumstances.

EC 5–20. A lawyer is often asked to serve as an impartial arbitrator or mediator in matters which involve present or former clients. He may serve in either capacity if he first discloses such present or former relationships. After a lawyer has undertaken to act as an impartial arbitrator or mediator, he should not thereafter represent in the dispute any of the parties involved.

DR 5–101. Refusing Employment When the Interests of the Lawyers May Impair His Independent Professional Judgement.

(A) Except with the consent of his client after full disclosure, a lawyer shall not accept employment if the exercise of his professional judgment on behalf of his client will be or reasonably may be affected by his own financial, business, property, or personal interests.

Canon 9. A lawyer should avoid even the appearance of professional impropriety.

OPINION:

A.R.S. § 25–314 (as added L.1973) provides that ". . . both parties to the marriage may initiate the proceeding." Petitions for dissolution of marriage in which both parties initiate the proceeding have come to be known as joint petitions. They, of course, are not the only way in which a petition for dissolution of marriage can be filed: either the husband or wife may file a petition for dissolution of the marriage without joining the other spouse as a joint petitioner.

Divorce law differs from much litigation in that divorces are frequently uncontested; often both parties want the matter to go by default because they both want the marriage terminated. There is, therefore, often not that adversity of interests which is more generally seen in civil litigation. However, the parties to a divorce obviously do have adverse interests unless the case is that rarity: a true no asset, short marriage, no children, no debt marriage. While those marriages are rare, they do occur.

Arizona lawyers are not uncommonly called upon to meet with a husband and wife both of whom say that the marriage is irretrievably broken and that they both want it dissolved. From there, the various fact situations become myriad. A rare few are true default dissolutions in which no property, debts, child custody, spousal maintenance or other issues exist. Most marriages, however, do entail the exercise of independent judgment on the part of a lawyer in some aspect of the marriage. Even though the parties say that they have fully agreed on everything and wish the lawyer to act as a mere scrivener, most often the lawyer is really being called upon to cast anointed water on the legitimacy of the agreement the parties have "worked out."

Some of the legal, ethical and practical considerations inherent in the question presented were considered by the court in Ishmael v. Mellington, 241 Cal.App.2d 520, 50 Cal.Rptr. 592 (1966), as follows:

Divorces are frequently uncontested; the parties may make their financial arrangements peaceably and honestly; vestigial chivalry may impel them to display the wife as the injured plaintiff; the husband may then seek out and pay an attorney to escort the wife through the formalities of adjudication. We describe these facts of life without necessarily approving them. Even in that situation the attorney's professional obligations do not permit his descent to the level of a scrivener. The edge of danger gleams if the attorney has previously represented the husband. A husband and wife at the brink of division of their marital assets have an obvious divergence of interests. Representing the wife in an arm's length divorce, an attorney of ordinary professional skill would demand some verification of the husband's financial statement; or, at the minimum, inform the wife that the husband's statement was unconfirmed, that wives may be cheated, that prudence called for investigation and verification. Deprived of such disclosure, the wife cannot make a free and intelligent choice. Representing both spouses in an uncontested divorce situation (whatever the ethical implications), the attorney's professional obligations demand no less. He may not set a shallow limit on the depth to which he will represent the wife.

The general standard of professional care described in Lucas v. Hamm . . . is appropriate to the garden variety situation, where the attorney represents only one of several parties or interests. It falls short of adequate description where the attorney's professional relationship extends to two clients with divergent or conflicting interests in the same subject matter. A more specific statement of the same rule is needed to guide the fact trier to the law's demands when the attorney attempts dual representation. In short, an attorney representing two parties with divergent interests must disclose all facts and circumstances which, in the judgment of a lawyer of ordinary skill and capacity, are necessary to enable his client to make free and intelligent decisions regarding the subject matter of the representation. Ishmael v. Millington, 241 Cal.App.2d 520, 50 Cal. Rptr. 592 (1966) noted in 8 Ariz.L.Rev. 343 (1967).

The dangers of a lawyer purporting to represent both spouses in a dissolution proceeding are well documented. See Opinion Number 207, Opinion of Committee on Legal Ethics Los Angeles Bar Association, Staedler v. Staedler, 6 N.J. 380, 78 A.2d 896 (1951); In re Rubin, 7 N.J. 507, 81 A.2d 776 (1951) [in which the lawyer who drafted the *Staedler* property settlement agreement and who did not advise the wife as to her rights "because she never asked him" was suspended from practicing as an attorney for one year]; Columbus Bar Association v. Grelle, 14 Ohio St.2d 208, 237 N.E.2d 298 (1968);

and "*Problems of Professional Ethics in Matrimonial Litigation*," 66 Harv.L.Rev. 443 (1953).

Recently, the Committee on Legal Ethics and Professional Conduct of the State Bar of Ohio was called upon to decide whether an attorney may represent both spouses in drafting a Separation Agreement and rendering professional advice and performing other duties relative to dissolution of marriage, including signing the petition for dissolution of marriage as counsel for both and appearing for both at the final hearing on the petition. The Ohio Committee decided that "a lawyer may not represent both spouses in a dissolution of their marriage as provided by the statute." The Ohio Committee went on to say:

[H]owever, we recognize that the purpose and nature of the dissolution of marriage proceedings is to avoid some of the usual adversary relationships in an action for divorce and that both parties may not choose to be represented by individual lawyers. Therefore, a lawyer may represent one party to the dissolution and prepare the Separation Agreement required by Section 3105.63, Revised Code, provided: (1) the second party is made fully aware that the lawyer does not represent him or her; (2) that the second party is given full opportunity to evaluate his or her need for representation free of any potential conflict and to obtain his or her own counsel; and (3) each spouse consents, in writing contained in or attached to the Separation Agreement, to the lawyer so proceeding. The lawyer shall not appear as counsel of record for both parties in the proceeding. (Formal Opinion No. 30, May 1975).

This Committee recognizes that the Ohio law relative to domestic relations in general and property rights in particular is vastly different from the applicable Arizona law.

EC 5–14, EC 5–15 and EC 5–16 clearly outline and define standards by which a lawyer may judge whether or not he should represent both spouses in a joint petition. There are many instances in which a lawyer may represent more than one client; he may form a corporation for many parties; he may form a partnership and, more closely analogous, he may dissolve a partnership. After a discussion with potential clients in these instances, the lawyer may discover a conflict and, therefore, by applying the EC's aforementioned may be unable to represent all parties concerned. . . .

(c) In the situations covered by DR–5–105(A) and (B), a lawyer may represent multiple clients if it is obvious that he can adequately represent the interest of each and if each consents to the representation after full disclosure of the possible effect of such representation on the exercise of his independent professional judgment on behalf of each.

The law of dissolution for married couples with no children and few assets is simple and uncomplicated. Many times the parties have used intelligent, adult judgment in the division of their few assets when amicably dissolving their marital bonds. Being unfamiliar with the legal system they seek some degree of counsel but have no desire or need to enter into an adversary proceeding. Often they can ill afford one lawyer. If no conflicts exist, then one lawyer should ethically be permitted to serve.

We emphasize that EC 5–15 draws a distinction between matters which involve litigation and those which do not. In an uncontested divorce where the attorney is representing both parties, any potential conflicts would probably surface prior to the filing of a joint petition for divorce. The actual proceeding is so short that it is not only unlikely that conflicts might occur at this stage, but if they did arise it would cause only slight disruption to the parties for the attorney to withdraw.

It is therefore the opinion of this Committee that it will be the *exception* rather than the *rule* for a lawyer to represent both parties in a dissolution proceeding. *Prima facie,* a lawyer should decline representation of both parties but there are undoubtedly some cases in which dual representation would not be improper. Should adversity of interest arise at some later time, the lawyer will presumably have to disqualify himself from representing either party and this should be clearly explained to both parties at the outset.

While not directly on point, this Committee is aware of the existing practice of some attorneys who represent only one of the spouses in a dissolution proceeding to use the mechanical device of a joint petition for dissolution of marriage. In doing so, the lawyer must appear as counsel for only one of the joint petitioners; the other joint petitioner either being designated as being in *propria persona* or appearing by other counsel. We approve of this practice.

NOTE ON LEGAL MALPRACTICE

Lawyers are becoming more and more concerned about being sued for legal malpractice—negligence in the performance of legal services for clients. In the following California case of Smith v. Lewis a Family Law client recovered $100,000 against her attorney for malpractice. California is a community property state.[3] What a spouse receives following a divorce in that state depends a great deal on what property can be classified as "community property" of the marriage as opposed to the "separate property" of one of the spouses. The issue in Smith v. Lewis dealt with the legal advice received on this important task of classification. As you read the opinion, you might reflect on what you might have done if you had worked

3. Infra p. 275.

for the attorney that represented the spouse. How do you think you might have helped this attorney avoid the malpractice liability that eventually resulted?

SMITH v. LEWIS

Supreme Court of California, In Banc, 1975.
13 Cal.3d 349, 118 Cal.Rptr. 621, 530 P.2d 589.

MOSK, Justice.

Defendant Jerome R. Lewis, an attorney, appeals from a judgment entered upon a jury verdict for plaintiff Rosemary F. Smith in an action for legal malpractice. The action arises as a result of legal services rendered by defendant to plaintiff in a prior divorce proceeding. The gist of plaintiff's complaint is that defendant negligently failed in the divorce action to assert her community interest in the retirement benefits of her husband.

Defendant principally contends, inter alia, that the law with regard to the characterization of retirement benefits was so unclear at the time he represented plaintiff as to insulate him from liability for failing to assert a claim therefor on behalf of his client.[1] We conclude defendant's appeal is without merit, and therefore affirm the judgment.

In 1943 plaintiff married General Clarence D. Smith. Between 1945 and his retirement in 1966 General Smith was employed by the California National Guard. As plaintiff testified, she informed defendant her husband "was paid by the state . . . it was a job just like anyone else goes to." For the first 16 years of that period the husband belonged to the State Employees' Retirement System, a contributory plan.[2] Between 1961 and the date of his retirement he belonged to the California National Guard retirement program, a noncontributory plan. In addition, by attending National Guard reserve drills he qualified for separate retirement benefits from the federal government, also through a noncontributory plan. The state and federal retirement programs each provide lifetime monthly bene-

1. Defendant alternatively contends the state and federal military retirement benefits in question cannot properly be characterized as community property, and hence his advice to plaintiff was correct. As will appear, the contention is manifestly untenable in light of recent decisions by this court. (In re Marriage of Fithian (1974) 10 Cal.3d 592, 111 Cal.Rptr. 369, 517 P.2d 449; Waite v. Waite (1972) 6 Cal.3d 461, 99 Cal.Rptr. 325, 492 P.2d 13; Phillipson v. Board of Administration (1970) 3 Cal.3d 32, 89 Cal.Rptr. 61, 473 P.2d 765.)

2. A contributory plan is one in which the member contributes to his retirement fund, normally through payroll deductions. A noncontributory plan is one in which no such contributions are made.

The State Employees' Retirement System is now referred to as the Public Employees' Retirement System (Gov. Code, § 20000 et seq.).

fits which terminate upon the death of the retiree. The programs make no allowance for the retiree's widow.

On January 1, 1967, the State of California began to pay General Smith gross retirement benefits of $796.26 per month. Payments under the federal program, however, will not begin until 1983, i. e., 17 years after his actual retirement, when General Smith reaches the age of 60. All benefits which General Smith is entitled to receive were earned during the time he was married to plaintiff.

On February 17, 1967, plaintiff retained defendant to represent her in a divorce action against General Smith. According to plaintiff's testimony, defendant advised her that her husband's retirement benefits were not community property. Three days later defendant filed plaintiff's complaint for divorce. General Smith's retirement benefits were not pleaded as items of community property, and therefore were not considered in the litigation or apportioned by the trial court. The divorce was uncontested and the interlocutory decree divided the minimal described community property and awarded Mrs. Smith $400 per month in alimony and child support. The final decree was entered on February 27, 1968.

On July 17, 1968, pursuant to a request by plaintiff, defendant filed on her behalf a motion to amend the decree, alleging under oath that because of his mistake, inadvertence, and excusable neglect (Code Civ.Proc., § 473) the retirement benefits of General Smith had been omitted from the list of community assets owned by the parties, and that such benefits were in fact community property. The motion was denied on the ground of untimeliness. Plaintiff consulted other counsel, and shortly thereafter filed this malpractice action against defendant.

Defendant admits in his testimony that he assumed General Smith's retirement benefits were separate property when he assessed plaintiff's community property rights. It is his position that as a matter of law an attorney is not liable for mistaken advice when well informed lawyers in the community entertain reasonable doubt as to the proper resolution of the particular legal question involved. Because, he asserts, the law defining the character of retirement benefits was uncertain at the time of his legal services to plaintiff, defendant contends the trial court committed error in refusing to grant his motions for nonsuit and judgment notwithstanding the verdict and in submitting the issue of negligence to the jury under appropriate instructions.[3]

3. The jury was instructed as follows: "In performing legal services for a client in a divorce action an attorney has the duty to have that degree of learning and skill ordinarily possessed by attorneys of good standing, practicing in the same or similar locality and under similar circumstances." "It is his further duty to use the care and skill ordinarily exercised in like cases by reputable members of his profession practicing in the same or a similar locality under similar circumstances, and to use reasonable diligence and his best judgment in the exercise of his skill and the ac-

The law is now settled in California that "retirement benefits which flow from the employment relationship, to the extent they have vested, are community property subject to equal division between the spouses in the event the marriage is dissolved." . . . Because such benefits are part of the consideration earned by the employee, they are accorded community treatment regardless of whether they derive from a state, federal, or private source, or from a contributory or noncontributory plan. . . . In light of these principles, it becomes apparent that General Smith's retirement pay must properly be characterized as community property.[4]

We cannot, however, evaluate the quality of defendant's professional services on the basis of the law as it appears today. In determining whether defendant exhibited the requisite degree of competence in his handling of plaintiff's divorce action, the crucial inquiry is whether his advice was so legally deficient when it was given that he may be found to have failed to use "such skill, prudence, and diligence as lawyers of ordinary skill and capacity commonly possess and exercise in the performance of the tasks which they undertake." (Lucas v. Hamm (1961) 56 Cal.2d 583, 591, 15 Cal.Rptr. 821, 825, 364 P.2d 685, 689.) We must, therefore examine the indicia of the law which were readily available to defendant at the time he performed the legal services in question.

The major authoritative reference works which attorneys routinely consult for a brief and reliable exposition of the law relevant to a specific problem uniformly indicated in 1967 that vested retirement benefits earned during marriage were generally subject to community treatment.[5] (See, e. g., Note, Pensions, and Reserve or Retired Pay, as Community Property, 134 A.L.R. 368; 15 Am.Jur.2d Community Property, § 46, p. 859; 38 Cal.Jur.2d, Pensions, § 12, p. 325; 10 Cal.Jur. 2d, Community Property, § 25, p. 692; 1 Cal.Family Lawyer (Cont.Ed. Bar 1962) p. 111; 4 Witkin, Summary of Cal.Law (1960) pp. 2723–2724; cf. 41 C.J.S. Husband and Wife § 475, p. 1010 & fn. 69 and 1967 Supp. p. 1011.) A typical statement appeared in The California Family Lawyer, a work with which defendant admitted general familiarity: "Of increasing importance is the fact that pension or retirement benefits are community property, even though they are not paid or payable

complishment of his learning, in an effort to accomplish the best possible result for his client."

"A failure to perform any such duty is negligence."

"An attorney is not liable for every mistake he may make in his practice; he is not, in the absence of an express agreement, an insurer of the soundness of his opinions."

4. The fact General Smith will not receive any portion of the federal benefits until he reaches the age of 60 does not affect their community character. Though his right to the payments remained unmatured at the time of the divorce, it had fully vested. . . .

5. In evaluating the competence of an attorney's services, we may justifiably consider his failure to consult familiar encyclopedias of the law. . . .

until after termination of the marriage by death or divorce." (1 Cal. Family Lawyer, supra, at p. 111.)

Although it is true this court had not foreclosed all conflicts on some aspects of the issue at that time, the community character of retirement benefits had been reported in a number of appellate opinions often cited in the literature and readily accessible to defendant. (Benson v. City of Los Angeles (1963) . . . 60 Cal.2d 355, 33 Cal.Rptr. 257, 384 P.2d 649; French v. French (1941) . . . 17 Cal.2d 775, 112 P.2d 235; Cheney v. City & County of San Francisco (1936) 7 Cal.2d 565, 61 P.2d 754; Williamson v. Williamson (1962) . . . 203 Cal.App.2d 8, 21 Cal.Rptr. 164; Estate of Manley (1959) 169 Cal. App.2d 641, 337 P.2d 487; Estate of Perryman (1955) 133 Cal.App.2d 1, 283 P.2d 298; Crossan v. Crossan (1939) supra, 35 Cal.App.2d 39, 94 P.2d 609.) In *Benson,* decided four years before defendant was retained herein, we stated directly that "pension rights which are earned during the course of a marriage are the community property of the employee and his wife." (60 Cal.2d at p. 359, 33 Cal.Rptr. at p. 259, 384 P.2d at p. 651.) In *French*, decided two decades earlier, we indicated that "retire[ment] pay is community property because it is compensation for services rendered in the past." (17 Cal.2d at p. 778, 112 P.2d at p. 236.) The other cases contain equally unequivocal dicta.

We are aware, moreover, of no significant authority existing in 1967 which proposed a result contrary to that suggested by the cases and the literature, or which purported to rebut the general statutory presumption, as it applies to retirement benefits, that all property acquired by either spouse during marriage belongs to the community. (Civ.Code, § 5110, as amended Jan. 1, 1970; formerly Civ.Code, § 164.)

On the other hand, substantial uncertainty may have existed in 1967 with regard to the community character of General Smith's *federal* pension. The above-discussed treatises reveal a debate which lingered among members of the legal community at that time concerning the point at which retirement benefits actually vest.[6] (See also Kent, Pension Funds and Problems Under California Community Property Laws (1950) 2 Stan.L.Rev. 447; Note, Community Property: Division of Expectancies as Community Property at Time of Divorce (1942) 30 Cal.L.Rev. 469.) Because the federal payments were contingent upon General Smith's survival to age 60, 17 years subsequent to the divorce, it could have been argued with some force that plaintiff and General Smith shared a mere expectancy interest in the future benefits. (See French v. French (1941) supra, 17 Cal.2d 775, 778, 112 P.2d 235; but see fn. 4 ante.) Alternatively, a reasonable contention could have been advanced in 1967 that federal retirement benefits were the personal entitlement of the employee spouse and were not subject to community division upon divorce in the absence of ex-

6. Indeed this debate may, to some extent, continue today. See, e. g., In re Marriage of Wilson (1974) 10 Cal.3d 851, 112 Cal.Rptr. 405, 519 P.2d 165.

press congressional approval. In fact, such was the conclusion reached in 1973 by Judge B. Abbott Goldberg in his scholarly article Is Armed Services Retired Pay Really Community Property? (1973) 48 State Bar Journal 12. Although we rejected Judge Goldberg's analysis in In re Marriage of Fithian (1974) supra, 10 Cal.3d 592, 597, 111 Cal. Rptr. 369, 517 P.2d 449, footnote 2, the issue was clearly an arguable one upon which reasonable lawyers could differ. (See Sprague v. Morgan (1960) 185 Cal.App.2d 519, 523, 8 Cal.Rptr. 347; Annot., 45 A.L.R.2d 5, 15.)

Of course, the fact that in 1967 a reasonable argument could have been offered to support the characterization of General Smith's federal benefits as separate property does not indicate the trial court erred in submitting the issue of defendant's malpractice to the jury. The *state* benefits, the large majority of the payments at issue, were unquestionably community property according to all available authority and should have been claimed as such. As for the *federal* benefits, the record documents defendant's failure to conduct any reasonable research into their proper characterization under community property law.[7] Instead, he dogmatically asserted his theory, which he was unable to support with authority and later recanted, that all noncontributory military retirement benefits, whether state or federal, were immune from community treatment upon divorce. The jury could well have found defendant's refusal to educate himself to the applicable principles of law constituted negligence which prevented him from exercising informed discretion with regard to his client's rights.

As the jury was correctly instructed, an attorney does not ordinarily guarantee the soundness of his opinions and, accordingly, is not liable for every mistake he may make in his practice. He is expected, however, to possess knowledge of those plain and elementary principles of law which are commonly known by well informed attorneys, and to discover those additional rules of law which, although not commonly known, may readily be found by standard research techniques. (Lucas v. Hamm (1961) 56 Cal.2d 583, 591, 15 Cal.Rptr. 821, 364 P.2d 685; Lally v. Kuster (1918) 177 Cal. 783, 786, 171 P. 961; Floro v. Lawton

7. At trial defendant testified that prior to the division of property in the divorce action, he had assumed the retirement benefits were not subject to community treatment, despite the fact General Smith had already begun to receive payments from the state; that he did not at that time undertake any research on the point nor did he discuss the matter with plaintiff; that subsequent to the divorce plaintiff asked defendant to research the question whereupon defendant discovered the *French* case which contained dictum in support of plaintiff's position; that the *French* decision caused him to change his opinion and conclude "that the Supreme Court, when it was confronted with this [the language in *French*] may hold that it [vested military retirement pay] is community property." On the basis of *French* defendant filed his unsuccessful motion to amend the final decree of divorce to allow plaintiff an interest in the retirement benefits. Defendant admitted at trial, "I would have been very willing to assert it [a community interest] on her behalf had I known of the dictum in the *French* case at the time."

(1960) 187 Cal.App.2d 657, 673, 10 Cal.Rptr. 98; Sprague v. Morgan (1960) . . . , 185 Cal.App.2d 519, 523, 8 Cal.Rptr. 347; Armstrong v. Adams (1929) 102 Cal.App. 677, 684, 283 P. 871.) If the law on a particular subject is doubtful or debatable, an attorney will not be held responsible for failing to anticipate the manner in which the uncertainty will be resolved. (See, e. g., Sprague v. Morgan (1960) supra.) But even with respect to an unsettled area of the law, we believe an attorney assumes an obligation to his client to undertake reasonable research in an effort to ascertain relevant legal principles and to make an informed decision as to a course of conduct based upon an intelligent assessment of the problem. In the instant case, ample evidence was introduced to support a jury finding that defendant failed to perform such adequate research into the question of the community character of retirement benefits and thus was unable to exercise the informed judgment to which his client was entitled. (See fn. 7, ante.)

We recognize, of course, that an attorney engaging in litigation may have occasion to choose among various alternative strategies available to his client, one of which may be to refrain from pressing a debatable point because potential benefit may not equal detriment in terms of expenditure at time and resources or because of calculated tactics to the advantage of his client. But, as the Ninth Circuit put it somewhat brutally in Pineda v. Craven (9th Cir. 1970) 424 F.2d 369, 372: "There is nothing strategic or tactical about ignorance . . . ." In the case before us it is difficult to conceive of tactical advantage which could have been served by neglecting to advance a claim so clearly in plaintiff's best interest, nor does defendant suggest any. The decision to forego litigation on the issue of plaintiff's community property right to a share of General Smith's retirement benefits was apparently the product of a culpable misconception of the relevant principles of law, and the jury could have so found.

Furthermore, no lawyer would suggest the property characterization of General Smith's retirement benefits to be so esoteric an issue that defendant could not reasonably have been expected to be aware of it or its probable resolution. (Lucas v. Hamm (1961) . . ., 56 Cal.2d 583, 15 Cal.Rptr. 821, 364 P.2d 685.) In *Lucas* we held that the rule against perpetuities poses such complex and difficult problems for the draftsman that even careful and competent attorneys occasionally fall prey to its traps. The situation before us is not analogous. Certainly one of the central issues in any divorce proceeding is the extent and division of the community property. In this case the question reached monumental proportions, since General Smith's retirement benefits constituted the only significant asset available to the community.[8] In undertaking professional representation of plaintiff, de-

8. It is undisputed that the only assets the parties had to show as community property after 24 years of marriage, aside from General Smith's retirement benefits, were an equity of $1,800 in a house, some furniture, shares of stock worth $2,800, and two automobiles on which money was owing.

fendant assumed the duty to familiarize himself with the law defining the character of retirement benefits; instead, he rendered erroneous advice contrary to the best interests of his client without the guidance through research of readily available authority.

Regardless of his failure to undertake adequate research, defendant through personal experience in the domestic relations field had been exposed to community property aspects of pensions. Representing the wife of a reserve officer in the National Guard in 1965, defendant alleged as one of the items of community property "the retirement benefits from the Armed Forces and/or the California National Guard." On behalf of the husband in a 1967 divorce action, defendant filed an answer admitting retirement benefits were community property, merely contesting the amount thereof. In 1965 a wife whom he was representing was so insistent on asserting a community interest in a pension, over defendant's contrary views, that she communicated with the state retirement system and brought to defendant correspondence from the state agency describing her interest in pension benefits. And representing an army colonel, defendant filed a cross-complaint for divorce specifically setting up as an item of community property "retirement benefits in the name of the defendant with the United States Government." It is difficult to understand why defendant deemed the community property claim to pensions of three of the foregoing clients to deserve presentation to the trial court, but not the similar claim of this plaintiff.

In any event, as indicated above, had defendant conducted minimal research into either hornbook or case law, he would have discovered with modest effort that General Smith's state retirement benefits were likely to be treated as community property and that his federal benefits at least arguably belonged to the community as well. Therefore, we hold that the trial court correctly denied the motions for nonsuit and judgment notwithstanding the verdict and properly submitted the question of defendant's negligence to the jury under the instructions given. (See fn. 3, ante.) For the same reasons, the trial court correctly refused to instruct the jury at defendant's request that "he is not liable for being in error as to a question of law on which reasonable doubt may be entertained by well informed lawyers." Even as to doubtful matters, an attorney is expected to perform sufficient research to enable him to make an informed and intelligent judgment on behalf of his client.[9]

. . .

The judgment is affirmed.

9. The principal thrust of the dissent is its conclusion . . . that "even assuming that defendant was negligent in failing to research the pension questions, the record does not furnish a balance of probabilities that his negligence—rather than the uncertain status of the law and the availability of uncontested alimony—caused plaintiff to lose a $100,000 pension award."

NOTE ON PARALEGAL LIABILITY

Like any worker, a paralegal can be liable for the harm s/he causes a client due to negligence in the performance of services. For paralegals that work for lawyers, this will usually mean that the injured client could also sue the paralegal's employer—the supervising attorney. This attorney will be liable for the negligence of his/her employees committed in the course of employment. The client will be able to sue either the supervising attorney or the employed paralegal. See Wade, J., "Tort Liability of Legal Paraprofessionals and Lawyers who Utilize their Services," 24 *Vanderbilt Law Review* 1133 (1971).

Whether defendant's negligence was a cause in fact of plaintiff's damage—an element of proximate cause—is a factual question for the jury to resolve. . . . Here the jury was correctly instructed that plaintiff had the burden of proving, inter alia, that defendant's negligence was a proximate cause of the damage suffered, and proximate cause was defined as "a cause which, natural and continuous sequence, produces the damage, and *without which the damage would not have occurred.*" (Italics added.) Under the strict standards governing appellate review of dispute questions of fact . . ., we see no reason on the present record to disturb the jury's implied finding of proximate cause.

Paralegal Interviewing a Client
Photo by Michael Diamond

Chapter Five

PRELIMINARY LEGAL INTERVIEW—BACKGROUND INFORMATION

This chapter consists of a large number of questions which could be asked during a preliminary interview of a client with a Family Law problem. Most of the questions focus on financial information since finances are crucial in a great many Family Law cases. Many lawyers feel that detailed background information is necessary for competent legal representation.[1] A number of observations need to be made about the questions:

—The questions are not necessarily listed in the order in which they would be asked.

—While most of the questions would be asked during an oral interview, some attorneys might prefer to send portions of the questions home with the client to be answered in a more relaxed setting where the client could check his/her records.

—For certain kinds of cases, some of the questions would not be relevant. In an adoption case, for example, the separation agreement questions (##439–496) would not be used.

—You will note that most of the questions do *not* deal with substantive issues such as whether one spouse can sue another in tort, how domicile is established, etc. Such questions will be presented in later chapters of this book where substantive issues are discussed. Some of the following questions (e. g., ##438–496) do deal with substantive issues, but only in an introductory way; they will be treated in greater depth later in the book.

The questions are organized as follows:

I.	Questions	1– 21.	Introductory Facts.
II.	Questions	22– 37.	Marital Facts.
III.	Questions	38– 58.	Prior Contracts Between the Spouses.
IV.	Questions	59–100.	Itemized Monthly Expenses.
V.	Questions	101–103.	Health Information.
VI.	Questions	104–126.	Information on Wills.
VII.	Questions	127–152.	Client's Business.

1. Many of the questions are adapted from Brown, L., "A Family Legal Information Check List," 3 *The Practical Lawyer* 60, No. 6 (Oct. 1957), and Barrett, L., "The Initial Interview with a Divorce Client," 23 *The Practical Lawyer* 75, No. 4 (June, 1977). Copyright by the American Law Institute. Reprinted with the Permission of *The Practical Lawyer*.

VIII. Questions 153–178. Spouse's Business.
IX. Questions 179–205. Client's Employment.
X. Questions 206–232. Spouse's Employment.
XI. Questions 233–254. Real Property.
XII. Questions 255–276. Personal Property (other than securities and cash).
XIII. Questions 277–327. Stocks/ Bonds/ Accounts/ Deposit Boxes.
XIV. Questions 328–393. Insurance.
XV. Questions 394–400. Miscellaneous Income.
XVI. Questions 401–407. Liabilities.
XVII. Questions 408–437. Tax Returns.
XVIII. Question 438. Conduct of Spouse.
XIX. Questions 439–496. Property Settlement and Separation Agreement.
XX. Questions 497–515. Persons Familiar With Client's Affairs.
XXI. Authorization to Represent and Compensation Agreement.

I. INTRODUCTORY FACTS

1. Client's full name ______________________________
2. Today's date ______________________________
3. Maiden name (if woman) ______________________________
4. Case file No. ______________________________
5. Other names used, if any ______________________________
____
6. Name of interviewer ______________________________
7. Current address of client ______________________________
7a. How long have you lived at this address ______________________________
7b. List every other residence you have had in this state and indicate how long you have lived at each address ______________________________
____
8. Home phone ______________________________
9. Business address ______________________________
10. Business phone ______________________________

I. INTRODUCTORY FACTS—Continued

11. Other addresses and phone numbers where you can be reached ______________________________

12. Spouses address ______________________________
13. Home phone ______________________________
14. Business address ______________________________
15. Business phone ______________________________
16. Other addresses and phone numbers where spouse can be reached ______________________________

17. Age of client ______________________________
18. Place of birth ______________________________
19. Certified copy of birth certificate kept at ______________________________
20. Have any other attorneys been contacted on this matter? ________
21. If so, their names and addresses and dates contacted ______________________________

II. MARITAL FACTS

22. Date of client's marriage ______________________________
23. Place of marriage ______________________________
(City) (County) (State)
24. To whom married ______________________________
25. Marriage license dated ______________________________
26. Marriage license granted by ______________________________
27. Certified copy of license kept at ______________________________
28. Marriage ceremony performed by ______________________________
29. Marriage certificate dated ______________________________
30. Certified copy kept at ______________________________
31. Names and addresses of witnesses to ceremony ______________________________

32. Have you ever had a common law spouse?[2] ______________________________

32a. Was this your first marriage? ______________________________

2. Infra p. 164.

II. MARITAL FACTS—Continued

33. If not, answer questions 22–31 as to each prior marriage ______

34. Indicate how each prior marriage terminated ______

35. Was your current spouse ever married before? ______

36. If not, give names of prior spouses and how each prior marriage terminated ______

37. In the space below, provide information on each child involved. For each child, give its full name, date of birth, current address, names of natural parents, names of adoptive parents, if any, names of guardians, if any ______

III. PRIOR CONTRACTS BETWEEN SPOUSES

38. Was there an antenuptial contract? [3] ______

39. If there was an antenuptial contract, state date ______

40. Contract prepared by (name of attorneys) ______

41. Contract kept at ______

42. Husband agreed to convey the following property ______

43. Is there a waiver by the wife of dower or other rights? ______

---

3. Infra p. 127.

III. PRIOR CONTRACTS BETWEEN SPOUSES—Continued

44. Is there agreement as to the manner of holding title to real property? ______

45. Is there provision for life insurance? ______

46. Is there waiver of future claims to each other's property? ______

47. Summarize other important provisions ______

48. Any separation agreement already in existence [4] ______

49. If so, date of the contract ______

50. Name of lawyer representing wife ______

51. Representing husband ______

52. Was contract made before marriage? ______

53. Or after marriage? ______

Brief description of contract:

54. Property division between spouses ______

55. Husband (or wife) to make payments to other spouse ______

56. Custody of children ______

57. Other significant provisions ______

58. Contract kept at ______

IV. ITEMIZED MONTHLY EXPENSES

In the following expense statement, it is important (e. g., for tax purposes) [5] to try to allocate expenses between yourself and your children. If you have difficulty making the allocation for any of the questions, leave it blank for now and check it with a supervising attorney as soon as possible.

4. Infra p. 245.

5. Infra p. 411.

IV. ITEMIZED MONTHLY EXPENSES—Continued

59. Costs for support of ______________________________
(client's name)

60. Name of dependents Ages

____

	Yourself	Children
Housing:		
61. Mortgage or rent		
62. Taxes		
63. Insurance		
Utilities:		
64. Gas/oil		
65. Electric		
66. Water & sewer		
67. Telephone		
68. Maintenance of house or apartment		
69. Maintenance of swimming pool		
Food:		
70. Groceries		
71. Milk		
72. Meat		
73. Clothing		
74. Shoes		
75. Maintenance for clothing—tailors, laundry, etc.		
76. Maid		
77. Babysitter		
Transportation:		
78. Gasoline for car		
79. Tolls		
80. License		
81. Registration		
82. Maintenance for car		
83. Depreciation		
84. Payments on car		

IV. ITEMIZED MONTHLY EXPENSES—Continued

Transportation: Continued	Yourself	Children
85. Insurance for self and children		
86. Insurance on car		
Medical expenses: 87. Doctor		
88. Drugs		
89. Dentist		
Personal: 90. Haircuts/hairdresser		
91. Miscellaneous toiletries—soap, cold cream, etc.		
92. Pets—care and food		
93. Entertainment		
94. Cash allowance		
95. Vacation allowance		
96. Contribution to church		
97. Charity		
98. YMCA		
99. Other		
100. Totals		

[B7962]

V. HEALTH INFORMATION

101. Describe your present health. Give details on prior health problems. Names of doctors. Dates of treatment ______

______

______

______

______

______

102. Same questions as to your spouse ______

______

______

______

______

V. HEALTH INFORMATION—Continued

103. Same questions as to each dependent child ____________________

____

____

____

____

____

VI. INFORMATION ON WILLS

104. Do you have your own will? ____________________

105. Date will signed ____________________

Lawyer who prepared will:

106. Name ____________________

107. Address ____________________
(Street) (City) (State)

Executors named in will:

108. Initial executor ____________________

109. Successor executor ____________________

110. Is guardian named for children? ____________________

111. Specific bequests, if any:

What property or amount ____________________

To whom ____________________

What property or amount ____________________

To whom ____________________

What property or amount ____________________

To whom ____________________

112. Remainder bequest:

To whom ____________________

If will contains testamentary trust:

113. Name of initial trustee ____________________

114. Successor trustee ____________________

115. Property to go into trust consists of ____________________

VI. INFORMATION ON WILLS—Continued

Beneficiaries of trust:

116. Lifetime beneficiaries ______________________

117. Remainder beneficiaries ______________________

118. Where is original will kept? ______________________

Codicils or amendments:

119. Date codicil signed ______________________

Lawyer who prepared codicil:

120. Name ______________________

121. Address ______________________
(Street) (City) (State)

122. General contents of codicil ______________________

123. Where is original codicil kept? ______________________

124. Does your spouse have a separate will? ______________________

125. Significant provisions in spouse's will ______________________
____
____
____
____

126. Do you and your spouse have a joint will? If so, questions 105–123 should be answered as to the joint will.

VII. CLIENT'S BUSINESS

127. Nature of business ______________________

If Sole Owner of Business:

128. Name of business ______________________

129. Address ______________________
(Street) (City) (State)

If partnership:

130. Name of partnership ______________________

131. Address ______________________
(Street) (City) (State)

132. Names of other partners ______________________

133. Percentage interest of client ______________________

134. Is there a written agreement? ______ If so, state: ______

135. General or limited partnership ______________________

VII. CLIENT'S BUSINESS—Continued

If partnership:—Continued

136. Date of Agreement ______

137. Termination provision ______

138. Any provision for purchase or sale of partnership interest during lifetime of partners ______

139. After death of a partner ______

If corporation:

140. Name of corporation ______

141. State of incorporation ______

142. Total issued shares ______

143. Number of shares client owns ______

144. Position in corporation ______

145. Member of board ______ Total number of members ______

146. Officer ______ Which office ______

147. Is there written agreement among stockholders? ______

148. If so, state:

149. Date of agreement ______

150. Names of parties and stock ownership of each ______

151. Is there provision for purchase or sale of stock during lifetime? ______

152. After death of a stockholder? ______

VIII. SPOUSE'S BUSINESS

153. Nature of business ______

If sole owner of business:

154. Name of business ______

155. Address ______
(Street) (City) (State)

If partnership:

156. Name of partnership ______

157. Address ______
(Street) (City) (State)

158. Names of other partners ______

159. Percentage interest of spouse ______

160. Is there a written agreement? ______ If so, state: ______

161. General or limited partnership ______

VIII. SPOUSE'S BUSINESS—Continued

If partnership:—Continued

162. Date of Agreement ______

163. Termination provision ______

164. Any provision for purchase or sale of partnership interest during lifetime of partners ______

165. After death of a partner ______

If corporation:

166. Name of corporation ______

167. State of incorporation ______

168. Total issued shares ______

169. Number of shares spouse owns ______

170. Position in corporation ______

171. Member of board ______ Total number of members ______

172. Officer ______ Which office ______

173. Is there written agreement among stockholders? ______

174. If so, state:

175. Date of agreement ______

176. Names of parties and stock ownership of each ______

177. Is there provision for purchase or sale of stock during lifetime?

______

178. After death of a stockholder? ______

IX. CLIENT'S EMPLOYMENT

179. Social Security Number ______

PRESENT EMPLOYMENT

180. Employer's name ______

181. Address ______
(Street) (City) (State)

182. Salary ______

183. Present employment started on ______
(Date)

184. Nature of present employment—brief job description—title.

Union membership:

185. Name of union ______

186. Address ______
(Street) (City) (State)

IX. CLIENT'S EMPLOYMENT—Continued

Union membership:—Continued

187. Date became member ____________

188. Dues ____________

189. Payable ____________

List and briefly describe employment benefits client may have, such as:

190. Life insurance ____________

191. Hospital insurance ____________

192. Medical insurance ____________

193. Paid vacations ____________

194. Paid holidays ____________

195. Illness leave ____________

196. Severance pay ____________

197. Credit union ____________

198. Pension plan ____________

199. Profit-sharing plan ____________

200. Other ____________

PREVIOUS EMPLOYMENT

201. Employer's name ____________

202. Address ____________
(Street) (City) (State)

203. Dates: from ____________ to ____________

204. Nature of employment—brief job description—title ____________

____

205. Add as many similar paragraphs for previous employment as may be necessary.

____

____

____

X. SPOUSES EMPLOYMENT

206. Social Security Number ____________

PRESENT EMPLOYMENT

207. Employer's name ____________

208. Address ____________
(Street) (City) (State)

X. SPOUSES EMPLOYMENT—Continued

PRESENT EMPLOYMENT—Continued

209. Salary ______

210. Present employment started on ______
(Date)

211. Nature of present employment—brief job description—title.
______

Union membership:

212. Name of union ______

213. Address ______
(Street) (City) (State)

214. Date became member ______

215. Dues ______

216. Payable ______

List and briefly describe employment benefits spouse may have, such as:

217. Life insurance ______

218. Hospital insurance ______

219. Medical insurance ______

220. Paid vacations ______

221. Paid holidays ______

222. Illness leave ______

223. Severance pay ______

224. Credit union ______

225. Pension plan ______

226. Profit-sharing plan ______

227. Other ______

PREVIOUS EMPLOYMENT

228. Employer's name ______

229. Address ______
(Street) (City) (State)

230. Dates: from ______ to ______

231. Nature of employment—brief job description—title ______
______

232. Add as many similar paragraphs for previous employment as may be necessary ______
______

XI. REAL PROPERTY

On separate sheets of paper you are to answer questions 233 to 254 for *each* item of real property owned by the client, the spouse or together. Examples of real property include: current residence(s), vacation home, fixtures on the land, undeveloped land, business buildings, land held for business, leased property, etc.

233. Describe the nature of the property ____________

____

234. Location of the property ____________

235. Original cost ____________

236. Was property received by will or via intestacy ____________

237. If so, from whom and to whom ____________

238. Who paid for the property ____________

239. Where did the money come from that was used to purchase the property ____________

____

240. In whose name was the property taken ____________

241. Where are the documents of sale located ____________

242. Date of the sale ____________

243. Name and address of seller ____________

244. Have any improvements been made to the property ____________

245. If so, what funds were used to pay for them ____________

246. Does any insurance exist on the property ____________

247. If so, who pays the premium, with what funds and who is the beneficiary ____________

____

248. Are any taxes paid on the property ____________

249. If so, who pays them and with what funds ____________

250. Is any money owed on the property ____________

251. If so, to whom ____________

252. Who pays and with what funds ____________

253. Who uses the property now ____________

254. Other information relevant to this property ____________

____

XII. PERSONAL PROPERTY (OTHER THAN SECURITIES AND CASH)

On separate sheets of paper you are to answer questions 255 to 276 for *each* item of personal property owned by the client, the spouse or together. Examples of personal property include: cars, trucks, boats, furniture, jewelry, clothing, business stock, business equipment, etc.

255. Describe the nature of the property ____________________

____

256. Location of the property ____________________
257. Original cost ____________________
258. Was property received by will or via intestacy ____________________
259. If so, from whom and to whom ____________________
260. Who paid for the property ____________________
261. Where did the money come from that was used to purchase the property ____________________

____

262. In whose name was the property taken ____________________
263. Where are the documents of sale located ____________________
264. Date of the sale ____________________
265. Name and address of seller ____________________
266. Have any improvements been made to the property ____________________
267. If so, what funds were used to pay for them ____________________
268. Does any insurance exist on the property ____________________
269. If so, who pays the premium, with what funds and who is the beneficiary ____________________

____

270. Are any taxes paid on the property ____________________
271. If so, who pays them and with what funds ____________________
272. Is any money owed on the property ____________________
273. If so, to whom ____________________
274. Who pays and with what funds ____________________
275. Who uses the property now ____________________
276. Other information relevant to this property ____________________

____

XIII. STOCKS/BONDS/ACCOUNTS/DEPOSIT BOXES

STOCKS

277. Name of corporation					
278. Name of owner as shown on certificate					
279. Number of shares					
280. Certificate number					
281. Date acquired					
282. Cost of shares					
283. Source of funds used to purchase					
284. Commission					
285. Sold—date					
286. Sales price					
287. Commission					

BONDS

288. Name of corporation or obligor					
289. Name of owner as shown on bond					
290. Face amount due at maturity					
291. Bond number					

XIII. STOCKS/BONDS/ACCOUNTS/DEPOSIT BOXES—Continued

BONDS—Continued

292.	Date acquired					
293.	Cost					
294.	Source of funds used to purchase					
295.	Commission					
296.	Maturity date					
297.	Rate of interest					
298.	When is interest payable					
299.	Are coupons attached					
300.	Sold—date					
301.	Sales price					
302.	Commission					
303.	Miscellaneous					

SAVINGS CERTIFICATES

304.	Name of bank or institution					
305.	Address					
306.	Type of certificate					
307.	Name(s) on certificate					
308.	Amount					

XIII. STOCKS/BONDS/ACCOUNTS/DEPOSIT BOXES—Continued

SAVINGS CERTIFICATES—Continued

309.	Rate of interest					
310.	Source of funds to purchase					
311.	Date purchased					
312.	Dates renewed					

SAVINGS AND CHECKING ACCOUNTS

313.	Name of bank or savings institution					
314.	Address of bank					
315.	Type of account					
316.	Name(s) on account					
317.	Persons authorized to draw on account					
318.	Date account opened					
319.	Amounts currently in account					

SAFE DEPOSIT BOXES

320.	Name of bank or institution					
321.	Address					
322.	Number of box					
323.	In whose name(s) is box					

XIII. STOCKS/BONDS/ACCOUNTS/DEPOSIT BOXES—Continued

SAFE DEPOSIT BOXES—Continued

324.	Who is authorized to enter box					
325.	Date box obtained					
326.	Date box rental terminated					
327.	Contents					

[B7967]

XIV. INSURANCE

LIFE INSURANCE

328. Insured (whose life) ____________________

329. Insurance company ____________________
(Name)

330. Address ____________________
(Street) (City) (State)

331. Where policy kept ____________________

332. Kind of policy ____________________

333. Date of issue ____________________

334. Face amount ____________________

335. Policy number ____________________

336. Premium ____________________

337. When payable ____________________

338. Who pays (what funds are used) ____________________

339. Beneficiary or beneficiaries ____________________

____

340. Owner of policy ____________________

341. Agent ____________________
(Name)

342. Address ____________________
(Street) (City) (State)

XIV. INSURANCE—Continued

LIFE INSURANCE—Continued

343. Has policy been assigned? If so, state when, and to whom ____

____

344. Loans against policy? If so, state when made and amount ____

____

ACCIDENT AND HEALTH INSURANCE

345. Company ____

346. Address ____
(Street) (City) (State)

347. Kind of policy ____

348. Date of issue ____

349. Number of policy ____

350. Premium ____

351. When payable ____

352. Who pays (what funds are used) ____

353. Agent ____
(Name)

354. Address ____
(Street) (City) (State)

FIRE OR HOMEOWNER INSURANCE

355. Name of insured ____

356. Company ____
(Name)

357. Address ____
(Street) (City) (State)

358. Kind of policy—coverages in addition to fire ____

359. Amount of coverage ____

360. Property covered ____

361. Date of issue ____

362. Date of expiration ____

363. Premium ____

364. Who pays (what funds are used) ____

365. Policy number ____

Notification requirements:

366. How soon after loss? ____

367. How must notification be sent? ____

367. How must notfication be sent? ____

XIV. INSURANCE—Continued

FIRE OR HOMEOWNER INSURANCE—Continued

Notification requirements:—Continued

368. Agent ______________________
(Name)

369. Address ______________________
(Street) (City) (State)

AUTOMOBILE INSURANCE

370. Name of insured ______________________

371. Company ______________________
(Name)

372. Address ______________________
(Street) (City) (State)

Automobile:

373. Make ______________________

374. Model ______________________

375. Year ______________________

Coverage:

376. Bodily injury liability ______________________

377. Each person ______________________

378. Each occurrence ______________________

379. Medical payments ______________________

380. Property damage liability ______________________

381. Comprehensive loss or damage ______________________

382. Collision ______________________

383. Other ______________________

384. Date of issue ______________________

385. Date of expiration ______________________

386. Premium ______________________

387. Who pays (what funds are used) ______________________

388. Policy number ______________________

Notification requirements:

389. How soon after loss or injury? ______________________

390. To whom must notification be sent? ______________________

391. How must notification be sent? ______________________

392. Agent ______________________
(Name)

393. Address ______________________
(Street) (City) (State)

XV. MISCELLANEOUS INCOME

394. Income from trusts (you) ______

395. Income from trusts (spouse) ______

396. Royalty income (you) ______

397. Royalty income (spouse) ______

398. Rental income (you) ______

399. Rental income (spouse) ______

400. Other income ______

______

XVI. LIABILITIES

401. Mortgages ______

402. On what ______

403. Who pays ______

404. Promissory notes or other credit transactions ______

______

405. On what ______

406. Who pays ______

407. Other debts ______

______

XVII. TAX RETURNS

INCOME TAX	Year	Year	Year	Year	Year	Year
Declaration						
408. Separate or joint						
409. Date filed						
410. City where filed						
411. Amount of estimated tax						
412. Amended—when						
413. Amended amount of tax						

XVII. TAX RETURNS—Continued

INCOME TAX	Year	Year	Year	Year	Year	Year
U. S. Return						
414. Separate or joint						
415. Date filed						
416. City where filed						
417. Amount of taxable income						
418. Amount of tax						
419. Return prepared by—Name of accountant, lawyer or other						
420. Address						
421. Has return been audited by government? (State result if audited)						
State Return						
422. Separate or joint						
423. Date filed						
424. City where filed						
425. Amount of taxable income						
425a. Amount of tax						
426. City return						
427. Separate or joint						
428. Date filed						
429. City where filed						
430. Amount of taxable income						
431. Amount of tax						
432. Return prepared by						
433. Address						
434. Has return been audited (if so, what result)						

XVII. TAX RETURNS—Continued

INCOME TAX	**Year**	**Year**	**Year**	**Year**	**Year**	**Year**
GIFT TAX						
435. Date filed						
436. Amount of gift or gifts						
437. Gift tax, if any						

[B7973]

XVIII. CONDUCT OF SPOUSE [6]

Date by month and year	**Unreasonable thing spouse did or did not do**	**Persons who knew or heard about it. State full names, mailing addresses, and telephone numbers**

438. ____

____

____

____

____

____

____

____

____

____

XIX. PROPERTY SETTLEMENT AND SEPARATION AGREEMENT [7]

General (You can obtain the information for the first set of questions from answers to prior questions):

439. Complete names and addresses of husband and wife:

____

____

---

6. Infra p. 307.

7. Infra p. 245.

XIX. PROPERTY SETTLEMENT AND SEPARATION AGREEMENT—Continued

440. Complete names, ages, and birth dates of all children:

____

____

____

441. Husband's current monthly gross salary: ______ Net monthly salary: ______

442. Wife's current monthly gross salary: Net monthly salary: ______

443. Place and date of marriage and name of person who married you:

____

Children:

444. Who shall have custody ______________________________

445. Who shall have custody if that person cannot serve as guardian. Give name and address. ______________________________

____

446. What visitation rights will other spouse have ______________________________

____

447. When will support cease for children ______________________________

Age 18 __ Marriage __ After college __ Entrance into service __

448. Amount of child support: ______________________________

449. Who claims children as income tax exemptions ______________

450. Support credit of $______ when child stays with ______ for ______ days.

451. Who carries medical insurance for children ______________

Blue Cross __ Blue Shield __ Major Medical __

452. Explain in detail if other types of medical insurance: ________

____

453. Who is responsible for minor medical bills (less than $25.00)__

____

454. For major medical bills ______________________________

455. Who pays for prescription drugs ______ For dentist ______

456. Who is responsible for children's religious training ____________

XIX. PROPERTY SETTLEMENT AND SEPARATION AGREEMENT—Continued

457. Who selects, is responsible, and pays for children's summer camp ____________________

458. Who selects, is responsible, and pays for college ____________

Wife:

459. How many years will alimony be paid ____________

460. When shall parties confer on important mutual matters ______

461. Shall parties agree not to cause children to dislike other spouse ______

462. What amount of alimony paid per month ____________

463. Should husband's alimony payment be lowered if wife works __ ____________________

464. If cost of living increases, should alimony or support increase __ ____________________

465. If husband earns more, should wife receive proportionately more alimony ______ How much more ____________

466. Should alimony be a lump sum payment ______ How much ____

467. Should payments be paid directly to spouse or through a third party ____________________

468. Should spouse be liable for prior joint tax returns ____________

469. Should parties agree that they will file a joint tax return for current year ____________________

Real estate:

470. Should house be sold and proceeds split now ____________

471. Who paid down payment for house ______ How much ______

472. When ____________________

473. Who made all payments ______ What monthly amount ______

474. What is house sale value ______ What is mortgage balance ____

475. Any other realty ____________________

476. Name and address of mortgage company: ____________ ____________________

477. Should wife continue to live in house ____________

XIX. PROPERTY SETTLEMENT AND SEPARATION AGREEMENT—Continued

477a. What amount is now owed to spouse for his/her interest in house

____

477b. Who is to pay mortgage ____________ Taxes ____________

478. Insurance ______ Water ______ Sewer ______

479. Repairs ______ Can husband make repairs ______

Personal property:

480. List all items husband will take. (Complete in detail on attached sheet.)

481. List all items wife will take. (Complete in detail on attached sheet.)

482. Value of wife's car: __________ Husband's car: __________

483. What is to be done with cars ______________________

484. List all bank accounts: ______________________

____

485. List all stocks, bonds, children's savings accounts, pets, house property, future income, and pensions: ______________

____

Insurance:

486. List all life insurance by company name, address, and policy number, amount, beneficiaries, and owners: ______________

____

487. Who pays ____________ Who keeps policies ____________

488. List all life insurance for children and provide data on policies:

____

489. Who pays ____________ Who keeps policies ____________

Other provisions:

490. Can both persons certify that they had independent legal advice

____

491. Who pays counsel fees ______________________

492. Can this agreement be changed if circumstances change ______

493. List all current outstanding obligations, household bills, debts, monthly and periodic payments, credit card debts, etc. on separate sheet.

XIX. PROPERTY SETTLEMENT AND SEPARATION AGREEMENT—Continued

494. Do both participants agree to have the Court approve this agreement and incorporate it in any subsequent divorce decree ______

495. Are there previous legal divorce, separation, or custody papers ________

496. Add any additional provisions you wish in this agreement. ______

____

____

XX. PERSONS FAMILIAR WITH CLIENT'S AFFAIRS

Business associate:

497. Name ____

498. Address ____
(Street) (City) (State)

499. General description of his knowledge of client's affairs__________

____

Lawyer:

500. Name ____

501. Address ____
(Street) (City) (State)

Doctor:

502. Name ____

503. Address ____
(Street) (City) (State)

Minister:

504. Name ____

505. Address ____
(Street) (City) (State)

Accountant:

506. Name ____

507. Address ____
(Street) (City) (State)

Banker:

508. Name ____

509. Address ____
(Street) (City) (State)

XX. PERSONS FAMILIAR WITH CLIENT'S AFFAIRS—Continued

Life insurance agent:

510. Name ______________________________

511. Address ______________________________
(Street) (City) (State)

Stockbroker:

512. Name ______________________________

513. Address ______________________________
(Street) (City) (State)

Others:

514. Name ______________________________

515. Address ______________________________
(Street) (City) (State)

XXI. AUTHORIZATION TO REPRESENT AND COMPENSATION AGREEMENT

Authorization to Represent and Compensation Agreement

1. I hereby request and authorize you to represent me as my Attorney in fact and in law as related to:

and against all additional persons, firms, or corporations who may appear to be related to this case.

2. As compensation for your services as my Attorney, I agree to pay you as follows:

3. I understand that it is impossible at this time to specify the exact nature, extent, and difficulty of the contemplated services and the time involved. You as my Attorney shall exert your best effort at all times to represent my interests and rights.

4. In connection with the services rendered, it is agreed that you as my Attorney shall be compensated for additional work not contemplated in the above noted estimate at a minimum hourly rate of $____ per hour. I understand that telephone calls and conferences are billed as office charges.

I understand I am to reimburse you in all events for any sums actually paid by you for investigation, preparing claims for trial, court costs, and your expenses.

Dated: ______________ ______________
Signature

We agree to act as Attorney on the above stated basis.

Dated: ______________ By ______________

Retainer paid __________

*

Chapter Six

BREACH OF PROMISE TO MARRY AND THE HEART BALM STATUTE

SECTION A. INTRODUCTION

There are a number of situations that pose legal problems when two parties make arrangements in contemplation of (i. e., while thinking about the possibility of) marriage. For example:

(1) Two parties exchange mutual promises to marry each other. One party breaks the promise. Can the other party sue? If so, for what?

(2) Two parties agree to be married and set a date. They exchange engagement rings. One party breaks the agreement and refuses to go through with the marriage. Can either get the ring back? Suppose they gave other property to each other, e. g., a house, in contemplation of a marriage which never materialized. If either party refuses to return the property, can the other party sue?

Problems such as these will be our concern in this chapter.

SECTION B. BREACH OF PROMISE TO MARRY

For centuries, one of the sacred principles in law has been the stability of contracts. It is not uncommon to find judges who claim that the "foundations of civilized society" depend upon the faithful performance of contractual agreements. Hence courts are available to force parties to live up to their contracts. In the business world, it is clear that thousands of contracts are made each day. Merchants invest large amounts of money and other resources in reliance upon these contracts. Because of this reliance, the law will not allow one merchant to avoid performing its contract simply because it is now having second thoughts about the agreement reached or because it can now obtain a better deal elsewhere. Our question here is whether all of this applies to a contract made between John and Mary to marry each other when one of them changes his or her mind and decides not to marry the other. A contract was made. What about the sacred principle of contractual stability? Are courts available to force people like John and Mary to honor their contracts? Before answering these questions, some understanding of the basic law of contracts is needed. What is a contract? What are the elements of a contract?

CONTRACT

DEFINITION: an agreement that is enforceable by law.

ELEMENTS:
(1) there must be an *offer*;
(2) there must be an *acceptance*;
(3) there must be *consideration* (consideration is something of value which is given[1]);
(4) the parties must have the *capacity*[2] to enter a contract;
(5) the contract may have to be in *writing* in order to comply with the Statute of Frauds;
(6) the contract must not be contrary to *public policy* or otherwise *illegal* within the state.

[B7961]

EXAMPLE:

John, age 34, goes to the XYZ Paint Co. and asks the manager how much it would cost to paint his fence. The manager says, "$857." John then says, "Fine, come as soon as you can." John and the manager sign an agreement that the job will be completed "within ten days" for $857. A contract exists which is enforceable by either John or the manager.

(1) *OFFER*: the manager offered to do the paint job for $857.

(2) *ACCEPTANCE*: John agreed to pay this amount for the job.

(3) *CONSIDERATION*: something of value was exchanged by both parties. The thing of value given by the manager was his *promise* to do the job for the amount specified and within the time specified. The thing of value given by John was his *promise* to pay the amount specified to do the job. Hence the consideration for this contract was an *exchange of promises*.

(4) *CAPACITY*: capacity refers to such factors as the age and mental stability of the parties.[3] There was no indication in the above example that John or the manager lacked the capacity to enter the contract; a minor or a mentally ill person, for example, may lack such capacity.

(5) *WRITING*: the paint agreement was in writing (note that not all contracts have to be in writing in order to be enforceable).

(6) *PUBLIC POLICY*: the paint contract is not in violation of any statute or public policy; it is not illegal.

1. See also p. 264.

2. See also p. 256.

3. For other factors that affect capacity see p. 177ff.

Compare the above example to the following:

John, age 34, has been dating Mary, age 33. Mary has independent wealth; John does not. Mary asks John to marry her. John says, "Yes," and they both agree on a wedding day. The next day Mary changes her mind and tells John that she no longer wants to marry him. Does a contract exist which is enforceable by John against Mary?

(1) *OFFER*: Mary offered to marry John.

(2) *ACCEPTANCE*: John agreed to marry her; he accepted her offer.

(3) *CONSIDERATION*: something of value was exchanged by both parties; they both exchanged *promises* to marry each other. This mutual *exchange of promises* was the consideration for the contract.

(4) *CAPACITY*: there was no indication in the example that either John or Mary lacked the capacity to enter this contract.

(5) *WRITING*: mutual promises to marry do not have to be in writing to be enforceable; the Statute of Frauds does not require such a contract to be in writing.[4]

(6) *PUBLIC POLICY*: ?

The sixth element raises the main question. Would it be against public policy to enforce this contract? Is there a statute in existence which states that such contracts are unenforceable? Should John have a *cause of action* [5] (i. e., a legally acceptable reason to sue) against Mary for breach of contract?

There was a time in our history when such contracts *were* enforceable in many of the states. A cause of action based upon a breach of a contract to marry was called a *heart balm action.*[6] A number of states, however, have abolished this cause of action. The pertinent statute in such a state might read as follows:

"Breach of contract to marry shall not constitute an injury or wrong recognized by law, and no action, suit or proceeding shall be maintained therefor."

Such a statute abolishing the right to sue for breach of a promise to marry is called a *heart balm statute.* These statutes were enacted for

4. Suppose, however, that more than mere promises to marry were exchanged. If one party promises to give the other party money in exchange for a promise of marriage, the agreement as to the money would have to be in writing in order to be enforceable. The Statute of Frauds does apply to such contracts. See also Calamari, J. & Perillo, J., *The Law of Contracts*, p. 460 (1970).

5. For more on the meaning of a cause of action, see Statsky, W. & Wernet, J., *Case Analysis and Fundamentals of Legal Writing*, pp. 125ff. (1977).

6. For a discussion of similar kinds of actions, see infra p. 480ff.

a number of reasons. It was felt that the tensions involving a refusal to marry were usually so personal, intense and possibly bitter that a court was not a proper forum to handle them. Courts were also afraid of being flooded with such lawsuits. Another major problem concerned the *remedy* or result that an aggrieved party would seek in a cause of action based on a breach of promise to marry. If there is a contract which is breached by an individual, one of the possible remedies may be to force this individual to perform the contract. For the marriage contract which is breached, the remedy would therefore be to force the reluctant party to go through with the contract since this is what performance would mean. The very concept of a compulsory marriage under these circumstances seemed quite inappropriate and as a result many states abolished the cause of action altogether. Another possible remedy is the payment of damages, i. e., money to compensate for the breach. As we shall see, many states have concluded that this remedy is equally inappropriate.

Assignment # 15

(a) Go to your state code and find statutes, if any, that tell you whether a heart balm action for breach of contract to marry is possible in your state. If such statutes exist, give their citation and summarize what they say. (See also General Instructions for the State Code Assignment, supra p. 14.)

(b) Find a court opinion written by a state court of your state which holds either that a heart balm action is possible in your state or that it is not possible. Briefly state the facts and conclusion of this opinion. (See also General Instructions for the Court Opinion Assignment, supra p. 26.)

(c) If your state allows heart balm actions for breach of contract to marry, draft a complaint alleging such a breach. On p. 111 above, you were given a hypothetical fact situation involving John and Mary. Assume that John is bringing the complaint against Mary for breach of contract to marry in your state. (See also General Instructions for the Complaint Drafting Assignment, supra p. 20.)

(d) If your state allows heart balm actions for breach of contract to marry, prepare a flow chart of the procedural steps necessary to bring such an action in your state. (See General Instructions for the Flow Chart Assignment, supra p. 33.)

If you live in a state that has abolished the cause of action for breach of promise to marry, is there any need for you to study such an action? Yes, for several reasons:

1. The heart balm statute may not be retroactive. If it is not retroactive, it will not apply to promises to marry made before the statute was passed; breach of promise actions may be

possible if the promise was made before the statute became effective.

2. At the time the promise to marry was made, the client may have lived in another state where a heart balm action *is* legal. A conflict of law [7] question may arise as to which state law applies: the law where the client currently lives (no heart balm actions allowed) or the law where the promise was made (heart balm actions allowed)?

3. As we shall see, even if a heart balm statute exists outlawing breach of promise causes of action, there is considerable dispute as to what these statutes mean in some states. The existence of the statute has not eliminated legal problems. Hence the need to know something about the area.

Assignment # 16

Assume that you live in a state where heart balm actions are legal. D asks C to marry D. C says yes. The date is set for the wedding. Two weeks before the wedding, C learns that D has just married X. At the time D was engaged to C, C was already married to Y. D did not know this. C was in the process of divorcing Y and hoped to have had the divorce finalized before C's marriage to D. C wanted to wait until the divorce was final before telling D about the prior marriage and divorce. D did not learn about any of this until after D's marriage to X. When C's divorce to Y became final, C sues D. The cause of action stated in C's complaint against D is breach of promise to marry. Should C be allowed to bring this action? Why or why not? (See also General Instructions for the Legal Analysis Assignment, supra p. 16).

Suppose that a woman is able to bring a cause of action for breach of promise to marry and wins. What does she win? She cannot obtain specific performance, i. e. she cannot have the court force the man to marry her (i. e., to force him to perform or carry out his promise). What then does a court victory mean? For what can she be compensated? What has she lost? What are her damages? The very difficulty of answering these questions has been partly responsible for the abolition of the cause of action in some states. Yet where the action can be brought, the jury must be given instructions on the standards to use in arriving at an amount of money (damages) the defendant must pay a plaintiff who has successfully convinced the

7. For more on conflicts of law, see supra p. 168.

court that the defendant breached his promise to marry the plaintiff. Four aspects of damages need to be considered:

(a) *Compensatory Damages:* What has the Plaintiff lost? The jury can consider:

—Out of pocket expenses. Moneys spent by plaintiff in purchasing a trousseau, a hall, rings, etc.

—Loss of income. If the plaintiff left a job in order to marry defendant.

—Destroyed financial expectations. If the defendant was wealthy and the plaintiff was poor, the plaintiff has obviously lost a great deal in terms of standard of living.

—Physical and mental health deterioration due to worry, publicity and humiliation.

—Injury to one's chances of getting a new marriage proposal and to one's reputation generally.

(b) *Aggravated Damages:* What special circumstances can the jury consider to increase the damage award?

—Sexual intercourse due to seduction.[8]

—Pregnancy, miscarriage.

—An unusual degree of publicity and hence humiliation.

(c) *Punitive* or *Exemplary Damages:* Are there reasons to increase the damage award in order to punish the defendant (and to deter others) such as:

—*Fraud.* The defendant never intended to marry the plaintiff in spite of the promise made.

—*Malice.* The defendant wanted to hurt and humiliate the plaintiff or recklessly disregarded the impact of the breach of promise.

(d) *Mitigation of Damages:* Some states will allow a jury to lessen the amount of damages it would otherwise impose on the defendant due to facts such as:

—The plaintiff never loved the defendant (wanted to marry for money only).

—The plaintiff was unchaste before meeting defendant.

—Although defendant broke the promise made, it was done with some sensitivity to the feelings of the plaintiff.

—The defendant is poor, physically sick or mentally unstable.

There was a time when juries returned very high verdicts against defendants in breach of promise actions, e. g., $250,000. More recently, however, the trend has been toward smaller verdicts. Some states will

8. For more on seduction, see infra p. 482.

limit damage awards to out-of-pocket losses, e. g., the cost of wedding preparation, and will not compensate the victim for the more speculative harm e. g., that caused by humiliation.

INTERVIEWING AND INVESTIGATION CHECKLIST

FACTORS RELEVANT TO THE PROMISE TO MARRY. (C IS THE CLIENT; D IS THE DEFENDANT)

Legal Interviewing Questions

1. On what date did you and D first agree to to be married?
2. Where were you at the time of this agreement? Were you in this state? If not, what state?
3. How old were you at the time? How old was D?
4. What specific language did D use when s/he promised to marry you? What specific language did you use when you accepted? (Try to get exact quotations.)
5. Was anyone present when this exchange occurred? If so, who? Did they hear or otherwise know about the engagement?
6. Was a date set for a wedding? If so, what date? If not, why not?
7. Were any preparations made, e. g., church or caterer contacted?
8. Did D send you any letters ("love letters") about the engagement? Did you send D any?
9. Did D ever repeat his/her promise to marry you? If so, state circumstances.
10. If D never used specific words to agree to marry you, what actions did D take to indicate to you that D wanted to marry you? How much time did you spend together? Did you live together? (Where? How long?) Did you talk about children? Did you have sexual relations? Did you meet each other's parents?
11. When did you first learn that D no longer wished to marry you? What specifically was said and done?
12. What reason did D give?
13. What did you say or do when you learned about this? Did you give any indication to D that you did not want to marry D? Were you angry? How was it expressed?
14. Was there anything about your life prior to the time that D asked you to marry him/her that D did not know, but which D now feels you should have revealed, e. g., information about a prior marriage, about your age, about your prior sex life?
15. What expenses did you have in order to prepare for the wedding? (clothes, church, etc.)
16. Were you employed before the engagement? Did you leave your job? How did the cancellation of the marriage affect your job, if at all?
17. Describe your standard of living before the cancellation, e. g., kind of dwelling, car, travel, entertainment interests, etc.

Possible Investigation Tasks

* Obtain birth certificates to verify ages.
* Try to reach anyone who may have heard D promise to marry C. Get witness statement.
* Contact church, caterer etc. to determine if wedding preparations were made. Get witness statements.
* Help C locate all letters from D.
* Locate all receipts of expenses due to wedding preparation. If no longer in existence or if never existed, contact merchants and others to whom money was paid in order to obtain new receipts or copies.
* Obtain financial records, e. g., bank statements, to show the financial worth and standard of living of C before the engagement was broken. Try to obtain the same kind of records on the financial standing of D.
* Obtain medical records to document the physical and mental strain caused C when D broke the promise to marry C, e. g., hospital records, doctor bills.
* Determine what kind of publicity, if any, accompanied the news that D broke the engagement, e. g., newspaper clippings.
* Attempt to determine whether D was ever engaged to others in the past and whether D broke any of those engagements.
* Draft an inventory of every gift in any way con-

INTERVIEWING AND INVESTIGATING CHECKLIST—Continued

FACTORS RELEVANT TO THE PROMISE TO MARRY. (C IS THE CLIENT; D IS THE DEFENDANT)

No.		
18.	Describe the standard of living of D.	nected with D's relationship with C. For each gift, identify the donor, donee, date of gift, kind and value of gift, the circumstances surrounding the gift, whether the donor has asked for the gift back, if so, the response of the donee, the present location of the gifts.
19.	If D had not broken the promise and you had married D, describe what you think your financial standing and standard of living would have been.	
20.	Describe the effect of D's breach of promise on your physical health and on your mental health, e. g., did you lose any sleep, were there any special problems of nerves?	
21.	When D broke the promise to marry you, who knew about it? Was there any publicity?	
22.	Were you humiliated? Describe all the reasons why.	
23.	Since the engagement to D was broken, have you been dating others? When they find out that you were once engaged to D and that D broke the engagement, what is their reaction? Do you think that your chances of getting married in the future are diminished because of D's breach of promise? Why?	
24.	Did you have relations with D? Were you seduced by D? Did D impregnate you? (If so, inquire into pregnancy problems, abortion, miscarriage, delivery.)	
25.	Do you have any reason to believe that at the time D promised to marry you, he never intended to do so? Explain.	
26.	Do you have any reason to believe that D wanted to hurt you? Explain.	
27.	Could D say that you never loved him?	
28.	Did D ever give you any gifts?	
29.	On what date did you get the gift? Was it before or after the engagement?	
30.	What were D's exact words when he gave you the gift? What did you say to him?	
31.	When did the gift come into your possession?	
32.	Answer the above three questions for every gift D gave you.	
33.	Did you receive any shower gifts or wedding gifts from others before the engagement was broken?	
34.	Make a list of every gift you gave D, i. e., kind, date, circumstances.	

IM–452

The calculation of damages is by no means a scientific determination as you can readily tell by examining the broad standards that juries use to assess damages and by reading the INTERVIEWING questions and INVESTIGATION tasks that are aimed at uncovering the facts that will become the basis for an award of damages. So imprecise is the calculation that the potential for abuse is apparent. Some have argued that the availability of the breach of promise cause of action is but a device for some plaintiffs to blackmail the defendant into agreeing to a substantial settlement to avoid the publicity of a trial.[9] In part for such reasons, a number of states have enacted a heart balm statute abolishing this cause of action altogether.

9. Clark, H., *The Law of Domestic Relations*, p. 3 (1968).

Some plaintiffs have tried to get around this statutory prohibition by bringing a *tort* cause of action for *fraud* rather than the breach of contract cause of action.

> **THE TORT OF FRAUD**
>
> (Sometimes called Misrepresentation or Deceit)
>
> ELEMENTS: (1) there must be a *false statement* of fact by the defendant (D);
> (2) the D must *know* that it is false;
> (3) the D must *intend* that the plaintiff (P) rely upon the statement;
> (4) the P must *rely* on the statement of the D and be reasonable in so relying;
> (5) the P must suffer *harm* due to the reliance.

[B7873]

In a broken engagement situation, the elements of the fraud cause of action could apply to a set of facts as follows: D told P that s/he wanted to marry P. At the time D made this *statement*, it was *false* because D never wanted to marry P. D *knew* that the statement was a lie and *intended* to use the statement to get P to do something (e. g., have sexual relations with D). P believed that D wanted to marry him/her and *relied* on D's statement (e. g., by giving D money). P suffered *harm* because of this reliance (e. g., humiliation, unwanted pregnancy).

What is the value, you might ask, of a state enacting a heart balm act designed to eliminate the *contract* cause of action for breach of promise to marry when a plaintiff can achieve almost the same result by bringing a *tort* cause of action for fraud? The question that must be answered is whether or not the heart balm statute was intended by the legislature to eliminate *both* causes of action even though the act may specifically mention only the contract action. States that have heart balm statutes have not all answered this question in the same way. When a legislature writes a heart balm act, there is clearly a need for some careful draftsmanship to avoid this problem.

Assignment # 17

On July 4, 1975 in your state, Jim Smith asks Linda Jones to marry him. Jim has a middle class background, while Linda is independently wealthy. Linda told Jim that she had never loved any other man in her life. This was not true, but she felt that unless she told this to Jim, he would never have proposed to her. On July 25, 1975, Linda tells Jim that she will marry him, but on August 19, 1975, she informs him that she has changed her mind. Jim is very upset. On October 4, 1977, he files suit against her in your state.

(a) On behalf of Jim, draft a complaint against Linda for breach of promise to marry. If you live in a state that has abolished breach of promise actions (e. g., Ala., Calif., Colo., Fla., Ind., Me., Md., Mass., Mich., Nev., N.H., N.J., N.Y., Pa., Wisc., Wy.,), then draft the complaint on a fraud cause of action. Assume that fraud causes of action were not abolished in such situations even though the breach of promise cause of action was abolished. (See also General Instructions for the Complaint Drafting Assignment, supra p. 20).

(b) Every state has statutes of limitations which specify the time limits within which suits must be brought. If they are not brought within the statutory time period, they will be barred forever. In the above assignment (a), you drafted a complaint. In Linda's answer to the complaint, would she be able to raise the defense that Jim's suit is barred by the statute of limitations? Check your state code to find out what the statute of limitations would be for this cause of action. (See also General Instructions for the State Code Assignment, supra p. 14.)

(c) Draft a set of interrogatories to be sent to Linda. Concentrate on those questions which are calculated to uncover facts that might be used to assess damages. (See General Instructions for the Interrogatories Assignment, supra p. 31).

SECTION C. THE PROBLEM OF GIFTS

It is not commonly known that once a gift is made, it is irrevocable—the giver (called the donor) cannot get the gift back from the person to whom it was given (called the donee). For a gift to be irrevocable in this way, all of the elements of a gift must be present:

GIFTS

ELEMENTS of an irrevocable gift:

(1) there must be a *delivery* of the property; [10]
(2) the transfer must be *voluntary*;
(3) the donor must intend to divest him or herself of *title* and *control* of what is given;
(4) there must be *no consideration* (e. g., payment by the donee);
(5) the donor must intend that the gift take effect *immediately*; there must be a *present* intention to give an *unconditional* gift;
(6) the donee must *accept* the gift.

[B7918]

10. The delivery of the gift of a house or the contents of a safety deposit box can be accomplished by a symbolic act such as the giving of the key to the donee.

If "A" says to "B", "I'll give you my car next year," no gift has occurred since there is no transfer which takes effect now and there is no delivery. If "A" says to "B," "you have borrowed my pen; maybe I'll give it to you tomorrow," there is no gift since there was no present intent by "A" to relinquish his control and dominion over the pen now. This is so even though "B" already had possession of the pen.

Suppose that "A" says to "B," "I'll give you this desk if it rains tomorrow." No gift has occurred because a condition exists which must be fulfilled before the gift becomes effective, i. e., it must rain tomorrow. There is no present intention to relinquish dominion and control. Suppose that Frank and Judy exchange engagement rings after they both agree to be married. One or both of them change their minds. Did a legally binding gift occur? It appears that all of the elements of a binding gift occurred so that if either Frank or Judy refuse to return the ring, they cannot be forced to do so. Yet, should we not *imply* a condition that the parties intended that there be no binding gift if the marriage does not occur? They never said this explicitly to each other, but it is reasonable to imply that this is what they had in mind, i. e., that this is what they would have intended if they thought about it. Courts often find such an implied intention as the theory of forcing a return of the purported gift in the situation of pre-marital gifts. Examine the following sequence of events:

January 1, 1970:	Mary and Bob meet.
January 2, 1970:	On a date, Bob gives Mary a bracelet.
March 13, 1970:	Mary and Bob become engaged and they exchange rings. The marriage date will be November 7, 1970.
March 26, 1970:	This is Mary's birthday, Bob gives Mary a new car.
June 5, 1970:	Bob and Mary change their minds about getting married.

Bob wants the bracelet, ring and car back. Mary refuses. Bob sues Mary on the theory that no gifts of these items took place—all the elements of a gift are not present. Bob wants the court to conclude that when he gave these items to Mary, he really meant that she should keep them only if they eventually married. Should the court imply this condition of marriage? The answer depends on what the court determines the intention of Bob to have been *at the time* he gave each of the items to Mary. For each of the items in question, the court must go through each of the elements of a gift to determine whether the transfer was irrevocable.

The exchange of *rings* poses the least problem. Most courts would imply a condition of marriage and permit the return of the rings. At the time the *bracelet* was given, however, the parties were not engaged. We can assume that Bob's intent was to please Mary, to win her favor but not necessarily to win her hand in marriage. The bracelet was given the day after they met and it is unlikely that marriage was on anyone's mind.[11] It would be rare, therefore, for a court to conclude that the gift of the bracelet was conditional; Bob would not be able to force Mary to return it. The birthday gift of the *car* is the most troublesome item. Again the central question is: what was Bob's intent at the time he gave her the car. Mary would argue that there was no condition of marriage attached to the gift. She would say that a birthday gift would have been given whether or not they were engaged. Bob, on the other hand, would argue that strong evidence exists to establish the presence of an unspoken condition of marriage. This evidence is the value of a new car. It is highly unlikely, according to Bob, that such an expensive gift would have been given as a birthday gift unconnected with the impending marriage. This argument of Bob is probably correct. Do you agree? What further factual inquiries would you want to make in order to be more sure of your answer? For example, would it help to know the relative wealth of Bob and Mary? Why or why not?

INTERVIEWING & INVESTIGATION: See Checklist Questions nos. 28–34 on establishing some of the facts that will be helpful to determine whether the gift was irrevocable. Supra p. 116.

[B7874]

Suppose in the above hypothetical, involving Bob and Mary, that Bob broke the engagement without any plausible reason or justification. In such a situation, Bob would be considered a wrongdoer who should not be able to "profit" by his wrong by getting any of the gifts back. Many courts so hold. The donor will be able to have the conditional gifts returned if the engagement ended by mutual agreement. If the donee was the one who broke the engagement without justification, and if the donor was without fault in the matter, the donor can have the gifts returned. Otherwise, s/he cannot in these states.

Third parties, e. g., relatives and friends, often send gifts in contemplation of the coming marriage. When the marriage does not take place, these parties can force a return of the gifts since courts almost always will conclude that such gifts were conditional.

11. On the other hand, the facts show that it was just over two months after the bracelet was given that the parties became engaged. This short time period does raise the possibility, however slight, that marriage *was* on Bob's mind when he gave Mary the bracelet, i. e., that the gift was conditional. More facts would be needed in order to determine whether this possibility has any merit. For more on legal analysis, see supra p. 16.

In the prior section we saw that some states passed heart balm statutes which abolished the cause of action for breach of promise to marry.[12] Some of these statutes are worded so broadly that courts might interpret them to mean that *any* cause of action growing out of a broken engagement will not be allowed, including a cause of action to obtain the return of gifts on the theory that the gifts were conditional.

SUMMARY

1. A donor cannot force a donee to return a gift of property if there was a present, unconditional, and voluntary transfer of the control and dominion of the property to the donee which the donee accepted and for which the donee paid no consideration.
2. A determination of whether or not a gift exchanged between formerly engaged individuals is conditional will depend upon the following factors:
   (a) the time of the gift (before or after the engagement);
   (b) whether the donor was at fault in terminating the engagement;
   (c) the kind of gift involved;
   (d) all other circumstances which will help a court determine what the donor's intent was at the time of the gift.
3. Third parties can force the return of wedding gifts they made when no wedding ever occurred.
4. If a heart balm statute exists in a state, an important question of interpretation will be whether the legislature, in enacting the statute, intended to bar any cause of action based upon a broken engagement. If so, a suit to force the return of a gift might be barred. The language of the statute would have to be closely examined to determine how broad or narrow its prohibition is.

[B7875]

NOTE

For a discussion of how the heart balm statutes affect the torts of alienation of affections, criminal conversation, and seduction, see infra p. 480.

12. Supra p. 111.

Assignment # 18

Examine the following sequence of events:

February 13, 1978: Jim says to Bob, "Please introduce me to Joan. I want to meet her because I know that she is the girl I want to spend the rest of my life with." Bob does so. Jim is so happy that he gives Bob a gold wristwatch and says to him, "I want you to have this and wear it to my wedding some day."

March 1, 1978: Joan brings Jim home to meet her mother. When the evening is over, Jim gives Joan's mother an expensive family bible.

June 23, 1978: Jim loans Joan $1,000 to pay a medical bill of Joan's youngest brother. Joan has one year to pay back the loan without any interest charge.

July 23, 1978: Joan pays back the $1,000.

September 5, 1978: They agree to get married on February 18, 1979. On the day that they agree to marry, Jim gives Joan a diamond bracelet and says, "I want you to have this no matter what happens."

December 14, 1978: They both agree to break the engagement.

Jim asks Bob for the wristwatch back. Bob refuses. Jim asks Joan's mother for the bible back. The mother refuses. Jim asks Joan for one months interest @ 6% on the $1,000 loan, and also asks for the bracelet back. Joan refuses both requests.

(a) Can Jim get any of these items from Bob, the mother and Joan? (See also General Instructions for the Legal Analysis Assignment, supra p. 16.)

(b) Draft a complaint against Joan in which Jim seeks the return of the bracelet and one month's interest. (See also General Instructions for the Complaint Drafting Assignment, supra p. 20.)

(c) Prepare a flow chart of the procedural steps that would be necessary to litigate the matter raised in the complaint that you drafted in assignment (b) above. (See also General Instructions for the Flow Chart Assignment, supra p. 33.)

Chapter Seven

CONTRACTS RESTRAINING MARRIAGE

A basic principle of free association is that you can marry whomever you please so long as certain conditions are met relating to age requirements, sanity requirements, etc.[1] Some feel that this principle is fundamental because of the importance of marriage in our society. Hence the law looks with disfavor on efforts to restrict one's ability to marry. Not all such restrictions, however, are invalid. A distinction must be made between a *general restraint* on marriage and a *reasonable limitation* on marriage.

1. GENERAL RESTRAINT

Consider the following situations:

—Mary agrees never to marry in exchange for a large sum of money to be given to her by her father.

—As John goes off to war, Jane says, "It is you that I want to marry, and even if you don't want to marry me, even if you marry someone else, even if you die, I promise you that I will never marry anyone else as long as I live." John leaves without promising to marry Jane.

A general restraint on marriage is a total or near total prohibition against marriage and such restraints are unenforceable. If Mary decides to marry, her father cannot sue her to hold her to her agreement never to marry. If Jane marries Bill, she cannot be sued by John for breach of her promise never to marry anyone but him. The law will not permit Mary, Jane or anyone to prohibit themselves from marrying in this way. They may decide on their own never to marry, but they cannot make an agreement that they will never marry and be forced by a court to abide by that agreement.

The John/Jane situation poses another difficulty. You will recall that for a contract to exist, there must be consideration.[2] Jane's consideration was her promise never to marry anyone but John. What consideration did John give in exchange? None. He gave up nothing. Hence, another reason Jane's promise is unenforceable is that she received no consideration, i. e., no contract existed.

2. REASONABLE LIMITATION

A reasonable limitation or restraint on marriage is one which (a) is a partial rather than a general prohibition, (b) serves what

1. For more on these requirements, see infra p. 156ff.

2. Supra p. 110.

the court feels to be a useful purpose and (c) is not otherwise illegal. Consider the following situations:

—John enters a contract in which he agrees that he will never marry a woman who is not of his religious faith.

—Mary enters a contract in which she agrees never to marry anyone who has a criminal record.

—Jane enters a contract in which she agrees that she will not marry before she turns eighteen, and that she will obtain the permission of her parent if she decides to marry between the ages of eighteen and twenty-one.

—Linda enters a contract in which she agrees that she will not marry until she completes her college education.

Are the above contracts valid? If John, Mary, Jane or Linda later change their minds and decide to marry contrary to their promises, can they be forced through litigation to abide by their contracts? Not all states will answer this question in the same way, but generally the answer will be *yes*. The restraints on marriage to which they agreed are enforceable, assuming that John, Mary, Jane and Linda received consideration for their promises. All of the restraints are *partial*: they do not totally prohibit marriage nor come near such a total prohibition. All of the restraints arguably serve a *useful purpose*: their purpose is to be protective of the person and/or of a valuable tradition. Do you agree? There is no *illegality* involved in any of the restraints, e. g., no one is being asked to refrain from marriage in order to engage in adultery or fornication which are crimes in some states. Hence, all of the restraints could be considered reasonable limitations on one's right to marry and are enforceable in most states.

Suppose that a school teacher signs a contract that s/he agrees to be terminated from the job if s/he marries. This is not a general restraint on marriage, but is it enforceable as a reasonable limitation? Is there a useful or beneficial purpose to the restriction? Many courts have said yes,[3] although this conclusion has been criticized.[4] Can you see any useful purpose to force a teacher to resign under these circumstances? Do not answer this question by saying that people should be forced to do what they have agreed to do. Answer it on the basis of whether you think any person, tradition, value, etc. is being protected by holding the teacher to his/her contract.

Thus far we have been examining *contracts* that restrain marriage:[5] what to do when a party at one time agreed to a restraint

3. See for example, Greco v. Roper, 145 Ohio St. 243, 61 N.E.2d 307, 30 O.O. 473 (1945).

4. See for example, Clark, H., *The Law of Domestic Relations*, p. 25 (1968).

5. Suppose that someone enters a contract which *promotes* rather than restrains marriage, e. g., a brokerage contract by which one person agrees to pay a fee to a third party for arranging a marriage. Such contracts are invalid.

on marriage. Suppose, however, that no such contract existed, but that the attempted restriction on marriage came as an attempted condition attached to a *gift*. For example:

—In Bob's will, he provides that he gives $10,000 to Fran so long as she remains unmarried. When Bob dies, Fran is not married. She is given the gift (bequest) of $10,000. One year later, Fran marries. Bob's estate brings a suit against Fran to have the money returned.

—John has a deed drafted which provides, "On my death I convey all my property to my wife, Joan to be owned and used by her until she remarries at which time all remaining property shall go to the Red Cross."

The same rules on marriage restrictions should apply to gifts and conveyances as apply to contracts. If a person is going to lose a substantial gift upon marriage, the gift obviously operates to restrain marriage. In theory, the same rules do apply. In fact, however, some courts are more inclined to find the restrictions to be reasonable (and hence enforceable) when gifts and conveyances are involved than when the restraint is embodied in a contract.

SUMMARY

1. A restraint imposed on marriage shall be valid and enforceable:
   (a) if there is consideration for the contract imposing the restraint;
   (b) if the restraint is partial rather than general;
   (c) if the restraint serves some useful purpose other than simply preventing the marriage;
   (d) if complying with the restraint would not otherwise involve a party in an illegal act.

   A restraint on marriage which meets these conditions is said to be a reasonable restraint.
2. Oddly, courts are sometimes more inclined to conclude that a restraint on marriage is reasonable when it is embodied in a gift and conveyance than when it is embodied in a contract even though the effect of the restraint appears to be the same regardless of how it is imposed.

[B7876]

Assignment # 19

Examine each of the following hypotheticals closely. Determine which restraints on marriage, if any, are enforceable. Give specific reasons why you think the restraint is or is not enforceable. (See also General Instructions for the Legal Analysis Assignment, supra p. 16.)

(A) John is married to Brenda. John enters a contract with Brenda's father that if children are born from the marriage and if Brenda dies before John, he will never remarry. In exchange, John is given the father's large farm to live in for life without having to pay any rent. Children are born, and Brenda does die first. John then marries Patricia. Brenda's father then sues to evict John from the farm. Does John have a defense to this suit?

(B) Joan enters a contract with her aunt that she will not have children before she turns twenty-one. In exchange, Joan is given a sum of money. Before she turns twenty-one, Joan has a baby (out of wedlock). The aunt sues Joan for breach of contract. Does Joan have a defense?

(C) Fred enters a contract with his father by which the father will pay for Fred's entire medical school education if Fred agrees never to marry a woman who is neither a doctor nor a medical student. When Fred becomes a doctor, at his father's expense, he marries a model. The father sues Fred for the cost of the medical education. Does Fred have a defense?

(D) Bill and Jean are not married. They live together, i. e., they share bed and board. They enter into a contract by which Jean promises to continue to live with Bill and to care for him. Bill agrees to put $500 per month in a bank account for Jean so long as she carries out her promise. Jean cannot get to the money until Bill dies. If Jean marries before Bill dies, however, Jean forfeits the right to all the money in the account. After living with Bill for twenty years, Jean leaves him to marry Tom. Can Jean sue Bill to recover $10,000, (plus interest), the amount in the account at the time she married Tom?

Chapter Eight

ANTENUPTIAL AGREEMENTS AND CONTRACT COHABITATION

SECTION A. ANTENUPTIAL AGREEMENTS

An antenuptial agreement is a contract made by two individuals before their marriage. Do you think it is a good idea for two people to sit down in advance of their marriage and agree in writing on what they want their rights and duties to be in the event that the two of them begin having marital problems later? Many antenuptial agreements are written by "senior citizens" contemplating marriage; although, it has recently been suggested that the concept is appropriate for anyone about to be married,[1] particularly a relatively young couple that needs to blend some reality with their romantic notions about the marital relationship. When both parties are entering second marriages, antenuptial agreements are often very useful in specifying respective property rights.

If the parties do not enter an antenuptial agreement, (and most people do not), a large body of laws will govern all problems involving personal and property matters that arise during and after the marriage. The parties *can* alter the effect of some of these laws through antenuptial agreements—but to what extent? Consider the following clauses in antenuptial agreements:

1. A clause that all property H (the prospective husband) and W (the prospective wife) now own in their individual names shall continue to be held individually during and after marriage.
2. A clause that all future savings and checking accounts shall be in their joint names.
3. A clause that property inherited by H or W during the marriage from their own families shall be held separately.
4. A clause that H and W will abstain from all sexual relations with each other.
5. A clause that the children will be raised in the Episcopalian religion and that the W (a Baptist) will not object to this.

1. See Sheresky, N. & Mannes, M., *A Radical Guide to Wedlock*, Saturday Review, 33ff. (July 29, 1972).

6. A clause that all disputes during their marriage will be submitted to their minister for resolution rather than to a court.
7. A clause that W will support herself through her own resources. If W ever needs funds from H, the latter will provide the funds in the form of a 6% loan to W.
8. A clause that if either party ever wants a divorce, the other party will not contest the right of that party to obtain the divorce.
9. A clause that if the parties ever obtain a divorce, the house and furnishings will go to H.
10. A clause renouncing any right of election,[2] dower[3] or curtesy[4] rights the parties may have.
11. A clause that H and W will make a joint will and that they will leave all their property to each other.
12. A clause that after five years of marriage the parties will live separately, and support each other individually.

Not all of these clauses are legal. In fact, all of them could be ineffective if certain standards are not met. That is our concern at this point: by what standards will the legality of antenuptial agreements be measured?

1. THE AGREEMENT MUST BE IN WRITING

The Statute of Frauds[5] requires that the agreement be in writing.

2. THE ELEMENTS[6] OF A VALID CONTRACT MUST EXIST

An antenuptial agreement cannot be imposed by one party on the other. As with any contract, there must be an offer, there must be an acceptance of the offer, consideration[7] must exist, the parties must have the capacity to enter a contract and the subject matter of the agreement must not be illegal.

2. The right of election refers to the wife's choice of either accepting what her husband provided for her in his will, or taking a share of his estate as designated by statute.

3. The right of a widow to the lifetime use of one third of the property her husband owned during the marriage. Many states have eliminated or modified dower rights.

4. The right of a widower to the lifetime use of the property his wife owned during the marriage. Many states have eliminated or modified curtesy rights.

5. See supra p. 111.

6. See supra p. 110.

7. The consideration for antenuptial agreements is often the contemplated marriage itself. On consideration, see also p. 110.

3. THE PROSPECTIVE HUSBAND MUST MAKE A FULL AND FRANK DISCLOSURE TO THE PROSPECTIVE WIFE OF ALL HIS ASSETS BEFORE SHE AGREES TO THE PROVISIONS OF THE ANTENUPTIAL AGREEMENT

This standard is one of the most important. The concern is that the wife will agree to certain property arrangements for her on the basis of her erroneous understanding of what the husband was worth at the time of the antenuptial agreement. The wife may have known that the husband was "well to do" or, alternatively, that his means enabled him to live "modestly." This degree of information, however, is generally not considered to be adequate. The husband must see to it that the wife has the details of his financial worth, his bank accounts, his holdings, his other property etc. Furthermore, when the husband makes these disclosures, there must be no under-valuation of assets. Some states require proof that the wife had the benefit of the advice of independent counsel before she accepted the terms of the agreement. In short, the husband must not deal with his prospective spouse at arm's length. He has the equivalent of a fiduciary or trust responsibility to her.

4. THE AGREEMENT MUST BE FAIR TO THE PROSPECTIVE WIFE

This standard is often viewed as an alternative to the third standard stated above. If there was a full and frank disclosure of everything to the prospective wife and she still agreed to the terms of the antenuptial agreement, she will be bound by those terms even if they later prove to have been unwise and unfair to her because of changed circumstances. Many courts, however, are not this strict; they will look for ways to relieve the wife from a burdensome agreement even if she was given all the facts at the time she signed the agreement. (See the next standard.)

5. THE AGREEMENT MUST NOT BE AGAINST PUBLIC POLICY

The clause mentioned in item 8 above is clearly against public policy. A party should not be asked to waive his or her right to object to the other party's attempt to obtain a divorce. If a party has a valid objection, it is in the interest of a just judicial proceeding to have that objection brought before the court. It is improper for the parties to make an agreement in advance to keep information from a court which that court must have; such an agreement would be a fraud on the court.[8] In many states, the husband has a duty

8. On collusion and connivance, see supra p. 307.

to support his wife.[9] It would be against public policy in such states to let a prospective wife sign away her right to be supported by her future husband as the clause in item 7 above attempts to do. Since a major purpose of marriage is to have children, some states might conclude that the clause in item 4 above is against public policy. A number of the clauses above (e. g., 8, 9, 12) refer to what will happen if the parties separate or obtain a divorce. Many states consider such clauses to be against public policy on the theory that they condone and perhaps might encourage the parties (or one of them) to end the marital relationship in order to obtain the benefits of the clauses.[10]

Different states may have different views of what public policy is. A particular clause in an antenuptial agreement, or in any contract, would have to be measured by the public policy of the state whose laws govern the interpretation and application of the agreement or contract. It is often said that realistic planning through an antenuptial agreement which takes account of the possibility of the dissolution of the marriage does not violate the state's public policy. The difficulty, again, is in defining exactly what a state's public policy is. It is entirely possible that an antenuptial agreement that is valid in one state would be considered invalid if entered into in another state.

INTERVIEWING AND INVESTIGATION CHECKLIST

FACTORS RELEVANT TO THE VALIDITY OF THE ANTENUPTIAL AGREEMENT

	Legal Interviewing Questions	**Possible Investigation Tasks**
1.	On what date did you begin discussing the agreement?	* Obtain copies of the antenuptial agreement and copies of all drafts of the agreement, if any, reflecting changes. * If the parties did not draft the agreement themselves, contact the individual who did draft it and interview that person as to the circumstances, e.g., dates, number of meetings, etc. * Contact and interview anyone else who was present during the discussions and/or signing of the agreement, or anyone else who has knowledge of the discussions or signing.
2.	Whose idea was it to have an agreement?	
3.	On what date did you first see the agreement?	
4.	Who actually wrote the agreement?	
5.	Did you read the agreement?	
6.	Did you understand everything in the agreement?	
7.	Describe in detail what you thought was in the agreement.	
8.	Did you sign the agreement? If so, why?	
9.	Were there ever any changes made in the agreement? If so, describe the circumstances, nature of the change, who proposed it, etc.	
10.	Do you recall anything that was said during the discussions on the agreement which is different from what was eventually written down?	
11.	Was there anyone present at the time you either discussed or signed the agreement?	

9. Infra p. 433.

10. On clauses that are conducive to divorce in separation agreements, see infra p. 253.

INTERVIEWING AND INVESTIGATION CHECKLIST—Continued

FACTORS RELEVANT TO THE VALIDITY OF THE ANTENUPTIAL AGREEMENT

	Legal Interviewing Questions	Possible Investigation Tasks
12.	Where was the agreement kept? Were you given a copy?	* Try to obtain bank records, tax records, etc. that would give some indication of the wealth and standard of living of D and of C at the time they signed the antenuptial agreement.
13.	Before you signed the agreement, did you consult with anyone, e.g., attorney, accountant, relative?	
14.	If you did consult with anyone, describe that person's relationship, if any, with your spouse.	
15.	What were you told by the individuals with whom you consulted? Did they think it was wise for you to sign the agreement? Why or why not?	* Prepare an inventory of every asset that C *thought* D owned at the time the agreement was signed and an inventory of every asset which your investigation has revealed that D in fact owned at the time of the signing whether or not C knew about it.
16.	How old were you when you signed the agreement? How old was your spouse?	
17.	How much did you know about your spouse's background before you agreed to marry? What generally did you think his/her wealth and standard of living was?	
18.	How did you obtain this knowledge?	
19.	While you were considering the antenuptial agreement, what specifically did you know about the following: D's bank accounts (savings, checking, trust), insurance policies, home ownership, business property, salary, investments (e.g., stocks, bonds), rent income, royalty income, inheritances (recent or expected), cars, planes, boats, etc.; D's debts and other liabilities. For each of the above items about which you had knowledge, state how you obtained the knowledge.	
20.	When did you first learn that D owned (______) at the time you signed the agreement? (Insert items in parentheses which C learned about only after the agreement was signed.)	
21.	Do you think you were given an honest accounting of all D's assets at the time you signed? Why or why not?	
22.	Do you think the agreement you signed was fair to you and to the children you and D eventually had? Why or why not?	

IM-453

6. SPECIAL TAX CONSEQUENCES

Normally, when two people enter a contract, they exchange something of value to each other; they clearly are not interested in making gifts to each other. If what they did, however, constituted a gift,[11] a gift tax would have to be paid even though they *appeared* to be entering into a contract. For tax purposes, therefore, the question must be asked as to whether the antenuptial agreement constitutes a contract or a gift. The answer depends upon the presence or absence of consideration.[12] More specifically, the answer depends

11. On the elements of a binding gift, see supra p. 118ff.

12. See supra p. 110.

upon the presence or absence of "full and adequate consideration" in money or money's worth. If such consideration exists, the exchange is a contract to which no gift tax attaches. If it does not exist, a gift tax must be paid by the "donor." What is the consideration for antenuptial agreements? Is such consideration sufficient to avoid the gift tax? No. Consider the following statement of the Internal Revenue Service in Rev.Rul. 69–347, 1969, 1 Cum.Bull. 227:

> "Although antenuptial agreements are enforceable under state law when consummated by marriage, transfers made pursuant to such agreements are not made for an adequate and full consideration in money or money's worth within the meaning of section 2512(b) of the Internal Revenue Code of 1954. Such consideration as love and affection, promise of marriage, or relinquishment of dower or other marital rights is to be wholly disregarded and the entire value of the property transferred constitutes a gift. Section 25.2512–8 of the Gift Tax Regulations." [13]

This result does *not* apply to exchanges made by spouses pursuant to a separation agreement. The tax consequences of such agreements will be discussed later.[14]

SUMMARY

1. Antenuptial or prenuptial agreements can determine the rights and obligations of the parties during and after marriage if:
   (a) the agreement is in writing;
   (b) the agreement fulfills all the conditions for a valid contract;
   (c) there has been a complete and open disclosure of all assets;
   (d) the agreement does not violate public policy.
2. If the antenuptial agreement is not effective because of a violation of the above conditions, then the rights and duties of the parties will be determined by applicable state statutes, court rulings, etc.
3. Simply because an antenuptial agreement may be valid under state law (because of compliance with the above conditions), the transaction may be considered a gift for tax purposes due to the possible absence of what the IRS considers "full and adequate consideration."

[B7877]

13. See also, Lowndes, C. & Kramer, R., *Federal Estate and Gift Taxes*, p. 687 (2nd Ed. 1962).

14. Infra p. 411.

Assignment # 20

(a) Find an opinion written by a court in your state which discusses the validity of antenuptial agreements in your state. Give the facts and result of the opinion. If no such opinion exists in your state, try to find one written by a neighboring state. (See also General Instructions for the Court Opinion Assignment, supra p. 26.)

(b) Pretend that you are about to be married and that you and your future spouse want to enter an antenuptial agreement. Draft this agreement. You can assume anything you want (within reason) about the financial affairs and interests of your spouse-to-be and yourself. Number each term or provision of the agreement separately and consecutively. In your agreement, try to anticipate as many difficulties as possible that could arise during the marriage and state how you want those difficulties to be resolved. (See also General Instructions for the Agreement Drafting Assignment, supra p. 25.)

(c) After your instructor makes note of the fact that you have drafted an agreement, you will be asked to exchange agreements with another member of the class. You are to analyze the agreement written by your classmate. Go through each numbered term or provision in the agreement and determine whether it is valid or invalid according to the standards identified in this chapter and/or according to the law governing antenuptial agreements in your state. When you cannot apply a standard, in whole or in part, because you need more facts, simply list the factual questions to which you would like answers in order to be able to assess the validity of the term or provision in question. (See also General Instructions for the Legal Analysis Assignment, supra p. 16.)

SECTION B. SAMPLE ANTENUPTIAL AGREEMENT CLAUSES

STONE, B., MODERN LEGAL FORMS

§§ 4493ff., p. 220ff., West Publishing Co. (1977)

Antenuptial Agreement—Release of Husband's Rights in Wife's Property [15]

Agreement made this ______ day of ______, 19__, between John Day, of ———, and Jane Kent, of ———.

Whereas a marriage is shortly to be solemnized between the parties hereto;

15. Construed in Appleby v. Appleby, 111 N.W. 305, 100 Minn. 408 (1907).

For another form, see Peet v. Monger, 56 N.W.2d 589, 244 Iowa 247 (1953).

For form of agreement entered into in contemplation of remarriage after divorce, see Kennett v. McKay, 57 N.W. 2d 316, 336 Mich. 28 (1953).

Whereas Jane Kent now owns a large amount of property and expects to acquire from time to time additional property under a trust established for her by her father, ______;

Whereas John Day has agreed that all of the property now or in the future owned by Jane Kent, or her estate, shall be free of all rights that he might acquire by reason of his marriage to her.

It is agreed as follows:

Wife Retains Full Control of Property

1. Jane Kent shall have full right and authority, in all respects the same as she would have if unmarried, to use, enjoy, manage, convey, mortgage, and dispose of all of her present and future property and estate, of every kind and character, including the right and power to dispose of same by last will and testament.

Husband Releases All Right in His Wife's Property

2. John Day releases to Jane Kent, her heirs, legal representatives and assigns, every right, claim, and estate, actual, inchoate, or contingent, that he might have in respect to said property by reason of his marriage to Jane Kent.

Deceased Minor Child's Property

3. In the event any child of said marriage shall survive Jane Kent and shall then die a minor, John Day releases every right, claim, and estate he might inherit by reason of the death of such minor child, and agrees that the property of such minor child shall be subject to any bequest or devise thereof made by Jane Kent.

Additional Instruments

4. John Day further agrees that upon the request of Jane Kent he will execute, acknowledge and deliver any additional instruments that may reasonably be necessary to carry out more effectually the purpose of this agreement.

Representatives Bound

This agreement shall bind the parties and their heirs, legal representatives and assigns.

In Witness Whereof, *etc.*

Clause Releasing Husband's Interest in Wife's Property for a Lump Sum Payable on Wife's Death [16]

Now, therefore, [*Wife*] agrees that she will, upon her decease, cause to be paid to [*Husband*], if he is then living, $______, within

16. See Lee v. Central Nat. Bank & Trust Co., 308 N.E.2d 605, 56 Ill.2d 394 (1974), holding that marriage is sufficient consideration for the settlement and that it is not lacking in mutuality because the intended wife did not release her claim against the intended husband's estate.

one year after her death; and [*Husband*] agrees that he will, upon the death of [*Wife*], take the said $______ in full of all rights of dower, homestead, survivorship, inheritance, separate maintenance, widower's award, or otherwise in or to her estate, and in full of all other rights, interests, claims or allowances which he might be entitled to but for this agreement, and that on payment to him of the said $______ he will release, quitclaim and discharge to her representatives or heirs all rights of dower, homestead, survivorship, inheritance, separate maintenance, widower's award, and all other rights, claims or interests which he might have in her estate but for this agreement.

Antenuptial Agreement—Release of Wife's Interest in Husband's Property—Present Payment of a Lump Sum [17]

Agreement made this ______ day of ______, 19__, between John Day, of ______, and Jane Kent, of ______, witnesseth:

Whereas the parties contemplate entering into marriage relations;

Whereas John Day is the owner of property listed on the memorandum attached hereto; and

Whereas John Day desires to make suitable provision for Jane Kent in lieu of dower or other interest in his property which she otherwise might have.

Now, therefore, the parties agree as follows:

Payment of Lump Sum

1. John Day agrees to pay to Jane Kent, immediately after the solemnization of said marriage, the sum of ______ dollars, the said sum to be her sole and separate property.

Wife Releases Rights in Husband's Property

2. Jane Kent agrees that she will accept the said sum in lieu of any and all claims of dower, inheritance and descent in and to the property of John Day, now owned or that may hereafter be acquired by him, and in lieu of any and all other claims which might otherwise arise or accrue to her by reason of said marriage.

17. Adapted from Commissioner of Internal Revenue v. Copley's Estate, 194 F.2d 364 (7th Cir. 1952). Held in this case that the antenuptial agreement executed in 1931 created a valid contractual debt in that year and transfers of property made in 1936 and 1944 pursuant thereto were mere discharges of the obligation and were not taxable under the gift tax statute enacted in 1932.

See also Hambleton v. Commissioner, 60 T.C. 567 (1973).

Management of Lump Sum

3. In view of the nature of the property set forth in the memorandum attached hereto, the nature and extent of which property is fully understood by Jane Kent, it is the desire of Jane Kent, and it is therefore agreed, that John Day shall take over the management of the ______ dollars this day given by him to the end that its value may be preserved and made productive.

Wife to Join in Conveyances

4. Jane Kent agrees that upon the request of John Day, she will execute all and any proper instruments of conveyance in order to enable John Day to sell or convey real estate now owned or afterward acquired by him.

In Witness Whereof, *etc.*

Antenuptial Agreement—Release of Marital Rights in Husband's Estate—Payment of Lump Sum Out of Husband's Estate [18]

This agreement, made this ______ day of ______, 19__, between John Day, of ______, and Jane Kent, of ______.

Whereas, a marriage is about to be solemnized between the parties to this agreement, who have made a full disclosure to each other as to their property, and are desirous that Jane Kent should have a cash payment instead of an interest in the estate of John Day.

Now, therefore, if Jane Kent survives John Day, Jane Kent agrees to accept from the estate of John Day the sum of ______ dollars in lieu of dower and her distributive share of the personal property, and John Day shall hold all the real estate which he now owns or may hereafter acquire free from any claim of dower, inchoate or otherwise; in consideration whereof John Day agrees that Jane Kent shall be paid said sum of ______ dollars as soon after his decease as may be practicable.

In Witness Whereof, *etc.*

18. The following provisions in an antenuptial agreement were held not sufficiently broad to relinquish widow's claim against estate of deceased husband for widow's award:

"3. That in consideration of Herman Guttman and Shirley Guttman Leibow joining in the execution of the within agreement, and of the covenants of Herman Guttman and Shirley Guttman Leibow herein contained, Rose Blair does hereby forever waive and release any and all rights which she, as the wife or widow of Samuel Guttman, might otherwise have either as dower in the real estate of Samuel Guttman, or by virtue of any statutory provision made for her benefit in lieu of dower, or might have to a distributive share in any personal property of Samuel Guttman, under any statutes now or hereafter in force and effect.

"4. That Samuel Guttman, his heirs or assigns, shall hold free from right of dower, inchoate or otherwise, on the part of Rose Blair, all real property which he may now or hereafter own, and Rose Blair, herewith covenants to execute or join as a party in any instrument which may be requested by Samuel Guttman, his heirs or assigns, for the purpose of divesting and quitclaiming any right of dower, inchoate, or otherwise, in said property." In re Guttman's Estate, 110 N.E.2d 87, 349 Ill.App. 58 (1952).

Clause Providing for Monthly Payment to Wife After Husband's Death [19]

Now, therefore, the Husband agrees that the representative of his estate shall pay to the Wife the sum of ______ dollars ($______), payable as follows: ______ dollars ($______) ______ days after the decease of the Husband and a like amount each ______ days thereafter, until the full sum is paid in full, which cash payment shall be a lien on any real estate owned by the Husband at the time of his decease, provided, however, that at his option the Husband, during his life, may purchase an annuity for a like sum payable in monthly installments in any good and solvent insurance company, which annuity shall be received by the Wife as a substitute for said cash payment. Provided also that if the Wife shall predecease the Husband, this agreement shall terminate upon her death.

Antenuptial Agreement Releasing Husband's Interest in Wife's Estate and Limiting Wife's Interest in Husband's Estate

Whereas, ______, of ______, herein called the Husband, and ______, of ______, herein called the Wife, contemplate entering into marriage relations; and whereas, the Husband has a large estate and has children by a former marriage; and whereas, the Wife is possessed of property in her own right and has a child by a former marriage; and whereas, the said parties desire to prescribe, limit, and determine the interest and control which each of them may have in the estate of the other party; therefore the following agreement is entered into:

Know all men by these presents: That we, ______ and ______, being about to enter into the marriage relations, do hereby agree:

Husband Releases His Rights in Wife's Estate

1. In the event of the death of the Wife during the continuance of said marriage relations, the Husband surviving her, then the Husband shall receive from the estate of the Wife the sum of five dollars; such sum when paid by the executors or administrators of the estate of the Wife to be in full for all claims and demands of every kind and character which the Husband shall have against the estate of the Wife.

Wife Limits Her Rights in Husband's Estate

2. In the event of the death of the Husband during the said marriage relations, the Wife agrees that her claim upon the estate of the Husband shall be limited to $______, and a payment by the executors or the administrators of the estate of the Husband to the

19. From In re Mosier's Estate, Ohio Prob., 133 N.E.2d 202 (1954).

Wife, her heirs or legal representatives, of the sum of $______ shall be in full for all claims and demands of every kind and character which the Wife shall have against the estate of the Husband.

During Marriage Each to Have Full Control of Own Property

3. During the continuance of said marriage relations, each of the parties is to have the full right to own, control, and dispose of his or her separate property the same as if the marriage relations did not exist, and each of the parties is to have the full right to dispose of and sell any and all real or personal property now or hereafter owned by each of them without the other party joining, and said transfer by either of the parties to this contract shall convey the same title that said transfer would convey had the marriage relations not existed. This contract limits the right of either party to participate in the estate of the other, whether the marriage relation is determined by death or legal proceedings.

Purpose of Contract to Limit Rights

4. The purpose of this agreement is to define and limit the claims and demands which each of the parties shall have against the estate of the other. Should either party die during the pendency of this contract, or should the contract be determined by legal proceedings, the claims herein stipulated and defined shall be the limit which either party may have against the other party or his or her estate.

Contract Made with Full Knowledge

5. This agreement is entered into with full knowledge that each of the parties has a separate estate, and no claim or demand can be predicated upon the fact that there has been any misrepresentation or concealment as to the amount and condition of said separate estate, it being expressly agreed that each of the parties considers the amount hereinabove fixed to be sufficient participation in the estate of the other, and it being expressly stated that each of the parties has sufficient general knowledge of the condition of the estate of the other to justify making and entering into this agreement.

In Witness Whereof, *etc.*

Antenuptial Agreement Each Relinquishing Interest in Other's Property

Agreement made the ______ day of ______, 19__, between John Day, of ______, and Jane Kent, of ______.

Whereas, the parties contemplate entering into the marriage relation with each other, and both are severally possessed of real and personal property in his and her own right, and each have children by former marriages, all of said children being of age and possessed of means of support independent of their parents, and it is desired by the parties that their marriage shall not in any way change their legal right, or that of their children and heirs, in the property of each of them.

Therefore it is agreed:

Home

1. John Day agrees that he will provide during the continuance of the marriage a home for Jane Kent, and that the two children of Jane Kent may reside in such home with their mother so long as said children remain unmarried.

Husband Releases Rights in Wife's Property

2. John Day agrees, in case he survives Jane Kent, that he will make no claim to any part of her estate as surviving husband; that in consideration of said marriage he waives and relinquishes all right of curtesy or other right in and to the property, real or personal, which Jane Kent now owns or may hereafter acquire.

Wife Releases Rights in Husband's Property

3. Jane Kent agrees, in case she survives John Day, that she will make no claim to any part of his estate as surviving wife; that in consideration of said marriage she waives and relinquishes all claims to dower, homestead, widow's award, or other right in and to the property, real or personal, which John Day now owns or may hereafter acquire.

Intent that Marriage Shall Not Affect Property

4. It is declared that by virtue of said marriage neither one shall have or acquire any right, title, or claim in and to the real or personal estate of the other, but that the estate of each shall descend to his or her heirs at law, legatees, or devisees, as may be prescribed by his or her last will and testament or by the law of the state in force, as though no marriage had taken place between them.

Agreement to Join in Conveyances

5. It is agreed that in case either of the parties desires to mortgage, sell or convey his or her real or personal estate, each one will join in the deed of conveyance or mortgage, as may be necessary to make the same effectual.

Full Disclosure between the Parties

6. It is further agreed that this agreement is entered into with a full knowledge on the part of each party as to the extent and probable value of the estate of the other and of all the rights conferred by law upon each in the estate of the other by virtue of said proposed marriage, but it is their desire that their respective rights to each other's estate shall be fixed by this agreement, which shall be binding upon their respective heirs and legal representatives.

In Witness Whereof, *etc.*

Antenuptial Agreement Each Relinquishing Interest in Other's Property—Another Form [20]

This Agreement made the ______ day of ______, 19__, between John Day, of ______, and Jane Kent, of ______.

Whereas, the parties contemplate legal marriage under the laws of the State of ______; and

Whereas, it is their mutual desire to enter into this agreement whereby they will regulate their relationships toward each other with respect to the property each of them own and in which each of them has an interest.

Now, therefore, it is agreed as follows:

1. That all properties of any kind or nature, real, personal or mixed, wherever the same may be found, which belong to each party, shall be and forever remain the personal estate of said party, including all interest, rents and profits which may accrue therefrom.

2. That each party shall have at all times the full right and authority, in all respects the same as each would have if not married, to use, enjoy, manage, convey and encumber such property as may belong to him or her.

3. That each party may make such disposition of his or her property as the case may be, by gift or will during his or her lifetime, as each sees fit; and in the event of the decease of one of the parties, the survivor shall have no interest in the property of the estate of the other, either by way of inheritance, succession, family allowance or homestead.

4. That each party, in the event of a separation, shall have no right as against the other by way of claims for support, alimony, attorney fees, costs, or division of property.

In Witness Whereof, *etc.*

Antenuptial Agreement Each Relinquishing Interest in Other's Property—Another Form [21]

This agreement is made the ______ day of ______, 19__, between ______, of ______, and ______, of ______.

Whereas, a marriage is intended to be shortly after the date hereof solemnized between the said ______ and ______; and

Whereas, each of the parties is possessed of considerable property, and has made a full and frank disclosure to the other in relation to its character and amount, and they have been advised as to

20. From In re Sayegh's Estate, 257 P.2d 995, 118 Cal.App.2d 327 (1953).

21. For another form, see Newton v. Pickell, 269 P.2d 508, 201 Or. 225 (1954).

their respective rights therein in the event of their marriage and in the absence of any agreement between them:

Now, therefore, the [*bridegroom*] and [*bride*], hereby declare it to be their intention that during their marriage each of them shall be and continue completely independent of the other as regards the enjoyment and disposal of all property, whether owned by either of them at the commencement of the marriage or coming to them or either of them during the marriage. Accordingly, they agree that all property belonging to either of them at the commencement of the marriage or coming to either of them during the marriage shall be enjoyed by him or her, and be subject to the dispositions of him or her, as his or her separate property, and after the death of either it shall be free from any claim by the other on account of dower, curtesy, or other statutory right, in the same manner as if the marriage had never been celebrated.

In Witness Whereof, *etc.*

Antenuptial Property Settlement Providing for Pooling of Property [22]

This agreement made this the ______ day of ______, 19__, between ______, of ______, and ______, of ______.

Whereas, the parties are contemplating marriage and establishing a home together; and

Whereas, the parties upon their marriage desire to pool their resources for the benefit of each other; and

Whereas, this agreement is made in order to avoid any future conflict as to their rights and interests in said property.

Now, therefore, the parties agree as follows:

1. The parties shall enter into the marriage relation and live together as husband and wife.

2. On or before the date of marriage all property belonging to the parties, including bonds, bank accounts and realty, shall be reissued, redeposited and deeds drawn so that each party shall be the joint owner, with right of survivorship, of all of the property at present owned and held by the parties individually.

3. Each party obligates himself to purchase and hold all property, present and future, jointly with the other party and agrees to execute any instrument necessary to convey, sell, or encumber any property, real or personal, when it is to the best interest of both parties that same be conveyed, sold, or encumbered.

22. From Sanders v. Sanders, 288 S.W. 2d 473, 40 Tenn.App. 20, 57 A.L.R.2d 932 (1955).

4. At the death of either party the property belonging to both shall become the absolute property of the other, free from claims of all other persons. To make effective this section of the agreement a joint will of the parties is made and is placed in their safety deposit box in the ______ Bank in the City of ______, ______.

5. Should either party file a divorce against the other, then the party so filing shall by such filing forfeit to the other all right, title, and interest in all the property, real, personal or mixed, jointly held and owned by them.

6. The parties agree that the original of this instrument shall be deposited in escrow with ______ to be held by him.

7. This agreement cannot be revoked except by written consent of both parties and the holder in escrow shall not deliver the original to any one except a court of competent jurisdiction or to the parties to this instrument upon their mutual demand for the surrender thereof.

8. This agreement is made in triplicate with each party hereto retaining a copy thereof, but the copy shall not be used in evidence or serve any legal purpose whatsoever if the original is available.

In Witness Whereof, *etc.*

NOTE

Clause no. 5 above appears to discourage spouses from using the court system. Property rights are forfeited upon the filing of a divorce. Does this violate public policy? Tom and Jane are married. Tom commits adultery. If Jane files for divorce on the ground of adultery, would she forfeit her property rights under clause # 5? The clause has been interpreted to mean that such a forfeiture will occur only if the divorce action is brought in bad faith, without reasonable grounds. Under this interpretation, Jane would not forfeit her rights so long as she is bringing the action in good faith and not simply to be malicious to Tom. See Annotation, "Validity, construction, and effect of provision in antenuptial contract forfeiting property rights of innocent spouse on separation or filing of divorce or other matrimonial action," 57 *American Law Reports* 2d 942 (1958).

Are there any other terms in any of the above clauses that might raise problems of legality?

SECTION C. CONTRACT COHABITATION

In many states, adultery (sex with a married person) and fornication (sex between unmarried persons) are crimes. Even if they are not considered crimes in a particular state, sexual intercourse outside of marriage is considered immoral behavior in all states. If two people enter a contract involving such immoral conduct, the courts will not enforce it because the consideration [23] for the contract is "meretricious sexual services." The courts will treat such a contract the same as or very similar to a prostitution agreement.

In today's society it is widely known that there are a great many couples who "live together" without being married.[24] If the couple lives in a state that allows common law marriages,[25] and if the parties fulfill all the requirements for a valid common law marriage (e. g., that they "hold themselves out" to the public as husband and wife even though they never go through a marriage ceremony), the result will be that the parties are legally married. In order to terminate their relationship, for example, they would have to go through the divorce procedure. Suppose, however, that the parties live in a state that has abolished common law marriages or that they fail to meet all the requirements for a valid common law marriage in a state that authorizes them. Do they acquire any rights in each other's property? If they enter into a contract (expressly or impliedly) to share their wealth equally, can this contract be enforced in a court of law? Would such a contract be any different from a prostitution contract?

EXAMPLE:

> George and Laura begin living together. They never go through a marriage ceremony. They buy a home together, they raise children, they use the same surname, they hold themselves out as husband and wife in every way. They live in a state that does not recognize common law marriages. Twenty years after they began cohabitating, they separate. Laura wants to sue George for an equitable share of the property they acquired during the marriage.

The traditional rule is that Laura is out of luck. Some of the arguments that would be used to prevent her from recovering anything from George include:

—Their living arrangement was meretricious, involving immoral sexual intercourse.

—Their was no express contract [26] between them as to property acquired during their relationship of cohabitation (whatever they gave each other during this time were gifts).

—To allow recovery would negate the purpose behind abolishing common law marriages.[27]

—To allow recovery would encourage people to live together and bypass the requirements for a ceremonial marriage.[28]

23. See supra p. 110.

24. See, for example, Lavori, N., *Living Together, Married or Single: Your Legal Rights* (1976).

25. Infra p. 164.

26. Supra p. 110.

27. Infra p. 166.

28. Infra p. 156.

On the other hand, there is a very small minority of states that *will* allow recovery. The basic argument of these states is that it would be grossly unfair to deny recovery.

—While the living arrangement has a meretricious component (i. e., the immoral sexual activity), the arrangement is not totally meretricious. The parties are also exchanging companionship, support, housekeeping services, etc. The baby should not be thrown out with the dirty bath water. In so far as, or to the extent that, there was no immoral activity, the contract should be enforced. Unless it can be shown that the entire reason for (i. e., the entire consideration for) the living arrangement was sex, the court should enforce the contract in whole or in part.

—Even if there is no express contract, the court may be able to imply the existence of a contract based upon the conduct of the parties, e. g., to imply a contract that the parties intended to have equal rights in all property (e. g., cash, land) that they acquire while they are living together. Another equitable solution may be to allow the woman to recover the value of her household services from her former lover.

The landmark case that recognized the rights of unmarried persons living together is Marvin v. Marvin. Excerpts from this California case are reprinted below since it has the potential of becoming a precedent in other states.[29]

MARVIN v. MARVIN

Supreme Court of California, 1976.
18 Cal.3d 660, 134 Cal.Rptr. 815, 557 P.2d 106.

TOBRINER, Justice.

During the past 15 years, there has been a substantial increase in the number of couples living together without marrying.[1] Such nonmarital relationships lead to legal controversy when one partner dies or the couple separates. . . . We take this opportunity to resolve that controversy and to declare the principles which should govern distribution of property acquired in a nonmarital relationship.

We conclude: . . . . (2) The courts should enforce express contracts between nonmarital partners except to the extent that the contract is explicitly founded on the consideration of meretricious sexual services. (3) In the absence of an express contract, the courts should inquire into the conduct of the parties to determine whether

29. See, for example, Carlson v. Olson, — Minn. —, 256 N.W.2d 249 (1977).

1. "The 1970 census figures indicate that today perhaps eight times as many couples are living together without being married as cohabited ten years ago." (Comment, *In re Cary: A Judicial Recognition of Illicit Cohabitation* (1974) 25 Hastings L.J. 1226.)

that conduct demonstrates an implied contract, agreement of partnership or joint venture, or some other tacit understanding between the parties. The courts may also employ the doctrine of quantum meruit, or equitable remedies such as constructive or resulting trusts, when warranted by the facts of the case.

In the instant case plaintiff and defendant lived together for seven years without marrying; all property acquired during this period was taken in defendant's name. When plaintiff sued to enforce a contract under which she was entitled to half the property and to support payments, the trial court granted judgment on the pleadings for defendant, thus leaving him with all property accumulated by the couple during their relationship. Since the trial court denied plaintiff a trial on the merits of her claim, its decision conflicts with the principles stated above, and must be reversed.

1. *The factual setting of this appeal*

. . . Plaintiff avers that in October of 1964 she and defendant "entered into an oral agreement" that while "the parties lived together they would combine their efforts and earnings and would share equally any and all property accumulated as a result of their efforts whether individual or combined." Furthermore, they agreed to "hold themselves out to the general public as husband and wife" and that "plaintiff would further render her services as a companion, homemaker, housekeeper and cook to . . . defendant."

Shortly thereafter plaintiff agreed to "give up her lucrative career as an entertainer [and] singer" in order to "devote her full time to defendant . . . as a companion, homemaker, housekeeper and cook;" in return defendant agreed to "provide for all of plaintiff's financial support and needs for the rest of her life."

Plaintiff alleges that she lived with defendant from October of 1964 through May of 1970 and fulfilled her obligations under the agreement. During this period the parties as a result of their efforts and earnings acquired in defendant's name substantial real and personal property, including motion picture rights worth over $1 million. In May of 1970, however, defendant compelled plaintiff to leave his household. He continued to support plaintiff until November of 1971, but thereafter refused to provide further support.

On the basis of these allegations plaintiff asserts two causes of action. The first, for declaratory relief, asks the court to determine her contract and property rights; the second seeks to impose a constructive trust upon one half of the property acquired during the course of the relationship.

. . .

2. *Plaintiff's complaint states a cause of action for breach of an express contract*

In Trutalli v. Meraviglia (1932) 215 Cal. 698, 12 P.2d 430 we established the principle that nonmarital partners may lawfully contract concerning the ownership of property acquired during the relationship. We reaffirmed this principle in Vallera v. Vallera (1943) 21 Cal.2d 681, 685, 134 P.2d 761, 763, stating that "If a man and woman [who are not married] live together as husband and wife under an agreement to pool their earnings and share equally in their joint accumulations, equity will protect the interests of each in such property."

In the case before us plaintiff, basing her cause of action in contract upon these precedents, maintains that the trial court erred in denying her a trial on the merits of her contention. Although that court did not specify the ground for its conclusion that plaintiff's contractual allegations stated no cause of action, defendant offers some four theories to sustain the ruling; we proceed to examine them.

Defendant first and principally relies on the contention that the alleged contract is so closely related to the supposed "immoral" character of the relationship between plaintiff and himself that the enforcement of the contract would violate public policy. He points to cases asserting that a contract between nonmarital partners is unenforceable if it is "involved in" an illicit relationship . . . or made in "contemplation" of such a relationship . . . . A review of the numerous California decisions concerning contracts between nonmarital partners, however, reveals that the courts have not employed such broad and uncertain standards to strike down contracts. The decisions instead disclose a narrower and more precise standard: a contract between nonmarital partners is unenforceable only *to the extent* that it *explicitly* rests upon the immoral and illicit consideration of meretricious sexual services.

In the first case to address this issue, Trutalli v. Meraviglia, . . ., 215 Cal. 698, 12 P.2d 430, the parties had lived together without marriage for 11 years and had raised two children. The man sued to quiet title to land he had purchased in his own name during this relationship; the woman defended by asserting an agreement to pool earnings and hold all property jointly. Rejecting the assertion of the illegality of the agreement, the court stated that "The fact that the parties to this action at the time they agreed to invest their earnings in property to be held jointly between them were living together in an unlawful relation did not disqualify them from entering into a lawful agreement with each other, so long as such immoral relation was not made a *consideration* of their agreement." (Emphasis added.) (215 Cal. at pp. 701–702, 12 P.2d 430, 431.)

In Bridges v. Bridges (1954) 125 Cal.App.2d 359, 270 P.2d 69, both parties were in the process of obtaining divorces from their erstwhile respective spouses. The two parties agreed to live together, to share equally in property acquired, and to marry when their divorces became final. The man worked as a salesman and used his savings to purchase properties. The woman kept house, cared for seven children, three from each former marriage and one from the nonmarital relationship, and helped construct improvements on the properties. When they separated, without marrying, the court awarded the woman one-half the value of the property. Rejecting the man's contention that the contract was illegal, the court stated that: "Nowhere is it expressly testified to by anyone that there was anything in the agreement for the pooling of assets and the sharing of accumulations that contemplated meretricious relations as any part of the consideration or as any object of the agreement." (125 Cal.App.2d at p. 363, 270 P.2d at p. 71.)

Croslin v. Scott (1957) 154 Cal.App.2d 767, 316 P.2d 755 reiterates the rule established in *Trutalli* and *Bridges*. In *Croslin* the parties separated following a three-year nonmarital relationship. The woman then phoned the man, asked him to return to her, and suggested that he build them a house on a lot she owned. She agreed in return to place the property in joint ownership. The man built the house, and the parties lived there for several more years. When they separated, he sued to establish his interest in the property. Reversing a nonsuit, the Court of Appeal stated that "The mere fact that parties agreed to live together in meretricious relationship does not necessarily make an agreement for disposition of property between them invalid. It is only when the property agreement is made in connection with the other agreement, or the illicit relationship is made a consideration of the property agreement, that the latter becomes illegal." (154 Cal.App.2d at p. 771, 316 P.2d at p. 758.)

. . .

Although the past decisions hover over the issue in the somewhat wispy form of the figures of a Chagall painting, we can abstract from those decisions a clear and simple rule. The fact that a man and woman live together without marriage, and engage in a sexual relationship, does not in itself invalidate agreements between them relating to their earnings, property, or expenses. Neither is such an agreement invalid merely because the parties may have contemplated the creation or continuation of a nonmarital relationship when they entered into it. Agreements between nonmarital partners fail only to the extent that they rest upon a consideration of meretricious sexual services. Thus the rule asserted by defendant, that a contract fails if it is "involved in" or made "in contemplation" of a nonmarital relationship, cannot be reconciled with the decisions.

The three cases cited by defendant which have *declined* to enforce contracts between nonmarital partners involved consideration that was expressly founded upon an illicit sexual services. In Hill v.

Estate of Westbrook, . . . , 95 Cal.App.2d 599, 213 P.2d 727 the woman promised to keep house for the man, to live with him as man and wife, and to bear his children; the man promised to provide for her in his will, but died without doing so. Reversing a judgment for the woman based on the reasonable value of her services, the Court of Appeal stated that "the action is predicated upon a claim which seeks, among other things, the reasonable value of living with decedent in meretricious relationship and bearing him two children . . . . The law does not award compensation for living with a man as a concubine and bearing him children. . . . As the judgment is, at least in part, for the value of the claimed services for which recovery cannot be had, it must be reversed." (95 Cal.App.2d at p. 603, 213 P.2d at p. 730.) Upon retrial, the trial court found that it could not sever the contract and place an independent value upon the legitimate services performed by claimant. We therefore affirmed a judgment for the estate. (Hill v. Estate of Westbrook (1952) 39 Cal. 2d 458, 247 P.2d 19).

In the only other cited decision refusing to enforce a contract, Updeck v. Samuel (1964), 123 Cal.App.2d 264, 266 P.2d 822, the contract "was based on the consideration that the parties live together as husband and wife." (123 Cal.App.2d at p. 267, 266 P.2d at p. 824.) Viewing the contract as calling for adultery, the court held it illegal.[6]

The decisions in the *Hill* and *Updeck* cases thus demonstrate that a contract between nonmarital partners, even if expressly made in contemplation of a common living arrangement, is invalid only if sexual acts form an inseparable part of the consideration for the agreement. In sum, a court will not enforce a contract for the pooling of property and earnings if it is explicitly and inseparably based upon services as a paramour. The Court of Appeal opinion in *Hill*, however, indicates that even if sexual services are part of the contractual consideration, any *severable* portion of the contract supported by independent consideration will still be enforced.

The principle that a contract between nonmarital partners will be enforced unless expressly and inseparably based upon an illicit

6. Although not cited by defendant, the only California precedent which supports his position is *Heaps v. Toy* (1942) 54 Cal.App.2d 178, 128 P.2d 813. In that case the woman promised to leave her job, to refrain from marriage, to be a companion to the man, and to make a permanent home for him; he agreed to support the woman and her child for life. The Court of Appeal held the agreement invalid as a contract in restraint of marriage (Civ. Code, § 1676) and, alternatively, as "contrary to good morals" (Civ.Code, § 1607). The opinion does not state that sexual relations formed any part of the consideration for the contract, nor explain how—unless the contract called for sexual relations—the woman's employment as a companion and housekeeper could be contrary to good morals.

The alternative holding in Heaps v. Toy, supra, finding the contract in that case contrary to good morals, is inconsistent with the numerous California decisions upholding contracts between nonmarital partners when such contracts are not founded upon an illicit consideration, and is therefore disapproved.

consideration of sexual services not only represents the distillation of the decisional law, but also offers a far more precise and workable standard than that advocated by defendant. Our recent decision in In re Marriage of Dawley (1976) 17 Cal.3d 342, 551 P.2d 323, offers a close analogy. Rejecting the contention that an antenuptial agreement is invalid if the parties contemplated a marriage of short duration, we pointed out in *Dawley* that a standard based upon the subjective contemplation of the parties is uncertain and unworkable; such a test, we stated, "might invalidate virtually all antenuptial agreements on the ground that the parties contemplated dissolution . . . but it provides no principled basis for determining which antenuptial agreements offend public policy and which do not." (17 Cal.3d 342, 352, 551 P.2d 323, 329.)

Similarly, in the present case a standard which inquires whether an agreement is "involved" in or "contemplates" a nonmarital relationship is vague and unworkable. Virtually all agreements between nonmarital partners can be said to be "involved" in some sense in the fact of their mutual sexual relationship, or to "contemplate" the existence of that relationship. Thus defendant's proposed standards, if taken literally, might invalidate all agreements between nonmarital partners, a result no one favors. Moreover, those standards offer no basis to distinguish between valid and invalid agreements. By looking not to such uncertain tests, but only to the consideration underlying the agreement, we provide the parties and the courts with a practical guide to determine when an agreement between nonmarital partners should be enforced.

. . .

Defendant's third contention is noteworthy for the lack of authority advanced in its support. He contends that enforcement of the oral agreement between plaintiff and himself is barred by Civil Code section 5134, which provides that "All contracts for marriage settlements must be in writing . . . ." A marriage settlement, however, is an agreement in contemplation of marriage in which each party agrees to release or modify the property rights which would otherwise arise from the marriage. (See Corker v. Corker (1891) 87 Cal. 643, 648, 25 P. 922.) The contract at issue here does not conceivably fall within that definition, and thus is beyond the compass of section 5134.[9]

Defendant finally argues that enforcement of the contract is barred by Civil Code section 43.5, subdivision (d), which provides that "No cause of action arises for . . . [b]reach of a promise of marriage." This rather strained contention proceeds from the premise that a promise of marriage impliedly includes a promise to support

9. Our review of the many cases enforcing agreements between nonmarital partners reveals that the majority of such agreements were oral. In two cases (Ferguson v. Schuenemann, . . . , 167 Cal.App.2d 413, 334 P.2d 668; Cline v. Festersen, . . . , 128 Cal.App.2d 380, 275 P.2d 149), the court expressly rejected defenses grounded upon the statute of frauds.

and to pool property acquired after marriage (see Boyd v. Boyd (1964) 228 Cal.App.2d 374, 39 Cal.Rptr. 400) to the conclusion that pooling and support agreements not part of or accompanied by promise of marriage are barred by the section. We conclude that section 43.5 is not reasonably susceptible to the interpretation advanced by defendant, a conclusion demonstrated by the fact that since section 43.5 was enacted in 1939, numerous cases have enforced pooling agreements between nonmarital partners, and in none did court or counsel refer to section 43.5.

In summary, we base our opinion on the principle that adults who voluntarily live together and engage in sexual relations are nonetheless as competent as any other persons to contract respecting their earnings and property rights. Of course, they cannot lawfully contract to pay for the performance of sexual services, for such a contract is, in essence, an agreement for prostitution and unlawful for that reason. But they may agree to pool their earnings and to hold all property acquired during the relationship in accord with the law . . . .[10] So long as the agreement does not rest upon illicit meretricious consideration, the parties may order their economic affairs as they choose, and no policy precludes the courts from enforcing such agreements.

In the present instance, plaintiff alleges that the parties agreed to pool their earnings, that they contracted to share equally in all property acquired, and that defendant agreed to support plaintiff. The terms of the contract as alleged do not rest upon any unlawful consideration. We therefore conclude that the complaint furnishes a suitable basis upon which the trial court can render declaratory relief. . . . The trial court consequently erred in granting defendant's motion for judgment on the pleadings.

. . .

In summary, we believe that the prevalence of nonmarital relationships in modern society and the social acceptance of them, marks this as a time when our courts should by no means apply the doctrine of the unlawfulness of the so-called meretricious relationship to the instant case. As we have explained, the nonenforceability of agreements expressly providing for meretricious conduct rested upon the fact that such conduct, as the word suggests, pertained to and encompassed prostitution. To equate the nonmarital relationship of today to such a subject matter is to do violence to an accepted and wholly different practice.

10. A great variety of . . . arrangements are possible. The parties might keep their earnings and property separate, but agree to compensate one party for services which benefit the other. They may choose to pool only part of their earnings and property, to form a partnership or joint venture, or to hold property acquired as joint tenants or tenants in common, or agree to any other such arrangement. (See generally Weitzman, *Legal Regulation of Marriage: Tradition and Change* (1974) 62 Cal.L.Rev. 1169.)

We are aware that many young couples live together without the solemnization of marriage, in order to make sure that they can successfully later undertake marriage. This trial period,[23] preliminary to marriage, serves as some assurance that the marriage will not subsequently end in dissolution to the harm of both parties. We are aware, as we have stated, of the pervasiveness of nonmarital relationships in other situations.

The mores of the society have indeed changed so radically in regard to cohabitation that we cannot impose a standard based on alleged moral considerations that have apparently been so widely abandoned by so many. Lest we be misunderstood, however, we take this occasion to point out that the structure of society itself largely depends upon the institution of marriage, and nothing we have said in this opinion should be taken to derogate from that institution. The joining of the man and woman in marriage is at once the most socially productive and individually fulfilling relationship that one can enjoy in the course of a lifetime.

We conclude that the judicial barriers that may stand in the way of a policy based upon the fulfillment of the reasonable expectations of the parties to a nonmarital relationship should be removed. As we have explained, the courts now hold that express agreements will be enforced unless they rest on an unlawful meretricious consideration. We add that in the absence of an express agreement, the courts may look to a variety of other remedies in order to protect the parties' lawful expectations.[24]

The courts may inquire into the conduct of the parties to determine whether that conduct demonstrates an implied contract or implied agreement of partnership or joint venture (see Estate of Thornton (1972) 81 Wash.2d 72, 499 P.2d 864), or some other tacit understanding between the parties. The courts may, when appropriate, employ principles of constructive trust (see Omer v. Omer (1974) 11 Wash.App. 386, 523 P.2d 957) or resulting trust (see Hyman v. Hyman (Tex.Civ.App.1954) 275 S.W.2d 149). Finally, a nonmarital partner may recover in quantum meruit for the reasonable value of household services rendered less the reasonable value of support received if he can show that he rendered services with the expectation of monetary reward. (See Hill v. Estate of Westbrook, . . ., 39 Cal.2d 458, 462, 247 P.2d 19.) [25]

23. Toffler, Future Shock (Bantam Books, 1971) page 253.

24. We do not seek to resurrect the doctrine of common law marriage, which was abolished in California by statute in 1895. (See Norman v. Thomson (1898) 121 Cal. 620, 628, 54 P. 143; Estate of Abate (1958) 166 Cal.App.2d 282, 292, 333 P.2d 200.) Thus we do not hold that plaintiff and defendant were "married," nor do we extend to plaintiff the rights which the Family Law Act grants valid or putative spouses; we hold only that she has the same rights to enforce contracts and to assert her equitable interest in property acquired through her effort as does any other unmarried person.

25. Our opinion does not preclude the evolution of additional equitable rem-

Since we have determined that plaintiff's complaint states a cause of action for breach of an express contract, and, as we have explained, can be amended to state a cause of action independent of allegations of express contract,[26] we must conclude that the trial court erred in granting defendant a judgment on the pleadings.

The judgment is reversed and the cause remanded for further proceedings consistent with the views expressed herein.

Assignment # 21

(a) Shepardize Marvin v. Marvin in order to determine whether the case has been cited by any opinion written by a court in your state. For every opinion, if any, in your state that has cited Marvin v. Marvin, state how the opinion used *Marvin*. Did it agree with, disagree with, expand upon *Marvin*? (If your state is California where *Marvin* was decided, you should shepardize *Marvin* in order to determine what other California cases have said about the Marvin v. Marvin. How have they expanded or narrowed *Marvin*?) (If you need help on how to shepardize, ask your teacher or a librarian. See also "Legal Research and Analysis" in Statsky, W., *Introduction to Paralegalism: Perspectives, Problems and Skills*, pp. 433ff (1974).)

(b) What crime or crimes, if any, can unmarried people in your state commit when they engage in sexual intercourse? (See also General Instructions for the State Code Assignment, supra p. 14.)

(c) Helen Smith and Sam Jones live together in your state. They are not married and do not intend to become married. They would like to enter a contract which spells out their rights and responsibilities. Specifically, they want it to be clear that the house in which they both live belongs to Helen even though Sam has done extensive remodeling work on the house. They each have separate bank accounts and one joint account. They want to make clear that only the funds in the joint account belongs to both of them equally. Next year they hope to have a child or to adopt a child. In any event, they want the contract to specify that the child will be given the surname, "Smith-Jones" which is a combination of their own last names. Draft a contract for them. Do not include any clauses in the contract which would be illegal in your state. (See also General Instructions for the Agreement Drafting Assignment, supra p. 25.) On a separate sheet of paper, make a list of clauses that you would include if they were not illegal. State why they are illegal. (See also General Instructions for the Legal Analysis Assignment, supra p. 16.)

edies to protect the expectations of the parties to a nonmarital relationship in cases in which existing remedies prove inadequate; the suitability of such remedies may be determined in later cases in light of the factual setting in which they arise.

26. We do not pass upon the question whether, in the absence of an express or implied contractual obligation, a party to a nonmarital relationship is entitled to support payments from the other party after the relationship terminates.

Assignment # 22

Richard and Lena have lived together for ten years without being married. This month they separated. They never entered a formal contract, but Lena says that they had an informal understanding that they would divide everything acquired during their relationship together equally. Lena sues Richard for one half of all property so acquired. You work for the law firm that represents Lena. Draft a set of interrogatories for Lena that will be sent to Richard in which you seek information that would be relevant to Lena's action. (See also General Instructions for the Interrogatories Assignment, supra p. 31.)

Jan Van Eyck, "Giovanni Arnolfini and His Wife," Reproduced by Courtesy of the Trustees, The National Gallery, London

Chapter Nine

THE FORMATION OF CEREMONIAL MARRIAGES AND COMMON LAW MARRIAGES

SECTION A. INTRODUCTION

Normally, a client will *not* walk into a law office and ask: "is my marriage valid?" The legality of a marriage will usually arise when a client is trying to achieve some other objective. Here are some examples of when the validity of a marriage might arise:

—The client wants to obtain a divorce (or the client is being sued for divorce) wherein one of the questions that always must be asked is: was there a valid marriage initially? If not, then there is no need to obtain a divorce since the parties were never married.

—The client wants to obtain a legal separation [1] or an annulment [2] (or is being sued for a separation or annulment) and again the question arises as to the validity of the marriage.

—The client is seeking some state agency benefit which is dependent, in part, on establishing the existence of a marriage, e. g., a state police officer dies with pension rights outstanding which are to go to his surviving wife; a person claiming to be the wife of the deceased may have to establish that she was validly married to him before he died.

—The client is seeking some federal agency benefit which is dependent, in part, on establishing the existence of a marriage, e. g., a woman dies leaving social security survivor benefits to her spouse; a person claiming to be her husband may have to establish that he was validly married to her before she died.

—The client is a minor who needs to know whether or not s/he is illegitimate, which in some states may be dependent upon whether or not his/her natural parents were validly married at the time of birth.[3]

—A woman dies and leaves a will which says I give my property "to my husband." A major problem here will be what the deceased meant by this phrase; [4] it may be that the person claiming to be her husband will have to establish the validity of the marriage.

1. Infra p. 405ff.

2. Infra p. 171ff.

3. Infra p. 449ff.

4. See also infra p. 281.

—A foreign born individual might be able to escape deportation if s/he can establish that s/he is now validly married to an American citizen.

—In many states, a wife is entitled to dower rights[5] to her husband's property when he dies (in spite of or in addition to whatever he puts into his will for her); the person claiming dower rights may have to establish the validity of the marriage.

—A client may be charged with the crime of bigamy: being married to two people at the same time;[6] one of his/her defenses to such a crime may be that the marriage that s/he attempted to enter with his/her first "spouse" was never valid.

Another way to phrase some of the above situations is to say that the party bringing the litigation may have the burden of proof to establish the existence of a valid marriage as a precondition to being able to obtain the ultimate objective of the pending or proposed litigation.

In this chapter, we begin to talk about the technical requirements for a marriage, specifically a ceremonial marriage and a common law marriage. In later chapters on annulment,[7] we will discuss other requirements for a valid marriage such as the legal capacity to enter any marriage at all.

SECTION B. CEREMONIAL MARRIAGE

There are two ways to become married: through a ceremonial marriage and through a common law marriage. The latter type of marriage, however, has been abolished in a number of states as we will see in the next section.

Certain requirements exist for a ceremonial marriage. These requirements are found within the statutory code[8] of your state. These requirements usually include:

(1) that there be a marriage license;

(2) that the ceremony be performed before a person authorized to perform the ceremony;

(3) that there be witnesses to the ceremony;

(4) that there be a waiting period between the time the license is applied for and issued, or between the date of issue and the date of the ceremony;

(5) that there be a physical examination of the two parties;

(6) that the license be recorded in a designated public office following the ceremony.

5. Supra p. 128.

6. Infra p. 177.

7. Infra p. 171ff.

8. On statutory codes, see supra p. 13ff.

Not all states have the same requirements, and some state codes may impose additional requirements. These technical requirements that relate to the ceremonial marriage are to be distinguished from those requirements or standards that relate to the intent to marry and the *legal capacity* to marry. As indicated, the latter requirements will be discussed later.[9]

INTERVIEWING AND INVESTIGATION CHECKLIST

FACTORS RELEVANT TO A CEREMONIAL MARRIAGE

	Legal Interviewing Questions	Possible Investigation Tasks
1.	On what date did you apply for the marriage license? On what date was it issued?	* Obtain a copy of the marriage license.
2.	Did you both go to fill out the application?	* Determine if a receipt exists for payment of the license fee, if any.
3.	Where did you go to obtain the license?	* You may be asked to obtain a statement (affidavit) from the witnesses and from the person performing the ceremony concerning the circumstances of the ceremony.
4.	Describe the person who issued the license to you.	* Go to where marriage records are kept in the county and copy all facts pertaining to the marriage.
5.	What happened after you obtained the license?	* Obtain copy of medical record of the physical examination.
6.	Who performed the wedding ceremony? State this person's address and phone number.	
7.	Who told you that this person was authorized to perform the ceremony?	
8.	Other than guests, who was present at the wedding ceremony and what was their role? Give the name, address and phone number of all witnesses.	
9.	On what date did the ceremony take place?	
10.	Did you both take medical examinations before you were issued the license? If so, where, who performed the exams and what were the results?	
11.	Do you know whether or not your marriage license was recorded?	
12.	Where, when and by whom was your license recorded?	

IM-453

9. Infra p. 177.

SAMPLE FORMS:

Number ______.

To ______, authorized to celebrate (or witness) marriages in the state of ______, greeting:

You are hereby authorized to celebrate (or witness) the rites of marriage between ______, of ______, and ______, of ______, and having done so, you are commanded to make return of the same to the clerk's office of ______ ______ within ten days under a penalty of fifty dollars for default therein.

Witness my hand and seal of said court this ______ day of ______, anno Domini ______.

______ Clerk.
By ______ Assistant Clerk.

Number ______.

I, ______, who have been duly authorized to celebrate (or witness) the rites of marriage in the state of ______ do hereby certify that, by authority of a license of corresponding number herewith, I solemnized (or witnessed) the marriage of ______ and ______, named therein, on the ______ day of ______, at ______, in said state.

Number ______.

I hereby certify that on this ______ day of ______, at ______, ______ and ______ were by (or before) me united in marriage in accordance with the license issued by the clerk of the ______.

Name ______,
Residence ______.

[B7912]

Prob. 641

Barrett Brothers, Publishers, Springfield, Ohio

Marriage License

NOT VALID After Sixty Days from Date

The State of Ohio, Adams County

To Any Person Legally Authorized to Solemnize Marriages in the State of Ohio:

I, the undersigned,

James W. Lang, Jr.

Judge of the Probate Court within and for the County and State aforesaid, have **Licensed**, *and do hereby License and Authorize*

Mr. Peter Steck *and*

*M*iss Patricia Jane Farrell

to be joined in **Marriage.**

In Witness Whereof, *I have hereunto subscribed my name and affixed the seal of said Court, at West Union, Ohio, this* 18th

day of June *A.D. 19*68

JAMES W. LANG, JR.

Judge of the Probate Court

By A. C. Bailey *Deputy Clerk*

The above marriage was solemnized by me this 22nd

day of June 1968

Rev. John J. Marquardt

[B779]

The next Assignment (# 23) asks you to go to your state statutory code and determine the requirements for a ceremonial marriage in your state. In preparation for that assignment, examine the following Utah statute (which we already looked at briefly in Chapter One[10]):

> **§ 1742. License prerequisite**—No marriage shall be solemnized without a license issued by the county clerk of any county of the state of Utah not more than thirty days prior to the date of solemnization of the marriage.

Whenever you are studying a statute, three questions should come to your mind:

(1) What does the statute tell you about the topic it treats?

(2) What is unclear or ambiguous about the statute?

(3) If you were interviewing a client, what questions would you ask of the client in order to be more sure of whether or not the statute applies?

The Utah statute tells us three things:

—A marriage license must exist.

—The license must be issued by a Utah county clerk.

—The license can't be used more than thirty days after it is issued.

What is unclear, unanswered, or ambiguous about section 1742?

—What does "solemnized" or "solemnization" mean? The statute does not tell us. It assumes that we know. The words probably refer to a ceremony of some kind, but we would not know for sure simply by reading this statute.

—What must the license contain? What statements or provisions must be in a marriage license in order for it to *be* a marriage license? This statute does not tell us.

—Do weekends and holidays count toward the thirty day period, or is the reference only to thirty business week days? This statute does not answer this question.

As you can see, one of the main objectives of going to a statute is to uncover *questions* about that statute.[11] It is a misconception to think that statutes sit in books waiting to give you answers. Often, before a statute can give you any answers to a client's problem, you must be able to raise the proper questions about that statute.[12]

Assuming that the right questions have been raised above about section 1742, where do you go to get answers to these questions? It may be that statutes near section 1742 in the Utah code will provide

10. Supra p. 29.

11. See generally, Statsky, W., *Legislative Analysis: How to Use Statutes and Regulations* (1975).

12. Another way of saying this is that you must be able to phrase issues of statutory construction. Id. at pp. 41ff. On legal analysis, see also supra p. 16ff.

some of the answers, e. g., there may be a definitions statute that defines "solemnization," there may be a statute that identifies everything that must be in a marriage license. For other questions, you may have to determine whether court opinions exist that provide the answer,[13] e. g., there may be a court opinion decided several years ago which held that in counting the thirty days of section 1742, you do not count weekends. If no such opinions currently exist, then it may be that new litigation must be instituted in order to resolve the questions left unanswered in the statutory code.

Suppose that you are talking to a client of the office where you work who recently went through a marriage ceremony in Utah and you are attempting to determine if and how section 1742 applies. A number of questions would have to be asked of this person: [14]

—Did you obtain a marriage license?

—Did you get the license from a Utah county clerk?

—On what date was the license issued to you?

—On what date were you married? (In handling the thirty day provision of section 1742, you will have to do some arithmetic: count the days between the date of license issue and the date of the ceremony).

Assignment # 23

Go to your state statutory code and determine whether there are statutes on the following topics (1) marriage licenses, (2) who can perform the ceremony, (3) whether witnesses to the ceremony must exist, (4) waiting periods, (5) physical examination and (6) the filing or the recording of the license (7) other technical requirements.

For *each* statute or portion of a statute on these topics, answer the following three questions:

(a) What does the statute tell you about the topic?

(b) What is ambiguous, unclear or unanswered in the statute?

(c) What specific questions would you ask a client in order to determine whether the statute applies?

(See also General Instructions for the State Code Assignment, supra p. 14.)

NOTE ON THE "QUICKY MARRIAGE"

A few states are experimenting with statutes that do not impose all the traditional requirements for the formation of a marriage. The

13. For more on how to find court opinions on point, see supra p. 26ff.

14. For more on the formulation of such checklist questions, see supra p. 29ff.

California statute, for example, is as follows (West's Ann.Calif.Civ. Code, sec. 4213, eff. 1973):

> When unmarried persons, not minors, have been living together as man and wife, they may, without a license, be married by any clergyman, without the necessity of first obtaining health certificates. A certificate of marriage shall be filled out by the parties to the marriage and authenticated by the clergyman performing the ceremony. The certificate shall be filed by the clergyman with the office of the county clerk in the county in which the ceremony was performed within four days after the performance of the ceremony. The county clerk shall maintain this certificate as a permanent record which shall not be open to public inspection except upon order of the superior court issued upon a showing of good cause.
>
> The form of the certificate of marriage shall be prescribed by the State Department of . . . Health. The form shall be furnished to any clergyman by the county clerk without charge.
>
> . . .

Assignment # 24

In Assignment # 23 above, you identified all of the requirements for a ceremonial marriage in your state. In this assignment, you are to interview someone who was married in your state in order to determine whether all the requirements for a ceremonial marriage were met. You can interview a married relative, a married friend, your spouse, a married classmate, etc. Ask the interviewee all the questions you need to ask in order to determine whether compliance with the requirements existed. Make a list of these questions before you conduct the interview. (In effect, you will be drafting a checklist of questions that could be part of a manual.) As you ask the questions, make notes of the interviewee's answers. For all answers, ask the interviewee if any documents or other evidence exists to substantiate (or corroborate) the answers given. (See also General Instructions for the Checklist Formulation Assignment, supra p. 29.) Hand in to your instructor a written account of the interview. Remember that one of the primary characteristics of such written work products must be specificity; the details of names, addresses, dates, who said what, etc. can be critical.

Suppose that the technical requirements for a ceremonial marriage have been violated? What consequences follow? Assume that a statute requires that there be a ten day waiting period between the date of the issuing of the license and the date of the ceremony. Joe and Mary want to be married right away and they find a minister who marries them on the same day they obtained the license. What result? Are they validly married? In most states, the marriage is *not* invalid when there has been a failure to comply with one of the requirements discussed in this chapter for a ceremonial marriage. In such states, noncompliance with the requirements for a ceremonial marriage cannot later be used as a ground for annulment [15] or divorce.[16] Again, keep in mind that we are *not* discussing requirements relating to the *legal capacity* of parties to marry, e. g., that they be of a specified age, that they not be related to each other as defined by statute, nor are we discussing the requirements on the necessary intent to marry. Violations of such requirements *can* be grounds for annulment or divorce.[17] Our concern here are those technical requirements of the ceremony that relate to the existence of a valid license, the presence of the required waiting days, etc.

As indicated, in most states noncompliance does not invalidate the marriage. In a few states, however, noncompliance *does* affect the validity of the marriage, thus creating grounds for annulment or divorce. Independent of the effect of noncompliance on the validity of the marriage, noncompliance with the requirements for a ceremonial marriage can have other consequences. The parties, for example, might be prosecuted for perjury if they have falsified any public documents. A person who performs a marriage ceremony without the authority to do so may be subjected to a fine or other criminal penalty. Different states may impose different sanctions.

Assignment # 25

(a) In your state, is the validity of the marriage affected by a violation of any of the technical requirements for a ceremonial marriage that you identified in Assignment # 23, supra p. 161?

(b) What penalties can be imposed for the violation of any of the technical requirements for a ceremonial marriage in your state?

(To answer the above two questions, you may have to check both statutory law and case law. See General Instructions for the State Code Assignment, supra p. 14, and for the Court Opinion Assignment, supra p. 26.)

Assignment # 26

Suppose that a statute in a state provides as follows:

Section 10: No marriage shall be invalid on account of want of authority in any person solemnizing the same if consummated with the full belief on the part of the persons so married, or either of them, that they were lawfully joined in marriage.

15. On the grounds for annulment, see infra p. 177ff.

16. On the grounds for divorce, see infra p. 307ff.

17. See infra p. 177ff.

George and Linda are married in this state, but the minister, Rev. Smith, who married them had no authority to marry anyone. The minister was in charge of the Triple Faith Church. George and Linda read a story in the paper a week before they were married that five of the seven ministers connected with the Triple Faith Church had been fined for illegally performing marriage ceremonies. George and Linda did not know that Rev. Smith was one of the five and they did not bother to ask. Can the validity of their marriage be called into question under section 10? (See also General Instructions for the Legal Analysis Assignment, supra p. 16.) Would it be invalid in your state?

SUMMARY

1. The main way by which people become married is through a ceremonial marriage.
2. Each state has statutory requirements for ceremonial marriages which usually involve the license, the authority of the person performing the ceremony, witnesses, waiting periods, medical examinations and recording the license or the facts involving the marriage ceremony.
3. In most states, the failure of anyone to follow these requirements will not void or invalidate the marriage, although the violators may be subjected to penalties. In a few states, however, the validity of the marriage *can* be effected by a violation of these technical requirements for a ceremonial marriage.
4. A distinction must be made between the technical requirements for a ceremonial marriage and the requirements which must exist before a person can have the legal capacity to marry and the requirements relating to the necessary intention to marry (the latter requirements will be discussed in later chapters.)

[B7881]

NOTES

1. In some states, a proxy marriage is possible where the marriage ceremony is carried out with one or both parties being absent at the time. A third party agent must be given the authority to act on behalf of the missing party during the ceremony.

2. For a discussion of what happens when a couple go to another state to be married solely to avoid the requirements for a ceremonial marriage in their own state, see infra p. 227ff.

SECTION C. COMMON LAW MARRIAGE

A common law marriage is a union of two people who have not gone through a wedding ceremony or complied with the requirements for a ceremonial marriage discussed in the preceding section. In our society, a vast number of people live together in what some of the religions refer to as "the state of sin." [18] The question before us is whether any of these individuals have entered a common law marriage even though they may never have heard of this kind of marriage. If the conditions of a common law marriage have been fulfilled, then the marriage is as valid as a ceremonial marriage. To end a valid common law marriage, for example, the parties must go through a divorce proceeding in the same manner as any other married couple seeking to dissolve its marriage.

Many states have abolished common law marriages. Even in such states, however, it is important to know something about common law marriages for the following reasons:

—Parties may enter a common law marriage in a state where such marriages are valid and then move to a state which has abolished such marriages. Under traditional conflict of law principles, as we shall see, the second state may have to recognize the marriage as valid.

—It may be that your state once recognized common law marriages as valid, but then on a certain date abolished all such marriages for the future. A number of people may still live in your state who entered valid common law marriages before the law was changed, and hence, their marriages may still be valid.

For people who have not entered ceremonial marriages, the question of whether they were married by common law usually arises after one of the parties has died and the survivor:

(a) wishes to claim a share of the deceased's will;

(b) seeks dower [19] or curtesy [20] rights;

(c) seeks an intestate share [21] if the deceased left no will;

(d) wants to sue for wrongful death of his/her "spouse";

(e) seeks social security benefits or workmen's compensation benefits through the deceased.

The question is also crucial for children: children born from a valid common law marriage are legitimate.[22]

Assignment # 27

Is there a statute in your state which abolishes common law marriages? If so, what is the effective date of this statute? If not, are common law marriages valid in your state? (See also General Instructions for the State Code Assignment, supra p. 14.)

18. See also supra p. 142.

19. Supra p. 128.

20. Supra p. 128.

21. To die intestate is to die without leaving a valid will. The spouse and the heirs of the deceased inherit his/her assets.

22. See infra p. 449ff.

What conditions must exist for a valid common law marriage (in states that recognize such marriages)? Not all states have the same requirements.[23] Generally, however, the following is applicable:

ELEMENTS OF A VALID COMMON LAW MARRIAGE
1. The parties must have the legal capacity to marry.[24] 2. There must be a present agreement to enter a marital relationship—to become husband and wife to each other. (Some states require an express agreement to this effect, while other states imply the existence of this agreement from the manner in which the man and woman relate to each other.) 3. The parties must actually live together as husband and wife, i. e., there must be cohabitation. 4. There must be an openness about the relationship; the parties must hold themselves out as husband and wife, i. e., they must make representations to the world that they are husband and wife.

[B7880]

In some states, there is a reluctance on the part of the courts to find that all of these elements are present in a particular case. Common law marriages may be disfavored by the court *even in a state where such marriages are legal.* The fear is as follows: two people will decide to live together solely for sexual reasons; one will die and the survivor will claim that they were really married in order to take advantage of benefits available only to surviving spouses. Such courts often require "clear and convincing" evidence that all the elements exist.

23. Furthermore, there is confusion in some states as to whether a particular requirement is a separate element of a common law marriage or is simply stated as evidence of one of the other elements. See Clark, H., *The Law of Domestic Relations*, p. 49 (1968).

24. On legal capacity, see also supra p. 110, and infra p. 177ff.

INTERVIEWING AND INVESTIGATION CHECKLIST

Factors Relevant to the Formation of a Common Law Marriage Between C (Client) and D (Defendant)

	Legal Interviewing Questions
1.	On what date did you first meet D?
2.	When did the two of you first begin talking about living together? Describe the circumstances. Who said what, etc.
3.	Did you or D ever discuss living together with anyone else?
4.	On what date did you actually move in together? How long have you been living together?
5.	In whose name was the lease taken? (Or, in whose name was the deed to the house taken in which you lived?)
6.	Do you have separate or joint bank accounts? If joint, what names appear on the account?
7.	Who pays the rent (or the mortgage)?
8.	Who pays the utility bills?
9.	Who pays the food bills?
10.	Since you have been living together, have you filed separate or joint tax returns?
11.	Have you ever made a written agreement that you and D were going to be married? Have you ever made an oral agreement to this effect?
12.	Why didn't you ever go through a marriage ceremony?
13.	When you and D went out and had to introduce each other to other people, how was this done? Did you ever introduce each other as "my husband" or "my wife?"
14.	Name any relatives, neighbors, business associates, friends etc. who think of you and D as husband and wife.
15.	Did you and D ever discuss making individual or joint wills?
16.	Did you and D ever separate for any period of time? If so, describe the circumstances.
17.	Did you and D ever have any children or adopt any? If so what last name did the children have?
18.	On any insurance policies, is either of you the beneficiary? How is the premium paid?
19.	During your life with D, what other indications exist that the two of you treated each other as husband and wife?

Possible Investigation Tasks

* If C indicates that C or D discussed their moving in together with anyone else, obtain a witness statement (affidavit) from such individuals.
* Obtain a copy of the lease. (Or, of the deed.)
* Obtain copies of bills, receipts, tax returns, etc. to determine how the names of C and D appear.
* Obtain copy of any agreements between C and D.
* Interview anyone C indicates would think of C and D as husband and wife.
* Obtain birth certificates of children, if any.

Two situations remain to be considered: the conflicts of law problem and the impediment removal cases.

CONFLICT OF LAW

> Bill and Pat live in state "X" where common law marriages are legal. They enter such a marriage. They then move to state "Y" where common law marriages have been abolished. A child is born to them in state "Y." Bill is injured on the job and dies. Pat claims workmen's compensation benefits as the "wife" of Bill. Will the state of "Y" recognize Pat as married to Bill? Is their child legitimate?

What law governs the validity of their "marriage"? The answer is that the law where the marriage was contracted will generally govern its validity. Pat and Bill's marriage was contracted in the state of "X" where it is valid. The state of "Y," therefore, will accept the marriage as valid even though it would have been invalid if it had been entered into in state "Y." Pat is married to Bill and their child is legitimate.[25] (Later we will discuss the separate problem of what happens when the parties move to another state solely to take advantage of the other state's more lenient marriage laws and then return to their original state after the marriage.[26])

IMPEDIMENT REMOVAL:

> In 1919, Ernestine enters a valid ceremonial marriage with Johnson. They begin having marital trouble and separate. In 1935, Ernestine and Henry begin living together. Ernestine never divorced Johnson. She and Henry cohabitate and hold each other out as husband and wife in a state where common law marriages are valid. But for the existence of the 1919 marriage to Johnson, it is clear that Ernestine and Henry would have been married by common law. In 1951, Johnson obtains a divorce from Ernestine. Henry and Ernestine continue to live together in the same manner as they had since 1935. In 1957, Henry dies. Ernestine claims death benefits under the Longshoremen's and Harbor Workers' Compensation Act as his surviving "wife." Was she ever married to Henry?

Ernestine and Henry never entered a ceremonial marriage. Up until 1951, a serious impediment existed to their being able to marry: Ernestine was already married to someone else and an attempted second marriage would probably be bigamous.[27] The impediment was the existence of a prior undissolved marriage. In 1951, however, that marriage was dissolved by the divorce, i. e., the impediment was removed. The issue is (a) whether Ernestine and Henry would be con-

25. See also infra p. 449.

26. Supra p. 227.

27. On bigamy, see also infra p. 177.

sidered to have entered a valid common law marriage at the time the impediment is removed (since, in effect, they had been living together as husband and wife for all these years) or, (b) whether at the time the impediment is removed they would have to enter a *new* common law marriage agreement, express or implied. In most states, they would not have to enter a new agreement. An earlier agreement to marry (by common law) will carry forward to the time the impediment is removed so long as the parties have continued to live together openly as husband and wife. Accordingly, Ernestine automatically became the wife of Henry when the impediment of the prior marriage was removed since she and Henry continued to live together openly as husband and wife after that time. As one court put it:

> "It is not to be expected that parties once having agreed to be married will deem it necessary to agree to do so again when an earlier marriage is terminated or some other bar to union is eliminated." [28]

In the states which reach this result, it makes no difference that either or both of the parties knew of the impediment at the time they initially agreed to live as husband and wife.

Assignment # 28

Examine the following sequence of events:

(a) Ann and Rich meet in state "Y" where they agree to live together as man and wife forever. They do not want to go through a marriage ceremony, but they agree to be married and openly represent themselves as such. The state of "Y" does not recognize common law marriages.

(b) Rich gets a job offer in state "X" and they both move there. State "X" recognizes common law marriages, i. e., they can be validly entered in State "X."

(c) After three years in state "X," Rich and Ann move back to state "Y." One year later, Rich dies. In his will, he leaves all his property "to my wife." Ann is not mentioned by name in his will.

(d) From the time they met up until the time of Rich's death, they lived together as husband and wife and everyone who knew them thought of them as such.

Can Ann claim under the will? State "Y" provides tax benefits to "widows." Can Ann claim these benefits? (See also General Instructions for the Legal Analysis Assignment, supra p. 16.)

28. Matthews v. Britton, 303 F.2d 408, 409 (1962).

NOTE ON PUTATIVE MARRIAGES

In a few states (e. g., Louisiana, Texas), putative marriages are recognized. "A putative marriage is one which has been contracted in good faith and in ignorance of some existing impediment on the part of at least one of the contracting parties. Three circumstances must occur to constitute this species of marriage: (1) There must be bona fides. At least one of the parties must have been ignorant of the impediment, not only at the time of the marriage, but must also have continued ignorant of it during his or her life. (2) The marriage must be duly solemnized. (3) The marriage must have been considered lawful in the estimation of the parties or of that party who alleges the bona fides." United States Fidelity & Guarantee Co. v. Henderson, 53 S.W.2d 811, 816 (Tex.Civ.App.1932).

SUMMARY

1. A common law marriage is one created by agreement of the parties without going through the statutory steps of a ceremonial marriage. Two thirds of the states do not recognize common law marriages unless they do so under conflict of law principles.
2. Not all states have the same requirements for a common law marriage. Generally, the following is required: legal capacity to marry, a present agreement to be married and open cohabitation.
3. If parties enter an otherwise valid common law marriage but for the existence of an impediment to the marriage, and that impediment is removed while the parties are still openly cohabitating, they will be considered to have validly entered a common law marriage at the moment of removal without the necessity of any new agreement to be married. Note, however, that not all states follow this rule; some states require proof that a new agreement to marry has been made by the parties after the removal of the impediment.

[B7879]

Chapter Ten

ANNULMENT: INTRODUCTION

In this introductory chapter on annulment, we will cover a number of topics:

1. Definitions: annulment, divorce and separation.
2. The void/voidable distinction.
3. Kinds of annulment actions.
4. Who can sue?
5. The conflicts problem.
6. Presumption that the marriage is valid.
7. Grounds: a summary.

1. DEFINITIONS: ANNULMENT, DIVORCE AND LEGAL SEPARATION

An *annulment* is a declaration that the marriage never existed. In a sense, it is technically incorrect to refer to an "annulled marriage." The word "marriage" means the legal union of two people as husband and wife. If reasons (i. e., grounds) exist to substantiate the initial illegality of the union, then no marriage ever existed in spite of the license, the ceremony, consummation and perhaps even children. While you will frequently see reference to the phrase, "suit to annul a marriage," it would be more technically correct to use the phrase, "suit to annul an attempted marriage," or "suit to declare the validity or invalidity of a marriage." A *divorce* is a legal dissolution of a marriage that once validly existed.[1] In a divorce, there is something to dissolve; in an annulment, there is simply a judicial statement or declaration that no marital relationship existed between the parties at the outset. A *legal separation* is a mutual agreement and/or a court order that the parties live apart, i. e., that there be a termination of the "bed and board" relationship between the parties.[2] Parties so separated are still legally married; they cannot remarry unless they later obtain a divorce.

When you are interviewing a client who wishes to dissolve his/her marital relationship, you must always be thinking of the three options of annulment, divorce and legal separation. This is so, even though, as we shall see later, the law covering the three options is becoming more and more blurred and the distinctions among them are no longer

1. Another phrase sometimes used for divorce is "divorce a vinculo matrimonii," or an "absolute divorce." See also infra p. 345.

2. Another phrase sometimes used for a legal separation is "divorce a mensa et thoro," or a "limited divorce." See also infra p. 345.

as important as they once were. There still, however, are separate suits or actions for annulment, divorce and legal separation in most states. Some of the practical reasons you must be alert to all three possibilities are as follows:

- —The procedural requirements for the three actions may differ, e. g., there may be different pleading rules for the three actions. One of the factors to be considered in deciding which action to pursue is the relative procedural burdens imposed by the three actions.[3]
- —It may be that an opposing party would not fight (i. e., contest) one action but would fight another. For example, a party might be willing to cooperate and not contest a legal separation action, but would contest a divorce or annulment action.
- —Different tax considerations may have to be considered.
- —Statutory grounds exist for each of the three actions. The grounds for the three actions are not always mutually exclusive. There are both similarities and differences among the grounds for the three actions. Sometimes a client can choose from among any of the three actions since his/her evidence would be sufficient to establish the grounds for all three. The choice might be dependent, in part, on local practice peculiarities, e. g., it may be that certain judges have a reputation for favoring one kind of action over another.

A good deal of our attention in the remaining chapters of this book will be devoted to an analysis of the grounds (and the defenses to these grounds) for annulment,[4] divorce [5] and separation,[6] and to an analysis of the interrelationship among the three actions.

2. THE VOID/VOIDABLE DISTINCTION

An *invalid* marriage is one that is not recognized by law; it is an illegal marriage. An "annulled marriage" is an invalid marriage. There are two kinds of invalid marriages:

A. The marriage is invalid *whether or not any court ever declares its invalidity* (VOID).

B. The marriage is invalid *only if a court declares that it is invalid* (VOIDABLE).

If no one brings an action to invalidate a *voidable* marriage, it will always be considered a valid marriage. No such court action, however, is necessary if the marriage is *void*. If a court declares a voidable marriage to be invalid, the invalidity generally relates back to the

3. In some states, the complaint (see supra p. 233) can ask for *either* a divorce or an annulment, i. e., they can be pleaded in the alternative.

4. Infra p. 177ff.

5. Infra p. 307ff.

6. Infra p. 406.

moment when the marriage was attempted.[7] Similarly, a void marriage is considered invalid from the time the parties tried to enter it. A void marriage is referred to as one *void ab initio,* i. e., invalid from the very beginning. As we study the grounds for annulment, we will see that certain grounds will render the marriage void, while other grounds will render it voidable only.

How can you determine whether a particular ground for annulment will render the marriage void or voidable? Generally, the answer can be found in the state's statutory code.[8] Different states may reach different conclusions on what is void and what is voidable. Unfortunately, a given state's code may not be clear on the subject. When we examine each of the grounds in detail in the next two chapters, you will be asked in the assignments to determine whether a particular ground renders the marriage void or voidable in your state.

3. KINDS OF ANNULMENT ACTIONS

States use different terminology to describe the proceeding:

—an action for annulment;

—a suit to annul;

—a libel for annulment;

—an action for declaratory judgment;

—an action to affirm the validity of a marriage;

—etc.

If the marriage is voidable, it is essential that an annulment action (or whatever the proceeding is called in your state) be brought. If it is not brought, as indicated above, the marriage will be considered valid. Suppose, however that the marriage is void. Technically, there is no need to bring any court action since the marriage is void whether or not a court has declared it so. Nevertheless, parties still use the courts to seek judicial declarations of void marriages in order to remove any doubt that the marriage is invalid. People feel a lot more secure when a court has ruled on the validity of the marriage.

4. WHO CAN SUE?

As we study each of the grounds for annulment, one of the questions we must ask ourselves is: who can be the plaintiff to bring the annulment action? It may be, for example, that the wrongdoer (i. e., the party who knowingly did the act which constituted the ground for the annulment) will *not* be able to bring the action. This party will lack *standing* to bring the action. If the *innocent* party refuses to bring the action, or if the innocent party is no longer living, it may be that the marriage can never be annuled. The wrongdoing party, in

7. For more on this "relation back" doctrine, see infra 213.

8. On statutes and statutory codes, see supra p. 14.

effect, is prevented (sometimes called *estopped*) from getting out of what might clearly be an invalid marriage. Such a marriage is sometimes referred to as a "marriage by estoppel." The wrongdoing party has "dirty hands" by reason of his/her wrongdoing and should not be allowed to "profit" by this wrongdoing through a court action seeking an annulment. As we shall see, however, whether or not a wrongdoing party will be estopped from bringing the annulment action may depend on whether the marriage is void or voidable. Prohibitions, if any, on who can initiate the litigation must be examined for each ground.

5. THE CONFLICTS PROBLEM

The facts constituting the ground for annulment may have occurred in more than one state, or the ground may occur in one state, but the annulment action may be brought in another state where one or both parties now reside. What law governs? This question can be of critical importance given the fact that there are some significant differences from state to state in the grounds for annulment and in the procedures followed to bring an annulment action.

6. PRESUMPTION THAT THE MARRIAGE IS VALID

Generally, the party claiming that the marriage is invalid has the *burden of proof*, meaning that this party must establish that the grounds for annulment exist. The law looks with disfavor on actions to invalidate marriages. Hence, to aid the party seeking to defend the validity of the marriage, the law has established a number of *presumptions*,[9] the most significant of which is that a marriage of parties living together as husband and wife is presumed to be valid. This presumption is *rebuttable* so that the party attacking the validity of the marriage can attempt to introduce evidence that the grounds for an annulment do in fact exist. If this party failed to introduce any such evidence, then the presumption would be conclusive. As we examine the grounds for annulment, this presumption that a marriage is valid should be kept in mind.

7. GROUNDS IN ANNULMENT ACTIONS: A SUMMARY

In the next two chapters, we shall look at the major grounds for annulment in the United States. There are essentially two kinds of grounds: those that relate to a party's *legal capacity* to marry and those that focus on whether or not a party with legal capacity to marry formed the requisite *intent* to marry. In addition, the defenses that apply to one or more of these grounds will also be explored.

9. For more on presumptions, see infra p. 180.

ANNULMENT GROUNDS: AN OVERVIEW (The page references are to pages in this text where the grounds and defenses are discussed.)	
GROUNDS RELATING TO LEGAL CAPACITY TO MARRY	**Page References**
1. Pre-existing marriage	Infra p. 177
2. Improper relationship by blood or by marriage	Infra p. 183
3. Nonage	Infra p. 186
4. Physical disabilities	Infra p. 190
5. Sex of the parties	Infra p. 194
GROUNDS RELATING TO THE INTENT TO MARRY	**Page References**
6. Sham marriages	Infra p. 195
7. Mental disabilities	Infra p. 198
8. Duress	Infra p. 203
9. Fraud	Infra p. 205

IM-455

NOTE

The Catholic Church has its own separate system of annulment and annulment procedure. Over 7,000 annulments are granted by the Church each year. The major ground for a Church annulment is "lack of due discretion." One or both of the parties to the marriage must have been mentally or emotionally unfit at the time they entered into marriage. The person or persons must be basically immature and incapable of marriage with anyone. Walker, L., "Divorce, Annulment, and the Alternatives—Catholics and Their Church," 1 *Family Law Reporter* 4057, No. 34 (July 15, 1975).

*

Chapter Eleven

ANNULMENT: GROUNDS RELATING TO THE LEGAL CAPACITY TO MARRY

SECTION A. PRIOR EXISTING MARRIAGE (BIGAMY)

In this section, we need to consider both the civil and the criminal consequences of entering a second marriage when the first marriage has not ended.

(a) Crime

Entering a second marriage, or even attempting to enter such a marriage, when the first marriage has not ended by death, annulment or divorce, is a felony in most states. Polygamy is a crime. It is not a defense that the party did not know that it is illegal to marry twice. Suppose, however, that John enters a valid common law marriage [1] with Mary and then marries Jane. As John understands the law, the second marriage was proper because the first marriage was invalid due to the fact that he and Mary never obtained a marriage license. Here again, ignorance of the law, or a mistake of law, would not be a defense unless the statute defining the crime specifically requires that there be a "knowing" violation of the prohibition.[2] Two special circumstances need to be considered:

- —Is it a defense to the crime that the spouse has disappeared and has not been heard from for a period of years (the Enoch Arden defense)?
- —Is it a defense to the crime that the party reasonably believed that the prior marriage had been validly terminated by divorce or annulment?

Some states allow the *Enoch Arden* defense which provides that after the passage of a designated number of years, the disappeared spouse will be presumed dead. Death established in this way will be a defense to a bigamy prosecution following the second marriage. States may differ on the elements of the Enoch Arden defense, e. g., differences as to the length of the disappearance, differences on the requirement of diligence in trying to locate the missing spouse, etc.

The second situation, involving a reasonable belief that the prior marriage ended in divorce or annulment, is more troublesome. Suppose that John obtains a divorce decree against Mary, and then proceeds to marry Jane. The divorce decree is invalid for one reason or

1. Supra p. 164ff.

2. See generally, Perkins, R., *Criminal Law*, 331, 836ff. (1957).

another, but John is unaware of this at the time he marries Jane. In some states, John's bona fide reliance on the divorce *would* be a defense, whereas in other states, the public policy favoring monogamy is so strong that it would *not* be a defense. In the latter states, it is the act of the second marriage that is crucial and not the intent of the party entering the second marriage.

Assignment # 29

(a) Is there a statute in your state defining the crime of bigamy? If so, give the citation to the statute and state each element of the crime.

(b) What defenses, if any, are listed in the statute to the crime of bigamy?

(See also General Instructions for the State Code Assignment, supra p. 14.)

(c) Draft a checklist of questions you would ask in order to determine whether the above statute(s) have been violated. (See also General Instructions for the Checklist Formulation Assignment, supra p. 29.)

(d) Draft a flow chart of the procedural steps that would constitute a criminal prosecution for this crime in your state. (See also General Instructions for the Flow Chart Assignment, supra p. 33.)

(b) ANNULMENT: THE CIVIL ACTION

Our next concern is the existence of a prior undissolved marriage as a ground for an annulment of a second (attempted) marriage. In most states, a bigamous marriage is void ab initio;[3] in only a few states is it voidable. Whether it is void or voidable, however, it is often wise to seek a declaration of invalidity from a court, even though such a declaration would technically not be necessary if the marriage is void.

As with our discussion of bigamy, we need to examine two special circumstances: (1) the spouse who has disappeared, and (2) the cloudy situation of whether the prior marriage ended in a divorce or annulment, or indeed whether the first marriage was ever validly contracted.

(1) The missing spouse

Again we must consider the effect of Enoch Arden laws. As indicated above, states have different requirements for calling into play the Enoch Arden provision which enables us to assume that the missing spouse is dead. We have already looked at Enoch Arden as a defense to a criminal prosecution for bigamy. We now examine a quite

3. Supra p. 173. On the consequences of a marriage being declared void or voidable, see infra p. 213.

separate question: what are the consequences of Enoch Arden on the second marriage in an annulment proceeding? Paul marries Cynthia. Cynthia disappears. Paul has not heard from her for fifteen years in spite of all his efforts to locate her. Paul then marries Mary in the honest belief that his first wife is dead. Mary does not know anything about Cynthia. Suddenly Cynthia reappears and Mary learns about the first marriage. Mary immediately brings an action against Paul to annul her marriage to him, on the ground of a prior existing marriage (bigamy). The question is whether or not Paul can raise the defense of Enoch Arden. Can Paul contest the annulment action against him by arguing that he had a right to presume that his first wife was dead? The states differ in their answer to this question. Here are some of the different ways that the states handle this question:

—Enoch Arden applies only to criminal prosecutions for bigamy; the presumption of death does not apply to annulment proceedings.

—Enoch Arden does apply to annulment proceedings; the missing spouse is presumed dead. The second marriage is valid and cannot be annulled even if the missing spouse later appears.

—Enoch Arden does apply to annulment proceedings; the missing spouse is presumed dead. If, however, the missing spouse later appears, the second marriage can be annulled. Hence, the Enoch Arden defense is effective only if the missing spouse stays missing.

Assignment # 30

(a) Is a ground for annulment in your state the existence of a prior undissolved marriage? If so, give the code citation and quote from the pertinent part of the statute which establishes this ground.

(b) Is the second marriage void or voidable in your state?

(c) Does your state have an Enoch Arden provision? If so, what are its elements and what effect, if any, does it have on the second marriage?

(See also General Instructions for the State Code Assignment, supra p. 14. You may also need to check case law on the latter two questions. See General Instructions for the Court Opinion Assignment, supra p. 26.)

(2) Was the prior marriage valid? Did it end in divorce or annulment?

When a claim is made in an annulment proceeding that the second marriage is invalid, one of the common responses (defenses) to this claim is that the first marriage was never valid or that the first marriage ended in a divorce or annulment. Marriage records, particularly old ones, are sometimes difficult to obtain,[4] and of course, for common law marriages,[5] there simply are no records. Divorce and annulment records can also be difficult to obtain.[6] Given this situation, it can be a monumental task to prove what the status of a prior marriage is, i. e., whether it was properly contracted, whether it was dissolved. To assist parties in this difficult situation, the law has created a number of presumptions: [7]

—a marriage is presumed to be valid [8] ;

—when more than one marriage exists, the latest marriage is presumed to be valid.

The effect of the second presumption is that the court will treat the first marriage as having been dissolved by death of the first spouse, by divorce or by annulment. Note, however, that the presumption is rebuttable which means that the party seeking to annul the second marriage can attempt to rebut (i. e., attack) the presumption by introducing evidence (a) that the first spouse is still alive, or (b) that the first marriage was *not* dissolved by divorce or annulment. The presumption favoring the validity of the latest marriage is so strong, however, that some states require considerable proof to overcome or rebut it.

One final point needs to be considered on this ground for annulment. In the preceding chapter it was pointed out that the law sometimes places prohibitions on who can be a plaintiff in annulment actions.[9] The party with "dirty hands," (i. e., the "guilty" party, the wrongdoer) is sometimes denied the right to bring the annulment action. When the ground for the annulment is prior existing marriage, the party with "dirty hands" is obviously the one who had a prior marriage outstanding at the time of the second marriage. Should the law permit this individual to invalidate the second marriage because of his/her own wrongdoing? In a few states, the answer is no; only the innocent party to the second marriage can seek to invalidate it. If the innocent party in these few states decides not to annul the marriage, it cannot be annulled. This, however, is a minority view. In most states, the second marriage is annulable by *either* party so long as the presumption of the validity of the second marriage is successfully rebutted, e. g., by introducing clear evidence of the continued existence of the first marriage.

NOTES

(1) In a few states, prisoners convicted of certain serious felonies are considered "civilly dead." See Singer, R. & Statsky, W., "Collater-

4. On where to write to obtain marriage records, see infra p. 522.

5. Supra p. 164.

6. On where to write to obtain divorce records, see infra p. 517.

7. On presumptions and the burden of proof, see also supra p. 174.

8. Supra p. 174.

9. Supra p. 173.

al Consequences of Conviction and Civil Adjudication," in *Rights of the Imprisoned: Cases, Materials and Directions*, p. 1096 (Bobbs-Merrill, 1974). One consequence of such a "death" is that the spouse of the inmate may be free to enter a second marriage. In most states certain kinds of imprisonment are grounds for divorce[10] rather than for annulment.

(2) In many states, the existence of a prior undissolved marriage is a ground for divorce as well as for annulment.[11]

(3) The existence of a prior undissolved marriage is an impediment to a second marriage. There are circumstances, however, as discussed in Chapter Nine when a valid common law marriage will arise at the moment this impediment ceases, e. g., by the death of the first spouse.[12]

SUMMARY GROUND FOR ANNULMENT: PRIOR EXISTING MARRIAGE	
DEFINITION: The existence of a prior valid marriage which has not been dissolved by divorce, annulment or the death of the first spouse.	
VOID OR VOIDABLE: In most states, the establishment of this ground renders the second marriage void.	
WHO CAN SUE: In most states, either party to the second marriage can bring the annulment action on this ground.	
MAJOR DEFENSES:	(1) the first spouse is dead (Enoch Arden); (2) the first marriage was not validly entered; (3) the first marriage ended by divorce or annulment; (4) the plaintiff has "dirty hands" (available in a few states); (5) statute of limitations or laches (the plaintiff waited too long to bring the annulment action, see infra p. 232); (6) the court lacks jurisdiction (see infra p. 223).
IS THIS ANNULMENT GROUND ALSO A GROUND FOR DIVORCE: yes, in most states (see infra p. 335).	

[B7878]

10. Infra p. 335.

11. Infra p. 335.

12. Supra p. 168.

INTERVIEWING AND INVESTIGATION CHECKLIST

FACTORS RELEVANT TO PRIOR EXISTING MARRIAGE AS A GROUND FOR ANNULMENT

(C = Client; S = Spouse; P = Plaintiff seeking annulment)

	Legal Interviewing Questions	Possible Investigation Tasks
1.	When were you married to S?	* Search marriage records in the county where C married S.
2.	Did you go through a marriage ceremony with S? (If not, ask questions nos. 1–19 supra 167 to determine whether C and S entered a valid common law marriage.)	* Contact the local police to determine whether S has ever been reported as a missing person.
3.	Is S alive now? If not, was S alive at the time you married P?	* Contact all of S's friends, relatives and co-workers, etc. to see if they knew where S was during the period after C last saw S.
4.	When did you last see S? How long ago was it?	* Contact court clerk in counties where C or S might have filed divorce or annulment papers to see if any such records exist.
5.	Describe the circumstances of the last time you saw S. Have the two of you phoned or written to each other since then?	* If S is alive and available, obtain a witness statement from S on the details of S's relationship with C.
6.	Describe everything you did to try to contact S. Did you speak with any of his friends, relatives or co-workers concerning his whereabouts? Did you call the police? Check with the military, social security, VA, Motor Vehicles Bureau, Internal Revenue Service, Union, etc.?	
7.	Did you and S ever discuss a divorce or annulment of your marriage? If so, did you consult an attorney? Were any court proceedings instituted? If so, what happened?	
8.	Do you have any reason to believe that S married someone else after you and S separated?	
9.	At the time you married P, did you think that your marriage with S was still valid?	
10.	At the time you married P, did P know about S?	
11.	How have you supported yourself since S's absence?	

IM–467

Assignment # 31

On December 10, 1960, Brenda entered a valid ceremonial marriage with Jim. On August 21, 1962, Jim goes on a sailing trip alone. He is never seen nor heard from again. Last month Brenda met Bob. They agree to be married. (Bob does not know anything about Jim.) Ten days ago, they were married. On the day after the wedding, Brenda tells Bob about Jim. Bob wants to annul his marriage with Brenda because of her prior marriage with Jim. Draft an annulment complaint for Bob on the ground of the prior existing marriage. (See also General Instructions for the Complaint Drafting Assignment, supra p. 20.)

SECTION B. CONSANGUINITY AND AFFINITY LIMITATIONS

There are two ways that you can be related to someone: by blood or by marriage. If you are related by blood, you are related by *consanguinity*; if you are related by marriage, you are related by *affinity*. State statutes prohibit certain individuals related by consanguinity and related by affinity from marrying. Violating these prohibitions can be a ground for annulment of the marriage. In most states, such marriages are void rather than voidable,[13] and either party can bring the action to annul the marriage.

States generally agree that certain relationships are *incestuous*: marriage of parent and child, brother and sister, grandparent and grandchild, etc. Most of the disagreement is in the area of cousin-cousin marriages, and in the area of affinity relationships.

The *crime* of incest [14] is committed mainly by designated individuals related by consanguinity. Surprisingly, however, the crime can also be committed in some states by designated individuals related by affinity.

The following assignment focuses on the legal capacity of related individuals to marry in your state:

Assignment # 32

In the following list, there are pairs of individuals mentioned. For each pair, go to your state code and answer three questions: can the individuals marry, what code section gives you the answer, and if the marriage is prohibited, is it void or voidable? (See also General Instructions for the State Code Assignment, supra p. 14.)

(a) Mother/son. Can they marry? __NO__ Void or voidable? __32__ Code section __205__.

(b) Father/daughter. Can they marry? __NO__ Void or voidable? __32__ Code section __205__.

(c) Brother/sister. Can they marry? __NO__ Void or voidable? __32__ Code section __205__.

(d) Grandparent/grandchild. Can they marry? __NO__ Void or voidable? __32__ Code section __205__.

(e) Uncle/niece or Aunt/nephew. Can they marry? __NO__ Void or voidable? __32__ Code section __205__.

(f) First cousin/first cousin. Can they marry? __NO__ Void or voidable? __32__ Code section __206__.

13. See also supra p. 172. On the consequences of a marriage being declared void or voidable, see infra p. 213.

14. The states differ on whether the crime of incest is committed only after sexual intercourse between the individuals, or whether it is sufficient that the prohibited individuals simply enter a marriage relationship.

(g) Second cousin/second cousin. Can they marry? ______ Void or voidable? ______ Code section ______.

(h) Half-brother/half-sister. Can they marry? ______ Void or voidable? ______ Code section ______.

(i) Father-in-law/daughter-in-law or Mother-in-law/son-in-law. Can they marry? ______ Void or voidable? ______ Code section ______.

(j) Brother-in-law/sister-in-law. Can they marry? ______ Void or voidable? ______ Code section ______.

(k) Step-parent/step-child. Can they marry? ______ Void or voidable? ______ Code section ______.

(*l*) Adoptive parent/adopted child. Can they marry? ______ Void or voidable? ______ Code section ______.

(m) God-parent/god-child. Can they marry? ______ Void or voidable? ______ Code section ______.

(If your state code does not provide a direct answer to any of the above questions, you may have to check court opinions. See General Instructions for the Court Opinion Assignment, supra p. 26.)

Assignment # 33

(a) Go to the sections in your state code that define criminal behavior. Determine how many, if any, of the marriages mentioned in Assignment # 32 (a to m) would subject the parties to criminal prosecution. (See also General Instructions for the State Code Assignment, supra p. 14.)

(b) Draft a flow chart of the procedural steps that would constitute a criminal prosecution for any of the crimes you identified in (a) above. (See also General Instructions for the Flow Chart Assignment, supra p. 33.)

(c) What questions would you ask the individuals mentioned in Assignment # 32 (a to m) in order to help determine whether any of them have violated the criminal code of your state? (See also General Instructions for the Checklist Formulation Assignment, supra p. 29.)

NOTES

(1) Since relationship by affinity depends upon marriage rather than blood, what happens to the prohibitions when the marriage ends by the death of the spouse who created the affinity relationship for the other spouse? Can the surviving spouse *then* marry his/her in-laws? Not all states agree. Some states allow such marriages, while others maintain the prohibition even after the death of the spouse who created the affinity relationship for the other spouse.

(2) The Uniform Marriage and Divorce Act [15] (section 207) would prohibit all marriages between ancestors and descendants, would pro-

15. Uniform Laws are a set of proposed laws which can be adopted, modified or rejected by any of the state legislatures.

hibit brother-sister marriages, would prohibit adopted brother-sister marriages, would *permit* first cousin marriages and would *permit* all affinity marriages.

(3) States differ on whether two adopted children in the same family can marry.

SUMMARY GROUND FOR ANNULMENT: PROHIBITED CONSANGUINITY OR AFFINITY RELATIONSHIP
DEFINITION: State statutes declare that persons lack the legal capacity to marry if they are related by consanguinity (blood) or by affinity (marriage) in the manner specified in those statutes.
VOID OR VOIDABLE: In most states, the prohibited marriage is void.
WHO CAN SUE: Either party can be the plaintiff in the annulment action.
MAJOR DEFENSES: (1) the parties are not prohibitively related by blood or marriage; (2) the spouse who created the affinity relationship for the other spouse has died (this defense is available only for affinity relationships and only in some states); (3) statute of limitations or laches (the plaintiff waited too long to bring the annulment action, see infra p. 232); (4) the court lacks jurisdiction (see infra p. 223).
IS THIS ANNULMENT GROUND ALSO A GROUND FOR DIVORCE: yes, in most states (infra p. 335).

[B7975]

INTERVIEWING AND INVESTIGATION CHECKLIST

Factors Relevant to Consanguinity and Affinity as a Ground for Annulment

(C = Client; P = Plaintiff)

	Legal Interviewing Questions	Possible Investigation Tasks
1.	Before you married P, what was your relationship to P?	* Obtain birth certificates, marriage records in order to substantiate who is related to whom. If helpful, draw a family tree graphically showing P's relationship to C.
2.	Are you related by blood (child, cousin, etc.)?	
3.	If so, through whom?	
4.	Are you related by marriage (brother-in-law, etc.)?	
5.	If so, through which marriage?	

IM-456

Assignment # 34

In Assignment # 32, supra p. 183, you identified marriages that would be prohibited in your state. Pick any one of the marriages that is prohibited in your state and draft a complaint for the plaintiff seeking its annulment. You can make up the names of the parties, their address, the date of their attempted marriage (which your complaint is going to try to annul) and any other facts that you need to draft the complaint. Assume that you want to have the complaint ready to file in a week. (See also General Instructions for the Complaint Drafting Assignment, supra p. 20.)

SECTION C. NONAGE

In order to marry, a party must be of a certain minimum age. This age may differ, however, depending upon:

—whether the party is a male and parental consent exists;

—whether the party is a female and parental consent exists;

—whether the party is a male and parental consent does not exist;

—whether the party is a female and parental consent does not exist;

—whether the female is already pregnant;

—whether a child has already been born out of wedlock.

In some states, a *court* may have the power to authorize a marriage of parties under age even if a parent or guardian has refused to consent to the marriage. In these states, the court will consider such factors as the maturity of the parties, their financial resources, whether children (to be born or already born) would be illegitimate if the marriage was not authorized, etc. Still another variation in some states is the authority in the courts to require that under-age individuals go through premarital counseling as a condition of their being able to marry.

In most states, a marriage contracted in violation of the statutory age limitations is voidable; in only a few states is it void. Oddly, in some circumstances, the failure to obtain parental consent may have *no* effect on the validity of the marriage as in the following hypothetical:

> Assume that a state requires a male to be 18 years of age in order to marry. If, however, the male is between 18 and 21 he must have parental consent to marry. Jim is 19. He marries without parental consent. In most states, Jim's marriage cannot be annulled because he did not get parental consent so long as he is over the minimum marriageable age. In a few states, however, this is not so; the failure to obtain parental consent is a ground for annulment even if the person is over the minimum age.

As we shall see in a later chapter, a minor has a right to *disaffirm* contracts s/he has made.[16] In this chapter, we are discussing the contract to marry. A minor can disaffirm the marriage contract through an annulment action if that minor is below the minimum marriageable age discussed above. It is also possible for a minor to *affirm* or *ratify* a contract. This affirmance or ratification will obligate the minor to perform the contract. A marriage contract can also be affirmed or ratified by a minor who otherwise could have the marriage annulled on the ground of nonage. The general rule is that if a person who is under age continues to cohabitate (i. e., live as husband and wife) after that person reaches the age of majority (as specified in the statute), the marriage has been affirmed or ratified, and thereafter cannot be annulled on the ground of nonage. An under-aged person can bring an annulment action after s/he has reached the statutory age to marry so long as there is no cohabitation after reaching that age.

Suppose that John, age 25, marries Mary, age 13. Mary is under statutory age; John is not. The parties separate a year after the marriage. The marriage is invalid in the state because of Mary's age. Clearly, Mary, the under-aged party, can bring an annulment action on the ground of nonage. Can John? In most states, he cannot. A person who was of proper age at the time of the attempted marriage will not be allowed to assert the nonage of his/her partner. Suppose that Mary lied about her age to the clerk issuing the marriage licenses and to the minister who performed the ceremony. Does this bar her from bringing the annulment action? Does this give her such "dirty hands" [17] that a court will refuse to permit her to sue for the annulment? Surprisingly, this defense does not operate as a bar to prevent the under-aged party from being the plaintiff in the annulment action.[18] (The effects of misrepresentation or fraud on annulment actions will be discussed in greater detail later.[19])

As indicated above, most states impose different age limitations for males and females; females are usually allowed to marry at a younger age than males. Is this anti-male and/or anti-female sexism? It is very likely that this discrimination between males and females will be held unconstitutional as a denial of the equal protection of the laws.[20]

16. Infra p. 456.

17. Supra p. 173.

18. The situation might be different, however, if the party lied about his/her age to his/her prospective spouse.

19. Infra p. 205.

20. See Stanton v. Stanton, 421 U.S. 7, 95 S.Ct. 1373, 43 L.Ed.2d 688 (1975) and Phelps v. Bing, 58 Ill.2d 32, 316 N.E.2d 775 (1974).

NOTES

1. At common law,[21] a male was allowed to marry at 14 and a female at 12. These ages, of course, have been changed by statute in the states.

2. In most states, statutory rape charges can be brought against men who have sexual intercourse with females under a specified age, e. g., 16.[22] Furthermore, if a parent tries to "marry off" a child at an unconscionably young age, the parent might be prosecuted for the crime of contributing to the delinquency of a minor.

3. Some public high schools discriminate against married students, particularly pregnant girls. They might be excluded from extracurricular activities or asked to leave school altogether. Landis, *Attitudes and Policies Covering Marriage Among High School Students*, 18 Marriage and Family Living 128 (1956).

Assignment # 35

The following questions are to be answered by examining the statutory code in your state. (See also General Instructions for the State Code Assignment, supra p. 14.)

(a) What is the citation of the statute that determines the minimum marriage age? ____________________

____

(b) How old does a male have to be to marry? __________

(c) How old does a female have to be to marry? __________

(d) When, if ever, is parental consent to marry needed? ______

____

(e) What effect, if any, does pregnancy or birth of a child born out of wedlock have on the age to marry? __________

(f) When, if ever, can a court give consent to marry? ______

____

(g) Is the marriage of under-aged individuals void or voidable?

____

(h) Can either party to the marriage sue to have it annulled? ___

____

(i) Under what circumstances, if any, can parents or guardians sue to annul a marriage on the ground of nonage? ________

(j) Under what circumstances, if any, can the parties to the marriage affirm or ratify it? ____________________

21. Common law is judge made law in the absence of controlling statutory law.

22. See Perkins, R., *Criminal Law*, p. 112 (1957).

(If your state code does not provide a direct answer to some of the above questions, you may have to check court opinions. See General Instructions for the Court Opinion Assignment, supra p. 26.)

SUMMARY GROUND FOR ANNULMENT: NONAGE
DEFINITION: At the time of the marriage, one or both of the parties was under the minimum age to marry set by statute.
VOID OR VOIDABLE: In most states, the marriage is voidable.
WHO CAN SUE: Usually, only the under-aged party is allowed to bring the annulment action. In some states, the parent or guardian of the under-aged party can also sue.
MAJOR DEFENSES: (1) the parties were of the correct statutory age at the time of the marriage; (2) the under-aged party affirmed or ratified the marriage by cohabitation after that party reached the statutory minimum age; (3) the wrong party is bringing the suit (only the under-aged party has standing to sue in most states; in some states, the parent or guardian of the under-aged person also has standing); (4) even though the parties failed to obtain the parental consent as specified in the statute, the absence of this consent is not a ground for annulment (note, however, that in a few states, it *is* a ground); (5) the male-female age distinctions in the statute are illegal because they violate the equal protection clause of the constitution; (6) statute of limitations or laches (the plaintiff waited too long to bring the annulment action, see infra p. 232); (7) the court lacks jurisdiction (see infra p. 223).
IS THIS ANNULMENT GROUND ALSO A GROUND FOR DIVORCE: yes, in some states (see infra p. 335).

[B7971]

INTERVIEWING AND INVESTIGATION CHECKLIST FACTORS RELEVANT TO NONAGE AS A GROUND FOR ANNULMENT		
	Legal Interviewing Questions	**Possible Investigation Tasks**
1.	How old were you when you married D? How old was D?	* Birth certificates to establish age will be critical.
2.	Did either of you lie about your ages to each other? to your parents? to the marriage license clerk?	* Obtain copies of the marriage license application and the marriage certificate.
3.	When did you stop seeing D? How old were you at the time?	* Determine whether D might be able to call anyone as a witness who will testify as to C's relationship to D after C reached the age of majority.
4.	Since you left D (or since D left you), have you had sexual intercourse with each other? If so, how old were you at the time?	
5.	Since the two of you have stopped living together, have you ever said or done anything that would indicate that you thought D and yourself could "make a go of it"? If so, describe the circumstances.	

IM-457

Assignment # 36

On January 15, 1977, George Smith marries Roberta Donaldson in your state. At the time of the marriage, Roberta was under the minimum statutory age to marry. On January 31, 1978, Roberta has a birthday on which she becomes old enough to marry in your state. A week before this birthday, however, George and Roberta have a fight and they agree that it made no sense to continue living together. They have never lived together since. On March 13, 1978, they had sexual intercourse. This has not happened again. Roberta brings an annulment action in your state. (No children exist from their union.) Does George have any defense? (See also General Instructions for the Legal Analysis Assignment, supra p. 16.)

SECTION D. PHYSICAL DISABILITIES

The major physical incapacities or disabilities mentioned in marriage statutes are communicable venereal disease and incurable impotence. While several other physical problems are sometimes involved,[22a] most of the litigation centers on VD and impotence.

As indicated in Chapter Nine,[23] most states have a statutory requirement that parties contemplating marriage go through a medical examination as a condition of obtaining a marriage license. A major objective of the medical exam is to determine whether either or both of the parties have communicable venereal disease. Suppose that the parties do have communicable venereal disease at the time of their marriage. It may be that the medical exam failed to show this, or that

22a. Most notably, epilepsy and pulmonary TB in advance stages.

23. Supra p. 156.

they failed to take the exam (and entered a common law marriage where such marriages are valid [24]) or that they were able to falsify the results of the medical exam.[25] The states differ as to what the consequences are of marrying where one or both of the parties have the disease. While in most states it does *not* invalidate the marriage, there are several states in which the contrary is true. In the latter states, a ground for annulment *can* arise as a result. Furthermore, a state may make it a crime to knowingly marry or have sexual intercourse with someone that has infectious venereal disease.

In discussing impotence, a number of different situations should be kept in mind:

(a) the inability to copulate—incurable;

(b) the inability to copulate—curable;

(c) the inability to have children (sterility);

(d) the refusal to have sexual intercourse.

In most states, only the first situation (a) is a ground for annulment. Copulation means having sexual intercourse. The standard for curability is not the impossibility of a cure; rather, it is the present unlikelihood of a cure. The standard for copulation is the ability to perform the physical sex act naturally and without pain or harm coming to the other spouse. The "mere" fact that a spouse does not derive pleasure from the act is not what is meant by an inability to copulate. The refusal to copulate is not an inability to copulate, although the refusal is sometimes used as some indication of (i. e., as evidence of) the inability to copulate. In most states, it makes no difference whether the inability is due to physical (organic) causes or to psychogenic causes, nor does it matter that the person is impotent only with his/her spouse. If normal coitus is not possible with one's spouse, whatever the cause, the ground exists. Finally, states usually do *not* make sterility a ground for annulment.

It is a defense to the annulment action that the party seeking the annulment knew of the other party's impotence at the time of the marriage and yet still went through with the marriage. Also, continued cohabitation (living as husband and wife) long after the party learned of the other partner's impotence may constitute the equitable defense of laches [26] and bar the annulment action. In most states, impotence will render the marriage voidable, rather than void, and either party to the marriage can be a plaintiff in the annulment action so long as the plaintiff did not have knowledge of the impotence at the time of the marriage.

24. Supra p. 164.

25. See also fraud as a ground for annulment, infra p. 205.

26. Supra p. 232. Laches is waiting an unreasonably long time to bring a suit.

NOTES

(1) The failure of one spouse to disclose to the other the existence of VD, impotence or other serious physical disability, may constitute the ground of fraud, entitling the innocent party to an annulment.[27]

(2) The refusal to have sexual intercourse, while not a ground for annulment, may be a basis for a divorce under the ground of cruelty.[28] Not all states, however, would agree that such refusal is sufficiently cruel to justify a divorce.

(3) According to the "doctrine of triennial cohabitation," applicable in some states, if the wife is a virgin "and apt" after three years of cohabitation, the husband will be presumed to be impotent. He can overcome the presumption by introducing evidence which proves that he is potent in spite of the virginity of his wife.[29]

Assignment # 37

Answer the following questions by examining the marriage statutes of your state. (See also General Instructions for the State Code Assignment, supra p. 14.)

(a) What happens if one of the parties has communicable venereal disease at the time of the marriage?

(b) Can you marry someone with epilepsy?

(c) Can you marry someone who is impotent?

(d) What defenses, if any, exist to an annulment action on the ground of impotence?

(e) Is the marriage with an impotent person void or voidable?

(If your state code does not answer some of the above questions, you may have to check court opinions. See General Instructions for the Court Opinion Assignment, supra p. 26.)

27. Infra p. 205.

28. Infra p. 321.

29. Tompkins v. Tompkins, 92 N.J.Eq. 113, 111 A. 599 (1920).

SUMMARY GROUND FOR ANNULMENT: PHYSICAL DISABILITIES (IMPOTENCE)
DEFINITION: The incurable inability to copulate naturally without pain or harm to the spouse.
VOID OR VOIDABLE: Voidable
WHO CAN SUE: Either party
MAJOR DEFENSES: (1) the impotence is curable; (2) the non-impotent party knew of the other's impotence at time of the marriage; (3) statute of limitations or laches: (the plaintiff has waited too long to bring this annulment action); (4) the court lacks jurisdiction (see infra p. 223).
IS THIS ANNULMENT GROUND ALSO A GROUND FOR DIVORCE: Yes, in some states (see infra p. 335).

[B7970]

INTERVIEWING AND INVESTIGATION CHECKLIST FACTORS RELEVANT TO IMPOTENCE AS A GROUND FOR AN ANNULMENT		
	Legal Interviewing Questions	**Possible Investigation Tasks**
1.	When did you first learn that D was impotent? Did you know this when you married D?	* It will be critical to try to obtain medical records pertaining to D's sexual capabilities. * If anyone else knew about D's impotence, they should be contacted and witness statements taken.
2.	Have you and D ever completed the act of sexual intercourse?	
3.	Describe the difficulties that you and D have had in attempting sexual intercourse.	
4.	Did you and D ever discuss this problem? If so, describe what was said.	
5.	To your knowledge, has D ever been to a medical doctor or to a psychiatrist about D's problem? Have you ever sought professional help?	
6.	To your knowledge, has D ever had an affair with anyone else?	
7.	If D made the claim that you were impotent, how would you answer it?	
8.	Do you now live with D? If not, when did you separate? How long did you live with D after you found out that D was impotent?	

IM–458

SECTION E. HOMOSEXUAL MARRIAGES

Given the recent movements for civil rights, gay liberation and sexual freedom generally, the question has arisen as to whether a man can marry a man and whether a woman can marry a woman. An examination of the traditional marriage statutes reveals that same-sex marriages are neither specifically prohibited nor approved. Such marriages have been denied by the courts on the theory that marriage has always contemplated a man and a woman. When the legislatures wrote the marriage statutes, they arguably had opposite-sex marriages in mind since this is what everyone assumed when they thought about marriage. If same-sex marriages were to be legal, then new legislation would have to be enacted specifically authorizing them.

The proponents of same-sex marriages countered that to deny homosexuals and lesbians the right to a same-sex marriage was to deny them the equal protection of the law contrary to the constitution. Since individuals of the opposite sex could marry, denying the right to those of the same sex would be treating two classes of people unequally. The courts have not been very receptive to this argument.

NOTES

1. Suppose that one of the parties is a transsexual, usually a man who has had a sex change operation. Can such an individual marry a man? Most courts would not permit the marriage, arguing that both parties to the marriage must have been *born* members of the opposite sex. There are a few courts, however, that take the opposite position and allow such marriages.

2. At one time in our history, a number of states prohibited marriages between members of different races. Such anti-miscegnation statutes have been declared unconstitutional.

Chapter 12

ANNULMENT: GROUNDS RELATING TO THE INTENT TO MARRY

SECTION A. SHAM MARRIAGES

An essential element of a contract is the intent to enter the contract, and an essential element of a marriage contract is the intent to enter a marriage. With this in mind, examine the following "marriages":

(a) Dennis and Janet enter a marriage solely to obtain permanent resident alien status for Dennis who is not a US citizen. Janet is a citizen. Dennis wants to avoid deportation by the immigration officials through the marriage.

(b) Edna dares Stanley to marry her following a college party. After a great deal of laughing and boasting, they go through all the formalities (obtaining a license, having the blood test, etc.[1]) and enter the marriage ceremony.

(c) Frank and Helen have an affair. Helen becomes pregnant. Neither parent wants the child to be born illegitimate. Hence, they decide to be married solely for the purpose of having the child born legitimate.[2]

(d) Robin and Ken have been dating for a number of months. They decide to get married "just to try it out." They feel that this is a more modern and rational way of determining whether they will want to stay together forever. It is fully understood by both that there will be "no hard feelings" if either of them wants to dissolve the marriage after six months.

All four of the above couples go through all the steps required to become married. To any reasonable outside observer of their outward actions, nothing unusual is happening. They all intended to go through a marriage ceremony; they all intended to go through the outward appearances of entering a contract, a marriage contract. Subjectively, however, they all had "hidden agendas." According to traditional contract principles, if the parties give clear outward manifestations of mutual assent to enter a contract, the law will bind

1. Supra p. 156.

2. This situation is quite different from one in which the father is forced or threatened to go through with the marriage. The latter involves duress which is a separate ground for annulment. On duress, see infra p. 203.

them to their contract even though their unspoken motive was *not* to enter a binding contract.[3] Most courts, however, apply a different principle when a marriage contract is involved. The situations involving the first three couples above (a to c) are total sham marriages. The parties never intended to live together as husband and wife; they had a limited purpose of avoiding deportation, of displaying braggadocio, or of "giving a name" to a child. Most courts would declare such marriages to be void and would grant an annulment to either party so long as the parties did not consummate their union or otherwise cohabitate *after* the marriage. If, in fact, they lived together as husband and wife even for a short period after the marriage, most courts would be reluctant to declare the marriage to be void. The subsequent cohabitation would be some evidence that at the time they entered the marriage, they *did* intend to live as husband and wife. The central question is always: what intention did the parties have at the time they entered the marriage? Did they intend to be married or not? It is, of course, very difficult to get into their heads to find out what they were thinking. Hence, the law relies on objective conduct as evidence of intent. If parties cohabitate after marriage, this is certainly some evidence that they intended to be married at the time they appeared to enter a marriage contract. In the first three hypotheticals above (a to c), assume that the couples did not cohabitate after they entered the marriage. Most courts would therefore find that at the time they entered the marriage contract, they did not have the intention to be married, i. e., to assume the duties of a marriage. It should be pointed out, however, that some courts would apply a *different* rule and hold that the marriage is valid whether or not cohabitation followed the marriage ceremony—so long as the parties went through all the proper procedures to be married.

What about the fourth hypothetical above—(d)? The parties entered a "trial marriage." The fact that the parties cohabitated is evidence that they did intend to be married at the time they entered the marriage contract. Most courts would find that this marriage is valid and deny an annulment to anyone who later claims that the parties never intended to assume the marital status. It cannot be said that they married in jest nor that they married for a limited purpose. The fact that they did not promise to live together as husband and wife forever does not mean that they lacked the intent to be married at the time they entered the marriage.

3. Ryan, P. & Granfield, D., *Domestic Relations: Civil and Canon Law*, p. 114 (1963).

SUMMARY GROUND FOR ANNULMENT: THE SHAM MARRIAGE
DEFINITION: The absence of an intention to marry (i. e., of a consent to be married) in spite of the fact that the parties voluntarily went through all the formalities of a marriage.
VOID OR VOIDABLE: Void.
WHO CAN SUE: Either party.
MAJOR DEFENSE: The parties did have the intention to marry at the time they entered the marriage ceremony. A major item of evidence that this intention existed is that they cohabitated after the ceremony. (NOTE: in some states, the annulment will be denied if the parties went through all the outward formalities of the marriage in spite of what their unspoken objective was.)
IS THIS ANNULMENT GROUND ALSO A GROUND FOR DIVORCE: Usually not.

[B7969]

INTERVIEWING AND INVESTIGATION CHECKLIST FACTORS RELEVANT TO DETERMINING WHETHER A MARRIAGE WAS A SHAM		
	Legal Interviewing Questions	**Possible Investigation Tasks**
1.	When did the two of you first discuss getting married? Describe the circumstances.	• Interview anyone who was aware of the circumstances of the marriage. Obtain witness statements.
2.	Who was around, if anyone, when the two of you discussed marriage?	
3.	Were you living together before you married?	
4.	Did you live together after you married?	
5.	Was your marriage consummated?	
6.	At the time you entered marriage with D, did you intend to live with D as husband and wife? Did D have this intention?	
7.	After the marriage ceremony, did you or D ever introduce each other to others as husband and wife (Mr. and Mrs.)?	

IM-459

Assignment # 38

(a) Elaine is 20 years old and Philip, a bachelor, is 75. Philip asks Elaine to marry him. Philip has terminal cancer and wants to die a married man. He and Elaine know that he probably has less than six months to live and that he will spend the rest of his life in a hospital bed. Under their arrangement, she does not have to continue as his wife after six months if he is still alive. They go through all the formal requirements to be married. On the day after the marriage ceremony, Elaine changes her mind and wants to end the marriage. Can she obtain an annulment? (See also General Instructions for the Legal Analysis Assignment, supra p. 16.)

(b) Draft a complaint for Elaine for her annulment action. (See also General Instructions for the Complaint Drafting Assignment, supra p. 20.)

(c) Draft a set of interrogatories from Philip to Elaine. (See also General Instructions for the Interrogatory Assignment, supra p. 31.)

SECTION B. MENTAL DISABILITIES

Two related reasons have been attributed to the existence of mental disability as a ground for annulment in most states. First, it is designed to prevent people from marrying who are incapable of understanding the nature of the marriage relationship. Second, it is designed to prevent or at least discourage such individuals from reproducing since it is argued that many mentally ill parents are likely to be poor parents and their children are likely to become public charges.[4] A great deal of difficulty exists in defining mental disability. The various state statutes use different terms to describe this condition: insane, idiot, weak-minded, feebleminded, unsound mind, imbecile, lunatic, incapable of consenting to a marriage, mentally ill or retarded, legally incompetent, mental defective, etc. One court provided the following definition:

> While there has been a hesitancy on the part of the courts to judicially define the phrase "unsound mind," it is established that such term has reference to the mental capacity of the parties at the very moment of inception of the marriage contract. Ordinarily, lack of mental capacity, which renders a party incapable of entering into a valid marriage contract, must be such that it deprives him of the ability to understand the objects of marriage, its ensuing duties and undertakings, its responsibilities and relationship. There is a general agreement of the authorities that the terms "unsound mind" and "lack of mental capacity" carry greater import than eccentricity or mere weakness of mind or dullness of intellect.[5]

Not all states would agree with every aspect of this definition of mental disability, although in general, it would be consistent with the definitions used by most courts. Suppose that a person was intoxicated or under the influence of drugs at the time the marriage contract was entered. In most states, this too, would be a ground for annul-

4. Brakel, S. & Rock, R., *The Mentally Disabled and The Law,* p. 226, Rev. Ed. (American Bar Foundation Study, 1971).

5. Johnson v. Johnson, 104 N.W.2d 8 (N.D.1960).

ment if the alcohol or drugs rendered the person incapable of understanding the marriage contract.

While the issue of mental health usually arises in annulment actions—when someone is trying to dissolve the marriage—it also becomes relevant in some states at the license stage. Before some state officials can issue a license to marry,[6] that person may be required by statute to inquire into the prior mental difficulties, if any, of the applicants for the license, e. g., to ask whether either applicant has ever been in a mental institution. Several states are concerned about the possibility of children. In these states, the license to marry may be denied to any mentally disabled person unless that person is sterilized [7] or the woman involved in the proposed marriage is over forty-five years old. It is generally conceded, however, that these license restrictions have been very ineffective in preventing the marriage of people with serious mental problems.[8]

Whenever the mental health question arises (at the license stage or as part of an annulment proceeding), the major difficulty that exists is trying to prove that the "right" amount of mental illness is present. All individuals are presumed to be sane unless the contrary has been demonstrated. Suppose that someone was once committed to a mental institution, and upon release, seeks to be married. Surely, the fact of prior institutionalization does not prove that the person is presently incapable of understanding the marriage contract and the marriage relationship at the time s/he attempts to marry.

Suppose that a person is mentally disabled, but gets married during a brief period of mental health before relapsing again to his/her prior state of mental disability. The marriage took place during what is called a "lucid interval," and many states will validate such a marriage if there was cohabitation. Furthermore, some states will deny the annulment if the parties cohabitated during a "lucid interval" at any time *after* the marriage was entered even if one or both parties was not "lucid" at the time of the marriage. The problems, however, of trying to prove that any "interval" was "lucid" can be enormous.

In most states, the marriage of a person who is mentally disabled is voidable rather than void,[9] and the suit to bring the annulment can be brought either by the mentally disabled or the mentally healthy partner. It might also be possible for the parent or guardian of the mentally disabled party to initiate the annulment proceeding.

NOTES

(1) At the time of the marriage, if one party conceals from the other the fact of prior mental institutionalization (or even prior men-

6. Supra p. 156.

7. See also infra pp. 439, 455.

8. Deutsch, *The Mentally Ill in America*, p. 377, 2nd Ed. (1949).

9. Supra p. 172.

tal illness not involving hospitals), a separate ground for annulment based on fraud may be present.[10]

(2) A state may have one standard of mental illness which will disable a person from being able to marry, another standard of mental illness which will disable a person from being able to enter an ordinary business contract, and still another standard of mental illness which will disable a person from being able to write a will.

(3) Later, we will discuss mental illness arising *after* the marriage begins as a ground for divorce.[11]

(4) Mental illness is, of course, also relevant in criminal proceedings where the defense of insanity is often raised in an attempt to relieve a defendant of criminal responsibility for what was done. Within criminal law, a great debate has always existed as to the definition of insanity. The *M'Naghten* Right/Wrong test is as follows: "at the time of the committing of the act, the party accused was laboring under such a defect of reason, from disease of the mind, as not to know the nature and quality of the act he was doing, or if he did know it that he did not know he was doing what was wrong."[12] The *Durham* Diseased-Mind test is as follows: "an accused is not criminally responsible if his unlawful act was the product of mental disease or mental defect."[13] The *Model Penal Code* test is as follows: "A person is not responsible for criminal conduct if at the time of such conduct as a result of mental disease or defect he lacks substantial capacity either to appreciate the criminality (wrongfulness) of his conduct or to conform his conduct to the requirements of the law."[14]

Assignment # 39

Answer the following questions by examining the marriage statutes of your state. (See also General Instructions for the State Code Assignment, supra p. 14.)

(a) What words or phrases are used in your state statute to describe the degree of mental illness which will disqualify a person from marrying in your state?

(b) What is the citation of this statute?

(c) If a mentally disabled person marries in violation of this statute, is the marriage void or voidable?

(d) Does your statute place any limitations on who can bring the annulment action on this ground? If so, what are they?

10. Infra p. 205.

11. Infra p. 336.

12. 10 Clark & F. 200, 8 Eng.Rep. 718 (1843).

13. Durham v. United States, 214 F.2d 862, 874–75 (D.C.Cir. 1954). See also United States v. Brawner, 471 F.2d 969 (1972).

14. American Law Institute, *Model Penal Code* section 4.01.

(If your state code does not provide answers to all of the above questions, you may have to check court opinions. See General Instructions for the Court Opinion Assignment, supra p. 26.)

Assignment # 40

On December 13, 1976, George Baylor married Jessica Framingham in your state. At the time, George was a patient at the State Mental Hospital where he had been institutionalized because he was a danger to himself and to others. On the day of the marriage, George was on a ten hour pass from the Hospital. Jessica knew everything about George's background and present condition, but still wanted to marry him. Both were residents of your state at the time of the marriage. Jessica now wants to have the marriage annulled. Draft a complaint for her which is to be filed in court in seven days from today. As the ground for the annulment, use mental disability (or whatever term your statute uses) at the time of the marriage. (See also General Instructions for the Complaint Drafting Assignment, supra p. 20.)

SUMMARY GROUND FOR ANNULMENT: MENTAL DISABILITY
DEFINITION: The inability to understand the marriage contract and the duties of marriage at the time the parties attempt to enter the marriage due to mental illness, the influence of alcohol or the influence of drugs.
VOID OR VOIDABLE: Voidable in most states.
WHO CAN SUE: In some states, only the mentally ill person (or his/her parent or guardian) can sue for the annulment. In other states, only the mentally healthy person can sue. In many states, either can sue.
MAJOR DEFENSES: (1) the person was never mentally disabled; (2) the marriage occurred during a lucid interval; (3) after the marriage began, a lucid interval was present during which the parties cohabitated; (4) the plaintiff has no standing to bring this annulment action; (5) statute of limitations or laches (the plaintiff waited too long to bring this annulment action); (6) the court lacks jurisdiction (see infra p. 223).
IS THIS ANNULMENT GROUND ALSO A GROUND FOR DIVORCE: in most states, mental disability is a ground for divorce if the disability arises after the marriage commences (see infra p. 336).

[B7913]

INTERVIEWING AND INVESTIGATION CHECKLIST FACTORS RELEVANT TO MENTAL DISABILITY AS A GROUND FOR ANNULMENT (C = Client; D = Defendant)		
	Legal Interviewing Questions	**Possible Investigation Tasks**
1.	When was the first time anyone told you that you were mentally ill?	* Have C sign a release giving you permission to obtain copies of all doctor and hospital records.
2.	Could you provide me with a list of every doctor who treated you and every hospital where you received care?	* Interview everyone who was present at the wedding ceremony (e.g., witnesses, guests, minister) and obtain witness statements on what they thought of C's condition.
3.	On the date you married D, were you under medical care?	
4.	Were you taking any drugs or alcohol?	
5.	Were you on out-patient care?	
6.	What do you remember, if anything, about the wedding ceremony?	* Obtain birth and marriage certificates.
7.	Besides D, who else was present at the ceremony? (e.g., witnesses, guests.)	* Have C sign a release giving you permission to obtain copies of school records, intelligence test scores, etc.
8.	How old were you when you married?	
9.	What was your occupation at the time?	
10.	What was the highest grade of school that you had completed at the time?	* Interview anyone who knew C and D after they married in order to determine whether anyone felt that C's mental health improved and whether C and D lived together as husband and wife during this period of improvement.
11.	Did you own property? Were you ever denied the right to sell any of it?	
12.	Did you manage your own property? Was there ever a guardian or conservator appointed for you? Was there ever any discussion of such an appointment?	
13.	Did you drive an automobile at the time of your marriage? Did you vote?	
14.	Were you engaged in any community activities at the time?	
15.	Had you written a will at the time? Do you have a will now?	
16.	Were you ever thought of as quarrelsome, senile or eccentric? If so, describe the circumstances.	
17.	Do you know what your IQ was at the time of your marriage? Do you know what your mental age was?	
18.	Who made the arrangements for the wedding ceremony?	
19.	Since the date of your marriage, describe all mental problems, if any. (Names and addresses of doctors, hospitals, etc.)	
20.	Have you lived with D since the marriage?	
21.	At any time after your marriage, did your mental health improve? If so, describe the circumstances, dates, doctors, etc.	
22.	During any time after your marriage when you were feeling healthy, did you have sexual intercourse with D, live with D, or otherwise treat each other as husband and wife?	

IM-466

SECTION C. DURESS

If someone has been forced to consent to marry, then it clearly cannot be said that that person had the requisite intent to be married. The major question is: what kind of force will be sufficient to constitute the ground for annulment? Applying physical force or threatening its use is sufficient. If an individual is faced with a choice between a wedding and a funeral, and chooses the wedding, the resulting marriage will be annulled as one induced by duress. The same is true if the choice is between bodily harm and marriage. Suppose that the choice does not involve violence nor the threat of violence. The most common example is as follows:

> George is courting Lena. They have had sexual relations several times. Lena becomes pregnant. Lena's father becomes furious at George and threatens to "turn him in" to the county district attorney to prosecute him for the crimes of seduction [15] and bastardy. (If Lena is under age, the charge of statutory rape may be involved as well.) Furthermore, Lena and her father will sue George in the county civil court for support of the child. On the other hand, no criminal prosecution will be brought and no civil action will be initiated if George agrees to marry Lena. George agrees and the "shotgun wedding" promptly takes place. After the wedding, it becomes clear that Lena was not pregnant; everyone made an honest mistake. George then brings an action to annul the marriage on the ground of duress.

Here the threat is of criminal prosecution and of bringing a civil support action. If such threats are made maliciously, they will constitute duress and be a ground for annulment. The threat is malicious if it has no basis in fact. If the threats are not malicious, no annulment action can be based on them.

In most states, marriages induced by duress are voidable rather than void, but only the innocent party will have standing to bring the annulment action on that ground. If, however, this innocent party voluntarily cohabitated with the "guilty" party (i. e., the one who did the coercing) after the effects of the duress have worn off, then the annulment action will be denied on the theory that the marriage has been ratified.

Assignment # 41

Do you think that any of the following marriages could be annulled on the ground of duress? (See also General Instructions for the Legal Analysis Assignment, supra p. 16.)

(a) Rita marries Dan after Dan threatened to kill Rita's second cousin if she did not marry him. The only reason Rita marries Dan is to save her cousin's life.

15. See also infra p. 482.

(b) Tom marries Edna after Tom's very domineering father orders him to marry her. Tom has been in ill health lately. Tom marries Edna solely because he has never been able to say no to his father.

(c) Paula marries Charles after Paula's mother threatens suicide if she does not marry him. Paula marries Charles solely to prevent this suicide.

Assignment # 42

Is duress a ground for annulment in your state? (See General Instructions for the State Code Assignment, supra p. 14.)

SUMMARY GROUND FOR ANNULMENT: DURESS
DEFINITION: The consent to marry was induced by (a) physical violence, or (b) threats of physical violence, or (c) malicious or groundless threats of criminal prosecution, or (d) malicious or groundless threats of civil litigation.
VOID OR VOIDABLE: Voidable in most states.
WHO CAN SUE: The party who was coerced.
MAJOR DEFENSES: (1) there was no physical violence or threat of it; (2) the plaintiff did not believe the threat of violence and hence was not coerced by it; (3) there was no threat of criminal prosecution nor of civil litigation; (4) the threat of criminal prosecution or of civil litigation was not malicious; it was made in the good faith belief that it could be won; (5) this is the wrong plaintiff (e. g., this plaintiff has "dirty hands" since this is the party who brought about the coercion); (6) the plaintiff freely cohabitated with the defendant after the effect of the duress had gone (ratification); (7) statute of limitations or laches (the plaintiff waited too long to bring this action); (8) the court lacks jurisdiction (see infra p. 223).
IS THIS ANNULMENT GROUND ALSO A GROUND FOR DIVORCE: **Yes, in some states (see infra p. 335).**

[B7968]

INTERVIEWING AND INVESTIGATION CHECKLIST FACTORS RELEVANT TO DURESS AS A GROUND FOR ANNULMENT		
	Legal Interviewing Questions	**Possible Investigation Tasks**
1.	Why did you marry D?	* Check court records to determine if civil or criminal proceedings were ever instituted against C before the marriage. * Interview anyone who may have had knowledge of the threatened civil or criminal proceedings to determine whether these proceedings were brought or were threatened maliciously.
2.	Did anyone physically abuse you or threaten to do so?	
3.	Did anyone threaten to sue you or to have you prosecuted?	
4.	Was pregnancy involved?	
5.	Did D seduce you?	
6.	Did D ever threaten you?	
7.	After you married D, did you have sexual intercourse with D? Did you treat each other as husband and wife in any way after the marriage?	

IM-468

SECTION D. FRAUD

The theory behind fraud as a ground for annulment is that if a party consents to a marriage where fraud was involved, the consent was not real. A party does not have an intent to marry if the marriage has a foundation in fraud. The party intends one thing and gets another! As with so many areas of the law, however, the difficulty is one of definitions: what is meant by fraud? Unfortunately, there is no clear answer to this question. Court opinions within the same state are often inconsistent. Various terms are used to define the kind of fraud which will justify an annulment, e. g., the fraud must relate to the "essentials" of the marriage, the fraud must be related to "vitals," the fraud must be "material," etc. The problem, however, is that the definitions need definitions. What is meant by "essential," "vital" or "material"?

One of the few clear principles in this area is that not every fraudulent representation will lead to an annulment. As one court put it:

> Surely every representation leading up to marriage cannot be material,—the fact that a brunette turned to a blond over night, or that the beautiful teeth were discovered to be false, or the ruddy pink complexion gave way suddenly to pallor, or that a woman misstated her age or was not in perfect health, would lead no court to annul the marriage for fraud.[16]

16. Ryan & Granfield, *Domestic Relations*, supra note 3 at p. 136.

There is more than one way to communicate as demonstrated by the following chart:

FORMS OF COMMUNICATION	
1. Just before their marriage, Joe tells Mary that he is anxious to have children with her. In fact, he intends to remain celibate after their marriage.	1. Joe's statement about children is an *intentional misrepresentation* of fact.
2. Joe says nothing about his planned celibacy since he knows that if he tells Mary, she will not marry him. He says absolutely nothing about children or celibacy and the subject never comes up prior to their marriage.	2. Joe's silence is an *intentional concealment* of fact.
3. Joe does not tell Mary that he intended to remain celibate because he incorrectly assumed that Mary already knew.	3. Joe's silence is *innocent* (or *good faith*) *nondisclosure* of fact.[17]
4. Just before their marriage, Joe tells Mary that since he is physically unable to have sexual intercourse, he will have to stay celibate. To his surprise, Joe later finds out that he is not impotent.	4. Joe's statement is an *innocent* (or *good faith*) *misrepresentation* of fact.
5. One hour after Joe marries Mary, he gets on a bus and disappears forever. They never had sexual intercourse before or after marriage and never discussed the subject.	5. From Joe's conduct, we can draw an *inference* that at the time he married Mary, he probably never intended to consummate the marriage.

IM-469

Generally, only the first two and the fifth (1, 2, 5) form of communication mentioned in the above chart will support an annulment on the ground of fraud. Innocent nondisclosure or innocent misrepresentation will not be sufficient in most states. It should be pointed out, however, that in some states the innocence of the communication is not relevant so long as the other elements of fraud are present.

The example used in the chart involving celibacy (where there was intentional misrepresentation or nondisclosure) will lead to an annulment in almost every court. What is the difference between fraud involving celibacy and fraud involving the color of the bride's hair which will not lead to an annulment in any court? It is at this point that we must turn to the two tests that the courts use to determine which facts can lead to an annulment if fraudulently communicated. The major ones are the essentials test and the materiality test.

The Essentials Test

Some courts argue that the fraud must involve the essentials of the marital relationship, usually defined as those aspects of the marriage that relate to sex and children.

17. Based upon the particular circumstances, it might be argued that Joe's silence constituted a *negligent nondisclosure* of fact if his assumption about what Mary already knew was silly or unreasonable.

The Materiality Test

Other courts say that the fraud must be material, meaning that "but for" the fraudulent representation (whether or not it relates to sex and children) the person deceived would not have entered the marriage. Furthermore, the person must have been reasonable in relying on the fraudulent representation.

Although, in theory, the essentials test is usually deemed to be the stricter of the two tests, in reality, the two tests often overlap and are frequently applied inconsistently by the courts. If children have been born from the union, for example, courts often strain the application of the tests in order to deny the annulment since preserving the marriage may be the only way to legitimize [18] the children in some states. Whether or not the marriage has been consummated prior to the annulment action may have a bearing on whether a court will find that fraud existed. If the marriage has never been consummated, courts tend to be more liberal in finding fraud than when the marriage has been consummated. Oddly, a few courts consider an unconsummated marriage to be little more than an engagement to be married.[19]

What follows is a list of representations, and how the courts have handled them. For each representation mentioned, you can assume that it was false when made and that the party deceived would not have married had s/he known that the representation was false. Also assume that the representation was *not* communicated innocently. (M=man; W=woman.)

(a) M tells W that he is a hard worker.

Insufficient fraud for an annulment. The misrepresentation does not relate to the essentials of the marriage. W acted unreasonably in relying on the representation. She could have checked M's background to see if he was a good worker.

(b) W tells M that she only drinks beer, not hard liquor.

Insufficient fraud for an annulment. Same reasons as in (a) above.

(c) M tells W that he is marrying her for love and not for her money.

Insufficient fraud for an annulment in most states. Same reasons as in (a) above. In extreme situations, however, the annulment might be granted.

(d) W tells M that she will give him a large amount of money when they marry.

States differ as to whether this fraud will lead to an annulment. Courts would probably disbelieve M that he relied

18. For more on legitimacy, see infra p. 451ff.

19. See, for example, Akrep v. Akrep, 1 N.J. 268, 63 A.2d 253 (1949).

on W's representation, especially if he cohabitated with her after he discovered that she did not have any money to give him. Cohabitation would tend to prove that he married her for reasons other than or in addition to the promise of money.

(e) M conceals from W the fact that he is a heroin addict, alcoholic, is impotent, has TB or VD.

Courts tend to grant to annulment for such intentional concealment, especially where the condition could effect W's sexual relationship with M.

(f) W conceals from M that she was once institutionalized in a mental hospital or that she has a criminal record.

Courts differ on whether either fraud will justify an annulment.

(g) M tells W that he has never been married before when in fact he was recently divorced.

Courts differ on whether this fraud will justify an annulment.

(h) W tells M that she is an orthodox Jew.

Many courts will grant the annulment for this fraud. (Do you think that this fraud is that much different from the fraud mentioned in example (a) above?)

(i) M tells W that after they are married in a civil ceremony, he will go through a second ceremony in the Catholic Church.

Most courts will deny the annulment for this fraud, although the result may be different if the marriage has not been consummated before W brings the annulment action.

(j) W conceals from M the fact that she does not intend to consummate the marriage or that she will never have sexual relations with M without using contraceptives even though they had both planned on having children.

Annulment always granted.

(k) M tells W that he is a virgin.

Annulment usually denied.

(*l*) W fails to tell M that she is pregnant by another man.

Annulment always granted. If, however, M had premarital sex with W, he may be denied the annulment on the theory that his illicit intercourse gives him "dirty hands" and he should not be allowed to sue. In addition, if W had premarital sex with him, he should not have been surprised to learn that she had premarital sex with another man.

(m) W is pregnant by another man, but tells M that he is the father.

Annulment usually granted.

(n) W tells M that she is pregnant by him. In fact, she is not pregnant.

Annulment usually denied.

As you can see by examining the results of these few examples (a to n), it is not easy to find a rational principle explaining why the courts have decided the cases the way they have. You cannot ask for consistency because it simply does not exist.

Once a court has determined that the fraud is sufficient to justify an annulment, the marriage is usually held to be voidable, rather than void. Generally, only the innocent party, i. e., the party deceived, has standing to bring the annulment action. If, however, this party waits too long to bring the action, s/he might be barred by the statute of limitations or by laches.[20] Furthermore, after the innocent party discovers the fraud, if s/he has sexual relations with the deceiver or otherwise cohabitates with him/her, the annulment action might be barred on the theory that the marriage has been ratified, i. e., the deception has been forgiven. Another theory for barring the action, in addition to ratification, is that the subsequent cohabitation is some evidence that the fraud was not material in the first place. If the innocent party cohabitated with knowledge of the fraud, then the fraud probably did not initially induce the innocent party to marry.

Assignment # 43

(a) Does your state code have a statute dealing with fraud as a ground for annulment? yes — I.C. 32-501 (4, 5, 6.)

(b) If so, quote that portion of the statute that deals with fraud. (See also General Instructions for the State Code Assignment, supra p. 14.) See in I. Code 32-501,(4, 5, 6)

Assignment # 44

At the end of this section, beginning on p. 207 supra, a number of examples of fraudulent communications are listed (a to n) with an overview of how courts have tended to treat these communications. This assignment asks you to find court opinions written by courts in your state which have dealt with these or similar communications. Go through the standard techniques of locating opinions written by courts of your state (see General Instructions for the Court Opinion Assignment, supra p. 26.) Give the citation to each opinion that you find, *briefly* state the facts of the opinion and how it handled the fraud.

20. Infra p. 232.

SUMMARY

GROUND FOR ANNULMENT: FRAUD

DEFINITION: The intentional misrepresentation or concealment of a fact which is essential or material to the marriage and which the person deceived reasonably relies upon in the decision to enter the marriage.

VOID OR VOIDABLE: Voidable in most states.

WHO CAN SUE: The innocent party only.

MAJOR DEFENSES:

(1) the fraud was not about an essential fact;
(2) the fraud was not material: the plaintiff did not rely on the fraud in his/her initial decision to marry;
(3) the fraud arose after the marriage was entered (again, no reliance);
(4) the plaintiff may have relied on the fraud, but s/he was unreasonable in doing so;
(5) after plaintiff discovered the fraud, s/he consummated the marriage or otherwise cohabitated with the fraudulent party (ratification);
(6) the misrepresentation or nondisclosure was innocent—made in good faith with no intention to deceive;
(7) this plaintiff has no standing to bring the annulment action since the plaintiff was the deceiver;
(8) this plaintiff has "dirty hands" (e. g., in a case involving fraud relating to pregnancy, the plaintiff had premarital sex with the defendant);
(9) statute of limitations or laches (the plaintiff waited too long to bring the annulment action, see infra p. 232);
(10) the court lacks jurisdiction (see infra p. 223).

IS THIS ANNULMENT GROUND ALSO A GROUND FOR DIVORCE? In a few states (see infra p. 335).

[B8803]

INTERVIEWING AND INVESTIGATION CHECKLIST FACTORS RELEVANT TO FRAUD AS A GROUND FOR ANNULMENT (C = Client; D = Defendant)		
	Legal Interviewing Questions	**Possible Investigation Tasks**
1.	On what date were you married?	* Obtain marriage records. * Interview anyone who has any knowledge about the reasons C married D, with specific reference to whether C relied on any representations made by D to C.
2.	What facts did D fail to tell you? What lies did D tell you?	
3.	How, if at all, were you influenced by what D failed to tell you, or by the lies D told you?	
4.	Would you have married D if you had known what you later learned about D?	
5.	What steps did you take, if any, to learn more about D's background and D's condition at the time of the marriage?	
6.	Do you think that you would have found out if you had taken more steps to inquire about D? Why or why not?	
7.	Do you think that D intentionally kept the truth from you? How do you know?	
8.	When did you find out the truth?	
9.	After you found out, did you have sexual relations with D? Did you live together as husband and wife?	
10.	Did you have premarital sex with D?	
11.	Was your marriage consummated?	
12.	Is there anything that *you* failed to tell D or that *you* lied about to D before you married?	

IM-470

*

Chapter Thirteen

ANNULMENT: THE CONSEQUENCES OF AN ANNULMENT DECREE

In theory, an annulled marriage never existed. The major question that always arises as a result of this theory is: what effect does the annulment have on events occurring after the "marriage?" The following chart summarizes these events:

QUESTIONS RAISED AS A RESULT OF THE ANNULMENT OF A MARRIAGE	
1. The parties give birth to children.	1. Are the children illegitimate?
2. While the parties lived together, the woman provided household services.	2. Is the woman entitled to compensation for the services she provided?
3. The parties separate.	3. Is the woman entitled to alimony? To a division of the property acquired during the time they lived together?
4. The parties exchange gifts with each other while living together. They also convey property to each other.	4. Must they return the gifts or any property conveyed to each other?
5. Assume that the annulled marriage was the woman's second marriage. She was receiving alimony from her first husband which ended when she married her second husband.	5. Does her first husband have to resume his alimony payments once the second marriage is annulled?
6. Same situation as in # 5 above except that the wife was receiving social security or workmen's compensation benefits through her first husband which ended when she married again.	6. Can she resume receiving social security or workmen's compensation benefits when her second marriage is annulled?
7. A party marries another even though the party's first spouse is still living and the first marriage has never been dissolved. The party is charged with bigamy.	7. Is it a defense to the criminal bigamy charge that the second marriage was annulled?
8. A couple have always filed joint income tax returns.	8. When their marriage is annulled, must they file amended returns so that each party will now file individual returns for each year that they were together on joint returns?

IM-471

The old rule was that once a marriage was declared invalid, the declaration "related back" to the time the parties attempted to enter the marriage. This "relation back" doctrine meant that the annulment decree was retroactive. The doctrine, when strictly applied, resulted in some very harsh consequences. Children born to parents before their marriage was annulled were, in effect, born out of wedlock and were illegitimate. Suppose that a woman lives with a man for forty years before their marriage is annulled. She would not be entitled to any alimony or support payments since a man has no duty to support someone who was never his wife. Clearly, these were unfair consequences, and steps were taken in many states to offset them. What follows is an overview of the present law in this area.

1. THE LEGITIMACY OF CHILDREN FROM AN ANNULLED MARRIAGE

With very few exceptions, the states have passed statutes which legitimize such children. Some of the statutes, however, are not absolute, e. g., the statute might say that the children are legitimate only if one or more of the parents honestly believed that their marriage was valid when they entered it, or the statute might legitimize all the children born from an annulled marriage *except* when the annulment was granted on the ground of a prior existing marriage [1] (bigamy).

2. ALIMONY AND THE DISPOSITION OF PROPERTY ACQUIRED BEFORE THE MARRIAGE WAS ANNULLED

In some states, alimony cannot be awarded in annulment proceedings. In other states, however, statutes have been passed which provide that alimony *can* be awarded in such actions: temporary alimony pending the final outcome of the action and permanent alimony following the annulment decree.[2] It may be, however, that alimony will be denied to the "guilty" party, e. g., the party who committed the fraud [3] or who forced [4] the other party to enter the marriage.

Another limitation on alimony in some states is that only defendants can receive it. By definition, the plaintiff seeking the annulment is saying that no marriage ever existed. A few courts say that it is inconsistent for the plaintiff to take this position and also to ask for alimony.

Where alimony is authorized, counsel fees are also awarded. The spouse able to pay, usually the husband, must pay the fees of the attorney for the other spouse in defending or initiating the annulment action.[5]

1. Supra p. 177.

2. For a discussion of temporary and permanent alimony in divorce proceedings, see infra pp. 365, 369.

3. On fraud as a ground for annulment, see supra p. 205.

4. On duress as a ground for annulment, see supra p. 203.

5. On attorney fees in divorce actions, see infra p. 430.

In the preceding two chapters dealing with the grounds for annulment, it was pointed out that some annulment grounds could also be grounds for divorce.[6] Temporary and permanent alimony can be granted in divorce actions.[7] Hence, if a party would like to receive alimony following an annulment, but the state's statute does not authorize it in annulment actions, the party might elect to sue for a divorce rather than for an annulment if there is a ground which the party can establish which could be the foundation for *either* an annulment or a divorce.[8]

Suppose that it is clear in a particular state that alimony cannot be awarded in the annulment action and the divorce option is not available, e. g., because the ground used to establish the annulment happens not to be a ground for divorce in that state. Courts have devised various theories to provide the woman with some kind of relief:

(a) The putative spouse theory in community property states.

A putative spouse is one whose marriage is invalid. In some community property states,[9] the *innocent* putative spouse (i. e., the one who believed in good faith that the marriage was valid) is entitled to a division of the property acquired during the marriage—sometimes referred to as the "quasi-marital property." [10]

(b) Quasi-contract theory.

The elements of a valid contract have been discussed earlier.[11] An annulled marriage is an invalid contract. Generally, a party whose contract has been wrongfully breached cannot recover any money (i. e., damages) if it turns out that the contract was invalid. This can be quite unfair to the innocent party, especially if this party has put in a good deal of time and resources, and if the other party has benefited thereby. To avoid such "unjust enrichment," the law establishes the fiction of a "quasi-contract" according to which the party who has been enriched must pay to the other party the reasonable value of the goods and/or services received. This doctrine has been applied to annulled marriages as a device to provide some resources to a wife who is not entitled to alimony. Some states require that the husband pay the wife the reasonable value

6. See the Summary charts on the annulment grounds, supra pp. 181–210.

7. Supra note 2.

8. In some states, it may be possible for the plaintiff's complaint to plead divorce or annulment in the alternative.

9. Verrall, H. & Sammis, A., *Cases and Materials on California Community Property*, p. 68, 2nd Ed. (1971).

10. See, for example, Cal.Civil Code, section 4452 (West, 1970).

11. Supra p. 110.

of the services she rendered during the marriage on a quasi-contract theory.

(c) Quasi-partnership or joint venture theory.

Here the theory is that during the marriage the husband and wife were somewhat like business partners engaged in a joint business venture. The partnership is over and there should now be a fair distribution of assets to the participants.

(d) Resulting trust or constructive trust theory.

A trust is property held by one person for the benefit of another. Carefully drafted trust agreements specify who the trustee is, what the trust res (i. e., the trust property) is, who the beneficiaries are, etc. When such trust instruments are not in existence, the law might imply the existence of a trust when fairness, justice and equity seem to require it. Such trusts are called resulting or constructive trusts. In states that use this device, the husband of the annulled marriage can be considered the "trustee" of property acquired during the marriage. The wife, as "beneficiary" of this "res" would receive whatever portion of the property deemed fair by the court.

As you can see, all of these theories rely upon fictions:

—a putative "spouse" is technically not a spouse;

—a quasi-"contract" is technically not a contract;

—a quasi-"partnership" is technically not a partnership;

—a resulting or constructive "trust" is technically not a trust.

Here is another instance where the law will "bend" in order to achieve an equitable result.

3. PROBLEMS OF REVIVAL

Assume that Bob is validly married to Elaine. They go through a valid divorce proceeding which provides that Bob will pay Elaine alimony until she remarries. One year later, Elaine marries Bill; Bob stops his alimony payments. Two years later, Elaine's marriage to Bill is annulled. What about Bob's obligation to pay alimony to Elaine? Several possibilities exist:

—Bob does not have to resume paying alimony; his obligation ceased forever when Elaine married Bill; the fact that the second marriage was annulled is irrelevant.

—Bob does not have to resume paying alimony; Bill must start paying alimony if the state authorizes alimony in annulment actions.

—Bob must resume paying alimony from the date of the annulment decree; the annulment of the second marriage *revived* his earlier alimony obligation.

—Bob must resume paying alimony and must pay back alimony from the date when Elaine married Bill; the annulment *revived* the alimony obligation.

The last option is the most logical since the technical effect of an annulment decree is to say that the marriage never existed; the decree is retroactive to the date when the parties entered the marriage that was later annulled. While the last option is perhaps the most logical of the four presented, it is arguably as unfair to Bob as the first option is unfair to Elaine. States take different positions on this problem. Most states, however, adopt the second or third option mentioned above.

4. CUSTODY AND CHILD SUPPORT

When children are involved, whether considered legitimate or not, courts will make temporary and permanent custody decisions in the annulment proceeding.[12] Furthermore, child support orders are inevitable when the children are minors.[13] Hence the fact that the marriage is terminated by annulment usually has little effect on the need of the court to make custody and child support orders.

5. SPECIAL TAX CONSIDERATIONS

The federal income tax law governing alimony and child support payments is complex. This law will be discussed in detail in Chapter 19.[14]

6. INHERITANCE

To die *testate* is to die leaving a will. Either spouse, of course, can make a will and leave property to each other [15] and/or to their children, whether considered legitimate or not. Suppose, however, that one of the spouses of the annulled marriage dies *intestate,* i. e., dies without a will. In this event, the state's intestacy laws operate to determine who inherits the property of the deceased. The intestacy statute will usually provide that so much of the deceased's property will go to the surviving spouse, so much to the children, etc. If the marriage has already been annulled, there will be no surviving spouse to take a spouse's intestate share of the decedent's estate. An annulment, as well as a divorce, terminates mutual intestate rights between the former spouses.

With respect to children of annulled marriages, whether they have intestate rights may depend upon whether they are legitimate or

12. On child custody in divorce proceedings, see infra p. 376.

13. On child support orders in divorce proceedings, see infra p. 382.

14. Supra p. 411.

15. On the right of a surviving spouse to elect a statutory share "against" the will, i. e., in lieu of what is provided for the spouse in the will, see infra p. 441.

illegitimate.[16] If the child is legitimate, s/he will take whatever intestate share is provided by statute. At common law, an illegitimate child had no right to inherit from his/her father or mother. In most states, however, this rule has been changed. Some states allow the illegitimate child to inherit from either parent, while others provide that the child can inherit from its mother but not from its father unless the latter acknowledges the child, e. g., by adoption.[17]

7. SOCIAL SECURITY AND WORKMEN'S COMPENSATION BENEFITS: THE REVIVAL PROBLEM AGAIN

In item 3 above, we discussed the problem of revival in connection with alimony payments. The same problem exists with respect to certain statutory entitlement benefits. Suppose, for example, that Jane is entitled to certain social security or workmen's compensation benefits following the death of her husband, Jim. These benefits will cease if and when she remarries. Jane then marries Tom and the benefits stop. The marriage with Tom, however, is subsequently annulled. Are the benefits now revived on the theory that Jane was never married to Tom? Case law is split on this question with some cases holding that the benefits do revive and others concluding the opposite.

8. CRIMINAL LAW CONSEQUENCES

Ed marries Diane. He leaves her without obtaining a divorce. He then marries Claire. He is charged with the crime of bigamy.[18] Is it a defense that his marriage with Claire is annulled so that it could be argued that he was never married to Claire? Most of the cases that have answered this question have said that the subsequent annulment is *not* a defense to the bigamy charge.

9. INTERSPOUSAL IMMUNITY IN TORT ACTIONS

As we shall see later,[19] in some states, one spouse cannot sue another for certain personal torts, e. g., if George assaults his wife, Paulene, she would not be able to sue him for the tort of assault. (She might be able to initiate a criminal action against him for the crime of assault and battery, but she could not bring a civil assault action against him.) An annulment of the marriage would not change this result. Even if George's marriage with Paulene was later annulled, she would still not be able to bring this tort action against him. The annulment does not have the effect of wiping out the remaining vestiges of the interspousal tort immunity.

16. Infra p. 449.

17. Infra p. 463.

18. On bigamy, see also supra p. 177.

19. Infra p. 477.

10. THE PRIVILEGE FOR MARITAL COMMUNICATIONS

At common law, one spouse was not allowed to give testimony concerning confidential communications that were exchanged between the spouses during the marriage. The details of this prohibition will be explained in greater detail later.[20] For now, our question is as follows:

> Sam is married to Helen. Their marriage is annulled. A year later Sam is sued by a neighbor who claims that Sam negligently damaged the neighbor's property. The alleged damage was inflicted while Sam was still married to Helen. At the trial, the neighbor calls Helen as a witness and asks her to testify as to what Sam told her about the incident while they were still living together. According to the privilege for marital communications, Helen would be prohibited from testifying about what she and her husband told each other during the marriage.[21] Their marriage, however, was annulled so that in the eyes of the law, they were never married. Does this change the rule on the privilege? Can Helen give this testimony?

The answer is not clear. Not many cases have considered the issue. Of those that have addressed the question, some have concluded that the annulment does not destroy the privilege, while other cases have reached the opposite conclusion.[22]

11. TAX RETURN STATUS

A husband and wife can enjoy the advantages of income splitting by filing a joint return so long as they were married during the taxable year. Suppose, however, that after ten years of marriage and ten years of filing joint returns, the marriage is annulled. Must the parties now file amended returns for each of those ten years? Should the returns now be filed as separate returns rather than joint ones, again on the theory that the annulment meant that the parties were never validly married? [23] According to Internal Revenue Service, Publication 504, *Tax Information for Divorced or Separated Individuals,* p. 1 (1977 Edition):

> "*If you obtain a decree of annulment* which holds that no valid marriage ever existed, you are not only considered unmarried for that tax year, but you must also file amended returns claiming unmarried status for all tax years not barred by the statute of limitations in which your filing status was determined by your annulled marriage."

20. Infra p. 447.

21. Not all marital communications are privileged. Ibid.

22. See McCormick, *Handbook of the Law of Evidence*, p. 167, 2nd Ed. (1972).

23. See Clark, H., *The Law of Domestic Relations*, p. 143, n. 39 (1968).

Assignment # 45

Answer the following questions by examining the statutory code of your state.

(a) Is there a statute on the question of whether the children of annulled marriages are legitimate? If so, give the citation to the statute and state how the statute resolves the question.

(b) Is there a statute on the question of whether temporary and permanent alimony can be granted in annulment proceedings? If so, give the citation to the statute and state how the statute resolves the question. (Include your answer in Step 8 of the Annulment Litigation Flow Chart, infra p. 242.) (See also General Instructions for the State Code Assignment, supra p. 14.)

Assignment # 46

Charles and Linda agree with each other that they want to be married, but that they do not wish to go through a marriage ceremony. A year later, they have a child, Kevin.

(a) Is Kevin legitimate if Charles and Linda live in a state where common law marriages [24] are illegal?

(b) Is Kevin legitimate if Charles and Linda live in a state where common law marriages are legal, but it is determined that they failed to enter a valid common law marriage because they did not hold themselves out to the public as husband and wife? [25] (See also General Instructions on the Legal Analysis Assignment, supra p. 16.)

Assignment # 47

(a) Fred and Jill are married. Fred is killed in an automobile accident with the ABC Tire Company. Jill brings a wrongful death action against the ABC Tire Company. The attorney of ABC learns that Jill was married to someone else at the time she married Fred. The attorney claims that Jill cannot bring the wrongful death action since she was never validly married to Fred.

(b) Bob and Mary are married. Bob dies intestate (i. e., without leaving a will). Mary claims Bob's estate (i. e., his property) pursuant to the state's intestate law. Bob's only other living relative, Fred, claims that he is entitled to Bob's estate. Fred

24. On common law marriages, see supra p. 164.

25. On the holding out requirement for common law marriages, see supra p. 166.

argues that Mary is not entitled to any of Bob's property because the marriage between Bob and Mary was invalid and should be annulled.

How would the above two problems be resolved in your state? You may have to check both statutory law and case law. (See General Instructions for the State Code Assignment, supra p. 26, and for the Court Opinion Assignment, supra p. 14.)

*

Chapter Fourteen

ANNULMENT: LITIGATION PROCEDURE

SECTION A. JURISDICTION

The word *jurisdiction* refers to the power of a court to render a binding decision.[1] In this section, we will consider how a court acquires jurisdiction in an annulment action or in an action to declare the validity of a marriage. Assuming that a court has jurisdiction, separate questions may arise involving *conflict of laws* (which state law will govern the validity of the marriage) and *venue* (in what county or district in the state should the case be tried). Conflict of laws [2] and venue [3] will be treated later in the chapter.

How does a plaintiff select a state court in which to bring the annulment action? Several possibilities exist:

(1) the state in which the marriage was celebrated;

(2) the state in which the plaintiff and/or the defendant is domiciled [4] at the time the annulment action is begun;

(3) the state in which the defendant is served with process.

If the same state is the state of celebration, the state of domicile and the state in which the defendant is served, no problems of jurisdiction arise. With rare exceptions, such a state has jurisdiction. In our mobile society, parties travel from state to state. It is quite possible for the marriage to have been celebrated in State I, for the plaintiff to be domiciled in State II, for the defendant to be domiciled in State III, and for the parties to be in State IV at the time one of the parties want to bring an annulment action. Which state has jurisdiction to hear the annulment action?

There are two main kinds of jurisdiction: jurisdiction over the *subject matter* [5] and jurisdiction over the *defendant*.

(1) Subject matter jurisdiction

The "subject matter" of the action is the annulment of the marriage or the declaration of its validity. A state's statute or constitution will usually indicate which court or courts in the state can hear annul-

1. Supra p. 22. Sometimes the word "jurisdiction" is used interchangeably with the word "state."

2. Infra p. 225.

3. Infra p. 231.

4. On domicile, generally, see infra p. 345.

5. On subject matter jurisdiction, and other kinds of jurisdiction, see Statsky, W. & Wernet, J., *Case Analysis and Fundamentals of Legal Writing* pp. 12ff. (1977).

ment actions. Factors considered in deciding which court can hear the action include:

—the marriage was contracted within the state;

—the plaintiff and/or defendant is domiciled in or is a resident [6] of the state at the time the action is brought;

—the plaintiff and/or defendant have been domiciliaries or residents of the state for a specified period of time up to the time the action is commenced;

—a combination of the above.

In a few states, subject-matter jurisdiction will be conferred if the parties were married in the state without the requirement of domicile of either or both of the parties. In most states, however, domicile of the plaintiff and/or the defendant is required.

Assignment # 48

(a) What is the name of the court in your state that can hear annulment actions? Write your answer in Step 1 of the Annulment Litigation Flow Chart, infra p. 241. See also Assignment 5, supra p. 43.

(b) How does this court acquire jurisdiction over the subject-matter of annulment actions, e. g., residence or domicile requirements, place of celebration, etc.? Write your answer in Step 2 of the Annulment Litigation Flow Chart, infra p. 241. (See also General Instructions for the State Code Assignment, supra p. 14, and for the Flow Chart Assignment, supra p. 33.)

(2) Jurisdiction over the defendant

In most litigation, it is not enough that a court has subject-matter jurisdiction. A method must exist to bring the defendant into the picture. Suppose that a court in California has the power to hear annulment actions, i. e., it has subject-matter jurisdiction, but the defendant is in Maine. It would obviously be unfair for the California court to litigate the case without giving the defendant notice and an opportunity to be heard. How is this done? Through *service of process.*

The two major kinds of service of process are (1) personal service, e. g., handing the summons [7] and complaint [8] directly to the defendant, and (2) substituted service (something is substituted for personal service), e. g., the publication of notice of the annulment action in a newspaper for a designated period of time. States differ on their

6. Residence is often used interchangeably with domicile. See supra p. 345.

7. A summons is an order requiring the defendant to appear in court. If the summons is ignored, a default judgment may be entered against the defendant.

8. A complaint is a pleading which begins the law suit. It states the grievance of the plaintiff against the defendant in the form of a cause of action. See supra p. 20.

service of process requirements. Some states may require personal service on the defendant in the annulment action, while in other states, substituted service may be authorized under designated circumstances.

Assignment # 49

Answer the following questions by examining the statutory code of your state. (See also General Instructions for the State Code Assignment, supra p. 14, and for the Flow Chart Assignment, supra p. 33.):

(a) Under what circumstances, if any, is service by publication or other substituted service authorized in annulment actions? Write your answer in Step 4 of the Annulment Litigation Flow Chart, infra p. 241.

(b) If service is by publication, what must be contained in the publication?

(c) If personal service is made, what must be served on the defendant? Writ your answer in Step 5 of the Annulment Litigation Flow Chart, infra p. 241.

(d) After service is complete, must an affidavit of compliance be filed? If so, where? Write your answer in Step 6 of the Annulment Litigation Flow Chart, infra p. 241.

NOTE

In some states, the jurisdictional requirements for an annulment action are exactly the same as those for a divorce action. Divorce jurisdiction will be discussed in Chapter Seventeen.[9]

SECTION B. CONFLICTS OF LAW

The conflicts-of-law question usually involves two states: the law where the parties were married (called the "law of celebration") and the law where the parties now live (called the law of domicile [10] or the domiciliary law). The question arises as follows:

> Jim and Jane marry in state "X" where their marriage is valid. They then move to state "Y." If they had married in state "Y," their marriage would not have been valid. Jim sues Jane in state "Y" for an annulment. What annulment law does the court in state "Y" apply? The law of "X" or the law of "Y?"

State "X" is the state of celebration or the state of contract, i. e., the state where the parties entered the marriage contract. State "Y" is the domiciliary state, i. e., the state where the parties are domiciled. State "Y" is also called the "forum state," meaning the state where the suit is being brought. Specifically, the forum is the court hearing the

9. Infra p. 343.

10. On domicile, see infra p. 345.

case. In the above example, the domiciliary state happens to be the same of the forum state.

Before examining the question of what law applies, we need to keep in mind the public policy favoring marriages. Legislatures and courts tend to look for reasons to validate a marriage, rather than create circumstances that make it easy to invalidate it. This is all the more so if the parties have lived together for a long time and if children have been born from the union. We have already seen that the law has imposed a presumption that a marriage is valid.[11] The public policy favoring marriage, however, is not absolute. Other public policies must also be taken into account. The conflict-of-law rules are a product of a clash of public policies.

GENERAL CONFLICTS-OF-LAW RULE IN ANNULMENT ACTIONS
If the marriage is valid in the state of celebration (even though it would have been invalid if it had been contracted in the domiciliary state), the marriage will be recognized as valid in the domiciliary state *unless* the recognition of the marriage would violate some strong public policy of the domiciliary state.

[B8802]

Hence, in the hypothetical involving Jim and Jane above, the general rule would mean that the state of "Y" would apply the law of the state of "X" unless to do so would violate some strong public policy of "Y." Assuming that no such policy would be violated, the annulment would be denied since the marriage was valid in the state of celebration, in "X." Assuming, however, that a strong public policy is involved, the state of "Y" would apply its own law and grant the annulment.

What do we mean by a strong public policy, the violation of which would cause a domiciliary state to apply its own marriage law? Some states provide that if the marriage would have been *void* [12] had it been contracted in the domiciliary state, then the latter state will not recognize the marriage even though the state of celebration recognizes the marriage as valid. In other words, it is against the strong public policy of a domiciliary state to recognize what it considers a void marriage regardless of the fact that other states would consider the marriage valid. Hence, whether a domiciliary state considers a marriage to be void or voidable may have a lot to do with whether it will recognize an out-of-state marriage. As we saw in Chapters Eleven and Twelve, states differ on which annulment grounds will render a mar-

11. Supra p. 174.

12. For a listing of each ground for annulment and whether a state considers a marriage in violation of that ground to be void or voidable, see supra pp. 177–210.

riage void or voidable.[13] A marriage which the domiciliary state would consider bigamous [14] or incestuous [15] are almost never recognized. In such cases, the domiciliary state will apply its own marriage law and grant the annulment even though the marriage may have been valid in the state of celebration. When other grounds for annulment are involved, states differ as to whether they, as domiciliary states, will apply their own marriage law or that of the state of celebration.

Marriage Evasion Statutes

Suppose that a man and woman live in a state where they cannot marry, e. g., they are under age.[16] They move from their domiciliary state to another state solely for the purpose of entering or contracting a marriage since they can validly marry under the laws of the latter state, e. g., they are not under age in this state. They then move back to their domiciliary state. If an annulment action is brought in the domiciliary state, what law will be applied? The marriage law of the domiciliary state or that of the state of celebration? If the annulment action is brought in the state of celebration, what law will be applied? Again the conflicts question becomes critical because the annulment will be granted or denied depending upon which state's marriage law will be applied. Note that the man and woman went to the state of celebration in order to *evade* the marriage laws of the domiciliary state. Several states have enacted marriage evasion statutes to cover this situation. In such states, the choice of law depends upon the presence or absence of an intent to evade. The statute might read as follows:

> § 1. If any person residing and intending to continue to reside in this state who is disabled or prohibited from contracting marriage under the laws of this state shall go into another state or country and there contract a marriage prohibited and declared void by the laws of this state, such marriage shall be null and void for all purposes in this state with the same effect as though such prohibited marriage has been entered into in this state.
>
> § 2. No marriage shall be contracted in this state by a party residing and intending to continue to reside in another state or jurisdiction if such marriage would be void if contracted in such other state or jurisdiction and every marriage celebrated in this state in violation of this provision shall be null and void.[17]

13. Ibid.

14. Supra p. 177.

15. Supra p. 183.

16. Supra p. 186.

17. National Conference of Commissioners on Uniform State Laws, "Uniform Marriage Evasion Act". The Uniform Commissioners withdrew the Uniform Marriage Evasion Act in 1943 because so few states had adopted it. There are, however, states that still have statutes the same as or similar to the Uniform Act quoted in the text.

It is sometimes very difficult to prove whether the parties went to the other state with the intent to evade the marriage laws of their domiciliary state. It may depend on how long they remained in the state of celebration, whether they returned to their initial domiciliary state or established a domicile in another state altogether. The INTERVIEWING AND INVESTIGATION CHECKLIST below is designed to assist you in collecting evidence on intent:

INTERVIEWING AND INVESTIGATION CHECKLIST

FACTORS RELEVANT TO THE INTENT TO EVADE THE MARRIAGE LAWS[18]

	Legal Interviewing Questions	Possible Investigation Tasks
1.	How long have the two of you lived in the state of "X?"	• Obtain copies of all records which tend to establish the kind of contact that the parties had with state "Y," e.g., motel receipts, bank statements, rent receipts, employment records. • Interview friends, relatives and associates of the parties to determine what light they can shed on the intent of the parties in going to the state of "Y."
2.	Why didn't you get married in "X?"	
3.	When did you decide to go to "Y?"	
4.	Have you or D ever lived in "Y?"	
5.	Do you or D have any relatives in "Y?"	
6.	Were you or D born in "Y?"	
7.	On what date did you and D go to "Y?"	
8.	Did you sell your home or move out of your apartment in "X?"	
9.	When you left "X," did you intend to come back?	
10.	After you arrived in "Y," when did you apply for a marriage license?	
11.	On what date were you married?	
12.	While you were in "Y," where did you stay? Did you have all your clothes and furniture with you?	
13.	Who attended the wedding ceremony in "Y?"	
14.	Did you and D have sexual relations in "Y?"	
15.	Did you or D work in "Y?"	
16.	How long did you stay in "Y?"	
17.	Did you ever vote or pay taxes in "Y?"	
18.	Did you open a checking account in any bank in the state of "Y?"	
19.	Where did you go after you left "Y?"	

IM-472

18. See also the INTERVIEWING & INVESTIGATION CHECKLIST for establishing domicile, infra p. 348.

Thus far, our focus has been on marriages which are valid in the state of celebration, but invalid and annullable in the domiciliary state if it had been contracted in the latter state:

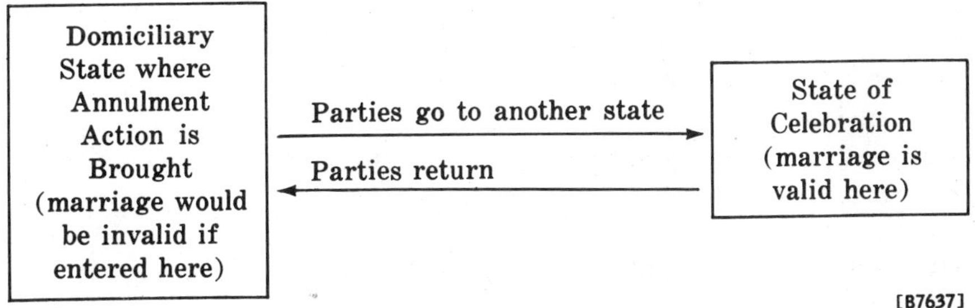

Suppose, however, that the marriage was invalid in the state of celebration. The parties then move to a new state where they establish a domicile.[19] If they had been married in their new domicile state, their marriage would have been valid. An annulment action is brought in their new domicile state:

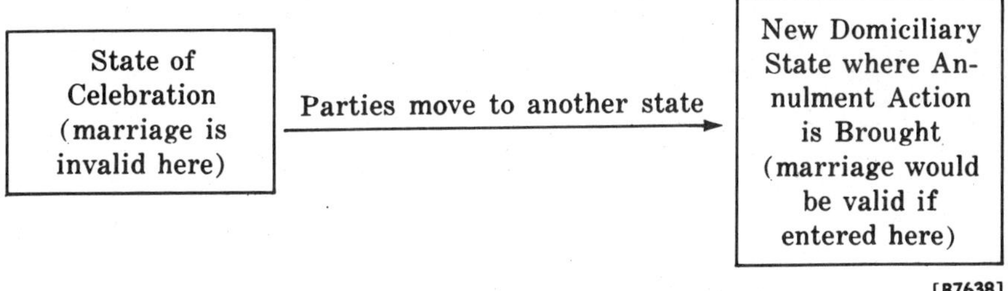

Our question now becomes: if a marriage is invalid where contracted, can it ever be considered valid in any other state? Will a present domiciliary state validate a marriage which is invalid according to the law of the state of celebration? Surprisingly, the answer is yes. In some states, a domiciliary state will *deny* an annulment of a marriage which would have been valid if contracted in the domiciliary state but which is clearly invalid in the state where it was actually contracted. Such states will take this position, in part, because of the public policy mentioned earlier (and indeed the presumption) favoring the validity of marriages.[20]

NOTE

On conflicts-of-law problems involving common law marriages, see earlier discussion.[21]

19. Infra p. 345.

20. Supra p. 174.

21. Supra p. 168.

Assignment # 50

(a) Is there a statute in your state which deals with marriages contracted out of state? If so, give its citation and state how it handles such marriages. (See also General Instructions for the State Code Assignment, supra p. 14.)

(b) Find a court opinion written by a state court in your state which involved an annulment action brought in your state concerning a marriage that was contracted in another state. (If no such action has ever been brought in your state, then you can pick an opinion from any state.) Answer the following questions about the opinion you found:

(i) In what state was the marriage contracted?

(ii) What was the ground for the annulment?

(iii) What marriage law was applied in the opinion?

(iv) What reason did the court give for applying that law?

(v) Was the annulment granted? Why or why not?

(See also General Instructions for the Court Opinion Assignment, supra p. 26.)

SUMMARY

1. A marriage will be considered valid in a domiciliary state if (a) the marriage is valid according to the state where it was contracted, and (b) recognizing the validity of the marriage would not violate any strong public policy of the domiciliary state. If both conditions are met, the domiciliary state will deny the annulment even though the marriage could have been annulled if it had been contracted in the domiciliary state.
2. Generally, if a marriage would have been void had it been contracted in the domiciliary state, the latter state will not apply the law of the state of celebration where the marriage is valid.
3. Some states have statutes which invalidate marriages contracted in other states solely to evade its marriage laws.
4. Some states have statutes which invalidate marriages contracted in their own state solely to evade the marriage laws of other states.
5. Some states will validate a marriage contracted in another state (even though the marriage is invalid in the state where it was contracted) so long as the marriage would have been valid if it had been contracted in the state where the parties are now domiciled. In effect, such a state will deny the annulment even though the state of celebration would have granted it.

[B7631]

SECTION C. A FLOW CHART OF ANNULMENT LITIGATION STEPS IN YOUR STATE

A Litigation Flow Chart, as pointed out in Chapter one,[22] is simply a list of the major steps involved in a particular litigation. At the end of this Chapter, you will be asked to compile such a Flow Chart for annulment litigation in your state.[23] We have already begun to identify pieces of the Flow Chart in prior assignments on temporary alimony and custody, and on jurisdiction. To complete the Flow Chart, we need briefly to consider the following topics:

(1) Venue.

(2) Statute of limitations and laches.

(3) Pleadings.

(4) Parties.

(5) Discovery.

(6) Standard of proof.

(7) Judgment.

(8) Appeal.

(1) Venue

A state's judicial system usually parallels its geographic breakdown into counties, districts, regions, etc. Each county, for example, may have its own county court. The word *venue* [24] refers to the place of the trial. Suppose there are twelve counties throughout the state, each with its own county court. The selection of the county in which to bring the suit is called the *choice of venue*. Venue should be distinguished from jurisdiction.[25] Jurisdiction is the *power* that a court has to hear a particular case. When we refer to a choice of venue, we mean the selection of one or more courts within the state or judicial system. Whichever court is chosen must also have jurisdiction. Statutes exist in almost every state which determine how venue is to be selected, e. g., according to the residence [26] of one or more of the litigants.

Assignment # 51

How is venue determined in your state in an annulment action? Your state code may have a specific statute on venue in annulment actions, or there may be a general venue statute governing all or most of the civil actions that can be brought in your state. Write your an-

22. Supra p. 33.

23. Infra p. 241.

24. Supra p. 223. See also Statsky, W., & Wernet, J., *Case Analysis and Fundamentals of Legal Writing*, p. 53 (1977).

25. Supra p. 223.

26. Infra p. 346.

swer in Step 3 of the Annulment Litigation Flow Chart, infra p. 241. (See also General Instructions for the State Code Assignment, supra p. 14, and the Flow Chart Assignment, supra p. 33.)

(2) Statute of limitations and laches

A statute of limitations is a specific time limit within which a party must commence a court action or be barred from ever being able to bring that action. The laches defense has the same effect, except that there is no set time which must elapse before the laches defense will bar the action. Laches applies when it would be unfair or inequitable to permit the annulment because of the length of time the plaintiff waited to commence the action and because of the particular circumstances of the case, e. g., the birth of children, the ill health and age of the defendant.

Most, but not all, states have statutes of limitation governing the time within which an annulment must be brought. The void/voidable distinction [27] might be relevant. If the marriage is considered void because of the particular ground used to challenge it, e. g., the marriage is incestuous,[28] then there may be no statute of limitations at all. The annulment action can be brought at any time, perhaps even after the death of one of the parties to the marriage! When there is a statute of limitations, the time period will usually begin to run from the date of the marriage or from the date of discovery of the particular impediment, e. g., the facts constituting the fraud.[29]

Assignment # 52

For each of the grounds for annulment listed below, you are to determine what statute of limitations, if any, applies in your state. (See also General Instructions for the State Code Assignment, supra p. 14.) Next to each of the grounds mentioned, place one of four answers:

—the general statute of limitation applies [30];

—no statute of limitation is provided;

—the time period is ____ years and begins to run from the date of the marriage;

—the time period is ____ years and begins to run from the date of discovery of the facts constituting the ground.

For each answer that you provide, give the citation to the state code section from which you obtained the answer.

(a) Bigamy [31] ______________________________

Citation ______________________________

27. Supra p. 172.

28. Supra p. 183.

29. Supra p. 205.

30. Supra p. 34.

31. Supra p. 177.

(b) Consanguinity and Affinity [32] ______________________

Citation ______________________

(c) Nonage [33] ______________________

Citation ______________________

(d) Physical Disabilities [34] ______________________

Citation ______________________

(e) Mental Disabilities [35] ______________________

Citation ______________________

(f) Duress [36] ______________________

Citation ______________________

(g) Fraud [37] ______________________

Citation ______________________

Select any one of the above answers and write it in Step 7 of the Annulment Litigation Flow Chart, infra p. 242. (If you cannot find the answers in the state code, you may have to check court opinions. See General Instructions for the Court Opinion Assignment, supra p. 26.)

(3) Pleadings

Annulment actions are like most other civil actions with respect to the rules governing pleading.[38]

Assignment # 53

Most of the following questions can be answered by examining your state statutory code and/or your court rules. (See also General Instructions for the State Code Assignment, supra p. 14, and for the Flow Chart Assignment, supra p. 33.) Some of the answers can be found in those sections of your state code that cover annulments, while others can be found in the procedure and practice sections that cover civil actions generally. Give the citation to the source where you got each answer.

(a) Must the complaint [39] for annulment be subscribed and/or verified? If so, who must do so? Write your answer in Step 9 of the Annulment Litigation Flow Chart, infra p. 242.

32. Supra p. 183.

33. Supra p. 186.

34. Supra p. 190.

35. Supra p. 198.

36. Supra p. 203.

37. Supra p. 205.

38. On divorce procedures, see infra p. 343. See also supra p. 33.

39. Supra p. 20.

(b) Where is the complaint filed? Write your answer in Step 10, infra p. 242.

(c) How many days does the defendant have to answer the complaint? Write your answer in Step 11, infra p. 242.

(d) Where and how is the answer filed and served? Write your answer in Step 12, infra p. 242.

(e) Must the answer be subscribed and/or verified? If so, by whom? Write your answer in Step 13, infra p. 242.

(f) How does the defendant raise a counterclaim? Write your answer in Step 14, infra p. 242.

(g) How many days does the plaintiff have to reply to the defendant's counterclaim? Write your answer in Step 15, infra p. 243.

(h) Where and how is the reply filed and served? Write your answer in Step 16, infra p. 243.

(i) Can there be a jury trial in an annulment action? If so, when must it be requested? Write your answer in Step 17, infra p. 243.

(j) How can a party go about getting more time to prepare a pleading? Write your answer in Step 18, infra p. 243.

(k) How does the plaintiff amend his/her complaint? Write your answer in Step 19, infra p. 243.

(4) Parties

As we surveyed each of the grounds for annulment in Chapters Eleven [40] and Twelve,[41] we briefly looked at the question of who had standing to bring the annulment action on that ground: the innocent spouse only, either spouse, the parent or guardian of one of the spouses? We also saw that certain parties were barred from bringing the annulment action if the defendant could successfully raise defenses such as ratification through cohabitation.[42] Another question concerning parties, mentioned briefly in the context of statute of limitations above,[43] is whether the annulment action can be brought after the death of one of the parties. For example:

> George and Karen are married. George leaves Karen and marries Diana. George and Karen never obtain a divorce. Diana then dies. There is a cloud over George's marriage with Diana because at the time he married her, Karen was still alive. To remove the cloud, George brings an annulment action against Diana's estate. (Assume that George has returned to Karen and wants the record clear that he was never married to Diana.)

40. Supra pp. 177–194.

41. Supra pp. 195–211.

42. E. g. supra p. 189.

43. Supra p. 232.

Whether the marriage can be annulled after the death of one of the parties may depend upon the ground asserted for the annulment. If the ground is one which would render the marriage void,[44] then the annulment action can usually be brought. If, however, the marriage would be voidable [45] only, the annulment action will usually be barred by the death of one of the parties.

Who the parties are in an annulment action is also relevant to problems of res judicata and collateral attack to be discussed below.[46]

(5) Discovery

The word *discovery* refers to the standard methods by which a party can obtain information from the other party prior to trial in order to assist in preparation for trial. These methods are:

—depositions [47];

—interrogatories [48];

—requests for admission [49];

—court ordered physical or mental examination.

Assignment # 54

The following questions are to be answered by examining your state statutory code and your court rules. (See also General Instructions for the State Code Assignment, supra p. 14, and for the Flow Chart Assignment, supra p. 33.) Check statutes and rules governing annulment actions in particular, as well as statutes and rules governing all civil actions in your state. Note all special limitations, if any, on the use of discovery in annulment actions.

(a) When must a deposition be requested in an annulment action in your state? How is the request made? Write your answer in Step 20, infra p. 243.

(b) When and on whom can interrogatories be filed? Write your answer in Step 21, infra p. 243.

(c) When must interrogatories be answered? Write your answer in Step 22, infra p. 243.

(d) When can a request (or demand) for admissions be made? Write your answer in Step 23, infra p. 244.

44. Supra p. 172.

45. Supra p. 172.

46. Infra p. 236.

47. Oral questions directed by one party in litigation to the other party or to a witness of the other party. The deposition is conducted outside the courtroom, usually in one of the lawyer's offices. A transcript (word-for-word account) is made of the questions and answers.

48. Supra p. 31. Written questions and answers.

49. Written statements of facts concerning the case which are submitted to an adverse party and which that party is required to admit or deny.

(e) When will the court order a physical or mental examination? Write your answer in Step 24, infra p. 244.

(6) Standard of proof

As we have seen, the law does not encourage the dissolution of marriage,[50] and one of the best indications of this is the presumption favoring the validity of a marriage.[51] In an annulment action, the burden of proof is on the plaintiff, and many states require that burden must be met by *clear and convincing* evidence which is a higher standard than the preponderance-of-evidence test.[52] Furthermore, many states require that there be corroboration [53] of the plaintiff's evidence.

(7) Judgment

(A) Jim marries Jane. Jim sues Jane for an annulment on the ground of bigamy. He loses on the merits [54], the annulment is denied.

One year later Jim again sues Jane for annulment on the ground of bigamy.

(B) Bill marries Claire. Claire sues Bill for a divorce and wins. One year later, Claire sues Bill for an annulment.

In both of these cases, the later actions will usually be barred by the defense of *res judicata.*[55] In the first case (A), Jim already had his day in court and will not be allowed to relitigate the same issue of whether Jane was married to someone else when she married him. The second case (B) is more difficult to analyze. In Claire's first action against Bill—the divorce action—there were no annulment issues explicitly raised. But recall the difference between an annulment and a divorce: an annulment means that the parties were never married, while a divorce is a dissolution of a marriage validly entered.[56] When

50. It may be argued, however, that the emergence of the "no-fault" divorce is a trend in the other direction, see infra p. 306.

51. Supra p. 174.

52. The preponderance test is simply that the evidence favoring the establishment of a disputed fact is more believable than the evidence favoring the non-establishment of that fact.

53. Infra p. 318. Corroboration "means that the testimony of the plaintiff has been made more credible or more probable by other evidence, either direct or circumstantial." Clark, H., *Cases and Problems on Domestic Relations*, p. 721, Second Edition (1974). See also Annotation, "Necessity and sufficiency of corroboration of plaintiff's testimony concerning ground for annulment of marriage," 71 A.L.R.2d 620 (1960).

54. The phrase "on the merits" means that the judgment was rendered on the substance of the claim, rather than on some procedural technicality.

55. Res judicata is a legal doctrine that a judgment on the merits will prevent the same parties from relitigating the same cause of action on the same facts. Sometimes the doctrine will also bar nonparties from relitigating. See infra p. 395.

56. Supra p. 171.

the court rendered its divorce judgment, it *impliedly* acknowledged that the marriage was valid, i. e., it dissolved a valid marriage. If Claire felt that the marriage was not validly entered, she should have raised this when she filed her divorce action. She probably could have sought a divorce, or in the alternative, an annulment in the same action.[57] She failed to do so; she sought a divorce only, and by doing so, she impliedly acknowledged the validity of the marriage. Hence, she has already had her day in court on the issue of the validity of the marriage, and her annulment action will be barred by the defense of res judicata.

(C) Fran marries Walter. They have one child, Kenneth. Walter sues Fran for an annulment on the ground of duress. Fran obtains a valid judgment denying the annulment.

Fran later brings a support action against Walter. Walter raises the defense that their marriage is invalid.

(D) Fran marries Walter. They have one child, Kenneth. Walter brings an annulment action against Fran. Fran obtains a valid judgment denying the annulment.

Fran dies. In a probate proceeding involving Fran's estate, Kenneth claims that Walter is not entitled to inherit from his mother because his mother and father were never validly married.

Both of these examples involve attacks on the validity of the marriage which are *not* raised in a proceeding directly challenging the marriage. The support action in (C) and the probate action in (D) do not directly challenge the marriage.[58] Again, res judicata will prevent Walter from claiming that the marriage is invalid in the support action (C), and it will prevent Kenneth from claiming the marriage was invalid in the probate proceeding (D). The issue of the validity of the marriage was already litigated in Walter's initial annulment action. Walter was a party to that action and he will not be allowed to relitigate the issue. Kenneth was not a party to the initial annulment action, but he will still be bound by the judgment in that action as to the issue of the validity of the marriage. Res judicata acts as a bar to parties and to non-parties of an annulment action on the issue of whether or not the marriage was valid.

(E) Fran marries Walter. They have one child, Kenneth. Walter suspects that he is not the father. Walter knew that Fran was pregnant at the time of their marriage, but Fran told Walter that he (Walter) was the father. Walter sues Fran for annulment on the ground of fraud since he now believes that Fran lied to him about who the father is. At the annulment trial, Fran insists that Walter is the father.

57. Supra p. 172.

58. See also infra p. 395.

The court finds that Walter is not the father, that Fran lied to him at the time of their marriage. The annulment is granted.[59]

Years later, Kenneth brings a support action against his "father," Walter. Walter's defense is that the prior annulment judgment determined that he was not Kenneth's father, and hence he owes him no duty of support.[60]

Is Kenneth's claim barred by the doctrine of res judicata? Kenneth was not a party to the annulment action. We said earlier that non-parties are bound by annulment judgments on the question of the *validity of the marriage*. But Kenneth is not taking a position on the validity of the marriage between Fran and Walter. He is making a claim separate from the validity of the marriage. His claim is that Walter is his father and owes him a duty of support. The annulment judgment *did* say that Walter was *not* Kenneth's father and it would seem that he should be bound by this determination and not be allowed to relitigate the issue of paternity in his support action. The law, however, is otherwise. While a non-party is barred by res judicata from relitigating the issue of the validity of the marriage which was settled in the earlier annulment action, res judicata will not bar a non-party from later relitigating facts (e. g., fatherhood) which were litigated as part of the annulment action. Hence, Walter's defense in the example above (E) will not work. Kenneth will be allowed to introduce evidence that Walter is his father. Res judicata will not bar him from doing so.

(F) Ida and Ralph are married in New York. Ida sues Ralph for an annulment and wins; the annulment is granted.

Ralph moves to New Jersey and claims that Ida, as his wife, has a duty to follow him and to live with him in New Jersey. When she refuses, he tries to sue her in a New Jersey court to force her to go with him.

A New Jersey court would not support Ralph's claim that Ida is his wife and that she has a duty to live with him. The New Jersey court would have to give *full faith and credit*[61] to the New York annulment judgment. Hence, Ralph would be barred by res judicata from relitigating the validity of the marriage. He is bound by the New York judgment unless he can show that the New York court did not have jurisdiction[62] when it issued the annulment judgment, e. g., by show-

59. Some courts might deny the annulment on the theory that Walter has "dirty hands" due to his own illicit intercourse with Fran before they were married, supra p. 208.

60. On the duty to support, see infra p. 433.

61. Infra p. 351.

62. Supra p. 223.

ing that he was never validly served with process [63] or by showing that the New York court lacked subject-matter jurisdiction [64] over the case.

One final aspect of judgments needs to be considered: the default judgment.

(G) Tom and Jessica are married. Tom decides to sue for an annulment. He files his complaint for annulment in a court with subject-matter jurisdiction. Jessica is properly served with process. On the date when Jessica is supposed to submit her answer to the court, nothing is heard from her. She completely ignores the proceeding.

In most civil actions, Jessica's non-response would have led to a default judgment against her, meaning that the plaintiff (Tom) would win what he sought without the necessity of going through a trial. In matrimonial actions, however, a different process usually takes place. A default judgment is not automatic in many states upon the failure of the defendant to appear. The plaintiff may be required to submit his/her evidence before the judge in order to demonstrate that the plaintiff is entitled to the relief sought, i. e., to prove that evidence supporting the cause of action exists. Other states are even more formal. A state attorney [65] may have to be notified whenever the defendant has defaulted, or whenever the action is uncontested. In effect, the state becomes a "party" to the matrimonial litigation. The attorney for the state acts in the best interests of the individuals involved, particularly the children. This is done to lessen the danger that the court will get a distorted picture from the plaintiff of what has happened in the marriage due to the fact that the defendant is not present to counter what the plaintiff is saying.

Assignment # 55

(a) Ida and Kevin are married. Ida sues Kevin for divorce. Kevin does not contest Ida's right to have the divorce decree in her favor. His main interest is to obtain favorable visitation rights for his children. Five years later, Kevin discovers that Ida had concealed from him the fact that she was already married to someone else at the time she married him. Kevin then brings an annulment action on the grounds of bigamy and fraud. Can Ida raise the defense of res judicata? Can she raise the defense of statute of limitations? (See also General Instructions for the Legal Analysis Assignment, supra p. 16.)

(b) Draft an annulment complaint for Kevin against Ida. (See General Instructions for the Complaint Drafting Assignment, supra p. 20.)

63. Supra p. 224.

64. Supra p. 223.

65. E. g., the "prosecuting attorney" in the state of Washington. Section 26.08.080, Rev.Code Wash.Ann. (1961).

Assignment # 56

Does your state have a statute on what happens when the defendant fails to appear or otherwise to pursue the annulment action brought against him/her? Is a default judgment automatic? Write your answer in Step 25 of the Annulment Litigation Flow Chart, infra p. 244. (See also General Instructions for the State Code Assignment, supra p. 14, and the Flow Chart Assignment, supra p. 33.)

(8) Appeal [66]

Assignment # 57

Answer the following questions after examining the statutory code and the court rules of your state. (See also General Instructions for the State Code Assignment, supra p. 14, and for the Flow Chart Assignment, supra p. 33.)

(a) Once an annulment judgment has been rendered by the trial court, to what court can the judgment be appealed? Write your answer in Step 26, infra p. 244.

(b) From the date of the judgment, how many days does the party have to file the appeal? Write your answer in Step 27, infra p. 244.

(c) Where and how is the notice of appeal filed and served? Write your answer in Step 28, infra p. 244.

Assignment # 58

In this assignment, you are asked to interview a paralegal, a lawyer or a legal secretary who has been involved in an annulment action in your state. (See also General Instructions for the Law Office Management Assignment supra p. 34.) Find out answers to the following questions:

(a) Approximately how many annulment cases have you worked on?

(b) When a client is first interviewed, does s/he usually know that s/he wants an annulment?

(c) What are the major steps that you have to go through to process an annulment in this state? Documents to be filed, court appearances, etc.

(d) What form or practice book, if any, do you use that is helpful?

(e) Does your office have its own internal manual that would cover any aspects of annulment procedure? If so, please describe it.

(f) In an annulment action, what is the division of labor among the attorney, the paralegal and the secretary? Who does what?

66. Supra p. 34 and infra p. 384.

Assignment # 59

ANNULMENT LITIGATION FLOW CHART FOR YOUR STATE

(Fill in each step after checking the law of your state, particularly your state statutory code. You may also need to refer to court rules and to judicial opinions. See also General Instructions for the Flow Chart Assignment, supra p. 33. For each step, give the citation to the statute, court rule or case that you used to fill in the answer.)

STEP 1[67]

Name the court that can hear annulment actions:
Citation:

STEP 2[68]

How does the court acquire subject-matter jurisdiction over the annulment action:
Citation:

STEP 3[69]

How is venue determined:
Citation:

STEP 4[70]

When, if ever, is substituted service of process allowed:
Citation:

STEP 5[71]

What must be personally served on the defendant:
Citation:

STEP 6[72]

After service is complete, must an affidavit of compliance be filed? If so, where:
Citation:

---

67. See Assignment #48(a), supra p. 224.
68. See Assignment #48(b), supra p. 224.
69. See Assignment #51, supra p. 231.
70. See Assignment #49(a), supra p. 225.
71. See Assignment #49(c), supra p. 225.
72. See Assignment #49(d), supra p. 225.

ANNULMENT LITIGATION FLOW CHART FOR YOUR STATE—Continued

STEP 7[73]

Select any ground for annulment and state the statute of limitations, if any, for bringing the annulment action on that ground:
Citation:

STEP 8[74]

Can an order for temporary alimony, custody and support be issued:
Citation:

STEP 9[75]

Must the complaint be subscribed and/or verified? If so, by whom:
Citation:

STEP 10[76]

Where is the complaint filed:
Citation:

STEP 11[77]

How many days does the defendant have to answer the complaint:
Citation:

STEP 12[78]

Where and how is the answer filed and served:
Citation:

STEP 13[79]

Must the answer be subscribed and/or verified? If so, by whom:
Citation:

STEP 14[80]

How does the defendant raise a counter-claim:
Citation:

73. See Assignment #52, supra p. 232.

74. See Assignment #45(b), supra p. 220.

75. See Assignment #53(a), supra p. 233.

76. See Assignment #53(b), supra p. 234.

77. See Assignment #53(c), supra p. 234.

78. See Assignment #53(d), supra p. 234.

79. See Assignment #53(e), supra p. 234.

80. See Assignment #53(f), supra p. 234.

ANNULMENT LITIGATION FLOW CHART FOR YOUR STATE—Continued

STEP 15[81]

How many days does the plaintiff have to reply to the defendant's counterclaim:
Citation:

STEP 16[82]

Where and how is the reply filed and served:
Citation:

STEP 17[83]

Can there be a jury trial in an annulment action? If so, when must it be requested:
Citation:

STEP 18[84]

How can a party go about getting more time to prepare a pleading:
Citation:

STEP 19[85]

How does the plaintiff amend his/her complaint:
Citation:

STEP 20[86]

When must a deposition be requested? How is the request made:
Citation:

STEP 21[87]

When and on whom can interrogatories be filed:
Citation:

STEP 22[88]

When must interrogatories be answered:
Citation:

81. See Assignment #53(g), supra p. 234

82. See Assignment #53(h), supra p. 234.

83. See Assignment #53(i), supra p. 234.

84. See Assignment #53(j), supra p. 234.

85. See Assignment #53(k), supra p. 243.

86. See Assignment #54(a), supra p. 235.

87. See Assignment #54(b), supra p. 235.

88. See Assignment #54(c), supra p. 235.

ANNULMENT LITIGATION FLOW CHART FOR YOUR STATE—Continued

STEP 23[89]

When can a request (or demand) for admissions be made:
Citation:

STEP 24[90]

When will the court order a physical or mental examination:
Citation:

STEP 25[91]

What happens if the defendant fails to answer the plaintiff's complaint? Is the default judgment automatic:
Citation:

STEP 26[92]

To what court can an annulment judgment be appealed:
Citation:

STEP 27[93]

How many days does the party have to file the appeal:
Citation:

STEP 28[94]

Where and how is the notice of appeal filed and served:
Citation:

IM-475

---

89. See Assignment #54(d), supra p. 235.
90. See Assignment #54(e), supra p. 236.
91. See Assignment #56, supra p. 240.
92. See Assignment #57(a), supra p. 240.
93. See Assignment #57(b), supra p. 240.
94. See Assignment #57(c), supra p. 240.

Chapter Fifteen

SEPARATION AGREEMENTS: LEGAL ISSUES AND DRAFTING OPTIONS

SECTION A. INTRODUCTION

The tax implications of separation agreements and divorce will be treated later in Chapter Nineteen.[1]

A separation agreement is a post nuptial contract [2] between a husband and wife governing their rights and obligations toward each other while they are separated.[3] Generally, a divorce is contemplated by both parties when they enter the agreement. This, however, is not always the case. Many separation agreements are written by parties who never become divorced, and hence, who never remarry. In most states, it is not necessary for a court to approve the separation agreement for it to be binding. Courts become involved, if at all, in the following kinds of situations:

—one party sues the other for breach of contract, i. e., for violation of the separation agreement; the plaintiff in this suit wants the original separation agreement enforced; [4]

—one party (after the divorce) brings a suit to set aside the separation agreement, e. g., because it is invalid [5] (a wife might try to bring such a suit after her husband dies in order to be able to take an election share of his estate [6] rather than be satisfied with what the separation agreement provided for her);

—the parties may later file for a judicial separation [7] and ask the court to use the separation agreement as the basis of the judicial separation decree;

—the parties may later file for a divorce and ask the court either (a) to approve the terms of the separation agreement, (b) to

1. Infra p. 411.

2. On contracts made by a man and woman before marriage, i. e., an antenuptial agreement, see supra p. 127. On contracts made between people living together who do not intend to marry (contract cohabitation) see supra p. 142.

3. In community property states (see infra p. 275), the separation agreement is often called the property settlement agreement.

4. See infra p. 282.

5. Infra p. 253.

6. Infra p. 281.

7. Infra p. 405.

approve them and to incorporate them into the divorce decree so that the decree and the agreement become merged.[8]

In many ways, the negotiation and drafting of the separation agreement are the most important and difficult tasks of the Family Law practitioner. The law encourages the parties to enter separation agreements. So long as certain basic public policy considerations (to be discussed below [9]) are not violated, the law gives a great deal of leeway to the parties to resolve their difficulties, and, in effect, to decide what their relationship will be toward each other on such vital matters as alimony, property division, custody and visitation of the children, etc. The role of the lawyer and paralegal is to assist the client in this large endeavor. If this role is not carried out effectively, one of the parties may be grossly taken advantage of and/or the difficulties between the spouses will have to be resolved by litigation.

At the very top of the Family Law practitioner's priority must be the avoidance of litigation. Litigation is often extremely time consuming, expensive and emotionally draining on the part of everybody. The marital breakdown of the parties was probably a most painful experience for the entire family. Litigation tends to remind the parties of old sores and to keep the bitterness alive. While a separation agreement will not produce abundant harmony between the spouses, it can keep the parties on a constructive level, and, to the extent that it is a substitute for litigation, the separation agreement can do a great deal to simplify and to tone down what can be a complex and strained set of circumstances.

Is there always a need for a written separation agreement? If one does not exist, will everything inevitably end up in litigation? Not necessarily. It is extremely unwise, however, for the parties to rely exclusively on their oral understandings of what they agreed to do about accumulated property, future expenses, custody and visitation of the children, etc. It makes good sense that they should deal with such matters *in writing* whenever possible. Misunderstandings can arise as to "who was supposed to get what," and "who was supposed to do what." A well drafted separation agreement can never eliminate all such controversies, but can avoid most of them. While it is conceivable that no controversies will ever arise after the parties separate, or that both parties, when separated, will be level headed enough to be able to work out any difficulties that do arise, this is highly unlikely. The safer course is for the parties to put everything down in writing in the form of a separation agreement. This is so even if the parties live in a state which would enforce an oral separation agreement.

8. Infra p. 283.

9. Infra p. 253.

SECTION B. NEGOTIATION FACTORS

What is a "good" separation agreement? Obviously, there is no absolute answer to this question. The individual circumstances of each couple, indeed, of each family, must be taken into consideration in drafting a separation agreement and in evaluating its effectiveness. Nevertheless, some general observations can be made:

CHARACTERISTICS OF AN EFFECTIVE SEPARATION AGREEMENT
1. COMPREHENSIVE: it covers all major matters; months or years later when something "new" arises, the parties will not have to say, "we never thought of that when we drafted the agreement." 2. FAIR: if the agreement is not fair to both sides, it may be unworkable which will force the parties into expensive and potentially bitter litigation; hence the worst kind of legal assistance may be to "outsmart" the other side into "giving up" almost everything. 3. ACCURATE: the agreement should accurately reflect the intentions of the parties; what they orally agreed to do in formal or informal bargaining sessions should be stated in the written agreement. 4. LEGAL: there are certain things that can and cannot be said in a separation agreement; the agreement must not attempt to do that which is illegal. 5. READABLE: it would help if the agreement was written in language that the parties can understand and refer to often without having to hire a lawyer every time some question arises.

[B7633]

An "effective" separation agreement is achieved through bargaining or negotiation. This is done by the parties on their own as well as through the lawyers representing them. Bargaining begins the moment the parties begin having serious marital difficulties. From a broader perspective, however, the "bargaining" begins much earlier. In large measure, the separation agreement is a product of who the parties are, what their personalities are, what their sensibilities tell them should or should not be done, what is and is not fair according to their upbringing and moral instincts. To be sure, many other factors also go into the formation of the separation agreement, such as the skill of the lawyers. At the core of the separation agreement, however, is the client him or her self.

The separation agreement can be a complex document. In the chart below, the myriad of factors that can influence the shape of the

FACTORS THAT INFLUENCE THE CONTENT OF A SEPARATION AGREEMENT

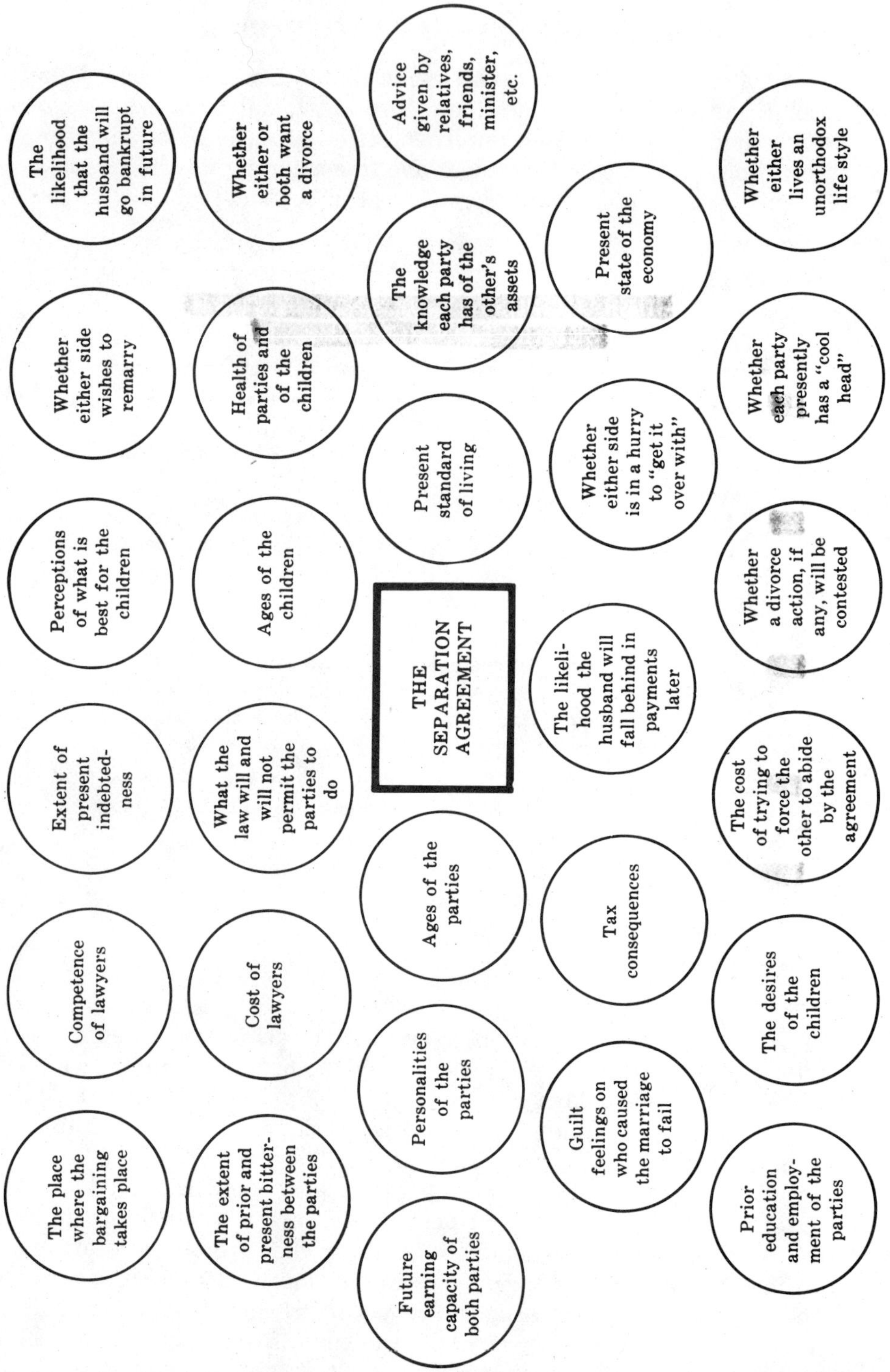

[B7639]

separation agreement are presented. As you can readily tell, there is an infinite variety of relationships that the factors can have with each other. In some cases, for example, certain factors predominate over others. In the next several chapters, we will examine the individual factors in greater detail in order to see how they are often played off against each other in the process of creating the agreement.

SECTION C. CHECKLISTS FOR THE PREPARATION OF THE SEPARATION AGREEMENT

Before an intelligent separation agreement can be drafted, a great deal of information is needed. First of all, a series of lists should be compiled:

PREPARING FOR THE SEPARATION AGREEMENT: LISTS THAT NEED TO BE COMPILED
Identify in detail: —all property held by the husband in his separate name; —all property held by the wife in her separate name; —all property in one person's name that really belongs to the other; —all property held jointly—in both names; —all property acquired during the marriage; —all insurance policies currently in force; —all debts currently outstanding (and incurred by whom); —all income from any source earned by the husband; —all income from any source earned by the wife; —all present living expenses of the husband; —all projected living expenses of the husband; —all present living expenses of the wife; —all projected living expenses of the wife.

[B7632]

In addition to such lists, the following data should be collected if relevant:

—names and addresses of both spouses and children;

—data on all prior litigation, if any, between the parties;

—name and address of spouse's current attorney;

—names and addresses of prior attorneys, if any, retained by either party;

—copies of tax returns filed in prior years;

—copy of ante-nuptial contract,[10] if any;

—character references (e. g., if needed on questions of custody);

—names and addresses of individuals who might serve as arbitrators[11] under the agreement;

—documentation of prior indebtedness;

—copy of will currently in force, if any.

The preliminary interview in Chapter Five identifies a large number of questions which will provide such background information.[12]

Before examining in some detail the law governing individual clauses of a separation agreement and the drafting options available for each clause, the following checklist should be examined. It is an overview of topics that need to be considered by the parties. Some or all of these topics may become part of the separation agreement.

PREPARING FOR THE SEPARATION AGREEMENT: TOPICS THAT NEED TO BE CONSIDERED BY THE PARTIES

ALIMONY

—who pays;
—how much;
—method of payment;
—frequency of payment;
—tax consequences;
—does it terminate on remarriage or death of either;
—does it fluctuate with income of husband;
—is it modifiable;
—security for payment;
—enforcement.

CHILD SUPPORT

—who pays;
—how much;
—method of payment;
—frequency of payment;
—tax consequences;
—does it terminate when the child reaches a certain age;
—does it terminate if the child is otherwise emancipated;
—college expenses.

CUSTODY

—who gets custody;
—visitation rights;
—summer vacations and special holidays;
—removal of child from state (temporary or permanent).

10. Supra p. 127.

11. Infra p. 285.

12. Supra p. 79.

PREPARING FOR THE SEPARATION AGREEMENT: TOPICS THAT NEED TO BE CONSIDERED BY THE PARTIES—Continued

HEALTH EXPENSES (wife and children)
- —medical;
- —dental;
- —who pays;
- —special payments to be made or included in regular support payments;
- —right to be consulted.

LIFE INSURANCE
- —wife as beneficiary;
- —children as beneficiaries.

WILLS
- —wills already in existence;
- —changes to be made in these wills.

DEBTS STILL TO BE PAID
- —who pays.

PERSONAL PROPERTY
- —cash;
- —joint and separate bank accounts (savings);
- —joint and separate bank accounts (checking);
- —stocks;
- —bonds;
- —motor vehicles;
- —art works;
- —household furniture;
- —jewelry;
- —rights to receive money in the future, e. g., retirement pay, stock options, court judgment awards.

REAL PROPERTY
- —residence;
- —vacation home;
- —business real estate;
- —leases.

INCOME TAX RETURNS

ATTORNEY FEES & COURT COSTS

INCORPORATION OF AGREEMENT IN DIVORCE DECREE

ARBITRATION

SECTION D. THE BEGINNING OF THE SEPARATION AGREEMENT

It is good practice in the drafting of a separation agreement to number each paragraph separately (1, 2, 3, etc.) with one number assigned to each major topic, e. g., alimony, custody. If a major topic requires sub-topics, each sub-topic should be assigned a separate letter, (a), (b), (c) etc. The major exception to this numbering and lettering system is the beginning of the agreement where no numbers or letters are used. For example:

SEPARATION AGREEMENT

THIS AGREEMENT, entered into this _______ day of _______, 19___, by Jim Jones (referred to in this agreement as the Husband), residing at _______, and by Linda Jones (referred to in this agreement as the Wife), residing at _______,

WITNESSETH:

WHEREAS, the parties were married on _______, 19___ in the state of _______, city of _______, and

WHEREAS, _______ children were born of this marriage: (here list each child and its date of birth), and

WHEREAS, as a result of irreconcilable marital disputes, the parties have been voluntarily living apart since _______, 19___ which both parties feel is in their own best interests and that of their children, and

WHEREAS, both parties wish to enter this agreement for the purpose of settling all custody, support and property rights between them and any other matter pertaining to their marriage relationship, and

WHEREAS, both parties acknowledge that they have had separate and independent legal advice from counsel of their own choosing on the advisability of entering this agreement, that they have not been coerced or pressured into entering the agreement and that they voluntarily decide to enter it.[13]

NOW THEREFORE, in consideration of the promises and the mutual commitments contained in this agreement, the parties agree as follows:

(the full text of the agreement goes here in numbered paragraphs; sample clauses are found at the end of this chapter, infra p. 288.)

[B7989]

13. This last "whereas" clause is sometimes placed at the end of separation agreements. It does not have to be placed at the end of the agreement. It is placed at the beginning here primarily for purposes of the discussion that follows.

A number of issues relating to the above introductory clauses need to be discussed:

(i) public policy and collusion;

(ii) capacity to contract;

(iii) duress and fraud;

(iv) consideration.

(i) Public policy and collusion

The above agreement between Jim and Linda Jones states that they are married, but that they have separated due to the fact that their marriage has fallen apart. As we have seen,[14] public policy strongly favors marriage and looks with disfavor on efforts to end it. If a husband and wife are still living together (and have not already decided to separate), the law would not recognize a contract between them to obtain a divorce. Such a contract would encourage the parties to seek a divorce; the contract would be *conducive to divorce*[15]. Hence the Jones agreement is careful:

—to point out that a separation has already occurred, and

—to avoid mentioning divorce—at least at the beginning of the agreement.

So long as the parties are still living together and separation is not imminent due to a recent decision to separate, the law operates on the assumption that there is still hope. By definition, a separation agreement attempts to provide *benefits* to the parties in the form of money, freedom, etc. The very existence of such an agreement is viewed as an inducement to obtain a divorce unless the parties have already separated or are about to do so shortly. If Mary said to her husband, Frank, "if you leave me now, I'll give you $25,000," and Frank does leave, the agreement is invalid because it is conducive to divorce, i. e., it encourages the parties to separate. If Frank later sues Mary for breach of her contract to pay him $25,000, she can successfully raise the defense that the contract is unenforceable because it violates public policy: it encourages divorce.

It is so often said that there are three parties to a marriage: husband, wife and the state. The parties are not free to do anything they want because the state has an interest in the marital relationship. It must, however, be admitted that parties do separate and disappear from each other without obtaining a divorce or involving the courts in any way. The parties might even marry someone else and have new families without letting it be known that they are already married to someone else who is still alive. If no suits are brought and if no investigation is undertaken, everything *appears* legal. Such situations are more common than most people think.

14. Supra p. 123.

15. See material on antenuptial agreements, supra p. 130.

Suppose that a husband and wife enter the following brief separation agreement:

> "We hereby declare that our marriage is over, and that we will have nothing to do with each other henceforth. As we part, we ask nothing of each other."

To permit parties to make such a contract would be to enable them to divorce themselves without the involvement of a court. At the time the parties attempted to enter this contract, it may have seemed fair and sensible. Suppose, however, that months or years later, the wife finds herself destitute. If she sues her husband for support or alimony,[16] he cannot defend the action by raising her contract commitment not to ask anything of him. If either of them later tries to marry someone else and is charged with the crime of bigamy,[17] they will not be able to defend the prosecution by arguing that they had privately divorced themselves and were therefore free to remarry.

Whenever a husband and wife discuss divorce and come to an agreement as to the results that should be achieved from the divorce proceeding, the spectre of *collusion*[18] is raised. Collusion is fraud committed on the court by agreeing on a story to be told to the court even though the parties know that the story is untrue, e. g., the plaintiff in a divorce action falsely claims that the defendant deserted her on a certain date, and the defendant falsely admits that he did desert her on this date. This is done, of course, in order to get the court to grant the divorce. Suppose that the separation agreement provides that if either party later seeks a divorce, the other party will not appear or will not raise any defenses to the divorce action even though such defenses may exist. Such an agreement would be invalid because it is collusive. A collusive separation agreement improperly induces divorce.

The rule that separation agreements are invalid if they are conducive to divorce has been criticized as unrealistic since it is difficult to imagine a mutually acceptable separation agreement involving future divorce that does *not* facilitate or encourage the parties to go through with the divorce. Nevertheless, courts continue to watch for improper facilitation and for collusion. It may be that the coming of no-fault divorce[19] will lessen a court's inclination to invalidate a separation agreement for these reasons. Since divorce has been made much easier to obtain by the no-fault ground,[20] courts should be more reluctant to save the marriage at all costs, and more willing to let the separation agreement be the vehicle through which the parties confront the inevitable. This is not to say that courts will no longer be

16. On the husband's duty to support his wife, see infra p. 265.

17. Supra p. 177.

18. Infra p. 338.

19. Infra p. 308.

20. E. g., living separate and apart for a designated period of time. See infra p. 308.

concerned with collusion and agreements that are conducive to divorce. These prohibitions are still on the books. The atmosphere, however, has changed with no-fault. Most of the court decisions on these prohibitions were decided before the extensive arrival of no-fault. It is questionable how willing a court may be to follow all of those decisions today.

Below there are a series of clauses sometimes found in separation agreements with comments on how the courts have treated the issues of divorce facilitation and collusion which are raised by the clauses.

> "The wife agrees that she will file for a divorce against the husband within three months."
>
> "None of the terms of this separation agreement shall be effective unless and until either of the parties are granted a divorce."

The first clause is invalid; a party cannot promise to file for a divorce. Not only does this encourage divorce, it makes it almost inevitable. It would appear that the second clause is as bad or worse than the first. Neither of the parties will obtain any of the benefits in the separation agreement unless one of them obtains a divorce. Arguably, this clause encourages one of the parties to file for divorce and the other party to refrain from contesting the divorce. Oddly, however, the courts have *not* interpreted the second clause in this way. It *is* legal to condition the entire separation agreement on the granting of a divorce. The logic of this result is not entirely clear, but the courts so hold.[21]

> "The wife agrees that if the husband files for divorce, she will not raise any defenses to his action."
>
> "In the event that the wife travels to another state to file for divorce, the husband agrees to go to that state, appear in the action and participate therein."

The first clause is collusive. If a party has a defense, it is improper to agree not to assert it. Even if you are not sure whether or not you have a defense, it is collusive to agree in advance to refrain from asserting whatever defense you *might* have. Courts consider this as improper as an agreement to destroy evidence which would defeat the plaintiff's case for a divorce or to conceal such evidence.

The second clause above is more troublesome. Here the parties are clearly contemplating an out-of-state divorce, perhaps because they both realize that they would have difficulty establishing the grounds for divorce in their own state. Such *migratory divorces* are not uncommon.[22] What often happens in such cases is as follows:

21. For the legal effect of a clause in an antenuptial agreement by which property rights are forfeited upon the obtaining of a divorce, see supra p. 142.

22. Infra p. 343.

(1) the defendant does *not* appear in the foreign (i. e., out-of-state) divorce action, (2) the plaintiff wins the divorce by default judgment [23] and returns to his/her original state, (3) upon return, s/he files an action to enforce the foreign divorce decree, i. e., s/he asks that the state give full faith and credit to the foreign judgment.[24] Do you think such a clause is conducive to divorce or collusive? Some states think that it is and invalidate the agreement. Other states take the opposite position and uphold the agreement containing this clause.[25]

Assignment # 60

Determine whether any of the following clauses are conducive of divorce or collusive. (See also General Instructions for the Legal Analysis Assignment, supra p. 16.)

(a) "In the event that the wife files a divorce action, the husband agrees not to file any defenses to said action if and only if it is clear to both parties that the husband has no defense."

(b) "In the event that the wife files a divorce action, the husband will pay in advance all expenses incurred by the wife in bringing said action."

(c) "In the event that the wife files for a judicial separation,[26] for separate maintenance,[27] or for an annulment,[28] the husband agrees to cooperate fully in the wife's action."

Assignment # 61

(a) Go to a digest containing small paragraph summaries of court opinions from your state. (On the kinds of digests that exist, see supra p. 27.) Find those parts of this digest that deal with separation agreements. List any ten (10) key topics and key numbers which cover any aspect of separation agreements. (For more on key topics and numbers, see supra p. 42. If you are using a digest that does not contain key topics and numbers, then simply list the topics and section numbers used by that digest.)

(b) Are there any statutes in your state code dealing with separation agreements? If so briefly summarize them. (See also General Instructions for the State Code Assignment, supra p. 14.)

(ii) Capacity to Contract [29]

There was a time in our history when the very thought of Linda Jones—a wife—entering a contract with her husband was anathema.

23. Infra p. 367.

24. Infra p. 351.

25. See Ploscowe, M., Foster, H., & Freed, D., *Family Law: Cases and Materials*, 798 (1972) and Clark, H., *The Law of Domestic Relations*, 527 (1968).

26. Infra p. 405.

27. Infra p. 433.

28. Supra p. 171.

29. See also supra p. 110 on contract capacity generally and supra p. 128 on contract capacity for purposes of entering an antenuptial contract.

A married woman lacked the capacity to contract with her husband.[30] At common law,[31] the husband and wife were one, and "the one" was the husband. You can't make a contract with yourself! This rule, of course, has been changed. A wife can enter a contract with her husband (although tax authorities and the husband's creditors are often suspicious of such contracts especially when the result is to place property purchased by the husband into the name of the wife). Linda Jones is no longer denied the right to enter a separation agreement with Jim Jones simply because she is his wife.

Today, the major question of capacity involves mental health. A separation agreement is invalid if either party lacked the capacity to understand the agreement and the consequences of signing it. The traditional test is as follows: when the person does not understand the nature and consequences of his/her act at the time of the transaction. This can occur due to insanity, mental retardation, senility, temporary delirium due to an accident, intoxication, drug addiction, etc.[32]

(iii) Duress and Fraud

In the excerpt from the Jones separation agreement above, you will note that several times at the beginning of the agreement the parties mention that they are entering it "voluntarily." [33] According to traditional contract principles, if a party entered a contract because of duress,[34] it would not be enforced. Suppose that a wife is physically threatened if she does not sign the separation agreement. Clearly the agreement would not be valid, e. g., the husband could not sue her for breaching it. Of course, simply because the separation agreement says that the parties enter it "voluntarily" does not necessarily mean that no duress existed: either spouse could have been forced to say s/he signed "voluntarily." Of what value it is to have the agreement say that it was "voluntarily" signed? It is some indication that no duress existed, but an aggrieved party can usually introduce evidence to the contrary if such evidence is available.

Fraud [35] is more difficult to analyze. Courts sometimes confuse fraud with the concept of fairness to the wife. If the husband lies about a major asset that he possesses and this lie has a material influence on the content of the separation agreement, the wife can have the agreement set aside for fraud. The more common situation involves nondisclosure rather than lies. The wife tries to invalidate the agreement when she later finds out that her husband failed to disclose to

30. Infra p. 439.

31. Common law is judge-made law in the absence of controlling statutory law.

32. Calamari, J., & Perillo, J., *The Law of Contracts*, 217 (1970).

33. Supra p. 252.

34. See also supra p. 203.

35. See also supra p. 117.

her all of his assets during the negotiations on the separation agreement. The courts have not been consistent on the issue. There are no absolute rules governing every situation. Whether the court will grant relief to a wife may depend on a number of factors:

—whether she is now destitute and about to become a public charge;

—whether the court feels that a fiduciary relationship existed between the husband and wife;

—whether she was advised to sign the separation agreement by someone other than her husband, i. e., whether she had the benefit of independent advice.

If the wife is in a destitute or near destitute position, many courts will come to her rescue and not let her suffer the consequences of the bad bargain that she made when she signed the agreement. Some courts will go so far as to *presume* that the husband has taken an unfair advantage of his wife until he demonstrates otherwise, e. g., by proving that she had independent advice, by proving that he disclosed everything to her (prior tax returns, bank statements, etc.). In most situations, a husband will not be allowed to treat his wife "at arm's length" as he would a competitor in a commercial transaction. Between a husband and wife, a *fiduciary* relationship exists which requires them to treat each other openly. This is not to say, however, that a wife will never have to suffer the consequences of not being as shrewd as she should have been in negotiation. Suppose that she is currently living comfortably, but that she would be able to live even more comfortably if she could renegotiate the separation agreement. Will a court allow her to do so? The answer is not clear even if it can be shown that the husband did not disclose everything to her before she signed the separation agreement. If she had the benefit of independent advice and if she does not face a serious financial crisis, many courts will leave the parties where they are and not force the husband to pay his wife more than the separation agreement provides.

The last WHEREAS clause of the beginning of the Jones separation agreement above recites that both Jim and Linda had the benefit of separate legal advice on the advantages and disadvantages of signing the agreement.[36] As indicated, this fact can be very significant in a court's deliberation on whether to set the agreement aside, e. g., on the ground of fraud. The husband is in a much better position if his wife has said that she had her own lawyer even though, as we shall see, the husband usually has to pay the legal expenses of the wife.[37]

In the following case of Bell v. Bell, you will examine some of the factors which a court will consider when the validity of a separation agreement is called into question:

36. Supra p. 252.

37. Infra p. 282.

BELL v. BELL

Court of Special Appeals of Maryland, 1977.
38 Md. 10, 379 A.2d 419.

Diane M. Bell, the appellant, appeals from an order from the Circuit Court for Montgomery County which dismissed her bill of complaint for cancellation of a separation and property settlement agreement between her and her husband, Stanley A. Bell, the appellee, and the cancellation of eleven deeds executed pursuant to that agreement. She raises [this question . . .] on appeal: was the chancellor's decision clearly erroneous when he found that the agreement and deeds were not obtained by duress or undue influence, ...

The facts that gave rise to this suit are as follows. Diane Bell consulted an attorney in July of 1975, concerning the preparation of a separation agreement. The agreement was prepared and Mrs. Bell presented it to Mr. Bell at home on the morning of August 27, 1975. After examining the agreement at his place of business Mr. Bell inserted several changes and gave it to his secretary for retyping. Two significant changes were made in the agreement. The original provided for child support in the amount of $700 per month. This figure in the amended agreement was reduced to $300. Mr. Bell's agreement also provided for the disposition of the eleven houses owned by the parties as tenants by the entireties. Under his agreement Mrs. Bell was to receive one of the houses while he retained the other ten. After his agreement was completed he telephoned the appellant and asked her to come to his office in Wheaton to sign the agreement. At that time no mention was made of the changes.

When Mrs. Bell arrived, Mr. Bell suggested that they go to the nearby offices of Ralph Duane Real Estate Co. so that they could discuss the agreement in private. Prior to Mrs. Bell's arrival Mr. Bell had prepared a series of sixteen 3 x 5 cards containing phrases such as "the man," "the kids," "his carrer," "your name," and "Ingrid (accessory)." During the course of the meeting he used these cards to inform the appellant of an investigation of her activities by private detectives and his knowledge of her adulterous affair with a police lieutenant. He also informed her that he knew that many of the contacts occurred at the apartment of her friend, Ingrid Gibson. He then presented his version of the separation agreement and made it clear that unless she signed it he would reveal her relationship to the Internal Affairs section of the police department and to the newspapers. Several times during the course of the conversation Mrs. Bell threatened to leave or requested an opportunity to consult with her attorney, but on each occasion, Mr. Bell threatened to "start the ball rolling" if such attempts were made before the agreement was signed. Mr. Bell placed a tape recorder in the office and recorded the entire conversation without the knowledge of Mrs. Bell. The tape was introduced into evidence.

After Mrs. Bell registered several protests, she read through the agreement and negotiated with Mr. Bell to make several changes. Among these changes was the receipt of a total of $15,000 in cash in addition to the one house. Under the agreement that was signed Mr. Bell received approximately $163,000 worth of property that was previously owned as tenants by the entireties while Mrs. Bell settled for approximately $45,000 in cash and property.[1]

The appellant argues that a confidential relationship existed between the parties and the burden was on the appellee to show the agreement was fair in all respects. In order to establish a confidential relationship one must show that by virtue of the relationship between them, he is justified in assuming the other party will not act in a manner inconsistent with his welfare. Unlike many jurisdictions, Maryland does not presume the existence of a confidential relationship in transactions between husband and wife. Owings v. Currier, 186 Md. 590, 47 A.2d 743 (1946). In Maryland there has been a presumption that the husband is the dominant figure in the marriage. In Manos v. Papachrist, 199 Md. 257, 262, 86 A.2d 474 (1951), the Court noted:

> "Ordinarily the relationship of husband and wife is a confidential one. Of course, in any given case it is a question of fact whether the marital relationship is such as to give the husband dominance over his wife or to put him in a position where words of persuasion have undue weight. Generally, however, on account of the natural dominance of the husband over the wife, and the confidence and trust usually incident to their marriage, a court of equity will investigate a gift from a wife to her husband with utmost care, especially where it strips her of all her property; and the burden of proof is on the husband to show that there was no abuse of confidence, but that the gift was fair in all respects, was fully understood, and was not induced by fraud or undue influence."

We noted the questionable foundation upon which this presumption rests in light of Article 46 of the Maryland Declaration of Rights, better known as the Equal Rights Amendment, in Trupp v. Wolff, 24 Md.App. 588, n. 15, 335 A.2d 171 (1975), cert. denied, 275 Md. 757. Since that decision, the Court of Appeals has held that sex classifications are no longer permissible under the amendment. Rand v. Rand, 280 Md. 508, 374 A.2d 900 (1977). Consequently, the presumption of dominance cannot stand.

When the presumption is disregarded the question of whether a confidential relationship exists between husband and wife becomes a question of fact. Among the various factors to be considered in

1. The property Mr. Bell received had a gross value of $597,000 but was subject to mortgages totalling $434,339.

determining whether a confidential relationship exists are the age, mental condition, education, business experience, state of health, and degree of dependence of the spouse in question. Treffinger v. Sterling, 269 Md. 356, 305 A.2d 829 (1973); Hoffman v. Rickell, 191 Md. 591, 62 A.2d 597 (1948); Gaggers v. Gibson, 180 Md. 609, 26 A.2d 395 (1942); Gaver v. Gaver, 176 Md. 171, 4 A.2d 132 (1939).

The testimony shows that Mrs. Bell was born in Europe, moved to this country when she was eleven years old, and left school at the age of fifteen. Although she is employed as a beautician, she has relatively little experience or expertise in business matters. On the other hand, Mr. Bell is an experienced businessman, possesses a real estate license, and has a college degree. The chancellor considered these facts, but found that no confidential relationship existed primarily because Mrs. Bell negotiated several changes in the agreement and questioned other provisions, as is clearly shown by the tape recording. He found there was a lack of trust and confidence in the other party necessary to the establishment of a confidential relationship. We are unable to say his decision on this issue was clearly erroneous. Md. Rule 1086.

Absent proof of a confidential relationship between the parties, separation agreements, not disclosing any injustice or inequity on their face, are presumptively valid and the burden is on the party challenging the agreement to show its execution resulted from coercion, fraud, or mistake. Cronin v. Hebditch, 195 Md. 607, 74 A.2d 50 (1950); Owings v. Currier, supra; Jackson v. Jackson, 14 Md.App. 263, 286 A.2d 778 (1972).

The only inequity claimed by the appellant is that she relinquished her one half interest in approximately $210,000 worth of real estate for approximately $45,000 in property and cash. This disparity in consideration is not sufficient to show that the agreement was unjust or inequitable. The cases which have found agreements to be unjust or inequitable on their face involved agreements that were completely lacking in any reasonable consideration. Cronin v. Hebditch, supra; Eaton v. Eaton, 34 Md.App. 157, 366 A.2d 121 (1976). In *Cronin* the wife signed an agreement releasing all her rights in property totalling more than $700,000 for a mere $10,000 and the Court of Appeals voided the agreement. More recently, in *Eaton* we struck down an agreement in which rights in $200,000 to $250,000 worth of property were released for $4,300. There we said:

> " '[The] defendant in this case has ostensibly purchased far more cheaply than a Court of Equity can condone all of the plaintiff's rights "of whatsoever kind or nature originating in and growing out of the marriage status." ' " 34 Md.App. at 162.

As we are unable to say the agreement in question was lacking in any reasonable consideration, *Cronin* and *Eaton* cannot be used to relieve the appellant from proving the agreement was the product of duress or undue influence.[2]

The appellant's claim of duress or undue influence rests on the threats of Stanley Bell to notify the Internal Affairs section of the Police Department and the newspapers of her adulterous relationship unless the agreement was signed. Mr. Bell also stated that such disclosures would ruin the career of her lover and Ingrid Gibson, as well as her reputation in the community. The chancellor construed these statements as being no more than a threat to institute a divorce action on the grounds of adultery.

In order to establish duress there must be a wrongful act which deprives a person of the exercise of his free will. See Central Bank v. Copeland, 18 Md. 305 (1862); Restatement (Second) of Contracts §§ 316–318 (Tent.Draft No. 12, 1977); 13 Williston on Contracts, §§ 1606–1607 (3d ed., W. Jaeger ed. 1970). Although we have found no Maryland case discussing the issue whether a threat to institute a civil suit can furnish a legally sufficient basis for duress, the question has been considered by a number of courts in other jurisdictions. Under these cases such suits do not form a legally sufficient basis for duress where the threat to institute the suit is made in good faith. Jack Winter, Inc. v. Koratron Co., 329 F.Supp. 211 (N.D.Calif.1971); Blalock v. Blalock, 51 Ala.App. 686, 288 So.2d 747 (1974); Dunbar v. Dunbar, 102 Ariz. 352, 429 P.2d 949 (1967); Del Carlo v. County of Sonoma, 245 Cal.App.2d 36, 53 Cal.Rptr. 771 (1966); Kaplan v. Kaplan, 25 Ill.2d 181, 182 N.E.2d 706 (1962); Eggleston v. Humble Pipe Line Co., 482 S.W.2d 909 (Tex.Civ.App.1972). The courts have stated the assertion of a claim with the knowledge there is no reasonable belief of success or that it is false, amounts to bad faith and is a sufficient basis for a claim of duress. Jack Winter, Inc. v. Koratron Co., supra; Kaplan v. Kaplan, supra; Louisville Title Insurance Co. v. Surety Title & Guaranty Co., 60 Cal.App.3d 781, 132 Cal.Rptr. 63 (1976). Even though a particular act is legal, if it is wrongful in the moral sense a number of authorities have held that it can be used to establish a claim of duress. Fowler v. Mumford, 48 Del. 282, 102 A.2d 535 (1954); Kaplan v. Kaplan, supra; Hochman v. Zigler's, Incorpo-

2. We are aware that some cases in other jurisdictions have created a presumption of invalidity where the consideration given is grossly disproportionate to the consideration received or is otherwise unfair. See Le Bert-Francis v. Le Bert-Francis, 194 A.2d 662 (D.C.1963) (where separation agreement is unfair it is presumed to be invalid and the burden is on the party seeking to enforce it to prove otherwise); Demaggio v. Demaggio, 317 So.2d 848 (Fla.App.1975) (presumption of fraud created where agreement was grossly disproportionate, husband concealed assets, and wife was unrepresented by counsel); Davis v. Davis, 24 Ohio Misc. 17, 258 N.E.2d 277 (1970) (where provisions are disproportionate burden is on party seeking to uphold agreement to show there was full disclosure and the agreement was signed voluntarily).

In the absence of a confidential relationship, we see no reason to shift the burden of proof because the parties were husband and wife and one of them made a bargain which now seems unfair, but is not grossly unfair.

rated, 139 N.J.Eq. 139, 50 A.2d 97 (1946); Link v. Link, 278 N.C. 181, 179 S.E.2d 697 (1971); Restatement (Second) of Contracts § 318 (Tent.Draft No. 12, 1977); 13 Williston on Contracts, §§ 1606–1607 (3d. ed. W. Jaeger ed. 1970).

The appellant argues that a threatened civil suit can be wrongful in a moral sense where it is used to coerce a settlement in a transaction unrelated to the subject matter of the suit. In support of this argument she relies on Link v. Link, supra. In *Link* the husband threatened to institute divorce proceedings against the wife and seek custody of their children unless the wife signed an agreement transferring her individual property to the husband. In deciding the case the Court noted that the general rule that threats to institute civil proceedings are not wrongful but went on to state:

> "The law with reference to duress has, however, undergone an evolution favorable to the victim of oppressive action or threats. The weight of modern authority supports the rule, which we here adopt, that the act done or threatened may be wrongful even though not unlawful, per se; and that the threat to institute legal proceedings, criminal or civil, which might be justifiable, per se, becomes wrongful, within the meaning of this rule, if made with the corrupt intent to coerce a transaction grossly unfair to the victim and not related to the subject of such proceedings." 179 S.E.2d at 705.

See Restatement (Second) of Contracts § 318 (Tent.Draft No. 12, 1977); 13 Williston on Contracts §§ 1606–1607 (3d ed. W. Jaeger ed. 1970).

We find the reasoning of *Link* to be persuasive. Applying this approach to the case before us we think there was a legally sufficient basis for a finding of duress.

Mr. Bell threatened an action for divorce on the grounds of adultery to force a property settlement between the parties. Although the threatened action and the separation agreement both relate to the marital status of the parties, their substance is significantly different. A court in an action for divorce does not have jurisdiction to settle the property rights of the parties to real estate. Md.Code, Courts and Judicial Proceedings Article § 3–603; Flage v. Flage, 35 Md.App. 619, 371 A.2d 729 (1977). Mr. Bell's threats of a civil suit for divorce were unrelated to the dispute over the property and were made to obtain Mrs. Bell's signature on an agreement.

Even though the chancellor concluded that there was no wrongful conduct he went on to note in his opinion that even if the actions were considered wrongful, they did not deprive Mrs. Bell of her free will, citing Treffinger v. Sterling, supra. In support of this finding he noted that Mrs. Bell actively negotiated with Mr. Bell concerning various provisions in the agreement. At one point in the conversation she stated:

> "Umn, I'm just trying to get you know as much as I can which is, you have to admit, you'd do the same thing."

Although there was testimony that Mrs. Bell was extremely upset after the agreement was signed, there was other testimony to the contrary. The chancellor considered this evidence and concluded:

> "[T]he negotiations and the tenor of the parties' meeting indicate quite clearly that the Plaintiff, in order to avoid an embarrassing incident involving her and close friends, freely and voluntarily negotiated with her husband."

The question of whether Mrs. Bell was deprived of her free will was one of fact and as there is ample evidence to support this finding, we are unable to say it was clearly erroneous. Md. Rule 1086. In other words, there is no rule of law that precludes a woman from giving away a substantial portion of her property to save her reputation, if it is her voluntary act. Although on the evidence we may have found the act involuntary, we must accept the chancellor's findings because of his superior position to make this subtle distinction.

. . .

As we have indicated, the chancellor found on the merits that the appellant did not act under duress or undue influence. We have accepted his finding because there was evidence to support it. . . .

DECREE AFFIRMED.

APPELLANT TO PAY THE COSTS.

(iv) Consideration

All contracts must be supported by consideration in order to be valid.[38] Consideration is something of value that is exchanged. The separation agreement is a set of promises or commitments by the parties of what they will do. The exchange of these promises (some of which may have already been performed, at least in part, at the time the agreement is signed) is the consideration for the separation agreement. A wife's promise to relinquish all claims that she may have against her husband's estate when he dies is an example of consideration that she gives to her husband. A husband's promise to transfer to his wife full title to land that he solely owns is an example of his consideration to her.

We have already seen, however, that certain kinds of consideration are improper. A couple, for example, cannot exchange promises that onc party will file for divorce and the other party will refrain

38. Supra p. 110.

from asserting any defenses s/he might have. Such consideration is illegal as collusive and as conducive to divorce.[39] So too, a few states will not allow a wife to promise in the separation agreement to release the husband from all support claims she may have against him. In most states, however, such a promise is valid consideration so long as the agreement is otherwise fair to the wife.

Perhaps the main consideration in the separation agreement involves the separation itself. A husband and wife have the right to live with each other as husband and wife, i. e., the right of cohabitation. By reason of the separation agreement, the parties promise each other that they will never again claim this cohabitation right.

SECTION E. ALIMONY PAYMENTS AND PROPERTY SETTLEMENT: INTRODUCTION

Alimony (sometimes referred to as *support* and *maintenance*) [40]: the funds provided by a husband to his wife following their separation to fulfill his legal obligation to support her (in many states, alimony can be awarded to the husband if the wife is the one with all or most of the resources [41])

Property Settlement (sometimes referred to as a *property division*): the distribution of property accumulated by the parties as a result of their joint efforts during the marriage

Unfortunately, there is often a good deal of confusion concerning alimony and property settlement. While the above definitions are generally accepted as accurate, sometimes even these concepts are blurred. A separation agreement (or a court opinion) may refer to alimony, but mean *both* support and property settlement. In part, the confusion may be due to the fact that in the minds of the husband and wife there may not always be a clear distinction between these two concepts.

The Significance of the Distinction Between Alimony and Property Settlement

In the following chart some of the major consequences of the distinction between alimony and property settlement are outlined.[42] These consequences must be understood, at least preliminarily, before examining the options available to the parties in drafting those clauses of the separation agreement that cover alimony and property settlement.

39. Supra p. 253.

40. The word "alimony" is often used interchangeably with the words, "support" and "maintenance" of the wife. Technically, alimony is *court ordered* support and maintenance for the wife.

41. Infra p. 369.

42. See also Krause, H., *Family Law: Cases and Materials*, pp. 1001ff (1976).

ALIMONY AND PROPERTY SETTLEMENT TERMS OF A SEPARATION AGREEMENT	
(A) EFFECT OF BANKRUPTCY	
Alimony	**Property Settlement**
If the husband goes into bankruptcy, his obligation to pay alimony is not discharged. (Same for wife if she has the alimony obligation to her husband.)	If either party goes into bankruptcy, the remaining property settlement obligations are discharged.
(B) EFFECT OF REMARRIAGE AND DEATH	
Alimony	**Property Settlement**
If the wife obtains a divorce and remarries, the alimony payments stop unless the separation agreement specifically provides otherwise. If the husband remarries, his alimony payments to his first wife must continue. If the husband or wife dies, alimony payments cease unless the separation agreement specifically provides otherwise.	Remarriage or death of either party does not effect the terms of the property settlement. All obligations under the property settlement must be fulfilled regardless of remarriage or death.
(C) AVAILABILITY OF CONTEMPT	
Alimony	**Property Settlement**
If a party fails to fulfill an alimony obligation and falls into arrears, the contempt power of the court can be used as an enforcement device if the separation agreement has been incorporated and merged into a later divorce decree.	If either party fails to fulfill the obligations under the property settlement, the contempt power of the court usually cannot be used as an enforcement device.
(D) THE COURT'S POWER TO MODIFY TERMS	
Alimony	**Property Settlement**
If the alimony terms of the separation agreement later prove to be seriously inadequate, the court often has the power to modify those terms in order to require that more alimony be paid.	If either party later becomes dissatisfied with the terms of the property settlement, the court will rarely modify those terms.
(E) FEDERAL INCOME TAX TREATMENT	
Alimony	**Property Settlement**
Alimony payments, if paid in the right form, are includible in the gross income of the wife, and are deductible to the husband. (Vice versa if the wife is paying alimony.)	Money or property paid pursuant to the terms of a property settlement are not deductible by the husband nor taxable to the wife. The division of property is not a taxable event unless appreciated property is transferred as part of the property settlement.

IM-476

(a) EFFECT OF BANKRUPTCY

Bankruptcy is a system to allow a person to eliminate all or most of his/her debts in order to make a fresh start. If a husband has fallen behind on his obligation under a separation agreement and/or a divorce decree, all arrears constitute a debt to his wife. Each time an alimony payment becomes due, a new debt is created. So too, all outstanding (i. e., unpaid) obligations under a property settlement agreement are debts. To have a debt "discharged" in bankruptcy means that the debt never has to be paid. As indicated, however, not all debts are discharged in bankruptcy. The Bankruptcy Act of Congress provides as follows:

> A discharge in bankruptcy shall release a bankrupt from all of his provable debts . . . except such as . . . are . . . for alimony due or to become due, or for maintenance or support of wife or child. . . .[43]

On the other hand, debts stemming from a property settlement are dischargeable. The effect of this law is to prevent a husband from agreeing to large alimony payments in order to induce his wife to give him what he wants, and then to declare bankruptcy after he signs the separation agreement. He cannot eliminate his alimony obligation in this way.

There are a number of practical consequences of this. If there is the slightest suspicion that the husband is in serious financial difficulties and that bankruptcy is a possibility (a fact that needs to be carefully investigated by the lawyer and paralegal representing the wife), then the wife may be advised in the negotiation stage of the separation agreement to accept a very low property settlement in exchange for a high alimony provision even though the wife will have to pay income taxes on what she receives for her support.[44] In the event that a bankruptcy does occur, she would lose everything still owed her under the property settlement, whereas the alimony debt survives the bankruptcy.

(b) Effect of Remarriage and Death

Normally a husband will want to stop paying alimony in the event that his wife remarries. His legal obligation to support her usually ends at that time.[45] If, however, alimony ends on the wife's remarriage, it can be argued that this operates as an incentive to the wife *not* to remarry. Hence, some separation agreements provide that alimony payments will continue after the remarriage of the wife (but at a much lower rate) in the hope that there will be at least some incentive to remarry. Of course, if the husband remarried, his obligation to support his first wife would continue.

If either husband or wife die, alimony payments cease unless the separation agreement specifically provides otherwise. It is possible, for example, that the separation agreement could provide that the alimony payments continue after the death of the husband, in

43. 11 U.S.C.A. § 35(a).

44. Infra p. 411.

45. Infra p. 433.

which event the wife would collect the alimony from the estate of the husband or from a trust [46] fund set up by the husband. Furthermore, the husband might take out a life insurance policy [47] payable on his death to his wife. This, in effect, continues some measure of support for the wife after the husband dies.

The situation is entirely different with respect to the property settlement commitments: they continue no matter who dies or remarries. As part of a property settlement (having nothing to do with support), John agrees to pay Mary $25,000. After John has paid Mary $1,000 of this amount, he dies. Mary can make a claim against John's estate for $24,000. If Mary died after John had paid her $1,000, Mary's estate could require John to pay the remaining $24,000 to it (i. e., to Mary's estate) for distribution according to Mary's will or according to the laws of intestacy.[48] The same is true if either party remarries. The funds or property due and owing under the property settlement provisions of the separation agreement remain due and owing no matter who remarries.

(c) Availability of Contempt

In examining what happens when one of the parties breaches a term of the separation agreement, we need to distinguish two situations: when the separation agreement is incorporated and merged into a subsequent divorce decree [49] and when it is not. If it is not incorporated and merged into the divorce decree, then the regular breach of contract remedies are available to the person who has suffered from the breach, e. g., suit for damages, possible rescission of the contract. The contempt sanction (e. g., fine, prison) is *not* available. The picture changes, however, if the divorce decree incorporates and merges with the separation agreement. Alimony provisions *can* be enforced by the contempt powers of the court when there is incorporation. The property settlement terms of the agreement, however, cannot be enforced by contempt even if incorporation and merger has occurred—with the possible exception of a term of the property settlement that requires a party to transfer (convey) property. If the party does not transfer the property, s/he can be held in contempt of court.

In summary, alimony terms are enforceable by contempt, property settlement terms are not (except for a property transfer term) when the separation agreement is incorporated and merged into the divorce decree.

46. See also infra p. 273.

47. Infra p. 270.

48. The inheritance laws—the laws that govern who receives property from a person who has died intestate, i. e., dies without leaving a will.

49. Infra p. 283.

(d) THE COURT'S POWER TO MODIFY TERMS

If for any reason either party becomes dissatisfied with the alimony terms of the separation agreement, will a court be available to modify those terms?[50] Usually not. A court will modify an alimony term only if the consequence of not doing so would be that the wife would become a public charge or would otherwise face serious financial difficulties due to a change of circumstances since the time she signed the separation agreement containing the original alimony term. A property settlement term, on the other hand, is rarely, if ever, modifiable by a court.

(e) FEDERAL INCOME TAX TREATMENT

The federal tax implications of alimony and property settlement in a separation agreement will be treated in detail in chapter nineteen.[51]

As you can see, it can make a great deal of difference whether a term of a separation agreement is classified as alimony or as a property settlement. The difficulty is that separation agreements do not always specify which is which. While alimony is usually paid in cash, the property settlement may also be "paid" in cash as well as in other kinds of property, e. g., house, car. In the heat of bargaining, the parties may not distinguish between alimony and property settlement. Even if the parties do clearly specify whether a term in the separation agreement is alimony or property settlement, a court may not be bound by the classification of the parties if it is otherwise apparent that the so-called property settlement provision is really alimony or vice versa. In chapter seventeen, we will examine a striking example of mis-classification through the opinion of Jones v. Flasted.[51a]

SECTION F. ALIMONY PROVISIONS FOR THE WIFE: DRAFTING OPTIONS

No individual provision of a separation agreement can be fully understood in isolation. As pointed out earlier, the negotiation process involves a large variety of factors.[52] A party may agree to a term in the agreement not so much because that term in and of itself gives the party what s/he wants, but rather because the party decided to concede that term in order to gain another term, e. g., a wife may accept a lower alimony provision in exchange for the husband's agreement to the term giving her custody of their child.

As just indicated, two separate financial arrangements need to be considered: *alimony* (a woman's right to be supported by her husband

50. On modification, see also supra p. 282.

51. Infra p. 411.

51a. Infra p. 372.

52. Supra p. 248.

unless she is the breadwinner and he is dependant on her), and *property settlement* or *property division* (the fair distribution of property acquired during the marriage based upon their mutual efforts in acquiring such property).

First, we consider alimony. (In the next section, we will examine property settlement terms in a separation agreement.) Here are some of the major options available:

PERIODIC PAYMENTS OR LUMP SUM?

In a few states, it is illegal for a husband and wife to agree on a lump sum payment in satisfaction of his duty to support her. In most states, however, it is permissible. The tax consequences, however, must be carefully weighed. Alimony payments are deductible to the husband if they are *periodic* as specifically defined by the Internal Revenue Service. If they are deductible to the husband, they are taxable to the wife, i. e., she must pay taxes on the alimony she receives.[53] Another important factor is collectibility. The wife may find it safer to take the lump sum now rather than have to hassle with periodic payments if there is any likehihood that he will fall behind in his payments. It can be expensive and psychologically draining to have to go after a delinquent husband.

FIXED OR FLUCTUATING PERIODIC PAYMENTS?

If periodic payments are decided upon, a number of questions need to be considered and resolved. Should the payments have a fixed dollar amount, e. g., $300 per month or per week? On what day of the month or week is each payment due? Another major option is the flexible periodic payment. The amount of the payment may fluctuate up or down depending upon the income of the husband, of the wife or both. An alimony payment of 25% of the husband's earnings, for example, provides an automatic fluctuating standard.

MEDICAL AND DENTAL EXPENSES OF THE WIFE

Does the alimony payment cover medical or dental expenses of the wife? Mental health expenses, e. g., psychiatrist? If not, do the parties want to include a term in the separation agreement on how these expenses are to be covered? If the husband pays these expenses and they qualify as periodic payments, he may be able to deduct them as alimony.[54]

LIFE INSURANCE

While the husband's duty to support his wife usually ends on his death or the death of his wife, the parties might agree that the support payments will continue after he dies. One way to do this is through a life insurance policy on his life with the wife as the beneficiary

53. Infra p. 411.

54. Ibid.

(and/or the children as beneficiaries). If the husband already has a life insurance policy, he may be required by the terms of the separation agreement to continue paying the premiums, to increase the amount of the policy, to name the wife as the irrevocable beneficiary, etc.[55] If no life insurance policy exists, the wife may try to negotiate with her husband to agree to take one out. When such a life insurance policy exists, the parties should decide whether it remains in force if the wife remarries.

RELATIONSHIP TO CHILD SUPPORT

A husband may try to get the wife to agree to a lower child support payment in exchange for a higher alimony payment. He cannot deduct child support payments,[56] but he can deduct alimony. One reason why the wife may resist this is that alimony payments are taxable to her, whereas child support payments are not. If a separation agreement fails to designate what payments are for alimony and what payments are for child support, the entire payment is treated as alimony for tax purposes, and hence deductible by him and taxable to her.[57]

MODIFICATION

The separation agreement may contain a clause that the terms of the agreement shall not be modified unless both parties agree in writing to do so. Courts, however, will rarely honor such a clause where children are concerned. Court will change custody and child support clauses when it feels the interests of the children warrant it.[58] This is so whether or not the separation agreement is later incorporated and merged into the divorce decree.

What about the alimony term of the separation agreement? Will a court modify this term if the separation agreement has been incorporated and merged into the divorce decree even though the agreement has a no-modification clause? States differ on their answer to this question. There are courts that *will* modify the alimony term if a change of circumstances since the divorce decree justifies it, e. g., the woman is about to become destitute.

Assignment # 62

Under what circumstances, if any, can an alimony provision be modified in your state? Determine whether your state code contains any statutes on this question. If not, try to find the answer in opinions written by courts of your state. (See also General Instructions for the State Code Assignment, supra p. 14, and for the Court Opinion Assignment, supra p. 26.)

55. Infra p. 278.

56. Infra p. 423.

57. Infra p. 424.

58. Infra p. 387.

TERMINATION OF SUPPORT PAYMENTS FOR THE WIFE

A separation agreement may provide that support or alimony payments to the wife will end:

(a) When she dies.

(b) When the husband dies.

(In some states, however, it is possible to force a husband's estate to continue supporting his wife even after he dies.)

(c) When the wife remarries.

(If the second marriage is later annulled, states differ on whether or not the original support obligation of the first husband revives.[59])

(d) When the wife commits adultery.

(Most courts will honor a separation agreement term providing that the wife's support payments end if she commits adultery or other act which would give him grounds for divorce [60] against her.)

(e) When the wife fails to abide by the custody terms of the separation agreement.

(Usually upheld.)

(f) When the wife competes with her husband in business.

(Not enforced. The wife's support payments cannot be conditioned on something which is not reasonably related to the marriage relationship.[61])

Of course, the separation agreement can provide the opposite. It may state, for example, that the wife's support payments continue:

(a) When the husband dies.

(The husband's estate would then have the obligation to continue the support payments. Life insurance is often used as a method of continuing support payments after the husband's death.[62])

(b) When the wife remarries.

(Rather than continue the support payments in full after the wife remarries, the separation agreement may provide for a reduced support payment in the event that the wife remarries. Some husbands fear that if the total support payment ends upon remarriage, the wife will have little incentive to remarry. It should be pointed out that there are a few states that forbid support payments to continue after the wife remarries.)

59. For more on this problem concerning annulments, see supra p. 216.

60. Infra p. 316ff.

61. Clark, H., *The Law of Domestic Relations*, p. 532 (1968).

62. Supra p. 270 and infra p. 427.

It is very unwise for the separation agreement to be silent on the circumstances that will terminate the husband's support obligation. These circumstances should be explicitly spelled out.

Whenever support payments are validly terminated, outstanding arrears are not affected. All delinquent payments which accrued before the support obligation terminated must be paid. If they terminated upon the death of the husband, for example, all payments which he failed to make before he died can be enforced against his estate.

SECURITY

When a husband fails to make a support payment, the wife can sue him,[63] but this is hardly an adequate remedy. Litigation can be expensive, lengthy and exhausting. Much more preferable is a term in the separation agreement that provides security to the wife for the performance of the husband's support obligation. This security can be provided in a number of forms:

—Escrow

The husband deposits a sum of money with an escrow agent, e. g., a bank, with instructions to pay the wife a designated amount of money in the event that the husband falls behind in a payment.

—Surety bond

The husband gives his wife a surety bond. The husband pays premiums to the Surety Company. The Surety Company guarantees the wife that if the husband fails to fulfill his support obligation, the Company will fulfill it up to the amount of the bond.

—Annuity

The husband purchases an annuity contract which provides a fixed income to the wife (annuitant) in the amount of the support obligation.

—Trust

The husband can transfer property (e. g., cash) to a trustee (e. g., a bank) with instructions to pay a fixed income to his wife (the beneficiary) in the amount of the support obligation.

The last two forms of security are *not* dependant upon a breach by the husband of his support obligation under the separation agreement in order to come into effect.

63. Infra p. 282.

SECTION G. PROPERTY SETTLEMENT: DRAFTING OPTIONS

As already indicated, it is unrealistic to view the provisions for property settlement in isolation from other terms of the separation agreement, especially those concerning support of one's spouse.[64] In the bargaining process, for example, a party might accept a lower support provision in exchange for a higher share of the property division or in exchange for any other term in the separation agreement that the party badly wants. In examining property settlements, we need to consider three questions:

1. What kind of property do the parties have?
2. With what resources was it acquired?
3. How is the property held, i. e., who has title?

1. WHAT KIND OF PROPERTY DO THE PARTIES HAVE?

There are two kinds of property: real property and personal property. Real property is land and those things attached or affixed to the land. The real property may consist of a main home, a vacation home, land and/or buildings used in a business, condominium, etc. Personal property consists essentially of movable items, e. g., cars, boats, cash, stocks, bonds, royalties, furniture, jewelry, art objects, books, records, clothes, photographic equipment, sports equipment, pets, business supplies (inventory), credits, accounts receivable, exclusive options to buy, insurance policies etc.

2. WITH WHAT RESOURCES WAS THE PROPERTY ACQUIRED?

There are a variety of ways that the above real and personal property could have been obtained:

—as a gift to one of the spouses;

—as a gift to both of the spouses;

—as a bequest (personal property given by will) to one or both spouses;

—as a devise (real property given by will) to one or both spouses;

—through intestate succession (an inheritance given to an heir of a person who died without leaving a valid will);

—through funds that a spouse brought with him/her to the marriage;

—through funds from the salary of one of the spouses;

—through funds from the salaries of both of the spouses;

—etc.

64. Supra p. 269.

3. HOW IS THE PROPERTY HELD? WHO HAS TITLE?

There are a number of ways that property can be held:

—*Solely Owned by One of the Spouses.* The title to the property is in the name of one of the parties only. This could be due to the fact that the property was purchased with the funds of that one spouse. Or, it may be that the property was purchased with the funds of one spouse, but placed in the name of the other spouse (perhaps in the hope of insulating the property from the claims of the creditors of the spouse that purchased the property).

—*Joint Tenancy.*[65] The ownership of the entire property by two or more individuals. Each joint tenant has an equal right to possess the entire property. They do not each own a piece of the property; each joint tenant owns it all. When one joint tenant dies, his/her interest passes to the surviving joint tenants (by the right of survivorship.) A husband and wife can own property as joint tenants.

—*Tenancy by the Entireties.*[66] In some states, a joint tenancy held by a husband and wife is called a tenancy by the entireties. Each spouse has a right of survivorship as with any joint tenancy.

—*Tenancy in Common.*[67] Each party has an equal right to possession of the property, but there is no right of survivorship. When one tenant in common dies, the property does not automatically pass to the surviving tenants in common. The property goes to whomever the deceased designated by will, or to the heirs of the deceased by intestate succession if the deceased died without leaving a valid will. Hence, the main distinction between (a) a joint tenancy and a tenancy by the entireties, on the one hand, and (b) a tenancy in common, on the other, is that the property of a deceased tenant passes through the estate of that tenant only in the case of a tenancy in common. In the other tenancies, the property passes immediately to the surviving tenant(s) by operation of law.

—*Community Property.*[68] In Arizona, California, Idaho, Louisiana, Nevada, New Mexico, Texas and Washington (the community property states), property acquired by either spouse during the marriage (except by gift, devise, legacy) is the property of both spouses.

65. Infra p. 419.

66. Infra p. 429.

67. Infra p. 429.

68. For more on community property, see 431.

Generally, a party will want to keep any property s/he obtained through his/her own resources or through his/her own relatives. Yet, even with respect to such property, a party might be willing to turn it over in exchange for some other objective.

There are a large number of options available to the parties in deciding how to divide their property. For example:

—the property could be sold with the proceeds divided equally or in any proportion agreed upon;

—some or all of the jointly owned property could be transferred into the name of one of the parties;

—one party may be allowed to remain living in the home for that party's life or the life of the children or until the children turn 18 (if this option is used, then the parties must also agree on who pays the mortgage, taxes, utilities, maintenance and repair costs, who takes the interest and property tax deduction, etc.);

—etc.

If the husband earned all the income while the wife stayed home to maintain the house and raise the children, she still has a strong equitable argument in favor of obtaining a significant share of the property since her efforts enabled him to spend the time away from the home earning his income.

SECTION H. CHILD CUSTODY AND SUPPORT [68a]

The parties have much less flexibility in deciding who gets the children and how they are to be supported than they do in deciding the questions involving the support of the wife and the property settlement. A court will not ignore the terms of a separation agreement on custody and child support, but it will be quick to disregard those terms in the event that the "best interests of the child" justify it.

In their deliberations, the parties must cover three major areas:

(i) Custody.

(ii) Visitation.

(iii) Support.

(i) Custody Considerations

—should only one parent be given custody;

—should the parents share custody;

—how old are the children;

—are they old enough to express an intelligent preference;

—which parent had greater contact (positive and negative) with the children during the marriage (have any special attachments or hostilities formed);

68a. See also infra pp. 376, 382.

—the health of the parents (physical and mental);

—the health of the children (physical and mental);

—who is to have final say on major decisions, e. g., school, health;

—does the other parent have the right to be consulted on the major decisions;

—if the mother has custody and remarries, will the children retain their father's surname;

—who will have custody in the event that both parents die;

—etc.

(ii) Visitation Considerations

—is the parent without custody to have visitation rights or is that parent to relinquish all rights in the children;

—how specific should the visitation right be (should it specify the day and time of pick up per week (month), the duration of the visit, etc.);

—should it be flexibly stated (once a month at any time so long as reasonable notice is given to the parent with custody in advance of the visit, once a week with notice, etc.);

—what happens during the major vacations, e. g., Christmas, Easter, Summer; do the parents alternate having the children during these times; is a new agreement to be reached each year, etc.;

—can the parent with custody move outside the city, state, country;

—what happens if the party with custody remarries and the new couple wishes to move out of the city, state, country;

—if the parent without custody moves out of the city, state, country, do the visitation terms of the separation agreement change;

—etc.

(iii) Support Considerations

—What standard of living were the children accustomed to during the marriage;

—does the father and/or the mother have the financial resources to maintain this standard of living;

—what are the tax factors [69] (child support payments are not deductible by the provider, nor includible in the income of the parent with custody—unlike alimony; [70] the provider of the support payments may try to have the parent with custody agree to a lower child support payment in exchange for a higher alimony to take advantage of the deduction);

69. Infra p. 423.

70. Infra p. 411.

—how many child support payments are to exist: one covering every-day expenses and a separate one covering large, emergency expenses, e. g., hospital expenses;

—are the children to be covered by medical insurance; who pays premiums;

—are the children to be beneficiaries of a life insurance policy on the life of the provider of their support; how much, who pays premiums, can the beneficiaries be changed;

—do the support provisions end or change when the children reach a certain age; what if they are disabled at that age;

—do the support payments fluctuate with the income of either of the parents;

—when the provider of child support payments dies, is his/her estate obligated to continue payments; must there be a will making provision for this;

—what educational expenses are anticipated: tutors, preparatory school, college, graduate/professional school, room, board, books, transportation, entertainment, etc.;

—while the child is away at school, does the provider of support have to continue sending support payments to the parent with custody;

—do the school payments go to the parent with custody or directly to the child away at school;

—etc.

SECTION I. INSURANCE

A number of questions have to be dealt with:

(1) What kinds of insurance do the parties now have?

(2) How have the insurance premiums been paid?

(3) Following the separation, what will happen to the policies?

(4) Is there a need for additional insurance?

There are several different kinds of insurance policies which could be in effect at the time the parties are drafting the separation agreement:

—life insurance;

—homeowner policy;

—hospitalization or other medical policy;

—liability insurance (for business);

—car insurance;

—etc.

Each kind of policy should be carefully identified with notations as to how much the premiums are, who has paid them, who the beneficiaries are, can the beneficiaries be changed and if so, by whom, etc. Unfortunately, parties often neglect such important details. Insurance policies can be as crucial and sometimes more crucial than other "property" items that must be divided or otherwise handled during the negotiations on the separation agreement. It may be that the parties want to leave the policies as they are with no changes or additions. This is fine if it is a conscious decision of both parties after all the facts are known about each policy, after the tax consequences of the policies are explained,[71] and after the economic advantages and disadvantages of the various ways of handling each policy are discussed.

Life insurance is or should be high on the agenda for the negotiations. Generally, a husband has no obligation to support his wife or children after he dies.[72] There is nothing, however, to prevent him from assuming this obligation if he does so freely and has the means to do so. Life insurance on his life is a common way of doing this. The beneficiaries can be his wife and/or his children. If such a life insurance policy already exists, then the husband will be agreeing to keep it effective (e. g., pay the premiums) after the separation. The wife and children, however, may not gain much protection from such an agreement if the husband can change the beneficiaries at his pleasure. Hence, as part of the bargaining process, the wife may ask that the designation of herself and the children as beneficiaries be made irrevocable.

SECTION J. DEBTS

The parties must discuss what to do with:

(a) debts outstanding (i. e., unpaid) at the time the separation agreement is signed, and,

(b) debts incurred after the separation agreement is signed.

A great variety of debts may be outstanding:

—debts between the spouses (e. g., a loan made by one spouse to the other during the marriage);

—business debts incurred by the husband (i. e., in his name);

—family debts incurred by the husband;

—business debts incurred by the wife (i. e., in her name);

—family debts incurred by the wife;

—business or family debts incurred by both the husband and wife (i. e., in both of their names so that they are jointly and severally liable on the debts—a creditor could sue the husband

71. Infra p. 427.

72. Infra p. 433.

and wife together on the debt, or could sue either the husband or the wife).

The parties must decide who is going to pay what debts, and once they have reached this determination, the separation agreement should specifically reflect what they have decided.

The extent to which the parties are in debt is relevant to (i) the necessity of using present cash and other resources to pay these debts, (ii) the availability of resources for support of spouse and children, and (iii) the possibility of bankruptcy now or in the immediate future. As to the husband's personal or business debts, for example, the wife should not take the attitude that such debts are "his problem," since the possibility of bankruptcy could mean that she loses whatever property settlement funds he owes her.[73]

As to future debts (i. e., incurred after the separation agreement is signed), the normal expectation of the parties is that they will pay their own debts. Except for the obligations that arise out of the separation agreement itself, the parties are on their own, e. g., a wife will not make a purchase of necessities [74] on the credit of her husband. A clause should be inserted in the agreement providing that each party promises not to attempt to use the credit of the other.[75]

SECTION K. TAXES

Elsewhere in this book the tax consequences of separation agreements are discussed.[76] Our focus here is on the question of who pays the taxes and who will be able to take advantage of certain tax benefits. The following are the kinds of situations that need to be anticipated:

—The Internal Revenue Service assesses a tax deficiency for a prior year during which the parties had filed a joint return—who pays this deficiency?

—For the current tax year, the parties file a joint return (the last such return that they ever file [77]); many months later, the Internal Revenue Service assesses a tax deficiency on that last tax return—who pays this deficiency?

—In the year in which the separation agreement is signed, if the wife files a separate return, with what resources are her taxes paid?

73. The husband's alimony obligations, however, are *not* discharged in bankruptcy. See supra p. 267.

74. Infra p. 435.

75. For example, see infra p. 288.

76. Infra p. 411.

77. For the law on when parties can no longer file joint returns, see infra p. 426.

—In the current and future years, who takes the tax deduction for the payment of interest on the mortgage, and for the payment of property taxes?

—In the current and future years, who takes the tax exemption for each of the dependent children?

—What happens to any tax refunds that might become available for the current tax year and for any prior year?

Often, the husband will agree to a clause in the separation agreement which indemnifies the wife against any tax deficiencies (or penalties) that may arise out of the last joint return filed and out of the joint returns filed in any prior year during their marriage. Under such a clause, he will have to pay the entire deficiency (or penalty) under which they are both jointly and severally liable.[78] Similarly, the parties must also agree on how tax refunds (usually payable by government check to both the parties) are to be divided.

With respect to interest, property tax deductions and exemptions, there are laws on who can take advantage of these benefits;[79] the parties do not have total freedom in deciding who can use these tax benefits. The point, however, is that one of the parties will be entitled to the benefits. This is an economic advantage which should be taken into consideration in the overall evaluation of who is getting what from the separation agreement. The parties make a big mistake when they fail to take account of such matters. The separation agreement may specify a dollar amount to be transferred pursuant to a support and/or a property settlement term. If, however, all the tax factors have not been considered, the parties may later be surprised about the discrepancy between such stated dollar figures and the *real* amounts that the parties later receive and pay out.

SECTION L. WILLS

There are a number of questions involving wills and estates that the parties must consider:

—Do the spouses already have wills naming each other as beneficiaries (if so, are these wills to be changed)?

—Have they named each other executor of their estates (if so, is this to be changed)?

—Is the husband going to agree to leave his wife and/or children something in his will (if so, and this requires a change in his will, when is this change to be made)?

—Is either spouse mentioned as a beneficiary in the will of a relative of the other spouse (if so, is this to be changed)?

78. For the law on when a wife will not be liable for back taxes, see infra p. 427.

79. Infra p. 428.

While the parties are still married, they may have rights of dower,[80] curtesy,[81] right to elect against the estate,[82] etc. Hence it may be important to know whether the parties are contemplating a divorce, and if so, how much time is anticipated between the signing of the separation agreement and the obtaining of the final divorce decree. The separation agreement will often contain a waiver of any rights that either party has in the estate of the other.[83]

SECTION M. MISCELLANEOUS PROVISIONS

A number of other items need to be considered:

(a) Counsel Fees

The husband is often ordered by the court to pay the attorney fees of the wife in a divorce action.[84] The parties may decide to specify this in the separation agreement itself. They should consider not only the legal costs (counsel fees, filing fees, etc.) of a potential divorce, but also the legal costs incurred by the wife in connection with the separation agreement itself. Of course, if the wife has separate means of her own, the parties may agree that she will pay her own legal bills.

(b) Non-Molestation Clause

Most separation agreements contain a "non-molestation clause" in which both parties agree, in effect, to leave each other alone. Specifically, they will not try to live with the other person, interfere with each other's life style or bother each other in any way.[85]

SECTION N. MODIFICATION AND ENFORCEMENT OF THE SEPARATION AGREEMENT

Generally a court has no power to alter the terms of a contract unless it finds that it was procured by fraud[86] or duress.[87] The same is true of a separation agreement with several important qualifications. As indicated, a court will not hesitate to modify the child custody and child support terms of the agreement when the best interests of the child require it.[88] So too, many courts will not allow a

80. Supra p. 128.

81. Supra p. 128.

82. The election right gives the surviving spouse a choice between provisions made for that spouse in the will of the deceased spouse and a fixed share of the deceased's estate as specified by statute.

83. For example, see infra p. 289.

84. Infra p. 365.

85. For example, see infra p. 293.

86. See also supra p. 257.

87. See also supra p. 257.

88. Supra p. 276 and infra p. 376.

wife to become destitute simply because she made a bad bargain in the separation agreement for her support.[89] Unlike the normal contract, a court will intervene in such situations, e. g., to require the husband to do things other than or in addition to what he initially agreed to do by contract with his wife.

The more troublesome problems concern (a) the property settlement provisions of the separation agreement,[90] and (b) support provisions for the spouse when they are not so inadequate that the wife is about to become a public charge. Can a court change these provisions? Most courts would say no—unless the parties included a clause stating that a court will have the power to modify any term in the agreement.

Another factor relevant to the question of whether a court can modify the terms of a separation agreement is what the parties ask the court to do with the agreement at the time they seek a divorce. A number of options are possible:

—they could say nothing about the separation agreement to the court; the court makes decisions about support, custody and property division independent of their agreement;

—they could ask the court to approve the separation agreement, but not issue an order that its terms be carried out;

—they could ask the court to *incorporate* the separation agreement into the divorce decree and *order* that its terms be carried out; the separation agreement *merges* into the divorce decree.[91]

When there has been an incorporation and merger, the agreement loses its separate identity; it becomes part of the divorce judgment. The question is no longer whether the separation agreement can be modified, but whether the *judgment* can be modified. A court may be more inclined to modify its own judgment than to modify a contract of the parties.

In summary:

—if the parties insert a clause authorizing a court to modify the terms of the separation agreement, they can be modified;

—if the parties say nothing about whether a court can modify the terms of the agreement or if they insert a clause forbidding a court from modifying the terms, a court will still have the power to modify those terms covering the custody and support of the children; this is so whether or not the separation agreement is merged into the divorce judgment;

—the provisions in the separation agreement on the support of the wife can usually be modified if the failure to do so would

89. Supra p. 258.

90. Supra p. 274.

91. See infra p. 385.

leave the wife destitute; in some states, this is so even if the parties have inserted a clause asking the court not to modify any terms, and whether or not the agreement has been merged into the judgment;

—if the wife is not about to become destitute, but could use additional funds to live more comfortably, a court may be more inclined to modify the support term if the agreement was merged into the judgment than if it was not merged, but in either case, will usually be reluctant to do so;

—the provisions in the separation agreement on property settlement cannot be modified by the court whether or not the agreement is merged into the divorce judgment unless the parties specifically provide that a court can modify the property division terms.

Again, it is an oversimplification to view property division and spousal support terms independently. They are often integrated or dependent on each other in the sense that the parties may have agreed to the property settlement in exchange for (and only because of) what is provided in the spousal support term, or vice versa. When this is evident, a court may be all the more reluctant to modify the support terms whether or not a merger has occurred.

Closely related to the question of whether separation agreements can be modified by a court is whether the agreement can be enforced by the contempt power (fine or imprisonment) of the court.[92] The answer depends upon the circumstances involved:

(a) Separation Agreement Where No Divorce Decree Is Involved

The separation agreement would be enforced by normal contract remedies. When the contract is breached, the injured party can obtain a judgment declaring that the breach has occurred and awarding damages (money) to the injured party. To collect this money, such party may have to seek *execution* of the judgment.[93] In some instances, the remedy of specific performance may be granted whereby the wrongdoing party is ordered to perform his/her contract as originally promised. The aggrieved party may also have the option of rescinding (canceling) the entire separation agreement.

92. See also supra p. 268.

93. After the judgment is rendered for a sum of money, an execution writ is issued out of the court clerk's office and given to the sheriff. The writ commands the sheriff to levy execution on the property of the defendant by taking possession of the property and selling it, using the proceeds of the sale to pay the plaintiff. Dobbs, D. *Handbook on the Law of Remedies*, p. 10 (1073).

Generally, if no divorce decree is involved, the separation agreement cannot be enforced by contempt.

(b) Separation Agreement Merged Into The Divorce Decree

—alimony and child support orders are enforceable by contempt;

—property settlement orders involving the payment of money are not enforceable by contempt;

—property settlement orders involving the transfer of property other than money, e. g., an order that the party transfer title to land to the other party, may be enforceable by contempt.

It is sometimes difficult to determine whether a court's award is alimony or is part of the property settlement.[94] If the terms are so blended, the problems of determining what can be enforced by contempt are obvious given the above rules which in part depend upon being able to distinguish alimony from property settlement terms.

(c) Separation Agreement Not Merged Into The Divorce Decree

Here, the divorce court makes decisions about custody, child support, alimony, etc., but does not incorporate and merge the separation agreement. The agreement may contain provisions for custody, child support and alimony which are different from what the divorce decree eventually provides. Since the separation agreement is not merged, it can be enforced through the same remedies as are available in (a) above. There is also a divorce decree ordering that certain things be done in reference to custody, child support and alimony. An aggrieved party can sue to enforce this judgment (if it is disobeyed) with the same remedies as are available in (b) above. This does *not* mean that the aggrieved party can recover twice—once under (a) the agreement and once under the decree. Only one recovery is possible.

SECTION O. ARBITRATION

Many separation agreements contain a clause that if disputes arise under the agreement, they shall be subject to arbitration. Normally, a professional arbitration organization, such as the American Arbitration Association, is specified as the arbitrator who will resolve the dispute. A professional group, however, is not necessary. The parties could select a mutually trusted friend or associate as the arbitrator.

94. See also supra p. 265.

SECTION P. RECONCILIATION

What happens if the parties become reconciled to each other after they execute the separation agreement? They clearly have the power to cancel or rescind their contract so long as both do so voluntarily. If this intention is put in writing or otherwise clearly indicated, no problem exists. The separation agreement goes out of existence legally. The problem arises when the parties say nothing about the separation agreement after they reconcile and resume cohabitation. Courts handle the problem in different ways:

—the reconciliation will cancel the alimony or spousal support terms of the separation agreement, but will not cancel the property settlement terms;

—the reconciliation will cancel the executory (unperformed as yet) terms of the separation agreement, but will not cancel the executed (already performed) terms.

What is meant by a reconciliation? The full resumption of the marital relationship is usually required; occasional or casual getting together will not be sufficient. The intent must be to abandon the separation agreement and to resume the marital relationship permanently.

INTERVIEWING AND INVESTIGATION CHECKLIST HAVE THE PARTIES RECONCILED?		
	Legal Interviewing Questions	**Possible Investigation Tasks**
1.	When did the two of you sign the separation agreement?	* Get a copy of the separation agreement in order to verify its date of execution. * Interview people who know the plaintiff (P) and defendant (D) well to find out what they know about the alleged reconciliation. * Obtain any documents executed after the separation agreement was signed which may indicate the extent to which P and D did things together during this time, e.g., rent receipts with both of their names on it, opening or continuing joint checking or savings accounts.
2.	When did you stop living together?	
3.	Where did you both live when you were separated?	
4.	Was your separation bitter?	
5.	After you signed the separation agreement, when did the two of you have your first contact? Describe the circumstances?	
6.	Have the two of you had sexual intercourse with each other since the separation agreement was signed?	
7.	Did you ever discuss getting back together again? If so, describe the circumstances, e.g., who initiated the discussion, was there any reluctance?	
8.	During this period, did the two of you abide by the terms of the separation agreement? Explain.	
9.	Did you move in together? If so, where did you both stay? Did one of you give up his/her house or apartment?	
10.	Did you discuss what to do with the separation agreement?	
11.	Did the two of you assume that it was no longer effective?	

INTERVIEWING AND INVESTIGATION CHECKLIST HAVE THE PARTIES RECONCILED? —Continued		
	Legal Interviewing Questions	**Possible Investigation Tasks**
12.	After you got together again, did either of you continue abiding by any of the terms of the separation agreement?	
13.	Did either of you give back whatever you received under the terms of the separation agreement?	
14.	When you got back together again, did you feel that the reunion was going to be permanent? What do you think your spouse felt about it?	
15.	Did either of you attach any conditions on your resuming your relationship again?	
16.	What have the two of you done since the two of you got together again to indicate that you both considered each other as husband and wife again, e.g., both signing joint tax returns, making joint purchases, spending a lot of time together in public, etc.?	
17.	Have you separated again? If so describe the circumstances.	

IM-477

Assignment # 63

Tom and Mary execute a separation agreement on February 17, 1978 in which they mutually release all rights (dower,[95] curtesy,[96] right of election,[97] etc.) in each other's estate. They stop living together on February 2, 1978. On March 13, 1978, Tom moves out of the city. He makes a long distance call to Mary in which he says, "This is ridiculous; why don't you come live with me. You know I still love you." Mary answers, "I guess you're right, but if we are going to live together again, I want you to come back here." Tom then says, "I'm sure we can work that out." They agree to meet next week to discuss it further. Before they meet, Tom dies. Tom's will makes no provision for Mary. Mary now seeks a share of his estate through the exercise of a right of election. What result? (See also General Instructions for the Legal Analysis Assignment, supra p. 16.)

95. Supra p. 128.

96. Ibid.

97. Supra p. 282.

SECTION Q. SAMPLE SEPARATION AGREEMENT CLAUSES

STONE, B., MODERN LEGAL FORMS

§ 4515ff., p. 274ff. (West Publishing Co. (1977)).

Separation Agreement—Significant Clauses [98]

Agreement made this 19th day of November, 19__, between John Jones, presently residing at 10 South Street, ______, hereinafter sometimes referred to as "the Husband," and Mary Jones, presently residing at 25 North Street, ______, hereinafter sometimes referred to as "the Wife."

Witnesseth:

Whereas, the parties are husband and wife and were married in ______, on June 15, 19__; and

Whereas, there are two children of the marriage, namely, a daughter, Elizabeth Ann Jones, hereinafter sometimes referred to as "Elizabeth," born on April 1, 19__, and a son, William Roe Jones, hereinafter referred to as "William," born on August 15, 19__ and

Whereas, in consequence of disputes and irreconcilable differences, the parties have separated, and are now living separate and apart, and intend to continue to live separate and apart for the rest of their natural lives; and

Whereas the parties desire to confirm their separation and make arrangements in connection therewith, including the settlement of all questions relating to their property rights, the custody of their children (which the parties recognize as paramount), and other rights and obligations growing out of the marriage relation;

Now, Therefore, in consideration of the premises and of the mutual covenants and undertakings herein set forth, the parties covenant and agree as follows:

1. *Separation.* The parties may and shall at all times hereafter live and continue to live separate and apart for the rest of their natural lives. Each shall be free from interference, authority and control, direct or indirect, by the other as fully as if he or she were single and unmarried. Subject to the provisions of this agreement, each may reside at such place or places as he or she may select. The parties shall not molest each other or compel or endeavor to compel the other to cohabit or dwell with him or her, by any legal or other proceedings for restitution of conjugal rights or otherwise.

2. *Wife's Debts.* The Wife covenants and represents that she has not heretofore incurred or contracted, nor will she at any time in

98. From a lecture by John Scully, Jr. on Significant Clauses in a Separation Agreement, published in Record of the Bar Association of the City of New York, Vol. 7, pp. 236–250.

the future incur or contract, any debt, charge or liability whatsoever for which the Husband, his legal representatives, or his property or estate is now or may become liable, and the Wife further covenants at all times to keep the Husband free, harmless and indemnified of and from any and all debts, charges and liabilities heretofore and hereafter contracted by her.

3. *Mutual Release.* Subject to the provisions of this agreement, each party has remised, released and forever discharged and by these presents does for himself or herself, and his or her heirs, legal representatives, executors, administrators and assigns remise, release and forever discharge the other of and from all cause or causes of action, claims, rights or demands whatsoever, in law or in equity, which either of the parties hereto ever had or now has against the other, except any or all cause or causes of action for divorce.

4. *Waivers of Claims Against Estates.* Subject to the provisions of this agreement, each of the parties may in any way dispose of his or her property of whatsoever nature, real or personal, and each of the parties hereto, for himself or herself, and for his or her heirs, legal representatives, executors, administrators and assigns, hereby waive any right of election which he or she may have or hereafter acquire regarding the estate of the other, or to take against any last will and testament of the other, whether heretofore or hereafter executed, . . . and renounces and releases all interest, right or claim of right of dower, or otherwise, that he or she now has or might otherwise have against the other, on the property of whatsoever nature, real or personal, of the other, under or by virtue of the laws of any State or country, and each will at the request of the other, or his or her legal representatives, executors, administrators and assigns execute, acknowledge and deliver any and all deeds, releases, or any other instruments necessary to bar, release or extinguish such interests, rights and claims, or which may be needful for the proper carrying into effect of any of the provisions of this agreement. Each of the parties renounces and relinquishes any and all claims and rights that he or she may have or may hereafter acquire to act as executor or administrator of the other party's estate.

5. *Division of Personal Property.* The parties have heretofore divided their personal property to their mutual satisfaction. Henceforth, each of the parties shall own, have and enjoy, independently of any claim or right of the other party, all items of personal property of every kind, nature and description and wheresoever situate, which are now owned or held by or which may hereafter belong or come to the Husband or the Wife, with the full power to the Husband or the Wife to dispose of same as fully and effectually, in all respects and for all purposes, as if he or she were unmarried.

6. *Custody of Children.* (a) The Wife shall have custody of Elizabeth and shall have custody of William, except that the Husband

may at his option have the custody of either child or both, concurrently or at different or overlapping periods, as follows:

(1) between the 1st day of June and the 30th day of September in each year for a continuous period not to exceed three months; and

(2) during the Christmas holidays each year, for a period of not more than 5 days; and

(3) during the Easter school vacations, for a period of not more than 5 days; and

(4) for one week end, consisting of Saturday and Sunday, in each calendar month.

(b) The Husband shall exercise his option by notifying the Wife in writing of his intention so to do at least 30 days before the beginning of any such period referred to in subparagraph (1) of paragraph 6(a) hereof and at least 10 days before the beginning of any such period referred to in subparagraphs (2), (3) or (4) of paragraph 6(a) hereof.

(c) It is the Husband's intent to exercise his right of partial custody each year and from time to time but the Husband's partial custody as provided in subparagraph 6(a) hereof shall be entirely optional with him and his waiver thereof on any occasion, and for any reason, shall not constitute a waiver of his right to insist thereafter upon compliance with the provisions thereof.

(d) The Husband shall have the right to meet with the children at any time on reasonable notice, and the Wife shall afford the Husband the opportunity to do so.

(e) Neither the Husband nor the Wife shall have the right to take or send the children or either of them outside of the continental territorial limits of the United States of America without obtaining the prior written consent of the other.

(f) Each of the parties agrees to keep the other informed at all times of the whereabouts of the children while the children or either of them are with the Husband or Wife respectively, and they mutually agree that if either of them has knowledge of any illness or accident or other circumstances seriously affecting the health or welfare of either of the children, the Husband or the Wife, as the case may be, will promptly notify the other of such circumstances.

(g) The parties shall consult with each other with respect to the education and religious training of the children, their illnesses and operations (except in emergencies), their welfare and other matters of similar importance affecting the children, whose well-being, education and development shall at all times be the paramount consideration of the Husband and the Wife.

(h) The parties shall exert every reasonable effort to maintain free access and unhampered contact between the children and each of the parties, and to foster a feeling of affection between the children and the other party. Neither party shall do anything which may estrange either child from the other party, or injure the opinion of the children as to their mother or father, or which may hamper the free and natural development of either child's love and respect for the other party.

7. *Support of Wife and Children.* If the Wife has not remarried (should the parties be divorced), the Husband shall make the following payments to the Wife for her life and for the support and maintenance of the Wife and for the support, maintenance and education of the children: [99]

> [The "payments" above referred to, will depend on the circumstances of each particular case. Frequently a percentage, or staggering percentages, of the Husband's income is used to measure the obligation. If so, consider the advisability of including minimum and maximum annual support and maintenance obligations. In any event, the term "income" must be clearly defined. However defined, the important thing is to be able to tie the "income" back in to the Husband's Federal income tax return. In these circumstances the Husband should be required to furnish the Wife with a true copy of his preceding year's Federal income tax return if the support and maintenance payments during such preceding year did not exceed the maximum provision.]

8. *Wife's Counsel Fees.* The Husband will pay the reasonable counsel fees and legal expenses of the Wife in connection with negotiation and preparation of this agreement.

9. *Acceptance and Release by Wife.* The Wife recognizes and acknowledges that the foregoing provisions for her benefit are satisfactory and that they are reasonable and adequate for her support and maintenance, past, present and future, and in keeping with her accustomed mode of living, reasonable requirements and station in life. The Wife accordingly releases and discharges the Husband, absolutely and forever, for the rest of her life from any and all claims and demands, past, present or future for alimony or for any other provision for maintenance and support except as contained in this agreement.

99. 26 U.S.C.A. § 71 makes separate maintenance payments taxable to the wife and 26 U.S.C.A. § 215 provides that the amounts so includible in the wife's income are deductible by the husband. These provisions do not apply if the husband and wife make a single return jointly. 26 U.S.C.A. § 71(a)(2). It is also important to note that these provisions do not apply to payments to support minor children. 26 U.S.C.A. § 71(b). The husband remains taxable on those amounts and they are not included in the wife's income. If, however, the agreement fixes one amount only for the support of the wife and children without specifying directly or indirectly any allocation of this amount as between the wife and the children, the full amount will be taxable to the wife and deductible by the husband.

Under the Tax Reform Act of 1976, periodic payments have been made a deduction in determining adjusted gross income for years beginning after 12–31–76. 26 U.S.C.A. § 62(13).

10. *Subsequent Divorce.* In the event that an action for divorce is instituted at any time hereafter by either party against the other in this or any other state or country, the parties hereto agree that they shall be bound by all the terms of this agreement and this agreement shall not be merged in any decree or judgment that may be granted in such action but shall survive the same and shall be forever binding and conclusive on the parties and nothing herein contained shall be construed to prevent the decree or judgment in any such action from incorporating in full or in substance the terms of this agreement.

11. *Entire Agreement.* Both the legal and practical effect of this agreement in each and every respect and the financial status of the parties has been fully explained to both parties by their respective counsel and they both acknowledge that it is a fair agreement and is not the result of any fraud, duress or undue influence exercised by either party upon the other or by any other person or persons upon either, and they further agree that this agreement contains the entire understanding of the parties. There are no representations, promises, warranties, covenants or undertakings other than those expressly set forth herein.

12. *Additional Instruments.* Each of the parties hereto agrees further at any time and from time to time to make, execute and deliver all instruments necessary to effectuate the provisions of this agreement.

13. *Notices.* For the purpose of this agreement, all notices or other communications given or made hereunder shall, until written notice to the contrary, be given or mailed to the Wife at 25 North Street, ______, and to the Husband at 10 South Street, ______.

Each party shall at all times keep the other party informed of his or her place of residence and business and shall promptly notify the other party of any change, giving the address of any new place of residence or business.

14. *Situs.* All matters affecting the interpretation of this agreement and the rights of the parties hereto shall be governed by the laws of the State of ______.

15. *Binding Effect.* All the provisions of this agreement shall be binding upon the respective heirs, next of kin, executors, administrators and assigns of the parties hereto.

16. *Counterparts.* This agreement shall be executed in triplicate, each of which so executed shall be deemed an original and shall constitute one and the same agreement.

In Witness Whereof, the parties hereto have hereunto set their respective hands and seals and initialed each page of this agreement the day and year first above written.

Witnesses:

_______________. _______________. [L.S.]

_______________. _______________. [L.S.]

[*Add acknowledgments*]

Separation Agreement—Fixed Monthly Payments—
Custody and Support of Children

This Agreement is made the ______ day of ______, 19__, between ______, herein called the Husband, and ______, his wife, herein called the Wife.

Whereas the Husband and Wife were married on the ______ day of ______, 19__, and have two children, ______ and ______;

Whereas differences have arisen between the Husband and Wife as the result of which they are now living separate and apart;

Whereas the Husband and Wife have entered into this Agreement freely, with the advice of counsel, and acknowledge that its provisions are fair.

The parties agree as follows:

1. *Separation.* The Husband and Wife may live apart from each other as if they were unmarried. Each shall be free from the control of the other and may reside at such place as he or she shall think fit.

2. *No Interference.* The Husband and Wife will not in any manner annoy, molest or disturb the other, or compel or endeavor to compel the other to cohabit or dwell with him or her.

3. *Wife's Debts.* The Wife will at all times keep the Husband indemnified against all debts and liabilities which she may hereafter contract and from all actions, claims, demands, costs, damages and expenses on account thereof. In case the Husband shall at any time be called on to and shall pay any debt or debts which she may hereafter contract, then it shall be lawful for the Husband to retain out of the next amount payable to the Wife hereunder the amount of such debt or debts with all costs and expenses which he may incur on account thereof.

4, *Division of Household Goods.* The Husband and Wife have divided between them to their mutual satisfaction the personal effects, household furniture and furnishings, and all other articles of personal property which have been used by them in common, in accordance with the Schedule attached hereto.

5. *Transfer of Home.* The Husband has conveyed to the Wife by deed, executed, acknowledged and delivered simultaneously with the execution of this Agreement, the property which was the former home of the parties and in which the Wife now resides.

6. *Support of Wife.* The Husband shall during the life of the Wife and until she remarries pay to the Wife, or to such person as she shall from time to time appoint in writing, the yearly sum of ______ dollars by equal monthly payments beginning on the ______ day of ______, 19__, for the support and maintenance of herself.

7. *Custody of Children in Wife.* The Wife shall have the sole custody and control of the children, ______ and ______, without any interference on the part of the Husband except as herein provided.

8. *Right of Husband to Visit Children.* The Husband shall have the right to visit the children or either of them one day every two weeks if he so desires at reasonable times and places. Further, the Husband shall at his option have the custody of the children or either of them during the summer school holidays for a continuous period of one month.

9. *Duty of Wife to Care for Children.* The Wife shall properly care for, educate and maintain the children until they respectively reach the age of 21 years.

10. *Support of Children.* The Husband shall pay to the Wife as long as she shall have custody of the children or either of them the sum of ______ dollars each month beginning on the ______ day of ______, 19__, for the support and education of each child so in the custody of the Wife until such child reaches the age of 21 years.

11. *Mutual Release.* Except as herein otherwise provided the Husband and Wife release and forever discharge the other of and from all causes of action, claims, rights or demands whatsoever in law or in equity which either of the parties hereto ever had or now has against the other except all cause of action for divorce.

12. *Subsequent Divorce.* If the Husband or Wife shall hereafter apply for a divorce and the court shall grant the same, this Agreement shall be submitted to the court for approval. If it is approved by the court, the terms thereof shall be carried into the decree of divorce and operate as a final determination of the property rights of the parties.[1]

13. *Wife's Attorney's Fees.* The Husband shall pay to ______ the sum of ______ dollars for his services as attorney to the Wife in connection with the negotiation and preparation of this Agreement.

1. If an alimony settlement agreement is to be embodied in or made a part of a decree for divorce, the provisions as to the duration of payments to the wife should be clear, if the intention is to bind the husband's estate to continue payments after his death. Garber v. Robitshek, 33 N.W.2d 30, 226 Minn. 398 (1948). See also 18 A.L.R. 2d 1101.

14. *Additional Instruments.* The Husband and Wife shall at the request of the other execute, acknowledge and deliver to the other party any and all further instruments that may be reasonably required to give full force and effect to the provisions of this Agreement.

15. *Binding Effect.* This Agreement shall be binding on the heirs, executors, administrators and assigns of the parties hereto.

In witness whereof the parties have signed and sealed this Agreement.

______________ [*Seal*]

______________ [*Seal*]

[*Add acknowledgments*]

Separation Agreement—Dismissal of Pending Action for Separation —Lump Sum Cash and Property Settlement—No Children

This agreement, made this ______ day of ______, 19__, between ______, the Husband, and ______, the Wife.

Whereas, the parties were married on ______ day of ______, 19__, and thereafter, on or about the ______ day of ______, 19__, separated and have since lived apart;

Whereas, an action was instituted by the Wife against the Husband in the ______ Court of ______, for a separation and provision for the maintenance of the Wife;

Whereas, the parties have agreed upon what is a reasonable provision for the support and maintenance of the Wife, past, present and for the remainder of her natural life; and

Whereas, the parties have agreed on a reasonable and just disposal of all of the property of the Husband, free and discharged of any and all past, present and future claims, demands, charges, dower estate rights, interests, liens, or other property rights of any kind whatsoever of the Wife.

Now, therefore, the parties agree as follows:

Separation

1. The parties agree to continue to live separate and apart from each other the same as if unmarried. Each may reside from time to time at such place or places, and, conduct, carry on and engage in any employment, business or trade which he or she shall deem fit, free from any control, restraint, or interference direct or indirect by the other.

Dismissal of Action

2. The parties agree that the said action for separation and maintenance now pending in the ______ Court shall be immediately dismissed without costs to either party.

Wife's Support

3. Simultaneously with the signing of this agreement the Husband agrees to pay to the Wife the sum of ______ dollars, and to pay her attorneys' bills and court disbursements in said action, amounting to ______ dollars, and further to convey to her by warranty deed the following described property: [*Description*]. It is understood that said money and property is given to the Wife for her support and maintenance.[2] The Wife agrees that such provision is ample and will in fact provide her with a support and maintenance befitting her station in life, and she accepts said money and property in full satisfaction and in lieu of support and maintenance by the Husband during her life.

No Future Liability

4. Neither party shall contract any debts in the name of the other, or in any way attempt to charge the other with liability therefor, nor will either party claim or demand maintenance or support from the other.

Each Spouse Releases Right in Property of Deceased Spouse

5. The Wife agrees that the estate of the Husband, after the payment of the consideration herein mentioned to the Wife, shall belong to the person or persons who would have become entitled thereto if the Wife had died during the lifetime of the Husband; and the Wife further agrees that she will permit any will of the Husband to be probated, and allow administration upon his personal estate to be taken out by the person or persons who would have been entitled so to do, had the Wife died during the lifetime of the Husband. The Husband agrees that the estate of the Wife, including the consideration herein mentioned, shall belong to the person or persons who would have become entitled thereto if the Husband had died during the lifetime of the Wife; and the Husband further agrees that he will permit any will of the Wife to be probated, and allow administration upon her personal estate to be taken out by the person or persons who would have been entitled so to do, had the Husband died during the lifetime of the Wife.

Further Assurance

6. The parties shall make, execute and deliver any and all such further assurances as the other of the parties shall reasonably require, for the purpose of giving full effect to the provisions of this agreement.

2. If property is transferred to the wife in consideration of her release of alimony and support, the difference between the value of the property at the time of the transfer and its cost to the husband, constitutes capital gain upon which the husband is taxed. Commissioner of Internal Revenue v. Mesta, 123 F.2d 986 (3d Cir. 1941). See also Gershman v. Finch, 454 F.2d 229 (4th Cir. 1971). (See infra p. 418.)

Effect of Divorce

7. The Wife agrees that in case the marriage between the parties should be dissolved by order of court, then the consideration passing to the Wife under this agreement shall stand as full satisfaction and discharge of alimony, counsel fees and other claims and demands which might be made by the Wife against the Husband for any cause whatever.

In Witness Whereof, *etc.*

Separation Agreement Incident to Divorce Action—Lump Sum Cash Settlement—No Children [3]

This agreement made ______, 19__, between ______, the Husband, and ______, the Wife.

Whereas on ______, 19__, the parties were married in ______ County, ______, and lived together as husband and wife until ______, 19__, and have reached the conclusion that it will be impossible for them to continue to live together;

Whereas a bill for divorce has been prepared and the parties are desirous of settling any and all claims for alimony that the Wife might have against the Husband; and

Whereas each party acknowledges that this agreement has been entered into freely with full knowledge of the facts, and each party believes that under the circumstances the sum of $______ is a fair and adequate settlement of all alimony;

Now, therefore, in consideration of the payment to the Wife of the sum of $______, the receipt of which is hereby acknowledged, the Wife does hereby release the Husband from any and all claims, now and hereafter, that might arise by way of alimony. The said settlement of alimony is hereby accepted as a full release of any and all liability, present and future, in so far as any alimony or property adjustment between the Husband and the Wife is concerned.

The foregoing settlement is approved by the undersigned ______ as attorney for the Wife.

[*Signatures*]

3. See Kirby v. Kent, 160 So. 569, 172 Miss. 457, 99 A.L.R. 1303 (1938).

In the preparation of settlement agreements between husbands and wives in connection with divorces, the amounts to be paid to the divorced spouse are either for alimony or in a lump sum property settlement. If the payments are in installments and are considered as alimony remarriage will stop all future payments, whereas, if there is a lump sum settlement of property rights, it is not subject to change even though the lump sum may be payable in installments. See 44 Illinois L.Rev. 382 (1949).

See also Gullo v. Brown, 483 P.2d 293, 34 A.L.R.2d 876 (1971).

Separation Agreement—Divorce Action Pending—Fixed Monthly Payments—Deposit of Property to Secure Such Payments—Release of Wife's Interest in Community Property—No Children [4]

This agreement made this ______ day of ______, 19__, between ______, herein called the Husband, and ______, herein called the Wife.

Whereas, the parties were united in marriage at ______, on or about the ______ day of ______, 19__, and lived together as husband and wife until about the ______ day of ______, 19__; and

Whereas, during the time the parties lived together as husband and wife they acquired certain real and personal property which comprises their community estate and which is not susceptible of partition; and

Whereas, on the ______ day of ______, 19__, the Wife filed her petition in the ______ Court of ______ County, ______, praying that the marriage relation between herself and the Husband be dissolved, and the parties have agreed that in the event said marriage relation is dissolved by judgment of said Court as prayed for in said petition, in lieu of a partition of said community estate the Husband shall pay to the Wife the sum of ______ dollars per month so long as she shall live, and the Wife shall transfer, assign and convey to the Husband all her right, title, and interest in and to said community estate;

Now, therefore, it is agreed as follows:

1. The Husband agrees to pay to the Wife the sum of ______ dollars on the first day of ______, 19__, and the sum of ______ dollars on the first day of each and every month thereafter so long as she shall live, said payments to be made by the Husband to the ______ National Bank of ______, with instructions to said bank to promptly

4. Adapted from the record in Farrell v. Commissioner of Internal Revenue, 134 F.2d 193 (C.C.A.Tex.1943) certiorari denied 64 S.Ct. 47, 320 U.S. 745, 88 L.Ed. 442, a proceeding to collect a deficiency in income taxes from one of the parties to this agreement.

The community property released in this contract consisted in part of oil leases that subsequently turned out to be very valuable. Shortly after this agreement was executed Mrs. Farrell secured a divorce from her husband and the decree embodied the terms of the contract with respect to the monthly payments and the transfer of the community interest to the husband. Four days later she married again.

About two years later she brought suit in the Texas courts to have the property provisions of the divorce decree set aside on the ground that she was induced to enter into this agreement by fraud. The Court of Civil Appeals in Burguieres v. Farrell, 85 S.W.2d 952 (1935), upheld the agreement, holding that the entire transaction was fair, that the wife was fully informed and there was no fraud. A petition for writ of error in the Supreme Court of Texas was dismissed, 87 S.W.2d 463, 126 Tex. 209 (1935), for lack of potential jurisdiction, and a motion for leave to file a petition for mandamus to require the Court of Civil Appeals to certify questions was overruled as was a motion for a rehearing of the motion.

pay the same to the Wife. For the purpose of guaranteeing such payments the Husband shall deposit with said bank the sum of ______ dollars in cash and ______ shares of the capital stock of ______ Corporation, of the approximate present value of ______ dollars; provided that the Husband shall have the right at any time to withdraw such shares of stock upon depositing with said bank the further sum of ______ dollars in cash in lieu thereof; and provided further that in the event the Husband shall fail to make any of the payments herein provided for, said ______ bank shall have the right to sell said shares of stock for cash and make such payments to the Wife out of such fund and in such event the Wife shall have the right to require the Husband to deposit the amount of such payment or payments with said bank in order that such fund shall at all times be maintained a the sum of ______ dollars or at the sum of ______ dollars and said ______ shares of the capital stock of ______ Corporation.

2. The Wife agrees that all property, belonging to the community estate of the parties, shall be and become the separate property of the Husband, and any and all rights, title and interest in and to said property now belonging to the Wife, or which might be claimed by her, shall be, and the same hereby is, transferred, assigned, and conveyed to the Husband, free from any and all liens or claims on the part of the Wife, and the Wife further agrees that she will, upon demand, execute and deliver to the Husband proper deeds, assignments or conveyances for any and all of such property conveying the title therein to the Husband.

In Witness Whereof, *etc.*

Separation Agreement—Divorce Action Pending—Lump Sum and Fixed Monthly Payments to Wife—Transfer of Community Property to Husband—Custody and Support of Children

This agreement made the ______ day of ______, 19__, between ______, herein called the Husband, and ______, herein called the Wife.

Whereas, disputes have arisen between the parties, and by reason thereof they have agreed to live separate and apart from each other during their natural lives; and

Whereas, the Husband as plaintiff filed a suit for divorce in the ______ Court of ______ County, ______, numbered ______ on the docket of said Court, which suit is now pending, and the Wife has filed her cross-action for divorce in said suit, and regardless of the outcome of the trial thereof, the parties recognize that their differences are so great that a reconciliation is impossible; and

Whereas, the Husband has furnished to the Wife a list of all principal assets and liabilities as of ______, 19__, and has also furnished additional information as to change of assets and liabilities as of this date, and the Wife has investigated and appraised these assets and liabilities with the aid of her legal counsel and is thoroughly conversant with all facts; and

Whereas, the parties desire to completely and forever settle their property rights in and to their community property, which is all of the property that either of them possesses.

The parties agree as follows:

Separation

1. They shall live separate and apart from each other the remainder of their natural lives, and neither shall have any right in any way to control the personal actions or conduct of the other, or to complain about such actions or conduct except in so far as the same may affect the right of custody of their children, and neither shall in any way molest, disturb or trouble the other.

Alimony to Wife

2. In full, final and complete settlement of all the rights of the Wife in and to the community property of the parties, as well as any and all other claims which she may now or hereafter have against the Husband arising out of the marriage relationship, the Husband has paid and promises to pay to the Wife the following amounts:

(a) **Lump Sum Payment.** The Husband has this day paid to the Wife the sum of $______, receipt of which is hereby acknowledged.

(b) **Fixed Monthly Payments.** The Husband promises to pay to the Wife at ______, the sum of $______ per month for ______ years, the first payment being due ______ and one payment being due on the ______ day of each month thereafter for ______ full years. Such payments may be made by check mailed to the Wife on or before the due dates, addressed to the last address that the Wife may have given in writing to the Husband.

(c) **Insurance Policies to Secure Monthly Payments.** The Husband shall at all times carry life insurance in solvent companies, payable to the Wife as beneficiary, for the amount of the then unpaid installments hereinabove provided, discounted at ____ per cent per year compounded for the period of prepayment; and upon the Husband's death, the Wife shall accept payment of said insurance money in full payment and satisfaction of all of the then unpaid monthly payments provided for in paragraph (b) hereof. The Husband shall have the right to discharge his obligations under said paragraph (b) at any time after the expiration of ______ years from date by paying the value of unmatured installments discounted at ______ per cent per year compounded for the period of prepayment.

(d) **Upon Death of Wife, Wife's Monthly Payments to be Made to Children.** Should the Wife die before the monthly installments are all paid, the then remaining installments shall be paid as they mature to the ______ children of the parties in equal parts, or to their guardian if they are then minors.

(e) **Transfer to Wife of Personal Belongings.** The Wife shall have as her property all of the silverware, dishes, glass-ware, linens, rugs, drapes, furniture, pictures and furnishings now in the home at ______, except ______, which excepted articles shall belong to the Husband. The Wife shall vacate the home on or before ______, 19__, but agrees that the Husband may keep all of her said personal property in the home until ______, 19__, at which time she shall remove the same, provided however that if the home is sold at an earlier date she shall upon demand remove her personal property.

Transfer of Community Property to Husband

3. All other property, rights, claims and choses in action belonging to the Husband or to their community estate, whether or not herein specifically mentioned, shall belong absolutely to the Husband, as his separate property, and the Wife agrees to execute to the Husband upon demand general warranty deeds covering her interest in all real property owned by them and bills of sale or other conveyances of title to such personal property. The principal items of property to be conveyed are as follows: [*Here list*].

Wife's Debts

4. The Wife agrees to pay promptly all bills incurred by her since ______, 19__. Should the Wife fail to pay any of such bills, and demand for payment is made on the Husband, he may pay same and deduct the amount so paid from the monthly payments owing by him to the Wife.

Community Debts

5. The Husband agrees to pay all of the community indebtedness of the parties not herein assumed by the Wife.

Custody of Children

6. The two children, ______ and ______, shall remain with the Wife, subject to the orders of the Court as is provided by law in such cases. The Husband shall have the right to visit his children and to have their company and companionship at reasonable times to be arranged.

Support of Children

7. The Husband shall pay to the Wife the sum of $______ per month for each child on the first day of each month for the support and maintenance of the two children, which payments shall continue

until the Husband's legal obligation to support them ends, or until changed as to amount by agreement of the parties or by order of the Court. Such payments shall cover all living expenses of the children that could be chargeable to the Husband, except tuition to schools to be selected by agreement of the parties which the Husband shall also pay, and such medical expenses as the Husband may first approve in writing. If one or both of the children shall at any time, by agreement of the parties, be sent to boarding schools or to summer camps, the Husband shall pay their reasonable expenses while there, but during such times he shall not be required to make the monthly payments otherwise required to be made to the Wife for their support and maintenance.

Mutual Release

8. In consideration of the payments now made and agreed to be hereafter made, the parties do each declare this to be a full, final and complete settlement of all of their property rights, and each party does hereby release and relinquish to the other all of his or her rights, title, claim, interest and demand, accrued or accruing in and to the property of the other whether now in being or hereafter acquired; and this shall be a full and complete settlement of the controversy over the property rights of the parties, involved in cause No. ______ in the ______ Court of ______ County, and, save the right of either party to prosecute his or her suit for complete divorce, this settlement shall be a bar to any suit at law or otherwise for anything growing out of the marriage relation of the parties as well as the property rights of the one against the other.

Witness our hands, in triplicate, at ______, this ______ day of ______, 19__.

____

____

Witnesses:

____

____

[*Add acknowledgments*]

Separation Agreement—Divorce Action Pending—Alimony Based on Oil Royalties—Custody and Support of Child [5]

This agreement, made this ______ day of ______, 19__, between ______, of ______, herein called the Husband, and ______, of ______, herein called the Wife, witnesseth:

Whereas, the parties are husband and wife, but are now living separate and apart from each other, and it is their intention to continue to live separate and apart; and,

5. Adapted from Harjo v. Harjo, 247 P.2d 522, 207 Okl. 73 (1952).

Whereas, the Wife has this day instituted suit for divorce against the Husband in the ______ Court of ______ County, ______, under cause numbered ______ in said Court, and has asked that she be awarded the custody, care, control and education of ______, minor child of the parties and for the ratification and approval of this property settlement and agreement concerning the support and maintenance of said child; and,

Whereas, the parties have this day reached a satisfactory agreement between themselves out of Court concerning the custody, support and maintenance of said child, and the support, maintenance and alimony of the Wife, as well as for a division of and settlement of property rights, claims or demands of any nature, either past, present or future, as hereinafter set out.

Now, therefore, the parties agree as follows:

Custody of Child

1. The Wife is to have the care, custody and control of ______, minor child of the parties, subject to the approval of the ______ Court of ______ County, ______, subject to any future orders of said Court concerning the custody of said child and subject to the right of the Husband to visit said child at any and all reasonable times and occasions; and the Wife, subject to the conditions hereinafter stated, accepts the custody of said child and agrees to properly care for, support, rear, train and educate said child to the best of her ability, it being understood that the Wife shall have the right to select the residence for said child at whatsoever place within the State of ______ she may desire, but that she will inform the Husband of any change in said place of residence.

Support of Wife and Child

2. The Husband shall turn over to the Wife for the support of and maintenance of herself and ______, minor child of the parties, until such time as the Wife may remarry, all of the proceeds arising from his interest in oil and gas royalties from wells now producing, and one half of all of the proceeds arising from his interest in oil and gas royalties from any wells which may be hereafter drilled upon any and all land now owned by the Husband, or in which he may own any interest, either legal or equitable, said land being particularly described as follows: [*Here describe*].

Remarriage or Death of Wife

3. It is further agreed that in the event of the remarriage of the Wife to any person other than the Husband during the lifetime of ______, minor child of the parties, then all of said oil and gas royal-

ties, oil and gas runs, or proceeds from same arising from said lands shall be paid to said child, or to her duly appointed guardian. In the event the Husband and the Wife remarry each other, or in the event the Wife marries someone other than the Husband during the lifetime of said child, and said child thereafter dies, or in the event of the remarriage of the Wife after the death of said child, or in the event of the death of the Wife at any time, then immediately upon the happening thereof, the Husband shall be entitled to, and shall have and receive all such oil and gas royalties, oil and gas runs, or other proceeds arising from the same not already paid over to the Wife or to said child under this agreement; and the Wife agrees that in the event of any such remarriage she will promptly make, execute and deliver any necessary and proper transfer orders, division orders, or other instruments necessary to enable such person as is entitled thereto under this agreement to collect and receive same, and that in the event she should refuse or neglect to do so, then this instrument shall be treated and construed as a compliance and assignment of said interests, runs and royalties.

Sale of Royalty Interest

4. It is further agreed that the Husband shall have the full and unrestricted use of all of the lands in any manner acquired by him and the rents and profits thereof, except the royalties and oil and gas runs above mentioned, but that in the event of the sale by the Husband of any of said real estate herein described during the lifetime of ______, minor child of the parties, the Husband shall pay over to said child, or to her duly appointed guardian, for her use, support, maintenance and education, one third of any and all sums realized from the sale of any or all of said property and that the Wife will, upon request, join with the Husband, or will execute, acknowledge and deliver any and all necessary and proper instruments in writing to effectuate the sale and conveyance of any such property; it being understood, however, that nothing in this paragraph shall be construed as conferring the right upon the Husband to make any sale or conveyance of any oil or gas royalty in, to or under any of the land above described, but that said oil and gas royalty interests in said land shall be held for the use, support and maintenance of the Wife and said child, as herein provided.

Release by Wife

5. The Wife agrees that she will not at any time undertake to hold the Husband liable for, or undertake to collect from him any sums for alimony, court costs, attorneys' fees, support and maintenance for herself or said child, and that this agreement may be pleaded in any suit as a defense to any action for alimony, court costs, attorneys' fees, support and maintenance.

Witness our signatures in duplicate the day and year above written.

____
Husband

____
Wife

[*Add acknowledgments*]

Assignment # 64

(a) Are any of the sample separation agreement clauses on the preceding pages illegal? If so, why? (b) Would you have advised any of the parties to these agreements against accepting any of the clauses? If so, why? (c) For each of the agreements on the preceding pages (beginning on pages 288, 293, 295, 297, 298, 299, 302) make a list of the items you think the parties failed to include in the agreement. (See also General Instructions for the Legal Analysis Assignment, supra p. 16.)

Assignment # 65

Two members of the class will role play a negotiation session involving a husband and wife who want to separate and enter a separation agreement. The spouses are representing themselves. They have two children, ages 2 and 3. The negotiation will be role played before the rest of the class. Each member of the class (including the two role players) will draft a separation agreement based upon the understandings reached at the negotiation session. The role players can improvise the facts as they go along, e. g., concerning matters such as bank accounts, amount of furniture. Use the checklist on page 250 supra as an overview of the topics to be negotiated. In the negotiation session, the role players should not act hostile toward each other. They should be courteous, but anxious to protect their own rights. Finally, they should not leave any matters hanging—everything discussed should result in some form of agreement through the process of bargaining and compromise. (See also General Instructions for the Agreement Drafting Assignment, supra p. 25.)

*

Chapter Sixteen

GROUNDS FOR DIVORCE

SECTION A. INTRODUCTION

Before examining the grounds for divorce, some general definitions of the *defenses* to some or all of those grounds are necessary since these defenses will be referred to during the discussion of the grounds. A more detailed treatment of these and other defenses will come at the end of this chapter after all the grounds have been surveyed.[1]

Collusion: fraud committed on the court by parties to a divorce by agreeing on a story to be told to the court even though both parties know that the story is untrue.

Connivance: a willingness or a consent that the marital wrong be done by the other spouse.

Condonation: an express or implied forgiveness by the innocent spouse of the marital fault committed by the other spouse.

Recrimination: the party seeking the divorce (the plaintiff) has also committed a serious marital wrong.

Provocation: the plaintiff provoked the acts constituting the marital wrong by the other party.

Statute of limitations: the plaintiff brought the divorce action too late (i. e., after a designated statutory time).

Laches: the plaintiff brought the divorce action too late (i. e., after the passage of such time that it would be unfair to the defendant to allow the action to be brought).

In order to obtain a divorce which dissolves the marital relationship, statutorily specified reasons or *grounds* must exist.[2] States differ on the grounds that will justify a divorce judgment. This difference among the states is part of the reason why married persons seeking a divorce will travel to other states to attempt to obtain the divorce; it may be much easier to establish a ground for divorce in one

1. Infra p. 337.

2. On the grounds for an annulment, see supra p. 175. On the grounds for a judicial separation, see infra p. 407. On the grounds for a separate maintenance judgment, see infra p. 433.

state than in another.[3] The following grounds are those most commonly found in the divorce statutes:

No-fault grounds:
1. Living apart.
2. Incompatibility.
3. Irretrievable breakdown.

Fault grounds:
4. Adultery.
5. Cruelty.
6. Desertion and abandonment.
7. Conviction of a crime.

In addition, there are a large number of miscellaneous grounds available in a number of states.

Assignment # 66

(a) Go to your state code and find the statute that lists the grounds for divorce in your state. Give the citation to this statute and list all the grounds for divorce provided therein. (See also General Instructions for the State Code Assignment, supra p. 14.)

(b) For each ground of divorce identified in (a), draft a checklist of questions to help determine whether those grounds exist. (See also General Instructions for the Checklist Formulation Assignment, supra p. 29.)

In your study of the remainder of this chapter, you may want to limit yourself to those grounds which apply to divorces in your state. You should keep in mind, however, that it is not uncommon for a lawyer or paralegal working in divorce law to have to be concerned about the grounds for divorce in other states. A client, for example, may come into the office and want to know if s/he can go into another state to obtain a divorce. Or, a client may have already been to another state and has returned with a foreign divorce judgment[4] seeking to enforce that judgment in your state.[5] Assisting such clients may require you to know something about divorce grounds in states other than your own.

SECTION B. LIVING APART

Living "separate and apart" is a ground for divorce in many states. The basis of the ground is the breakdown of the marriage, and not the *fault* of either spouse, although as we shall see, fault may still be relevant. The statutes authorizing this ground must be care-

3. For more on out-of-state (foreign) divorces, see infra p. 343.

4. The word "foreign" refers to any state other than your own.

5. For a discussion of the enforcement of such judgments, see infra p. 390.

fully read since slight differences in wording may account for major differences in meaning. A number of specifications often exist for this ground.

(a) TIME

All the statutes require that the parties live apart for a designated period of time, ranging from a period of months to ten years. The purpose of the time limitation is, in effect, to force the parties to think seriously about whether a reconciliation is possible.

(b) CONSECUTIVENESS

If the parties have separated off and on over a period of time, the living-apart ground will not be established, even if the sum total of the time the parties were actually separated exceeded the designated time required for separation under the statute. The separated time must be consecutive and it must continue right up to the time one of the spouses brings the divorce action on the ground of living apart. Hence, if the parties reconcile and resume cohabitation, even if only temporarily, the period of separation will not be considered consecutive. If, following cohabitation, the parties separate again, the requisite consecutiveness of the period of living apart will be calculated as of the time when the most recent cohabitation ended.

(c) CONSENT

Several states require that the period of separation be consensual or voluntary on the part of both spouses. Hence, if one spouse is drafted into the service or is hospitalized for an extended period of time, the separation is surely not by consent. A question that sometimes arises is whether the *cause* of the separation is relevant when marital fault is involved. Suppose, for example, that Bob deserts his wife Linda and they live apart for a period in excess of that required by the statute. Here the cause of the separation is relevant to its voluntariness. The parties did not separate voluntarily; they separated as a result of the fault of Bob. States handle such a situation differently. Some states will deny the divorce on the ground of living apart because the separation was not voluntary. Some states will deny the divorce on this ground only if the plaintiff is the "guilty" party. Most states, however, will grant the divorce to either party on the basis that voluntariness and marital fault are irrelevant so long as there was a living apart for the requisite period of time.

INTERVIEWING AND INVESTIGATION CHECKLIST
DIVORCE ON THE GROUND OF LIVING APART

	Legal Interviewing Questions	Possible Investigation Tasks
1.	How long have you lived apart?	* Collect evidence that the parties have lived separate and apart, e.g., rent receipts from the apartments of C and D, statements from landlords. * Obtain copy of separation decree, separate maintenance decree (if any).
2.	On what date did you separate?	
3.	Since that date, what contact have you had with D?	
4.	Have you ever asked D to live with you again? Has D ever asked you?	
5.	Have you had sexual intercourse with D since you separated?	
6.	Describe the circumstances of your separation with D?	
7.	When you separated, did you intend a permanent separation? If so, what indications of this did you give?	
8.	Did D intend a permanent separation? If so, what indications did D give?	
9.	What was the condition of your marriage at the time of the separation?	
10.	Did you leave D? Did D leave you? Did you both leave at the same time by mutual agreement?	
11.	When the separation occurred, did either of you protest? Were either of you dissatisfied with the separation?	
12.	Since you separated, have either of you asked or suggested that the two of you get back together again? If so, what was the response of the other?	
13.	Have either of you ever obtained a judicial separation or a decree of separate maintenance? If so, when? Have you been living separate since that time? Have both of you abided by the terms of the judicial separation or of the maintenance decree?	
14.	Are you now living separate from D?	
15.	Since you separated, at what addresses have you lived? Same question about D.	
16.	Have you and D entered into a separation agreement?	

IM-478

Assignment # 67

Assume that the statute provides that one of the grounds for divorce is voluntary separation for a period of two consecutive years. This "living apart" ground is the only one authorized in the state. Apply this statute to the following three situations. Could a divorce be granted on the ground of living apart? (See also General Instructions for the Legal Analysis Assignment, supra p. 16.)

(a) Fred and Gail are married. On June 10, 1975, they agree to separate. On May 15, 1977, Fred learns that Gail is thinking about filing for divorce. Fred calls Gail and pleads with her to let him come back. She refuses. On July 25, 1977, she files for divorce on the ground of living apart.

(b) Tom and Diane are married. On November 1, 1975, Diane deserts Tom. Tom did not want her to go. On March 13, 1976, Tom meets Karen. They begin seeing each other regularly. On June 14, 1976, Tom tells Karen that he hopes he never sees Diane again. On December 28, 1977, Tom files for divorce on the ground of living apart.

(c) Bill and Susan are married. For over three years they have been living separate lives due to marital difficulties, although they have continued to live in the same house. They have separate bedrooms and rarely have anything to do with each other. One of them files an action for divorce on the ground of living apart.

Assignment # 68

In your answer to Assignment # 66, supra p. 308, you made a list of the grounds for divorce in your state. If one of the grounds for divorce in your state is "living apart", determine whether the divorce actions sought above in Assignment # 67(a), (b) and (c) would be granted in your state. (See also General Instructions for the Legal Analysis Assignment, supra p. 16.) In doing this, you should try to find opinions written by courts in your state that have interpreted the law governing the same facts or facts similar to those involving Fred and Gail, Tom and Diane, Bill and Susan. (See also General Instructions for the Court Opinion Assignment, supra p. 26.)

Assignment # 69

Pick one of the three fact situations involved in Assignment # 67, above: (a), (b) or (c). Draft a complaint for the party seeking the divorce. (See also General Instructions for the Complaint Drafting Assignment, supra p. 20.)

As we shall see in Chapter Nineteen, many states enable parties to seek a judicial separation which is a court authorization that the parties can live separate under specified terms, e. g., alimony, custody order.[6] See Assignment # 113, infra p. 406, on whether your state has a judicial separation proceeding. In some states, this judicial separation can be "converted" into a divorce after the judicial separation has been in existence for a designated period of time. Similarly, a decree of separate maintenance [7] can often be converted into a divorce after this period of time. In some states, it is not necessary to obtain a judicial separation or a separate maintenance decree. So long as the parties lived separate and apart for the statutory period, a divorce ground will arise whether or not the parties have been to court before.

6. Infra p. 405.

7. Infra p. 433.

NOTES

(1) Following a decree of divorce on the ground of living apart, questions of permanent alimony must be resolved. Fault may be very relevant to the alimony determination even though in many states, fault is not relevant to the establishment of the living-apart ground for the underlying divorce.[8]

(2) When a spouse has disappeared for a certain period of time, Enoch Arden statutes presume that the missing spouse is dead, and in some states, this enables the spouse left behind to remarry without being charged with bigamy or without having the second marriage annulled if the missing spouse returns after the statutory period.[9]

SUMMARY GROUND FOR DIVORCE: LIVING APART
DEFINITION: Living separate and apart for a designated, consecutive period of time. (In some states, the separation must be voluntary.)
WHO CAN SUE: In most states, either party. In a few states, the party at fault cannot bring the divorce action, i. e., the party who wrongfully caused the separation.
MAJOR DEFENSES: (1) the parties have never separated; (2) the parties have not been separated for the period designated in the statute; (3) the parties reconciled and cohabitated before the statutory period was over, i. e., the separation was not consecutive; (4) the separation was not voluntary (this defense is available in only a few states); (5) recrimination (available in only a few states); (6) the agreement to separate was obtained by fraud or duress; (7) at the time the divorce action was filed, the parties were not separated; (8) the court lacks jurisdiction, see infra p. 352. (9) res judicata, see infra p. 395; (10) statute of limitations or laches, see infra p. 342; (11) collusion or connivance.
IS THIS ALSO A GROUND FOR ANNULMENT: no.
IS THIS ALSO A GROUND FOR JUDICIAL SEPARATION: yes, in many states.
IS THIS ALSO A GROUND FOR SEPARATE MAINTENANCE: yes, in many states.

[B7990]

8. Infra p. 369.

9. Supra p. 177.

SECTION C. INCOMPATIBILITY

A few states list "incompatibility" as a ground for divorce. It is often pointed out that "petty quarrels and minor bickerings" is not enough to grant the divorce on this ground.[10] There must be such rift or discord that it is impossible to live together in a normal marital relationship. For most of the states that have this ground, fault is not an issue: to obtain a divorce on this ground, the plaintiff does not have to show that the defendant was at fault in causing the incompatibility, and the defendant cannot defend the action by introducing evidence that the plaintiff committed marital wrongs (recrimination). This is not true, however, in every state. Some courts *are* concerned about the defendant's fault and the plaintiff's recrimination.

Suppose that the plaintiff alleges that the parties are incompatible. Can the defendant defend by disagreeing? Do both husband and wife have to feel that the marriage is in such a state that it is impossible to live together? Assuming that the plaintiff is able to establish that more than "petty quarrels" are involved, most courts will grant the divorce to the plaintiff even though the defendant insists that they can still work it out.

As we shall see later, there appears to be a good deal of similarity between the ground of incompatibility and the ground of cruelty.[11] Even though cruelty is considered a fault ground while incompatibility generally is not, the same or similar kinds of evidence is used to establish both grounds. (Compare Checklist Questions nos. 1–13, below, with Questions nos. 1–37, supra p. 326.) The major difference in most states is that for cruelty, unlike incompatibility, the plaintiff must show that the acts of the defendant have endangered the plaintiff's physical health.

INTERVIEWING AND INVESTIGATION CHECKLIST

DIVORCE ON THE GROUND OF INCOMPATIBILITY

(This checklist is also relevant to the Breakdown ground, infra p. 315. See also the Cruelty checklist, infra p. 326.

	Legal Interviewing Questions	Possible Investigation Tasks
1.	Are you and D now living together? If not, how long have you been separated?	* Get copy of separation judgment, separate maintenance decree, police report, hospital records, if any.
2.	Have you ever sued D or been sued by D for separate maintenance or for a judicial separation? If so, what was the result?	
3.	Describe your relationship with D at its worst.	
4.	How often did you argue? Were the arguments intense or bitter? Explain.	
5.	Did you ever have to call the police?	

10. Burch v. Burch, 195 F.2d 799, 806–807 (3rd Cir. 1952).

11. Infra p. 328.

INTERVIEWING AND INVESTIGATION CHECKLIST—Continued DIVORCE ON THE GROUND OF INCOMPATIBILITY (This checklist is also relevant to the Breakdown ground, infra p. 315. See also the Cruelty checklist, infra p. 326.)		
	Legal Interviewing Questions	**Possible Investigation Tasks**
6.	Did you ever receive medical attention as a result of arguments or fights with D?	
7.	Did D have any drinking or drug problem?	
8.	How did D act toward the children?	
9.	Have you and D had any sexual problems?	
10.	Do you feel that there is any possibility that you and D could reconcile your differences?	
11.	Do you think D feels that the two of you can solve your problems?	
12.	Have you or D, individually or together, ever sought counseling or mental health help?	
13.	Are you now interested in any such help in order to try to save the marriage? Do you feel it would work? How do you think D feels about this?	

IM-279

Assignment # 70

One married partner says to the other, "I no longer love you." By definition, are they incompatible for purposes of this ground for divorce? (See also General Instructions for the Legal Analysis Assignment, supra p. 16.)

SUMMARY GROUND FOR DIVORCE: INCOMPATIBILITY
DEFINITION: The impossibility of two parties being able to continue to live together in a normal marital relationship because of severe conflicts and personality differences.
WHO CAN SUE: Either party in most states.
MAJOR DEFENSES: (1) the differences between the parties are only minor; (2) the defendant was not at fault in causing the incompatibility (this defense is *not* available in most states); (3) recrimination, see infra p. 337 (this defense is *not* available in most states); (4) the court lacks jurisdiction, see infra p. 352; (5) res judicata, see infra p. 395; (6) statute of limitations or laches, see infra p. 342; (7) collusion or connivance.
IS THIS ALSO A GROUND FOR ANNULMENT: no.
IS THIS ALSO A GROUND FOR JUDICIAL SEPARATION: yes in many states.
IS THIS ALSO A GROUND FOR SEPARATE MAINTENANCE: yes in many states.

IM-480

SECTION D. IRRECONCILABLE DIFFERENCES, IRRETRIEVABLE BREAKDOWN OF MARRIAGE

The newest and most popular version for the no-fault ground of divorce adopted in many states provides that the marriage can be dissolved for "irreconcilable differences" which has caused the irremediable breakdown of the marriage." The quote in the preceding sentence is from the California statute.[12] Statutory language from other states is similar: [13]

—discord or conflict of personalities that destroys the legitimate ends of marriage and prevents any reasonable expectation of reconciliation;

—irretrievable breakdown of the marriage;

—breakdown of marriage to such an extent that the legitimate objects of marriage have been destroyed and there remains no reasonable likelihood that the marriage can be preserved;

—substantial reasons for not continuing the marriage which make it appear that the marriage can be dissolved.

This ground for divorce is quite similar to the incompatibility ground just considered.[14]

The intention of the legislatures that have enacted the "irremediable breakdown" ground has been:

—to eliminate fault as a consideration in the dissolution proceeding (except to the extent that fault might still be relevant to alimony [15] and child custody [16] issues)

—to focus on the central question of whether it makes any sense to continue the marriage: can this marriage be saved?

Some states have even tried to eliminate the word "divorce," and to replace it with the word "dissolution" as a symbolic gesture that a new day has arrived.

What happens if the defendant denies that the breakdown of the marriage is irremediable and feels that marriage conciliation [17] or counseling would help? In most states, this is simply one item of evidence which the court must consider in deciding whether remediation is possible. It would seem, however, that if one party absolutely refuses to participate in any reconciliation efforts, a court would be justified in concluding that the breakdown of the marriage is total even if the other party expresses a conciliatory attitude.

12. Cal.Civil Code, section 4506 (West, 1970).

13. See Paulsen, M., Wadlington, W. & Goebel, Jr., *Cases and Materials on Domestic Relations*, p. 869 (1974) and Clark, H., *Cases and Problems on Domestic Relations*, p. 695 (1974).

14. Supra p. 314.

15. Infra p. 369.

16. Infra p. 376.

17. Infra p. 363.

When the divorce is sought on no-fault grounds, the courts are less concerned about the dangers of collusion [18] and connivance.[19] These traditional defenses, however, will still apply if it can be established that the parties have committed a fraud on the court in an effort to obtain the dissolution.

SUMMARY GROUND FOR DIVORCE: IRREMEDIABLE BREAKDOWN
DEFINITION: The breakdown of the marriage to the point where the many differences and conflicts between the spouses are beyond any reasonable hope of conciliation.
WHO CAN SUE: Either party.
MAJOR DEFENSES: (1) the breakdown is remediable; (2) the court lacks jurisdiction, see infra p. 352; (3) res judicata, see infra p. 395; (4) statute of limitations or laches, see infra p. 342; (5) collusion or connivance.
IS THIS ALSO A GROUND FOR ANNULMENT: no.
IS THIS ALSO A GROUND FOR JUDICIAL SEPARATION: yes, in many states.
IS THIS ALSO A GROUND FOR SEPARATE MAINTENANCE: yes, in many states.
INTERVIEWING & INVESTIGATION: See Checklist Questions nos. 1–13 on establishing incompatibility as a ground for divorce. Supra p. 313. Many of the questions on incompatibility are also relevant to the irremediable breakdown ground. See also the Checklist Questions 1–37 for the cruelty ground, infra p. 326.

[B7995]

SECTION E. ADULTERY

Adultery is voluntary sexual intercourse between a married person and someone to whom s/he is not married. The intercourse is not voluntary, of course, if the defendant was raped, or if the defendant was insane at the time. States differ on their definition of insanity in this context. A "mental disease" or "mental defect" may be sufficient in some states, whereas in others, the defense of insanity

18. Infra p. 338. Although the California statutes no longer make reference to the traditional defense of collusion, the California Supreme Court has stated that the parties cannot fabricate evidence and commit fraud on the court. McKim v. McKim, 6 Cal.3d 673, 100 Cal.Rptr. 140, 493 P.2d 868 (1972).

19. Infra p. 340.

will fail unless it can be established that at the time of the intercourse the defendant did not know the difference between right and wrong.[20]

There are statutes that specifically include homosexual acts (sodomy) within the definition of adultery, although homosexuality is more often raised in a divorce action where the plaintiff is using the cruelty ground.[21] When a man and woman engage in sexual acts short of intercourse, adultery does not exist unless the statutory definition of adultery includes such behavior, which it seldom does.

Adultery is not often used as a ground for divorce in America today. It is obviously difficult to prove by direct evidence.[22] Even when the *corespondent* (the third party who allegedly had intercourse with the defendant) testifies at the trial, courts are reluctant to grant a divorce on this ground. Adultery is, however, frequently raised by plaintiffs seeking a divorce on other grounds, e. g., as evidence of cruelty.[23]

Since direct evidence is seldom available, circumstantial evidence must be relied upon. Specifically, the plaintiff will try to prove:

(a) defendant had the *opportunity* to commit adultery, and

(b) defendant had the *inclination* to commit adultery.

Suppose that the plaintiff is able to introduce evidence that the defendant checked into a motel (single room) with another woman. These two individuals certainly had the opportunity to have intercourse, and seeking the privacy of a motel bedroom suggests the strong possibility that the defendant wanted to do so (inclination). The situation might be different, however, if the evidence showed that a defendant spent a few late evenings a week at the office with his secretary. It is difficult to find much indication or opportunity on these facts alone. It must be remembered that there is no mathematical formula on what constitutes sufficient evidence. A great deal depends upon the sensibilities of the persons listening to and evaluating the evidence: the judge and/or jury. It can be argued that there are times in our history and there are sections of our country in which the slightest suggestion of scandal and impropriety in the conduct of an individual can lead to harsh consequences for that individual. Some say that this is all the more so if that individual is a woman. To the extent, however, that sexual mores are becoming more "loose," or "liberal," it may be that a plaintiff will have greater difficulty in convincing a court that the circumstantial evidence of adultery is convincing.

Courts are always concerned about the danger of collusion[24] between the husband and wife in a divorce action. Hence the re-

20. For the definitions on insanity in criminal cases, see supra p. 200.

21. Infra p. 321.

22. See also infra p. 367.

23. Infra p. 321.

24. Supra p. 254, and infra p. 338.

quirement in many states that there be *corroboration* of evidence. Corroboration is the introduction of evidence other than the testimony of the plaintiff which supports the plaintiff's testimony. A state might require corroboration only when the defendant "confesses" to having done what the plaintiff has charged, or, more broadly, corroboration might be required to support the testimony of *both* husband and wife. How much corroboration is needed? There is no definite answer to this question. Every fact alleged in the testimony of a spouse does not have to be corroborated. Generally, whatever facts are material or essential to establish a case must be corroborated by evidence other than the testimony of the spouse trying to establish that case. Hence, in many states, if the only evidence that the defendant had sexual intercourse with a third party is the testimony of the plaintiff to this effect, the case will be dismissed because of the absence of corroboration. In many states, the same result follows even if the defendant-spouse admits that s/he committed the adultery since the admission itself would have to be corroborated. The testimony of one spouse is not sufficient corroboration for the testimony of the other spouse.

One of the common examples of the attempted use of the adultery ground is when the husband brings the action when he discovers that his wife is pregnant and he knows that he is not the father, or when he discovers that a child he thought was his is not his. While all children born to a married woman are presumed to be legitimate,[25] it is possible for the husband to prove that he could not be the father by blood grouping tests and very substantial evidence of *nonaccess* to the mother during the time of conception and gestation. If a husband is successful in winning a divorce action on the ground of such adultery, one consequence in many states is that the child is illegitimate.[26] The stigma of illegitimacy can be substantial. Hence courts are extremely reluctant to permit the husband to obtain the divorce in these circumstances. The evidence of non-paternity has to be almost absolute.

When an issue as emotionally charged as paternity is not involved, however, most courts will grant the divorce to the plaintiff if his/her allegation of adultery has been proven (with corroboration) by a *preponderance of the evidence*.[27] Other courts require a higher standard of proof of the adultery: clear and convincing evidence.

25. Infra p. 453.

26. Infra p. 449.

27. Something has been established by a "preponderance of evidence" when it is more convincing than not.

INTERVIEWING AND INVESTIGATION CHECKLIST DIVORCE ON THE GROUND OF ADULTERY		
	Legal Interviewing Questions	**Possible Investigation Tasks**
1.	How do you know that D has committed adultery?	* If C claims that D committed the adultery at a specific place, e.g., a hotel, interview people at that place, try to obtain records or anything that would indicate that D was there and under what circumstances. * Try to obtain information about D's lover, e.g., name, address, employer.
2.	With whom has D done it? How often?	
3.	When did you first find out?	
4.	Since that time, have you had sexual intercourse with D?	
5.	Have you indicated to D in any way that you forgave D, that you were going to give D another chance?	
6.	Who else knows about this? How do they know?	
7.	To your knowledge, when was the last time D committed adultery?	
8.	Where was D at the time?	
9.	Who was with D?	
10.	Does D come home late often? Does D ever stay out all night?	
11.	Does D spend a lot of time with the person you suspect is D's lover?	
12.	Have you ever spoken to this person?	
13.	Do you know where this person lives or works?	
14.	Has D ever spoken to you about this person?	
15.	Do you think this person would admit to being D's lover?	
16.	Has D confessed everything to you?	
17.	If D had never admitted it, how would you have known? What specific things would make you suspicious?	
18.	Have you and D ever discussed getting a divorce?	
19.	Do you both want a divorce?	
20.	Did you and D ever discuss what evidence you or your attorney would introduce to prove adultery?	
21.	Could D claim that you committed any wrongs toward D, e.g., adultery, desertion, nonsupport?	

IM-481

Assignment # 71

Tom is married to Mary. They no longer live together. Tom wants to sue Mary for divorce on the ground of adultery. His evidence is as follows: a man visited Mary's apartment one night until midnight. When he left, he kissed her good night at the front door.

(a) Has adultery been established? (See also General Instructions for the Legal Analysis Assignment, supra p. 16.)

(b) Draft a set of interrogatories which Tom would send to Mary. (See also General Instructions for the Interrogatory Assignment, supra p. 31.)

(c) Draft a complaint for Tom for the divorce on this ground. (See also General Instructions for the Complaint Drafting Assignment, supra p. 20.)

Assignment # 72

In the following four situations, assess any difficulties the plaintiff may have in obtaining a divorce on the ground of adultery. (See also General Instructions for the Legal Analysis Assignment, supra p. 16.)

(a) Jim is married to Helen. One day when Helen is so drunk that she does not know where she is nor with whom, she has sexual intercourse with Bob. Jim sues Helen for divorce on the ground of adultery.

(b) Paul and Jill are married. They want a child, but Jill is having difficulty getting pregnant. Jill consults a doctor who recommends artificial insemination using the semen of an anonymous donor. Jill agrees and does so without telling Paul. When Paul finds out, he sues Jill for divorce on the ground of adultery.

(c) Charles and Georgia are married. Georgia divorces Charles and marries Bill. Later, the divorce is declared invalid with the consequence that during the time that Georgia was living with Bill, she was still married to Charles. Charles sues Georgia for divorce on the ground of adultery.

(d) Nora is married to Ted. They have never used contraceptives. One day Nora discovers a package of prophylactics in Ted's pocket. She sues him for divorce on the ground of adultery. The only evidence she introduces at trial is the package that she found.

NOTES

(1) In most states, adultery is a crime. Similarly, many states make fornication and illicit cohabitation a crime. Adultery is committed by the married person with someone not his/her spouse. Fornication is sexual intercourse between unmarried persons.[28] Illicit cohabitation is fornication between two individuals who live together. It is rare, however, for the state to prosecute anyone for these crimes.

(2) Criminal conversation is a tort which is brought against a third party who has had sexual intercourse (adultery) with the plaintiff's spouse.[29]

28. In some states, both the married and the unmarried persons who have sex together are guilty of adultery. In other states, the unmarried person is guilty of fornication.

29. See infra p. 480. See also, Prosser, W., *Handbook of the Law of Torts*, pp. 896ff. (3rd 1964).

Assignment # 73

Are the following crimes in your state:

(a) Adultery.

(b) Fornication.

(c) Illicit cohabitation.

(See also General Instructions for the State Code Assignment, supra p. 14, and for the Court Opinion Assignment, supra p. 26.)

SUMMARY GROUND FOR DIVORCE: ADULTERY	
DEFINITION: Voluntary sexual intercourse between a married person and someone not married to that person.	
WHO CAN SUE: The innocent spouse.	
MAJOR DEFENSES:	(1) the intercourse was not voluntary, e. g., rape; (2) the defendant was insane at the time of the intercourse; (3) there was no sexual intercourse; (4) the defendant is not married to the plaintiff; (5) recrimination, see infra p. 337; (6) collusion, see infra p. 338; (7) connivance, see infra p. 340; (8) condonation, see infra p. 340; (9) statute of limitations or laches, see infra p. 342; (10) the plaintiff's testimony has not been corroborated; (11) the court lacks jurisdiction, see infra p. 352. (12) res judicata, see infra p. 395.
IS THIS ALSO A GROUND FOR ANNULMENT: no, see supra p. 175.	
IS THIS ALSO A GROUND FOR JUDICIAL SEPARATION: yes, in most states.	
IS THIS ALSO A GROUND FOR SEPARATE MAINTENANCE: yes, in most states.	

[B7986]

SECTION F. CRUELTY

In most marriage ceremonies, the parties take each other "for better or worse." This concept was viewed quite literally early in our history, particularly when the woman was the one claiming to have received too much of the "worse." It was to be expected that a good deal of fighting, nagging and mutual abuse would occur within the institution of marriage. The concept of permitting the marriage to be dissolved because of "mere" cruelty or indignities was alien to our legal system for a long time. The change in the law came slowly. When cruelty was allowed as a ground for divorce, the statute would often require that the cruelty be "extreme" or "inhuman" before the divorce could be granted on this ground. Furthermore, some states limited the ground to actual or threatened physical violence. Then inflicted mental anguish came to be recognized as a form of cruelty and indignity, but there was often a requirement that the psychological cruelty must result in some impairment of the plaintiff's health. Some courts will accept a minimal health impairment e. g., a loss of sleep. Other courts require more serious impairment. Whether a court will accept a minimal impairment or will require something close to hospitalization, the fact is that most courts will insist that at least *some* physical effect result from the cruelty. Only a few states will authorize a divorce on the ground of cruelty or indignity where the mental suffering does not produce physical symptoms.

It has been pointed out that there is considerable discrepancy between the law of cruelty as it is technically defined on the books, and as it is practiced in the courtroom—particularly when the divorce proceeding is uncontested.[30] If the defendant is not objecting to the plaintiff's petition for divorce on the ground of cruelty, or is simply not appearing in the action (resulting in a default judgment) [31] courts have been known to grant the divorce with little attention or scrutiny given to the severity or consequences of the alleged cruelty. Some courts tend to use the ground of cruelty loosely as a way to end a marriage that should be ended when the other divorce grounds do not seem to fit the facts. This is not to say that cruelty can mean anything you want it to mean. There are many courts that continue to adhere strictly to the technical definition of cruelty, requiring, for example, that there be a significant health impairment as a result of the defendant's cruelty or indignities toward the plaintiff.

In short you will find that courts are not consistent in defining and applying the ground of cruelty. The consequence for the practitioner representing plaintiffs is clear: prepare the case with the most conservative judge in mind. Assume that the court is going to be reluctant to grant the divorce on the ground of cruelty unless you can demonstrate a case bordering on outrage.

30. Clark, H., *The Law of Domestic Relations*, p. 341 (1968). An uncontested divorce is one where the defendant does not appear or does not dispute the plaintiff's claim.

31. Infra p. 367.

The following is a listing of facts that courts have held to be insufficient to amount to cruelty and facts which have been found to be cruel. Of course, it is always dangerous to look at a small number of facts separate from the entire context of the marital relationship. Courts may find cruelty not so much on the basis of isolated facts alone, but in the context of the totality of facts.[32] In fact, some courts require a *pattern* of conduct that is cruel; for such courts, isolated acts of cruelty will not be sufficient for the granting of the divorce. For other courts, however, individual or isolated facts may be so outrageous as to amount to cruelty no matter how well the defendant treats the plaintiff otherwise.

FACTS COURTS HAVE HELD TO BE INSUFFICIENT TO CONSTITUTE CRUELTY [33] (in the following list, the court found that the facts in and of themselves were not serious enough and/or that the plaintiff did not suffer health or other damage as a result of what the defendant did):

—the wife nagged a lot;

—the husband sat around with his sweater around his neck;

—the wife modeled a topless bathing suit at a party;

—the wife was a poor housekeeper;

—the husband was a penny-pincher;

—the husband insisted that the wife take birth control pills;

—the wife accused the husband of infidelity and often ordered him out of the house;

—the wife refused to have sexual relations for a long period of time;

—the husband spanked his wife twice in bed;

—the husband abandoned his wife;

FACTS COURTS HAVE HELD SUFFICIENT TO CONSTITUTE CRUELTY (in the following list, the court found that the facts in and of themselves were serious enough and/or that the plaintiff suffered health or other damage as a result of what the defendant did):

—the husband beat the wife;

—the husband tries to hit his wife with car in driveway;

—the husband threatens to kill his wife and children;

—the wife nagged her husband for 18 years, poured hot coffee on him and threatened to shoot him;

—the wife refused to have sexual relations for a long period of time;

32. See Statsky, W. & Wernet, J., "The Totality of Facts as Key," in *Case Analysis and Fundamentals of Legal Writing*, pp. 171ff. (1977).

33. See Ploscowe, M., Foster, H. & Freed, D., *Family Law: Cases and Materials*, pp. 397ff. (1972), and Clark, supra note 30 at 345ff.

—the husband wanted sex all the time;

—the husband wanted to be flagellated;

—the wife was a public lesbian;

—the husband showed obscene pictures to visitors in the presence of his wife;

—the wife constantly ridiculed her husband's religion;

—the wife constantly drank and used foul language;

—the wife threw out the TV set so that her husband could not watch football games;

—the wife gave VD to her husband;

—the husband would not speak to his wife for long periods of time;

—the wife constantly criticized her husband to his relatives and business associates;

—the husband has not supported his wife.

Again, it must be pointed out that there is not a great deal of consistency in these lists. It is quite possible that two different courts will reach opposite results on the same set of facts. It should also be pointed out that while a certain set of facts may not be sufficient to constitute cruelty, they might constitute another ground, e. g., desertion [34] or adultery.[35]

Suppose that the defendant claims that what s/he did was done innocently, without any intent to harm his/her spouse. There are courts that take this factor into consideration. They will deny the divorce unless the plaintiff can show that the defendant was malicious toward the plaintiff. Most courts, however, do not take this position. The issue is seldom raised, however, either because it is obvious that the defendant intended to hurt his/her spouse, or because of the application of the traditional intent doctrine that we are presumed to intend the natural consequences of our acts. The natural consequence of what someone does may be to hurt someone whether or not the harm is intended.

The test used to determine whether the defendant's actions are cruel and had an adverse effect upon the health of the plaintiff is often said to be subjective: were these acts perceived as cruel by *this* plaintiff, and did they result in damage to the physical (and in some states, the mental) health of *this* plaintiff? It cannot be said, however, that courts do not also use an objective standard. If the court determines that no reasonable person would have reacted the way this plaintiff did to the behavior of the defendant, it is unlikely that the court would find cruelty or indignities.

34. Infra p. 328.

35. Supra p. 316.

Most courts require that the plaintiff's evidence of cruelty be corroborated before allowing the divorce.[36]

Sample Complaint on the Ground of Cruel and Inhuman Treatment

Appendix C, infra p. 499.

[B7987]

INTERVIEWING AND INVESTIGATION CHECKLIST

DIVORCE ON THE GROUND OF CRUELTY OR INDIGNITIES

	Legal Interviewing Questions	Possible Investigation Tasks
1.	How long have you been married to D (defendant)? Number of children?	* Obtain all of C's (client's) medical records, if any, from doctors, hospitals etc. that have treated her as a result of what D has done.
2.	How does D get along with the children?	* If the children are old enough and it is determined that it would not be harmful to them, they should be interviewed to see how they viewed D's relationship with C, and specifically, how D treated them.
3.	How often do you and D communicate?	* Obtain police records, if any, resulting from any fights or disturbances.
4.	Does D insult you? If so, how?	* Friends, neighbors, business associates, relatives may have to be interviewed to determine what they know about how D treated C, especially if D ever said anything derogatory to these people about C.
5.	Does D ridicule your religion, your political views, your family?	
6.	Does D do this in front of anyone? Who else knows that D does this? How do they know?	
7.	Has D ever ridiculed or criticized you to your friends, relatives or other associates?	
8.	Do you think that D has ever tried to turn the children against you? If so, how do you know? What specifically have the children or others said or done to make you think so?	
9.	Does D drink? If so, how much and how has it affected your marriage?	
10.	Does D take any drugs? If so, what kind, how often and how has it affected your marriage?	
11.	Has D ever hit you? If so, describe the circumstances. How often has D done this? Did the children see it? Has anyone else ever seen it?	
12.	Were there any other major events or scenes that were unpleasant for you? Describe the circumstances, particularly whether or not anyone else observed it.	
13.	How would you describe your sexual relationship with D?	
14.	Has D ever refused your request for sex? Has D ever made any unreasonable sexual demands on you?	
15.	Has D ever accused you of infidelity?	
16.	Does D stay away from home often? Does D ever not come home at night?	

36. For a discussion of corroboration, see supra p. 367.

INTERVIEWING AND INVESTIGATION CHECKLIST—Continued DIVORCE ON THE GROUND OF CRUELTY OR INDIGNITIES		
	Legal Interviewing Questions	**Possible Investigation Tasks**
17.	Have you ever had to call the police because of what D did? Explain.	
18.	Has D ever sued you, or have you ever sued D?	
19.	How often do you fight or argue with D?	
20.	Is D now living with you? If not, explain the circumstances of the separation.	
21.	Has D's behavior affected your health in any way?	
22.	Have you had to see a doctor?	
23.	Have you seen or have you considered seeing a psychiatrist or some other person in the field of mental health?	
24.	How old are you? Prior education?	
25.	Have you ever experienced any behavior like this before?	
26.	How was your health before D started behaving this way?	
27.	Do you have any difficulty sleeping?	
28.	Any difficulty doing your regular work because of D?	
29.	When D feels worse about you, what do you think D would say about you?	
30.	What would D claim was the worst thing you ever did to D?	
31.	Is there any possibility that it could be said you provoked D's behavior?	
32.	Have you ever said or done anything to indicate that you approved of D's behavior or that you had forgiven D?	
33.	Since the last time that D was cruel to you, have you had sexual intercourse with D?	
34.	Have you and D discussed getting a divorce?	
35.	If you sue D for divorce on the ground of cruelty, would D contest the action? Would D admit the cruelty?	
36.	Have you and D ever discussed the evidence that would or would not be introduced in the divorce action?	
37.	Could D claim that D's behavior could not be avoided, that D's acts were not intentional, that D never meant to hurt you?	

IM–482

Assignment # 74

On a sheet of paper, write down three things which one spouse could do to another that the spouse would consider cruel but which the other spouse (the one who performed the act) could honestly think is not cruel. Don't pick any obvious examples of cruelty, e. g., violence, bitter and constant arguments. Be more subtle. Try to put yourself in the position of both spouses to determine how they would feel about each of your three examples. After you write down your examples, your instructor may want to have a class discussion on whether cruelty does or does not exist in any of the examples, what further facts might be needed in order to be better able to determine whether cruelty exists and how you would go about obtaining those facts. Also, the instructor might select one example for role playing in which the client is interviewed for more facts stemming from the example.

Assignment # 75

(a) If cruelty or indignities are grounds for divorce in your state, find one opinion decided by a court in your state on this ground. Give the citation of the opinion and state the facts of the opinion. Did the court find that cruelty existed? Why or why not? (See also General Instructions for the Court Opinion Assignment, supra p. 26.)

(b) Draft a complaint based upon the set of facts you stated in (a) above. Assume that the opinion had never been written and that a complaint was being brought for the first time. Limit yourself to those facts that you think would be necessary to allege in a complaint for a divorce on the ground of cruelty. (See also General Instructions for the Complaint Drafting Assignment, supra p. 20.)

Assignment # 76

H sues W for divorce on the ground of cruelty. They no longer live together. During the trial, W learns that H has been living and having sexual relations with a third party. Can W raise the latter conduct as a defense to H's divorce action? Assume that W does not want to dissolve the marriage. (See also General Instructions for the Legal Analysis Assignment, supra p. 16.)

SUMMARY GROUND FOR DIVORCE: CRUELTY OR INDIGNITIES
DEFINITION: Conduct by the defendant that endangers the health or safety of the plaintiff.
WHO CAN SUE: The injured party.
MAJOR DEFENSES: (1) defendant's acts were not serious; (2) defendant's act was isolated and not part of a pattern of offensive behavior (this defense is not available in every state); (3) plaintiff has suffered no physical or mental health impairment; (4) recrimination, see infra p. 337; (5) provocation, see infra p. 338; (6) condonation, see infra p. 340; (7) statute of limitations or laches (undue delay in bringing the suit), see infra p. —; (8) collusion, see infra p. 338; (9) connivance, see infra p. 340; (10) the defendant's actions were unintentional, e. g., due to insanity; (11) the plaintiff's testimony has not been corroborated; (12) res judicata, see infra p. 395; (13) the court lacks jurisdiction, see infra p. 352.
IS THIS ALSO A GROUND FOR ANNULMENT: no.
IS THIS ALSO A GROUND FOR JUDICIAL SEPARATION: yes, in most states.
IS THIS ALSO A GROUND FOR SEPARATE MAINTENANCE: yes, in most states.

[B7988]

SECTION G. DESERTION AND ABANDONMENT

Almost all states list desertion or abandonment as a ground for divorce. (Review your answer to Assignment # 66 supra p. 308 to be sure of the exact language of the statute in your state on this ground.) Desertion is:

1. Voluntary separation of spouses.
2. For an uninterrupted statutory period of time.
3. With the intent not to return.
4. Where the separation was without the consent of the other spouse, and,
5. Where there was no justification for the separation.

(1) Voluntary separation of the spouses

The separation must be voluntary. If a party is drafted into the service, for example, or is hospitalized, the separation is clearly not voluntary. If the defendant is imprisoned, most states will deny the divorce on the ground of desertion, although the imprisonment may give rise to a separate ground for divorce in some states.[37]

Separation normally means that the defendant leaves the home completely, and this is what happens in the vast majority of desertion cases. It is certainly possible, however, for two people to continue living under the same roof but for their marriage to be over for all practical purposes.

Suppose that one spouse requests and is denied sexual intercourse. Has the spouse who refused sex deserted the other? Are parties living under such circumstances "separated?" Most states would answer no. In only a few states does the refusal to have sexual intercourse constitute desertion. For the majority of states, separation means the end of cohabitation, i. e., the end of living together as husband and wife.

(2) For an uninterrupted statutory period of time

The statute will specify the period of time the separation must occur in order for the divorce to be granted on this ground, e. g., two years. The period must be uninterrupted. Suppose that one party leaves the other, returns, leaves again, returns, etc. You cannot add up all the time the parties have been separated in order to achieve the requisite statutory period.

Suppose that immediately after the parties separate one party sues the other for divorce (on a ground other than desertion), or for judicial separation,[38] or for separate maintenance[39] or for annulment[40] and loses. The parties continue to live separate during the litigation. It would appear logical that if a divorce action is later brought on the ground of desertion, the time the parties spent in litigation over the earlier action should count toward the statutory separation time. Not so, however. Litigation time is *not* counted in most cases.

(3) With no intent to return

One spouse can walk out in a fit of anger without having the intention of abandoning the other forever. For desertion to exist, however, the separation must be with the intent never to resume cohabitation. The individual facts must be carefully scrutinized in order to determine whether this intent exists. It is certainly possible for a spouse to leave without the intent to stay away permanently, but yet

37. Infra p. 335.

38. Infra p. 405.

39. Supra p. 433.

40. Supra p. 223.

to formulate such an intent *while* s/he is away. The plaintiff may not always be able to introduce evidence as clear as a defendant's statement, "I'm never coming back." The overall circumstances of the departure and separation, however, may make reasonably clear what the defendant's intention was upon departure or what it later became. On the other hand, even a statement such as, "I'm never coming back," must be looked at from the perspective of whether the defendant "really" meant these words as opposed to whether they were more indicative of a high temper than a serious determination.

(4) Without consent

Suppose that the parties enter into a separation agreement,[41] obtain a judicial separation[42] or a separate maintenance decree.[43] It can be said that by participating in any of these events, the parties are consenting to each other's separation. As to the latter two events, the court, in effect, officially sanctions the separation. Hence either party should not be allowed to bring a divorce action on the ground of desertion since there was consent, and perhaps justification (see discussion below). The divorce may be available on other grounds, e. g., living separate and apart,[44] but the desertion ground should not be available. The living separate-and-apart ground[45] is applicable when the separation is by mutual consent.

After the defendant leaves, if the plaintiff makes a genuine request of the defendant to return (i. e., an offer of reconciliation), which the defendant refuses, the fact that the plaintiff made the request is strong evidence that the defendant's separation was *not* with the consent of the plaintiff. On the other hand, if the defendant makes a genuine request of the plaintiff *to be allowed to return* which the plaintiff refuses, the evidence shows that the separation *is* with the plaintiff's consent. In such a case, the plaintiff would be denied the divorce on this ground. Furthermore, as we shall see shortly, the plaintiff's refusal under these circumstances could amount to *constructive desertion* by the plaintiff meaning that the defendant could sue the plaintiff for divorce on the ground of the plaintiff's desertion. The plaintiff cannot refuse a genuine offer of reconciliation during the statutory period.

Courts sometimes place a good deal of significance on the amount of resistence or the lack of resistence on the part of the plaintiff to the departure of the defendant. If there was no resistence, or if it was minimal, it may be interpreted as an indication that the plaintiff consented to the separation.

41. Supra p. 245.

42. Infra p. 405.

43. Infra p. 433.

44. Supra p. 308.

45. Ibid.

(5) Without justification

Justification is sometimes defined as "reasonable cause." If the defendant had a reasonable cause to leave the plaintiff, the ground of desertion will not exist. What do we mean by reasonable cause? Courts differ on their answer to this question. Two different standards are possible:

—a defendant has reasonable cause to leave the plaintiff if the conduct of the plaintiff would give the defendant grounds to sue the plaintiff for a divorce;

—a defendant has reasonable cause to leave the plaintiff if the conduct of the plaintiff seriously disrupts the marriage relationship.

The first standard is certainly stricter than the second. Under the second standard, one spouse would be justified in leaving the other if what the plaintiff did amounted to something less than cruelty, adultery, or any of the other grounds for the divorce. If, however, you live in a state that applies the stricter standard, you need to review the material earlier in this chapter on the grounds for divorce [46] in order to be able to determine what conduct of the plaintiff would justify the defendant in leaving, and hence would defeat the plaintiff's divorce action on the ground of desertion.

Constructive desertion exists (1) when the conduct of the spouse who stayed home justified the other spouse's departure, *or* (2) when the spouse who stayed home refuses a sincere offer of reconciliation (within the statutory period) from the other spouse who initially left without justification. In effect, the spouse who stayed home becomes the deserter! The spouse who left would be allowed to sue the other spouse for divorce on the ground of desertion.

In many states, the husband still has the right to select the domicile [47] of the family. If he acts reasonably in selecting a domicile,[48] his wife must follow him. If she does not, and he goes to the new domicile anyway, she has constructively deserted him, enabling him to sue her for divorce on the ground of desertion. Similarly, in some states the refusal of a spouse to have sexual relations, or to have sexual relations without contraceptives, would justify the other spouse in leaving, giving the latter the right to sue for divorce on the ground of desertion (constructive desertion).

Finally, as already indicated, an initially innocent spouse (innocent because the other spouse left without justification) becomes a deserter the moment s/he refuses the request of the other spouse to be allowed to return home so long as (a) this request is made within the time prescribed by statute (see discussion of this time period above), and (b) the request is genuine and not simply a tactic to try to brand the other spouse a constructive deserter.

46. Supra p. 308.

47. Infra p. 345.

48. Infra p. 347.

INTERVIEWING AND INVESTIGATION CHECKLIST

DIVORCE ON THE GROUND OF DESERTION OR ABANDONMENT

(C = Client; D = Defendant)

	Legal Interviewing Questions	Possible Investigation Tasks
1.	When did D (defendant) leave you?	• Interview anyone who may have been present when D left C (client).
2.	Why did D leave?	• If necessary, try to obtain evidence that D lived separately from C during the statutory period, e.g., interview D's landlord, try to get copies of D's lease or payment receipts.
3.	What precisely did D say when s/he left?	• Obtain copies of any court papers or judgments that may exist from prior litigation between C and D, e.g., earlier divorce action, judicial separation, separate maintenance decree.
4.	What did you say?	• Obtain police reords, if any, resulting from any fights or disturbances involving D and C.
5.	Was anyone present to see and hear what happened? Children? Neighbors? Relatives?	
6.	What indications, if any, did D give that s/he was not coming back?	
7.	Where did D go to live?	
8.	Did D take his suit case, any furniture, etc?	
9.	Has D ever walked out before? If so, what were the circumstances?	
10.	Had D ever threatened to walk out before?	
11.	Have you ever walked out on D or threatened to do so? If so, what were the circumstances?	
12.	When D walked out this last time, did you approve of his/her going? Did you let D know how you felt?	
13.	Have you told anyone else that you would like D to come back?	
14.	Did you write any letters to D or did D write any letters to you about your relationship after D left? If so, what were they about?	
15.	How long has D been away?	
16.	Since D left, has s/he told you that s/he would like to come back? Has D in any other way indicated that s/he would like to come back? (Describe in detail.)	
17.	Since D left, describe every contact that you and D have had.	
18.	Has D supported you during this period? Have you supported him/her?	
19.	Since D left, have the two of you had sexual intercourse? If so, when?	
20.	What has D's relationship with the children been during this period?	
21.	Has D ever said that s/he was going to sue you for divorce? If so, what has D said that you have done to warrant this action against you?	
22.	Have you and D ever sued each other before, e.g., prior divorce attempt, judicial separation, separate maintenance?	
23.	Since D left, have you had sexual intercourse with anyone else?	
24.	Could D say that you have ever been cruel to D?	
25.	Did you ever refuse to have sexual intercourse with D? If so, what was D's reaction?	
26.	Did D ever refuse to have sexual intercourse with you? If so, what was your reaction?	
27.	Did D ever ask you to move somewhere else with him/her? If so, what was your reaction?	

INTERVIEWING AND INVESTIGATION CHECKLIST -Continued DIVORCE ON THE GROUND OF DESERTION OR ABANDONMENT (C = Client; D = Defendant)		
	Legal Interviewing Questions	**Possible Investigation Tasks**
28.	Did you ever ask C to move somewhere else with you? If so, what was his/her reaction?	
29.	Have you and D discussed the present divorce action? Is D going to contest the suit? Have the two of you ever discussed what evidence would be introduced in order to establish D's desertion of you?	

IM-482

Assignment # 77

Examine the following set of facts to determine whether either Robert *or* Karen could obtain a divorce on the ground of desertion. (See also General Instructions for the Legal Analysis Assignment, supra p. 16.)

Karen and Robert were married in 1950. In 1951, Karen decided to enter the Navy out of a sense of duty to her country. Robert was torn about the matter. He wanted her to be fullfilled, but he really didn't want her to leave. He told her, "I hope you don't go, but I guess I can't stop you." During her first year away, Karen told Robert by phone and letter that she was beginning to go out with other men, but that there was no sexual involvement with them. Robert was upset and brooded about this, but for a long time he never said anything about it to Karen in his letters and phone conversations. In early 1953, Karen called Robert and told him that her leaving was all a mistake. She was going to quit the Navy and come home. Robert was distressed by the news, and for the first time told her how upset he was about her going out with other men and about her having left him in the first place. "I'm not going to live with you unless you've changed completely," he told her. Furthermore, he told her that if he does let her come back, she and he were going to move in with his mother because his mother was ill and he wanted to be with her. Karen then decided to stay in the Navy. She never saw Robert again.

Assignment # 78

Draft a complaint (for either Karen or Robert) based upon the facts in Assignment # 77 above. The complaint is for a divorce on the ground of desertion. (See also General Instructions for the Complaint Drafting Assignment, supra p. 20.)

SUMMARY

GROUND FOR DIVORCE: DESERTION OR ABANDONMENT

DEFINITION: The voluntary separation of the spouses where the spouse who leaves does so without justification, without the consent of the other spouse and with the intent never to return. The parties must remain separated for an uninterrupted period of time specified by statute.

WHO CAN SUE: The innocent party (the party who did not desert the other—actually or constructively).

MAJOR DEFENSES:
(1) the separation was not voluntary;
(2) there was no separation—no one moved out;
(3) there was no separation during the entire statutory period, e. g., the period was interrupted by reconciliations;
(4) the defendant never had the intent to leave permanently and never formulated this intent while away;
(5) the plaintiff consented to the separation;
(6) the defendant was justified in leaving—the plaintiff constructively deserted the defendant;
(7) the plaintiff's testimony has not been corroborated;
(8) the plaintiff refused a genuine offer of reconciliation before the statutory period ended;
(9) the plaintiff's request that the defendant return was a sham;
(10) collusion, see infra p. 338;
(11) connivance, see infra p. 340;
(12) condonation, see infra p. 340;
(13) recrimination, see infra p. 337;
(14) the court lacks jurisdiction, see infra p. 352.
(15) res judicata, see infra p. 395;
(16) statute of limitations or laches, see infra p. 342.

IS THIS ALSO A GROUND FOR ANNULMENT: no.

IS THIS ALSO A GROUND FOR JUDICIAL SEPARATION: yes.

IS THIS ALSO A GROUND FOR SEPARATE MAINTENANCE: yes.

SECTION H. MISCELLANEOUS GROUNDS

While the grounds surveyed on the preceding pages of this chapter are the ones most commonly found in state statutes, there are a good number of other grounds specified by various other states:

—Bigamy,
—Impotence,
—Nonage,
—Fraud,
—Duress,
—Incest,
—Conviction of a crime,
—Insanity,
—Habitual drunkenness,
—Drug addiction,
—Non-support,
—Neglect of duty,
—Obtaining an out- of-state divorce,
—Venereal disease,
—Unchastity,
—Pregnancy by someone else at the time of the marriage,
—Treatment injurious to health,
—Deviate sexual conduct,
—For any other cause deemed by the court sufficient, if satisfied that the parties can no longer live together.

BIGAMY,[49] IMPOTENCE,[50] NONAGE,[51] FRAUD,[52] DURESS,[53] INCEST[54]

These grounds for divorce are also grounds for annulment. In the chapters on annulment in this book,[55] these grounds were discussed and they should be reviewed now if they are also grounds for divorce in your state (see your answer to Assignment # 66, supra p. 308.)

CONVICTION OF A CRIME

States differ on the kind of conviction that will justify a divorce on this ground. The statute may specify that the crime must be a "felony," a "crime of moral turpitude," an "infamous crime," etc. Infamous crimes or those of moral turpitude usually involve crimes such as rape, murder, drug sales, etc. In order to determine what a felony is, you may have to refer to the penal code section of the

49. Supra p. 177.

50. Supra p. 190.

51. Supra p. 186.

52. Supra p. 205.

53. Supra p. 203.

54. Supra p. 183.

55. Chapters Ten-Fourteen, supra pp. 171–244.

state's statutes. In some states, it is not enough to be convicted of such a crime; a specified time in prison may have to be served.[56]

INSANITY

We have already seen that insanity at the time of the marriage ceremony is a ground for annulment.[57] In many states, it is also a ground for divorce whether it occurred at the time of the marriage or whether it developed during the marriage. The statute may specify that the divorce will not be granted unless defendant has been institutionalized in a hospital for a designated period of time. The insanity may also have to be "incurable."

HABITUAL DRUNKENNESS AND DRUG ADDICTION

The use of alcohol or drugs must be habit forming; occasional or even heavy use will not suffice for the divorce to be granted. It may be a defense that the plaintiff knew that the defendant drank before s/he married him/her. If the plaintiff did not know about the defendant's drinking or drug problem at the time of the marriage because the defendant concealed it from him/her, there may be grounds to annul the marriage for fraud.[58]

NON-SUPPORT

While non-support is most frequently a ground for judicial separation[59] or separate maintenance,[60] it is also a ground for divorce in some states if the non-support was willful and continued for a set period of time. Recrimination is often a defense.[61] The ground will not exist if the spouse (usually the husband) is providing support to the best of his ability.

NEGLECT OF DUTY

Neglect of duty or gross neglect usually constitutes a combination of the cruelty, desertion and incompatibility grounds when the acts of the defendant are considered extremely serious.[62]

OBTAINING AN OUT-OF-STATE DIVORCE

If one spouse leaves his/her state, obtains a valid divorce judgment in another state, and returns to his/her original state, the foreign (i. e., out-of-state) judgment is entitled to full faith and credit (i. e., it can be enforced) in any other state.[63] Suppose, however, that the foreign judgment is not valid, e. g., because the foreign

56. On the consequences of a conviction see also supra p. 181.

57. Supra p. 201.

58. Supra p. 205.

59. Infra p. 405.

60. Infra p. 433.

61. Infra p. 337.

62. See Clark, H., *The Law of Domestic Relations*, p. 354 (1968).

63. Infra p. 351.

court lacked jurisdiction.[64] In a few states, when the party returns to his/her original state with an invalid divorce judgment, not only will it *not* be enforced against the other spouse, but also the latter is given the right to sue for divorce on the ground that his/her spouse attempted to obtain an out-of-state divorce.

SECTION I. DEFENSES TO DIVORCE ACTIONS

There are a fair number of defenses that can be raised by a defendant in a divorce action:

1. Recrimination.
2. Provocation.
3. Collusion.
4. Connivance.
5. Condonation.
6. Insanity.
7. Statute of limitations and laches.
8. The parties are not married.
9. Res judicata.
10. The court lacks jurisdiction.
11. Improper venue.

All but the last three defenses will be discussed in the remainder of this chapter. The last three will be treated in Chapter Eighteen.

Assignment # 79

Are there any statutes in your state which specify the defenses to any of the grounds for divorce? If so, what are these defenses? Have any of the defenses been abolished or limited? If so, which ones? (See also General Instructions for the State Code Assignment, supra p. 14.)

1. RECRIMINATION

Recrimination is a serious marital wrong committed by the plaintiff. Since the plaintiff does not have "clean hands,"[65] s/he may not be allowed to have the divorce no matter what marital wrongs the defendant committed. For the plaintiff to lose the action because of recrimination, many courts say that the plaintiff's marital wrong must be serious enough to justify a finding that the defendant has grounds for divorce against the plaintiff. Other courts, however, find recrimination when the plaintiff's conduct, although serious, does not amount to an independent ground for divorce.

Recrimination does not have the same effect in every state. In a few states, it is *not* an absolute bar to the plaintiff's action. The court may have discretion on whether or not to permit the divorce in spite of the plaintiff's wrongdoing, or, the court may be allowed to

64. Infra p. 350.

65. See also p. 174.

compare the wrongdoing of the plaintiff and of the defendant and grant the divorce to the party who was least at fault. Finally, the court may have the power to grant the divorce to *both* plaintiff and defendant if both can establish grounds.

2. PROVOCATION

One spouse may commit a marital wrong in retaliation against provocative conduct of the other spouse. If the latter spouse later brings a divorce action, some states allow the other spouse to defeat the action through the defense of provocation. If, however, the retaliatory action of the defendant is out of proportion to the provocative conduct of the plaintiff, the latter's provocation will not be a defense. Provocation is similar to the recrimination defense except that the provocative conduct need not amount to an independent ground for divorce for the defendant. As indicated above, many courts require that the conduct constituting recrimination amount to an independent ground for divorce in favor of the defendant.[66]

3. COLLUSION[67]

Parties cannot agree to get a divorce and then "conspire" on what they will or will not say to the judge when they know that the judge will not receive a true picture of their marital relationship.

The collusion defense is considered by many to be the pinnacle of absurdity and hypocrisy. It is well known that collusion is rampant in divorce actions, particularly in so called uncontested actions. The difficulty is that there is almost no way to prevent collusion. If both parties are conspiring to make it appear to the court that grounds exist (e. g., the plaintiff and defendant agree that plaintiff will falsely claim that the defendant beat her and the defendant will pretend that he did so, or will simply not deny such cruelty), who is going to raise the defense of collusion? Not the plaintiff or defendant since their goal is to get the divorce at any cost even if it means defrauding the court.

Collusion mainly surfaces, if at all, long after the divorce has been granted. One of the parties later becomes dissatisfied with one of the terms of the divorce, e. g., a child custody or payment order, and tries to attack the divorce judgment. Should such a party be allowed to attack a divorce decree on the basis of collusion, and in effect say to the court: "that divorce that you gave in the action involving me and my ex-spouse should really be invalidated because I want to tell you now that we defrauded you into thinking that we had grounds for the divorce, when in fact, we were lying." Many

66. See Moore, *Forgotten Defenses to Divorce Suits*, 9 Journal of Family Law 149 (1969) and Ploscowe, M., Foster, H. & Freed, D., *Family Law: Cases and Materials*, p. 489 (1972).

67. See also supra p. 254.

courts will deny standing to such a spouse to attack the divorce; it would amount to a reward for wrongdoing. There are some courts, however, that *will* give such wrongdoing spouses the right to challenge their own divorce decrees on the basis of their own collusion!

The essence of collusion is the *agreement* between husband and wife that they will falsely let it appear to the court that grounds for the divorce exist. This can be done by affirmatively saying things to the court that are not true, or by refusing to deny what is untrue. *One* party can lie or fail to object to what is untrue and still *not* commit collusion. In fact, both parties can lie or otherwise conceal the truth without committing collusion. No collusion exists unless the fraud is by *mutual understanding.* Of course, if a party defrauds the court, s/he can be sanctioned, e. g., by contempt, but no collusion exists without an agreement.

Of course, the essence of the separation agreement [68] when it is presented to the court for approval or incorporation [69] in the divorce decree is that the document is the mutually-agreed-on position of the husband and wife on issues critical to the divorce proceeding. Isn't the separation agreement collusive? No, so long as the parties in the agreement do not conspire, e. g., to refrain from raising a defense.[70]

It is quite proper for husband and wife to want a divorce and to refrain from asserting all of their defensive rights in the divorce action—so long as they do not mislead the court and so long as they act unilaterally.

Assignment # 80

H and W sue each other for divorce on the ground of irremediable breakdown.[71] Immediately before and after the divorce decree is awarded, the parties have had sexual intercourse with each other. Does this conduct constitute collusion? (See also General Instructions for the Legal Analysis Assignment, supra p. 16).

Assignment # 81

Richard and Paula are married. They both want a divorce. Richard convinces Paula to fabricate evidence of her own adultery. He will sue her for adultery on the basis of false evidence and she will not object. The plan goes as scheduled. The divorce is granted on the adultery ground. To Paula's surprise, however, custody of their two children is awarded to Richard. She is very angry about this. In your state, can she attack the divorce judgment on the theory that it was procured through collusion? (See also General In-

68. Supra p. 245.

69. Supra p. 283.

70. For more on the issue of collusion in separation agreements, see supra p. 254.

71. Supra p. 315.

structions for the Legal Analysis Assignment, supra p. 16. You will also need to check statutory and case law for your state. See General Instructions for the State Code Assignment, supra p. 14, and for the Court Opinion Assignment, supra p. 26.)

4. CONNIVANCE

Connivance may be defined by statute. For example:

> Connivance is the corrupt consent of one party to the commission of the acts of the other constituting the cause of divorce. Corrupt consent is manifested by passive permission with intent to connive at or actively procure the commission of the acts complained of.

In effect, the plaintiff is consenting to the marital wrong, e. g., adultery, of the defendant, and should not be allowed to sue the defendant later for a divorce on the basis of that wrong. Connivance can occur:

(a) by the plaintiff's active participation in the defendant's marital wrong, e. g., the plaintiff hires a third party to seduce the defendant so that adultery can be established,

(b) by the plaintiff's passive consent: knowing that the defendant is about to commit a marital wrong, the plaintiff takes no steps to prevent it.

Everything depends upon the state of mind of the plaintiff since it is his/her consent that is the essence of connivance. If a spouse is spying in order to gather evidence of possible adultery, and indeed finds such evidence, there has been no consent to the adultery and hence no connivance. If one spouse constantly drinks with the other, there is no connivance unless the plaintiff-spouse tried to make the defendant spouse into an habitual drunkard in order to sue the latter for divorce on the ground of habitual drunkardness or cruelty due to such drinking. It is obvious that in connivance cases, it is often very difficult to prove what plaintiff's intention was.

Connivance, of course, is very similar to collusion. The major difference is that collusion involves the corrupt consent or agreement of both parties, while connivance is the corrupt consent of only one of the parties.

5. CONDONATION

Condonation is forgiveness by the plaintiff of the marital wrong of the defendant barring the plaintiff's divorce action on the basis of that wrong. The plaintiff must have knowledge of the defendant's wrong; a mere suspicion of wrongdoing would not be enough in most states. Suppose that the plaintiff has heard rumors that the defendant has committed adultery and yet continues to live with the defendant. Does the continued cohabitation constitute a forgiveness by the plaintiff of the adultery if the rumor later turns out to be true? It may depend upon whether or not it could be proven that the plaintiff *believed* the rumor. Knowledge of a rumor may not be sufficient in and of itself.

Having sexual intercourse with the defendant after learning of the latter's wrong is usually interpreted as condonation by the plaintiff, although some states require evidence of forgiveness in addition to (or in place of) the plaintiff's participation in the sex act. Without a resumption of sexual relations, however, or other significant signs of cohabitation,[72] courts have difficulty finding the requisite forgiveness.

The plaintiff's forgiveness, express or implied, must be voluntary. If the wrongdoing spouse pressures or tricks the innocent spouse into resuming cohabitation, there may be no forgiveness at all.

Suppose that the plaintiff knowingly and voluntarily forgives the defendant's marital wrong (either expressly—"I forgive you," or impliedly—by a resumption of sexual intercourse), and the defendant then repeats the same or a similar wrong. Is the earlier ground for divorce revived? Was the plaintiff's forgiveness impliedly conditioned on a promise of the defendant to treat the plaintiff with conjugal kindness? Many states do imply such a condition and, upon defendant's misconduct, revive the plaintiff's original ground for divorce. Some states, however, make the forgiveness absolute. If the defendant does not display conjugal kindness to the plaintiff, the latter cannot sue for divorce unless the defendant's conduct would amount to a new ground for divorce; there is no revival of the old ground in these states.

6. INSANITY

If the defendant was insane[73] at the time s/he committed the marital wrong (e. g., adultery, cruelty, desertion), most courts would deny the divorce to the plaintiff. When the marital wrong involves fault, e. g., adultery, the courts are more inclined to hold that insanity is a defense than when the plaintiff is seeking a divorce on one of the no-fault grounds, e. g., incompatibility,[74] living separate and apart.[75]

72. Living together as husband and wife.

73. On the definition of insanity, see p. 200.

74. Supra p. 313.

75. Supra p. 308.

7. STATUTE OF LIMITATIONS AND LACHES

A statute of limitations is a specific period of time within which a party must bring an action or be barred from bringing it at all. States often have statutes of limitations for grounds such as:

ADULTERY DIVORCES:	the statute of limitations usually begins to run after the plaintiff discovers the defendant's adultery;
DESERTION DIVORCES:	the statute of limitations usually begins to run after the statutory period for the separation [76] is over (note, however, that some states have no statute of limitations for the divorce on the ground of desertion);
CRUELTY DIVORCES:	the statute of limitations usually begins to run whenever the defendant's misconduct is serious enough to warrant a finding of cruelty.

Laches means that there has been undue delay on the part of the plaintiff in bringing the divorce action. The courts obviously have a great deal of discretion in deciding when laches will bar a plaintiff's action. The concern is fairness to the defendant. If the plaintiff waits too long to sue, some of the defendant's witnesses, for example, might move away. It may be much more difficult for the defendant to defend the action if the plaintiff waits too long. In deciding whether to apply the defense of laches, the court must weigh, on the one hand, the harm that may have resulted to the defendant because of the delay, and, on the other hand, the reasonableness of the cause of the delay, e. g., the plaintiff's sickness, ignorance of the law, desire to stay together for the sake of the children, hope for a reconciliation.

8. THE PARTIES ARE NOT MARRIED

Of course, the defendant has a good defense to the plaintiff's divorce action if s/he can show that s/he is not married to the plaintiff; there is no marriage to dissolve.

9. RES JUDICATA [77]

10. THE COURT LACKS JURISDICTION [78]

11. IMPROPER VENUE [79]

76. Supra p. 328.

77. Infra p. 395.

78. Infra p. 350.

79. Infra p. 361.

Chapter Seventeen

DIVORCE PROCEDURE, ALIMONY, PROPERTY DIVISION, CHILD SUPPORT AND CUSTODY

SECTION A. OVERVIEW

Over 90% of the divorce cases are uncontested, i. e., the parties are in agreement (legally or by collusion [1]) on the termination of the marital relationship, alimony, property division, child custody and child support. If the parties are able to agree on the terms of the separation agreement,[2] the actual steps of divorce procedure are frequently a matter of ritual. If the bitterness of the past has not subsided, however, the technicalities of procedure can occupy center stage in costly and complicated proceedings.

The following terms are often found in connection with divorce procedure:

MIGRATORY DIVORCE:	The husband and/or wife travels (migrates) to another state in order to obtain a divorce—usually because it is procedurally easier to obtain the divorce in the other state. Then there is a return to the "home" state and an attempt to enforce the "foreign" divorce.
FOREIGN DIVORCE:	A divorce decree obtained in a state other than the state where an attempt is made to enforce that decree.
"QUICKIE" DIVORCE:	A migratory divorce obtained in what are often called "divorce mill states," i. e., a state where the procedural requirements for divorce are very slight in order to encourage out-of-state citizens to come in for a divorce, and while there, to spend some tourist dollars.

1. Supra p. 338.

2. Supra p. 245.

COLLUSIVE DIVORCE: An agreement or "conspiracy" between a husband and wife to commit fraud on the court by falsely letting it appear that they have grounds for divorce.

DEFAULT DIVORCE: A divorce granted to the plaintiff because the defendant failed to appear to answer the complaint of the plaintiff. (In most states, the divorce is not granted automatically; the plaintiff must still show the court that the grounds for divorce exist.)

DIVISIBLE DIVORCE: A divorce decree does two things: (1) dissolves the marital relationship, and (2) resolves the questions of support, property division and child custody/care. The divorce decree is divisible or "divide-able" into these two objectives. A *divisible divorce* is a divorce decree granted in one state but enforceable in another state only as to the dissolution of the marriage. The part of the divorce decree that deals with support, property division, etc., is not enforceable in another state (i. e., the other state does not have to give full faith and credit to this part of the divorce decree). The divorce is divisible in that only part of it must be recognized in another state.

BILATERAL DIVORCE: One rendered by a court when both parties were present before the court. The opposite of a bilateral divorce is an ex parte divorce.

EX PARTE DIVORCE: One rendered by a court when only one party was present before the court.

DUAL DIVORCE:	The divorce is granted to both husband and wife. Normally when a divorce decree is awarded, it dissolves the marriage, but the decree is usually given to *one* party only—to the plaintiff, or to the defendant if the latter has filed a counterclaim [3] for divorce against the plaintiff. A dual divorce is granted to *both* parties.
UNCONTESTED DIVORCE:	The defendant does not appear at the divorce proceeding (see default divorce above), or does appear without disputing any of the plaintiff's claims.
CONTESTED DIVORCE:	The defendant appears and disputes any or all of the claims made by the plaintiff at the divorce proceeding.
DIVORCE A MENSA ET THORO:	A judicial separation. A limited divorce. The parties are *not* free to remarry since they are still married after receiving this kind of "divorce."
LIMITED DIVORCE:	A judicial separation. Divorce a mensa et thoro.
DIVORCE A VINCULO MATRIMONII:	An absolute divorce. The parties are no longer married. They are free to remarry.

One of our objectives in this chapter is to have you prepare a flow chart [4] of divorce procedure for your state. There will be a number of individual assignments to be answered mainly by reference to your state code, to the court rules of your state, and, to a lesser degree, by reference to court opinions of your state. The answers to these assignments on pieces of the procedural picture will also be used to complete Assignment # 112, infra p. 398, at the end of this chapter on the divorce flow chart.

SECTION B. DOMICILE

The word domicile is often confused with the word residence. In many divorce statutes the word residence is used, but the meaning

3. Supra p. 34 and infra p. 362.

4. Supra p. 398. For other flow charts, see p. 241.

intended for this word is domicile.[5] Except for such oddities, there are distinct differences between the two words:

RESIDENCE: where someone is living at a particular time; a person can have many residences, e. g., a home in the city plus a beach house plus an apartment in another state or country.

DOMICILE: the place (a) where someone has physically been in (b) with the intention to make that place his/her permanent home. It is the place to which one would intend to return when away. A person can have only one domicile.

For a number of reasons it is important to be able to determine where one's domicile is, particularly in a society where people are so mobile:

—a court does not have jurisdiction to divorce parties unless one or both spouses are domiciled in the state where that court sits;[6]

—a few courts refuse to grant child custody orders unless the child is domiciled in the state; [7]

—liability for inheritance taxes may depend upon the domicile of the decedent at the time of death.

Generally, a child cannot acquire a domicile of his/her own until the child reaches majority (e. g., 21 years of age) or is otherwise emancipated.[8] In effect, a child acquires a domicile by *operation of law* rather than by *choice*. The law operates to impose a domicile on the child regardless of what the child may want (if the child is old enough to form any opinion at all). What is the domicile that is so imposed on an unemancipated child?

—the domicile of a legitimate child is that of his/her father;

—the domicile of an illegitimate child [9] is that of his/her mother;

—if the mother and father are divorced, the child's domicile is that of whatever parent is awarded custody by the court;

—if the father abandons his legitimate child, the domicile of the child is that of the mother;

—if the father of a legitimate child dies, its domicile is that of its mother.

Once a child's domicile has been determined in the above manner, the child cannot force a change in his/her own domicile simply by moving. For example, suppose that Jim is the legitimate child of

5. See infra p. 359.

6. Infra p. 352.

7. Infra p. 376.

8. Infra p. 455. Emancipation is freedom from the control and discipline of one's parents.

9. Infra p. 449.

George. Assume that Jim is not emancipated and that George has never abandoned him. Hence Jim's domicile is that of George even though Jim may be living with his mother in another state. Similarly, if George moves to another state, Jim's domicile becomes that of the new state even if Jim never sets foot in that state. His presence in the new state is not necessary for that state to be his new domicile so long as he is the legitimate, unemancipated child of a father who has never abandoned him.

What is the domicile of a married woman? At common law, as soon as a woman married, she acquired the domicile of her husband. This domicile was imposed on her by operation of law; she had no domicile of choice. If the husband moved and she refused to move with him without any justification for refusing, she has deserted him and the husband could sue her for divorce on this ground.[10] The rule that a married woman must take the domicile of her husband exists in most states today, although some courts have taken the position that it is an unconstitutional denial of equal protection of the law for a married woman to be forced to take the domicile of her husband when the latter is not required to take the domicile of his wife. There are some exceptions to the rule that the wife takes the domicile of her husband:

—if the wife is the spouse who earns the income for the family, a few courts conclude that she can acquire her own domicile independent of her husband;

—if the husband consents, many courts allow the wife to acquire her own domicile;

—if the husband has deserted his wife, or has otherwise given her grounds to divorce him,[11] most courts will permit her to acquire her own domicile;

—so long as the wife has not deserted her husband, a few courts permit her to acquire her own domicile whether or not she has grounds to divorce him.

What is the domicile of a man, of a single woman or of an emancipated child? They can all pick any domicile they want (domicile by *choice*) so long as they are physically present in a place (even if only momentarily) and have the intention to make that place their permanent home at the time of their presence there. The major difficulty that exists is in determining when that intention exists. Intention is a state of the mind, and the only way to prove a state of mind is by looking at external acts and determining what those acts tell us by implication about the state of mind of the person performing the acts. Verbal statements are not necessarily conclusive as to what the state of mind is of the person making those statements. Suppose, for example, that Bill is domiciled in Ohio, and while visit-

10. Supra p. 328.

11. Supra p. 308.

ing California, becomes violently ill. Assume that if Bill dies domiciled in California, his beneficiaries will pay a lower inheritance tax than if he had died domiciled in Ohio. Assume further that Bill knows this. While lying in a California sick bed, Bill openly says just before he dies "I hereby declare that I intend California to be my permanent home." This statement in itself does *not* prove that Bill was domiciled in California at the time of his death. Other evidence may show that he made the statement simply to give the *appearance* of changing his domicile and that if he had gotten better, he would have returned to Ohio. If this is so, then his domicile at death is Ohio in spite of his declaration, since he never intended to make California his permanent home.

In the following chart, you will gain an insight into some of the factors that courts will consider in determining whether the requisite state of mind on intention existed.

INTERVIEWING AND INVESTIGATION CHECKLIST
HOW TO DETERMINE WHEN A PERSON HAS ESTABLISHED A DOMICILE

	Legal Interviewing Questions	Possible Investigation Tasks
1.	When did you move to that state?	* Interview persons to whom the interviewee (client) may have discussed the move to that state, e. g., relatives, neighbors, business associates. * Obtain copies of records that would indicate the extent of contact with that state, e. g., state tax returns, bank statements, land ownership papers, leases, voting records.
2.	How often have you been in that state in the past? (Describe the details of these contacts with the state.)	
3.	Why did you move to that state?	
4.	Was it your intention to stay there for a short period of time? A long period of time? Indefinitely? Forever?	
5.	While you were in that state, did you also have homes elsewhere in the state, and/or in another state, and/or in another country? If so, give details, e. g., addresses, how long you spent at each home, etc.	
6.	Where do you consider your permanent home to be?	
7.	Have you ever changed your permanent home in the past? (If so, give details.)	
8.	Do you own a home in the state? Do you rent a home or apartment?	
9.	How long have you had the home or apartment?	
10.	Where are you registered to vote?	
11.	Where is your job or business?	
12.	In what state is your car registered?	
13.	What state issued your driver's license?	
14.	In what states do you have bank accounts?	
15.	In what states do you have club memberships?	
16.	In what states do you own land?	
17.	Where do your relatives live?	

IM-483

Assignment # 82

Make a list of the times that your state code refers to domicile. Specify where domicile is relevant in domestic relations as well as in other areas of law in your state. (See also General Instructions for the State Code Assignment, supra p. 14.)

Assignment # 83

Try to find an individual (e. g., relative, friend, classmate) who now lives or who in the past lived in more than one state at the same time, e. g., for business purposes, for school purposes, for vacation purposes, etc. Interview this individual with the objective of determining where that person's domicile is (or was). List all the facts that would tend to show that the person's domicile was in one state, and then list all the facts that would tend to show that the person's domicile was in another state.

Assignment # 84

In each of the following situations, determine in what state the person was domiciled at the time of death. (See also General Instructions for the Legal Analysis Assignment, supra p. 16.)

(a) Tom's permanent home is Florida. He decides to leave Florida for good and go find a place to live in Canada. He sells all his belongings, buys a trailer and heads north. While traveling through North Carolina, he dies in a traffic accident.

(b) Gloria lives in New York because she attends New York University. Her husband lives in Montana. Gloria finishes school in six months when she will rejoin her husband in Montana. Two months before graduation, her husband decides to move to Oregon. Gloria is opposed to the move and tells him that she will not rejoin him if he does not return to Montana. Her husband refuses to move back to Montana. One month before graduation, Gloria dies in New York.

(c) Fred lives in Illinois. He hears about a high paying job in Alaska. He is tired of Illinois and decides to move to Alaska. He sell everything he owns in Illinois and rents an apartment in Alaska. While there he discovers that jobs are not that easy to find. He decides to leave if he cannot find a job in three months. If this happens, he arranges to move in with his sister in New Mexico. Before the three months are over, Fred dies jobless in Alaska.

SECTION C. JURISDICTION

Some definitions:

Full Adversarial Proceeding:

Both the plaintiff and the defendant appear at the hearing to contest the issues.

Ex Parte Proceeding:

Only one party appears at the hearing; the defendant is not present.

Direct Attack:

A challenge to the validity of a judgment made in a proceeding brought specifically for that purpose such as an appeal of that judgment brought immediately after it was rendered by the trial court.[12]

Collateral Attack:

A non-direct attack or challenge to the validity of a judgment. X obtains a judgment against Y. X then brings a separate action against Y to enforce the judgment. In this action, Y claims that the judgment was invalid because the court had no jurisdiction to render it. This is a collateral attack by Y against the judgment. A collateral attack is an attempt to challenge a judgment in a proceeding other than the proceeding which issued the judgment.

Res Judicata:

When a judgment on its merits has been rendered, the parties cannot relitigate the same dispute (i. e., the same cause of action); the parties have already had their day in court.

Estop or Estoppel:

Preventing a person from questioning the validity of a judgment because it would be unfair or inequitable to allow this person to do so.

Foreign:

Another state or country. A foreign divorce decree, for example, is one rendered by a state other than the state where one of the parties is now seeking to enforce the decree.

Forum State:

The state in which the parties are now litigating, e. g., in an action to enforce a foreign divorce decree.

12. Casad, R., *Res judicata in a Nutshell*, p. 271 (1976).

Full Faith and Credit:

According to the United States Constitution, the valid public acts of a state (e. g., a judgment of one of its courts) must be recognized by other states.

Service of Process:

Providing formal notice to a defendant that orders him/her to appear in court to answer the allegations made by the plaintiff. The notice must be delivered in a manner exactly prescribed by law.

Substituted Service:

Service of process other than by handing the process in person to the defendant, e. g., service by mail, service by publication in a local newspaper.

The word "jurisdiction" has two main meanings: a "geographic" meaning and a "power" meaning.[13] A specific geographic area of the country is referred to as the jurisdiction. A Nevada state court, for example, will often refer to its entire state as "this jurisdiction." The more significant definition of the word relates to power—the power of a court to resolve a particular controversy. (As we shall see, there are a number of different kinds of jurisdiction relating to power.) If a citizen of Maine wrote to a California court and asked for a divorce through the mail, the California court would be without jurisdiction (without power) to enter a divorce decree if the husband and wife had never been to California nor had any contact with that state. Our central question in this section is: how does a court acquire jurisdiction to hear a divorce case? The issue is a complicated one. The following chart presents an overview of the factors determining divorce jurisdiction. Some of the factors will be treated in greater depth throughout the remainder of the chapter.

13. For more on the different kinds of jurisdiction, see Statsky, W. & Wernet, J., "Judicial Systems" in *Case Analysis and Fundamentals of Legal Writing*, pp. 11ff. (1977).

FACTORS DETERMINING DIVORCE JURISDICTION

I. Kind of Jurisdiction.
II. What Part of the Divorce Decree is Being Attacked.
III. Who is Attacking the Divorce Decree.
IV. In What Court is the Divorce Decree Being Attacked.
V. Kind of Service of Process.

I. Kind of Jurisdiction

1. *Subject-Matter Jurisdiction*

The power of the court to hear cases of this kind. A criminal law court would not have subject-matter jurisdiction to hear a divorce case. If a court renders a divorce decree without having subject-matter jurisdiction over divorces, the decree is void.

2. *In Rem Jurisdiction*

The power of the court to make a decision affecting the *res* or thing. In divorce actions, the *res* is in any state where one or both of the spouses are domiciled. When a state has in rem jurisdiction because of this domicile, it has the power to terminate the marriage. (Without personal jurisdiction over the defendant, however—see below—a court will not have the power to grant alimony or a property settlement; it can only dissolve the marriage. Quasi-in-rem jurisdiction—see below—may be a basis for partial alimony or property settlement.) A court that renders a divorce judgment even though neither party is domiciled in that state can be challenged on jurisdictional grounds.

3. *Personal Jurisdiction* (also called *In Personam Jurisdiction*)

The power of the court over the person of the defendant. Personal jurisdiction is acquired by proper service of process. If a court has personal jurisdiction over a defendant, it can order him/her to pay alimony and to divide the marital property in a designated way. If a court makes such an order without personal jurisdiction, the order can be attacked on jurisdictional grounds. (For a discussion of how a state can acquire personal jurisdiction over a non-domiciliary defendant through its "long-arm" statute, see the note at the end of this chart.)

4. *Quasi-In-Rem Jurisdiction*

The power of the court over particular property that the defendant has in the state. If the plaintiff cannot obtain personal jurisdiction over the defendant, but the latter has property in the state, the plaintiff can have an alimony or property division award satisfied out of that property—but only to the extent of that property.

II. What Part of the Divorce Decree is Being Attacked

A divorce decree usually accomplishes three objectives:

1. *Dissolves the Marriage*

For a court to have jurisdiction to dissolve a marriage, one or both of the spouses must be domiciled in the state. A court can have personal jurisdiction over both of the parties without either of them being domiciled in the state where that court sits. Generally, personal jurisdiction is not enough to give the court the power to dissolve the marriage; domicile must exist.

2. *Alimony and Property Division*

Alimony and property division cannot be ordered by the court unless it has personal jurisdiction over the defendant (quasi-in-rem jurisdiction is effective for this purpose only to the limit of any property that the defendant has in the state). Hence, it is possible for the court to have jurisdiction to dissolve the marriage (because of domicile) but not have jurisdiction to make alimony and property division awards (because the plaintiff could not obtain personal jurisdiction over the defendant). This is the concept of the divisible divorce: a divorce which is effective for some purposes but not for others.

3. *Child Custody*

Generally, a court has jurisdiction to grant a custody order if the child is domiciled in that state. Courts, however, do not always adhere to this rule. They tend to take jurisdiction if the welfare of the child warrants it and if they will be able to enforce their order no matter where the domicile of the child is.

III. Who is Attacking the Divorce Decree

1. *The Person Who Obtained the Divorce*

A person should not be allowed to attack a divorce decree on jurisdictional grounds if that person was the plaintiff in the action that resulted in the divorce. A person will be estopped to deny the validity of a divorce that same person obtained. (The effect of this rule, which is followed by most states, can be to prevent a person from attacking a divorce decree that is clearly invalid, e. g., someone lied to the court about being domiciled in the state. Because of this troublesome result, there are a few courts that do *not* follow the rule, i. e., they *will* allow the person to attack the divorce s/he obtained earlier.)

2. *The Person Against Whom the Divorce Was Obtained*

If the person now attacking the divorce on jurisdictional grounds was the defendant in the action that led to the divorce and if that person made a personal appearance in that divorce action, s/he will not be allowed to attack the divorce. S/he should have raised the jurisdictional attack in the original divorce action.

If the original divorce was obtained ex parte (i. e., no appearance by the defendant), the defendant *will* be able to attack the divorce on jurisdictional grounds, e. g., the plaintiff was not domiciled in the state that granted the divorce, or the court that granted the divorce had no subject-matter jurisdiction.

If the person against whom the divorce was obtained has accepted the benefits of the divorce, e. g., alimony payments, most courts would estop that person from now attacking the divorce on jurisdictional grounds.

[B8860]

If the person against whom the divorce was obtained has remarried, s/he will be estopped from denying the validity of the second marriage on the ground that the divorce to his/her first spouse was invalid due to jurisdictional defects in the divorce decree. (There are some states, however, that will allow the jurisdictional attack on the divorce if the person making this attack did not know about the jurisdictional defect, e. g., no domicile, at the time s/he married the second time.)

3. *A Person Who was Not a Party to the Divorce Action*

A second spouse who was not a party to the prior divorce action cannot challenge the validity of that divorce on jurisdictional grounds. This second spouse relied on the validity of that divorce when s/he entered the marriage and should not now be allowed to upset the validity of that marriage by challenging the validity of the divorce.

A child of one of the parties of the prior divorce action cannot challenge the validity of the divorce on jurisdictional grounds if that child's parent would have been estopped from bringing the challenge.

IV. In What Court is the Divorce Decree Being Attacked

Full Faith and Credit

Many of the disputes in this area arise when a divorce decree is obtained in one state and brought to another state for enforcement and recognition. Whether the forum state (where enforcement of the divorce decree is being sought) must give full faith and credit to the foreign divorce may depend on which of the three aspects of the divorce decree a party is attempting to enforce:

1. *The Dissolution of the Marriage*

If the plaintiff was domiciled in the state where the divorce was granted, every other state must give full faith and credit to that part of the divorce decree which dissolved the marriage. The forum state must decide for itself whether there was a valid domicile in the foreign state. The person attacking the foreign divorce decree has the burden of proving the jurisdictional defect, i. e., the absence of domicile in the foreign state.

2. *Alimony and Property Division Awards*

If the state where the divorce was obtained did not have personal jurisdiction over the defendant, then that state's award of alimony and property division is not entitled to full faith and credit in another state. Again we see the divisible divorce concept: only part of the divorce decree need be recognized in another state if the court had jurisdiction to dissolve the marriage because of domicile, but had no jurisdiction to grant alimony and a property division due to the absence of personal jurisdiction over the defendant.

3. *Custody Award*

A custody award which was rendered without personal jurisdiction over the defendant in the action that awarded custody is not entitled to full faith and credit in another state.

[B8863]

#14 Even if there was personal jurisdiction over the defendant, however, most states will not give full faith and credit to a foreign custody award if the circumstances have changed since the award which justifies a different custody award.

V. Kind of Service of Process

1. *Personal Service*

   Each state has its own rules on how personal service is made. Generally, it is done by delivering "process" in person to the defendant in the forum state. A court acquires personal jurisdiction over the defendant in this way. (See Note following this chart on another way to acquire personal jurisdiction.)

2. *Substituted Service on a Defendant Domiciled in the Forum State*

   It is possible to acquire personal jurisdiction over a defendant domiciled in the forum state (where the action is being brought) through substituted service (e. g., by mail or newspaper publication). Local rules control as to when this can be done.

3. *Substituted Service on a Defendant Not Domiciled in the State*

   When personal jurisdiction is not required, (e. g., for that part of the divorce that dissolves the marriage when the plaintiff is domiciled in the forum state), the defendant who is not a domiciliary must still be served with process, but it need not be personal service. The service can be substituted so long as it is reasonably calculated to give a non-resident defendant actual notice of the action and an opportunity to be heard.

4. *Appearance*

   If a non-resident defendant appears in the action solely to contest the jurisdiction of the court, it is generally not possible for the plaintiff to then serve the defendant with process in person in order to acquire personal jurisdiction over him/her. So long as the defendant limits him/herself to the jurisdictional issue, the court does not obtain personal jurisdiction over him in most states.

[B8862]

NOTE: PERSONAL JURISDICTION ACQUIRED BY THE LONG-ARM STATUTE

A number of states have "long-arm" statutes which provide a method of acquiring personal jurisdiction over a defendant who is not domiciled in the forum state. The New York statute, for example, is as follows (New York Civil Practive Law and Rules, Section 302(b) (1972)):

> (b) *Personal jurisdiction over non-resident defendant.* A court in any matrimonial action or family court proceeding involving a demand for support or alimony may exercise personal jurisdiction over the respondent or defendant notwithstanding

the fact that he or she no longer is a resident or domiciliary of this state, or over his or her executor or administrator, if the party seeking support is a resident of or domiciled in this state at the time such demand is made, provided that this state was the matrimonial domicile of the parties before their separation, or the defendant abandoned the plaintiff in this state, or the obligation to pay support or alimony or alimony accrued under the laws of this state or under an agreement executed in this state.

States have different requirements for the exercise of their long-arm statute as indicated by the following survey by a New York court in Lieb v. Lieb, 53 A.D.2d 67, 385 N.Y.S.2d 569, 574 (1976):

California, by judicial interpretation of its statute, requires that the marital domicile must have been in California at the time the defendant left the plaintiff . . . Idaho and Illinois require the maintenance within the State of a matrimonial domicile at the time of the commission of any act which gives rise to the cause of action for divorce or separate maintenance. Kansas requires the parties to have been living in a marital relationship within the State as to all obligations arising from alimony, child support or property settlement, plus the added proviso that the other party to the marital relationship "*continues* to reside in this state" (emphasis supplied). Oklahoma requires that the defendant be shown to be "maintaining any other relation to this state or to persons or property including support for minor children, who are residents of this state which affords a basis for the exercise of personal jurisdiction by this state consistently with the Constitution of the United States." The Supreme Court of Oklahoma, in Hines v. Clendenning, 465 P.2d 460, ruled that its statute justified the court's taking personal jurisdiction of a nondomiciliary defendant husband who had abandoned the plaintiff wife, whom he had married in Oklahoma, with whom he had twice resided in Oklahoma under circumstances strongly indicating domicile, who had attended college in Oklahoma and had obtained a license to practice medicine there, had registered to vote and did vote there, and who sent his wife back to Oklahoma, her home State and the home of her parents, and who refused to permit her to return to him in California.

Wisconsin, the State which established the least restrictive test, requires not merely that the defendant have resided in the State in marital relationship with the plaintiff, but also that the marital residence within the State have lasted not less than six consecutive months within the six years next preceding the commencement of the action.

EXAMPLES (not involving the long-arm statute):

1. Tom and Mary are married. Both are domiciled in Massachusetts. Mary moves to Ohio which is now her state of domicile. She obtains a divorce decree from an Ohio state court. Tom is notified of the action by mail but does not appear. The decree awards Mary $500-a-month alimony. Mary travels to Massachusetts and brings an action against Tom to enforce the alimony award of the Ohio court.

JURISDICTIONAL ANALYSIS

—The Ohio court had jurisdiction to dissolve the marriage because of the domicile of Mary in Ohio. This part of the divorce decree is entitled to full faith and credit in Massachusetts, i. e., Massachusetts *must* recognize this aspect of the Ohio divorce decree if Massachusetts determines that Mary was in fact domiciled in Ohio at the time of the divorce decree.

—The Ohio court did not have jurisdiction to render an alimony award since it did not have personal jurisdiction over Tom. This part of the divorce decree is not entitled to full faith and credit in Massachusetts, i. e., the Massachusetts court does not have to enforce the Ohio alimony award.

—Suppose that Tom had procured the out-of-state divorce in a state where he was domiciled. Suppose further, that the divorce decree provided that Mary was not entitled to alimony. If this court did not have personal jurisdiction over Mary, she would not be bound by the no-alimony decision even though she would be bound by the decision dissolving the marriage.

---

2. Bill and Pat are married in New Jersey. Bill brings a divorce action against Pat in a New Jersey state court. Bill is awarded the divorce. Pat was not served with process or notified in any way of this divorce action. Bill then marries Linda. Linda and Bill begin having marital difficulties. They separate. Linda brings a support action (separate maintenance action) against Bill. Bill's defense is that he is not married to Linda because his divorce with Pat was invalid due to the fact that Pat had no notice of the divorce.

JURISDICTIONAL ANALYSIS

—Bill is bringing a collateral attack against the divorce decree. He is attacking the jurisdiction of the court to award the divorce because Pat had no notice of the divorce action.

—Bill is the person who obtained the divorce decree and in most states he will be estopped from attacking the decree on jurisdictional grounds. This is so whether or not the court in fact had jurisdiction to render the divorce decree. Bill will not be allowed to challenge it. He relied on the divorce when he married Linda. He took the benefits of the divorce when he decided to marry Linda. He should not be allowed to undo it all now by attacking the very thing he tried to accomplish.

---

3. Joe and Helen are married in Texas. Helen goes to New Mexico and obtains a divorce decree against Joe. Joe knew about the action but did not appear. Helen was never domiciled in New Mexico. Joe marries Paulene. Helen dies. Joe wants to claim part of Helen's estate as her surviving husband. His position is that he is still married to Helen because the New Mexico court had no jurisdiction to divorce Helen and him since neither of them were ever domiciled in New Mexico.

JURISDICTIONAL ANALYSIS

—Joe was not the party who sought the New Mexico divorce. The divorce proceeding was ex parte. Normally, he would be allowed to attack the divorce decree on the ground that no one was domiciled in New Mexico at the time of the divorce.

—Since Joe relied upon the divorce, however, and accepted its benefits by marrying Paulene, it would be inconsistent to allow him to change his mind now and it could be unfair to Paulene. Hence, Joe will be estopped from attacking the divorce on jurisdictional grounds.

Assignment # 85

John and Sandra are married in Georgia. John goes to Nevada and obtains a divorce decree against Sandra. Assume that the decree is subject to jurisdictional attack because there was no domicile in Nevada. The decree awards Sandra alimony. John marries Irene. Irene later brings a support (separate maintenance) action against John. His defense is he has no duty to support Irene since he is still married to Sandra because the Nevada court had no jurisdiction to divorce him and Sandra. What result? John falls behind in his alimony payments to Sandra. She sues him for the arrears. Does he have a defense? (See also General Instructions for the Legal Analysis Assignment, supra p. 16.)

In the remaining assignments of this section on divorce jurisdiction, we focus on the mechanics of jurisdiction. Specifically, what courts have subject-matter jurisdiction over divorce, what are the residency requirements and service of process rules for your state?

Most states require that the plaintiff have been a resident of the forum state for a designated period of time before a divorce can be granted, e. g., six weeks, a year. In a few states, it is sufficient that the defendant is a resident even if the plaintiff is not. While the word "residence" is frequently used in the state statutes, the meaning intended by most of the statutes is domicile: one's permanent home at which one intends to stay indefinitely.[14] As we saw in the preceding pages, for a court to have jurisdiction to divorce a couple, domicile must exist. The statutes on residency (domicile) state the length of time during which there must be residence (domicile) in the state.

Assignment # 86

What court has subject-matter jurisdiction over divorces in your state? If more than one court can dissolve marriages, identify each court with this power. Write your answer in Step 1 of the Divorce Litigation Flow Chart, infra p. 398. (See also General Instructions for the State Code Assignment, supra p. 14, and for the Flow Chart Assignment, supra p. 33.)

Assignment # 87

(a) What is the residency requirement for a divorce action in your state? Write your answer in Step 2 of the Divorce Litigation Flow Chart, infra p. 398. (See also General Instructions for the State Code Assignment, supra p. 14, and for the Flow Chart Assignment, supra p. 33.)

(b) If your state code uses the word "residence" in its divorce statute, find a court opinion in your state that defines the word "residence." (See also General Instructions for the Court Opinion Assignment, supra p. 26.)

Assignment # 88

Answer the following questions by examining your statutory code. Your answers will also become part of the Divorce Litigation Flow Chart, infra p. 398. (See also General Instructions for the State Code Assignment, supra p. 14, and the Flow Chart Assignment, supra p. 33.)

(a) Who may serve process in your state? Write your answer in Step 3, infra p. 398.

(b) How is personal service made on an individual? Write your answer in Step 4, infra p. 398.

(c) In a divorce action, when can substituted service be used?

(d) How is substituted service made? Summarize your answer in Step 5, infra p. 398.

(e) How is proof of service made? Write your answer in Step 6, infra p. 399.

(f) Does your state have a long-arm statute? If so, when can it be used?

14. Supra p. 345.

SUPERIOR COURT OF THE DISTRICT OF COLUMBIA
FAMILY DIVISION
DOMESTIC RELATIONS BRANCH
451 Indiana Avenue, N.W., Washington, D.C. 20001

SUMMONS

TO:

Jacket Number: ....
.... : Plaintiff
vs.
.... :Defendant

You are hereby SUMMONED and required to file an answer to the complaint, which is herewith served upon you, at the office of the Clerk of this Court in Room 220, 451 Indiana Avenue, N.W., within twenty (20) days after service of this summons upon you, exclusive of the day of service, and to serve a copy of said answer upon the plaintiff's attorney, indicated below. If you fail to do so, action may be taken against you for the relief demanded in the complaint. It is recommended that you seek the advice of an attorney to assist you in this case.

PLAINTIFF'S ATTORNEY:

Name:	Address:

Witness, the Honorable Chief Judge of the Superior Court of the District of Columbia and seal of said Court.

Clerk of the Superior Court of the District of Columbia

SEAL

Date: .... By: ....
Deputy Clerk

FOR USE OF U.S. MARSHAL OR PROCESS SERVER

I hereby certify and return that I served the within Summons and Complaint upon

Name: ....

Address: ....

on the ...... day of ...., 19.... at ..... AM/PM

- ☐ Personally.
- ☐ Individual served is a person of suitable age and discretion then abiding in the defendant's usual place of abode.
- ☐ I further certify that defendant is not a resident of the District of Columbia.
- ☐ I hereby certify and return that after diligent investigation I am unable to serve the individual, company, corporation, etc., named above.

Dates of Endeavor and/or Remarks:	Time: AM/PM

OFFICE OF THE U.S. MARSHAL DISTRICT OF COLUMBIA By: .... Signature of Marshal Representative

PROCESS SERVER'S CERTIFICATION

I hereby certify that I am a competent person over eighteen years of age residing or maintaining a regular place of business in the District of Columbia with no interest in the subject matter of this suit nor am I party thereto and that I have served this SUMMONS and COMPLAINT as indicated above.

Signature of Process Server: .... Age: ......

Business Address: ....

Residence: ....

Subscribed and sworn to before me this ..... day of ...., 19....

....
Notary Public (Deputy Clerk)
District of Columbia

LEGAL RECORD COPY

[B7974]

SECTION D. MISCELLANEOUS PRE-TRIAL MATTERS

1. PROCTOR

In many states, a government official, sometimes called a proctor, is appointed to protect the interests of children, to watch for collusion [15] between the husband and wife and to play the general role of a party to the divorce litigation.

Assignment # 89

Is a government official appointed in divorce cases in your state? If so what is the function of this individual? Write your answer in Step 7, infra p. 399. (See also General Instructions for the State Code Assignment, supra p. 14, and for the Flow Chart Assignment, supra p. 33.)

2. GUARDIAN AD LITEM

If the husband or wife is a minor or if the defendant is insane [16] at the time of the divorce action, the court may require that the individual be represented by a guardian ad litem or conservator in order to insure that the interests of the individual are protected during the proceeding.

Assignment # 90

Under what circumstances can a guardian ad litem be appointed in a divorce action in your state? Write your answer in Step 8, infra p. 399. (See also General Instructions for the State Code Assignment, supra p. 14, and for the Flow Chart Assignment, supra p. 33.)

3. VENUE

Venue refers to the place of the trial.[17] Within a state, it may be that the divorce action could be brought in a number of different counties or districts. The choice of venue is the choice of one county or district among several where the trial could be held. The state's statutory code will usually specify the requirements for the selection of venue. The requirements often relate to the residence (usually meaning domicile) of the plaintiff or defendant.

Assignment # 91

In a divorce action in your state, how is venue determined? Write your answer in Step 9, infra p. 399. (See also General Instructions for the State Code Assignment, supra p. 14, and for the Flow Chart Assignment, supra p. 33.)

15. Supra p. 338.

16. Supra p. 336.

17. See also supra p. 231.

4. PLEADING

The complaint must contain a concise statement of the elements of the action including a statement that the parties are married, the basis of the court's jurisdiction, the grounds for the divorce, the relief sought, etc.[18] Affirmative defenses (i. e., a defense that raises new facts other than those raised by the plaintiff in the complaint) usually must be specifically pleaded in the defendant's answer. In most states, the defendant can counterclaim for divorce in his/her answer. This is so when the defendant is being sued for annulment [19] and legal separation [20] as well as for a divorce. (A counterclaim is a cause of action by the defendant against the plaintiff.)

SAMPLE COMPLAINTS
Chapter One, supra p. 20.
Appendix C, infra p. 499.

[B8806]

Assignment # 92

Answer the following questions on pleading after examining your state code and your court rules. (See also General Instructions for the State Code Assignment, supra p. 14, and for the Flow Chart Assignment, supra p. 33.)

(a) What must a complaint for divorce contain? Write your response in Step 10, infra p. 399.

(b) Must the complaint be subscribed and/or verified? If so, by whom? Write your response in Step 11, infra p. 399.

(c) Where is the complaint filed? Write your response in Step 12, infra p. 400.

(d) How many days does the defendant have to answer the complaint? Write your response in Step 13, infra p. 400.

(e) Where and how is the answer filed and served? Write your response in Step 14, infra p. 400.

(f) Must the defendant specifically plead affirmative defenses in the answer? Write your response in Step 15, infra p. 400.

(g) Must the defendant's answer be subscribed and/or verified? If so, by whom? Write your response in Step 16, infra p. 400.

18. See also supra p. 20.

19. Supra p. 171.

20. Infra p. 405.

(h) How many days does the plaintiff have to reply to the defendant's counterclaim? Write your response in Step 17, infra p. 400.

(i) Where and how is the plaintiff's reply filed and served? Write your response in Step 18, infra p. 401.

5. WAITING PERIOD

In many states, there is a compulsory waiting period (e. g., for 60 days) that usually begins to run from the time the divorce complaint is filed. During this period of time, no further proceedings are held in the hope that tempers might calm down, producing an atmosphere of reconciliation. In a few states, the parties *must* attempt marital counseling.

Assignment # 93

Answer the following questions after examining your statutory code and your court rules. (See also General Instructions for the State Code Assignment, supra, p. 14, and for the Flow Chart Assignment, supra p. 33.)

(a) Is there a waiting period in your state? If so, how long is it and when does it begin to run? Write your answer in Step 19, infra p. 401.

(b) Is marital counseling compulsory in your state? Write your answer in Step 20, infra p. 401.

SECTION E. DISCOVERY

Discovery refers to a series of devices designed to assist the parties to prepare for trial. The standard devices are as follows:

Interrogatories: [21]

A series of written questions to be answered in writing on matters relevant to the litigation. For example, when the plaintiff is the wife who needs to have alimony, she might send interrogatories to her defendant-husband concerning his assets.

Deposition

A deposition is an in-person, question-and-answer session outside the court room, e. g., in one of the attorney's offices. Some states have limitations on the use of depositions at trial in divorce cases.

Request for Admissions

If a party believes that there will be no dispute over a certain fact at trial, s/he can request that the other party admit

21. Supra p. 31.

(or stipulate) the fact so that the expense and delay of having to prove the fact at trial can be avoided. The other party, of course, need not make the admission if s/he feels that there is some dispute over the fact.

Mental and Physical Examination

If the mental or physical condition of a party is relevant to the litigation, many courts can order a person to undergo an examination. If paternity, for example, is at issue, the court might order the husband to undergo a blood-grouping test.[22]

No discovery devise can be a substitute for a trial, or at least a hearing, in a divorce case. If, for example, the defendant admits the existence of the grounds for divorce in an answer to an interrogatory or during a deposition, the plaintiff cannot simply submit the answer or a transcript of the deposition to the court and ask for the divorce without the need for any hearing whatsoever. In most states, the plaintiff must make an appearance in court and prove that the grounds for divorce exist even if the defendant does not appear. While the plaintiff's appearance may be rather perfunctory, a default judgment[23] in the traditional sense (automatic judgment for plaintiff when the defendant fails to appear), is usually not possible in divorce actions.

Assignment # 94

Answer the following questions after examining your statutory code and your court rules. (See also General Instructions for the State Code Assignment, supra p. 14, and for the Flow Chart Assignment, supra p. 33.)

(a) When must a deposition be requested? How must the request be made? Write your response in Step 21, infra p. 401.

(b) Are there any restrictions on the use of depositions in divorce actions? Write your response in Step 22, infra p. 401.

(c) When and on whom can interrogatories be filed? Write your response in Step 23, infra p. 401.

(d) When must interrogatories be answered? Write your response in Step 24, infra p. 402.

(e) When can a request for admissions be made? Write your response in Step 25, infra p. 402.

(f) When will a court order a physical or mental examination? Write your response in Step 26, infra p. 402.

22. Infra p. 454.

23. Supra p. 322.

(g) What sanctions can be imposed if a party improperly refuses to comply with valid discovery requests? Summarize your response in Step 27, infra p. 402.

Assignment # 95

Assume that you work for the law firm that is representing the wife in a divorce action against her husband. You are asked to draft a set of interrogatories to be sent to the husband in which you attempt to find out as much information as possible relevant to his personal finances. The firm wants to use this information in its representation of the wife on the alimony and property division issues. Draft the interrogatories. (See also General Instructions for the Interrogatories Assignment, supra p. 31.)

SECTION F. PRELIMINARY ORDERS

Obtaining a divorce can be a time consuming undertaking even where the matter is uncontested. The court's calendar may be so crowded that it may take months to have the case heard. If the case is contested and some bitterness between the parties remain, the litigation can be seemingly endless. While the litigation is going on (or to use the latin phrase, *pendente lite*), the court may be asked to make a number of *preliminary* rulings:

—granting custody of the children;

—granting a child support order;

—granting alimony;

—granting attorney's fees and related court costs in the divorce action;

—enjoining (preventing) the husband from molesting the wife and children;

—enjoining the husband from transferring any of his property which might make it unavailable for the support of the wife and children;

—enjoining the defendant from leaving the state;

—etc

Assignment # 96

In a divorce action in your state, what preliminary orders can be granted by the court pendente lite? Summarize your response in Step 28, infra p. 402. (See also General Instructions for the State Code Assignment, supra p. 14, and for the Flow Chart Assignment, supra p. 33.)

Temporary alimony, attorney's fees and other litigation costs (e. g., filing fees) can be granted to the wife whether she is the plaintiff or the defendant in the divorce proceeding. The major factors are her need for this assistance and her husband's financial ability to provide it.[24] After the trial court renders its decision grant-

24. Infra p. 369.

ing or denying the divorce, states differ on whether or not the husband must continue to pay temporary alimony and attorney's fees while the trial court's decision is being appealed.

SUPERIOR COURT OF THE DISTRICT OF COLUMBIA
FAMILY DIVISION
DOMESTIC RELATIONS BRANCH

-- *Plaintiff*

v. Jacket No. ----------------------

-- *Defendant*

MOTION AND AFFIDAVIT

NOTE:
FINANCIAL STATEMENT REQUIRED
FILL OUT AND ATTACH HERETO.

For ☐ TEMPORARY ALIMONY, MAINTENANCE OR SUPPORT
☐ CUSTODY OF MINOR CHILDREN

Now comes ☐ Plaintiff ☐ Defendant and moves the Court that -- (name)

be required to pay such amount as seems just and reasonable for the support and maintenance of the ☐ Plaintiff ☐ Defendant (and ------ minor children) pending the final disposition of this cause (and to award ☐ her ☐ him the temporary custody of said minor children). Note: *Strike out portions of the preceding that do not apply.*

The following facts are submitted in support of the above motion:

1. Marriage:	Date:	Place:	2. Are you agreeable to a reconciliation: ☐ Yes ☐ No

3. Children by this marriage:		Living with			Amounts Contributed to family
Name	Age	Name	Address	Relation	

4. WIFE			5. HUSBAND		
Age:	Married before: ☐ Yes—How terminated? ☐ No		Age:	Married before: ☐ Yes—How terminated? ☐ No	
Occupation:	Employer:		Occupation:	Employer:	
Living with	Name:	Relation:	Living with	Name:	Relation:
	Address:			Address:	

6. Wife asks for support of self (and -------- minor children):	Amount: $ Per: ☐ Week ☐ Month	7. Husband willing to contribute as such support:	Amount: $ Per: ☐ Week ☐ Month
8. Husband's support to family:	Before Separation: $ After Separation: $	9. Previous divorce proceedings between parties. ☐ Yes ☐ No Alimony awarded: ☐ Yes ☐ No	
10. Juvenile Court proceedings: ☐ Yes ☐ No Explain:		11. Remarks	

DISTRICT OF COLUMBIA, ss:

________________, being first duly sworn, deposes and says that he/she has read the foregoing statement and subscribed to the same and that it is a true and correct statement of fact.

____
Plaintiff (Defendant)

Subscribed and sworn to before me this ________ day of ________________, 19___.

____
Notary Public, D.C.

My commission expires ________________

____
Attorney

____
Address

FORM DR-4/SEPT. 71 IM-484

SECTION G. TRIAL

Corroboration [25] is reinforcing evidence. Most of the plaintiff's evidence will probably be his/her oral testimony. In many states, this will not be enough in a divorce action. The plaintiff's testimony must be corroborated by evidence other than or in addition to his/her testimony. The same is usually true of the defendant's testimony: it too must be corroborated. If, for example, the defendant admitted that s/he deserted the plaintiff, this admission would have to be corroborated. Corroboration is one technique used by the courts to try to prevent collusion.[26]

Within the marriage there is a privilege for marital communications [27] meaning that one spouse cannot disclose in court any confidential communications that occurred between the spouses during the marriage. If this privilege were strictly applied in divorce actions, the results could be quite harsh. In an action by the wife for divorce on the ground of desertion, for example, the wife might not be able to testify that her husband said to her as he left the home, "I'm never coming back again." In most states, however, the privilege for marital communications is not applicable in divorce actions or in any action between a husband and wife. Its application is limited mainly to actions by third parties against a spouse where the third party attempts to introduce into evidence what one spouse may have said to the other.

States differ as to whether the questions of fact in a divorce trial can be tried by a jury. In some states, no juries are allowed; the entire case is tried by the judge.

Default judgments [28] are not automatic in most states when the defendant fails to appear to answer the complaint of the plaintiff. Again the fear is that the non-appearance by the defendant is due to collusion between the spouses who have both agreed to get the divorce and feel that the least troublesome way to do it is by the

25. Supra p. 318.

26. Supra p. 338.

27. Infra p. 447.

28. Supra p. 364.

defendant's staying away from the courtroom. A weak effort by the court to try to combat this is to refuse to grant automatic default judgments when the defendant does not appear. The plaintiff must appear and give at least some evidence to the court that grounds for divorce exist and that the court has jurisdiction to grant the divorce. The effort is weak because the plaintiff's evidence rarely is questioned by the court; the process is more ritual than substance.

Assignment # 97

Answer the following questions after examining your state code and court rules. (See also General Instructions for the State Code Assignment, supra p. 14, and for the Flow Chart Assignment, supra p. 33.)

(a) In a divorce action, what evidence, if any, must be corroborated? Write your response in Step 29, infra p. 402.

(b) In a divorce action, are there any limitations on testimony that one spouse can give against the other? Write your answer in Step 30, infra p. 403.

(c) Can there be a jury trial in a divorce case? If so, when must the request for one be made? Write your response in Step 31, infra p. 403.

(d) What happens if the defendant fails to appear? Can there be a default judgment? Write your response in Step 32, infra p. 403.

Assignment # 98

In your state, can one spouse use wiretap evidence against the other spouse at the divorce hearing, e. g., the wife taps her husband's phone and wants to introduce into evidence the conversation he had with his paramour. Check the code of your state as well as the federal code: the *United States Code* or the *United States Code Annotated.* (See also General Instructions for the State Code Assignment, supra p. 14.)

Assignment # 99

In this assignment, you are to go to a court hearing in your state on divorce. In Assignment # 86, supra p. 359 you are identified what court(s) in your state have the power to grant divorces. Attend a divorce hearing and answer the following questions on what you observe:

(a) What court was hearing the case?

(b) What was the name of the case?

(c) Were both sides represented by counsel?

(d) Were both parties present?

(e) What kind of evidence, if any, was introduced?

SECTION H. ALIMONY

Alimony [29] is often said to be a substitute for a man's obligation to support his wife. There are statutes in some states, however, that authorize alimony to be paid to the husband if he is in need and the wife has the means to provide it. The need for support and the means to provide it are not the only factors involved in making the alimony decision. As we shall see, in some states the presence or absence of marital fault is relevant to whether or not alimony is awarded. While the trend is toward the irrelevance of fault in the decision of whether or not the divorce should be granted, marital fault continues to play a role in the alimony decision in some areas of the country. The fear of the ex-husband is usually that his alimony payments will be used by his ex-wife to help support her live-in lover. He then tries to have those payments terminated or substantially reduced because of this alleged misconduct of his former wife. We will cover the modification of alimony awards in greater detail later.[30]

Alimony is usually awarded in the form of periodic payments. In some states, a lump sum payment is not allowed. When the parties draft their separation agreement, they may provide formulas for the payment of alimony, e. g., the payments increase or decrease as the husband's income fluctuates, and ask the court to incorporate their agreement into the divorce decree.[31] For income tax purposes, great care must be given to the form of the support provision. The tax code has precise definitions of what constitutes a "periodic payment" in order to determine whether the husband can deduct the alimony payments and whether the wife must pay income taxes on the alimony payments received.[32]

29. See also the discussion of support in the separation agreement, supra p. 269.

30. Infra p. 385.

31. Supra p. 283.

32. Infra p. 411.

CONSIDERATIONS OF THE COURT IN THE ALIMONY DECISION
1. *The Needs of the Wife* —Alimony should enable the wife to continue to live at substantially the same standard of living she enjoyed during the marriage. —Her needs may vary according to her age and health. —Some, but not all, courts will provide a lower alimony award, or none at all if she has independent income and property sufficient for her needs. —A few courts consider her present employability, although many courts say that she does not have to go out and obtain work as a condition of her being able to receive alimony. —Some courts grant "rehabilitative alimony" which is alimony for a limited period until the wife can "get back on her feet" to become self-sufficient. In most states, however, the alimony award is granted for an indefinite period until modified by court order.
2. *The Ability of the Husband to Pay* —Present income. —Future earnings. —Property other than cash. —His own standard of living. —His age and health. —Present debts and other financial responsibilities. —Anticipated debts and other financial responsibilities.
3. *Marital Fault* —In most states, marital fault of the wife will not disqualify her from receiving alimony, although it will be taken into consideration in determining the amount of the alimony award. —In some states, only if the wife was granted the divorce will she be entitled to alimony. If the husband was granted the divorce and she was found at fault, she would not receive any alimony in such states. —In some states, if the husband is found at fault, his alimony obligation may be increased.

[B8807]

Assignment # 100

Answer the following questions after examining your state code. (See also General Instructions for the State Code Assignment, supra p. 14.)

(a) What standards will a court use in awarding alimony, e. g., is marital fault relevant?

(b) When, if ever, can alimony be awarded to a man?

(c) Are there any limitations on the form that alimony can take, e. g., periodic payments, lump sum, etc.

(d) When alimony is awarded, is it always for an indefinite period?

(e) If the court denies the divorce to both parties, can alimony still be awarded?

Assignment # 101

Find an opinion from a court in your state which awarded alimony. List all the considerations that the court used in making its alimony decision. Try to find an opinion in which the court mentioned a specific dollar amount as alimony. If you cannot find such an opinion written by a court sitting in your state, select a neighboring state. (See also General Instructions for the Court Opinion Assignment, supra p. 26.)

SECTION I. PROPERTY DIVISION

As pointed out in the chapter on separation agreements, for tax, bankruptcy and other reasons, it is extremely important to distinguish between (a) alimony and (b) property division or property settlement.[33] Alimony is a substitute for the obligation (usually of the husband) to support one's spouse. Property division is the fair distribution of the property accumulated by the spouses during the marriage due to their joint efforts. The factors considered by the court in dividing the property are:

—the terms of a separation agreement in which the parties conclude what a fair distribution would be;

—whether the property was inherited by one of the parties;

—whether the property was acquired by joint earnings;

—the extent to which the wife's being at home taking care of the house and children enabled the husband to earn a living outside the home.

In spite of the importance of keeping alimony separate from property division, the fact is that the parties *and the courts* often blur the distinction with the result that it is sometimes impossible to determine what is alimony and what is part of the property settlement. The distinction cannot always be made on the basis of form alone. While alimony payments, for example, are usually periodic and property divisions usually are paid in lump sums and/or in the form of property other than cash, the reverse is also possible, i. e., alimony might be paid in a lump sum and/or in the form of property other than cash.

The following court opinion illustrates the difficulties that can occur in distinguishing a property settlement from alimony.

33. Supra p. 265.

JONES v. FLASTED

Supreme Court of Montana, 1976.
— Mont. —, 544 P.2d 1231.

DALY, Justice.

This is an appeal from a judgment of the district court, Carter County, sitting without a jury, construing the terms of a divorce agreement entitled "PROPERTY SETTLEMENT", the terms of which were incorporated in the decree of divorce.

On September 27, 1960, Esther Flasted and Merle Flasted were divorced. In that decree the district court found that Merle and Esther had entered into a written property settlement. The court decreed:

> ". . . that the Court adopts the property settlement agreement and that the plaintiff [Esther] is allowed the sum of $250.00 a month for her support commencing September 1, 1960, as alimony . . . ."

The remaining portion of the decree merely reiterated the terms of the agreement.

Inasmuch as the wording of that agreement is the basis for the action now under consideration, we set forth the agreement in full:

> "PROPERTY SETTLEMENT
>
> "This agreement between Esther Flasted and Merle Flasted:
>
> "WITNESSETH:
>
> "As a property settlement the Defendant agrees to pay to the Plaintiff the sum of $250.00 a month commencing September 1, 1960, for a term of 20 years as alimony, regardless of the statutes and whether she remarries or the Defendant's death, with the first three (3) years of the monthly payments payable in advance forthwith in the lump sum of $9,000. In addition, the Plaintiff is to receive one half of all income from any oil or mineral leases including royalty, bonus, and rentals from real estate standing of record in the defendant's name.
>
> "In addition, IT IS FURTHER AGREED that the defendant shall deliver to the Plaintiff the possession, on or before October 10, 1960, certain personal property belonging to the Plaintiff consisting of: Dishes, Silverware, Linens, Television set, and bric-a-brac, choice of any bed and chair. After the lump sum payment the $250.00 a month payments to commence October 1, 1963 and on the first day of each month thereafter, and
>
> "IT IS FURTHER AGREED that the payments herein provided shall be a lien upon any real estate of record in the name of the Defendant."

Merle, the husband, abided by the terms of the agreement up to the time Esther, the wife, died on April 23, 1971. Since then Merle has ceased making any installment or periodic payments. Ella Jones, sister of Esther Flasted, was appointed administratrix of Esther's estate. Ella commenced this action claiming the estate was entitled to receive Esther's interest under the above agreement.

The administratrix contends that the agreement: (1) conveys an undivided one-half ownership in all mineral rights held by the Flasteds at the time of the divorce in 1960; and (2) is a contract to give the divorced wife an amount equal to one-half of the value of the Flasted property at the time of the divorce and is therefore not terminable upon Esther's death but is now payable to Esther's estate.

Defendant Merle contends that the agreement was merely an agreement to provide support or alimony for his ex-wife and his obligations under the contract terminated when the object of the support became deceased.

After trial, the district court entered these conclusions of law:

"I. That the alimony provision contained in the agreement is a contractual and integral part of the agreement arising from claims of the parties at the time of divorce, and the same cannot be ignored or modified without the consent of the parties thereto.

"II. That the words, 'as alimony" were intended to cover the contingency of Esther Flasted's death, specific reference to that contingency having not otherwise been spelled out in the agreement.

"III. That the benefits conferred upon Esther Flasted by the agreement and decree of divorce were for her support until her death, or for a period of twenty years, whichever occurred first.

"IV. That the phrase 'regardless of statutes' is not inconsistent with the provision made by the parties and the divorce decree for support of Esther Flasted.

"V. While the agreement recites that it constitutes a 'property settlement,' the provisions contained therein refer only to matters concerning Esther Flasted's support. This same objective is also expressed in the complaint and decree filed in the divorce action. The Court concludes that the label 'property settlement' must yield to the expressions variously claimed and made for support of Esther Flasted.

"VI. That the provisions giving Esther Flasted one-half of the income from oil and mineral leases does not convey a fee title to minerals, but assigned only what the agreement provides, a one-half interest in the income, and that this was intended as additional support for Esther Flasted during her life time, but not to exceed twenty years.

"Now Therefore, It Is Hereby Adjudged and Decreed

"1. That the plaintiff take nothing by her complaint.

"2. That the defendant have his costs.

"3. That the interest of Esther Flasted of mineral income from defendant's property provided for in the annexed agreement terminated on her death and as of April 23, 1971.

"4. That the obligation of support of Merle K. Flasted toward Esther Flasted terminated on her death, April 23, 1971."

Plaintiff filed exceptions to the district court's findings of fact and conclusions of law. The exceptions were disallowed except for the correction of a minor error and plaintiff appealed to this Court from the final judgment.

The issue presented for review is whether the above quoted agreement passed permanent and continuing property rights to the ex-wife Esther or gave Esther only alimony rights terminating upon her death.

At the outset, we note in examining the agreement of the parties, the language of 17 Am.Jur.2d, Contracts, §§ 242, 245, pp. 627, 633:

> ". . . It must be construed and enforced according to the terms employed, and a court has no right to interpret the agreement as meaning something different from what the parties intended as expressed by the language they saw fit to employ. . . .
>
> ". . .
>
> ". . . the object to be attained in construing a contract is to ascertain the meaning and intent of the parties as expressed in the language used and to give effect to such intent if it does not conflict with any rule of law, good morals, or public policy."

In regard to the oil leases the administratrix contends that exhibits and testimony before the district court showing that Esther signed at least three oil and gas leases and the fact that she had received rentals on these leases points to a conclusion that Merle and Esther by their conduct interpreted the agreement as conveying an undivided one-half interest in the mineral rights.

Merle's testimony on this point is to the effect that Esther "didn't have to sign them. There was a lot of them she didn't sign." It was never shown that Esther signed *all* leases. The fact that Esther received rents from the leases indicates nothing more than that the terms of the agreement were being abided by—it indicates no proof of ownership.

In any case, this is not sufficient to transfer the claimed interest to the divorced wife. In Hochsprung v. Stevenson, 82 Mont. 222, 234, 266 P. 406, 408, this Court observed:

> "It is as a general rule necessary that a deed contain operative words of grant . . .; that a deed without words of convey-

ance passes no title . . .; and that, if an instrument has no words of conveyance, the courts have no right to put them in by interpretation . . .. The intention of the grantor in a deed is to be gathered from a consideration of the entire instrument, taking into consideration all of its provisions, and every part must be given effect if reasonably practicable and consistent with its evident purpose and operation, 'not, indeed as it is presented in particular sentences or paragraphs, but according to its effect when viewed as an entirety.' R. M. Cobban Realty Co. v. Donlan, 51 Mont. 58, 149 P. 484 . . . ."

Taking this agreement by its four corners, we do not find either words or meaning evidencing an intent to convey an undivided one-half interest in mineral rights. Rather, the language is clear and unambiguous—the ex-wife was to receive one-half the income from the mineral rentals for her support and not to exceed 20 years.

The administratrix further contends that (1) the title of the agreement, i. e., "PROPERTY SETTLEMENT", (2) the phrase "as a property settlement" in the first sentence, (3) the phrase "regardless of the statutes or whether she remarries or the defendant's death", and (4) the fact that the payments total $60,000 over a 20 year period ($60,000 allegedly being one-half the value of the Flasted property at the time of the divorce) all taken together lead to the conclusion that the agreement is a division of property, a property settlement, and not merely an agreement for support.

There is a distinction between a property settlement on the one hand, and a contract to pay stated sums periodically in lieu of alimony on the other hand. This Court stated in Stefonick v. Stefonick, 118 Mont. 486, 501, 167 P.2d 848, 855:

> "It is well settled that in this jurisdiction alimony is in no way a property settlement, but is the provision made for the support of the wife. . . ."

This is true whether the alimony award is made payable in installments or in a lump sum. Alimony payable in installments is preferred under Montana case law. . . .

On the other hand, a property settlement settles property rights and may or may not mention the additional item of alimony. In 24 Am.Jur.2d, Divorce and Separation, § 883, p. 1003, it is stated:

> " . . . Commonly, such a settlement (1) determines the rights of the parties in jointly owned property and states the disposition to be made of it; (2) settles all claims of each spouse in the property of the other and claims of each spouse to title to property held in the name of the other; (3) mutually releases all past and present claims except as established by the agreement; (4) waives and releases all future rights as spouse in the property of each other; (5) surrenders the rights of each on the death of the other, including rights of inheritance, homestead, dower, and the right to administer the estate of the other and to have exemptions

and allowances from the estate; and (6) agrees that each will execute all documents necessary or desirable to carry out the purposes of the agreement."

The administratrix cites Washington v. Washington, 162 Mont. 349, 512 P.2d 1300, as a "case practically on all fours with the instant case." We do not agree. The six elements commonly found in a property settlement agreement [24 Am.Jur.2d, Divorce and Separation, § 883, p. 1003] are all in *Washington.*

In contrast the "PROPERTY SETTLEMENT" agreement here involved satisfies none of the six named elements. Except for the disposition of certain minor personal property, there is no mention of the parties' rights in the ranch, livestock, house, debts, etc. Notwithstanding the agreement's title, and notwithstanding the administratrix's other contentions, this agreement—by its own language—does not transfer any property rights. It is purely and simply a contract to provide support for the ex-wife, the support to continue for 20 years if she should live that long. The contract therefore, by its very nature, is personal to the ex-wife and must terminate upon her death.

The judgment of the district court is affirmed.

Assignment # 102

(a) What guidelines will a court use in your state to make its property division decision?

(b) How will a court in your state divide a joint bank account containing commingled funds of the spouses?

(c) How, if at all, will a court divide a husband's pension rights if he is still employed?

(d) Find a court opinion in your state that distinguishes property division from alimony. What was the basis of the court's decision? (If you cannot find such an opinion in your state, try a neighboring state.)

(See also General Instructions for the State Code Assignment, supra p. 14, and for the Court Opinion Assignment, supra p. 26.)

SECTION J. CHILD CUSTODY

The primary concern of the court in awarding custody is the welfare of the child. The courts will give careful consideration to how the parents wish to handle the custody question as reflected in the separation agreement,[34] but will not hesitate to disregard what the parents want if it is in the "best interests" of the child to do so. It may even be possible for the divorce court to bypass both natural parents and award custody to a third party, e. g., relative.

34. Supra p. 276.

The general practice is to award custody to one of the parents—with fairly generous visitation rights to the other parent. A lot of the details, e. g., who gets the child at Christmas vacation, is the non-custody parent entitled to be consulted on major decisions affecting the child's welfare, etc., are usually worked out in the separation agreement and presented to the court for approval and/or incorporation and merger into the divorce decree.[35] While it is possible for the court to order that the custody of the child be shared by both parents, joint custody is often frowned upon as too disruptive of the child's life. Equally disruptive would be efforts of one parent to alienate the affections of the child against the other parent and courts are anxious to do whatever possible in designing the custody-visitation arrangement to minimize this.

In Wisconsin, some judges make use of the following guidelines: [36]

RELATION TOWARD CHILDREN

Although the Court does have the power to dissolve the bonds of matrimony, the Court does not have the power to dissolve the bonds that exist between you as parents and your children. Both of you, therefore, are to continue your responsibility to emotionally support your children. You are to cooperate in the duty and right of each other to love those children. By love, the Court means the training, the education, the disciplining and motivation of those children. Cooperation means to present the other party to the children with an attitude of respect either for the mother or for the father. Neither of you should in any way downplay, belittle or criticize the other in the presence of those children; because you may emotionally damage your children and/or you may develop a disappointment or hatred in the minds of those children for the party that attempts to belittle or demean the other in the presence of those children. It is of utmost importance you both recognize your children's right to love both parents without fear of being disloyal to either one of you.

In support of this admonition, the Courts have drafted written guidelines on your future conduct relating to the best interest of your children. I sincerely urge that you preserve them, periodically read them and always be guided by them.

GUIDELINES FOR SEPARATED PARENTS

As you know, your children are usually the losers when their parents separate. They are deprived of full-time, proper guidance that two parents can give—guidance and direction essential to their moral and spiritual growth.

It is highly desirable that you abstain from making unkind remarks about each other. Recognize that such remarks are not about

35. Supra p. 276.

36. 1 Family Law Reporter 3029 (No. 15, February 25, 1975).

a former spouse but are about a parent of your children. Such comments reflect adversely upon the children.

It is urged that both parties cooperate to the end that mutual decisions concerning the interest of the children can be made objectively. Parents should remember that the mother who has custody should urge the children to find time to be with the father and encourage them to realize that their father has affection for them and contributes to their support. The father should recognize that his plans for visitation must be adjusted from time to time in order to accommodate the planned activities of the child. Visitation should be a pleasant experience rather than a duty. Cooperation in giving notice and promptness in maintaining hours of visitation are important to avoid ruffled feelings.

Although there is probably some bitterness between you, it should not be inflicted upon your children. In every child's mind there must and should be an image of two good parents. Your future conduct with your children will be helpful to them if you will follow these suggestions.

I. *Do Not's*

A. Do not poison your child's mind against either the mother or father by discussing their shortcomings.

B. Do not use your visitation as an excuse to continue arguments with your spouse.

C. Do not visit your children if you have been drinking.

II. *Do's*

A. Be discreet when you expose your children to any member of the opposite sex with whom you may be emotionally involved.

B. Visit your children only at reasonable hours.

C. Notify your spouse as soon as possible if you are unable to keep your visitation. It's unfair to keep your children waiting—and worse to disappoint them by not coming at all.

D. Make your visitation as pleasant as possible for your children by not questioning them regarding the activities of your spouse and by not making extravagant promises which you know you cannot or will not keep.

E. Minimize the amount of time the children are in the care of strangers or relatives.

F. Always work for the spiritual well-being, health, happiness and safety of your children.

III. *General*

A. The parent with whom the children live must prepare them both physically and mentally for the visitation. The children should be available at the time mutually agreed upon.

B. If one parent has plans for the children that conflict with the visitation and these plans are in the best interests of the children, be adults and work out the problem together.

C. Arrangements should be made through visitation to provide the mother with some time "away" from the family. She needs the time for relaxation and recreation. Upon her return, she will be refreshed and better prepared to resume her role as mother and head of the household. Therefore, provide for extended periods of visitation such as weekends and vacations.

BILL OF RIGHTS FOR CHILDREN IN DIVORCE ACTION

1. The right to be treated as important human beings, with unique feelings, ideas and desires and not as a source of argument between parents.

2. The right to a continuing relationship with both parents and the freedom to receive love from and express love for both.

3. The right to express love and affection for each parent without having to stifle that love because of fear of disapproval by the other parent.

4. The right to know that their parents' decision to divorce is not their responsibility and that they will live with one parent and will visit the other parent.

5. The right to continuing care and guidance from both parents.

6. The right to honest answers to questions about the changing family relationships.

7. The right to know and appreciate what is good in each parent without one parent degrading the other.

8. The right to have a relaxed, secure relationship with both parents without being placed in a position to manipulate one parent against the other.

9. The right to have the custodial parent not undermine visitation by suggesting tempting alternatives or by threatening to withhold visitation as a punishment for the children's wrongdoing.

10. The right to be able to experience regular and consistent visitation and the right to know the reason for a cancelled visit.

Written by: Dane County Family Court Counseling Service Staff, City-County Building, Madison, Wisconsin 53709.

October, 1974

CONSIDERATIONS OF THE COURT IN MAKING THE CHILD CUSTODY DECISION
1. *The Court's Own Discretion* —The custody decision is one of the most difficult that a court has to make. There are few, if any, formulas that will work in every situation. Because the judge has so much discretion in deciding where the child should go, the judge's own philosophy of the family, child rearing, etc. will have a lot to do with how that judge views the "best interests of the child."
2. *Where the Child has been Living up to Now* —It may make a great deal of difference if one of the parents has not seen the child for a long period of time or has abandoned the household. The court will tend to look with disfavor on a parent whose interest in the child is fairly recent.
3. *Legal Preferences* —In most states, neither parent is deemed to be better suited to have custody than the other. Some fathers have complained, however, that this norm is not observed in fact. In their view, courts have a bias in favor of mothers. —Some courts feel that very young children of either sex should be with their mother (this is referred to as the "tender years" presumption) but that a boy of some maturity should be with his father.
4. *Who is Seeking Custody* —It may be one thing if the two parents are seeking custody and quite another if a third party (e. g., a relative who has been caring for the child) and one of the parents are fighting for custody. As between a parent and a third party, most courts say that the parent has the right to custody unless that parent is proven to be unfit. A few states, however, say the only issue is the welfare of the child irrespective of anyone's rights to that child.[37]
5. *The Wishes of the Parties* —Most separation agreements contain clauses on which parent should have custody. As indicated, courts will respect such clauses only if they feel that the parties' wishes are in the best interest of the child. Courts will be anxious to know about these clauses dealing with custody, visitation rights, child support, etc. as some indication of how the parties feel about the children.
6. *The Life Style of the Parties* —A court will be concerned with the living arrangements of the child: what would home life be like if the child went to live with either parent? —What other adult or adults, if any, would be living with the

37. See Clark, H., *The Law of Domestic Relations*, p. 592 (1968), and Weinman, "The Trial Judge Awards Custody," 10 *Law and Contemporary Problems* 721 (1944).

parent awarded custody? Some courts would frown on the parent having an open sexual relationship. In most courts, homosexuality would automatically render a parent unfit.

—In some states, if the divorce was granted on the ground of adultery, the adulterer, by definition would be deemed unfit for custody.

7. *The Wishes of the Child*

—If the child is mature enough to express an unpressured preference, a court will be anxious to consider what the preference is and how strongly it is held.

8. *Miscellaneous Factors*

—The age and health of each parent.

—Whether the parent with custody intends to remain in the state or move to another state (most courts would prefer that the child remain in the state subject to its jurisdiction unless it is clearly in the interests of the child to move to another state).

[B8808]

Assignment # 103

(a) What standards exist in your state code to guide the judge on the decision to grant custody? (See General Instructions for the State Code Assignment, supra p. 14.)

(b) Find an opinion written by a court in your state in which the court granted custody to one of the parents following a divorce or legal separation. State the factors that the court used in making this decision. Why did the judge decide not to give custody to the other parent? Do you agree with the judge's decision on the custody issue? Are there other facts that you would have liked to have known, but which were not provided in the opinion? Did the investigators for each side do a good job of gathering all the facts? If you cannot find a custody opinion written by a court in your state which will enable you to answer this question, try the court opinions of neighboring states. (See also General Instructions for the Court Opinion Assignment, supra p. 26.)

(c) Can a court in your state render a custody decision in a divorce action even though the court does not grant a divorce to either spouse? (See General Instructions for the State Code Assignment, supra p. 14, and for the Court Opinion Assignment, supra p. 26.)

NOTE ON THE "PSYCHOLOGICAL PARENT"

With the publication in 1973 of *Beyond the Best Interests of the Child* by Goldstein, Freud and Solnit, a good deal of discussion and controversy centered on the concept of the "psychological parent." The concept is particularly relevant when the controversy over who should obtain custody over the child involves a biological parent and a variety of other individuals who have actually cared for the child: an uncle, grandmother, foster parent, sister, neighbor, etc. As pointed out above, many courts will grant custody to the biological parent unless the latter has been found to be unfit, e. g., by abandoning the child. A painful question that a court must often face is what weight will it give to the fact that the child has lived with, has been cared for by, and has developed strong psychological bonds with someone else—the "psychological parent" who is not the biological parent. Suppose that such a "psychological parent" exists who is seeking custody of the child in opposition to a biological parent who has *not* been found to be unfit. Recently the United States Supreme Court made the following observation:

> We have little doubt that the Due Process Clause would be offended "[i]f a State were to attempt to force the breakup of a natural family, over the objections of the parents and their children, without some showing of unfitness and for the sole reason that to do so was thought to be in the children's best interest." Quilloin v. Walcott, —— U.S. ——, ——, 98 S.Ct. 549, 555, 54 L.Ed.2d 511, 520 (1978) quoting Smith v. Organization of Foster Families for Equality and Reform, 431 U.S. 816, 861–863, 97 S.Ct. 2094, 2119, 53 L.Ed.2d 14, 46–47 (1977) (Concurring opinion of Justice Stewart).

(On the factors that a court will take into consideration in determining whether a parent is unfit, see infra p. 469.) The above Supreme Court quote does not answer every question that can arise. Suppose, for example that the "natural family" has already broken up, that the biological parent has had little or intermittent contact with the child. If this parent has not been technically declared to be unfit, does it offend Due Process for a court to grant custody to someone else—the "psychological parent?" There are no clear answers to this question. As already indicated, the custody decision is one of the most agonizing for a court to make.

SECTION K. CHILD SUPPORT

In most states, it is the father's duty to support his children; the mother has a duty to support them if he does not do so. (Many feel that this is an unconstitutional discrimination based on sex.) In other states, the parents are equally liable for their support. In addition, it may be a crime for either parent to fail to support his/her children.

The parties usually draft a separation agreement in which they specify how much is to be paid for child support, when the support ends (e. g., on the death of the father, when the child reaches twenty-one), whether the father will carry life insurance with the children as beneficiaries, whether there will be regular support payments for everyday expenses and special support payments for large medical and educational expenses, whether the support payments continue while the child is away at college if the father is paying all college expenses, etc.[38] While the divorce court is not bound by these clauses in the separation agreement, it will give them considerable weight. Absent a commitment in the separation agreement to pay college expenses, the courts are not uniform in their decision as to whether the father must do so. Similarly, unless the father agrees otherwise, the child support obligation usually cannot be enforced against the father after the child is no longer a minor except where the adult child is disabled or otherwise incapable of caring for his/her own financial needs.

If the husband in the divorce action refuses to support a child because of his claim that he is not the father of the child, the question of paternity must be resolved since a father has no duty to support someone else's children. In the event that the wife's child is found to be illegitimate, but the child is not made a party to the divorce proceeding, the child will *not* be bound by this finding of illegitimacy; s/he can relitigate the paternity issue later. On the other hand, if in the divorce proceeding the husband is found to be the father of the child, he will not be able to bring an action later claiming that he is not the father.

Before a support order can be enforced against a father, the court must have personal jurisdiction [39] over him similar to the enforcement of alimony orders.[40] Quasi-in-rem jurisdiction, however, can be used to satisfy any support order but only to the extent of property in the state.[41]

Assignment # 104

(a) Is it a crime in your state for a parent to willfully fail to support his/her child?

(b) In a divorce action in your state, can a child support order be issued even if no divorce is granted?

(See General Instructions for the State Code Assignment, supra p. 14, and for the Court Opinion Assignment, supra p. 26.)

38. Supra p. 277.

39. Supra p. 352.

40. Supra p. 365 and infra p. 390.

41. Supra p. 352.

SECTION L. THE DIVORCE JUDGMENT

An interlocutory decree (or a *decree nisi*) is one which will not become final until the passage of a specified period of time. In some states, after the court has reached its decision to grant a divorce, an interlocutory decree of divorce will be issued. During the period that this decree is in force, the parties are still married. The divorce decree could be set aside if the parties reconcile or if the person who won the divorce action commits a marital wrong that would justify the loser to sue for divorce.

In many states, the parties may not remarry while the trial court's divorce judgment is being appealed. Finally, in a few states, even a final divorce judgment will not automatically enable a party to remarry. The court may have the power to prohibit one or both of the parties from remarrying for a period of time or forever.

Assignment # 105

Answer the following questions after examining your state code. (See also General Instructions for the State Code Assignment, supra p. 14, and for the Flow Chart Assignment, supra p. 33.)

(a) Is there an interlocutory decree or a decree nisi in your state? If so, how long is it effective and how does the divorce become final? Write your answer in Step 33, infra p. 403.

(b) After the divorce becomes final, can the court forbid either party to remarry?

(c) While the divorce decree is being appealed, can the parties remarry?

(d) To what court can the divorce decree be appealed? Write your answer in Step 34, infra p. 403.

(e) How many days does a party have to appeal? Write your answer in Step 35, infra p. 403.

(f) Where and how is the notice of appeal filed and served? Write your answer in Step 36, infra p. 404.

SECTION M. MODIFICATION OF DIVORCE DECREES

Attempts to modify a divorce decree occur mainly in three areas:

1. The alimony award,
2. The child support award,
3. The child custody award.

Rarely, if ever, is the property division portion of the divorce decree modifiable especially if it was based on the parties' separation agreement.[42]

42. Supra p. 269.

Before examining the topic of alimony modification, you should review the discussion of this topic in reference to separation agreements particularly concerning the incorporation/merger of such agreements in the divorce decree.[43]

1. MODIFICATION OF THE ALIMONY AWARD

After the divorce decree has become final, either party may try to go back into court to ask for a change in the alimony award: to increase it because the ex-wife needs more and the ex-husband can afford to pay more, or to reduce it because the ex-wife needs less and/or the ex-husband cannot afford to pay what he was originally ordered to pay. The authority of the court to modify an alimony award may be due to a statute which specifically provides this authority, or it may be due to the fact that the divorce court retained jurisdiction over the case in order to handle an eventuality such as the need for alimony modification. This assumes that there is something to modify. If the divorce decree dissolved the marriage, but refused to allow any alimony because neither party was entitled to it, it will not be possible to modify the divorce decree by *adding* alimony.

The central question is: since the time of the original alimony award, have circumstances so changed as to warrant a modification of the award? Some of the circumstances that could change are as follows:

a. The ex-husband becomes sick and earns substantially less.

   Most courts would modify the decree to lessen the amount he must pay—at least during the period when his earning capacity suffered during the illness.

b. The ex-husband suddenly starts earning a great deal more.

   The ex-wife will usually not be able to increase her alimony award simply because her ex-husband becomes more wealthy than he was at the time of the divorce decree.

c. The ex-wife is about to become destitute.

   Most courts would modify an alimony award if it becomes clear that it is totally inadequate, e. g., due to unexpected, substantial medical bills.

d. The ex-wife violates the terms of the separation agreement relating to the visitation rights of the ex-husband/father.

   Some courts feel that alimony payments and visitation rights are interdependent. If the ex-wife interferes with the father's visitation rights with the children, these courts will reduce or terminate her alimony. For such a result, however, the interference would have to be substantial.

e. The ex-wife engages in "immoral" conduct, e. g., has a live-in lover.

43. Supra p. 283.

When the ex-husband finds out about the lover, his concern is that his alimony payments are being used to support his ex-wife's lover. Most states will not reduce the alimony payments for this reason. In those states that do reduce it, the ex-wife's affair usually must be flagrant and on-going.

f. The ex-husband wants to retire, change jobs or go back to school.

When his income is reduced in this way, the courts will consider a downward modification of the alimony obligation only if the proposed change in life style is made in good faith and not simply as a way to avoid paying the original amount of alimony. A rich executive, for example, cannot "drop out" and become a poor farmer. Such an executive, however, may be able to take a lower paying job if this is required for his health.

g. The ex-husband remarries.

In most states, his alimony obligation to his first wife is not affected by his remarriage. There are a few states, however, that are sympathetic of his burden of supporting two families and will consider a reduction if it is clear that he cannot meet both obligations.

h. The ex-wife remarries.

If the ex-wife remarries, most courts will permit her first husband to petition the court to terminate his alimony obligation unless the parties agreed in the separation agreement that alimony would continue in some form after she remarried.[44]

i. The ex-husband dies.

Alimony usually ends on the death of the ex-husband unless the separation provides for its continuance,[45] and/or the divorce decree imposes this obligation on the ex-husband's estate.

NOTE

For a discussion of whether *accrued* (unpaid) alimony payments can be modified, see the next section.[46]

Assignment # 106

Find authority (e. g., a statute or a court opinion) in your state for the court's power to modify an alimony award. When will such a modification be made? (See also General Instructions for the State Code Assignment, supra p. 14, and the Court Opinion Assignment, supra p. 26.)

44. Supra p. 270.

45. Supra p. 279.

46. Infra p. 390.

Assignment # 107

Karen and Jim obtain a divorce which awards Karen $500 a month in alimony "until she dies or remarries." A year after the divorce decree becomes final, Karen marries Paul. Jim stops the alimony payments. A year later, this marriage to Paul is annulled.[47] Karen now wants Jim to resume paying her $500 a month alimony and to pay her $6,000 to cover the period when she was "married" to Paul ($500 x 12). What result? (See also General Instructions for the Legal Analysis Assignment, supra p. 16.)

2. MODIFICATION OF THE CHILD SUPPORT AWARD

Legal technicalities rarely are allowed to interfere with the court's power to modify child support orders. When the child's welfare is at stake, the court will go out of its way to be sure that the parents, particularly the father, respond.

If the financial needs of the child increase, e. g., due to medical or educational expenses, a court will order the father to increase the support payment *if the father is able to pay more.* It obviously makes no sense to order a father to make payments beyond his earning capacity. The real difficulty arises when the father remarries and has children by the second marriage. Is this a change in circumstances which would convince a court to reduce his payments for the support of the children of his first marriage? Usually not, although as indicated above, there are a few states that will consider a reduction on these facts. The remarriage of the mother is almost never a basis for modifying the child support payments downward unless the second husband adopts the children. The second husband cannot be forced to support the children fathered by someone else.

When the father dies, most courts take the position that they have no power to order the father's estate to continue making child support payments unless the father specifically agreed to do so in a separation agreement.[48]

If the child reaches majority, is emancipated,[49] e. g., through marriage, the father is almost always able to have the court terminate the child support payments unless the child, although an adult, is physically or mentally unable to earn his/her own living.

3. MODIFICATION OF THE CHILD CUSTODY AWARD

Generally speaking, child custody orders are easily modifiable if a court is convinced that it would be in the interests of the child's welfare to take custody away from the parent originally granted custody in the divorce action and to give it to someone else, usually

47. See supra p. 216.

48. Supra p. 276.

49. Infra p. 455.

the other parent. A change in circumstances that might warrant such action would be when the parent with custody has neglected the child, or when, because of health or financial reasons, that parent is no longer able to care for the child adequately.

Normally a court of one state will be reluctant to modify a judgment issued by a court in another state. The reluctance, however, is much less if the judgment is a child custody order. Since states are willing to modify the child custody arrangements ordered by other states, the rather bizarre practice of "child snatching" has become all too frequent. The sequence is as follows:

—in a divorce action in New Jersey, Mary is awarded custody of her daughter, much to the dissatisfaction of Fred, the father;

—while the child is in a playground, Fred drives up and "snatches" the child without ever telling Mary;

—Fred then takes the child from state to state looking for a court that would be willing to modify the New Jersey custody order on the basis of changed circumstances (Fred is engaged in what is called "forum shopping").

This obviously dangerous practice will be encouraged so long as states continue to be willing to modify custody orders. It is not an answer, however, to simply require all states to refrain from modifying custody orders of other states since there are circumstances when it *is* clearly in the best interests of the child to have the order modified. Some courts handle the problem by refusing to modify if the person seeking the modification has violated the custody order of the court that originally made the order, e. g., by taking the child out of state in direct violation of the original custody order. The National Conference of Commissioners on Uniform State Laws has proposed that each state adopt the Uniform Child Custody Jurisdiction Act and a number of states have done so. Not enough states have adopted it, however, to eliminate the problem caused by "the shifting of children from state to state with harmful effects on their well being." One of the objectives of the proposed Act is to "avoid relitigation of custody decisions of other states" by having the forum state "decline the exercise of jurisdiction when the child and his family have a closer connection with another state." Section 8(b) would provide:

> (b) Unless required in the interest of the child, the court shall not exercise its jurisdiction to modify a custody decree of another state if the petitioner, without consent of the person entitled to custody, has improperly removed the child from the physical custody of the person entitled to custody or has improperly retained the child after a visit or other temporary relinquishment of physical custody. If the petitioner has violated any other provision of a custody decree of another state

the court may decline to exercise its jurisdiction if this is just and proper under the circumstances.

Again, however, the problem is that only a handful of states have adopted this Uniform Child Custody Jurisdiction Act.

Sample affidavits in support of motions to modify custody decrees. See Appendix B, infra p. 493.

[B8805]

Assignment # 108

(a) When will a court in your state modify a child support award?

(b) When will a court in your state modify a child custody award when the child has not been removed from the state?

(You may have to check statutes and case law to answer the above questions. See General Instructions for the State Code Assignment, supra p. 14, and for the Court Opinion Assignment, supra p. 26.)

Assignment # 109

(a) Has your state adopted the Uniform Child Custody Jurisdiction Act? If so, what is the citation to the Act?

(b) Have any of the states that border on your state adopted this Act? If so, give the citations to the Act in each state that has adopted it.

(See also General Instructions for the State Code Assignment, supra p. 14.)

(c) If your state has not adopted the above Act, how does it handle the problem of "child snatching?"

SECTION N. ENFORCEMENT

What happens if the party ordered to pay alimony and child support payments (usually the ex-husband) fails to make these payments? What enforcement options can be brought against the delinquent party? The possibilities include:

- Civil contempt (jail until comply).
- Execution (an order to the sheriff to carry out the judgment, e. g., to sell the property of the delinquent party—called the judgment debtor—and turn the proceeds over to the party who has not been paid—called the judgment creditor).
- Garnishment (reaching moneys or other property of the judgment debtor that is in the hands of a third party, e. g., the employer or bank of the judgment debtor).
- Attachment (seizing one's property to bring it under the control of the court so that it can be used to satisfy a judgment).
- Posting Security (requiring the ex-husband to post a bond which is forfeited if he fails to meet his alimony or child support obligation).
- Receivership (a receiver might be appointed over all the ex-husband's property to prevent him from squandering it or otherwise making it unavailable to satisfy his alimony or child support obligation).
- Criminal non-support (in some states it is a crime to willfully fail to meet one's support obligation).

Perhaps the most potent enforcement mechanism is contempt:[50] putting the delinquent party in jail until he complies with the alimony and/or child support order. Inability to pay does not simply mean burdensome to pay or inconvenient to pay. Using all resources currently available or which could become available with reasonable effort, he must be unable to comply with the alimony or child support orders in whole or in part. If he is so unable, then he does not have to go to jail. When and if he becomes able, however, he must meet all past and future obligations.

50. Supra p. 268.

SUPREME COURT OF THE STATE OF NEW YORK

COUNTY OF ____________

____________, Plaintiff, –against– ____________, Defendant.	AFFIDAVIT IN SUPPORT OF MOTION TO PUNISH FOR CONTEMPT Index No. ______

STATE OF NEW YORK } ss.: ____________

COUNTY OF ____________

______, being duly sworn, deposes and says:

That I am the plaintiff in the above entitled action and make this application to punish the defendant for contempt of Court for willfully neglecting and refusing to comply with the Judgment of this Court dated ______, 19__, directing the defendant, among other things, to pay to the plaintiff the sum of ______ ($______) Dollars per week as alimony, plus the sum of ______ ($______) Dollars per week per child for the maintenance and support of the infant children ______, ______, and ______, for a total sum of ______ ($______) Dollars per week by check or money order at the residence of the plaintiff.

That hereto annexed is a copy of the Judgment of Divorce herein. That the defendant was duly personally served with a copy of said Judgment on the ______ day of ______, 19__.

That defendant has failed, neglected, and refused to pay me the amounts of money set forth in said Judgment of Divorce during the period commencing ______, 19__ to date.

That the above named defendant has willfully neglected and failed to comply with said Judgment of this Court and he is now in arrears in the sum of ______ ($______) Dollars, and no part of which has been paid although duly demanded. That the neglect and refusal of the above named defendant to comply with said Judgment of the Court was calculated to and did defeat, impair, impede, and prejudice the rights and remedies of the above named plaintiff.

That the arrears are computed as follows:

DATE	AMOUNT DUE	AMOUNT PAID	ARREARS
______	$______	$______	$______
______	$______	none	$______
______	$______	$______	$______
______	$______	none	$______
______	$______	none	$______
______	$______	$______	$______
______	$______	none	$______
______	$______	$______	$______
______	$______	none	$______
______	$______	$______	$______
______	$______	none	$______
		TOTAL ARREARS	$______

That total arrears are therefore due me in the sum of ______ ($______) Dollars.

That it is respectfully submitted that the defendant deliberately does this to defeat and prejudice the rights and remedies of myself and my infant children.

That defendant is employed as a school teacher with the same position that he held at the time of the trial on ______, 19__, which was only ______ months ago. His income is at least as much as he was earning then, if not more. The defendant is also engaged in private tutoring.

That no order of sequestration has been made herein for the reason that there is no property to sequestrate.

That no bond or security has been given for the payment of said alimony.

That your deponent has been unable to obtain steady employment and is in dire financial straits by reason of the defendant's willful refusal to comply with said Judgment of Divorce.

That no previous application for the relief herein prayed for has been made.

That the reason that an order to show cause herein is requested is that the same is required on an application of this matter by virtue of section 245 of the Domestic Relations Law.

WHEREFORE, an order to show cause is respectfully prayed requiring the defendant to show cause why he should not be punished for contempt for willfully disobeying the Judgment of this Court.

[*Signature*]

____

[*Type Name of Deponent*]

[B7635]

SOURCE: Marvins, J., *McKinney's Forms*, 13:131A (West Publishing Co. 1976).

The other major enforcement device is execution. Execution is usually possible only with respect to alimony and child support orders that are final and non-modifiable. There are two ways in which such orders can become *final* and *non-modifiable*:

—In some states, each unpaid alimony or child support installment automatically becomes a final and non-modifiable judgment as to which execution will be available.

—In other states, each unpaid alimony or child support installment does not become a final and non-modifiable judgment until the wife makes a specific application for a judgment and one is entered. Execution is available only after the judgment is so entered or docketed.

As we shall see below, this distinction is also relevant to the application of the Full Faith and Credit Clause.

Suppose that the delinquent ex-husband leaves the state. What options are available to the ex-wife? The Uniform Reciprocal Enforcement of Support Act may be available. Under the terms of this Act, the following sequence occurs:

—the ex-wife commences the action in her own state—the initiating state;

—the initiating state makes a determination of how much the ex-husband owes;

—the initiating state sends this determination to a court in the state where the husband is residing—the responding state;

—the prosecuting attorney in the responding state will represent the interests of the wife who does not have to appear in the responding state;

—the prosecuting attorney of the responding state shall take steps to acquire jurisdiction over the husband, e. g., by personal service of process in the responding state;

—after a hearing, the responding state can enter a judgment against the husband which can be enforced by contempt, execution or any other enforcement remedy available in the responding state.

Under the Full Faith and Credit Clause [51] of the United States Constitution, one state must give effect to the public acts, e. g., the court judgments, of another state. Assume the following facts:

> Phyllis obtains a divorce from Ralph in Ohio. Ralph falls behind in the alimony and child support payments he is obligated to make under the terms of the Ohio divorce judgment. Ralph then moves to Kentucky. Phyllis goes to Kentucky to bring a suit against Ralph to collect all unpaid installments.

The question is: can Kentucky re-litigate the alimony and child support issues, or most Kentucky give *full faith and credit* to the Ohio judgment by allowing Phyllis to sue on the Ohio judgment? The answer depends upon the status of the Ohio divorce judgment:

—Did the Ohio court have subject matter jurisdiction [52] over divorce actions?

—Did the Ohio court have personal jurisdiction [53] over Ralph?

51. Supra p. 351 and infra p. 396.

52. Supra p. 352.

53. Supra p. 352.

—In Ohio, would each unpaid installment (of alimony and child support) be considered a final and non-modifiable judgment?

If the answer to each of these questions is yes, then the Kentucky court *must* give full faith and credit to the Ohio judgment and permit Phyllis to enforce it against Ralph and not allow Ralph to re-litigate the alimony and child support obligation. Suppose, however, that no Ohio final judgment exists on unpaid installments until Phyllis makes specific application to an Ohio court for such a judgment and that at the time she brought her Kentucky action, she had not obtained such a judgment. Under these circumstances, a Kentucky court would not be *obliged*, under the Full Faith and Credit Clause, to force Ralph to make good all unpaid installments. Under the doctrine of *comity*, however, a state can decide to give full faith and credit to a foreign judgment even though it is not obliged to do so. To reduce the burden on a wife seeking back alimony and child support payments, a court might enforce a foreign judgment that it is not required to enforce.

Another example of the application of the comity doctrine involves foreign land decrees. Suppose that as part of the Ohio divorce decree, the Ohio court ordered Ralph to transfer title to land he owned in Kentucky to Phyllis. Phyllis then brings an action in Kentucky to force Ralph to convey his Kentucky land to her. As a general rule, the forum state (e. g. Kentucky) does not have to give full faith and credit to the judgment of a foreign state (e. g., Ohio) which affects the title of land in the forum state. The latter state, however, may nevertheless decide to enforce that foreign judgment affecting its land as a matter of comity.[54]

Assignment # 110

Answer the following questions after examining your state code. (See also General Instructions for the State Code Assignment, supra p. 14, and for the Flow Chart Assignment, supra p. 33.)

(a) What remedies (enforcement devices) exist to collect unpaid alimony and child support payments?

(b) What procedures must be followed to seek enforcement of an alimony or child support order by contempt? Write your answer in Step 37, infra p. 404.

(c) Has your state enacted the Uniform Reciprocal Enforcement of Support Act? If so, give the citation of the Act.

(d) What is the statute of limitations for bringing an action to enforce an alimony or child custody award? Write your answer in Step 38, infra p. 404.

54. See Clark, H., *The Law of Domestic Relations*, p. 477 (1968).

(e) What procedures must be followed to set aside a divorce judgment on the ground that it was obtained by fraud? Write your answer in Step 39, infra p. 404.

SECTION O. RES JUDICATA AND COLLATERAL ESTOPPEL

RES JUDICATA: When a judgment on its merits has been rendered, the parties cannot relitigate the same dispute (i. e., the same cause of action); the parties have already had their day in court. The second action based on the same cause of action is barred by the defense of res judicata.

EXAMPLES:

A. Mary sues Harry for divorce on the ground of adultery. Mary's action is dismissed because she brought it in the wrong court. (The court had no subject-matter jurisdiction to dissolve a marriage.[55]) Mary then brings the same cause of action in the right court.

Her second action is not barred by res judicata because the first judgment (against her) was not on the merits. She lost on a procedural matter (jurisdiction); she has not yet received a judgment on the substance of her claim: adultery. She has not yet had her day in court on this cause of action.

B. Same facts as in the "A" example above except that Mary lost the first judgment because she could not prove Harry's adultery. One year later, she again brings a divorce action on the ground of adultery.

Is her second cause barred by res judicata? It depends upon when the alleged adultery occurred. If the second action is based on the same adultery claim that she used in the first action (she brings up the same facts, the same date, the same alleged paramour, etc.), then the second action is barred by the defense of res judicata. She already had her day in court on this cause of action. She obtained a judgment on the merits and it would be unfair to force Harry to relitigate the issue. If, however, Mary is alleging adultery that has occurred since the first action was concluded, then res judicata does not apply. She is alleging a new cause of action, a new marital wrong involving new facts. She has not had her day in court on this cause of action.

55. Supra p. 352.

(NOTE: This same result would also apply if Mary brought her second action in another state. One state must give full faith and credit to the final judgments of other states. Mary had a final judgment on the merits involving the "first" adultery; another state must give full faith and credit to this judgment and not allow her to relitigate the divorce on that ground. If the adultery alleged in the second action occurred after the first action, then Mary could bring this action in another state so long as the other state had jurisdiction over the action and the parties.[56])

C. Tom sues Jill for divorce on the ground of desertion and loses. A month later, Tom sues Jill for divorce on the ground of adultery which allegedly occurred six months ago. Tom knew of this adultery at the time he brought his first action but did not raise it in that action; he limited himself to the desertion cause of action.

The normal res judicata rule would be that the second action would be barred: if a party knew of a cause of action at the time of the first action, but failed to raise it, the party is barred by res judicata from raising it later. States differ, however, as to whether this rule applies in divorce actions. Some states say that it does. Tom would be barred from bringing the second cause of action on the ground of adultery in these states since he could have raised it in the first action and did not. There are other states that do *not* apply this rule. In these states, Tom could bring the divorce action on the ground of adultery whether or not he knew about this ground at the time he brought and lost the action on the ground of desertion.

COLLATERAL ESTOPPEL: When an issue of fact or issue of law has been litigated in a prior action, it cannot be relitigated in a later action whether or not the two actions were based on the same cause of action.

EXAMPLE:

D. George sues Karen for a legal separation[57] on the ground of desertion. The judgment is for Karen on the merits; no legal separation is awarded. George later sues Karen for divorce on the ground of desertion.

56. Supra p. 352.

57. Infra p. 405.

> In the legal separation action, it was concluded that Karen did not desert George. In the divorce action, if George is relying on the same facts that allegedly constitute desertion that he used in the separation action, then he will be collaterally estopped from relitigating the desertion issue in the divorce action. He had his day in court on this desertion issue. If he relies on other facts allegedly constituting desertion, then collateral estoppel may not be a bar.

(It should be kept in mind that courts sometimes use the words, res judicata, collateral estoppel and bar interchangeably.)

Assignment # 111

In this assignment, you are asked to interview a paralegal, a lawyer or legal secretary who has been involved in divorce actions in your state. (See also General Instructions for the Law Office Management Assignment, supra p. 34.) Obtain answers to the following questions:

(a) Approximately how many divorce cases have you worked on?

(b) How many of them have been uncontested?

(c) Approximately how long does it take to process an uncomplicated, uncontested divorce?

(d) Is there a difference between working on a divorce case and working on another kind of case in the law office?

(e) What are the major steps that you have to go through to process a divorce action in this state? What documents have to be filed? What court appearances must be made? etc.

(f) What form or practice book do you use, if any, that is helpful?

(g) Does your office have its own internal manual that would cover any aspect of divorce practice?

(h) In a divorce action, what is the division of labor among the attorney, the paralegal and the legal secretary?

Assignment # 112

DIVORCE LITIGATION FLOW CHART FOR YOUR STATE

(Fill in each Step after checking the law of your state, particularly your state statutory code. You may also need to refer to court rules and to judicial opinions. See General Instructions for the Flow Chart Assignment, supra p. 33. For each Step, give the citation to the statute, court rule or opinion that you are relying upon as authority for your answer.)

STEP 1[58]

Name the court or courts that have subject-matter jurisdiction over divorces: 5th District -
Citation: I.C. 1-806 I.C. 32-715

STEP 2[59]

What is the residency requirement for a divorce action: 6 full Weeks
Citation: I.C. - 32-701

STEP 3[60]

Who may serve process:
Citation:

STEP 4[61]

How is personal service made on an individual: in person -
Citation: I.C.

STEP 5[62]

In divorce actions, how is substituted service made: by certified mail
Citation: I.C. 12-501 - 12-503

58. See Assignment # 86, supra p. 359.

59. See Assignment # 87(a), supra p. 359.

60. See Assignment # 88(a), supra p. 359.

61. See Assignment # 88(b), supra p. 359.

62. See Assignment # 88(d), supra p. 359.

DIVORCE LITIGATION FLOW CHART FOR YOUR STATE—Continued

STEP 6[63]

How is proof of service made:
Citation:

STEP 7[64]

If a government official, e.g., a proctor, is appointed as part of divorce actions, what is the role of this person:
Citation:

STEP 8[65]

When can a guardian ad litem be appointed in a divorce action:
Citation:

STEP 9[66]

In a divorce action, how is venue determined:
Citation:

STEP 10[67]

What must a complaint for divorce contain:
Citation:

STEP 11[68]

Must the complaint be subscribed and/or verified? If so, by whom:
Citation:

63. See Assignment # 88(e), supra p. 359.

64. See Assignment # 89, supra p. 361.

65. See Assignment # 90, supra p. 361.

66. See Assignment # 91, supra p. 361.

67. See Assignment # 92(a), supra p. 362.

68. See Assignment # 92(b), supra p. 362.

DIVORCE LITIGATION FLOW CHART FOR YOUR STATE—Continued

STEP 12[69]

Where is the complaint filed:
Citation:

STEP 13[70]

How many days does the defendant have to answer the complaint:
Citation:

STEP 14[71]

Where and how is the answer filed and served:
Citation:

STEP 15[72]

Must the defendant specifically plead affirmative defenses in the answer:
Citation:

STEP 16[73]

Must the defendant's answer be subscribed and/or verified? If so, by whom:
Citation:

STEP 17[74]

How many days does the plaintiff have to reply to the counterclaim of the defendant:
Citation:

---

69. See Assignment # 92(c), supra p. 362.

70. See Assignment # 92(d), supra p. 362.

71. See Assignment # 92(e), supra p. 362.

72. See Assignment # 92(f), supra p. 362.

73. See Assignment # 92(g), supra p. 362.

74. See Assignment # 92(h), supra p. 363.

DIVORCE LITIGATION FLOW CHART FOR YOUR STATE—Continued

STEP 18[75]

Where and how is the plaintiff's reply filed and served:
Citation:

STEP 19[76]

Is there a waiting period? If so, how long is it and when does it begin to run:
Citation:

STEP 20[77]

Is marital counseling compulsory in your state:
Citation:

STEP 21[78]

When must a deposition be requested? How is the request made:
Citation:

STEP 22[79]

Are there any restrictions on the use of depositions in divorce actions:
Citation:

STEP 23[80]

When and on whom can interrogatories be filed:
Citation:

---

75. See Assignment # 92(i), supra p. 363.

76. See Assignment # 93(a), supra p. 363.

77. See Assignment # 93(b), supra p. 363.

78. See Assignment # 94(a), supra p. 364.

79. See Assignment # 94(b), supra p. 364.

80. See Assignment # 94(c), supra p. 364.

DIVORCE LITIGATION FLOW CHART FOR YOUR STATE—Continued

STEP 24[81]

When must interrogatories be answered:
Citation:

STEP 25[82]

When can a request for admissions be made:
Citation:

STEP 26[83]

When will a court order a physical or mental examination:
Citation:

STEP 27[84]

What sanctions can be imposed if a party improperly refuses to comply with valid discovery requests:
Citation:

STEP 28[85]

In a divorce action, what preliminary orders can be granted by the court pendente lite:
Citation:

STEP 29[86]

In a divorce action, what evidence, if any, must be corroborated:
Citation:

81. See Assignment # 94(d), supra p. 364.

82. See Assignment # 94(e), supra p. 364.

83. See Assignment # 94(f), supra p. 364.

84. See Assignment # 94(g), supra p. 365.

85. See Assignment # 96, supra p. 365.

86. See Assignment # 97(a), supra p. 368.

DIVORCE LITIGATION FLOW CHART FOR YOUR STATE—Continued

STEP 30[87]

Are there any limitations on testimony that one spouse can give against the other:
Citation:

STEP 31[88]

Can there be a jury trial in a divorce case? If so, when must the request for one be made:
Citation:

STEP 32[89]

What happens if the defendant fails to appear? Can there be a default judgment:
Citation:

STEP 33[90]

Is there an interlocutory decree or decree nisi? If so, how long is it effective, and how does the divorce become final:
Citation:

STEP 34[91]

To what court can the divorce decree be appealed:
Citation:

STEP 35[92]

How many days does a party have to appeal:
Citation:

---

87. See Assignment # 97(b), supra p. 368.

88. See Assignment # 97(c), supra p. 368.

89. See Assignment # 97(d), supra p. 368.

90. See Assignment # 105(a), supra p. 384.

91. See Assignment # 105(d), supra p. 384.

92. See Assignment # 105(e), supra p. 384.

DIVORCE LITIGATION FLOW CHART FOR YOUR STATE—Continued

STEP 36[93]

Where and how is the notice of appeal filed and served:

Citation:

STEP 37[94]

What procedures must be followed to seek enforcement of an alimony or child support order by contempt:

Citation:

STEP 38[95]

What is the statute of limitations for bringing an action to enforce an alimony or child custody award:

Citation:

STEP 39[96]

What procedures must be followed to set aside a divorce judgment on the ground of fraud:

Citation:

IM–488

93. See Assignment # 105(f), supra p. 384.

94. See Assignment # 110(b), supra p. 394.

95. See Assignment # 110(d), supra p. 394.

96. See Assignment # 110(e), supra p. 395.

Chapter Eighteen

JUDICIAL SEPARATION

SECTION A. INTRODUCTION

A judicial separation [1] is a decision by a court (a) that two people can live separately—from bed and board—while still remaining husband and wife, and (b) what the rights and obligations of the parties are while they are separated. A judicial separation may also be known as:

—a legal separation;

—a limited divorce;

—divorce a mensa et thoro;

—separation from bed and board.

Parties subject to this judicial decree (by whatever label it is called in a particular state) are *not* free to remarry. The marriage relationship remains until it is dissolved by the death of one of the parties,[2] by annulment,[3] or by divorce [4]—an absolute divorce, or a divorce a vinculo matrimonii,[5] as the "full" divorce is called.[6]

→ We should distinguish a judicial separation from a "separation agreement." [7] The latter is a private contract between a husband and wife. The agreement may or may not become part of (i. e., incorporated or merged in) the judicial separation decree, or part of the absolute divorce decree if one is later sought.[8] Also, it is important that the word "separated" or "separation" be used carefully. The words are often used to mean a physical separation between the husband and wife without involving a judicial decree. If, however, a court-sanctioned or court-ordered separation is involved, then the reference should be to a *legal* or *judicial* separation.

1. Supra p. 171.

2. By actual death, or by presumed death via Enoch Arden, supra p. 177.

3. Supra pp. 171–244.

4. Supra pp. 307–404.

5. Supra p. 345.

6. In some community property states (see infra p. 431), the "community estate" is dissolved by a separation from bed and board. See Internal Revenue Service, *Community Property and the Federal Income Tax*, p. 1 (1977 Edition).

7. Supra p. 245.

8. Supra p. 283.

Assignment # 113

Answer the following questions by examining your state code. (See also General Instructions for the State Code Assignment, supra p. 14.)

(a) Does your state have an action for a judicial separation?

(b) If so, what is the action called?

(c) What is the citation of the statute authorizing this action?

NOTE

In addition to the action for judicial separation, many states have an action for separate maintenance which accomplishes essentially the same result. The separate maintenance action will be discussed later.[9]

SECTION B. GROUNDS FOR A JUDICIAL SEPARATION

Parties cannot obtain a judicial separation simply by asking for it. Specifically designated *grounds* must exist before the court can order the decree.

Often the statute on grounds will provide that the grounds for judicial separation are the same as the grounds for an absolute divorce[10] with the addition of a catch-all ground that, in effect, gives the court considerable (but not absolute) discretion in granting the decree. For example:

> Separation from bed and board may be adjudged for any cause which is by law made ground for granting absolute divorce, or for conduct on the part of the husband toward his wife which renders it unsafe and improper for her to cohabit with him.[11]

Oddly, however, there are some states that have adopted no-fault grounds for divorce[12] while retaining fault grounds for a legal separation. Since we have already studied the grounds for divorce in detail,[13] we will not examine them closely here. The chart below lists the standard grounds for divorce with page references to where the grounds are discussed in this book. In addition, the chart gives references to the pages where the INTERVIEWING and INVESTIGATION CHECKLISTS are that can be of assistance in determining whether the facts supporting a particular ground exist.

9. Infra p. 433.

10. The grounds for separate maintenance are also often the same as the grounds for divorce, infra p. 407.

11. Section 25-332 Ariz.Rev.Stats.Ann. (1956).

12. Supra p. 308ff.

13. Supra p. 307.

GROUNDS FOR JUDICIAL SEPARATION WHICH IN MANY STATES ARE THE SAME AS THE GROUNDS FOR DIVORCE[14]		
Ground	Pages where discussed	INTERVIEWING AND INVESTIGATION CHECK-LIST to aid in determining whether the facts exist to substantiate the ground
Living apart	Supra p. 308	Questions 1–16 Supra p. 310
Incompatibility	Supra p. 313	Questions 1–13 Supra p. 313
Irreconcilable differences; irretrievable breakdown	Supra p. 315	Questions 1–13 Supra p. 313
Adultery	Supra p. 316	Questions 1–21 Supra p. 319
Cruelty	Supra p. 321	Questions 1–37 Supra p. 325
Desertion and abandonment	Supra p. 328	Questions 1–29 Supra p. 332
Bigamy	Supra p. 177	Questions 1–11 Supra p. 182
Impotence	Supra p. 190	Questions 1–8 Supra p. 193
Incest	Supra p. 183	Questions 1–5 Supra p. 185
Nonage	Supra p. 186	Questions 1–5 Supra p. 190
Duress	Supra p. 203	Questions 1–7 Supra p. 205
Fraud	Supra p. 205	Questions 1–12 Supra p. 211
Insanity	Supra p. 198	Questions 1–22 Supra p. 202
Conviction of a crime	Supra p. 335	
Habitual drunkenness and drug addiction	Supra p. 336	
Non-support	Supra p. 336	
Neglect of duty	Supra p. 336	

IM-489

14. You will note that the chart also contains six grounds for judicial separation which are also grounds for annulment (bigamy, impotence, incest, nonage, duress and fraud). The reason is that in some states these six annulment grounds are also grounds for divorce.

Assignment # 114

What are the grounds in your state which can be the basis for a judicial separation? Are there any grounds for judicial separation which are *not* grounds for divorce? (See also General Instructions for the State Code Assignment, supra p. 14.)

As indicated in the following chart, many of the defenses applicable in divorce actions also govern judicial separation actions. The defenses were discussed in the context of divorce:

DEFENSES TO JUDICIAL SEPARATION WHICH IN MANY STATES ARE THE SAME AS THE DEFENSES TO DIVORCE	
Defense	Pages where discussed
Recrimination	Supra p. 337
Provocation	Supra p. 338
Collusion	Supra p. 338
Connivance	Supra p. 340
Condonation	Supra p. 340
Statute of limitations and laches	Supra p. 342
Insanity	Supra p. 341
The parties are not married	Supra p. 342
Res judicata	Supra p. 395
The court lacks jurisdiction	Supra p. 350
Improper venue	Supra p. 361

IM-490

SECTION C. CONSEQUENCES OF A JUDICIAL SEPARATION JUDGMENT

As a consequence of a judicial separation proceeding, the court can award alimony,[15] can issue custody [16] and child support [17] orders,

15. On the factors a court will consider in awarding alimony, see supra p. 369. On the factors that will justify a modification of an alimony order, see supra p. 385.

16. Supra p. 376ff.

17. Supra p. 365.

all of which are enforceable through traditional execution [18] and contempt [19] remedies. States differ as to whether property divisions [20] can be awarded a spouse pursuant to a judicial separation judgment. Some states authorize it, while others do not. The argument against it is that the spouse will be entitled to a property division on the death of the other spouse through dower [21] rights, intestate shares,[22] etc., (assuming the parties are not divorced before death), and should not be given another property division through the judicial separation. The alimony order should suffice according to this argument.[23] Very often, the parties will draft a separation agreement.[24] Courts will consider incorporating the terms of this agreement into the judicial separation judgment. The separation agreement, of course, will reflect the wishes of the parties on the critical issues of alimony, custody and child support.

After a judicial separation judgment has been rendered, the fact that the parties reconcile and resume cohabitation does not mean that the judgment becomes inoperative. The judgment remains effective until a court declares otherwise. Hence, a husband who is under an order to pay alimony to his wife pursuant to a judicial separation judgment must continue to pay alimony even though the parties have subsequently reconciled and are living together again. To be relieved of this obligation, a petition must be made to the court to change the judgment.

The major consequence of a judicial separation judgment in many states is its conversion feature into a divorce—an absolute divorce. In effect, the existence of the judgment can become a ground for divorce. As we saw in Chapter Sixteen, states differ on the conditions which will trigger the conversion, particularly with respect to the length of time that the judicial separation judgment must have been in effect before an application for the conversion to the divorce will be considered by the court.[25]

Assignment # 115

Prepare a flow chart of the procedural steps that are necessary for a judicial separation in your state. (See General Instructions for the Flow Chart Assignment, supra p. 33.)

18. Supra p. 390.

19. Supra p. 268.

20. Supra p. 265.

21. Infra p. 441.

22. Supra p. 217, and infra p. 441.

23. See Clark, H., *The Law of Domestic Relations*, p. 199 (1968).

24. Supra pp. 245–305.

25. Supra p. 311.

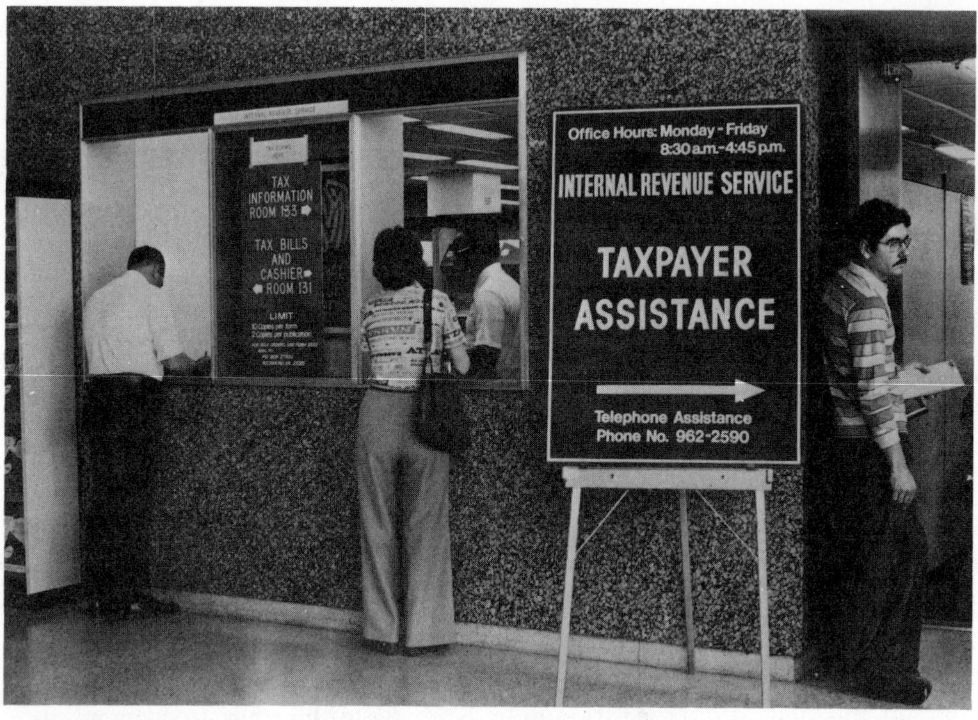

Internal Revenue Service

Chapter Nineteen

TAX CONSEQUENCES OF SEPARATION AND DIVORCE

SECTION A. ALIMONY: WHAT IS A PERIODIC PAYMENT?

Tax law greatly influences the practice of Family Law. When parties are given legal advice on the drafting of a separation agreement,[1] for example, if they are not also given tax counseling, the result can be devastating. What the clauses in the separation agreement say the parties are to receive may have little relationship to reality once the tax consequences of those clauses are assessed.

Alimony [2] or separate maintenance [3] payments are *income* and generally must be included within the gross income of the recipient. If in a particular year, for example, a woman receives $5,000 as alimony, she must include this amount as income on her tax return and pay taxes on it in the same manner that taxes are paid on a salary. As we shall see, however, this tax consequence does *not* apply to every payment.

Alimony or separate maintenance payments, if they meet certain requirements, are *deductible* by the person making those payments. Child support payments [4] and property settlement payments,[5] however, are not deductible.

> Suppose that a husband has a total income of $20,000. Pursuant to a separation agreement, he pays his wife $4,000 in the current year for her support. If this $4,000 qualifies as an alimony payment under the tax rules (to be discussed), he can take a deduction for this payment. If this were his only deduction for the current year, he would pay taxes on $16,000.

Alimony or separate maintenance payments are taxable to the recipient and deductible to the payor if the payments are:[6]

(a) required under the terms of a divorce or separation decree, or required under the terms of a written instrument incident to such a decree, e. g., a separation agreement;

(b) paid in discharge of a legal obligation based on the marital or family relationship (a husband's duty to support his wife

1. Supra p. 245.

2. Supra p. 369.

3. Infra p. 433.

4. Infra p. 423.

5. Infra p. 418.

6. 26 U.S.C.A. § 71(a).

is such a legal obligation; a husband's repayment of a loan he took from his wife is not);

(c) paid after the divorce or separate maintenance decree or after the separation agreement is executed;

(d) periodic payments (defined below).

If the payments are pursuant to a separation agreement, they are includable in the gross estate of the recipient and deductible by the payor if:

(a) the husband and wife are separated,

(b) the payments qualify as periodic,

(c) the payments are made after the execution of the agreement,

(d) the payments result from the marital or family relationship, and

(e) the husband and wife do not file a joint return.[7]

Of course, it is quite possible that the parties never execute a separation agreement and that the alimony obligation is set by the court. Payments pursuant to this obligation are includable in the gross estate of the recipient and deductible by the payor if:

(a) the payments for support and maintenance are required by the court,[8]

(b) the payments qualify as periodic,

(c) the husband and wife are separated, and

(d) the husband and wife do not file a joint return.

So much depends upon the meaning of the critical word, *periodic.* Too often, this word is confused with the word, installment. The distinction between the two concepts need to be kept in mind.

What is a *periodic payment*?

PERIODIC ALIMONY PAYMENTS FOR TAX PURPOSES
Periodic payments are: (a) payments of a fixed amount (e. g., \$50.00 per week) for an indefinite period, *or,* (b) payments of an indefinite amount (e. g., 10% of a fluctuating income) for *either* (i) a fixed period, *or,* (ii) an indefinite period.

[B7636]

7. A sixth requirement is that the separation agreement must have been executed after 1954.

8. After 1954.

An "indefinite" period is one whose duration is not known at the time. In the following examples, the payments qualify as periodic and hence are included in the income of the recipient and deductible by the payor:[9]

—A divorce decree obligates Harry to pay Jane, his former spouse, $200.00 per month for life.

—A divorce decree obligates Susan to pay Fred, her former spouse, now an invalid, one fourth of her income (she works on sales commissions) every month for a total of six years, or, for as long as Fred lives.

The payments do *not* have to be made at regular intervals in order to qualify as periodic.

As indicated above, sometimes separation agreements and even courts do not always clearly differentiate alimony from property settlements.[10] In the event that this occurs, the Internal Revenue Service will have to examine the obligations of the parties to determine what amounts are pursuant to a legal obligation of support regardless of the labels used in the separation agreement and/or by the court.[11] If these amounts otherwise fit within the requirements for periodic payments, they will be included in the income of the recipient and will be deductible by the payor.

At times a separation agreement and/or a court decree will give a spouse a *lump sum* payable in *installments* as the alimony provision, e. g., $30,000, payable $5,000 a year for the next six years. The "principal sum" to be paid is $30,000. A principal sum is a definite amount of money or property. An installment is a payment toward a principal sum. Our question is: when can an installment payment be a periodic payment? The answer depends mainly upon the *period* over which the installment is to be paid:

9. See Internal Revenue Service, *Tax Information for Divorced or Separated Individuals* (Pub. 504, 1977), Taggart, J., *Some Tax Aspects of Separation and Divorce* (American Bar Association, 1975), and Commerce Clearing House, Inc., 177 U.S. Master Tax Guide (1976).

10. Supra p. 265.

11. See Jones v. Flasted, supra p. 372.

WHEN DO INSTALLMENT PAYMENTS QUALIFY AS PERIODIC PAYMENTS?
(1) If the principal sum payable in installments is to be paid over a period of ten years or less, the installment payments are not periodic payments *unless* the installment payments are subject to one of the following three contingencies: (a) the court has the power to modify, alter or amend the installment payments, (b) the installment payments are to end or change in amount upon the remarriage of the recipient spouse, or, (c) the installment payments are to end or change in amount upon death or a change in the economic status of either spouse.
(2) If the principal sum payable in installments is to be paid over a period of more than ten years, and if the installment payments are not subject to contingencies, these installment payments will be considered periodic payments, but only to the extent of 10% of the principal sum per taxable year of the recipient. (The 10% per year limitation applies to installment payments made *in advance*, but not to delinquent installment payments received during the recipient's taxable year.)

[B7640]

EXAMPLES:

A. Under the terms of a separation agreement incorporated later into a divorce decree, Tom is to pay $19,000 for the support of his ex-wife Rita. Of this amount, $14,000 is payable upon entry of the divorce decree, and the remaining $5,000 is payable at the rate of $200 a month for 25 months, subject to termination on Rita's death or remarriage.

TAX ANALYSIS:

—The $14,000 is a lump sum payment not payable in installments. Hence it does not qualify as a periodic payment. Tom cannot deduct it. Rita does not have to pay taxes on it—it is not included in her gross income.

—The $5,000 is payable in installments ($200 a month for 25 months). The principal sum is $5,000 and it is payable over a period of less than ten years. The installment payments are subject to a contingency: they end if Rita dies or remarries. Hence, each installment payment is a periodic payment on which Rita must pay taxes and which Tom can deduct.

—If the $5,000 were payable over a period of more than ten years, the installment payments would not be periodic payments because they are subject to a contingency.

B. Under a divorce decree, Leo must pay Paula $150,000 for her support as follows: $20,000 a year for five years, and $5,000 a year for the next ten years. The court cannot modify, alter or amend these payments. They do not end or change if Paula remarries. Nor do they end or change on her death or that of Leo. Nor do they end or change upon any other condition.

TAX ANALYSIS:

—The $150,000 is a lump sum payable in installments over a period of more than ten years. The installment payments are not subject to any contingencies. Hence, each installment payment is a periodic payment—but the 10% rule applies.

—10% of $150,000 is $15,000. In no one year will more than $15,000 qualify as a periodic payment. Hence, during the first five years, $15,000 per year is a periodic payment deductible by Leo and taxable to Paula. During the last ten years, the 10% limit is not exceeded in any year. Hence, for each of the last ten years, $5,000 is deductible to Leo and taxable to Paula.

—Of the $150,000, the total amount deductible to Leo and taxable to Paula is $125,000 ($75,000 during the first five years and $50,000 during the last ten years). Paula received the other $25,000, but did not have to include it in her gross income and pay taxes on it, and Leo could not deduct it on his return because $25,000 of the $100,000 received during the first five years did not qualify as periodic payments.[12]

Assignment # 116

A separation agreement provides that Brenda is to pay Robert a total of $48,000 for his support. The money is to be paid as follows: $800 a month for five years until Robert dies or remarries, at which time Brenda can stop paying. What amounts, if any, are includable in Robert's gross income and deductible to Brenda? (See also General Instructions for the Legal Analysis Assignment, supra p. 16.)

Assignment # 117

A divorce decree requires that Donald pay his ex-wife Fran, $150,000 alimony. The money is to be paid as follows: $10,000 a year for 15 years. The payments continue regardless of the death, remarriage

12. See Internal Revenue Service, *Tax Information*, supra note 9 at p. 8.

or change in economic status of Donald or Fran. There are no contingencies. In 1976, Donald failed to make a payment. In 1977, Donald gave Fran $30,000 which represented $10,000 back alimony for 1976, $10,000 for 1977, and $10,000 for 1978. What amounts, if any, are includable in Fran's gross income and deductible by Donald? Answer this question separately for 1976, 1977 and 1978. (See also General Instructions for the Legal Analysis Assignment, supra p. 16.)

SECTION B. TRANSFER OF APPRECIATED PROPERTY AS ALIMONY

First, some basic terminology:

Tom buys a house in 1950 for $10,000. He spends $1,000 to add a new room. In 1978, he sells the house for $20,000 to a stranger.

Appreciation: increase in value. Tom's house appreciated by $10,000 (from $10,000 to $20,000). He has made a profit, called a gain.

Depreciation: decrease in value. If no one wanted to buy Tom's house for more than $7,000 and he sold it for that amount, the house depreciated by $3,000. He obviously has suffered a loss.

Realize: to benefit from, receive or enjoy. Normally, income is realized when it is received. Suppose that it is quite clear that Tom could sell his house for $20,000, but he decides not to do so. He has not realized any income. He has a "paper" gain only. He does not have to pay taxes on profit until he has realized a profit, e. g., by selling the house.

Fair market value: the price which could be obtained on an open market between a willing buyer and a willing seller. A sale between a parent and child will usually not be at fair market value. The fact that they are related probably affected the price paid in a manner that would not have occurred if they had been merchants dealing at arm's length. It is possible for a happily married husband and wife to sell something to each other for fair market value, but the likelihood is that they did not. Tom sold his house for $20,000 to a stranger. There is no indication that either party was pressured into the deal nor that they had any special relationship to each other. $20,000, therefor, is probably the fair market value.

Basis: the initial capital investment, usually the cost of the property. The basis of Tom's house is $10,000. If the property was acquired other than through a purchase, (e. g., as a gift or through a will) special rules exist to determine the basis of such property.

Adjusted basis: the basis of the property after adjustments are made. The basis is either adjusted upward (increased) by the amount of capital expenditures (structural improvements on the property) or adjusted downward (decreased). Tom added a room to his house—a structural improvement. His basis ($10,000) is increased by the amount of the capital expenditure ($1,000) giving him an adjusted basis of $11,000.

When Tom sold the house for $20,000, he *realized* income. The amount of income for tax purposes is determined as follows:

SALE PRICE	minus	ADJUSTED BASIS	=	TAXABLE GAIN

The sale price of Tom's house was $20,000. His adjusted basis was $11,000. He, therefore, realized a taxable gain of $9,000 ($20,000 less $11,000). He must declare this amount on his federal tax return.[13] Of course, if the sale price was *less* than the adjusted basis, he would have suffered a loss. If, for example, he had sold the house for $5,000, his loss would have been $6,000 ($11,000 minus $5,000).

Now, let us put this in the context of a marital separation. Suppose that Tom had not sold the house in 1978 to a stranger, and that the following events occurred:

> Tom marries Mary. Two years later, they decide to separate. In their separation agreement, Tom is required to give Mary a lump sum alimony payment [14] of $20,000. In satisfaction of this obligation, he transfers to Mary the house he bought in 1950 for $10,000 (which he solely owns) and which now has a fair market value of $20,000. His adjusted basis in the house is $11,000.
>
> TAX ANALYSIS:
>
> —When appreciated property, which is separately owned, is transferred from one spouse to another in satisfaction of marital rights, the transferring spouse realizes a taxable gain to the extent that the fair market value of the property exceeds its adjusted basis. The excess in Tom's case is $9,000.
>
> —Hence, when Tom transfers the house to Mary, two tax consequences for Tom result: (a) he must declare $9,000 on his next tax return,[15] and (b) he *cannot* deduct the $20,000 alimony payment because it was not a periodic payment.[16]

13. As well as on possible state and local tax returns.

14. Supra p. 270.

15. He might even have to pay an estimated tax, which is, in effect, an advance tax paid before the end of the tax year.

16. Supra p. 412.

SECTION C. TRANSFER OF APPRECIATED PROPERTY AS PART OF A PROPERTY SETTLEMENT

Recall the distinction between alimony and property settlement: [17]

Alimony: payment to fulfill the obligation to support a spouse (or an ex-spouse)

Property Settlement: the division of property between the spouses which fairly accounts for their mutual efforts in obtaining the property during the marriage.

The tax consequences of the two are substantial:

Alimony: taxable to the recipient and deductible by the payor, if the payments are periodic [18]

Property Settlement: not taxable to the recipient nor deductible by the payor.

Suppose that a husband transfers $100,000 to his ex-wife as part of a property settlement. Why, you might ask, is this $100,000 not income to the wife? The reason is that the law assumes that what she gave up in exchange for the $100,000 is equal to the value of what she got—the $100,000. What did she give up? Claims on personal property, e. g., a car, the right to be supported, etc. It is very difficult to put a price tag on what the wife gives her husband as part of the property settlement, i. e., it is difficult to value the *consideration* [19] she gives him. The Internal Revenue Service assumes that the separated parties are operating at arm's length and are not giving anything to each other for nothing. The consideration provided by the wife is deemed to be equal to the consideration provided by the husband. Hence, no taxable income is realized. The transaction has the same tax effect as exchanging one $100 bill for another $100 bill. No income has been earned.

The picture changes, however, if *appreciated* property is exchanged as part of a property settlement:

Stella divorces Stanley. As part of the property settlement, Stella transfers to Stanley title to a yacht which she had inherited from her mother. When she received the yacht, it was worth $25,000. When she gave it to Stanley its fair market value was $60,000.

TAX ANALYSIS

—Stella has transferred separately owned property as part of a property settlement.

—The property she transferred has appreciated in value by $35,000.

17. Supra p. 265.

18. Supra p. 412.

19. Supra p. 110.

—Stella has realized a $35,000 taxable gain which she must declare on her next tax return.

—Stanley has not realized any taxable income since the value of what he gave Stella, i. e., the release of his marital rights in her property, is assumed to be equal in value to what he received, i. e., $60,000.

—If Stanley now sold the yacht, his basis will be $60,000. For example, if he sold the boat for $100,000, he would have a taxable gain of $40,000.

Assignment # 118

George divorces Charlene. George owns a bakery shop in his own name which he purchased before he married Charlene. He purchased the business for $10,000. His adjusted basis in it is $23,000. As part of the property settlement, George transfers the bakery to Charlene. At the time of the transfer, its fair market value is $47,000. Ten years later, Charlene decides to sell the bakery. Her adjusted basis in it is $52,000. She sells it for $46,500.

(a) When George transferred the bakery to Charlene, could he deduct anything?

(b) Did George realize any taxable gain at this time?

(c) In the year Charlene received the bakery, did she have to include anything in her tax return?

(d) When she obtained the bakery from George, what was her basis in the bakery?

(e) When she sold the bakery ten years later, what were the tax consequences to her?

(See also General Instructions for the Legal Analysis Assignment, supra p. 16.)

SECTION D. JOINTLY OWNED PROPERTY

During the marriage, the parties may have acquired a variety of property [20] which they hold in their joint names:

—savings account;

—checking account;

—stocks, bonds, certificates;

—home;

—business property;

—etc.

20. Supra p. 275.

If each party owns one half of the property and it is split accordingly through the separation agreement and/or divorce, no taxable event occurs. Similarly, in a community property state,[21] when the community property is divided equally following a divorce, the division is a non-taxable event.

If there is an unequal division of jointly owned property (or an unequal division of community property in a community property state), a taxable gain may result to the extent that the fair market value exceeds the adjusted basis of the property.

Tom and Mary are divorced. Their total assets have a fair market value of $110,000 at the time of the divorce as follows:

—jointly owned property:	$70,000 (fair market value)
—separately owned property of Tom:	$40,000 (fair market value)
	$110,000

Mary has no separately owned property. The divorce decree provides the following property settlement:

TO TOM:

—jointly owned property:	$15,000 (fair market value)
—separately owned property:	$40,000 (fair market value)

TO MARY:

—jointly owned property:	$55,000 (fair market value)

The adjusted basis of the property received by Mary is $29,500, of which $4,000 is attributable to personal furniture with a fair market value of $2,000.[22]

TAX ANALYSIS

—The jointly owned property has been divided unequally. There was $70,000 in jointly owned property. If it had been divided equally, each would have received $35,000. Instead, Tom received $15,000 and Mary received $55,000.

—Since Tom received $15,000 rather than $35,000, he gave Mary $20,000 worth of his share of the jointly owned property ($35,000 less $15,000).

—What did Tom receive when he gave Mary $20,000 of his share of his jointly owned property? What did he receive in exchange for this $20,000? He received a release of Mary's marital rights

21. Infra p. 431.

22. *Tax Information*, supra note 9 at pp. 10–11.

in the $40,000 worth of separately owned property that he owned. This was a taxable exchange.

—What was Tom's taxable gain in this exchange? To answer this question we must compare the fair market value of Tom's share of the jointly owned property that he gave to Mary ($20,000) with the adjusted basis of this share.

Fair market value of Tom's share of jointly owned property he gave to Mary	−	Adjusted basis of Tom's share of jointly owned property he gave to Mary	=	Tom's taxable gain

—Tom's adjusted basis in the excess jointly owned property received by Mary is determined by the following formula:

Fair market value of excess jointly - owned property received by Mary / Fair market value of all jointly - owned property received by Mary	×	Adjusted basis of all jointly-owned property received by Mary	=	Adjusted basis of excess jointly-owned property received by Mary

—The fair market value of the jointly owned property received by Mary was $55,000. What was the adjusted basis of this property? We are given the figure $29,500 by the facts, but this figure includes the adjusted basis of personal furniture which exceeds its fair market value. The personal furniture has an adjusted basis of $4,000 and a fair market value of $2,000. The adjusted basis of the personal furniture exceeds its fair market value by $2,000. In such situations the tax rule is as follows:

> The adjusted basis of all jointly owned property cannot include that portion of the adjusted basis of the personal furniture which exceeds its fair market value since a loss deduction would not otherwise be allowable on property held for personal use.

There is a $2,000 unallowable loss on the furniture. This amount must be subtracted from the overall adjusted basis of the jointly owned property received by Mary:

	$29,500	adjusted basis of jointly owned property received by Mary
less	$ 2,000	unallowable loss deduction for the property (the furniture) held for personal use
	$27,500	

$27,500 is the adjusted basis of the jointly owned property Mary received. We can now apply the above formula:

$$\frac{\$20{,}000}{\$55{,}000} \times \$27{,}500 = \$10{,}000$$

—We now have the adjusted basis of Tom's share of the jointly owned property he gave to Mary ($10,000). We must subtract this from the fair market value of Tom's share of the jointly owned property he gave to Mary which we already determined to be $20,000 ($35,000 less $15,000). Tom's taxable gain, therefore, is $10,000 ($20,000 less $10,000).

SECTION E. TRUSTS

A *trust* is a fiduciary relationship in which one person holds property for the benefit of another. For example:

John transfers $10,000 to the ABC Bank (the trustee) in trust for his children (the beneficiaries).

Suppose that the beneficiary of the above trust was not John's children, but his ex-wife and that the income from the trust was to be paid to her in fulfillment of John's alimony obligation. According to the Internal Revenue Service, the tax consequences are as follows:

"*Trust property.* If you have placed income-producing property in trust to discharge your alimony obligation, you neither include nor deduct payments from income on the trust property. They are taxable to your spouse, who must report them as income received from a trust on Schedule E (Form 1040)." [23]

23. *Tax Information,* supra note 9 at p. 9. Cf. Lindey, A., *Separation Agreements and Ante-Nuptial Contracts* p. 19–27 (1964).

SECTION F. CHILD SUPPORT PAYMENTS

A separation agreement and/or divorce decree will always make provision for minor children who are dependent on their parents for support. The tax implications of this are as follows:

THE TAXATION OF CHILD SUPPORT PAYMENTS
1. Child support payments are not includible in the income of the parent with custody of the children. 2. Child support payments are not deductible by the parent making the payments. 3. If the separation agreement and/or divorce decree does not specifically designate how much goes for child support and how much goes for alimony (support of spouse), then the entire amount payed is treated as alimony (taxable to the parent with custody and deductible by the parent making the payments). This is so even if the parent with custody in fact uses some of the money received to support the children. 4. If both alimony and child support payments are required, but less than the required amount is paid, the payments will be applied first to the child support obligation and then to the alimony obligation. 5. Child support payments that are used to pay medical expenses of the children are deductible by the parent making the support payments if: (a) the parent making the payments is entitled to the dependency exemptions for the children, and (b) the support money was actually used for the medical expenses. (These medical deductions cannot exceed the limitations for such deductions applicable to taxpayers generally.) 6. The parent who has custody of the child for the greater part of the year is treated as the parent who furnished more than half of the child's support, and hence is the parent who is entitled to the dependency exemption for that child. There are, however, some exceptions (not covered here) which allow the dependency exemption to go to the parent who does not have custody or who has custody for the lesser part of the year.[24]

[B8859]

EXAMPLES:

A. A divorce decree requires that Bob pay $100 a week to Helen, his ex-wife, for the support of their two children until the children die or reach majority age. In addition, Bob is to pay all the education expenses of the children until they die or reach majority.

24. See 26 U.S.C. 152(e) (1967), and Chommie, J., *The Law of Federal Income Taxation*, pp. 155–56 (1968).

TAX ANALYSIS

—The $100 a week received by Helen for the support of the two children plus all funds Bob gives her for their education are not deductible by Bob and are not taxable to Helen.

B. A divorce decree requires Tom to pay Pat his ex-wife, $400 a month for the support of Pat and of their child, David. When David dies, marries or reaches majority (whichever occurrs first), the payments are reduced to $300 a month.

TAX ANALYSIS

—The divorce decree fails to specifically designate how much of the $400 a month was to go for Pat's support and how much was to go for the support of David.

—When a divorce decree and/or separation agreement fails to make such a designation, the Internal Revenue Service treats the *entire* payment as alimony. Hence each $400 payment received is taxable to Pat and deductible by Tom.

—The fact that the $400 is reduced to $300 when David dies, marries or reaches majority suggests that $100 of the $400 was for child support which is no longer needed when the child dies, marries or reaches majority. This is not significant, however, since Pat was free to use the $400 any way she wanted to. She was not expressly told by the court and/or by the separation agreement what amount of the $400 was to go for child support, and as a consequence, the entire $400 is taxable to her, i. e., the entire $400 is treated as alimony.

—The separation agreement (which is often later incorporated into the divorce decree [25]) must be drafted with care. Do the parties want the child support payments to have the same tax consequences as alimony payments? [26] If not, a commingling of funds for support of spouse and of child without a clear indication of who is getting what will frustrate the intention of the parties.

C. A separation agreement which is later incorporated into a divorce decree provides that Ed must pay Kelly, his ex-wife, $700 a month for her support until she remarries, and $300 a month for the support of their child, Frank. In 1978, the total amount of money received from Ed for her and Frank's support was $7,000.

25. Supra p. 283.

26. Supra p. 411.

TAX ANALYSIS

—If Ed had paid his entire support obligation for 1978, he would have given Kelly $12,000. $8,400 for the support of Kelly ($700 x 12), and $3,600 for the support of Frank ($300 x 12).

—In fact, Ed paid only $7,000. He is $5,000 in arrears. What are the tax consequences of the $7,000? To whom is it taxable? What deduction, if any, can be taken? If Ed had not fallen into arrears, he would have had an $8,400 deduction for his alimony payments to Kelly. The $8,400 would have been taxable to Kelly. The $3,600 child support would not have been deductible by nor taxable to anyone.

—If less than the required amount is paid, the payments apply first to child support and then to alimony. Hence, the $7,000 paid is first applied to the $3,600 child support obligation, leaving $3,400 to be applied to the alimony obligation. Of the $7,000 paid, $3,600 is deemed to have been paid for child support, and $3,400 is deemed to have been paid for alimony.

—Ed gets an alimony deduction of $3,400. Kelly must pay taxes on $3,400. No deduction can be taken for the $3,600 and it is not taxable.

Assignment # 119

Discuss the tax consequences of the following two situations. What amounts, if any, are taxable? What amounts, if any, are deductible? (See also General Instructions for the Legal Analysis Assignment, supra p. 16.)

(a) Sam is divorced from Diane. Under the terms of the separation agreement, later incorporated into the divorce decree, Diane must pay Sam $475 a month alimony until he remarries of which $125 a month is for the support of their child, Charles, who is in the custody of his father. In 1978, Diane runs into financial difficulties at her work and accumulates $4,195 in arrears with respect to Sam and Charles.

(b) Amanda is divorced from Len. Under the terms of the divorce decree, Len must pay Amanda $100,000 of which 75% is for her support and 25% is for the support of their child, Jill, who is nineteen years old. Amanda is to receive the funds as follows: $15,000 a year for the first four years, and $5,000 a year for the next eight years. The payments are not subject to any contingencies. In the first year, Len pays $6,000; he falls $9,000 in arrears.

SECTION G. FILING STATUS

Is there a tax advantage to a husband and wife filing a joint return as opposed to separate returns? Generally yes. There may be circumstances, however, when separate returns can be more advantageous, e. g., if both spouses have income, but one has moderate income and substantial medical expenses, while the other has little or no medical expenses.[27] It is always advisable for a couple to determine what their tax liability would be if they filed *either* way to determine whether a joint return or separate returns would be more advantageous.

Who can file a joint return? The answer depends upon what relationship the parties have to each other at the end of the tax year (which for most people is December 31st). Here are some of the possibilities.

1) the parties are living together as husband and wife;
2) the parties have separated, but they have not entered any separation agreement nor has any court decree been rendered concerning their marriage;
3) the parties have separated and entered a separation agreement, but no court decree has been rendered concerning their marriage;
4) an interlocutory divorce decree [28] has been issued;
5) a final divorce decree has been issued;
6) a separate maintenance decree [29] has been issued;
7) a judicial separation decree [30] has been issued;
8) an annulment decree [31] has been issued.

In the first four situations above, the parties can file a joint return if both parties are willing to sign the return. Separation agreements sometimes have a clause in which the parties are required to cooperate in the filing of a joint return.[32] If the last four situations (5–8) have occurred before the end of the tax year, the parties are considered unmarried for tax purposes and cannot file a joint return.

Suppose that the parties separate toward the end of the year and complete a separation agreement. If it is possible for them to delay the divorce decree until the beginning of the next year, they will be able to file a joint return in the year of their separation [33] (so long as events (6) and (7) above have not occurred).

27. Internal Revenue Service, *Tax Information* supra note 9 at p. 1.

28. Supra p. 384.

29. Infra p. 433.

30. Supra p. 405.

31. Supra p. 236.

32. Supra p. 280.

33. See Lindey, A., *Separation Agreements and Ante-Nuptial Contracts*, p. 19–2 (1977).

If the parties are allowed to file a joint tax return and decide to do so, both parties are liable for all taxes due, i. e., the Internal Revenue Service can go after *either* party for the entire tax (and possible penalty) due, even though only one of the parties generated all of the income. There is one major exception to this rule:

A spouse will not have to pay any tax liability or penalty if:

(a) it was caused by an omission of items on the joint return of an amount in excess of 25% of gross income on the return, and

(b) the spouse did not know of the omission, and,

(c) had no reason to know of the omission, and,

(d) the spouse did not significantly benefit from the items omitted.

The concern is for the wife who happens to be unfamiliar with the finances of the husband and also unfamiliar with tax law. The above exception to the joint and several liability rule, (i. e., that both are responsible together and individually) gives her some measure of protection. Another form of protection is a clause in the separation agreement which provides that the husband will pay any tax liability or penalty which results from the last joint return that they file together. Such a clause is often called an "indemnity" or "hold harmless" clause.[34]

SECTION H. LIFE INSURANCE PREMIUMS AS ALIMONY

It is not uncommon for a husband to be required pursuant to a separation agreement and/or a divorce decree to take out or maintain a life insurance policy on his life with the wife as beneficiary.[35] What are the tax consequences of the premiums paid on such a policy?

Premiums paid by a husband on a life insurance policy are deductible by the husband and taxable to the wife if:

(a) the husband is required to do so by a divorce decree and/or separation agreement as a support provision and not merely as security[36] for the support payments, and,

(b) the husband absolutely assigns the policy to his wife, and,

(c) the wife is the irrevocable beneficiary under the policy.

When the policy is "assigned" (i. e., when one's rights under the policy are transferred to someone else), and when the beneficiary is irrevocable, then the husband has no "incidents of ownership" over the policy. He cannot reduce the amount of the insurance, he cannot use

34. Supra p. 281.

35. Supra p. 279.

36. Supra p. 273.

the cash surrender value of the policy, he cannot change the beneficiary. All he does is pay the premiums. Simply to name his wife as beneficiary and to pay the premiums is not enough. For him to be able to deduct the premiums, he must assign the policy to his wife and name her as irrevocable beneficiary.

If the beneficiaries of the life insurance policy are the children of the marriage, no deduction for the premiums is allowed and the premiums are not taxable to the spouse with custody.

SECTION I. PAYMENT OF TAXES, MORTGAGE, INSURANCE AND UTILITIES ON A RESIDENCE

The separation agreement and/or divorce decree may obligate an ex-spouse to pay any of the following bills on the residence occupied by the other ex-spouse: [37]

—utilities;

—real estate taxes;

—interest on the mortgage;

—principal on the mortgage;

—home insurance premiums.

We have two tax questions:

(a) Who can take the deduction for the payment of real estate taxes and of mortgage interest payments available to all taxpayers who itemize their deductions? (These deductions are separate from the alimony deduction.)

(b) When can an *alimony* deduction be taken for the payment of utilities, property taxes, interest and principal, and insurance?

In the following discussion assume the following facts:

Ted and Clara are divorced. Clara is living in the home alone. Ted is making the payments attributable to the home.

First, we consider the payment of utility bills. If Ted pays the utility bills (gas, electric, etc.), the payments are considered periodic payments and are deductible by Ted and taxable to Clara. This is so no matter who owns the home so long as Clara is entitled to sole and exclusive possession of the home.

The tax treatment of the real estate taxes, mortgage, and insurance premiums is more complex. A great deal depends upon how the home is owned. Several possibilities exist:

1) the home is solely owned by Clara;

2) the home is solely owned by Ted;

37. Supra p. 276.

3) the home is owned by both as joint tenants or as tenants by the entirety;

4) the home is owned by both as tenants in common.

1. HOME SOLELY OWNED BY CLARA

Ted's agreement to pay the real estate taxes, mortgage payments and real estate premiums are deductible by Ted as alimony if they are taxable to Clara as periodic payments under the separation agreement and/or divorce decree.

When Clara files her return, if she itemizes her deductions, she can deduct the amounts Ted paid for real estate taxes and for the interest on the mortgage.

2. HOME SOLELY OWNED BY TED

If Clara is living in the home solely owned by Ted without paying any rent to Ted, he cannot deduct the mortgage payments he makes, nor can he deduct the fair rental value of the home as alimony. If, however, Ted itemizes his deductions, he can deduct interest payments and the property tax payments.

3. JOINT TENANTS OR TENANTS BY THE ENTIRETY

A joint tenancy is a form of ownership. The individual owners (called joint tenants) own the entire property together. They do not own parts of it; they own it all together. When one party dies, the property does not pass through the estate of the deceased. It passes immediately to the survivor tenant. When a husband and wife own property as joint tenants, it is called a tenancy by the entirety.

Since Ted and Clara own the home as tenants by the entirety, both are responsible for the principal and interest payments on the mortgage. If the divorce decree requires that Clara must pay the principal and interest on the mortgage out of the money she receives from Ted for her support, then the following tax consequences follow:

a) Ted can deduct one-half of each principal and interest payment as alimony.

b) Ted can deduct the other one-half of the interest payment as an interest deduction if he itemizes his deductions.

c) Ted can deduct all real estate taxes that he pays as a real estate deduction if he itemizes his deductions.

d) Clara must include in her gross income one-half of each principal and interest payment.

4. TENANTS IN COMMON

A tenancy in common is a form of ownership. The individual owners (called tenants in common) own pieces or parts of the property, e. g., each owns one half. When one party dies, his/her share does not pass to the surviving tenant. The deceased tenant's share passes through the estate of the deceased, e. g., to his/her designated heirs. When a husband and wife hold property as tenants in common, they usually each own a one-half interest. Hence, Ted and Clara each own a one-half interest in the home. When Ted makes payments for principal and interest on the mortgage, for insurance and for property taxes, he can do so either on Clara's one-half of the home, or on his own one-half. The tax consequences differ depending on which one-half the payments are being made for.

(a) Payments on Clara's one-half can be deducted by Ted as alimony. Such payments made by Ted are taxable to Clara.

(If Clara itemizes her deductions, she can deduct as "taxes" and "interest" the portion allocated to real estate taxes and mortgage interest payments on her one-half of the property.)

(b) Payments on Ted's one-half of the property are not deductible as alimony and are not taxable to Clara.

(If Ted itemizes his deductions, he can deduct as "taxes" and "interest" the portion he pays for real estate taxes and mortgage interest on his one-half of the property.)

SECTION J. LEGAL COSTS

The general rule is that legal expenses, e. g., counsel fees, paid in reference to divorce or separation are *not* deductible by either spouse. There are, however, several important exceptions that involve:

—legal fees for tax advice, and

—legal fees incurred for the production or collection of income.

TAX ADVICE

When a lawyer is consulted about a divorce, only a portion of the counsel and representation provided relates to tax matters. Yet, only that portion of the legal fee that relates to tax matters is deductible by the husband. It obviously is very important that the bill from the law firm specify what part of the bill is for tax advice and representation. If this is not made clear on the bill, the Internal Revenue Service will allow a reasonable allocation between tax matters and non-tax matters.

A husband *cannot* deduct the legal fees that he pays to *his wife's lawyer* even though such fees are specifically designated for tax advice to her.

PRODUCTION OR COLLECTION OF INCOME

While the husband cannot deduct the cost of the legal fees he incurs in fighting his wife's financial claims pursuant to a separation agreement and/or divorce, his wife *can* deduct legal fees connected with obtaining and collecting alimony from her husband. Her legal fees in obtaining or in resisting the divorce itself are *not* deductible. The deduction must relate to legal assistance pertaining to matters of income, specifically the income she seeks as alimony.

SECTION K. COMMUNITY PROPERTY

Some slightly different tax rules apply to property settlements in community property states:[38] Arizona, California, Idaho, Louisiana, Nevada, New Mexico, Texas and Washington. No taxable income is realized in these states if there is an *equal* division or an *approximately equal* division of the community property.[39] Regardless of which spouse holds title to the property, if it is considered community property (not separate property) and is divided equally, the division following a divorce is not a taxable exchange.

This does not mean that every item of community property must be "split down the middle," half and half. This may be impractical or impossible given the nature of the particular property in question. What is important is an equal or approximately equal division of the total fair market value of all the community property. It is not significant that title to some of the community property goes completely to one spouse so long as the other spouse gets other property of equivalent value.

The basis of each asset received in an equal division of community property is the same as its basis to the community. Where a particular asset is partitioned between the spouses, each spouse's basis for the portion received is the allocable share of the community basis.[40]

Suppose, however, that there is *not* an equal division of the community property. The tax consequences of such an event are the same as those discussed above when there is an unequal division of jointly owned property in a non-community property state.[41]

SECTION L. FEDERAL GIFT TAX

A gift is a voluntary transfer of property without consideration.[42] To avoid a federal gift tax on such transfers, the person receiving the property must have provided an "adequate consideration" for it.

38. Supra p. 144.

39. Oklahoma is a non community property state, although it treats property accumulated during marriage as similar in conception to community property, and regards such property as held by a type of community ownership even though title is in the name of only one of the spouses. State property law will control. For federal tax purposes, a division of property will be treated in the same way as a division of community property. See Internal Revenue Service, *Tax Information*, supra note 9 at p. 11.

40. Ibid.

41. Supra p. 149.

42. Supra p. 110.

Transfers of property between spouses pursuant to a written separation agreement in settlement of their marital and property rights are deemed to be for adequate consideration and therefore exempt from the gift tax *if they obtain a final decree of divorce within two years after entering into the separation agreement.* This is so whether or not the separation agreement is approved or incorporated into the divorce decree.[43] The same is true if the separation agreement provides property or funds (reasonable in amount) for the support of minor children. The transfer of the property or funds for this purpose is not subject to a gift tax if the parents obtain a final divorce within two years after executing the separation agreement that contains these provisions for the children.

If one spouse transfers property to the other spouse when there is no legal obligation to do so, e. g., because neither the separation agreement nor the divorce decree require it, a gift tax may have to be paid. Suppose that a husband pays his wife's legal fees even though he is not required to do so under the terms of the separation agreement and/or the divorce decree. A gift tax will probably have to be paid.

43. Supra p. 283.

Chapter Twenty

SEPARATE MAINTENANCE AND OTHER REMEDIES TO ENFORCE THE SUPPORT DUTY

States provide a variety of ways for a child and/or spouse to enforce the right to be supported—usually against the father-husband:

—in a divorce action; [1]

—in a judicial separation action; [2]

—in an annulment action; [3]

—in a paternity action; [4]

—via the Uniform Reciprocal Enforcement of Support Act; [5]

—in a separate maintenance action;

—in a criminal non-support or desertion action;

—in an action for necessities;

—etc.

SEPARATE MAINTENANCE

An action for separate maintenance (sometimes called an action for support) is a proceeding brought by a spouse (usually the wife) to secure support. Like the judicial separation decree,[6] a separate maintenance decree does not alter the marital status of the parties: they remain married to each other while living separately.

Since the main objective of the separate maintenance action is to reach the property (e. g., cash, land) of the defendant for purposes of support, the court must have personal jurisdiction over the defendant,[7] unless the plaintiff wants to reach only the property owned by the defendant in the forum state (where the action is being brought), in which case, quasi-in-rem jurisdiction [8] is sufficient.

The major ground for a separate maintenance decree is the refusal of the husband to support his wife without just cause. In addition, most states provide that all of the grounds for divorce [9] will also be grounds for a separate maintenance award. The interplay between divorce and separate maintenance can also be seen in the fact

1. Supra p. 343.
2. Supra p. 405.
3. Supra p. 223.
4. Infra p. 452.
5. Supra p. 393.
6. Supra p. 405.
7. Supra p. 352.
8. Supra p. 352.
9. Supra pp. 307–337.

that in many states if the court refuses to grant either party a divorce, it may still enter an order for separate maintenance.

If the defendant makes a good faith offer to reconcile with his spouse before or after the separate maintenance decree is awarded which the plaintiff refuses, the plaintiff becomes a wrongdoer which may justify the defendant in refusing to support her. If the separate maintenance action is still pending, the plaintiff will lose it. If a separate maintenance decree has already been awarded, the defendant can usually discontinue making payments under it. Similarly, if the wife commits other acts of serious marital misconduct, e. g., adultery, she may forfeit her right to be supported by her husband through actions such as one for separate maintenance.

The way that a court determines the amount and form of the separate maintenance award is very similar to the alimony determinations made by a divorce court.[10] If needed, the court can also make child support and child custody decisions in the separate maintenance action.

Assignment # 120

(a) Does your state have an action for separate maintenance or its equivalent? If so, on what grounds will the action be granted?

(b) Prepare a flow chart of all the procedural steps required in a proceeding for separate maintenance or its equivalent.

(See also General Instructions for the State Code Assignment, supra p. 14, for the Court Opinion Assignment, supra p. 26, and for the Flow Chart Assignment, supra p. 33.)

CRIMINAL NON-SUPPORT

In most states it is a crime for a man to desert and/or to fail to support his wife and/or his children, and it is a crime for a woman to desert and/or to fail to support her children. The defendant must act intentionally or willfully. This means that the desertion and/or failure to support must be "curable" by the defendant. If a man, for example, fails to support his children because he is hospitalized and unable to earn any income, the failure to support is clearly not willful. One must have the ability to support before s/he can be guilty of non-support. Of course, many different levels of non-support can exist. The objective of most of the criminal statutes on desertion and non-support is to prevent the needy spouse and children from going on welfare or otherwise becoming public charges. Hence the level of non-support that will lead to criminal prosecution usually must be such that the defendants are destitute as a result of the defendant's neglect. If this is the objective, however, it may seem

10. Supra p. 369.

odd that in some states a husband has a defense to the charge of not supporting his wife (no matter how destitute the wife is left thereby) if the latter engages in improper conduct (e. g., adultery).

An obvious practical problem with the remedy of criminal penalties to enforce the support duty is that if the defendant is jailed, s/he is not likely to be in a position to earn income to meet the support obligation. One way out of this dilemma for an individual convicted of desertion and/or non-support is for the judge to agree to suspend the jail sentence so long as the defendant fulfills the support obligation. In such situations, the defendant may be required to post a bond which will be forfeited in the event that the defendant defaults on the support obligation. Another consequence of such a default could be the imprisonment of the defendant.

Assignment # 121

(1) Is it a crime in your state for an individual to desert and/or to fail to support his/her spouse and/or children? If so, give the citation to the statute that so provides.

(2) When is the crime committed, i. e., what are the elements of the crime?

(3) Prepare a checklist of questions which you would ask in order to help determine whether this crime was committed.

(4) Prepare a flow chart of all the procedural steps required in a criminal prosecution of this crime.

(See also General Instructions for the State Code Assignment, supra p. 14, for the Checklist Formulation Assignment, supra p. 29, and for the Flow Chart Assignment, supra p. 33.)

NECESSITIES

Another way for the wife and children to enforce the support duty of the husband/father is to go out and purchase "necessities" on credit—charging everything to the husband/father. The latter must pay the bills whether or not he knows about them or authorizes them:

—if they are in fact for necessities, and,

—if the husband/father has not provided these necessities for his family.

Since the definition of necessities is not precise, and since a merchant has difficulty knowing whether or not a husband/father has already made provision for the necessities of his family, there are not many merchants who are willing to extend credit in these circumstances without express authorization from the husband/father. If such authorization exists, the theory of recovery would be *agency* rather than the doctrine of necessities. The merchant would recover from the husband/father on the theory that the wife or children made the purchases as the *agents* of the husband/father.

What is a necessity? Generally, it is whatever is necessary to maintain the family at the standard of living to which it was accustomed before the husband/father stopped providing necessities on his own, e. g., home, food, medical care, clothing, furniture. The educational expenses of minor children are necessities. A college education, on the other hand, is not considered a necessity in most states. As college becomes more and more widespread and common, however, it may be that some states will consider it as much a necessity as food and shelter.

Assignment # 122

(a) Find two opinions written by courts in your state which involved the doctrine of necessities. Try to find opinions divided as follows: one which reached the conclusion that the husband or father was liable and one which reached the opposite conclusion. (If you cannot find such opinions written by courts in your state, try neighboring states.)

(b) Would a college education be considered a necessity in your state so that a father would be required to pay the expenses of the education?

(c) Suppose that a wife wishes to complete her undergraduate degree. Would a husband in your state have to pay for it?

(See also General Instructions for the Court Opinion Assignment, supra p. 26.)

INTERVIEWING AND INVESTIGATION CHECKLIST

SUPPORT

	Legal Interviewing Questions	Possible Investigation Tasks
1.	Are you now living with your husband?	* Assist client in collecting records, e. g., receipts, of expenditures made since the support stopped or was interrupted. * Obtain court records of all prior court proceedings, if any.
2.	If not, when did you separate?	
3.	Do the two of you have a separation agreement that specifies how much support he is to provide you and the children?	
4.	Have you ever sued him for support? If so, give the details of the suit(s).	
5.	Describe your standard of living while your husband was supporting you and the children, e. g., value of home, cars, education expenses, kind of clothing, vacations.	
6.	When did he stop providing support? Did it stop completely? Occasionally? Give details.	
7.	How old were the children when the support stopped or became sporatic?	
8.	Do the children live with you?	
9.	Where does your husband live?	
10.	Does your husband have the means to support you and the children?	
11.	Why do you think that he is not fulfilling his support obligation?	
12.	Is he doing it intentionally, e. g., to hurt you and the children?	
13.	Have you made any purchases for food, clothing, shelter, medical care, etc. and charged such purchases to your husband? If so, give the specifics.	
14.	Are there any other purchases which you have refrained from making for any reason? If so, explain.	
15.	In the past, has your husband given you or the children permission to make purchases on his credit? If so, give the details.	

IM-491

Assignment # 123

(a) In your state, when, if ever, does a wife have to support her husband (or ex-husband)?

(b) In your state, when, if ever, does a child have to support his/her parents? When, if ever, does a grandparent have to support a grandchild, or vice versa? When, if ever, does a niece/nephew have to support an aunt/uncle, or vice versa?

(See also General Instructions for the State Code Assignment, supra p. 14, and for the Court Opinion Assignment, supra p. 26.)

NOTE

Some states have tried to enforce the support obligation through their marriage formulation statutes. The statute may provide, for example, that no individual will be allowed to enter a marriage if that person has failed to support his/her child in the custody of someone else. The United States Supreme Court has recently held, however, that such statutes are an unconstitutional invasion on the fundamental right to marry. Zablocki v. Redhail, —— U.S. ——, 98 S.Ct. 673, 54 L.Ed.2d 618 (1978).

Chapter Twenty-One

THE LEGAL RIGHTS OF WOMEN

Today, a married woman would probably consider it condescending to be told that she has the right:

—to make her own will;

—to own her own property;

—to make a contract in her own name;

—to be a juror;

—to vote;

—to bring a suit and to be sued;

—to execute a deed.

The fact is, however, that there was a time in our history when a married woman could not engage in any of the above activities at all, or could not engage in them without the consent of her husband, e. g., she could not bring a suit against a third party unless her husband agreed to join in the suit. At common law, the husband and wife were considered one person, and the one person was the husband!

While a great deal happened to change the status of women, particularly married women, all of the discrimination has not been eliminated.

1. PROPERTY

Most states have enacted what are called Married Women's Property Acts which remove almost all of the disabilities that married women suffered at common law. Under the terms of most of these statutes, women are given the right to own and dispose of property in the same manner as men enjoy this right.

2. CONTRACTS AND CONVEYANCES

Similarly, women in most states have been given the power through the Married Women's Property Acts to enter into all forms of contracts and conveyances (i. e., transfers of land) in their own name independent of their husbands. If, however, both spouses owned the property together, then, of course, before the wife could convey the property to someone else, she would normally have to have the consent of her husband—and vice versa.

What about contracts and conveyances between the spouses? Are there any restrictions on the ability of one spouse to enter into agreements with the other? If they are still living together, they cannot enter a contract concerning the husband's duty to support his wife (although such a contract may be valid after the parties have separated.[1]) It would be illegal for spouses to agree (collusively) to obtain a divorce by misrepresenting evidence to the court on the grounds for divorce or on a procedural matter.[2] In most states, the wife owes a duty to provide "services" to her husband, usually household services, which cannot be the subject of a contract between the spouses. A husband, for example, cannot agree to pay his wife for the services she renders since she already has a duty to provide these services.

Courts tend to be very suspicious of conveyances of property between husband and wife. Suppose, for example, that a husband transfers all of his property into his wife's name for which she pays nothing so that when he is sued by his creditors, he technically does not own any assets from which they can satisfy their claims. The transfers would be considered fraudulent and would be invalidated by a court.

Two other situations can cause difficulty:

A. The husband buys property with his own funds but puts the title in his wife's name. (Assume this is not a fraudulent transfer—he is not trying to defraud his creditors.)

B. The wife buys property with her own funds but puts the title in her husband's name.

Courts treat the above two situations differently. In "A" above, many courts presume that the husband intended to make a gift of the property to his wife. In "B," however, many courts do *not* presume a gift of the wife to her husband. The presumption is that the husband is holding the property in trust for his wife. Some have argued that this is an unconstitutional discrimination based on sex.

Assignment # 124

For the following questions, you will need to consult the statutory code of your state and/or the opinions of the courts sitting in your state. See General Instructions for the State Code Assignment, supra p. 14, and for the Court Opinion Assignment, supra p. 26.

(a) What is the citation for the Married Women's Property Act in your state?

(b) In your state, does a husband have to consent or join his wife when the latter wishes to convey her separately owned property to a third person?

(c) What restrictions, if any, exist in your state on the capacity of one spouse to enter into a contract with the other?

(d) Suppose that a wife works for her husband in the latter's business in your state. Does the husband have to pay her or would such work be considered part of the "services" that she owes him?

1. Supra p. 253.

2. Supra p. 338.

3. DEATH OF THE HUSBAND

At common law, when a husband died, the surviving wife had a dower right.[3] This consisted of:

(a) her right during her life time [4] to use;

(b) one third of all the real estate; [5]

(c) owned or acquired by her husband during the marriage.[6]

Dower has been abolished in most states. In place of dower, states protect the wife by giving her a share of her husband's estate, often called a "forced share" because the wife may be able to *elect* to take this share in place of and in spite of what her husband may have provided for her in his will.

Assignment # 125

For the following questions, examine the statutory code of your state. See also General Instructions for the State Code Assignment, supra p. 14.

(a) Has dower been abolished in your state? If so, give the citation to the statute that abolished it.

(b) If a widow is not satisfied with the property left her in the will of her deceased husband, what can she do in your state? Can she elect against the will?

(c) If her husband dies intestate (i. e., without leaving a valid will), what proportion of his estate will his widow receive in your state?

4. EMPLOYMENT

There are a good many laws which in theory have eliminated job discrimination against women. The Equal Protection Clause of the United States Constitution provides that:

> "No State shall . . . deny to any person within its jurisdiction the equal protection of the laws."

If a state passes a law which treats women differently from men, it will be invalidated unless there is a reasonable purpose for the differentiation. Only *unreasonable* discrimination violates the constitution. Title VII of the 1964 Civil Rights Act provides that:

> "It shall be an unlawful employment practice for an employer . . . to fail or refuse to hire or to discharge any individual, or otherwise to discriminate against any individual with respect to

3. Supra p. 282.

4. The right to use property during one's lifetime is called a life estate.

5. Or more specifically, one third of all real estate which could pass to the children of the marriage by inheritance.

6. The corresponding right which the husband had in the property of his wife when she died was called curtesy. Supra p. 128.

> his compensation, terms, conditions, or privileges of employment, because of such individual's . . . sex; . . . .[7]

Again, this does not mean that all sex discrimination in employment is illegal. Sex discrimination is permitted if it is "job related." More precisely, discrimination based on sex is valid if sex is a "Bona Fide Occupational Qualification" (BFOQ) reasonably necessary to the operation of a particular business or enterprise. If men and women are doing the same job in a company but are being paid differently, the practice would be invalid. Since they are both performing the same job, sex cannot be a BFOQ. On the other hand, it would be proper for a state prison to exclude all women from being guards in all-male prisons where a significant number of the inmates are convicted sex offenders. It is reasonable to anticipate that some of the inmates would attack the female guards, creating a security problem. In this instance, sex (i. e., being a male) in an all-male prison would be a BFOQ.

The major complaint leveled against the laws outlawing sex discrimination in employment is that they have been very inadequately enforced. The law of discrimination can be complex and confusing. Bringing a discrimination case is usually time consuming and expensive. In the view of many, we have a long way to go before the problem is solved.

5. NAME

Most women change their name to that of their husband at the time of marriage. This is done for one of several reasons:

—the law of the state requires that she take the surname of her husband;

—the law of the state gives her a choice on keeping her maiden name or taking her husband's name, and she chooses the latter;

—the law of the state gives her a choice which she does not know about; she uses her husband's surname simply because that is the way that it is done in her environment.

If the state law requires her to use her husband's surname and she does not wish to do so, she will have to go through a statutorily defined procedure to change her name from her husband's to her maiden name or to another name. If she has a choice and she decides not to use her husband's surname, she does not have to go through any special steps to exercise this choice. Once she is married, she simply continues using her maiden name or she starts using a totally new name (other than her husband's). In such states, her legal name is whatever name she uses after her marriage so long as she is not trying to defraud anyone (e. g., to make it difficult for her creditors to locate her), and so long as her use of the name is exclusive and consistent.

7. 42 U.S.C.A. § 2000e–2(a)(1)(1974).

Once there has been a divorce, most states permit the woman to request that the court allow her to resume using her married name or another name. There are some states, however, that place restrictions on this. She may not be able to resume her maiden name or to select a new name if there are children of the marriage, or if the divorce court has found her to have been the "guilty" party in the breakup of the marriage.

Suppose that she makes the request that her children's name be changed to her maiden name, or to the name of her new husband. Many courts will be reluctant to authorize this change unless it can be shown that the change is in the best interests of the child.

What happens if a woman changes her name improperly, e. g., by failing to use her husband's surname after marriage in a state that requires her to do so, or by resuming her maiden name following divorce without court permission in a state that requires such permission? The issue can arise in a number of contexts. A woman must sign her name to register to vote, to register a car, to sign a deed, to obtain a passport, to obtain a social security number, to obtain credit, etc. If a woman fails to use her proper legal name, she may run into substantial difficulty. The Motor Vehicle Department, for example, may refuse to issue her a driver's license, or the county may deny her the right to vote.

As indicated, the main time that a woman must go through a formal, statutorily defined change-of-name procedure is when the state requires her to take her husband's surname upon marriage, but she wishes to resume using her maiden name or to use some other name. This statutory procedure involves several steps, e. g., filing a petition to change one's name in the appropriate state court, stating the reasons for the change request, paying a fee to the court, publishing a notice of the court proceeding in a local newspaper. This process is usually not complicated so long as the court is convinced that the name change will not mislead anyone who may need to contact the individual, e. g., police officials, a former spouse, creditors.

Assignment # 126

For most of the following assignments, you will need to examine your state statutory code. You may also need to check opinions written by state courts of your state. See General Instructions for the State Code Assignment, supra p. 14, and for the Court Opinion Assignment, supra p. 26.

(a) When a woman marries in your state, does she have to take her husband's surname?

(b) Following a divorce, how can a woman have her name changed back to her maiden name?

(c) Make a list of every administrative agency situated in your state which involves the filling out of some kind of application e. g., for a driver's license, for state employment, for food stamps, for workmen's compensation, etc. Assume that a woman who has just been married is filling out all of these applications. She wants to use her maiden name, not her husband's surname on the application. She has not been through any change-of-name statutory procedure. Contact each of these agencies and ask if a woman can use her maiden name on the application. If there are a large number of agencies in the area, perhaps the class could be divided up so that each student will have the responsibility of contacting a set number of agencies. At a designated time, there will be a class discussion in which the students will report on the responses they received from the agencies they contacted.

(d) Prepare a Flow Chart of all the steps that an individual must go through to change his/her name in your state through the statutory procedure. (See also General Instructions for the Flow Chart Assignment, supra p. 33.)

(e) Assume that you want to change your name. Pick a new name. Draft all the court papers which would be needed for you to acquire your new name via the statutory procedure outlined in the Flow Chart prepared in Assignment (d).

(f) Mary Jones married Tom Smith in your state. Her name then became Mary Smith. They had one child, Paul Smith. Tom abandons Mary. Can Mary have Paul's name changed to Paul Jones in your state? Assume that Paul is five years old and that Mary does not want to bring a divorce proceeding against Tom.

6. ABORTION

There was a time when abortions were permitted only when the health of the mother necessitated it (usually to preserve her life) or when special circumstances warranted it, e. g., when the pregnancy was caused by rape or incest. The law was dramatically changed in 1973 by Roe v. Wade [8] in which the United States Supreme Court held:

(a) For the stage prior to approximately the end of the first trimester, the abortion decision and its effectuation must be left to the medical judgment of the pregnant woman's attending physician.

(b) For the stage subsequent to approximately the end of the first trimester, the State, in promoting its interest in the health of the mother, may, if it chooses, regulate the abortion procedure in ways that are reasonably related to maternal health.

8. 410 U.S. 113, 93 S.Ct. 705, 35 L.Ed. 2d 147 (1973).

> (c) For the stage subsequent to viability, the State in promoting its interest in the potentiality of human life may, if it chooses, regulate, and even proscribe, abortion except where it is necessary, in appropriate medical judgment, for the preservation of the life or health of the mother.[9]

Hence, during the first trimester, a state cannot prohibit abortions. If a woman wants an abortion during this period, she can have one if a doctor agrees to perform it. To deny her this right is to infringe upon her constitutional right to privacy. During the period between the end of the first trimester and the beginning of the child's viability (a child is viable after about six months of pregnancy), the state can regulate medical procedures to make sure that abortions are performed safely—but the state cannot prohibit abortions altogether. Once the child is viable, abortions can be prohibited unless they are necessary to preserve the life or health of the mother.

If the woman is poor and cannot afford an abortion which she wants for non-health reasons (a non-therapeutic abortion), the state is *not required* to pay for it, although a number of states have decided to set aside funds for such abortions.

A husband who does not want his wife to have an abortion cannot prevent the abortion, i. e., his consent is not necessary. Similarly, parents of a minor daughter cannot prevent her from having an abortion if the daughter and her doctor have decided to terminate the pregnancy, i. e., parental consent cannot be made a precondition to the availability of an abortion to the minor daughter of the parents.

9. 410 U.S. 113, 164–165, 93 S.Ct. 732, 733.

*

Chapter Twenty-Two

THE PRIVILEGE FOR MARITAL COMMUNICATIONS

A number of evidence terms need to be distinguished:

COMPETENCY TO TESTIFY

At one time, both spouses were disqualified from ever giving testimony for or against each other in a court proceeding. Today, this is not so in civil cases. In some states, however, the rule still applies in criminal cases so that a prosecutor could not call the spouse of the accused as a witness (unless the spouse is the victim of the alleged crime) without the consent of the accused spouse.

Also, according to Lord Mansfield's rule "the declarations of a father or mother cannot be admitted to bastardize the issue born after marriage." Hence, if a wife becomes pregnant during the marriage and the husband knows that he is not the father because he stopped having sex with his wife long before the child was conceived, many states will *not* permit him to introduce evidence that he had no access to his wife during the critical time because such evidence, if true, would "bastardize" the child. Courts are very reluctant to admit evidence which would cast doubt on the legitimacy of children. As we shall see later, however, many states have either eliminated or have limited Lord Mansfield's rule.[1]

PRIVILEGE FOR MARITAL COMMUNICATIONS[2]

During the marital relationship, a spouse has a privilege to refuse to disclose and to prevent another from disclosing confidential communications with his/her spouse while they were husband and wife. For example:

> David and Leslie are married. David tells Leslie that he just chopped down his neighbor's tree. The neighbor sues David and calls Leslie as a witness to ask her whether she and David ever spoke about the tree.

Leslie can refuse to give testimony on what her husband told her or on what she told her husband during marriage. Even if Leslie wanted to give such testimony, David could object and prevent her from doing so. This is the effect of the privilege for marital communications.

In most states, the privilege is limited to communications in the sense of something spoken or written. In several states, however, the privilege has been broadened to include any act or transaction that occurs during the marriage. For example, a spouse in such a state

1. Infra p. 454.

2. See *McCormick's Handbook of the Law of Evidence*, pp. 161ff. 2d Ed. (1972).

would not be allowed to testify that she saw her husband drinking or that he was sick on a certain day.

The spouses must intend that the communication be private. Most conversations between spouses, however, are assumed to be private except perhaps those that relate to business agreements between the spouses. The parties probably intend conversations about such agreements to be non-private since others would have to know about them if they had to be enforced.

If a third party hears the conversation or reads the letter between the spouses, the privilege is lost. This is so even though the third person is a member of the family (other than a very young child), and even though the third person may have intentionally intercepted the conversation, e. g., by eavesdropping, or may have accidentally heard it or read what was written.

The privilege does not apply in certain situations:

1. In criminal proceedings for alleged crimes committed by one spouse against the other or against the children.
2. When one spouse is suing the other, e. g., divorce, legal separation, conversion actions.

The theory supporting the existence of the privilege is the encouragement of openness in marriage. If the parties thought that what they said to each other during marriage could later be used as evidence in court, they arguably would be reluctant to communicate. Of course, in the case of criminal behavior by a spouse or civil litigation between the spouses, there is very little marital communication and openness left to protect. This is the reason for the above exceptions to the applicability of the privilege.

Assignment # 127

(a) What is the privilege for marital communications in your state? Cite a statute or court opinion that defines the privilege.

(b) Give three examples of marital communications that were held privileged by courts in your state. Use a neighboring state if you cannot find three examples from court opinions of your state.

(See also General Instructions for the State Code Assignment, supra p. 14, and for the Court Opinion Assignment, supra p. 26.)

Chapter Twenty-Three

ILLEGITIMACY AND PATERNITY PROCEEDINGS

SECTION A. CONSEQUENCES OF ILLEGITIMACY

At common law, the illegitimate child (still referred to as a "bastard" in many legal texts) was *filius nullius,* the child of nobody. The central disability imposed by this status was that the child had no right to inherit from either of its parents. In addition, the child had no right to be supported by its father. Fortunately, the pronounced discrimination that has existed for centuries between the legitimate and the illegitimate child is beginning to erode. This is not to say, however, that the discrimination has ended.

(1) Inheritance

Statutes have been passed in most states permitting an illegitimate child to inherit from his/her mother when the latter dies intestate (i. e., dies without leaving a will). A number of states have also passed statutes permitting an illegitimate child to inherit from his/her intestate father. In most states, however, such statutes do not exist with respect to the father. In these states, the main way that an illegitimate child can share in the estate of his/her deceased father is when the latter leaves a will (i. e., dies testate rather than intestate) making provision for such child. (Some states will allow an illegitimate child to inherit from his/her intestate father if the latter has acknowledged [1] the child or has been found to be the father of the child in a paternity action.[2]) The United States Supreme Court has held that a state statute can prefer legitimate children over illegitimate children in the disposition of the property of their father who dies intestate.[3]

(2) Testate distribution

When the father of an illegitimate child dies testate (i. e., leaving a will), a clause may be found in which property is given "to my children" or "to my heirs." If the father has legitimate and illegitimate children living when he dies, the question sometimes arises as to whether he intended to include his illegitimate children within the word "children" or "heirs." In order to resolve this question of intent, the court must look at all of the circumstances (e. g., how much con-

1. Infra p. 451.

2. Infra p. 452.

3. Labine v. Vincent, 401 U.S. 532, 91 S.Ct. 1017, 28 L.Ed.2d 288 (1971). Trimble v. Gordon, 430 U.S. 762, 97 S.Ct. 1459, 52 L.Ed.2d 31 (1977). See also Annotation, "The Supreme Court's View as to the Status and the Rights of Illegitimate Children," 41 L.Ed.2d 1228 (1975).

tact did the illegitimate child have with the father at the time the latter wrote the will and at the time he died). A surprisingly large number of cases exist in which the court concluded that the illegitimate child was *not* included within the words "children" or "heirs."

(3) Support

There was a time when many state laws did not obligate a father to support his illegitimate children. Such laws have been invalidated as an improper discrimination between legitimate children (who must be supported by their father) and illegitimate children (who did not have to be supported by him). Hence, so long as paternity can be established, a father has an equal duty to support *all* of his children.

(4) Wrongful death action

When a parent dies due to the wrongful act of another, who can sue? Legitimate and illegitimate children have an equal right to bring wrongful death actions against defendants who have caused the death of one or both of their parents.

(5) Workmen's compensation

When a father dies due to injury on the job, the workmen's compensation laws of the states permit the children of the deceased to recover benefits. If any state gives a preference to legitimate children over illegitimate children in claiming these benefits, the state is unconstitutionally denying equal protection of the law to the illegitimate child.

(6) Social Security

Social Security laws discriminate against illegitimate children in various phases of the social security system. Some of these discriminatory provisions have been declared unconstitutional while others have been allowed to stand. For example, while it is unconstitutional to deny social security survivorship benefits to a child solely because that child is illegitimate, it may be permissible to impose greater procedural burdens on illegitimate children than on legitimate children in applying for benefits. For example, if the law requires that a child be "dependent" on the deceased father as a condition of receiving survivorship benefits, an illegitimate child can be forced to prove that s/he was dependent on the father whereas no such requirement will be imposed on the legitimate child—the law will presume that the legitimate child was dependent on the father without requiring specific proof of it.

(7) Custody

In most states, when the father and mother both want separate custody of their illegitimate child, the mother is preferred over the father unless the mother is found to be unfit.[4] This preference has been challenged as an unconstitutional discrimination based on sex.

4. See also supra p. 376.

Assignment # 128

Answer the following questions by examining your state code. (See also General Instructions for the State Code Assignment, supra p. 451.)

(a) What are the inheritance rights of an illegitimate child in your state? From whom can an illegitimate child inherit?

(b) Who can inherit from an illegitimate child?

(c) Make a list of every mention of legitimacy/illegitimacy in your state code other than in the area of inheritance rights. Explain each reference, e. g., in what context and for what purpose is legitimacy/illegitimacy mentioned? Do not include references to how an illegitimate child is legitimated or how paternity is proved. Focus instead on those instances, if any, in which your state code differentiates between a person of legitimate origin and one of illegitimate origin.

SECTION B. LEGITIMATION AND PATERNITY

Legitimation is the process by which an illegitimate child becomes a legitimate child. A paternity proceeding is a process by which the fatherhood of a child is determined. In most states, a finding of paternity does not necessarily lead to the legitimation of the child.

LEGITIMATION

States have different methods by which illegitimate children can be legitimated:

—*Acknowledgement.* The father publicly recognizes or acknowledges the illegitimate child as his. States differ on how this acknowledgement must take place. In some states, it must be in writing and witnessed. In others, no writing is necessary if the man's activities strongly indicate that he is the father of the child, e. g., the father takes the child into the family and treats it the same as the children who were born legitimate.

—*Marriage.* If the mother and father of the illegitimate child marry, the child may be legitimated automatically.

—*Combination of acknowledgement and marriage.* Some states require both marriage of parents and some form of acknowledgement by the father.

—*Legitimation proceeding.* A few states have special proceedings by which illegitimate children can be legitimated.

—*Paternity proceedings.* Although most paternity proceedings deal with fatherhood only, in a few states, a finding of paternity also legitimates the child.

—*Legitimation by birth.* In a very few states, all children are legitimate whether or not its parents were married at the time of birth.

As indicated earlier, children of annulled marriages are considered legitimate according to special statutes even though technically the parents were not validly married at the time the children were born.[5]

Assignment # 129

(a) In what way(s) can an illegitimate child be legitimated in your state? (See also General Instructions for the State Code Assignment, supra p. 14.)

(b) Tom and Mary are married. Tom is sterile. They both agree to have Mary artificially inseminated with the semen of an anonymous donor. They do so and a child is born. Is this child legitimate in your state? (See also General Instructions for the Legal Analysis Assignment, supra p. 16, for the State Code Assignment, supra p. 14, and for the Court Opinion Assignment, supra p. 26.)

PATERNITY

The major method by which a father is forced to support his illegitimate child is through a paternity proceeding, sometimes called a filiation proceeding or a bastardy proceeding. Once fatherhood is determined, the support obligation is imposed. In addition, some states impose criminal penalties for a father's unjustified refusal to support his illegitimate child.

The paternity proceeding itself looks a good deal like a criminal proceeding in many states, e. g., a warrant is issued for the arrest of the putative (i. e., alleged) father, the jury renders a guilty or not guilty verdict. States differ on whether the proceeding is criminal, civil or neither.

The mother of the child is the one who usually initiates the paternity proceeding, although the child is often also given standing to sue through a specially appointed representative, e. g., a guardian ad litem. When the mother brings the action, it is important to know whether the child was made a party to the proceeding and was represented. If not, then in some states, the child will *not* be bound by the judgment. For example:

> Mary, the mother of Sam, brings a paternity proceeding against Kevin, alleging that Kevin is the father of Sam. Sam is not made a party to the proceeding. A guardian ad litem is not appointed for him and he is not otherwise represented in court. The court finds that Kevin is not the father of Sam. Ten years later, Sam

5. Supra p. 214.

brings his own action against Kevin for support, alleging that he is the son of Kevin.

Is Sam's support action ten years later barred by the defense of res judicata,[6] i. e., was the fatherhood issue already resolved in the paternity proceeding? States differ in their answer to this question. Many will only bar the later suit of the child if the latter was a party to the earlier case that decided the fatherhood issue. In such states, Sam *would* be able to re-litigate the paternity issue against Kevin.

A related question is whether or not the mother can enter into a settlement with the putative father under which she agrees to drop the paternity proceeding in exchange for defendant's agreement to pay a certain amount for the support of the child and for the mother's expenses in giving birth to the child. In some states, it is illegal to enter into such a settlement agreement. In other states, however, the settlement is permitted if the child is represented and/or the settlement is approved by the court.

The paternity proceeding is considered an in personam[7] action requiring personal jurisdiction over the defendant-putative father. This generally means that service of process must be made on the defendant in person within the forum state, i. e., the state where the paternity proceeding is being brought. If the defendant is not a resident of the forum state, can personal jurisdiction be obtained over him under the state's long-arm statute on the basis of his not having supported his alleged child in the forum state?[8] States differ in their answer to this question. Many will not authorize personal jurisdiction unless the defendant is served in the forum state. Others, however, permit out-of-state service.

Once the trial on the paternity issue begins, the defendant is faced with a presumption of legitimacy. A child born to a married woman is presumed to be legitimate unless conclusively proven otherwise. This means that if the defendant is the husband of the mother and denies paternity, he must introduce very strong evidence that he is not the father, e. g., evidence that he is sterile. Furthermore, according to Lord Mansfield's rule, neither spouse can introduce evidence that they had no sexual intercourse around the time of conception (i. e., evidence of non-access) if such evidence would tend to "bastardize" the child.[9] Hence, if a defendant has not had sexual intercourse with his wife in years he cannot introduce evidence to this effect since it would tend to "bastardize" the mother's recently born child. It is obviously very difficult for a husband to deny that he is the father of his wife's child. The harshness of this rule has been criticized. A

6. Supra p. 395.

7. Supra p. 352.

8. Supra p. 355. "Long-Arm Statute: Obtaining Jurisdiction over Non-Resident Parent in Filiation or Support Proceeding, Annotation", 76 A.L.R.3d 708 (1977).

9. Supra p. 447.

number of states have either eliminated or have substantially limited Lord Mansfield's rule.

In many states, parties can be required to take blood-grouping tests. Such tests cannot conclusively establish who the father is, but they are known to be very reliable, if properly administered, to establish non-paternity, i. e., to eliminate certain men as possible fathers. In most states, the test results can only be admitted into evidence if they show non-paternity. If the father refuses to take the blood test, the court might resolve the paternity issue against him or permit the mother's attorney to let the jury know that he did refuse to take it, leaving them with the obvious implication that he had somehing to hide.

Assignment # 130

(a) In what way(s) can the fatherhood of a child be determined by a court in your state?

(b) Select the main way that fatherhood is established in your state, e. g., in a paternity proceeding, and prepare a flow chart of all the procedural steps of the process.

(c) What is the statute of limitations for paternity actions in your state?

(d) How, if at all, can blood grouping tests be used in your state?

(e) Assume that you work for the law firm that represents the defendant-putative father in a paternity proceeding in your state. The defendant has not lived with the plaintiff-mother for two years, although they are still married. Draft a set of interrogatories to be sent by the defendant to the plaintiff in which you attempt to obtain as much information as possible that will be relevant to the defense of the case.

(f) Does Lord Mansfield's rule apply in your state?

(See also General Instructions for the State Code Assignment, supra p. 14, for the Flow Chart Assignment, supra p. 33, for the Court Opinion Assignment, supra p. 26, and for the Interrogatories Assignment, supra p. 31.)

Chapter Twenty-Four

THE LEGAL STATUS OF CHILDREN

Generally, an adult is an individual twenty-one years of age or older. A minor (or a child) is anyone under twenty-one. (Note: a person reaches twenty-one on the day *before* his/her twenty-first birthday.) Once this age arrives, *majority* is achieved. The difficulty, however, is that not all states use twenty-one as the age of majority. Many states set the age at eighteen. Furthermore, a person may be a minor for one purpose, but not for another. Hence, one cannot always rely on twenty-one as the critical age to determine rights and obligations. For purposes of clarity, three questions must always be asked:

a. What is the individual trying to do, e. g., vote, enter a contract, get out of a contract?

b. Does the state set a specific age that is relevant to that task or objective?

c. Has the individual been emancipated? If so, does the emancipation mean that the person is no longer a minor for purposes of that particular task or objective?

Emancipation is the relinquishment of parental control over the child. A child can be emancipated before the age of majority if certain events take place which clearly indicate that the individual is living independent of his/her parents with the consent of the latter. Such events include the marriage of the individual, entering the service, the abandonment of the individual by his/her parents, an explicit agreement between the parents and individual that the latter will live independently, etc. As we discuss the various rights and obligations of "minors," we will see that it will sometimes be important to know whether emancipation has occurred.

Assignment # 131

Find one opinion written by a court in your state in which the court held that emancipation had occurred. (If you cannot find an opinion written by a court of your state, try the courts of a neighboring state.) State the facts of the opinion. What specific events led the court to conclude that emancipation had occurred? (See also General Instructions for the Court Opinion Assignment, supra p. 26.)

1. CONTRACTS

As a general rule (to which there are exceptions), a minor does not have legal capacity to enter a binding contract. More specifically, a minor does not have to perform a contract s/he has entered if s/he repudiates or disaffirms the contract at any time before the minor reaches majority or within a reasonable time after reaching majority.

> Tom is fifteen years of age—clearly a minor. He goes to the ABC Truck Co. and purchases a truck. The sales contract calls for a small down payment (which Tom pays) with the remainder to be paid in installments—on credit. Two months later, Tom changes his mind about the truck and decides to take it back to the dealer. The truck is still in good working order.

If Tom were an adult, he would be bound by his contract. Once the contract had been formed by Tom, the adult, and the company,[1] they both would be bound by it. Neither party could rescind the contract simply because of a change of mind. The difference, however, in our hypothetical is that Tom is a minor. Most states give minors the right to *disaffirm* their contracts so long as they do so while they are still minors or within a reasonable time (e. g., several months) after they have reached majority. In Tom's case, this would mean that he is not bound by the contract to buy the truck. He can take it back and perhaps even force the company to return the money he had paid on it thus far (although in some states, the merchant may be able to keep all or part of the purchase price paid thus far to cover the depreciation resulting from the minor's use of the item.)

Why is it that minors are given this right to disaffirm? The objective of the law is to protect young people from their immaturity. Merchants are put on notice that if they deal with minors, they do so at their own risk.

This does not mean that every contract entered into by a minor is invalid. If the minor does not disaffirm, the contract is valid and can be enforced against the minor. Similarly, if a minor tries to disaffirm too late, the contract will be enforced against him/her. Suppose that Tom tried to disaffirm the truck sales contract when he was twenty three years old (and that the age of majority in his state is twenty-one). He must disaffirm before he reaches majority or within a *reasonable* time thereafter. Most courts would probably find that a two year wait to disaffirm is unreasonable.

What happens if the minor commits fraud in order to induce the merchant to enter the contract, e. g., lies about his/her age via a forged birth certificate. Some courts take the position that such wrongdoing by the minor prevents (i. e., estops) him/her from being able to disaffirm. Other courts, however, argue that the policy in favor of protecting minors against their own immaturity is so strong that even their own fraud will not destroy their right to disaffirm.

Special statutes have been passed in many states to limit the minor's right to disaffirm, particularly with respect to certain kinds of contracts. In some states, for example, some contracts of employ-

1. On the elements of a contract, see supra p. 110.

ment are binding on minors, such as sports and show business contracts. Similarly, contractual arrangements with banks and other lending institutions cannot be disaffirmed in many states. When a minor makes a contract with a merchant for a necessity,[2] the contract can rarely be disaffirmed.

When a guardian has been appointed over a minor and the guardian enters a contract on behalf of that minor, the contract generally cannot be disaffirmed by the minor. Suppose, for example, that a minor is involved in litigation and an offer of settlement is made. A settlement is a contract. If a court appoints a guardian over the minor and the guardian negotiates a settlement contract on behalf of the minor, the latter cannot later disaffirm the settlement if the court finds that the settlement was a fair one. Most states have enacted the Uniform Gifts to Minors Act pursuant to which gifts of securities can be made to minors through custodians of the securities. The custodian can sell and reinvest the securities on behalf of the minor. Contracts made by the custodian for this purpose cannot be later disaffirmed by the minor.[3]

Suppose that a minor has become emancipated before reaching the age of majority, e. g., by marrying or by being abandoned by his/her parents. Does this end his/her power to disaffirm? There is no absolute answer to this question. A minor so emancipated may be denied the power to disaffirm in some states, while in others, it will not affect the power.[4]

Assignment # 132

Answer the following questions by examining the statutory code of your state and/or the opinions of the courts in your state. (See also General Instructions for the State Code Assignment, supra p. 14, and for the Court Opinion Assignment, supra p. 26.)

(a) What is the minimum age to enter a contract that cannot be disaffirmed in your state?

(b) Are there specific kinds of contracts which a minor cannot disaffirm in your state? If so, what are they?

(c) If a minor lies about his/her age in entering a contract, does this misrepresentation affect the minor's power to disaffirm the contract in your state?

(d) If the minor in your state still has the item purchased through the contract, must s/he return the item to the merchant as a condition of the exercise of the power to disaffirm?

2. For the definition of a necessity, see supra p. 435.

3. Calamari, J., & Perillo, J., *The Law of Contracts*, p. 202 (1970).

4. See Clark, H., *The Law of Domestic Relations*, p. 244 (1968).

(e) Does your state have the Uniform Gifts to Minors Act? If so, give the citation and state how it works.

2. DOMICILE

The domicile of a minor is the domicile of his/her parents—even in some instances when the minor lives in a different state from his/her parents.[5] With parental consent, however, a minor can acquire his/her own separate domicile. Similarly, if a minor who has not yet reached the age of majority is emancipated, many states give that individual the power to acquire his/her own domicile.

3. WILL

States have specified certain minimum ages for the disposition of property by a will. Some states have different minimum ages for the disposition of personal property (e. g., clothes, cash) and of real property (e. g., land). In a few states, the emancipation of the minor by his/her marriage will enable the minor to make a valid will before reaching the minimum age.

Assignment # 133

Answer the following questions by examining the statutory code of your state and/or the opinions of the courts of your state. See also General Instructions for the State Code Assignment, supra p. 14, and for the Court Opinion Assignment, supra p. 26.

(a) What is the minimum age for an individual to execute a valid will in your state?

(b) When a minor dies without leaving a valid will (i. e., dies intestate) either because s/he never attempted to write a will or because the will s/he attempted was invalid due to being under age, what happens to his/her property? Who gets it?

4. TORT

On the tort liability of a minor, see Chapter Twenty-six.[6]

5. VOTING

Twenty-one has been the traditional minimum voting age, although many states have recently lowered this to eighteen.

Assignment # 134

What is the minimum voting age in your state? (See also General Instructions for the State Code Assignment, supra p. 14.)

5. See supra p. 346 for a discussion of what happens when the child's parents are domiciled in different states.

6. Infra p. 477.

6. PROPERTY AND EARNINGS

A minor can own real and personal property in his/her own name. The parents of a minor do not own and cannot dispose of the minor's property. A minor, on the other hand, does not have a right to keep his/her own earnings. The parent who has the duty to support the child [7] has a right to keep the earnings of the child. If the child had not yet reached the age of majority, but had been emancipated (e. g., by express agreement with the parents, by marriage, by abandonment by the parents), the parents would not be entitled to the earnings of the child.

7. SCHOOL

If a parent does not wish to send his/her child to a public or private school, can the child be kept at home and be taught by the parents or some other individual in the home? A few states permit this. In other states, the compulsory attendance law requires that the child be sent to an approved school.

Can a child force his/her parent to pay for his/her college education? It depends upon whether the child can convince the court that a college education is a "necessity." [8]

Assignment # 135

Can a parent educate his/her child at home in your state? (See General Instructions for the State Code Assignment, supra p. 14.)

8. NEGLECT AND ABUSE

Statutes exist protecting children who have been neglected or abused by their parents. Neglect is often defined as failing to give support, education, medical care or other care necessary for the child's welfare, e. g., the refusal of a parent to give a child a needed operation, leaving a young child unattended at home. Abuse often involves physical harm inflicted by the parent on the child.[9]

If a court finds that a child has been neglected or abused, a number of options are usually available. Criminal penalties might be imposed. The court may have the power to terminate the parent's parental rights,[10] the child may be placed in the custody of the state's child welfare agency, e. g., for foster care placement.

7. Supra p. 382.

8. Supra p. 436.

9. See generally Fox, S., *Juvenile Courts in a Nutshell* Second Edition (1977).

10. Infra p. 463.

Assignment # 136

Answer the following questions after examining your state statutory code. (See General Instructions for the State Code Assignment, supra p. 14.)

(a) What is the definition of a neglected, abandoned, dependent or abused child in your state?

(b) What court has jurisdiction to determine whether a child is neglected, abandoned, dependent or abused?

(c) What can the court do once it determines that a child is neglected, abandoned, dependent or abused?

Assignment # 137

Prepare a checklist of questions which you could use to help determine whether a child has been neglected, abandoned, etc. (See General Instructions for the Checklist Formulation Assignment, supra p. 29.)

Assignment # 138

Draft a flow chart of the procedural steps that are necessary in your state to determine whether a child has been neglected, abandoned, etc. (See also General Instructions for the Flow Chart Assignment, supra p. 33.)

9. DELINQUENCY

At common law, a minor below the age of seven was incapable of committing a crime—or so the law conclusively presumed. A minor between the ages of seven and fourteen could be guilty of a crime if the prosecution could show that the minor was mature enough to have formed the criminal intent necessary for the particular crime. A rebuttable presumption existed that a minor between these ages did not possess the requisite criminal intent. Minors over fourteen were treated and tried the same as adults.

Today, the trend is to remove the stigma of criminality from the misconduct of minors. The terms "juvenile delinquency," "PINS" (Person In Need of Supervision), etc. are often used. A juvenile delinquent may be defined as a person under a certain age, e. g., sixteen, who does any act which if done by an adult would constitute a crime. A PINS might be defined as a person under a certain age who is incorrigible, ungovernable or habitually disobedient.

A full range of options are available to a court that finds that the child is a juvenile delinquent, or a PINS, e. g., institutionalization,[11] probation, foster home placement.

11. See Singer, R. and Statsky, W., *Rights of the Imprisoned: Cases, Materials and Directions*, pp. 66ff. (1974).

Assignment # 139

Most of the following questions can be answered by examining your state statutory code. (See General Instructions for the State Code Assignment, supra p. 14.)

(a) What is a juvenile delinquent in your state?

(b) What court has jurisdiction to determine juvenile delinquency?

(c) Is any classification other than juvenile delinquent used in your state to describe a minor who has misbehaved, e. g., the classification of PINS? If so, define the classification.

(d) Draft a Flow Chart of the procedural steps required in your state for the processing of a juvenile delinquency case. (See also General Instructions for the Flow Chart Assignment, supra p. 33.)

(e) Once a minor has been found to be a juvenile delinquent, what disposition options are available to the court in your state?

*

Chapter Twenty-Five

ADOPTION

SECTION A. DEFINITIONS

A number of important words should be defined and distinguished:

CUSTODY:

The control and care of an individual.

GUARDIANSHIP:

The legal right to the custody of an individual.

WARD:

An individual who is under guardianship.

TERMINATION OF PARENTAL RIGHTS:

A judicial declaration that a parent shall no longer have any right to participate in decisions affecting the welfare of the child.

ADOPTION OF A CHILD:

The legal process by which an adoptive parent assumes all the rights and duties of the natural parents.

PATERNITY:

The fatherhood of a child.

FOSTER CARE:

A child welfare service which provides substitute family care for a child when his/her own family cannot care for him/her for a temporary or extended period and when adoption is neither desirable nor possible.[1]

Assignment # 140

(a) Find statutes or court opinions that define the words "custody" and "guardianship" in your state. For each word, try to find at least one statute or opinion that defines the word. If either or both words have more than one meaning in your state, give each meaning. (See also General Instructions for the State Code Assignment, supra p. 14, and for the Court Opinion Assignment, supra p. 26.)

1. Child Welfare League of America, *Standards for Foster Family Care*, p. 5 (1959).

(b) Write a flow chart of guardianship procedures in your state involving a minor child. If there is more than one kind of such guardianship in your state, you may select any one. (See also General Instructions for the Flow Chart Assignment, supra p. 33.)

(c) Draft a custody agreement under which your best friend agrees to care for your child while you are in the hospital for six months. (See also General Instructions for the Agreement Drafting Assignment, supra p. 25.)

SECTION B. ADOPTION PROCEDURE

A rather elaborate set of procedures exist in the field of adoption; it is not easy to adopt a child. Courts are very concerned about protecting the interests of the child, the natural parents and the adoptive parents. When the most sought after babies are in short supply, the temptation to "buy" a baby on the black market becomes considerable. The adoption procedures are in part designed to combat this temptation.

1. JURISDICTION

Subject-matter jurisdiction refers to the power of the court to hear a particular kind of case.[2] Generally, not every court in a state has subject-matter jurisdiction to issue adoption decrees. The state constitution or state statutes will designate one or perhaps two courts that have authority to hear adoption cases, e. g., the state family court or the state juvenile court.[3] There are also specifications as to the county in which the adoption proceeding must be brought. The question of which county has jurisdiction usually depends upon the residence (or occasionally on the domicile[4]) of one or more of the participants, usually the adoptive parents or the child.

Assignment # 141

(a) What court or courts in your state have the power to hear adoption cases?

(b) In what county or section of your state must the adoption proceeding be initiated? Does your answer depend upon the residence or domicile of any of the participants? If so, what is the definition of residence or domicile?

(To answer the above questions, you may have to check your state constitution, state statutory code, and perhaps opinions of your state courts. See General Instructions for the State Code Assignment, supra p. 14, and for the Court Opinion Assignment, supra p. 26.)

2. Supra p. 352.

3. See Clark, H., *The Law of Domestic Relations*, p. 605 (1968).

4. Supra p. 345.

2. PETITION

States differ on the form and content of the adoption petition which is filed by the adoptive parents to begin the adoption proceeding. The petition will contain data such as, names of the petitioners, their ages, whether they are married, if so, whether they are living together, name of child, age, religion, etc. Not all states require that the names of the natural parents be mentioned in the petition itself. If a state does not require that they be named, it does not, of course, mean that the natural parents are not notified or are not part of the adoption proceeding.

Assignment # 142

(a) What must a petition for adoption contain in your state? Must it name the natural parents? (See also General Instructions for the State Code Assignment, supra p. 14. You may also need to check the court rules of the court(s) that have subject-matter jurisdiction over adoptions.)

(b) Draft an adoption petition. Assume that you are seeking to adopt the one (1) year old baby of your best friend who has recently died. This friend has no other relatives and no living spouse. You can make up facts which you need to draft the petition. (Although an adoption petition is not a complaint, you may find some of the suggestions on drafting complaints to be useful, supra p. 20.)

3. NOTICE

For due process purposes, it is fundamental that the natural parents be given *notice* of the petition by the prospective adoptive parents to adopt the child. This usually does not mean that the natural parents must be served with process personally within the state where the adoption petition is brought.[5] Substituted service,[6] e. g., registered mail, is often adequate.

There was a time when the father of an illegitimate child[7] was not entitled to notice of the adoption proceeding; only the mother of such a child was given notice. The situation has changed, however, due to recent decisions of the United States Supreme Court.[8] While the full scope of the rights of the father of an illegitimate child have not yet been fully defined by the courts,[9] it is clear that he can no longer be ignored in the adoption process. As we shall see, however,

5. Clark, supra note 3 at p. 610.

6. Supra p. 351.

7. Supra p. 449.

8. E. g., Stanley v. Illinois, 405 U.S. 645, 92 S.Ct. 1208, 31 L.Ed.2d 551 (1972).

9. It is not clear, for example, whether a father who has abandoned or otherwise ignored his illegitimate child is entitled to notice of the adoption proceeding. See also Quilloin v. Walcott, — U.S. —, 98 S.Ct. 549, 54 L.Ed. 2d 511 (1978).

there is a difference between a parent's right to notice of the adoption proceeding and the parent's right to prevent the adoption by refusing to consent to it.

Assignment # 143

(a) In your state, who must receive notice of an adoption proceeding?

(b) When can substituted service of process (e. g., mail, publication) be used in your state on persons who must receive notice of adoption proceedings?

(See also General Instructions for the State Code Assignment, supra p. 14, and for the Court Opinion Assignment, supra p. 26.)

4. CONSENT

Adoption occurs in essentially two ways: with or without the consent of the natural parents. When consent is necessary, the state's statute will usually specify the manner in which the consent must be given, e. g., whether it must be witnessed, whether it must be in writing, whether the formalities for consent differ when an agency is involved in the adoption as opposed to an adoption involving only the natural parents and the adoptive parents,[10] whether the consent form must mention the names of the parties seeking to adopt the child, etc.

Both natural parents must consent to the adoption unless one of the parents has lost the right to prevent the adoption, e. g., through the abandonment of the child. Although many state statutes say that the consent of the father of an illegitimate child is not necessary for the adoption of the child, this does not mean that the father of such a child can have no role in the adoption proceeding. As indicated earlier, he probably has a right to present his views on the propriety of the proposed adoption. This requires that he be given notice of the adoption proceeding unless he has abandoned the child.[11]

Often a child welfare agency will place the child in a foster home. Foster parents are not legal guardians [12] and therefore cannot prevent the adoption of the child by someone else, i. e., the consent of foster parents is not necessary. This does not mean that the foster parents can be ignored entirely. When an agency attempts to remove the child from the foster home, many states give the foster parents the right to object to the removal and to present their arguments against the removal.[13] While foster parents may have a right to be heard on the removal, they cannot veto the adoption of the child.

10. Clark, supra note 3 at p. 620.

11. Supra note 9.

12. See definitions, supra p. 463.

13. For a discussion of the constitutional dimensions of the foster parent's right to be heard, see Smith v. Organization of Foster Families for Equality, 431 U.S. 816, 97 S.Ct. 2094, 53 L.Ed.2d 14 (1977).

CONSENT TO ADOPTION

We, the undersigned, being the father and mother, respectively, of A______ C______, who was born on ______, 19__, in ______ County, California, and being the persons entitled to the sole custody of said child, do hereby give our full and free consent to the adoption of said child by B______ D______ and E______ D______, his wife, and do hereby relinquish to said persons forever all of our rights to the care, custody, control, services, and earnings of said child.

Each of us hereby promises that, as soon as adoption proceedings are commenced in the state of ______, we will properly execute any further instruments or papers necessary to effectuate the adoption of said child by said persons.

Each of us hereby authorizes said persons, or either of them, to procure and provide any and all medical, hospital, dental, and other care needed for said child, it being understood by us that said persons have agreed to, and will pay, such expenses without seeking reimbursement from us prior to the adoption of said child.

Each of us fully understand that, upon the signing of this instrument, we have irrevocably relinquished and waived all right to withdraw the consent and authority herein given.

DATED: ______, 19__.

____

G______ C______

____

F______ C______

SOURCE: Adams, D. California Code Forms, p. 297 (West Publishing Co., 1960).

Assignment # 144

(a) What is the citation to the statute in your state that sets out the formalities necessary for consent to adoption in your state?

(b) Who must give consent?

(c) Is it necessary to obtain the consent of a natural parent who is mentally ill in your state?

(d) Is it necessary to obtain the consent of a natural parent who previously was not awarded custody of the child in a divorce proceeding?

(e) Is there a minimum age for giving consent in your state? Can a minor parent consent to adoption in your state?

(f) When, if ever, does the child who is being adopted have to consent to his/her own adoption in your state?

(g) In what form or with what formalities must the consent be given in your state? Does your answer differ depending upon whether or not a child welfare agency is involved? If so, explain the difference.

(h) Does the consent form have to mention the names of the prospective adoptive parents in your state?

(See also General Instructions for the State Code Assignment, supra p. 14. You may also need to check court opinions for some of the above questions. See General Instructions for the Court Opinion Assignment, supra p. 26.)

Assignment # 145

In Assignment #142(b), supra p. 465, you drafted an adoption petition based primarily on facts that you invented yourself. Using those facts, draft a consent form (to be signed by the best friend) which complies with the statutory requirements for consent in your state.

Once a natural parent (or a guardian or an agency) consents to the adoption, can the consent be changed assuming that it was given according to the requisite formalities? Once the adoption decree has been entered, most states will not allow the consent to be revoked. Before the decree, however, some states permit revocation:

(a) if the court determines that the revocation would be in the best interests of the child;

(b) if the court determines that the consent was obtained by fraud or duress.

STATE OF NEW YORK
__________ COURT
COUNTY OF __________
ADDRESS __________

In the Matter of the Adoption of __________ Adoptive Child	NOTICE OF HEARING ON ISSUE OF REVOCATION AND DISPOSITION AS TO CUSTODY, PRIVATE PLACEMENT ADOPTION

PLEASE TAKE NOTICE that the ______ Court, ______ County, New York, on the ______ day of ______, 19__, at ______ o'clock in the ______ noon of that day, or as soon thereafter as counsel can be heard, will hear and determine whether the revocation of consent of the parent in the above entitled matter shall be permitted and, in any event, hear and determine what disposition should be made with respect to the custody of said child.

____
Chief Clerk of the ______ Court

To: ______________
Adoptive Parent(s)

____
Parent(s)

______________, Esq.
Attorney for Adoptive Parent(s)

______________, Esq.
Attorney for Parent(s)

____
Law Guardian

SOURCE: Marino, J. McKinney's Forms, New York (West Publishing Co. 1976).

Assignment # 146

When, if ever, can consent to adoption be revoked in your state? (See also General Instructions for the State Code Assignment, supra p. 14. You may also have to check court opinions of your state if no statutes on revocation exist. See General Instructions for the Court Opinion Assignment, supra p. 26.)

5. INVOLUNTARY TERMINATION OF PARENTAL RIGHTS

It would obviously be illogical to permit a natural parent to prevent the adoption of his/her child by withholding consent if that parent has abandoned the child. Many statutes, therefore, provide that abandonment, extreme cruelty, conviction of certain crimes, etc. will mean that the consent of a parent engaged in such conduct is not necessary. The difficulty, however, is the absence of any clear definition of terms such as abandonment or extreme cruelty. Many cases take the position that a parent does not lose his/her right to withhold consent to an adoption unless a clear intention to relinquish all parental duties can be shown. Non-support in itself, for example, may not be enough if the parent has made some effort to see the child, at least occasionally.

As demonstrated in the following chart, many factors are relevant to the question of whether or not a parent had the intention to abandon or otherwise relinquish all rights in his/her child. A court will consider all of these factors in combination; no one factor may be determinative.

INTERVIEWING AND INVESTIGATION CHECKLIST FACTORS RELEVANT TO WHETHER AN INTENT TO ABANDON THE CHILD EXISTED		
	Legal Interviewing Questions	**Possible Investigation Tasks**
1.	How old are you now?	* Interview relatives, friends, strangers who knew that you visited the child.
2.	With whom is your child living?	* Interview anyone with whom the client may have discussed the reasons for leaving the child with someone else.
3.	Is the person caring for the child your relative, a friend, a stranger?	* Prepare an inventory of all the money given by the client for the support of the child while living with someone else.
4.	How did the child get there?	* Collect receipts, e. g., cancelled check stubs, for all funds given by the client for such support.
5.	How long has the child been there?	* Locate all relevant court records, if any, e. g., custody order in divorce proceeding, neglect or juvenile delinquency proceeding.
6.	When is the last time you saw your child?	
7.	How often do you see your child per month?	
8.	How often do you speak to your child on the phone per month?	
9.	How often do you write to your child?	
10.	Did you ever tell anyone that you did not want your child or that you wanted your child to find a home with someone else? If so, explain.	
11.	Did you ever tell anyone that you wanted your child to live with someone else just temporarily until you got back on your feet again? If so, explain.	
12.	Have you ever placed your child in an adoption agency? Have you ever discussed adoption with anyone?	
13.	Have you ever been charged with neglecting, abandoning or failing to support your child?	
14.	Has your child ever been taken from you for any period of time?	
15.	Have you ever been found by a court to be mentally ill?	
16.	How much have you contributed to the support of your child while your were not living with the child?	
17.	Did you give the child any presents?	
18.	While your child was not with you, did you ever speak to the child's teachers or doctors?	
19.	Were you on public assistance while the child was not living with you? If so, what did you tell the public assistance workers about the child?	
20.	How well is the child being treated now?	
21.	Could anyone claim that the child ever lived under immoral or unhealthy circumstances while away from you and that you knew of these circumstances?	
22.	Has the child ever been charged with juvenile delinquency or been declared a person in need of supervision?	

IM–492

Many states have separate proceedings to terminate parental rights for misconduct which are not necessarily part of adoption process. If, for example, a parent has been found to have abandoned his/her child, the child may be taken away from the parent in a separate legal proceeding to terminate parental rights. The child is usually then placed in a child welfare agency where it might be put up for adoption. If so, a separate adoption proceeding would then take place. The consent of the parent whose parental rights had previously been terminated would not be needed to effectuate the adoption.

Assignment # 147

(a) When is the consent of a natural parent *not* necessary in your state for the adoption of his/her child?

(b) Is there a proceeding to terminate parental rights in your state which is separate from the adoption process? If so, explain.

(See General Instructions for the State Code Assignment, supra p. 14.)

(c) Prepare a flow chart of all the procedural steps necessary to terminate parental rights in your state. (See General Instructions for the Flow Chart Assignment, supra p. 33.)

6. PLACEMENT

Once a petition for adoption has been filed, many states authorize the court to ask a public or private child welfare agency to investigate the case and make a recommendation to the court. The agency, in effect, assumes a role which is very similar to that of a social worker or a probation officer in many juvenile delinquency cases.

Assignment # 148

(a) What is the role of child welfare agencies in your state after an adoption petition has been filed?

(b) Once an agency files a report in your state containing the results of its investigation and its recommendation on the proposed adoption, who has access to the report? Can the prospective adoptive parents have access to it? Can they question the person who wrote the report?

(See also General Instructions for the State Code Assignment, supra p. 14. You may also need to check court opinions of your state. See General Instructions for the Court Opinion Assignment, supra p. 26.)

What factors go into a court's decision on whether a particular adoption is appropriate? The major standard used is "the best interests of the child." This leaves a great deal of discretion in the trial judge who in turn usually relies a great deal on the professional judgment of the child welfare agency that has investigated the case. The petitioner seeking to adopt the child must be an adult, but in many states, s/he need not be married. If the petitioner is married, however, most states require that his/her spouse join in the petition.[14] Beyond these factors, the court is concerned with the environment which the prospective adoptive parents (i. e., the petitioners) will provide the child if the adoption is granted. This involves considerations such as:

—standard of living;

—health of child and of the petitioners;

—age of child and of petitioners;

—compatibility of race and religion of child and of petitioners;

—compatibility between child and other children of petitioners;

—maturity of petitioners;

—the desires of the child if old enough to formulate an intelligent preference;

—the alternatives available (what will happen to the child if this petition to adopt is denied?).

Assignment # 149

(a) In your state, who is eligible to adopt children? Who is not eligible?

(b) What standards exist to guide a judge's decision in your state on whether to approve a particular adoption?

(c) Mary Jones is a Baptist. She wants to place her one year old child for adoption. Mr. and Mrs. Johnson want to adopt the child and file the appropriate petition to do so in your state. The Johnsons are Jewish. Mary Jones consents to the adoption. What effect, if any, will the religious difference between Mary Jones and the Johnsons have on the adoption? Assume that Mary has no objection to the child being raised in the Jewish faith.

(d) Same facts as in (c) above except that the Johnsons are professed atheists. Mary Jones does not care.

(e) Would it be legal for the Johnsons to pay Mary $25,000 to influence her to give her consent to the adoption? For purposes of this question, assume that there is no religious difference between Mary and the Johnsons.

(See also General Instructions for the State Code Assignment, supra p. 14. You may also need to check court opinions. See General Instructions for the Court Opinion Assignment, supra p. 26.)

Assignment # 150

(a) Contact a *private* child welfare agency in your state involved in adoption placement. Ask the agency what criteria it uses in recommending an adoption. If available, ask the agency to send you any

14. Clark, supra note 3 at p. 641.

literature which lists such standards, e. g., pamphlets, applications. Compare these standards with your answers to the questions in the preceding assignment (# 149). Is the agency's practice in conformity with the standards that exist in the law of your state?

(b) Same question as in (a) above except that this time a *public* child welfare agency involved in adoption in your state should be contacted.

NOTE

On the meaning of the "psychological parent," see supra p. 382 and Goldstein, J., Freud, A., and Solnit, A., *Beyond the Best Interests of the Child* (1973).

7. CHALLENGES TO THE ADOPTION DECREE

In some states, an adoption decree does not become final immediately. An interlocutory (temporary) decree of adoption is first issued in such states which becomes final after a set period of time. During the interlocutory period, the child is placed with the adoptive parents to give the court a chance to evaluate the adoption before it becomes final.[15] Once the child has been placed with the adoptive parents, there is an obvious need for stability in the placement; it would be very unhealthy for the child to be moved from place to place as legal battles continue to rage among any combination of adoptive parents, natural parents and agencies. Hence, state statutes place time limitations within which challenges to the adoption decree must be brought, e. g., two years. (The time limitation may differ depending upon the nature of the challenge to the decree.) In most states, if the challenge (e. g., lack of notice of the adoption proceeding, fraud in procuring the consent of the natural parent) is not brought within the designated period of time, the challenge can never be brought.

Assignment # 151

(a) It there an interlocutory period in your state which must pass before the adoption can become final? If so, what is this period?

(b) After the trial court in your state issues a final adoption decree, to what court can the decree be appealed?

(c) If someone wants to challenge an adoption decree in your state, within what period of time must the challenge be brought? What happens if the challenge is not brought within this time?

(See also General Instructions for the State Code Assignment, supra p. 14. You may also need to check the court rules of your state courts, and perhaps court opinions as well. See General Instructions for the Court Opinion Assignment, supra p. 26.)

15. Id. at p. 659.

Assignment # 152

Draft a flow chart of all the procedural steps involved in an adoption proceeding in your state. (See also General Instructions for the Flow Chart Assignment, supra p. 33.)

Assignment # 153

Contact a paralegal, an attorney or a legal secretary in your state who has worked on adoption cases in the past. Obtain answers to the following questions:

(i) Approximately how many adoption cases have you worked on?

(ii) How many of them have been uncontested?

(iii) Approximately how long does it take to process an uncomplicated, uncontested adoption?

(iv) Is there a difference between working on an adoption case and working on another kind of case in the law office?

(v) What are the major steps that you have to go through to process an adoption in this state? What documents have to be filed? What court appearances must be made? etc.

(vi) What form or practice book do you use, if any, that is helpful?

(vii) Does your office have its own internal manual that would cover any aspect of adoption practice?

(viii) In an adoption case, what is the division of labor among the attorney, the paralegal and the legal secretary?

(See also General Instructions for the Law Office Management Assignment, supra p. 34.)

SECTION C. CONSEQUENCES OF ADOPTION

Once the adoption becomes final, the adopted child and the adoptive parents have almost all the rights and obligations toward each other that natural parents and children have toward each other. The major exception involves the death of a relative of the adoptive parent. For example:

> Kevin is the adopted child of Paul. Paul's brother, Bill, dies intestate (i. e., without leaving a will.) Can Kevin inherit from Bill?

In some states, the answer would be no: an adopted child cannot take an intestate share of a relative of his/her adopted parents. Other states do not impose this limitation.

In most other respects, an adopted child is treated the same as a natural child:

—the adopted child can take the name of his/her adopted parents;

—the birth certificate can be changed to reflect the new parents;

—the adopted child can inherit from his/her adopted parents (and in a few states, can continue to inherit from his/her natural parents);

—the adopted parents have a right to the services and earnings of the adopted child; [16]

—the adopted parents must support the adopted child;

—the adopted child is entitled to workmen's compensation benefits due to the on-the-job injuries of his/her adopted parent;

—if an adopted parent dies leaving a will which leaves property to "my heirs" or to "my children" or to "my issue," without mentioning any individuals by name, most (but not all) courts are inclined to conclude that the intention of the deceased adopted parent was to include his/her adopted children as well as his/her natural children within the designation of "heirs" "children" or "issue."

Assignment # 154

(a) What rights and obligations are assumed by adopted parents and children in your state?

(b) Re-examine the hypothetical in the text immediately above involving Kevin, Paul and Bill. Could Kevin inherit from Bill in your state?

(c) Suppose that Kevin's natural parent dies intestate. Can Kevin inherit from this natural parent in your state?

(Check statutory law and case law on the above questions. See General Instructions for the State Code Assignment, supra p. 14, and for the Court Opinion Assignment, supra p. 26.)

SECTION D. EQUITABLE ADOPTION

It is possible for a natural parent and a third party to enter into a contract that the latter will adopt the child of the natural parent. The agreement may be in writing or simply be an oral understanding among the parties. Suppose that the third party takes the child and treats him/her as a member of the family, but never goes through the formal adoption procedures. The third party dies without leaving a will. Technically, the child cannot inherit from the deceased because the adoption never took place. This argument may be used

16. Supra p. 459.

by the deceased's natural children to prevent the non-adopted child from sharing in the deceased's estate. Many feel that this is a very unfair result. The child should not be denied inheritance benefits simply because the deceased failed to abide by the agreement to adopt the child. While alive, the deceased treated the child as his/her own in every way. The deceased acted as if the child had been adopted even though technically this was not so. To avoid the unfairness, some courts conclude that such a child was adopted under the doctrine of *equitable adoption*, and hence is entitled to inheritance and all other rights of adopted children. The doctrine is also referred to as *adoption by estoppel*: challengers will be estopped (i. e., prevented) from denying that such a child has been adopted.

Assignment # 155

To what extent, if at all, does your state recognize equitable adoption or adoption by estoppel? (See also General Instructions for the Court Opinion Assignment, supra p. 26.)

SECTION E. ADOPTION OF ADULTS

In most states, it is possible to adopt an adult. This is usually done so that the adult will be able to inherit from the adopting person. The procedure for adopting an adult is usually much simpler than that for adopting a child. The only real concern that a court might have would be that the adoption was the free act of the adopting person.

Assignment # 156

Can a younger person adopt an adult in your state? If so, how does this adoption differ from the adoption of a child? (See also General Instructions for the State Code Assignment, supra p. 14.)

Chapter Twenty-Six

INTRAFAMILY TORTS

A tort is a private wrong. It is separate from the breach of contract [1] cause of action and from wrongs that are crimes. Torts can be classified as follows:

INTENTIONAL TORTS AGAINST PROPERTY

Trespass: a wrongful entry on the property of another.

Conversion: to deprive someone of their property without authorization.

Fraud: harm caused by a false statement known to be untrue and relied upon by the person injured.[2]

Nuisance: the use of one's property in such a way as to interfere with someone else's property.

INTENTIONAL TORTS AGAINST THE PERSON

Assault: the attempt to inflict harmful or offensive contact on a person, placing that person in fear or apprehension of the contact.

Battery: harmful or offensive contact with a person.

False imprisonment: detaining or restraining a person without authorization (this tort does not necessarily involve prisons, jails, police, etc.; a person, for example, can falsely imprison his/her neighbor on the sidewalk).

Malicious prosecution: bringing a civil or criminal action against someone for malicious reasons when no reasonable basis or probable cause exists for the action.

Slander: oral statements that are false and that injure the reputation of another.

Libel: written statements that are false and that injure the reputation of another.

UNINTENTIONAL TORTS

Negligence: injury to person or property caused by a failure to act with reasonable care.

Vicarious Liability: the tort liability of a person or company that is due entirely to the wrongful or tortious acts of someone else, e. g., an employer who is liable for the torts of his/her employee committed within the scope of employment.

1. Supra p. 110.

2. Supra p. 117.

Our question in this section is as follows: when, if ever, will parents, children and other relatives be liable to each other in tort. Are they immune from such tort liability? As we shall see, there is a considerable reluctance on the part of the courts to permit intrafamily tort actions. A major reason used to justify this reluctance is that family harmony would be seriously disrupted if family members knew that they could sue each other. This rationale has been seriously criticized, however, on the ground that there is not much family harmony left to preserve if a family member has committed an act on another member which would lead to court liability if it had been committed by a stranger.[3] The other great fear of intrafamily torts is fraud, especially where insurance is involved. A husband, for example, who is covered by automobile insurance, would fraudulently agree with his wife that she would pretend to have been injured by him in a car accident. At common law, there was a serious logical problem in allowing a wife to sue her husband: the husband and wife was considered one person and that person was the husband; to permit the spouses to sue each other, therefore, would be like one person suing himself!

Today, intrafamily tort suits are possible—but not all torts and not in every state. The following chart provides an overview of the law:

INTRAFAMILY TORTS
I. Husband and Wife
1. In most states, spouses can sue each other for intentional or negligent injury to their property, e. g., trespass, conversion, fraud.
2. In many states, spouses cannot sue each other for intentional or negligent injury to their person, e. g., assault, battery, false imprisonment.
3. Exceptions—some states will permit personal tort actions if the man and woman are divorced.
4. Some states will permit intentional tort actions for injury to the person to be brought by spouses against each other, but continue to forbid negligence actions for injury to the person.
5. Each spouse is liable for his/her own torts; they are not vicariously liable for each other's torts.
II. Parent and Child
1. In all states, a child can sue his or her parent for intentional or negligent injury caused by the parent to the child's property, e. g., trespass, conversion, fraud.
2. In most states, a child cannot sue his/her parent for intentional or negligent injury caused by the parent to the child's person, e. g., assault, battery, false imprisonment.

3. See Prosser, W., *Handbook of the Law of Torts*, pp. 879ff., 3rd Ed. (1964), and Clark, H., *The Law of Domestic Relations*, pp. 252ff. (1968).

3. Exceptions—if the child is emancipated[4] (e. g., married, joined the armed forces, supporting him/herself), the child in all states can sue his/her parent for intentional or negligent injury caused by the parent to the child's person, e. g., assault, battery.
4. Some states will permit any child (emancipated or not) to sue his/her parent for intentional tort actions for injury to the person, but continue to forbid negligence actions for injury to the person.
5. A few states allow the child to sue the parent for all intentional tort actions against the person except where the tort arises out of the parent's exercise of discipline over the child.
6. In most states, the child is liable for his/her own torts. In several states, however, parents are vicariously liable for the torts of their children, but only up to a certain amount of damages, e. g., $1,000.
7. Automobile use by children poses special problems. In many states, the owner of the family automobile (e. g., a parent) is liable for the negligence of anyone whom s/he permits to use the car (e. g., the child). This is a form of vicarious liability.
8. If a parent knows the child can be dangerous to other people and fails to take steps that would have been effective to prevent harm, the parent will be liable, not on a theory of vicarious liability, but on a theory of the parent's own negligence.

III. Other Related Persons

Brothers and sisters, aunts and uncles, grandparents and grandchildren, etc. can sue each other in tort. The restrictions imposed on husband-wife suits, and on parent-child suits do not apply to tort actions involving other relatives.

Assignment # 157

To answer the following questions, you may have to check both the state code and the opinions of courts sitting in your state. (See also General Instructions for the State Code Assignment, supra p. 14, and for the Court Opinion Assignment, supra p. 26.)

(a) Under what circumstances, if any, can one spouse bring a tort action against the other spouse in your state?

(b) Can divorced spouses sue each other in tort?

(c) Under what circumstances, if any, can a child bring a tort action against his/her parent in your state?

(d) Pick any tort action that one family member can bring against another in your state. Draft a complaint in which the cause of action is this tort. (See also General Instructions for the Complaint Drafting Assignment, supra p. 20.)

4. Supra p. 455.

CONSORTIUM

Consortium refers to the nature of the relationship between a husband and wife. Consortium is what each is entitled to have from the other. Specifically:

companionship;

love and affection;

sexual intercourse;

services.

When someone interferes with these characteristics of a marital relationship, a tort may have been committed entitling the injured party (i. e., the spouse who has been deprived of the consortium of the other spouse) to damages (i. e., money) to compensate for the loss. There are several causes of action in existence which are designed to remedy the interference with consortium:

1. ALIENATION OF AFFECTIONS

This cause of action supposedly is the answer to the "eternal triangle." When a "lover" "steals" the affections of one's spouse, the lover can be sued for alienation of affections. If, however, the spouse seduced the lover, the latter will not be liable for alienation of affections. It is not necessary to prove that adultery occurred since sexual intercourse is only one of the components of the loss of consortium that the alienation of affection suit is supposed to remedy. The plaintiff-spouse can win simply by showing that the defendant wrongfully persuaded the plaintiff's spouse to cease providing affection and attention to the plaintiff. The defendant could be a relative of the spouse, e. g., the mother-in-law. It must be proven, however, that the relative acted with malice before the relative will be liable for alienation of affections. This is not always easy to prove since there is often a thin line between the advice of a relative that is given with malice (with the intent to harm someone) and advice that is given in good faith (with the intent to protect).

Given the nature of this cause of action, other problems of proof are evident. How does one prove who caused the alienation? How does one measure damages? How can a dollar tag be placed on the suffering that one endures when consortium is taken away or impaired? Because of such difficulties, a number of states (in their heart balm statutes [5]) have abolished the alienation of affection cause of action.

2. CRIMINAL CONVERSATION

Committing adultery with a married person is a clear interference with the exclusive consortium right of sexual intercourse that the "innocent" spouse is supposed to enjoy. The innocent spouse can sue

5. Supra p. 111.

the paramour for criminal conversation which is a *civil* action in spite of the use of the word "criminal." For this tort, it is no defense that the spouse seduced the paramour. All the innocent spouse has to prove is that the defendant had sexual intercourse with the plaintiff's spouse.

As with alienation of affections, a number of states have abolished the criminal conversation cause of action.

3. LOSS OF CONSORTIUM

In most states, a more common way to remedy an injury to consortium than the two mentioned above is a direct action for loss of consortium. Strangely, a few states permit the husband to recover for the loss of his wife's consortium, but deny the wife the right to sue for the loss of her husband's consortium. A few courts have ruled that this form of discrimination against women is an unconstitutional denial of equal protection.

The cause of action works as follows:

—Rich and Ann are married;

—Paul, a stranger, injures Ann, e. g., by negligently hitting her with his car (or by one of the intentional torts such as battery);

—Ann sues Paul for negligence. She receives damages to cover her medical bills, lost wages, if any, pain and suffering, punitive damages,[6] if any;

—Rich then brings a separate suit against Paul for loss of his wife's consortium. He receives damages to compensate him for whatever loss or impairment he can prove to the companionship he had with Ann before the accident—to the love, affection, sexual intercourse, and services that she gave him as his wife before the accident.

In Rich's action against Paul, he cannot recover for injuries sustained by Ann. Ann must recover for such injuries in her own action against Paul. Paul's liability to Rich is limited to the specific injuries sustained by Rich—the loss or impairment of his wife's consortium. Of course, if Ann loses her suit against Paul, e. g., because she was contributorily negligent, Rich will not be able to bring his consortium suit.

NOTE ON CHILDREN

(1) A parent (usually the father) can bring an action in many states for the abduction or enticement of his child by someone else. He can also bring a seduction action against the male who seduced his daughter.

(2) Very few states allow a child to sue a third party for alienating the affections of one of the parents.

(3) A parent has a right to the services of his/her unemancipated child, e. g., the child can be asked to help with the chores, the parent

6. Supra p. 114.

can keep the earnings of a child.[7] When a third party has wrongly injured the child, the child, of course, can sue for damages. The parent can also bring a separate suit for loss of the child's services.

(4) Although a husband can sue for the loss of his wife's consortium, and in many states, the wife can sue for the loss of her husband's consortium, a child *cannot* sue for the loss of consortium caused by a third party's injury to the child's parent.

Assignment # 158

To answer the following questions, you may have to check both the state code and the opinions of courts sitting in your state. (See also General Instructions for the State Code Assignment, supra p. 14, and for the Court Opinion Assignment, supra p. 26.)

(a) Under what circumstances, if any, can an action for alienation of affections be brought in your state?

(b) Under what circumstances, if any, can an action for criminal conversation be brought in your state?

(c) Under what circumstances, if any, can an action for loss of consortium be brought in your state? Can a wife bring the action?

(d) Under what circumstances, if any, can actions be brought for enticement, abduction, of seduction of a child in your state?

(e) Is it a crime in your state to seduce a child?

7. Supra p. 459.

Appendix A

SAMPLE CHECKLISTS

STATE BAR OF WISCONSIN, A HANDBOOK OF DIVORCE PROCEDURE

Revised Edition (June, 1970).

(The following is presented as an *example* of a format for checklists. Since these checklists were written the law in Wisconsin has changed. The purpose of presenting these checklists is *not* to cover Wisconsin law, but to examine one way to write checklists. See also supra p. 29.)

STATE BAR OF WISCONSIN CHECKLIST SERIES

ANNULMENT

1. SERVE SUMMONS, COMPLAINT AND ORDER TO SHOW CAUSE

A. Prepare Chapter 262 summons and complaint (Contents of Complaint—Sec. 247.085).

B. If necessary, prepare order to show cause for custody of minor children restraining defendant, etc., and submit the proposed order, together with a supporting affidavit or verified complaint, to the family court commissioner or court for signing. Sec. 247.-23.

C. Serve summons, complaint and order to show cause upon the defendant.

1. Service within the state—Serve summons and complaint personally within state or at defendant's usual place of abode and within 20 days thereafter a copy of the summons shall be served upon the family court commissioner. Then file the summons with the clerk of court before any pre-trial proceeding or hearing is held either by the court or the family court commissioner. Sec. 247.061, 247.14.
2. Personal service outside the state—Personally serve summons and a copy of the verified complaint on defendant and within 20 days thereafter file the summons and verified complaint in court and serve a copy of the summons and verified complaint on the family court commissioner. Sec. 247.062(1).
3. Publication—(1) File with the court the summons and verified complaint and affidavit describing efforts to make per-

sonal service. (2) Mail a copy of the summons and complaint to the defendant. (3) Publish summons. (4) Prior to trial the plaintiff or plaintiff's counsel must file an affidavit in court describing efforts to make personal service upon the defendant within or without the state. (5) Within 20 days following the first publication, serve copy of summons and complaint on family court commissioner. Sec. 247.062(2).

D. Jurisdiction and residence.

1. To acquire jurisdiction in an annulment action to determine questions of status, one of the parties must be a bona fide resident of the state and of the county where the action is commenced for at least 30 days prior to the commencement of the action; or if both parties are nonresidents, the marriage must have been contracted within the state and the action must be commenced within a year after such marriage. Sec. 247.05.
2. To acquire jurisdiction in annulment action where there is personal claim for support or property division—see Sec. 247.055, 247.06.
3. Annulment action may be commenced at any time while either of the parties has a husband or wife living. Sec. 247.03(2).

II. HEARING ON ORDER TO SHOW CAUSE

A. Prepare temporary order, have family court commissioner sign it and serve copy on defendant.

Default Procedure

III. PRE-HEARING MATTERS—STIPULATION, NOTICE OF DEFAULT MOTION, ORDER REQUIRING DEFENDANT TO APPEAR

A. Draft stipulation with defendant or his attorney, if possible.

B. Set hearing date (judgment cannot be granted until the family court commissioner has made his investigation and advised the court as to the merits of the case and the efforts made toward reconciliation). Sec. 247.15(1).

C. Serve notice of motion for default.

1. If defendant, either in person or by attorney, has appeared in the action (entering into a stipulation is such an appearance), serve notice of motion for default upon him at least 8 days before the hearing. Sec. 270.62(2). Sec. 269.31.
2. If there is a stipulation, waiver of notice should be incorporated therein.

D. Prepare order requiring defendant to appear at the trial, have the judge or the family court commissioner sign it and serve upon the defendant personally before the trial. Sec. 247.125.

E. Prepare proposed findings, conclusions and the judgment. Also prepare affidavit of no answer and affidavit re military service.

IV. CONDUCT HEARING

A. Proof showing jurisdiction.

1. Proof of service—Sec. 247.061, 247.062, as amended by Chapters 46 and 500.

2. Proof of required residency (must be corroborated by evidence other than the testimony of the parties). Sec. 247.05, 247.18(2).

B. Affidavit of no answer.

C. Affidavit of non-military service. May be waived in stipulation.

D. Plaintiff's testimony as to grounds for annulment.

E. Corroborating evidence as to grounds for annulment. Sec. 247.18 (2).

F. Proof as to custody, property division, etc.

G. If non-residence in state or other good cause prevented service upon the defendant of the order requiring him to appear, introduce competent evidence showing such non-residence or other circumstances preventing service. Sec. 247.125.

Contested Procedure

V. NOTICE CASE FOR TRIAL (Sec. 270.115)

1. Serve order on defendant for appearance at trial. Sec. 247.125.

VI. CONDUCT TRIAL

A. Proof of residence in state and county where action is commenced within a year after such marriage. Sec. 247.05, 247.18(2).

B. Plaintiff's testimony as to grounds of annulment.

C. Corroborating evidence as to grounds for annulment. Sec. 247.18 (2).

D. Proof as to custody, property division, etc.

E. Obtain, prepare and file Vital Statistics form.

VII. SUBMIT FINDINGS, CONCLUSIONS AND JUDGMENT

A. Submit findings, conclusions and judgment to the court.

B. After entry to judgment, serve a copy of findings, conclusions and judgment upon the defendant or his attorney.

C. If judgment affects title to real property, record a certified copy of the judgment in the office of the register of deeds of the county in which the real estate is located. Sec. 247.26. (Judgment assigning real estate must contain a description of such real estate.)

D. Chapter 55, Laws of 1965, repeals Sec. 247.235 and creates Sec. 247.25, relating to support of the children by the wife.

STATE BAR OF WISCONSIN CHECKLIST SERIES

DIVORCE ACTION

I. JURISDICTION

A. To determine question of marital status—To acquire jurisdiction in divorce action to determine question of status, one of the parties must be a bona fide resident of the state for at least two years next preceding the commencement of the action and one of the parties must be a bona fide resident of the county where the action is commenced for at least 30 days prior to the commencement of the action; and defendant must be served pursuant to Secs. 247.061, 247.062 or 247.063. (See III A–D) Sec. 247.05(3).

1. Separation action does not require two year state residency—only 30 days in county. Sec. 247.05(1).

B. Over claims for support, alimony or property division—Where plaintiff has a personal claim against the defendant for support, alimony, or property division, court has jurisdiction to grant such relief only if defendant:

1. Is personally served with a summons within the state; or
2. Being domiciled within the state, cannot with reasonable diligence be personally served under (1), is served by having a copy of the summons left at his usual place of abode within the state in the presence of some competent member of the family of at least 14 years of age; or
3. Being domiciled within the state cannot with reasonable diligence be served under (1) or (2) is personally served with a summons without the state pursuant to Sec. 247.062 or 247.063 (See III B–D); or
4. Makes a general appearance in the action. Sec. 247.06. If, with reasonable diligence, personal jurisdiction over the defendant cannot be acquired by the above four methods, but property belonging to the defendant is found within the state when the action is commenced, the court may enter a judgment quasi in rem determining the personal claims and order them satisfied out of such property. Sec. 247.055(2).
5. Defendant resided in marital relationship with plaintiff for at least 6 months in last 6 years and plaintiff continued to live in state and defendant cannot be served in state but is personally served without state. Sec. 247.057.

C. But court has jurisdiction for property division only where there has been a prior or concurrent judgment of divorce or legal separation. Jezo v. Jezo, 19 Wis.2d 78.

D. Action must be brought within 10 years after the cause of action arose. The court may exclude from the time period, time which either party has been committed to a mental institution. Sec. 247.03(2).

II. OBTAIN ORDER TO SHOW CAUSE AND DRAFT SUMMONS

A. If temporary alimony, support, custody or attorneys' fees are needed, prepare summons and an order to show cause, together with a supporting affidavit, submit both to the family court commissioner for signing. Sec. 247.23(1), (2), (3).

1. The affidavit cannot set forth any of the grounds for divorce or any details which form the basis for such grounds, but shall state only that it is necessary and for the best interests of the affiant, and any minor children of the parties that the relief specified in the affidavit be granted. Sec. 247.23(2).

B. Form of summons where summons served within state personally or at usual place of abode. See Sec. 247.066(1).

1. Where summons served personally outside state or by publication, the general provisions of Chap. 262, respecting the content and form of summons in regular civil actions applies. Sec. 247.066(2).

III. SERVE ORDER TO SHOW CAUSE, SUMMONS (and complaint where defendant cannot be served within state)

A. Service within the state—Serve summons and order to show cause together with supporting affidavit personally within the state or summons only at defendant's usual place of abode pursuant to Sec. 247.06(1)(b), and within 20 days serve a copy of the summons on the family court commissioner, and thereafter file it with the clerk of court prior to any hearing. Sec. 247.061.

B. Personal service outside the state—When the defendant cannot with reasonable diligence be served within the state under (A) above, personally serve the summons and a copy of the verified complaint on defendant outside the state, and within 20 days thereafter file the summons and verified complaint in court and serve a copy of the summons and verified complaint on the family court commissioner. Sec. 247.062(1).

C. Publication—If with reasonable diligence, the defendant cannot be served personally within or without the state, serve by publication and mailing as follows:

1. Give sheriff a Sec. 247.066 summons and get a not found return.

2. If you have an address for defendant outside state, prepare a Chapter 262 summons and attach complaint and attempt service outside state.

3. File with court the above summons(es) and publication summons (Sec. 262.11) and complaint prior to mailing and publication.
4. Prior to trial the plaintiff or plaintiff's counsel must file an affidavit in court describing efforts to make personal service upon the defendant within or without the state.
5. If defendant's post office address is known or can with reasonable diligence be ascertained, mail a copy of the summons and complaint to the defendant, at or immediately prior to the first publication.
6. Publish summons. 247.062(2).
7. Within 20 days following the first publication, serve a copy of the summons and complaint on family court commissioner. Sec. 247.062(2).

D. Serving person under disability—Serve a person under disability by serving summons and complaint as provided by A–C above, and, in addition, where prescribed by Sec. 262.06(2)(a) or (b), upon a person designated therein. Sec. 247.063.

IV. FOR HEARING ON ORDER TO SHOW CAUSE

A. Prepare temporary order and have family court commissioner or court sign it.

B. Serve copy of temporary order on defendant; file original with clerk of court.

V. SERVE COMPLAINT (unless already served by personal service outside the state or publication)

A. Sixty days after service of the summons upon the defendant serve a copy of the complaint upon the defendant or his attorney of record.

1. When a defendant appears in action by an attorney of record, service of the complaint shall be made upon said attorney.
2. When a defendant has not appeared by an attorney of record, service of the complaint shall be made upon the defendant. Sec. 247.061(1)(a).

B. Within 20 days following the service of the complaint upon the defendant serve a copy upon the family court commissioner, and then promptly file the complaint in court. Sec. 247.06(1)(c), 247.14. (No judgment will be granted without compliance with this section.)

C. Upon good cause shown that such waiting period will be injurious to the health or safety of either of the parties or any child of the marriage or that some other emergency exists, and after consideration of the recommendation of the family court commissioner, the court may issue an order waiving the 60-day waiting period. Sec. 247.06(1)(a).

D. If the complaint is not served upon the defendant or upon the defendant's attorney of record, after 60 days following the service of the summons, defendant in person or by attorney may serve a demand in writing on plaintiff's attorney for a copy of the complaint and a copy of the complaint shall be served within 20 days thereafter accordingly. Sec. 247.061(1)(b).

E. If complaint is not served within 120 days after service of summons, the action may be dismissed upon motion of either party or of the family court commissioner, or the defendant may prior to any order of dismissal, serve upon the plaintiff's attorney a pleading for relief under s. 247.05 or 247.055 which shall be designated a counterclaim and the defendant within 20 days thereafter shall serve a copy thereof on the family court commissioner and file the original counterclaim in court. Sec. 247.061 (1)(d).

F. Contents of complaint—Sec. 247.085. Specify data required under Sec. 247.085(1)(a) and (b).

   1. If either party was previously divorced, the name of the court in which the divorce was granted and the time and place the divorce was granted, must be specifically alleged in complaint. Sec. 247.085(1)(c).

   2. If legal separation is sought, must allege reason only legal separation is desired. Sec. 247.085(4).

VI. SERVE OR DEMAND BILL OF PARTICULARS

A. If the defendant makes a written demand within 20 days after the service of the complaint for the facts relied upon as the statutory ground, prepare a verified bill of particulars setting forth such facts and serve upon defendant within 10 days after demand. Sec. 247.085(2).

   1. If the bill of particulars is not furnished within 10 days, the complaint may be dismissed upon motion of defendant or of the family court commissioner. Sec. 247.085(2).

B. If the defendant counterclaims, plaintiff may make a written demand within 20 days after the service of the counterclaim for the facts relied upon as the statutory ground. Sec. 247.085(2).

C. Where a bill of particulars has been demanded, the time to answer or reply begins to run from the time the bill of particulars is furnished. Sec. 247.085(2).

VII. WAITING PERIOD BEFORE TRIAL (Sec. 247.081(2))

A. Whether contested or not, the action cannot be brought to trial until the family court commissioner has, within 120 days after service of the summons or 5 days after the action is set for trial, whichever is sooner, certified to the court that a reconciliation effort has been made, and until the happening of whichever of the following events occurs first:

1. The expiration of 60 days after filing of complaint when summons is served within the state under Sec. 247.061. (See V above).
2. The expiration of 120 days after the filing of the complaint when the summons is served without the state under Sec. 247.062(1). (See III B above).
3. The expiration of 120 days after the first day of publication when the summons is served by mailing and publication under Sec. 247.062(2). (See III C above).
4. An order by the court after consideration of the recommendation of the family court commissioner, directing immediate trial of such action for protection of the health and safety of either of the parties or any child of the marriage or for other emergency reasons. The court must specify the grounds for granting the order. Sec. 247.081(2)(d).

B. Make certain that your client responds to family court commissioner's inquiries.

VIII. PRE–HEARING MATTERS—STIPULATION, NOTICE OF DEFAULT MOTION, ORDER REQUIRING DEFENDANT TO APPEAR

A. Draft stipulation with defendant or his attorney, if possible.

B. Set hearing date.

C. Serve Notice of Motion for Default.

1. If defendant, either in person or by attorney, has appeared in the action (entering into a stipulation is such an appearance), serve notice of motion for default upon him at least 8 days before the hearing. Sec. 270.62(2), 269.31.
2. If there is a stipulation, waiver of notice should be incorporated therein.

D. Prepare order requiring defendant to appear at the trial, have the judge or family court commissioner sign it and serve upon defendant personally before the trial. Sec. 247.125.

E. Prepare affidavit of no answer and affidavit re military service.

IX. CONDUCT HEARING

A. Proof of service upon defendant.

1. Proof of 2 years residence in state and 30 days in county prior to the commencement of the action (must be corroborated by evidence other than by testimony of the parties). Sec. 247.05(3), 247.18(2). (Separation action requires only 30 days in the county.)

B. Affidavit of no answer and affidavit re military service.

C. Plaintiff's testimony as to grounds for divorce.

D. Corroborating evidence as to grounds (unless cruel and inhuman and no corroborating evidence is available.) Sec. 247.18(2).

E. Proof as to alimony, support, property division, custody, etc.

F. If stipulation, present for approval.

G. If nonresidence in the state or other good cause prevented service upon defendant of the order requiring him to appear, introduce competent evidence showing such nonresidence or other circumstances preventing service. Sec. 247.125.

H. Wife to announce preference as to restoration of former name or alimony, if choice available. Sec. 247.20 (Omit in legal separation action).

I. If conscientious objection to divorce is the reason for demanding legal separation, such objection should be confirmed. Sec. 247.09.

J. Obtain Bureau of Vital Statistics form from clerk of court, fill it out, and leave it with clerk. This must be done where the action has been dismissed, but not where it has been dropped.

K. Where cruel and inhuman treatment is ground, have corroborating evidence of effect on mental or physical health of plaintiff. Jacobs v. Jacobs, 42 Wis.2d 507.

X. NOTICE CASE FOR TRIAL (Sec. 270.115)

1. Serve order for appearance at trial on defendant. Sec. 247.-125.

XI. CONDUCT TRIAL

A. Proof of 2 years residence in state and 30 days in county prior to the commencement of the action (must be corroborated by evidence other than by testimony of the parties). Sec. 247.05(3), 247.18(2). (Separation action requires only 30 days in the county).

B. Plaintiff's testimony as to grounds for divorce.

C. Corroborating evidence as to grounds (unless cruel and inhuman and no corroborating evidence is available). Sec. 247.18(2) and effect on health.

D. Proof as to alimony, support, property division, custody, etc.

E. Wife to announce preference as to restoration of former name or alimony, if choice available. Sec. 247.20. (Omit in legal separation action).

F. If conscientious objection to divorce is the reason for demanding legal separation, such objection should be confirmed. Sec. 247.09.

G. File Vital Statistics form.

XII. SUBMIT FINDINGS, CONCLUSIONS AND JUDGMENT

A. Attorney for prevailing party must submit to the court and file with the clerk of court within 30 days after judgment is granted, the findings, conclusions and the judgment. Sec. 247.37(1) (a); (b) and (c), as amended 1965 by Chapter 480.

1. If the action has been uncontested, they must first be submitted to opposing counsel, if any, and if the family court commissioner has appeared in the action, such original papers, together with copies thereof, shall also be sent to him for examination before submission to the court. Sec. 247.37(1) (a).
2. Findings of fact and judgment should state thereon the last known address of each party to aid clerk of court in mailing copies of judgment.

B. In addition the written judgment for divorce must state, in a separate paragraph, that where either party to the marriage being so dissolved is obligated under such judgment or by other judgment or court order to support any minor issue of the marriage not in his custody, he is prohibited by s. 245.10 from marrying again in this state or elsewhere after such judgment becomes effective unless permission to marry is granted by order of either the court of this state which granted such judgment or support order, or the court having divorce jurisdiction in the county of this state where such minor issue resides or where the marriage license application is made. Sec. 247.37(1) (b).

C. If the judgment affects title to real estate, record a certified copy of the judgment in the office of the register of deeds of the county in which the real estate is located. Sec. 247.26. (Judgment assigning real estate must contain a description of such real estate.)

XIII. ASSIGNMENT BY EMPLOYEE FOR SUPPORT

A. After judgment of divorce the court may order the father to assign such salary or wages due him or to be due him in the future from his employer or successor employers to the clerk of the court where the judgment of divorce was granted.

B. The amount assigned shall be sufficient to pay the weekly allowance, as adjudged by the court, for the support, maintenance and education of the minor children of the parties. Sec. 242.265.

C. See Sec. 247.235, relating to support of the children by the wife.

Appendix B

AFFIDAVITS CONNECTED WITH MOTIONS TO MODIFY CUSTODY DECREE

MARINO, J., McKINNEY'S FORMS, Form 14:24B and Form 14:33A

West Publishing Co. (1976).

SUPREME COURT OF THE STATE OF NEW YORK
COUNTY OF ____________

[Add title of cause]

AFFIDAVIT IN SUPPORT OF CROSS-MOTION

Index No. ______

STATE OF NEW YORK } ss.:
COUNTY OF ____________ }

______, being duly sworn, deposes and says:

1. That I am the defendant in the above entitled proceeding and submit this affidavit in support of my cross-motion (based in part on events that took place after the hearing in the above matter) for a modification of the Court's judgment herein, by (a) directing the posting of a ______ ($______) Dollar bond by plaintiff as a condition to plaintiff removing the infant children from the jurisdiction of the Court; (b) modifying the terms of plaintiff's visitation with the infant children by reducing the frequency of over-night weekend visits as presently provided for in the judgment of this Court dated ______, 19__; and (c) granting me counsel fees in the sum of ______ ($______) Dollars.

2. That the Court granted me custody of my [*two*] daughters, ages [7½] and [*6*], and it is my understanding that plaintiff is not contesting that decision.

3. That it is further requested that this Court reconsider its determination not to include in its judgment the provision for the posting of adequate security by plaintiff during periods of extended visitation. That in this connection, I strenuously oppose plaintiff's application for visitation with the children in [*Italy*] during the months of [*July*] and [*August*]. That the children are nationals of this country and have a right to be raised, educated, and to spend their summer vacations here. That it cannot be overstressed that plaintiff has no real ties or roots

in this country to warrant his remaining in this jurisdiction once the children are under his control. That this is all the more apparent now that he intends to remain in [*Italy*]. That for these reasons it is respectfully submitted that I should have adequate protection to insure against plaintiff fleeing from this jurisdiction with the children. Consequently, I would ask that this Court order the posting of security in the amount of ______ ($______) Dollars if it should allow plaintiff's request for summer visitation in [*Italy*]. That plaintiff's statement that he has no present intention of disregarding this Court's order and that he will return the children will be of little avail to me without this protection once they are in [*Italy*].

4. That I would also request that this Court review its determination regarding overnight visitation. That if I may remind the Court, as testified to by the plaintiff, he has never taken care of the children by himself for any significant length of time. That moreover, he admitted that at least on one occasion in [*Italy*] he had a maid accompany them in order to attend to the needs of the children. That it should, also, be borne in mind that the older child, ______, has an asthmatic condition which requires medication and supervision.

5. That, similarly, I would ask the Court upon reconsideration to modify the terms of visitation by reducing the frequency of overnight weekend visits. That under the judgment—if plaintiff elects to remain in the United States—he would have overnight weekend visitation with the children every weekend. That I would, also, respectfully ask that provision be included therein directing plaintiff to advise me of the place or places where he intends to remain with the children and a description of the accommodations. That as the mother, I am naturally concerned with the welfare of the children when they are away from ______, New York, on any extended visitation.

6. That finally, it is respectfully requested that the Court grant me counsel fees in connection with these motions. That the papers filed on my behalf amply demonstrate the work entailed in the presentation of my defense in connection with the motions brought by plaintiff and myself. That it is respectfully submitted that upon reconsideration, this Court should award counsel fees to me. That I believe that was the Court's intent and that the award to plaintiff in the judgment dated ______, 19__ was due to a typographical error. That Court is asked to award me ______ ($______) Dollars for counsel fees, which is considerably less than the cost of the proceedings to me. That it is respectfully submitted that this Court clearly has the power to grant this application in light of all of the circumstances herein.

7. That upon the return date of this motion, the Court will be requested to refer plaintiff's motion and my cross-motion to Mr. Justice ______ for determination. That it is further requested that upon such

review and reconsideration, the Court should deny the relief sought by plaintiff and grant the relief requested by this cross-motion.

[*Signature*]

____

[*Type Name of Deponent*]

AFFIDAVIT IN SUPPORT
Index No. ______

STATE OF NEW YORK
COUNTY OF ______________ } ss.

______, being duly sworn, deposes and says:

I am defendant herein. This affidavit is submitted in support of an application for reconsideration of the decision of the court made in this action on ______, 19__, insofar as custody of my children is concerned.

Custody of the children has been awarded to my ex-wife, plaintiff. I did not contest her claim to a divorce. When I reported this to the children, they became extremely upset. My son told me that he did not want to live with his mother and that he felt it was unfair for a boy of his age to be forced to live with a parent contrary to his desires. My daughter had a similar reaction.

I tried to convey the situation to the Court by an informal application for reconsideration, on the strength of simple notes written to the Court by my children. My attorney advised me that the Court would not alter its determination.

I love my children very much. A history of prior proceedings between my wife and myself indicates that she had been awarded custody of the children under a Family Court order several years ago. At that time, she lived with the children in our house in [*Peekskill*]. I paid support, as directed for the children and my wife, and for the upkeep of the house. About two years ago my wife ousted my son from the house and sent him to live with me. At that time, I occupied a small apartment in [*Peekskill*] so that I could be near the children. I would see them quite often and would take them to school on many mornings. When my son came to me, I made room for him and we lived together until ______ came to live with us about a year ago. We made room for ______. My wife made no objections to the children living with me and made no attempts to get them to come back to her. While we all lived in my small apartment, my wife continued to live in the [*Peekskill*] house all by herself. I continued paying the upkeep on the house, although my wife permitted it to fall into a state of deteriorating disrepair. I contributed to her support.

I took care of my children as best I could. They were grown and attended school most of the day. In the evenings we enjoyed a family life. We were together on week-ends. There were many week-ends when their mother would not attempt to spend any time with them. My son stayed away from the [*Peekskill*] house. ______ visited there with her mother on occasion. I know that on many occasions my wife stayed away from the [*Peekskill*] house for days at a time.

I have devoted my non-working hours to my children. I altered my schedule so that I would see them off to school each morning when I was not away from the City. If I was to be away, I would arrange adult supervision. I worked with my children on their homework and on anything else where they sought my participation. We shopped together and played together. My children were encouraged to maintain their friendships and to bring their friends to our home. Because of cramped quarters, my children would often visit with their friends and I encouraged them to maintain relationships with companions of their respective ages. I shared their problems and their joys. I tried to set responsible examples for them. My son had demonstrated to me that he is growing into a responsible young man who aspires to attend [*Massachusetts Institute of Technology*]. I am proud of his seriousness and of his healthy outlook in times like this. I have tried to maintain a closely knit family between my children and myself so that they should know the advantages of love, companionship, and security. I know that they did not find any such relationship at their mother's bosom.

My children have revealed to me that they were wrong in not having made a definite choice during their interview with the court on the matter of their preference of a home. I understand that they still love their mother and I have not attempted to sway them from that plateau. They told me that they wanted the court to decide the problem for them and that they had hoped that they could be the force which could solve the rift between plaintiff and myself. They were unaware that at the time of the interview my wife's prayer for divorce had already been granted. My son told me that he indicated to the court that he preferred to live with me although he did not state, unequivocally, that he did not desire to live with his mother.

I gather from my children's reaction and from what they have told me that they misunderstood what was required of them during their interview with the court. I submit that another interview should be granted if the court feels that my children's affidavits are insufficient to establish their desires. Had I not seen the effect of the custody decision on my children and had they not indicated their grief over it, I would sit back and abide by the will of the court.

I seriously question my wife's fitness as our children's custodian. She voluntarily relinquished their custody, as aforesaid. Under adverse living conditions (craped quarters), my children have thrived and demonstrated a progression toward adulthood. I believe that my wife's having been competitive instead of being cooperative with the children operated to compromise their welfare. I believe that by using the children as a pawn against me my wife has lost our children's respect. I feel that my pleasures must be subservient to the welfare of my children. They deserve as real a home as can be possible under the circumstances. They are entitled to eat a meal in peace and one which shows concern in its preparation. I believe that my children deserve some security in the knowledge that they have the genuine care and love of a parent. I believe that they cannot get this from their mother.

WHEREFORE, I respectfully pray that this application be granted and that upon reconsideration I be awarded custody of my children.

[*Signature*]

____

[*Type Name of Deponent*]

*

Appendix C

SAMPLE COMPLAINT *

COMPLAINT FOR DIVORCE ON THE GROUND OF CRUEL AND INHUMAN TREATMENT—N.Y.

MARINO, J., McKINNEY'S FORMS, Form 9:11A

West Publishing Co. (1977).

[*Add title of court and cause*]

COMPLAINT

Index No. ______

The plaintiff for his complaint herein shows to this court and alleges:

FIRST: That the plaintiff and the defendant were married on ______, 19__, by a religious ceremony performed at ______, located at ______, New York.

SECOND: That the plaintiff and the defendant have been residents of the State of New York for a continuous period of at least one year immediately preceding the commencement of the above entitled action, to wit: from on or about ______, 19__ to the present time.

THIRD: That the parties hereto have resided in this state as husband and wife and both parties hereto still are residents thereof when this action was commenced and have been residents thereof for a continuous period of one year immediately preceding the action herein.

FOURTH: That there is no issue of this marriage.

FIFTH: That the plaintiff has always conducted himself as a faithful and loyal husband toward the defendant and the conduct of the defendant hereinafter complained of, was without just cause or provocation on the plaintiff's part and despite the fact that he at all times fully discharged his conjugal obligations.

SIXTH: That commencing in or about the summer of 19__ and continuing up to about ______, 19__, the defendant has engaged in a course of cruel and inhuman treatment of the plaintiff and has subjected him to vilification and abuse, in treating him with hatred, aversion, and contempt; in withholding from and denying him of normal affection and society and refusing to cohabit with him; in subjecting

* See also supra pp. 20, 321.

him to the humiliation of compelling him to sleep in a bed in their apartment at No. ____ ______ Avenue, in the City of ______, State of New York, separate and apart of the plaintiff; in refusing to have marital relations with plaintiff; in compelling the plaintiff to move from a one bedroom apartment at No. ____ ______ Avenue, ______, New York, which they occupied and was ample and consistent with their means to a two bedroom apartment at No. ____ ______ Avenue, ______, New York, in order that the plaintiff not invade the privacy of the defendant and also for the purpose of restraining the plaintiff in all attempts for conjugal relations with defendant, his wife; that in said period the defendant without cause wilfully and wrongfully has refused, failed, and neglected to live with the plaintiff as his wife; that said defendant has ordered plaintiff to stay out of her room and has continuously in said period refused to occupy the same bed with the plaintiff.

SEVENTH: That all of the foregoing acts of cruel and inhuman treatment have made it impossible for the plaintiff to live with the defendant; that such acts have greatly disturbed the plaintiff both mentally and physically and caused him mental anguish and that because of defendant's wilful refusal to cohabit with plaintiff as man and wife and to have normal sexual relations with him, although both plaintiff and defendant are both physically capable of engaging in same, the plaintiff's health has become impaired.

EIGHTH: That upon information and belief no previous action has been commenced by either of the parties hereto, no decree of annulment or divorce or any other decree dissolving the said marriage between the parties hereto has ever been obtained by the defendant against the plaintiff in any of the courts of any of the States or territories of the United States or any court of this State or in any other territory or nation.

WHEREFORE, the plaintiff demands judgment of absolute divorce against the defendant, that the bonds of matrimony between the plaintiff and the defendant be forever dissolved; that appropriate allowance be made for the maintenance and support of the defendant consistent with the financial means of the parties hereto, and that the plaintiff have such other and further relief as to the court shall seem just and proper in the premises.

____

Attorney for Plaintiff
P. O. Address
Tel. No.

[*VERIFICATION*]

Appendix D

RECIPROCAL SUPPORT LAWS

COUNCIL OF STATE GOVERNMENTS, RECIPROCAL STATE LEGISLATION TO ENFORCE THE SUPPORT OF DEPENDENTS LEXINGTON, KENTUCKY

1971 Edition

Table I

CITATIONS TO RECIPROCAL SUPPORT LAWS (As of July 1971)

State or other jurisdiction	*Citations to Reciprocal Support Laws*
Alabama	Act 879, 1951, as amended by Act 823, 1953; Code of Ala. Title 34, §§ 105 to 123
Alaska	A.S. 25.25.010-270, as amended by Chap. 19, SLA 1960
American Samoa	P.L. 9-20, 1965; Rev. Code Title V, Ch. 5.04
Arizona	Laws 1970, Ch. 90; A.R.S. §§ 12-1651 to 12-1691
Arkansas	Act 182, 1969; Ark. Stats. §§ 34-2401 to 34-2448
California	Code Civ. Proc., §§ 1650 to 1697, as amended by Stats. 1970, Ch. 1126
Colorado	43-2-17 C.R.S. 1963 (1969 Supp.)
Connecticut	Conn. Gen. Stats., Title 17, Ch. 308, Part IV, §§ 17-327 to 17-355b
Delaware	Ch. 6, Title 13, Del. Code
District of Columbia	Act of July 10, 1957; Ch. 94
Florida	FSA §§ 88.011 to 88.371
Georgia	Ga. Laws of 1958, Page 34; Ga. Code, §§ 99-901a to 99-932a
Guam	Title X, Part III, Guam Code of Civil Procedure
Hawaii	Ch. 576, Hawaii Rev. Stat.
Idaho	Title 7, Ch. 10, Idaho Code, as amended 1969
Illinois	P.A. 76-1090, 1969; Ill. Rev. Stats., Ch. 68, §§ 101 to 142
Indiana	Ch. 309, Acts of 1961; Burns Ann. Stat. §§ 3-3101 to 3-3139
Iowa[1]	Ch. 252A, Code of Iowa, 1971
Kansas	KSA 1970 Supp. §§ 23-451 to 23-491
Kentucky	Ch. 190, Ky. Acts of 1954; K.R.S. Ch. 407
Louisiana	Acts 1966, No. 288, §§ 1, 2; R.S. §§ 13:1641 to 1699
Maine	M.R.S.A. 1964, T. 19, §§ 331 to 410
Maryland	Ch. 295, 1965; Md. Code Article 89c
Massachusetts	M.G.L.A. Ch. 273A
Michigan	Act 8, P.A. 1952, as amended 1953, 1955, 1957, 1959, 1960; MCLA §§ 780.151 to 780.172
Minnesota	Minn. Stats. 1969, §§ 518.41 to 518.53
Mississippi	Laws of 1954, Ch. 211; Code 1942 §§ 456-01 to 456-34
Missouri	Ch. 454, R.S. Mo. 1969
Montana	Ch. 237, Laws of 1969; §§ 93-2601-41 to 93-2601-82, RCM
Nebraska	R.R.S. Neb., §§ 42-722 to 42-761
Nevada	Ch. 44, 1955, as amended by Ch. 61, 1961 and Ch. 346, 1969; Ch. 130 NRS
New Hampshire	Ch. 546, N.H.R.S.A., Vol. 5
New Jersey	N.J.S. 2A: §§ 4-30.1 to 4-30.23
New Mexico	Ch. 242, Laws 1969; Ch. 22, Art. 19, Vol. 5, N.M.S.A. 1953, §§ 22-19-25 to 22-19-68
New York[1]	N.Y.U.S.D.L. Art. 3A, §§ 30 to 43, Dom. Rel. Law, as amended 1958, 1959, 1960, 1962, 1966, 1968
North Carolina	Ch. 52A, N.C. Gen. Stats., as amended
North Dakota	N.D.C.C. 14-12.1, as amended 1969
Ohio	§§ 3115.01 to 3115.22 Rev. Code of Ohio
Oklahoma	12 O.S.A. §§ 1600.1 to 1600.38
Oregon	O.R.S. 110, as amended 1957, 1959, and 1969
Pennsylvania	62 P.S. § 2043.1 *et seq*
Puerto Rico	Act No. 71 of 1956; 32 L.P.R.A. §§ 3311 to 3313v
Rhode Island	Gen. Laws Ch. 15 to 11 *et seq*, as amended by Ch. 287, 1970
South Carolina	§ 20-311, Code of 1962, as amended
South Dakota	Ch. 41, SL 1951, as amended by Ch. 43, SL 1953; S.D.C.L. 25-9

[1]Iowa and New York still retain the language of the "Support of Dependents Law" as originally developed by New York; all other jurisdictions follow, in whole or in part, the 1952, 1958 or 1968 version of the Uniform Reciprocal Enforcement of Support Act, as promulgated by the National Conference of Commissioners on Uniform State Laws.

[B7798]

Table I—Continued

State or other jurisdiction	*Citations to Reciprocal Support Laws*
Tennessee	Tenn. Code Ann. §§ 36-901 to 36-929
Texas	1965, Ch. 679, p. 1561; Vernon's Tex. Civ. Stats., Art. 2328b-4, §§ 1 to 42
Utah	Title 77, Ch. 61a, Utah Code Ann. 1953
Vermont	No. 191 Adj. Session 1969; 15 VSA 385-428
Virginia	Title 20, Ch. 5.2 Code of Virginia
Virgin Islands	16 V.I.C. §§ 391 to 429
Washington	Ch. 45, Laws of 1963; R.C.W.A. 26.21.010 *et seq*
West Virginia	Ch. 48, Article 9, W.Va. Code, 1953, as amended
Wisconsin	§ 52.10 Wisc. Stats., as amended 1959, 1961 and 1968
Wyoming	Wyoming Stats. 1957, §§ 20-77 to 20-104

Table II

STATE INFORMATION AGENTS FOR UNIFORM RECIPROCAL ENFORCEMENT OF SUPPORT

State or other jurisdiction	*Information Agency**
Alabama	Ruben K. King, Commissioner State Department of Pensions and Security 64 North Union Street Montgomery 36104
Alaska	Department of Health and Social Services Division of Family and Children Services Pouch H Juneau 99801
American Samoa	The Attorney General Territory of American Samoa Pago Pago 96920 Attn.: James Kingzett, Assistant Attorney General
Arizona	The Attorney General State Capitol Phoenix 85007 Attn.: Frances Nelson Wallace
Arkansas	Department of Public Welfare Capitol Mall, P. O. Box 1437 Little Rock 72201 Attn.: Ivan H. Smith
California	The Attorney General 600 State Building San Francisco 94102 Attn.: Arlo E. Smith
Colorado	The Attorney General State Capitol, Room 104 Denver 80203 Attn.: Douglas Doane
Connecticut	Joseph J. Keefe, Executive Secretary Judicial Department State Library and Supreme Court Bldg. P. O. Box 1350 Hartford 06101
Delaware	Kenneth Singleton, Master Family Court Public Building Wilmington 19801

*In most States the reciprocal law officially designates an office of the State which shall act as "state information agency" to assist officials within and without the State in securing information about the operation of the reciprocal support laws. In other States this is done informally, and to the extent possible, by the listed agency. Individual names are listed here so that mail will be routed as promptly as possible to the person actually doing such work.

Table II—Continued

State or other jurisdiction	*Information Agency**
District of Columbia	Corporation Counsel Special Litigation Division Support Section 601 Indiana Ave., N.W. Washington 20001 Attn.: Ms. Judith Ann Dowd, Acting Senior Attorney
Florida	The Attorney General Department of Legal Affairs State Capitol Tallahassee 32304
Georgia	Attorney General Arthur K. Bolton 132 State Judicial Building Atlanta 30303
Guam	The Attorney General Government of Guam Agana 96910
Hawaii	Legislative Reference Bureau University of Hawaii State Capitol Honolulu 96813
Idaho	B. Child Commissioner of Public Assistance Box 1189 Boise 83701
Illinois	Illinois Department of Public Aid 618 East Washington Street Springfield 62706 Attn.: Arthur C. Zimmerman, State Information Agent
Indiana	Department of Public Welfare 100 North Senate Avenue Indianapolis 46204 Attn.: Oscar C. Crawford
Iowa	State Dept. of Social Services Lucas State Office Building Des Moines 50319 Attn.: Ron Marvelli
Kansas	Charles V. Hamm, General Counsel State Department of Social Welfare 6th Floor, State Office Building Topeka 66612
Kentucky	Ann T. Hunsaker, Attorney State Information Agent Department of Economic Security Frankfort 40601
Louisiana	Department of Public Welfare P. O. Box 44065 Baton Rouge 70804 Attn.: Lucas S. Conner, Jr., General Counsel
Maine	Department of Health and Welfare State House Augusta 04330 Attn.: Ruth L. Crowley, Assistant Attorney General
Maryland	State Department of Employment and Social Services Social Services Administration 1315 St. Paul Street Baltimore 21202 Attn.: John M. Williams
Massachusetts	Department of Welfare 600 Washington Street Boston 02111 Attn.: Catherine M. Loughlin
Michigan	William H. Meyer Michigan Department of Social Services Legal Liaison Unit 300 South Capitol Avenue Lansing 48926

Table II—Continued

State or other jurisdiction	*Information Agency**
Minnesota	Department of Public Welfare Centennial Office Building St. Paul 55101
Mississippi	The Attorney General State Capitol Jackson 39205 Attn.: R. Hugo Newcomb, Sr.
Missouri	Division of Welfare State Office Building Jefferson City 65101 Attn.: Proctor N. Carter
Montana	Division of Family Services State Department of Public Welfare P. O. Box 1723 Helena 59601
Nebraska	Director Department of Public Welfare State Capitol Lincoln 68509 Attn.: E. D. Warnsholz
Nevada	The Attorney General State Capitol Carson City 89701
New Hampshire	Division of Welfare State House Annex Concord 03301 Attn.: Thomas L. Hooker
New Jersey	Administrative Director of the Courts State House Annex Trenton 08625 Attn.: Mr. Fred D. Fant
New Mexico	Miss Julia Southerland, Chief Attorney Health and Social Services Department P. O. Box 2348 Santa Fe 87501
New York	State Department of Social Services 1450 Western Avenue Albany 12203 Attn.: Felix Infausto
New York City	Family Court 135 East 22nd Street New York 10010 Attn.: Administrative Judge
North Carolina	Clifton M. Craig Commissioner of Public Welfare P. O. Box 2599 Raleigh 27602 Attn.: Family Support Services
North Dakota	Legal Counsel Public Welfare Board Capitol Building Bismarck 58501
Ohio	The Attorney General State Capitol Annex Columbus 43215 Attn.: Leo J. Conway, Assistant Attorney General
Oklahoma	L. E. Rader Director of Public Welfare P. O. Box 25352 Oklahoma City 73125
Oregon	The Attorney General Welfare Recovery Division 630 Oregon Pioneer Building 320 S. W. Stark Street Portland 97204 Attn.: Walter N. Fuchigami

Table II—Continued

State or other jurisdiction	*Information Agency**
Pennsylvania	Department of Public Welfare P. O. Box 2675 Harrisburg 17105 Attn.: Robert Stewart
Puerto Rico	Miguel A. Martinez Nieves, Chief Division of Social Service Office of Court Administration Vela Street, Stop 35½ Hato Rey, San Juan 00919
Rhode Island	John J. O'Neil Court Administrator Family Court 22 Hayes Street Providence 02908
South Carolina	R. Archie Ellis, Director State Department of Public Welfare Wade Hampton State Office Building Columbia 29201
South Dakota	The Attorney General State Capitol Pierre 57501 Attn.: Lloyd B. Peterson, Assistant Attorney General
Tennessee	Fred E. Friend, Commissioner State Department of Public Welfare State Office Building Nashville 37219
Texas	Burton G. Hackney, Commissioner State Department of Public Welfare Austin 78701
Utah	The Attorney General 236 State Capitol Salt Lake City 84114 Attn.: Welfare Division
Vermont	Commissioner Department of Social Welfare State Office Building Montpelier 05602
Virginia	Department of Welfare and Institutions 429 South Belvidere Street Richmond 23220 Attn.: J. Luther Glass, Legal Consultant
Virgin Islands	The Attorney General Department of Law Government of the Virgin Islands St. Thomas 00801
Washington	The Attorney General Temple of Justice Olympia 98501 Attn.: Walter E. White, Assistant Attorney General
West Virginia	Division of Family Services Department of Welfare State Capitol Building Charleston 25305 Attn.: Mrs. Lelia H. Fay
Wisconsin	The Attorney General State Capitol Madison 53702 Attn.: Ward L. Johnson
Wyoming	The Attorney General State Capitol Cheyenne 82001

[B7834]

Table III

COURTS: OFFICIAL TO WHOM INITIATING STATE SHOULD MAIL PETITION; AND OFFICIAL RESPONSIBLE FOR HANDLING PAYMENTS

State or other jurisdiction	*Courts handling cases*	*Petition to:*	*Officials handling payments*
Alabama	Circuit Court	Register of the Circuit Court in Equity	Register of the Circuit Court in Equity
Alaska	Superior Court	Dept. of Health and Social Services, Div. of Family and Children Services	Court Clerk
American Samoa	High Court of American Samoa	High Court	Clerk of Court
Arizona	Superior Court	Clerk of Court	Clerk of Court
Arkansas	Chancery Court	Clerk of Court	1
California	Superior Court	Clerk of Court	Officer designated by the Court
Colorado	District Court	Clerk of Court	Clerk of Court or Probation Dept., depending on judicial district
Connecticut	Court of Common Pleas	Clerk, Bureau of Support, Court of Common Pleas	Bureau of Support, Court of Common Pleas
Delaware	Family Court	State Info. Agent	Family Court Support Dept.
District of Columbia	Superior Court	Chief Deputy Clerk	Chief Deputy Clerk
Florida	Circuit Court	State Attorney	Clerk of Court
Georgia	Superior Court	District Attorney	Court Probation Dept.
Guam	Island Court	Clerk of Court	Clerk of Court
Hawaii	Family Court	Clerk of Court	Chief Clerk
Idaho	District Court	Clerk of Court	Clerk of Court
Illinois	Circuit Court	State's Attorney	Circuit Clerks and Probation Officers
Indiana	Circuit Court	Clerk of Court	Clerk of Court
Iowa	District Court	Clerk of Court	Clerk of Court
Kansas	District Court	Clerk of Court	Clerk of Court
Kentucky	Circuit Court County Court	County Attorney	No Information
Louisiana	Juvenile Court	District Attorney	Division of Probation and Parole
Maine	Superior or District Courts	Clerk of Court	Clerk of Court
Maryland	Circuit Court Juvenile Court Trial Magistrates and People's Courts	Clerk of Court	Clerk of Court or Probation Dept.
Massachusetts	District Court	Clerk of Court	Probation Officers
Michigan	Circuit Court	County Clerk	Friend of the Court

[1]In Arkansas, those handling payments are: Master in Chancery (Pulaski County), Clerks of Courts in most counties, and the Welfare Director in 12 counties.

[B7800]

Table III—Continued

State or other jurisdiction	*Courts handling cases*	*Petition to:*	*Officials handling payments*
Minnesota	District Court	Clerk of Court	Clerk of Court and Directors, County Welfare Depts.
Mississippi	Chancery Court	Chancery Clerk	Clerk of Court
Missouri	Circuit Court	Clerk of Court	Clerk of Court
Montana	District Court	County Attorney	Clerk of Court
Nebraska	District Court	Clerk of Court	Clerk of Court
Nevada	District Court	Clerk of Court	Clerk of Court or other appropriate agency
New Hampshire	Superior Court	Clerk of Court	Probation Officers
New Jersey	Juvenile and Domestic Relations Court	Clerk of Court	Probation Officers
New Mexico	District Court	Clerk of Court	Clerk of Court
New York	Family Court	Clerk of Court	Court Probation Officers
North Carolina	District Court	Clerk of Court	Clerk of Court or Dept. of Social Services
North Dakota	District Court	Clerk of Court	Clerk of Court
Ohio	Court of Common Pleas	Clerk of Court	Clerk of Court
Oklahoma	District Court	Clerk of Court	Clerk of Court
Oregon	Circuit Court	Clerk of Court	Clerk of Court
Pennsylvania	Court of Common Pleas	Prothonotary	2
Puerto Rico	Superior Court	Information Agent	Information Agent
Rhode Island	Family Court	Manager of Collections	Manager of Collections
South Carolina	Family Courts, Court of Common Pleas	Information Agent	Clerk of Court
South Dakota	Circuit Court	Information Agent	Clerk of Court
Tennessee	Circuit Court or Criminal Court	Clerk of Court	Clerk of Court
Texas	District Court	Clerk of Court	Clerk of Court or Probation Dept.
Utah	District Court	Clerk of Court	County Clerk
Vermont	District Court	Clerk of Court	Clerk of Court
Virginia	Juvenile & Domestic Relations Court	Clerk of Court	Clerk of Court
Virgin Islands	Municipal Court	Clerk of Court	Clerk of Court
Washington	Superior Court	Prosecuting Attorney	Clerk of Court
West Virginia	Several Courts (usually criminal or intermediate)	Clerk of Circuit Court	Clerk of Circuit Court
Wisconsin	Circuit Court, Milwaukee County; Family Court Branch of County Court in other counties	District Attorney	No Information
Wyoming	District Court	Clerk of Court	Clerk of Court

[2]Allegheny County — Director, Family Division, Court of Common Pleas; Philadelphia County — Dept. of Accounts, Family Division, Court of Common Pleas; all other counties — Domestic Relations Division, Court of Common Pleas, Probation Officer.

[B7835]

Table IV

PETITIONER'S REPRESENTATIVES AND PETITIONER'S REPRESENTATIVE SERVICES

State or other jurisdiction	*Public petitioner's representatives*[1]	*When you are the responding State, what petitioners may secure services of public petitioner's representative?*
Alabama	Circuit Solicitor or other prosecuting attorney[2]	Decision entirely up to court
Alaska	Attorney General	Any petitioner requesting it
American Samoa	Attorney General	Any petitioner requesting it
Arizona	County Attorney[2]	Any petitioner requesting it
Arkansas	Assistant Welfare Attorney	Any petitioner requesting it except when court orders case handled by private counsel
California	District Attorney[2]	Any petitioner requesting it
Colorado	District Attorney[2]	Any petitioner requesting it
Connecticut	Petitioner's representative for each 10 bureaus to which petitions are forwarded	Any petitioner requesting it
Delaware	None	No public petitioner's representative as such
District of Columbia	Corporation Counsel	Only for persons on public assistance or liable to become so
Florida	State Attorney	Any petitioner requesting it
Georgia	District Attorney	Any petitioner requesting it
Guam	Island Attorney[2]	Ordinarily handles actions only where petitioner has established inability to employ private counsel
Hawaii	County Attorneys for Maui & Kauai counties; otherwise Corporation Counsel	Any petitioner requesting it
Idaho	County Prosecuting Attorney	Any petitioner requesting it
Illinois	State's Attorney	Any petitioner requesting it
Indiana	County Prosecuting Attorney[2]	Any petitioner requesting it
Iowa	County Attorney[2]	Any petitioner requesting it
Kansas	County Attorney[2]	Decision entirely up to court
Kentucky	County Attorney[2]	Any petitioner requesting it
Louisiana	District Attorney	Any petitioner requesting it
Maine	County Attorney	Any petitioner requesting it
Maryland	State's Attorney or Counsel to the County Council or Commissioners	Any petitioner requesting it
Massachusetts	Court may appoint	When there appears to be a need for counsel, court may appoint counsel
Michigan	County Prosecuting Attorney	Any petitioner requesting it
Minnesota	County Attorney[2]	Ordinarily handles action only for needy persons on public assistance or in danger of becoming a public charge
Mississippi	County Attorney, but District Attorney when county has no County Attorney[2]	No public petitioner's representative as such
Missouri	Prosecuting Attorney[2]	Only handles action which has been initiated through a public official in another State

[B7826]

Table IV—Continued

State or other jurisdiction	*Public petitioner's representatives*[1]	*When you are the responding State, what petitioners may secure services of public petitioner's representative?*
Montana	County Attorney	Any petitioner requesting it
Nebraska	County Attorney	Decision entirely up to court
Nevada	District Attorney	Decision entirely up to court
New Hampshire	County Attorney	Ordinarily handles action only for needy persons on public assistance or in danger of becoming a public charge
New Jersey	County Adjuster[3]	Any petitioner requesting it
New Mexico	District Attorney	Any petitioner requesting it
New York	County Attorney or District Attorney — Corporation Counsel in New York City	Any petitioner requesting it
North Carolina	District Solicitor	Any petitioner requesting it
North Dakota	State's Attorney[2]	Decision entirely up to court
Ohio	Prosecuting Attorney[2]	Decision entirely up to court
Oklahoma	District Attorney or Assistant District Attorneys	Any petitioner requesting it
Oregon	District Attorney or Attorney General[4]	Any petitioner requesting it
Pennsylvania	District Attorney[2]	Ordinarily handles actions only where petitioner has established inability to employ private counsel
Puerto Rico	District Prosecuting Attorney	Any petitioner requesting it
Rhode Island	If welfare case, counsel is furnished; if private, judge acts as counsel	Any petitioner requesting it
South Carolina	Act names several	Any petitioner requesting it
South Dakota	State's Attorney[2]	Decision entirely up to court
Tennessee	District Attorney General	Any person filing for support of minor children
Texas	Prosecuting Attorney	The plaintiff who obtains a request from the court or the State Dept. of Public Welfare
Utah	State Information Agent[2]	Ordinarily handles action only for needy persons on public assistance or in danger of becoming a public charge
Vermont	State's Attorney	Decision rests with court or with Dept. of Social Welfare in certain cases
Virginia	Commonwealth's Attorney	Ordinarily handles action only for needy persons on public assistance or in danger of becoming a public charge
Virgin Islands	Attorney General	Any petitioner requesting it
Washington	Prosecuting Attorney[2]	Generally all
West Virginia	Prosecuting Attorney[2]	Decision entirely up to court
Wisconsin	District Attorney	Any petitioner requesting it
Wyoming	Court may appoint	Decision entirely up to court

[1] Not all the statutes are clear in the duty placed upon the listed official to represent the petitioner.
[2] When ordered by the court, or upon notice, or upon other request.
[3] In some counties other officials serve as petitioner's representative.
[4] By 1957 amendment, Oregon Attorney General has statewide concurrent jurisdiction.

[B7836]

Table V

CENTRAL STATE LOCATION SERVICES*

State or other jurisdiction	Agency	Extent of Service
Alabama	Dept. of Pensions & Security	Full Service
Alaska		No Central Unit
Arizona	Dept. of Public Welfare	AFDC Only
Arkansas	Dept. of Public Welfare	Full Service
California	Office of Attorney General	Full Service
Colorado	Dept. of Social Services	AFDC Only
Connecticut	Dept. of Finance and Control	Full Service
Delaware		Plans Underway
District of Columbia	Dept. of Human Resources	Full Service
Florida		No Central Unit
Georgia		No Central Unit
Hawaii		No Central Unit
Idaho	Dept. of Public Assistance	AFDC Only
Illinois	Dept. of Public Aid	Full Service
Indiana		No Central Unit
Iowa	Dept. of Social Services	Full Service
Kansas	Dept. of Social Welfare	AFDC Only
Kentucky	Dept. of Economic Security	AFDC Only
Louisiana		No Central Unit
Maine	Dept. of Health and Welfare	Full Service
Maryland	Baltimore Dept. of Social Service	Full Service
Massachusetts		No Central Unit
Michigan	Dept. of Social Services	AFDC Only
Minnesota	Dept. of Public Welfare	AFDC Only
Mississippi		No Central Unit
Missouri	Dept. of Health, Educ. & Welfare	AFDC Only
Montana	Dept. of Public Welfare	Full Service
Nebraska	Dept. of Public Welfare	AFDC Only
Nevada		No Central Unit
New Hampshire		Plans Underway
New Jersey	Div. of Public Welfare	AFDC Only
New Mexico	Health & Social Service Dept.	Full Service
New York	Dept. of Social Service	Full Service
North Carolina	Dept. of Social Services	Being Established
North Dakota		No Central Unit
Ohio	Dept. of Public Welfare	AFDC Only
Oklahoma	Dept. of Public Welfare	Full Service
Oregon		Plans Underway
Pennsylvania	Dept. of Public Welfare	Full Service
Rhode Island	No Answer	
South Carolina		No Central Unit
South Dakota		No Central Unit
Tennessee	Dept. of Public Welfare	AFDC Only
Texas	Dept. of Public Welfare	AFDC Only
Utah	Div. of Family Services	AFDC Only
Vermont	Dept. of Social Welfare	Full Service
Virginia	Dept. of Welfare & Institutions	Full Service
Washington	Dept. of Public Assistance	Full Service
West Virginia	Dept. of Welfare	AFDC Only
Wisconsin	Dept. of Health & Social Services	Full Service
Wyoming	Dept. of Health & Social Services	AFDC Only

*Information taken from report prepared by Committee on Location of the National Conference on Uniform Reciprocal Enforcement of Support.

[B7827]

Table VI
WAIVER OF FEES AND COSTS FOR PETITIONER BY RESPONDING STATE

Alabama	1½% of collections withheld as fees for receiving and paying out monies. Regular equity costs and fees taxed, but at court's discretion may be paid by State. Pauper's affidavit required.
Alaska	Fees may be waived. Affidavit required.
American Samoa	No fees
Arizona	No fees
Arkansas	No fees
California	No fees
Colorado	No fees
Connecticut	No fees
Delaware	Court assesses 25¢ charge on each payment from defendant only
District of Columbia	Fees may be waived on reciprocal basis. Pauper's affidavit required.
Florida	No fees
Georgia	No fees
Guam	No fees. Pauper's affidavit suggested.
Hawaii	No fees
Idaho	No fees
Illinois	Fees may be waived. Pauper's affidavit suggested.
Indiana	No fees
Iowa	Fees may be waived. Pauper's affidavit suggested.
Kansas	Fees may be waived and paid by county. Pauper's affidavit required.
Kentucky	Fees may be waived. Pauper's affidavit suggested.
Louisiana	No fees
Maine	Fees may be waived
Maryland	Fees may be waived. Pauper's affidavit required.
Massachusetts	Fees may be waived on reciprocal basis. Pauper's affidavit required.
Michigan	No fees
Minnesota	Fees waived when County Attorney represents petitioner. Pauper's affidavit required.
Mississippi	Fees may be waived and paid by county. Pauper's affidavit suggested.
Missouri	No fees required
Montana	Fees may be waived. Pauper's affidavit suggested.
Nebraska	No fees
Nevada	No fees required
New Hampshire	No fees
New Jersey	Fees may be waived. Pauper's affidavit required.
New Mexico	No fees
New York	No fees
North Carolina	Fees may be waived. Pauper's affidavit suggested.
North Dakota	Fees may be paid by county in the discretion of court. Pauper's affidavit suggested.
Ohio	Fees may be waived. Pauper's affidavit suggested.
Oklahoma	Fees may be waived
Oregon	No fees
Pennsylvania	No fees
Puerto Rico	No fees
Rhode Island	No fees
South Carolina	Fees may be waived. Pauper's affidavit suggested.
South Dakota	Court may direct payment of fees by county. No filing fee required when action is brought by State or by an agency thereof.
Tennessee	No fees to petitioner when petition filed by State or accompanied by pauper's affidavit
Texas	No fees
Utah	Fees may be waived. Pauper's affidavit required.
Vermont	No fees
Virginia	No fees if case sent to Juvenile and Domestic Relations Court
Virgin Islands	No fees
Washington	No fees
West Virginia	No fees
Wisconsin	No fees
Wyoming	Fees may be waived

[B7828]

Table VII

BASIC DUTIES OF SUPPORT IMPOSED BY STATE LAW

Code

A—Husband liable for support of wife.
B—Wife liable for support of husband unable to support himself.
C—Both mother and father liable for support of minor legitimate children.
D—Father alone liable for support of minor legitimate children.
E—Both mother and father liable for support of minor illegitimate children.
F—Father alone liable for support of minor illegitimate children.
G—Mother alone liable for support of minor illegitimate children.
H- Children liable for support of needy parent or parents.
I —Brother liable for support of needy brother or sister.
J —Sister liable for support of needy brother or sister.
K—Grandparent liable for support of needy grandchild.
L—Grandchild liable for support of needy grandparent.
M—Other support liability (such as guardians, etc.).
Note: In many States parents are liable for support of children of any age unable to support themselves. See Table VIII.

State	Code
Alabama	A,C,E,H,I,K,L,M
Alaska	A,B,C,E,H,I,J,K,L,M
American Samoa	No Information.
Arizona	A,C,E
Arkansas	A,B,C,E
California	A,B,C,E,H
Colorado	A,B,C,E,H,I,J,K,L
Connecticut	A,B,C,E,H (Children's liability for supporting needy parent or parents terminates when parent reaches age 65.)
Delaware	A,B,C,E,H,I,J
District of Columbia	A,B,C,E
Florida	A,D,G
Georgia	A,C,E,H,M
Guam	A,B,C,E,H
Hawaii	A,B,C,E,G
Idaho	A,B,C,E,H,M
Illinois	A,B,C,E,H (for parents in a mental health facility)
Indiana	A,B,C,E,F,G,H
Iowa	A,C,E,H,K,L
Kansas	A,B,C,E
Kentucky	A,C,E,H,
Louisiana	A,B,C,E,H,K,L
Maine	A,B,C,G,H
Maryland	A,C,E,H
Massachusetts	A,C,E,H
Michigan	A,B,C,E,M
Minnesota	A,C,F,H,I,J,K,L (if receiving public assistance)
Mississippi	A,C,E
Missouri	A,C,E
Montana	A,B,C,E,H
Nebraska	A,B,C,E
Nevada	A,B,C,E,H,M
New Hampshire	A,B,C,E,H,K
New Jersey	A,B,C,E,H,K (if under 55), M
New Mexico	A,B,C,E
New York	A,B,C,E
North Carolina	A,B,C,E,H
North Dakota	A,B,C,E,G,H
Ohio	A,B,C,D,F,H
Oklahoma	A,B,C,E
Oregon	A,B,C,E,H
Pennsylvania	A,B,C,E,H,M
Puerto Rico	A,B,C,E,H,I,J,K,L
Rhode Island	A,B,C,E,F,H
South Carolina	A,C,E,K,M
South Dakota	A,B,C,E,H
Tennessee	A,C,E
Texas	A,B,C,G
Utah	A,B,C,E,M
Vermont	A,C,E,H
Virginia	A,C,F,G,H
Virgin Islands	A,B,C,E,H,I,J,K,L
Washington	A,C,E,M
West Virginia	A,B,C,E,H,I,J
Wisconsin	A,B,C,E,H,M
Wyoming	A,C,E

[B7829]

Table VIII

AGE AT WHICH SUPPORT OF CHILDREN LEGALLY TERMINATES

Alabama. Under Alabama case law the father has a duty to support his minor children until they reach 21, the common law age of majority. By statute, legitimate and illegitimate minor children under the age of 18 are entitled to support from parents or other persons who have legally acquired custody. Failure to provide such support for needy children is a misdemeanor. Title 34, Sections 89-104 and Title 27, Sections 12(1)-12(9), Code of Alabama 1940, as recompiled 1958, as amended. Parents are liable for the support of adult handicapped children only if such children meet the statutory definition of "poor persons unable to maintain themselves." Title 44, Section 8, Code of Alabama 1940, as recompiled 1958.

Alaska. Age of majority 19 years. Female arrives at majority upon marriage. Parents are bound to maintain children who are poor and unable to work. Children must maintain parents who are poor and unable to work. If a minor who has a father living has property providing sufficient maintenance in a manner more expensive than the father can reasonably afford, the child's maintenance may be defrayed in whole or in part from such income (25.20.030 and 040).

American Samoa. Both parents have a legal obligation to support children during their minority. A boy becomes of age at 21; a girl at 18.

Arizona. On reaching 21 (age of majority under Arizona Revised Statutes, Title 1, Ch. 2, Art. 2, Sec. 1-215). There is no statutory authority as to the liability of either parent to support an adult handicapped child. However, if either parent is able to contribute support every effort is made to obtain it.

Arkansas. From a civil standpoint, a father and a mother have both a legal and a moral obligation to support their minor children within their means and ability during a child's minority. A boy becomes of age at 21; a girl at 18. Liability of parents to illegitimate children is enforced only until child's 16th birthday. Many times, the court will consider whether the child has been emancipated in making the determination as to support when the minor child is living outside the home. Under an old law, the father and mother of poor, impotent or insane persons must maintain them at their own charge if of sufficient ability, and the children and grandchildren of poor, impotent or insane persons or grandparents must maintain them at their own charge. This law is seldom used but in a few cases the courts have enforced liability for support of adult handicapped children.

California. Parents entitled to custody must support and educate the child (Cal. Civ. Code, Sec. 196). Duty ends with child's majority, child's marriage or appointment of guardian (Cal. Civ. Code, Sec. 204), but parents must support adult needy child who is unable to support himself (Cal. Civ. Code, Sec. 206). Failure to provide support for a minor child is a criminal offense (Pen. Code §270).

Colorado. Court may enter a support order for children under 18 (22-7-1 et seq. CRS 1963) but parents must support adult children who are indigent and cannot support themselves (36-10-7, CRS 1963). There is a criminal penalty for failure to support children under 16 (43-1-1 CRS, 1963).

Connecticut. On reaching 21, regardless of whether the person is handicapped. Duty to support a married child is subject to primary responsibility of child's spouse.

Delaware. 18 years. In cases of handicapped children over the age of 18 the parents are liable for the support of said persons.

District of Columbia. Age 21 unless sooner emancipated by marriage or employment. In some instances parents are liable for support of adult children who are unable to support themselves.

Florida. Right ends with majority, but parents must support adult children who are physically or mentally incapable of supporting themselves. *Perla* v. *Perla*, 58 So. 2d 689, 690 (Fla. Sup. Ct.).

Georgia. Both mother and father liable for support of adult disabled children. Parents liable for support of children until age of majority (21 years of age).

Table VIII—Continued

Guam. Reciprocal duty, parents and children. It is the duty of the father, the mother, and the children of any poor person who is unable to maintain himself by work, to maintain such person to the extent of their ability. The promise of an adult child to pay for necessaries previously furnished to such parent is binding (Sec. 206, Civil Code of Guam). Both mother and father liable for support of adult disabled children.

Hawaii. On reaching 20 (age of majority under Sec. 557.1, Hawaii Revised Statutes).

Idaho. On reaching 18 for females, 21 for males. Both mother and father liable for support of adult disabled children.

Illinois. Age 18, with the following exceptions: (1) Age 21 for the unemancipated male in divorce unless the decree provides otherwise. (2) Age 21 for children receiving public assistance. (3) No age limitation for children who are patients of a mental health facility, although liability is limited to $50 monthly for 12 years.

Indiana. On reaching 21 (common law unless sooner emancipated). Desertion of child of any age is a felony if he is left without reasonable means of support, and failure to provide for a child under 14 is a felony (Acts of 1913, Ch. 358, Sec. 1 and 2, Burns, 1956 Repl., Secs. 10-1401 and 1402). It is a misdemeanor to neglect to support a boy under 16 and a girl under 17 (Acts of 1915, Ch. 73, Sec. 1, Burns, 1956 Repl. Sec. 10-1405).

Iowa. No specific statutory provision defining the age of the minor other than Chapter 252A which specifies the age of 17 except where a child is unable to maintain himself and likely to become a public charge. Both mother and father liable for support of adult disabled child.

Kansas. K.S.A. 1970 Supp. 38-101. A child is self-supporting at age 21, or age 18 for one who is or has been married. No provision for parental responsibility due to disability beyond age of minority.

Kentucky. Parents liable for support of child to age 18 or adult child mentally or physically handicapped. KRS 405.020.

Louisiana. Usually 21 years, but with the following exceptions: (1) If the child is emancipated, but if divorced the latter does not reinstate the disabilities incidental to minority. (2) Mentally or physically incompetent child retains his right of support from his parents. (3) Before 21 years there has to be a need.

Maine. Age 20. M.R.S.A. 1964, Title 19, Sections 441-453, Uniform Civil Liability for Support.

Maryland. Parents of a child are responsible for support until 21, unless married in the case of a female. Liability for an adult handicapped child's support is that of both parents, whether legitimate or illegitimate.

Massachusetts. Both mother and father are liable for support of minor children (Ch. 117, General Relief, and 118A, AFDC). Both mother and father under 65 liable for support of minor children under 21 years (Ch. 118D) and widowed mother under 62, liable for support of minor children under 21.

Michigan. On reaching 21, but adult children are entitled to support under responsible relative laws.

Minnesota. On reaching 21 years, but parent must support adult child who is physically or mentally unable to support himself (M.S.A. 518.54).

Mississippi. Age 16. Code 1689 and 2087.

Missouri. The general rule is that a father is liable for support of minor child (under 21 years), and if for any reason that duty is abrogated, it becomes the duty of the mother to care for and support the minor child. If, however, a minor child who is physically and mentally able to take care of himself abandons the parental home and becomes emancipated the parent is under no obligation to support him.

Table VIII—Continued

Montana. On reaching 19 years or at marriage, whichever is first (Sec. 61-118). Where a child, after attaining majority, continues to serve and to be supported by the parent, neither party is entitled to compensation in the absence of an agreement therefor.

Nebraska. On reaching 20. (18 for married females.)

Nevada. Duty of support of both parents of both legitimate and illegitimate children during minority. Minority of females continues to 18, minority of males to 21. Both parents liable for support of disabled adult child.

New Hampshire. The duty to support children is imposed upon both the father and the mother. Children are defined in the statute to encompass those under 16 years of age and those under 21 who, by reason of physical or mental infirmity, are incapable of supporting themselves (RSA 460:23 and 24, Supp.). Also, courts may order reimbursement for support of children under 18 who are neglected or deprived of support as a result of the death, continued absence or incapacity of parents (RSA 169:2, Supp. 10 and 11 and RSA 167:2,3, and 6-e, Supp.). Support of minor children may be ordered by a court in connection with a divorce decree or when parents are living apart (RSA 458:17 and 35).

New Jersey. Parents who have custody must support child until he reaches 21 except for married females (N.J.S. 9:2-13 b and c). It is a misdemeanor for a father to desert or neglect a minor child (N.J.S. 2A: 100-1, N.J.S. 9:6-1). Both mother and father liable for support of adult disabled child.

New Mexico. 18 years for girls; 21 for boys; unresolved for adult handicapped children.

New York. There is no liability on either parent to support a child over 21.

North Carolina. Illegitimate children to age 18. Legitimate children to age 21. Parents have a continuing liability for support of adult handicapped children.

North Dakota. On reaching 21 for boys, 18 for girls. Sec. 1409-10 of the NDCC provides it is the duty of the father, the mother, and the children of any poor person who is unable to maintain himself by work, to maintain such person to the extent of the ability of such father, mother, or children.

Ohio. Criminal liability extends only to 18; except to 21 for handicapped.

Oklahoma. 18 for girls, 21 for boys. Both mother and father liable for support of disabled adult child.

Oregon. On reaching 21 or being emancipated. Both mother and father liable for support of some adult disabled children.

Pennsylvania. The phraseology of Section 3 (a) of the Support Law of 1937, as amended, has governed the activities of the courts and the regulations of the Pennsylvania Department of Public Welfare. The courts are able to exercise considerable discretion in placing an order of support upon parents for the support of a child because they are not bound by any statutory limitation relative to the age of the child. In Pennsylvania, a child becomes of age at 21. The appellate courts have held that while ordinarily a parent is not required to support his adult child, where a child is too feeble mentally or physically to support himself, the duty on the parent continues after the child has attained his majority.

Puerto Rico. Both parents have a duty to support unemancipated minors (Sec. 153, Civil Code, 1930, 31 L.P.R.A., Sec. 601) in a manner appropriate to the family's social position (Sec. 42 Civil Code, 1930, 31 L.P.R.A., Sec. 971) until they reach 21 years of age (Civil Code 1930, 31 L.P.R.A., Sec. 901; Sec. 247 Civil Code 1930, 31 L.P.R.A., Sec. 971). Emancipation may take place at 18 years (Sec. 233 Civil Code of 1930, 31 L.P.R.A., Sec. 911) through parental exercise of patria potestas, marriage or judicial order. In certain circumstances the father may be liable for the support of children over 21 (*Molini* v. *District Court,* 72 P.R.R. 884 (1961)); *Garcia* v. *Acevedo,* 78 P.R.R. 580, 585 (1955).

Table VIII—Continued

Rhode Island. 21 unless emancipated. Both mother and father liable for support of adult disabled child.

South Carolina. Parents liable for child's support until he becomes 21. Support also ceases if a child marries before 21 or is emancipated before 21.

South Dakota. 21 for males, 18 for females. Both mother and father liable for support of adult disabled child.

Tennessee. Criminal liability for minor children ceases at age 18, but civil liability continues until age 21 unless emancipated at an earlier age. Under case decisions, both parents are also liable for handicapped adult children.

Texas. Either parent may be ordered to support child(ren) until the child has reached 18 (Articles 4639a and 4639b, Vernon's Texas Civil Statutes) and in divorce actions court may require support for mentally or physically unsound child(ren), whether minor or not (Article 4639a-1, Vernon's Texas Civil Statutes). For criminal penalties regarding desertion, see Articles 602 and 602-A, Vernon's Texas Penal Code.

Utah. On reaching 18 for girls, 21 for boys. Both mother and father liable for support of adult disabled child.

Vermont. 15 VSA 201/202 require support of children to age of 18 or if in school or vocational training until 21. Children includes stepchildren. 33 VSA 931 dealing with support of destitute children regardless of age has been repealed.

Virgin Islands. Under the age of 17 years. Parents and children are liable for adult handicapped children.

Virginia. On reaching 18 years, but parents must support children of any age who are crippled or otherwise incapable of making a living.

Washington. Ordinarily a child is entitled to support from both parents until 21 or until emancipated. (The effect of H.B. 309 passed by the Legislature on May 10 including comprehensive revisions to the laws affecting 21 year olds and lowering the general age of majority to 18 has not yet been determined.) Adult children incapable of self-support by reason of physical or mental infirmities are entitled to support from both parents.

West Virginia. A child is entitled to support from both parents if under 18. No provision is made for adult handicapped children. Support in bastardy cases can be ordered until the child reaches the age of 21.

Wisconsin. Both parents have civil liability for support of children under 21 years (Sec. 52-01, Wisc. Stats.). Civil liability under Sec. 52.01 may possibly apply to adult children who are unable to support themselves, but this question is still open in Wisconsin. Criminal liability ceases when the child becomes 18 (Sec. 52.05 and 52.055, Wisc. Stats.).

Wyoming. Statutes do not set forth the maximum age at which a child is entitled to support and confusion exists during current legislative session, but the age is probably 18.

[B7840]

Appendix E

DIVORCE, MARRIAGE, BIRTH AND DEATH RECORDS

Where to write for DIVORCE RECORDS

An official record of every divorce or annulment of marriage should be available in the place where the event took place. These records may be filed permanently either in a State vital statistics office or in a city, county, or other local office.

A copy may be obtained by writing to the appropriate office listed below. Fees listed are subject to change.

When writing for a copy, it is suggested that a money order or certified check be enclosed since the office cannot refund cash lost in transit. The following information will also be needed (type or print all names and addresses):

1. **Full names of husband and wife (including nicknames).**
2. **Present residence address.**
3. **Former addresses (as in court records).**
4. **Ages at time of divorce (or dates of birth).**
5. **Date and place of divorce or annulment of marriage.**
6. **Type of final decree.**
7. **Purpose for which copy is needed.**
8. **Relationship to persons whose record is on file.**

Place of divorce	*Cost of copy*	*Address and remarks*
Alabama	$3.00	Records since January 1950: Bureau of Vital Statistics, State Department of Public Health, Montgomery, Alabama 36104. Fee includes search and report, or copy of record if found.
	$1.50	Clerk or Registrar of Court of Equity in county where divorce was granted.
Alaska	$3.00	Records since 1950: Bureau of Vital Statistics, Department of Health and Welfare, Pouch "H", Juneau, Alaska 99801.
	Varies	Clerk of the Superior Court in judicial district where divorce was granted: Juneau and Ketchikan (First District), Nome (Second District), Anchorage (Third District), Fairbanks (Fourth District), Alaska.
American Samoa	$0.50	Registrar of Vital Statistics, Pago Pago, American Samoa 96799.
Arizona	Varies	Clerk of Superior Court in county where divorce was granted.
Arkansas	$2.00	Coupons since 1923: Division of Vital Records, Arkansas Department of Health, 4815 W. Markham, Little Rock, Arkansas 72201.
	Varies	Full certified copy may be obtained from circuit or chancery clerk in county where divorce was granted.
California	$2.00	For final decree entered since January 1, 1962 or initial complaint filed since January 1, 1966: Vital Statistics Section, Department of Health, 410 N Street, Sacramento, California 95814.
	Varies	Clerk of Superior Court in county where divorce was granted.
Canal Zone	$2.00	License section, Box "L", Balboa Heights, Canal Zone.
		Cristobal Division (Atlantic Area), Clerk, U.S. District Court, Box 1175, Cristobal, Canal Zone.
Colorado	*	Statewide index of records for all years except 1940-1967: Records and Statistics Section, Colorado Department of Health, 4210 East 11th Avenue. Denver, Colorado 80220. Inquiries will be forwarded to appropriate county office.
	Varies	Clerk of District Court in county where divorce was granted.

*Certified copies not available.

SOURCE: DHEW Publication No. (HRA) 76–1145 (Rev.1976).

Place of divorce	Cost of copy	Address and remarks
Connecticut	*	Index of records since June 1, 1947: Public Health Statistics Section, State Department of Health, 79 Elm Street, Hartford, Connecticut 06115. Inquiries will be forwarded to appropriate office.
	$3.00	Clerk of Superior Court in county where divorce was granted.
Delaware	*	Records since March 1932: Bureau of Vital Statistics, Division of Public Health, Department of Health and Social Services, State Health Building, Dover, Delaware 19901. Inquiries will be forwarded to appropriate office. Search made and essential facts of divorce verified (fee $2.50).
	$2.00	Prothonotary in county where divorce was granted.
District of Columbia	Varies	Records since September 16, 1956: Clerk, Superior Court for the District of Columbia, Family Division, 451 Indiana Ave., Washington, D.C. 20001. Records prior to September 16, 1956: Clerk, U.S. District Court for the District of Columbia, Washington, D.C. 20001.
Florida	$2.00	Records since June 6, 1927: Bureau of Vital Statistics, State Division of Health, P.O. Box 210, Jacksonville, Florida 32201. If year is unknown, the fee is $2.00 for the first year searched and $1.00 for each additional year to a maximum of $25.00. Fee includes a copy of the record found.
	Varies	Clerk of Circuit Court in county where divorce was granted.
Georgia	*	Centralized State records since June 9, 1952: Vital Records Unit, State Department of Human Resources, Room 217-H, 47 Trinity Avenue, S.W., Atlanta, Georgia 30334. Inquiries will be forwarded to appropriate office.
	Varies	Clerk of Superior Court in county where divorce was granted.
Guam	Varies	Clerk, Superior Court of Guam, Agana, Guam, M.I., 96910
Hawaii	$2.00	Records since July 1, 1951: Research and Statistics Office, State Department of Health, P.O. Box 3378, Honolulu, Hawaii 96801.
	Varies	Circuit Court in county where divorce was granted.
Idaho	$2.00	Records since January 1947: Bureau of Vital Statistics, State Department of Health and Welfare, Boise Idaho 83720.
	Varies	County Recorder in county where divorce was granted.
Illinois	*	Records since January 1, 1962: Office of Vital Records, State Department of Public Health, Springfield, Illinois 62761. Some items may be verified (fee $2.00).
	Varies	Clerk of Circuit Court in county where divorce was granted.
Indiana	Varies	County Clerk in county where divorce was granted.
Iowa	*	Brief statistical record only since 1906: Division of Records and Statistics, State Department of Health, Des Moines, Iowa 50319. Inquiries will be forwarded to appropriate office.
	Varies	County Clerk in county where divorce was granted.
Kansas	$2.00	Records since July 1951: Bureau of Registration and Health Statistics, 6700 S. Topeka Ave., Topeka, Kansas 66620
	Varies	Clerk of District Court where divorce was granted.
Kentucky	$2.00	Records since July 1, 1958: Office of Vital Statistics, State Department of Health, 275 East Main Street, Frankfort, Kentucky 40601.
	Varies	Clerk of Circuit Court in county where divorce was granted.
Louisana	*	Records since 1946: Division of Public Health Statistics. State Board of Health, P.O. Box 60630, New Orleans, Louisana 70160. Inquiries will be forwarded to appropriate office. All items may be verified.
	Varies	Clerk of Court in parish where divorce was granted.

*Certified copies not available.

Place of divorce	Cost of copy	Address and remarks
Maine	$2.00	Records since January 1, 1892: Office of Vital Statistics, State Department of Health and Welfare, State House, Augusta, Maine 04333.
	$1.00	Clerk of District Court in the judicial division where divorce was granted.
Maryland	•	Records since January 1961: Division of Vital Records, State Department of Health and Mental Hygiene, State Office Building, 201 West Preston Street, P.O. Box 13146, Baltimore, Maryland 21203. Inquiries will be forwarded to appropriate office. Some items may be verified.
	$2.00	Clerk of the Circuit Court in county where divorce was granted.
Massachusetts	$1.50	Index only from 1952: State Registrar of Vital Statistics, Room 103, McCormack Building, 1 Ashburton Place, Boston, Massachusetts 02108. Inquirer will be directed where to forward request.
	$1.50	Registrar of Probate Court in county where divorce was granted.
Michigan	$2.00	Records since 1897: Office of Vital and Health Statistics, Michigan Department of Health, 3500 North Logan Street, Lansing, Michigan 48914.
	Varies	County Clerk in county where divorce was granted.
Minnesota	•	Index since January 1, 1970: Minnesota Department of Health, Section of Vital Statistics, 717 Delaware Street, S.E., Minneapolis, Minnesota 55440
	Varies	Clerk of District Court in county where divorce was granted.
Mississippi	•	Records since January 1, 1926: Division of Public Health Statistics, State Board of Health, P.O. Box 1700, Jackson, Mississippi 39205. Inquiries will be forwarded to appropriate office.
	$2.00	Chancery Clerk in county where divorce was granted.
Missouri	•	Indexes since July 1948. Division of Health, Bureau of Vital Records, Jefferson City, Missouri 65101. Inquiries will be referred to apprpriate Circuit Clerk of the county in which the decree was granted.
	Varies	Clerk of Circuit Court in county where divorce was granted.
Montana	•	Records since July 1943: Division of Records and Statistics, State Department of Health, Helena, Montana 59601. Inquiries will be forwarded to appropriate office. Some items may be verified.
	Varies	Clerk of District Court in county where divorce was granted.
Nebraska	$3.00	Records since January 1909: Bureau of Vital Statistics, State Department of Health, Lincoln Building, 1003 'O' Street, Lincoln, Nebraska 68508.
	Varies	Clerk of District Court where divorce was granted.
Nevada	•	Indexed since January 1, 1968. Department of Human Resources, Division of Health - Vital Statistics, Capitol Complex, Office of Vital Records, Carson City, Nevada 89710. Inquiries will be forwarded to appropriate office.
	Varies	County Clerk in county where divorce was granted.
New Hampshire	$2.00	Records since 1880: Department of Health and Welfare, Division of Public Health, Bureau of Vital Statistics, 61 South Spring Street, Concord, New Hampshire 03301. Fee includes search and one copy.
	Varies	Clerk of the Superior Court which issued the decree.
New Jersey	$2.00	Superior Court, Chancery Division, State House Annex, Room 320 Trenton, New Jersey 08625.
New Mexico	Varies	Clerk of District Court in county where divorce was granted.
New York	$2.00	Records since January 1, 1963: Bureau of Vital Records, State Department of Health, Empire State Plaza, Tower Building, Albany, New York 12237.
	Varies	County Clerk in county where divorced was granted.

*Certified copies not available.

Place of divorce	Cost of copy	Address and remarks
North Carolina	$2.00	Department of Human Resources, Division of Health Services, Vital Records Branch, P.O. Box 2091, Raleigh, North Carolina 27602.
	Varies	Clerk of Superior Court where divorce was granted.
North Dakota	*	Index of records since July 1, 1949: Division of Vital Records, State Department of Health, Bismarck, North Dakota 58505. Inquiries will be forwarded to appropriate office. Some items may be verified.
	Varies	Clerk of District Court in county where divorce was granted.
Ohio	*	Records since 1948: Division of Vital Statistics, Ohio Department of Health, G-20 Ohio Departments Building, 65 S. Front Street, Columbus, Ohio 43215. Inquiries will be forwarded to appropriate office. All items may be verified.
	Varies	Clerk of Court of Common Pleas in county where divorce was granted.
Oklahoma	Varies	Court Clerk in county where divorce was granted.
Oregon	$3.00	Records since May 1925: Vital Statistics Section, State Health Division P.O. Box 231, Portland, Oregon 97207. Fee includes search and first copy. Additional copies of the same record ordered at the same time are $2.00 each.
	Varies	County Clerk in county where divorce was granted.
Pennsylvania	*	Records since January 1946: Division of Vital Statistics, State Department of Health, Central Building, 101 South Mercer Street, P.O. Box 1528, New Castle, Pennsylvania 16103. Inquiries will be forwarded to appropriate office.
	Varies	Prothonotary, Court House, in county seat where divorce was granted.
Puerto Rico	$0.60	Superior Court where divorce was granted.
Rhode Island	*	Records since January 1962: Division of Vital Statistics, Rhode Island Department of Health, Room 101, Davis Street, Providence, Rhode Island 02908. Inquiries will be forwarded to appropriate office.
	$1.00	Clerk of Family Court in county where divorce was granted.
South Carolina	$2.00	Records since July 1, 1962: Division of Vital Records, Department of Health and Environmental Control, 2600 Bull Street, Columbia, South Carolina 29201.
	Varies	Records since April 1949: Clerk of county where petition filed.
South Dakota	$2.00	Records since July 1, 1905: Division of Publice Health Statistics, State Department of Health, Pierre, South Dakota 57501.
	Varies	Clerk of Court in county where divorce was granted.
Tennessee	$2.00	Records since July 1945: Division of Vital Statistics, State Department of Public Health, Cordell Hull Building, Nashville, Tennessee 37219.
	Varies	Clerk of Court where divorce was granted.
Texas	Varies	Clerk of District Court in county where divorce was granted.
Trust Territory of the Pacific Islands	Varies	Clerk of Court in District where divorce was granted.
Utah	Varies	County Clerk in county where decree was granted.
Vermont	$1.50	Records since January 1860: Secretary of State, Vital Records Department, State House, Montpelier, Vermont. 05602.
	$3.00	Clerk of County Court where divorce was granted.
Virginia	$2.00	Records since January 1918: Bureau of Vital Records and Health Statistics, State Department of Health, James Madison Building, P.O. Box 1000, Richmond, Virginia 23208.
	Varies	Clerk of Court in county or city where divorce was granted.

*Certified copies not available.

Place of divorce	*Cost of copy*	*Address and remarks*
Virgin Islands (U.S.)		
St. Croix	$2.40	Deputy Clerk of District Court, Christiansted, St. Croix, Virgin Islands 00820.
St. Thomas and St. John	$2.40	Clerk of District Court, Charlotte Amalie, St. Thomas, Virgin Islands 00802
Washington	$3.00	Records since January 1, 1968: Bureau of Vital Statistics, Health Services Division, Department of Social and Health Services, P.O. Box 709, Olympia, Washington 98504.
	Varies	County Clerk in county where divorce was granted.
West Virginia	Varies	Clerk of Circuit Court, Chancery Side, in county where divorce was granted.
Wisconsin	$4.00	Records since October 1, 1907: Bureau of Health Statistics, Wisconsin Division of Health, P.O. Box 309, Madison Wisconsin 53701.
Wyoming	$2.00	Records since May 1941: Vital Records Services, Division of Health and Medical Services, State Office Building West, Cheyenne, Wyoming 82002.
	Varies	Clerk of District Court in county where divorce was granted.

*Certified copies not available.

[B7359]

Where to write for
MARRIAGE RECORDS

An official record of every marriage should be available in the place where the event occurred. These records may be filed permanetly either in a State vital statistics office or in a city, county, or other local office.

A copy may be obtained by writing to the appropriate office listed below. Fees listed are subject to change.

When writing for a copy, it is suggested that a money order or certified check be enclosed since the office cannot refund cash lost in transit. The following information will also be needed (type or print all names and addresses):

1. **Full names of bride and groom (including nicknames).**
2. **Residence addresses at time of marriage.**
3. **Ages at time of marriage (or dates of birth).**
4. **Date and place of marriage.**
5. **Purpose for which copy is needed.**
6. **Relationship to person whose record is on file.**

Place of marriage	*Cost of copy*	*Address and remarks*
Alabama	$2.00	Records since August 1936: Bureau of Vital Statistics, State Department of Public Health, Montgomery, Alabama 36104. Fee includes search and report, or copy of record if found.
	$1.00	Probate Judge in county where license was issued.
Alaska	$3.00	Records since 1913: Bureau of Vital Statistics, Department of Health and Welfare, Pouch H, Juneau, Alaska 99801.
American Samoa	$1.00	Registrar of Vital Statistics, Pago Pago, American Samoa 96799.
Arizona	Varies	Clerk of Superior Court in county where license was issued.
Arkansas	$2.00	Records since 1917: Division of Vital Records, Arkansas Department of Health, 4815 W. Markham, Little Rock, Arkansas 72201.
	$2.00	Full certified copy may be obtained from county clerk in county where license was issued.
California	$2.00	Vital Statistics Section, State Department of Public Health, 410 N Street, Sacramento, California 95814.
Canal Zone	$2.00	License Section, Civil Affairs Bureau, Box "L", Balboa Heights, Canal Zone.
Colorado	*	Statewide index of records for all years except 1940-1967: Records and Statistics Section, Colorado Department of Health, 4210 East 11th Avenue, Denver, Colorado 80220. Inquiries will be forwarded to appropriate county office.
	Varies	County Clerk in county where license was issued.

*Apply to county where license was issued if it is known. Certified copies not available from State health department.

SOURCE: DHEW Publication No. (HRA) 76–1144 (Rev.1976).

Place of marriage	*Cost of copy*	*Address and remarks*
Connecticut	$2.00	Records since July 1, 1897: Public Health Statistics Section, State Department of Health, 79 Elm Street, Hartford, Connecticut 06115.
	$2.00	Registrar of Vital Statistics in town where license was issued.
Delaware	$2.50	Bureau of Vital Statistics, Division of Public Health, Department of Health and Social Services, Jesse S. Cooper Memorial Bldg., Dover, Delaware 19901.
District of Columbia	$2.00	Marriage Bureau, 440 G Street, N.W., Room 337, Washington, D.C. 20001. Fee for proof of marriage, $1.00. Fee for application only, $1.00. Complete record, $2.00.
Florida	$2.00	Records since June 6, 1927: Bureau of Vital Statistics, State Division of Health, P.O. Box 210, Jacksonville, Florida 32201. If year is unknown, the fee is $2.00 for the first year searched and $1.00 for each addtional year up to a maximum of $25.00. Fee includes a copy of the record if found.
	$2.00	Clerk of Circuit Court in county where license was issued.
Georgia	*	Centralized State records since June 9, 1952: Vital Records Unit, State Department of Human Resources, Room 217-H, 47 Trinity Avenue, S.W., Atlanta, Georgia 30334. Inquiries will be forwarded to appropriate office.
	$2.00	County Ordinary in county where license was issued.
Guam	$1.00	Office of Vital Statistics, Department of Public Health and Social Services, Government of Guam, P.O. box 2816, Agana, Guam, M.I. 96910.
Hawaii	$2.00	Research and Statistics Office, State Department of Health, P.O. Box 3378, Honolulu, Hawaii 96801.
Idaho	$2.00	Records since 1947: Bureau of Vital Statistics, State Department of Health and Welfare, Statehouse, Boise, Idaho 83720.
	Varies	County Recorder in county where license was issued.
Illinois	*	Records since January 1, 1962 Office of Vital Records, State Department of Public Health, Springfield, Illinois 62761. All items may be verified (fee $2.00).
	$2.00	County Clerk in county where license was issued.
Indiana	*	Records since 1958: Division of Vital Records, State Board of Health, 1330 West Michigan Street, Indianapolis, Indiana 42606 No certification. Inquiries will be forwarded to appropriate office.
	Varies	Clerk of Circuit Court, or Clerk of Superior Court, in county where license was issued.
Iowa	$2.00	Division of Records and Statistics, State Department of Health, Des Moines, Iowa 50319.
Kansas	$2.00	Records since May 1913: Bureau of Registration and Health Statistics, Kansas State Department of Health and Environment, 6700 S. Topeka Ave., Topeka, Kansas 66620.
	Varies	Probate Judge in county where license was issued.
Kentucky	$2.00	Records since July 1, 1958: Office of Vital Statistics, State Department of Health 275 East Main Street, Frankfort, Kentucky 40601.
	Varies	Clerk of County Court in county where license was issued.
Louisiana	*	Records since 1946: Bureau of Vital Statistics, State Department of Health, P.O. Box 60630, New Orleans, Louisana 70160. Inquiries will be forwarded to appropriate office.
	$2.00	Certified copies are issued by the Clerk of Court in parish where license was issued.

*Apply to county where license was issued if it is known. Certified copies not available from State health department.

Place of marriage	Cost of copy	Address and remarks
Maine	$2.00	Office of Vital Records, State Department of Health and Welfare, State House, Augusta, Maine 04333.
	$2.00	Town Clerk in town where license was issued.
Maryland	$2.00	Records since June 1, 1951: Divsiion of Vital Records, State Department of Health and Mental Hygiene, State Office Building, P.O. Box 13146, 201 West Preston Street, Baltimore, Maryland 21203.
	Varies	Clerk of Circuit Court in county where license was issued or Clerk of Court of Common Pleas of Baltimore.
Massachusetts	$2.00	Records since 1841: Registrar of Vital Statistics, Room 103 McCormack Bldg., 1 Ashburton Place, Boston, Massachusetts 02108. Earliest Boston records are for the year 1848.
Michigan	$2.00	Records since April 1867: Office of Vital and Health Statistics, Michigan Department of Public Health, 3500 North Logan Street, Lansing, Michigan 48914.
	$2.00	County Clerk in county where license was issued.
Minnesota	*	Statewide index since January 1958: Section of Vital Statistics, State Department of Health, 717 Delaware Street, S.E., Minneapolis, Minnesota 55440. Inquiries will be forwarded to appropriate office.
	$2.00	Clerk in District Court in county where license was issued.
Mississippi	$2.00	Statistical Record only from January 1926 to July 1, 1938, and from January 1, 1942 to present: Vital Records Registration Unit, State Board of Health, P.O. Box 1700, Jackson, Mississippi 39205.
	$2.00	Circuit Clerk in county where license was issued.
Missouri	Free	Indexes since July 1948. Division of Health, Bureau of Vital Records, Jefferson City, Missouri 65101. Correspondent will be referred to appropriate Recorder of Deeds of the county where the license was issued.
	Varies	Recorder of Deeds in county where license was issued.
Montana	*	Records since July 1943: Bureau of Records and Statistics, State Department of Health and Environmental Sciences, Helena, Montana 59601. Inquiries will be forwarded to appropriate office.
	Varies	Clerk of District Court in county where license was issued.
Nebraska	$3.00	Records since January 1909: Bureau of Vital Statistics, State Department of Health, Lincoln Bldg., 1003 O Street, Lincoln, Nebraska 68508.
	Varies	County Court in county where license was issued.
Nevada		Indexed since January 1, 1968: Department of Human Resources, Division of Health - Vital Statistics, Capitol Complex, Office of Vital Records, Carson City, Nevada 89710. Inquiries will be forwarded to appropriate office.
	Varies	County Recorder in county where license was issued.
New Hampshire	$2.00	Records since 1640: Department of Health and Welfare, Division of Public Health, Bureau of Vital Statistics, 61 South Spring Street, Concord, New Hampshire 03301.
	$1.00	Town Clerk in town where license was issued.
New Jersey	$2.00	State Registrar, State Department of Health, P.O. Box 1540, Trenton, New Jersey 08625. If year is unknown, the fee is an additional $0.50 for each calendar year to be searched.
	No fee	For records from May 1848 thru May 1878 write to the Archives and History Bureau, State Library Division, State Department of Education, Trenton, New Jersey 08625.
New Mexico	Varies	County Clerk in county where marriage was performed.

*Apply to county where license was issued if it is known. Certified copies not available from State health department.

Place of marriage	Cost of copy	Address and remarks
New York (except New York City)	$2.00	Records from January 1880 to December 1907 and since May 1915: Bureau of Vital Records, State Department of Health, Empire State Plaza. Tower Building, Albany, New York 12237.
	Varies	Records from January 1908 to April 1915: County Clerk in county where license was issued.
	$2.00	Records from January 1880 to December 1907: Write to City Clerk in Albany or Buffalo and Registrat of Vital Statistics in Yonkers, if marriage occurred in these cities.
New York City	$4.00	Records from 1847 to 1865: Municipal Archives and Records Retention Center, New York Public Library, 23 Park Row, New York, New York 10038, except Brooklyn records for this period, which are filed with County Clerk's Office, Kings County, Supreme Court Building, Brooklyn, New York 11201. Additional copies of the same record ordered at the same time all $2.00 each.
	**	Records from 1866 to 1907: City Clerk's Office in borough in which marriage was performed.
	**	Records from 1908 to May 12, 1943:Residents-City Clerk's Office in borough of bride's residence; non-residents-City Clerk's Office in borough in which license was obtained.
	**	Records from May 13, 1943, to date: City Clerk's Office in borough in which license was issued.
Bronx Borough		Office of City Clerk, 1780 Grand Concourse, Bronx, New York 10457. Records for 1908-1913 for Bronx are on the file in Manhattan Office.
Brooklyn Borough		Office of City Clerk, 208 Joralemon Street, Brooklyn, New York 11201.
Manhattan Borough		Office of City Clerk, Chambers and Centre Streets, New York, N.Y. 10007.
Queens Borouጎh		Office of City Clerk, 120-55 Queens Boulevard, Borough Hall Station, Jamaica, New York 11424.
Richmond Borough		Office of City Clerk, Borough Hall, St. George, Staten Island, New York 10301.
North Carolina	$2.00	Department of Human Resources, Division of Health Services, Vital Records Branch, P.O. Box 2091, Raleigh, North Carolina 27602.
	Varies	Registrar of Deeds in county where marriage was performed.
North Dakota	$1.00	Records since July 1, 1925: Division of Vital Records, State Department of Health, Bismarck, North Dakota 58505. Inquiries will be forwarded to appropriate office.
	Varies	County Judge in county where license was issued.
Ohio	*	Records since September 1949: Division of Vital Statistics, Ohio Department of Health, G-20 Ohio Departments Building, 65 S. Front Street, Columbus, Ohio 43215. Inquiries will be forwarded to appropriate office. All items may be verified.
	Varies	Probate Judge in county where license was issued.
Oklahoma	Varies	Clerk of Court in county where license was issued.
Oregon	$3.00	Records since January 1907: Vital Statistics Section, State Health Division. State Board of Health, P.O. Box 231, Portland, Oregon 97207. Fee includes search and first copy. Additional copies of the same record ordered at the same time are $2.00 each.
	Varies	County Clerk of county where license was issued.
Pennsylvania	*	Records since January 1941: Division of Vital Statistics, State Department of Health, Central Building, 101 South Mercer Street, P.O. Box 1528, New Castle, Pennsylvania 16103. Inquiries will be forwarded to appropriate office.
	Varies	Marriage License Clerks, County Court House in county seat where license was issued.

*Apply to county where license was issued if it is known. Certified copies not available from State health department.

**$4.00 when exact year of marriage is submitted. (Add $0.50 for the 2d year of search and $0.25 for each additional year). Certificate will show names, ages, dates of birth, and date and place of marriage. For additional information-names and countries of birth of parents, matrimonial history, etc.-express request must be made. Mail requests must also include the cost of return postage.

Place of marriage	Cost of copy	Address and remarks
Puerto Rico	$0.50	Division of Demographic Registry and Vital Statistics, Department of Health, San Juan, Puerto Rico 00908.
Rhode Island	$2.00	Records since January 1853: Division of Vital Statistics, Rhode Island Department of Health, Room 101, Health Building, Davis Street, Providence, Rhode Island 02908.
	$1.00	Town Clerk in town, or City Clerk in city, where marriage was performed.
South Carolina	$2.00	Records since July 1, 1950: Division of Vital Records, Department of Health and Environmental Control, 2600 Bull Street, Columbia, South Carolina 29201.
	Varies	Records since July 1, 1911: Probate Judge in county where license was issued.
South Dakota	$2.00	Records since July 1, 1905: Division of Public Health Statistics, State Department of Health, Pierre, South Dakota 57501.
	$2.00	County Treasurer in county where license was issued.
Tennessee	$2.00	Records since July 1945: Division of Vital Records, State Department of Public Health, Cordell Hull Building, Nashville, Tennessee 37219.
	Varies	County Court Clerk in county where license was issued.
Texas	Varies	County Clerk in county where license was issued.
Trust Territory of the Pacific Islands	Varies	Clerk of Court in district where marriage was performed.
Utah	Varies	County Clerk in county where license was issued.
Vermont	$1.50	Records since 1857: Secretary of State, Vital Records Department, Montpelier, Vermont 05602.
	$2.00	Town Clerk in town where license was issued.
		For information on vital statistics laws, how to correct a record, etc., write to: Public Health Statistics Division, Department of Health, Burlington, Vermont 05401.
Virginia	$2.00	Records since January 1853: Bureau of Vital Records and Health Statistics, State Department of Health, James Madison Building, P.O. Box 1000, Richmond, Virginia 23208.
	Varies	Court Clerk in county or city where license was issued.
Virgin Island (U.S.)	*	Bureau of Vital Records and Statistical Services, Virgin Islands Department of Health, Charlotte Amalie, St. Thomas, Virgin Islands 00801. Inquiries will be forwarded to appropriate office.
St. Croix	$1.00	Clerk of Municipal Court, Municipal Court of the Virgin Islands, Christiansted, St. Croix, Virgin Islands 00820.
St. Thomas and St. John	$1.00	Clerk of Municipal Court, Municipal Court of the Virgin Islands, Charoltte Amalie, St. Thomas, Virgin Islands 00801.
Washington	$3.00	Records since January 1, 1968: Bureau of Vital Statistics, Health Services Division, Department of Social and Health Services, P.O. Box 709, Olympia, Washington 98504.
	$2.00	County Auditor in county where license was issued.
West Virginia	*	Records since 1921: Division of Vital Statistics, State Department of Health, Charleston, West Virginia 25305. Inquiries will be forwarded to appropriate office. Some items may be verified (fee $1.00).
	Varies	County Clerk in county where license was issued.

***Apply to county where license was issued if it is known. Certified copies not available from State health department.**

Place of marriage	Cost of copy	Address and remarks
Wisconsin	$4.00	Records since April 1835: Bureau of Health Statistics, Wisconsin Division of Health, P.O. Box 309, Madison, Wisconsin 53701.
Wyoming	$2.00	Records since May 1941: Vital Records Services, Division of Health and Medical Services, State Office Building, West Cheyenne, Wyoming 82002.
	Varies	County Clerk in county where license was issued.

*Apply to county where license was issued if it is known. Certified copies not available from State health department.

[B7366]

Where to write for

BIRTH AND DEATH RECORDS

United States and Outlying Areas

For every birth and death, and offical certificate should be on file in the place where the event occurs. These certificates are prepared by physicians, funeral directors, other professional attendents, or hospital authorities. The Federal Government does not maintain files or indexes of these records. They are permanently Filed in the central vital statistics office of the State, independent city, or outlying area where the event occurred.

To obtain a certified copy of a certificate, write or go to the vital statistics office in the State or area where the birth or death occurred. The offices are listed below.

In writing for a certified copy, it is suggested that a money order or certified check be enclosed since the office cannot refund cash lost in transit. Fees listed are subject to change.

The letter should give the following facts (type or print all names and addresses):

1. **Full name of the person whose record is being requested.**
2. **Sex and race.**
3. **Parents' names, including maiden name of mother.**
4. **Month, day, and year of the birth or death.**
5. **Place of birth or death (city or town, county, and State; and name of hospital, if any).**
6. **Purpose for which copy is needed.**
7. **Relationship to person whose record is being requested.**

Place of birth or death	*Cost of full copy*	*Cost of short form*	*Address of vital statistics office*	*Remarks*
Alabama	$3.00	Not issued	Bureau of Vital Statistics State Department of Public Health Montgomery, Alabama 36104	Additional copies at same time are $1.00 each. State office has records since January 1, 1908. Fee for special searches is $3.00 per hour.
Alaska	$3.00	$3.00	Bureau of Vital Statistics Department of Health and Welfare Pouch "H" Juneau, Alaska 99801	State office has records since 1913.
American Samoa	$1.00	Not issued	Office of the Territorial Registrar Government of American Samoa Pago Pago American Samoa 96799	Registrar has records on file since before 1900.
Arizona	$2.00	$2.00	Division of Vital Records State Department of Health P.O. Box 3887 Phoenix, Arizona 85030	State office has records since July 1, 1909, and abstracts of records filed in the counties before that date.

NOTE: Births occurring before birth registration was required or births not registered when they occurred may have been filed as "delayed birth registrations." Keep this in mind when seeking a copy of a record.

SOURCE: DHEW Publication No. (HRA) 76–1142 (Rev.1976).

Place of birth or death	Cost of full copy	Cost of short form	Address of vital statistics office	Remarks
Arkansas			Division of Vital Records Arkansas Department of Health 4815 West Markham Street Little Rock, Arkansas 72201	State office has records since February 1, 1914, as well as some original Little Rock and Fort Smith records from 1881.
Birth......................	$2.00	$2.00		
Death	$3.00			
California	$2.00	$2.00	Vital Statistics Section State Department of Health 410 N Street Sacramento, California 95814	State office has records since July 1, 1905. For records before that date, write to County Recorder in county of event.
Canal Zone	Not issued	$2.00	Vital Statistics Clerk Health Bureau Balboa Heights, Canal Zone	Central office has records since May 1904.
Colorado	$2.00	$2.00	Records and Statistics Section Colorado Department of Health 4210 East 11th Avenue Denver, Colorado 80220	State office has death records since 1900 and birth records since 1910. State office also has birth records for some counties for years prior to 1910. $2.00 fee is for search of files and one copy of record if found.
Connecticut	$2.00	$1.00	Public Health Statistics Section State Department of Health 79 Elm Street Hartford, Connecticut 06115	State office has records since July 1, 1897. For records before that date write to Registrar of Vital Statistics in town or city where birth or death occured.
Delaware	$2.50	$2.50	Bureau of Vital Statistics Division of Public Health Department of Health and Social Services Jesse S. Cooper Memorial Building Dover, Delaware 19901	State office has records for 1861 to 1863 and since 1881 but no records for 1864 through 1880.
District of Columbia...	$1.00	$1.00	Department of Human Resources Vital Records Section Rm 1022 300 Indiana Avenue, NW. Washington, D.C. 20001	Death records on file beginning with 1885 and birth records beginning with 1871, but no death records were filed during the Civil War.
Florida	$2.00	$2.00	Department of Health and Rehabilitative Services Division of Health Bureau of Vital Statistics P.O. Box 210 Jacksonville, Florida 32201	State office has some birth records since April 1865 and some death records since August 1877. The majority of records date from January 1917. (If the exact date is unknown and more that 1 year has to be searched, the fee is $2.00 for the first year searched and $1.00 for each additional year searched up to a maximum of $25.00. Fee includes a copy of the record if found.)
Georgia	$3.00	$3.00	Vital Records Unit State Department of Human Resources Room 217-H 47 Trinity Avenue, SW. Atlanta, Georgia 30334	The State office has records since January 1, 1919. For records before that date in Atlanta or Savannah, write to the County Health Department in place where birth or death occurred. Additional copies of same record ordered at same time are $1.00 each.
Guam	$1.00	$1.00	Office of Vital Statistics Department of Public Health and Social Services Government of Guam P.O. Box 2816 Agana, Guam, M.I. 96910	Office has records on file since October 26, 1901.
Hawaii.......................	$2.00	$2.00	Research and Statistics Office State Department of Health P.O. Box 3378 Honolulu, Hawaii 96801	State office has records since 1853.

NOTE: Births occurring before birth registration was required or births not registered when they occurred may have been filed as "delayed birth registrations." Keep this in mind when seeking a copy of a record.

Place of birth or death	*Cost of full copy*	*Cost of short form*	*Address of vital statistics office*	*Remarks*
Idaho	$2.00	$2.00	Bureau of Vital Statistics State Department of Health and Welfare Statehouse Boise, Idaho 83720	State office has records since 1911. For records from 1907 to 1911, write to County Recorder in county where birth or death occurred.
Illinois	$3.00	$3.00	Office of Vital Records State Department of Public Health 535 W. Jefferson Street Springfield, Illinois 62761	State office has records filed since January 1, 1916. For records filed before that date and for copies of State records since January 1, 1916, write to the County Clerk in county where birth or death occurred. ($3.00 fee is for search of files and one copy of the record if found. Additional copies of the same record ordered at the same time are $2.00 each.)
Indiana	$3.00	Not issued	Division of Vital Records State Board of Health 1330 West Michigan Street Indianapolis, Indiana 46206	State office has birth records since October 1, 1907, and death records since 1900. For records before that date, write to Health Officer in city or county where birth or death occurred. Additonal copies of same record ordered at same time are $1.00 each.
Iowa	$2.00	$2.00	Division of Records and Statistics State Department of Health Des Moines, Iowa 50319	State office has records since July 1, 1880.
Kansas	$2.00	$2.00	Bureau of Registration and Health Statistics 6700 S. Topeka Avenue Topeka, Kansas 66620	State office has records since July 1, 1911. For records before that date, write to County clerk in county where birth or death occurred.
Kentucky	$2.00	$2.00	Office of Vital Statistics State Department of Health 275 East Main Street Frankfort, Kentucky 40601	State office has records since January 1, 1911 and for Louisville and Lexington before that date. If birth or death occurred in Covington before 1911, write to City Health Department.
Louisiana	$2.00	$2.00	Office of Vital Records State Department of Health P.O. Box 60630 New Orleans, Louisana 70160	State office has records since July 1, 1914. Birth records available for City of New Orleans from 1790, and death records from 1803.
Maine	$2.00	$2.00	Office of Vital Records State Department of Health and Welfare State House Augusta, Maine 04333	State Office has records since 1892. For records before that year write to the municipality where event occurred.
Maryland	$2.00	$2.00	Division of Vital Records State Deparment of Health State Office Building 201 West Preston Street P.O. Box 13146 Baltimore, Maryland 21203	State office has records since 1898. Records for the City of Baltimore are available from January 1, 1875.
Massachusetts	$2.00	Free	Registrar of Vital Statistics Rm. 103 McCormack Bldg. 1 Ashburton Place Boston, Massachusetts 02108	State office has records since 1841. For records prior to that year, write to the City or Town Clerk in place where birth or death occurred. Earliest Boston records available in this office are for 1848.
Michigan	$2.00	$2.00	Office of Vital and Health Statistics Michigan Department of Public Health 3500 North Logan Street Lansing, Michigan 48914	State office has records since 1867. Copies of records since 1867 may also be obtained from County Clerk. Detroit records may be obtained from the City Health Department for births occuring since 1893 and for deaths since 1897.

NOTE: Births occurring before birth registration was required or births not registered when they occurred may have been filed as "delayed birth registrations." Keep this in mind when seeking a copy of a record.

Place of birth or death	*Cost of full copy*	*Cost of short form*	*Address of vital statistics office*	*Remarks*
Minnesota.................	$2.00	$2.00	Minnesota Department of Health Section of Vital Statistics 717 Delaware Street, S.E. Minneapolis, Minnesota 55440	State office has records since January 1908. Copies of records prior to 1908 may be obtained from Clerk of District Court in county where birth or death occurred or from the Minneapolis or St. Paul City Health Department if the event occurred in either city.
Mississippi.................	$2.00	$2.00	Vital Records Registration Unit State Board of Health P.O. Box 1700 Jackson, Mississippi 39205	
Missouri.....................	$1.00	$1.00	Bureau of Vital Records Division Of Health State Department of Public Health and Welfare Jefferson City, Missouri 65101	State office has records beginning with January 1910. If birth or death occurred in St. Louis (city), St. Louis County, or Kansas City before 1910, write to the City or County Health Department; copies of these records are $2.00 each.
Montana.....................	$2.00	$2.00	Bureau of Records and Statistics State Department of Health and Environmental Sciences Helena, Montana 59601	State office has records since late 1907.
Nebraska	$3.00	$3.00	Bureau of Vital Statistics State Department of Health Lincoln Building 1003 "O" Street Lincoln, Nebraska 68508	State office has records since late 1904. If birth occurred before that date, write the State office for information.
Nevada	$2.00	$1.00	Department of Human Resources Division of Health - Vital Statistics Office of Vital Records Capitol Complex Carson City, Nevada 89710	State office has records since July 1, 1911. For earlier records, write to County Recorder in county where birth or death occurred.
New Hampshire	$2.00	$2.00	Department of Health and Welfare Division of Public Health Bureau of Vital Statistics 61 South Spring Street Concord, New Hampshire 03301	Copies of records may be obtained from State office or from City or Town Clerk where birth or death occurred. ($2.00 fee is for search of files and copy of the record if found.)
New Jersey	$2.00	$2.00	State Department of Health Bureau of Vital Statistics Box 1540 Trenton, New Jersey 08625	State office has records since June 1878. ($2.00 fee is for search of files and one copy of the record if found. Additional copies of same record ordered at same time are $1.00 each. When the exact date is unknown the fee is an additional $0.50 per year searched.)
			Archives and History Bureau State Library Division State Department of Education Trenton, New Jersey 08625	For records from May 1848 through May 1878, write State Department of Education.
New Mexico	$2.00	$2.00	Vital Records New Mexico Health and Social Services Department PERA Building Room 118 Santa Fe, New Mexico 87501	State office has records since 1880 ($2.00 fee is for search of files and one copy of the record is found).

NOTE: **Births** occurring before birth registration was required or **births** not registered when they occurred may have been filed as "delayed birth registrations." Keep this in mind when seeking a copy of a record.

Place of birth or death	Cost of full copy	Cost of short form	Address of vital statistics office	Remarks
New York (except New York City) ..	$2.00	$2.00	Bureau of Vital Records State Department of Health Empire State Plaza Tower Building Albany, New York 12237	State office has records since 1880. For records prior to 1914 in Albany, Buffalo, and Yonkers or before 1880 in any other city, write to Registrar of Vital Statistics in the city where birth or death occurred. For the rest of the State, except New York City, write to State office.
New York (all boroughs) .... Birth.................... Death	 $3.00 $2.50	 $3.00	Bureau of Records and Statistics Department of Health of New York City 125 Worth Street New York, New York 10013	Records on file since 1898. Additional copies of birth records ordered at same time are $1.50 each. For Old City of New York (Manhattan and part of the Bronx) birth and death records from 1865-1897, write to the Municipal Archives and Records Retention Center of New York, 23 Park Row, New York, New York 10038.
North Carolina	$2.00	$2.00	Department of Human Resources Division of Health Services Vital Records Branch P.O. Box 2091 Raleigh, North Carolina 27602	State office has records since October 1, 1913, and some delayed records prior to that date.
North Dakota	$2.00	$2.00	Division of Vital Records Office of Statistical Services State Department of Health Bismarck, North Dakota 58505	State office has some records from July 1, 1893; years from 1894 to 1920 are incomplete.
Ohio	$1.00	$1.00	Division of Vital Statistics Ohio Department of Health G-20 Ohio Departments Building 65 S. Front Street Columbus, Ohio 43215	State office has records since December 20, 1908. For records before that date; write to Probate Court in county where birth or death occurred.
Oklahoma	$2.00	$2.00	Vital Records Section State Department of Health Northeast 10th Street & Stonewall P.O. Box 53551 Oklahoma City, Oklahoma 73105	State office has records since October 1908.
Oregon	$3.00	$3.00	Vital Statistics Section Oregon State Health Division P.O. Box 231 Portland, Oregon 97207	State office has records since July 1903. State office has some earlier records for the City of Portland dating from approxiamtely 1880. Additional copies of the same record ordered at the same time are $2.00 each.
Pennsylvania	$2.00	$1.00	Division of Vital Statistics State Department of Health Central Building 101 South Mercer Street P.O. Box 1528 Newcastle, Pennsylvania 16103	State office has records since January 1, 1906. For records before that date, write to Register of Wills, Orphans Court, county seat where birth or death occurred. Persons born in Pittsburgh from 1870 to 1905 or in Allegheny City, now part of Pittsburgh, from 1882 to 1905 should write to the Office of Biostatistics, Pttsburgh Health Department, City-County Building, Pittsburgh, Pennsylvania 15219. For births and deaths occurring in the City of Philadephia from 1860 to 1915, apply to Vital Statistics, Philadelphia Department of Public Health, City Hall Annex, Philadelphia, Pennsylvania 19107.
Puerto Rico...............	$0.50	$0.50	Division of Demographic Registry and Vital Statistics Department of Health San Juan, Puerto Rico 00908	Central office has records since July 22, 1931. Copies of records prior to that date may be obtained by writing to local Registrar (Registrador Demografico) in municipality where birth or death occurred or to central office.

NOTE: Births occurring before birth registration was required or births not registered when they occurred may have been filed as "delayed birth registrations." Keep this in mind when seeking a copy of a record.

Place of birth or death	Cost of full copy	Cost of short form	Address of vital statistics office	Remarks
Rhode Island	$2.00	$2.00	Division of Vital Statistics State Department of Health Room 101 Health Building Davis Street Providence, Rhode Island 02908	State office has records since 1853. For records before that year, write to Town Clerk in town where birth or death occurred.
South Carolina	$2.00	$2.00	Division of Vital Records Bureau of Health Measurement S.C. Department of Health and Analysis Environmental Control 2600 Bull Street Columbia, South Carolina 29201	State office has records since January 1, 1915. City of Charleston births from 1877 and deaths from 1821 on file at Charleston County Health Department. Ledger entries of Florence City births and death from 1895 to 1914 on file at Florence County Health Department. Ledger entries of Newsberry City births and deaths from late 1800's on file at Newberry County Health Department. Early records are obtainable only from County Health Departments listed.
South Dakota............	$2.00	$2.00	Division of Public Health Statistics State Department of Health Pierre, South Dakota 57501	State office has records since July 1, 1905, and access to other records for some births and deaths which occurred before that date.
Tennessee..................	$2.00	$2.00	Division of Vital Statistics State Department of Public Health Cordell Hull Building Nashville, Tennessee 37219	State office has birth records for entire State from January 1, 1914, to date and records from June 1881 for Nashville, July 1881 for Knoxville, and January 1882 for Chattanooga. State office has death records for entire State from January 1, 1914, to date and records from July 1874 for Nashville, March 6, 1872, for Chattanooga, and July 1, 1887, for Knoxville. Birth and death enumeration records by school districts from July 1, 1908, through June 30, 1912. Memphis birth records are from April 1, 1874, through December 1887; records continue November 1, 1898, to January 1, 1914. Death records date from May 1, 1848, to January 1, 1914. Apply to Memphis-Shelby County Health Department, Division of Vital Statistics, Memphis, Tennessee.
Texas	$2.00	$2.00	Bureau of Vital Statistics Texas Department of Health Resources 410 East 5th Street Austin, Texas 78701	State office has records since 1903.
Trust Territory of the Pacific Islands	$0.25 plus $0.10 per 100 words	$0.25 plus $0.10 per 100 words	Clerk of Court of district where event occurred. (If not sure of the district in which event occurred, write to the Director of Medical Services, Department of Medical Services, Saipan, Mariana Islands 96950, to have the inquiry referred to the correct district.)	Courts have records since November 21, 1952. Beginning 1950 a few records for various islands are temporaily filed with the Hawaii Bureau of Vital Statistics.
Utah	$3.00	$3.00	Division of Vital Statistics Utah State Department of Health 554 South Third East Salt Lake City, Utah 84113	State office has records since 1905. If birth or death occurred from 1890 through 1904 in Salt Lake City or Ogden, write to City Board of Health. For records elsewhere in the State from 1898 through 1904, write to County Clerk in county where birth or death occurred.
Vermont			Town or City Clerk of town where birth or death occurred.	
	$1.50		Secretary of State Vital Records Department State House Montpelier, Vermont 05602	
			Public Health Statistics Division Department of Health Burlington, Vermont 05401	For information on vital statistics laws, how to correct a record, etc., write to Department of Health.

NOTE: **Births occurring** before birth registration was required or births not registered when they occurred may have been filed as "delayed birth registrations." Keep this in mind when seeking a copy of a record.

Place of birth or death	Cost of full copy	Cost of short form	Address of vital statistics office	Remarks
Virginia	$2.00	$2.00	Bureau of Vital Records and Health Statistics State Department of Health James Madison Building Box 1000 Richmond, Virginia 23 208	State office has records from January 1853 through December 1896 and since June 4, 1912. For records between those dates, write to the Health Department in the city where birth or death occurred.
Virgin Islands (U.S.) St. Thomas	$2.00	Not issued	Registrar of Vital Statistics Charlotte Amalie St. Thomas, Virgin Islands 00802	Registrar has birth records on file since July 1, 1906, and death records since January 1, 1906.
St. Croix	$2.00	Not issued	Registrar of Vital Statistics Charles Harwood Memorial Hospital St. Croix, Virgin Islands	Registrar has birth and death records on file since 1840.
Washington	$3.00	$3.00	Bureau of Vital Statistics Health Services Division Department of Social and Health Services P.O. Box 709 Olympia, Washington 98504	State office has records since July 1, 1907. In Seattle, Spokane, and Tacoma a copy may also be obtained from the City Health Department. For records before July 1, 1907, write to Auditor in county where birth or death occurred.
West Virginia	$1.00	Not issued	Division of Vital Statistics State Department of Health State Office Building No. 3 Charleston, West Virginia 25305	State office has records since January 1917. For records prior to that year, write to Clerk of County Court in the county where birth or death occurred.
Wisconsin	$4.00	$4.00	Bureau of Health Statistics Wisconsin Division of Health P.O. Box 309 Madison, Wisconsin 53701	State office has some records since 1814; early years are incomplete.
Wyoming	$2.00	$2.00	Vital Records Services Division of Health and Medical Services State Office Building West Cheyenne, Wyoming 82002	State office has records since July 1909.

NOTE: Births occurring before birth registration was required or births not registered when they occurred may have been filed as "delayed birth registrations." Keep this in mind when seeking a copy of a record.

[B7845]

INDEX

References are to Pages

References are to Pages

WEST
KEY NUMBER SYSTEM